Maps, Myths, and Men

Kirsten A. Seaver

Maps, Myths, and Men

The Story of the Vinland Map

STANFORD UNIVERSITY PRESS

STANFORD, CALIFORNIA   2004

Stanford University Press
Stanford, California

Printed in the United States of America on acid-free paper

Library of Congress Cataloging-in-Publication Data
Seaver, Kirsten A., date–
    Maps, myths, and men : the story of the Vínland map /
Kirsten A. Seaver.
        p.   cm.
    Includes bibliographical references and index.
    ISBN 0-8047-4962-0 (cloth : alk. paper)—
ISBN 0-8047-4963-9 (pbk : alk paper)
1. Vinland map.   I. Title.
GA308.Z6S43 2004
912—DC22   2004001197

Original Printing 2004

Last figure below indicates year of this printing:
13   12   11   10   09   08   07   06   05   04

Designed by Janet Wood
Typeset by BookMatters in 10.75/14 Adobe Garamond

In loving memory of Helen Wallis

Oh, what a tangled web we weave,
When first we practice to deceive!

Sir Walter Scott, *Marmion,* Canto VI

Contents

Illustrations

Acknowledgments

This volume is dedicated to the memory of Helen Wallis, whose death on February 7, 1995, was a tremendous loss to her many friends and colleagues around the world. My gratitude to this passionate and erudite map scholar is both professional and personal. Helen taught me how to use early maps in my research on medieval and early Renaissance voyages of exploration in the northwestern Atlantic region, and she encouraged my research on the Vínland Map, placing at my disposal all the material she herself had collected on the subject.

As R. A. Skelton's deputy in the British Museum Map Room, Helen became suspicious of the Vínland Map's claim to authenticity when the volume containing the map and the "Tartar Relation" was briefly shown at the museum in 1957. By the time she succeeded Skelton as superintendent of what was soon to become The British Library Map Library, she was convinced that the map was a fake. This conviction rested on her own experience with medieval maps, combined with the results of the scientific investigations made at the British Museum in 1967, when A. E. Werner (keeper of the Research Laboratory) and A. D. Baynes-Cope (principal scientific officer) reported that the map's ink was quite unlike that used in its sister manuscript and also unlikely to be medieval iron gallo-tannate ink. Like Helen, I have benefited greatly from personal contact with both scientists and from the kindness of Sheridan Bowman, the present keeper of what is now called the British Museum Department of Scientific Research, who gave me access to her department's archives concerning the 1967 Vínland Map investigation. In addition, Baynes-Cope was for many years endlessly patient and generous with his scientific advice and explanations. I mourn his death on December 27, 2002.

Indeed, throughout my ten years of research on this book I have often been

xv

given reason to marvel at the generosity of other scholars in sharing their knowledge. For sheer willingness to suffer greatly in order that unknown readers may suffer less, it would be hard to surpass my valued London friend Andrew S. Cook, who has shared his wide interest in—and knowledge of—early maps and exploration. Andrew's patient commentaries on my work in progress have led to much rewriting on my part; I owe him more than I can express.

Much valuable information has also come from people responding by mail to my inquiries, especially as I felt my way through the ink jungle. I am particularly grateful to Th. DeBeer at the Oudt Hollandse Olieverven Makerij, Driebergen, The Netherlands, for his carefully formulated responses. Direct contact with all the scientists responsible for important Vínland Map ink studies subsequent to the 1967 one in London helped me immeasurably as I studied each new report. While Jacqueline Olin (now retired from the Smithsonian Institution in Washington, D.C.) and I have different opinions about the authenticity of the Vínland Map, we have maintained our friendship, and I owe much to her grasp of current research on iron gallo-tannate inks. The late Walter McCrone and his wife Lucy as well as Kenneth Towe have all given freely of their expertise; Thomas Cahill has been informative about his own ink research; and Robin J. H. Clark responded most kindly to my early inquiry about his and Katherine L. Brown's recent ink study.

Like the McCrone study, the Brown and Clark ink analysis detected modern, industrially modified anatase crystals in the matrix of the yellow ink line on the map. This circumstance suggests a post-1923 date for the creation of the Vínland Map and places the spotlight on the properties of this form of anatase.

As it happens, the chemical process by which titanium dioxide in the form of anatase is converted into smooth globules, suitable for suspension in paints and inks, was first developed and subsequently refined in my Norwegian hometown. I am grateful to my brother, Per-Olaf Andresen, for putting me in touch with Truls Tandberg and Per Thoen, the past and present chief executive officers of Kronos Titan A/S in Fredrikstad, who made arrangements to send—for comparative studies as well as for experimentation—two samples each of their laboratory's 1923 and 1968 anatase products. Thanks in no small part to generous networking by Carl Djerassi and Richard Zare of the Stanford University Chemistry Department, studies were kindly undertaken by Peter Buseck and Li Jia at Arizona State University and subsequently also by J. Victor Owen at St. Mary's University, Halifax, Nova Scotia. I am truly grateful to them all.

Equally warm thanks are due to Erik Lund in Fredrikstad and to Torstein Bryn in Sandefjord, both of them Norwegian specialists within the pigment industry. Lund, who worked as a chemical engineer at Kronos Titan A/S until his retirement, provided me with the historical and technical framework necessary to understand the significance of the analyses performed by Buseck, Jia, and Owen. Bryn, the official historian of the large Norwegian paint firm Jotun A/S, not only supplied much valuable information concerning the modern use of pigments in paints and inks but also gave me an informative tour of Jotun's technical museum.

Other Nordic friends and institutions have helped in innumerable ways to unravel the Vínland Map story. I am very grateful to Thorsteinn Hallgrímsson at the National and University Library of Iceland in Reykjavík for sending me copies of archival material, and to Karen Arup Seip and Benedicte Gamborg Briså for providing copied archival material from the Map Collection at the Norwegian National Library in Oslo. This material included newspaper clippings that tell a story not available from any other source. The staff of the Manuscript Department at the same library made it possible for me to examine A. A. Bjørnbo's letters to Fridtjof Nansen during the limited time I had at my disposal on a brief visit to Oslo.

Henrik Dupont, curator of maps and prints at the Royal Library in Copenhagen, also searched his archives with significant results. In addition, he has provided samples of various types of the parchment paper that map scholars used for tracing maps before the advent of Xerox copies. Before the method of drawing the Vínland Map had become obvious, it seemed worth exploring the possibility that residue from the coating of such paper might transfer to an object underneath. Henrik also revealed that his library has a number of letters written by Father Josef Fischer, S.J., to A. A. Bjørnbo and called my attention to a file containing Bjørnbo's correspondence with Nansen. In addition, with Henrik's kind permission I inspected several early map treasures, including the fragile original of the 1605 Resen map that is normally reproduced as an 1887 redrawing. I am deeply indebted to Henrik.

At Wolfegg Castle, Count Maximilian zu Waldburg-Wolfegg and his archivist, Dr. Bernd Mayer, generously allowed me to examine Father Fischer's letters and a number of their priceless manuscript maps. I am very grateful both to them and to Sadie Holland, who directed the filming at Wolfegg of a

Granite Productions program on the Vínland Map and shared valuable information with me.

In Switzerland, Germany, and Austria, a number of Jesuit institutions showed me exemplary kindness that enabled me to collect information about many aspects of the Jesuit college of Stella Matutina as well as about the holdings of the Jesuit Archives in Munich. Father Hans Grünewald, S.J., archivist at the Jesuit provincial archive in Munich, and his successor, Dr. Rita Haub, helped me both with personal recollections and with a search through their archives. Frau Isolde Listmayer, the recently retired administrator at Stella Matutina, tirelessly replied to my various appeals for information and also sent much printed material used in the present book.

My search for information about the former Mikulov Castle Library in general and for a fifteenth-century *Speculum Historiale* manuscript fragment in particular also involved a number of people in Europe: To Olle Ekstedt in Malmö, Sweden, to Eva Handler-Wajntraub in Vienna, Dorothea McEwan at the Warburg Institute in London, to the Moravian Public Archives in Brno, to the Czech National Library in Prague, as well as to Elizabeth Hoffmann at the Gilhofer Antiquariat in Vienna, and E. Frederick Schwab at the Gilhofer & Ranschburg Antiquariat in Lucerne, I have expressed my gratitude individually, but I repeat my thanks here.

In London, where the bulk of my research took place, I have benefited from the superb collections of The British Library and from the knowledge of its curatorial specialists past and present. Every member of the Map Library and Humanities reading rooms staff has at one time or another made my life easier. Michelle Brown in the Department of Manuscripts provided many useful comments on the paleography and orthography of the Vínland Map; Graham Nattrass of the German Section let me benefit from his antiquarian expertise; and during a series of illuminating discussions, Peter C. Hogg of the Scandinavian Section uniquely combined Norse literary knowledge with a keen interest in old maps.

The present keeper of the public record, Sarah Tyacke, has been a constant source of encouragement and of the cartographic expertise to which she has been adding ever since she began her career under Skelton's stewardship in the British Museum Map Room. The Map Library at the new British Library carries on the tradition of scholarly sharing and helpfulness that I first encountered in the old Map Room at the British Museum under the guidance of

Helen Wallis. Readers interact in a helpful way, and the staff will go to great lengths to track down needed items. Karen S. Cook was often my last great hope while she was at The British Library; now her detective skills are serving her well in Kansas. In the past few years, Geoffrey Armitage has had the job of saving my sanity with his skill and patience. Tony Campbell, in charge of the Map Library until his recent retirement, has always been supportive of my work and has dealt deftly with arguments for overlooking the Vínland Map's lack of provenance.

Peter Barber, the current head of the Map Library, has been a source of both miscellaneous and specialized information for many, many years and deserves my warmest thanks not only for sharing his knowledge of the library's vast holdings, but for his unflagging support of my research. A dedicated scholar, he has also made certain that I connected with people able to recall the early days of the Vínland Map debate. Among them is the medieval map specialist P. D. A. Harvey, who very kindly sent me a copy of the notes he made after examining the Vínland Map and its sister manuscripts in 1967. T. C. Skeat, the keeper of manuscripts at the British Museum in 1967, has also shared with me a number of astute observations of his own that he made while going over these works years ago. Last, but certainly not least, Peter Schofield has provided several vivid recollections of the comments that his father Bertram Schofield (at that time keeper of manuscripts) made in 1957 on the occasion of the Vínland Map's visit to the museum.

No list of London assets and pleasures would be complete without mentioning Francis Herbert, the Royal Geographical Society's map curator, who has gone out of his way to assist me over the years, and who is known (and feared) among map scholars everywhere for his attention to detail and for his willingness to help others pull up their standards.

Help has truly come from everywhere. William W. Fitzhugh at the Smithsonian's Arctic Studies Center was always ready to answer questions about North American natives. Other archaeologists—Jette Arneborg in Copenhagen, Georg Nyegaard in Qaqortoq, Greenland; Patrick Plumet in Paris; Peter Schledermann in Calgary, Alberta; Kevin Smith in Providence, Rhode Island; Patricia Sutherland in Hull, Quebec; and Birgitta L. Wallace in Halifax, Nova Scotia—have all contributed valuable insights gleaned from their work. Solveig Zempel at St. Olaf College in Northfield, Minnesota, has sent me newspaper clippings and has been supportive in other ways during my long investigative journey. Robert Babcock, curator of the Vínland Map and its related volumes at Yale University's Beinecke Library, went out of his way to be helpful while I was in New Haven.

Kari Ellen Gade at Indiana University has repeatedly helped me through difficult Old Norse interpretations. By providing expert translations of key Latin legends on the Vínland Map, F. Donald Logan, formerly at Emmanuel College in Boston, and Philippe Buc at Stanford University have confirmed my misgivings about the treatment that these passages received in *The Vinland Map and the Tartar Relation* (Yale University Press, 1965, 1995). Indeed, one of my many advantages here in California is my continued access to the Stanford University libraries and to the richness of its academic community, including to my husband's colleagues in the History Department.

My husband Paul has been an inexhaustible source of advice about thorny historical problems. He has also joined me on journeys to which an historian of Tudor and Stuart England would not normally have subjected himself, but on which he has gamely trudged through Greenland scrub, Icelandic lava fields, and Newfoundland bogs. Our daughter Hannah has remained as encouraging as she is outspoken, and our graphic-designer son David has yet again been willing to provide me with illustrations for my work.

The message behind my individual and collective thanks is that only with the help of a large number of people was it possible to write this book. If it contains mistakes, they are my own.

Note to the Reader

In the text, Old Norse phrases and citations will not be Anglicized, but the thorn will be represented by "th" and a hooked "o" will be written as ö. Writing in English about the medieval Norse, one must decide whether their names should conform to Old Norse or to English practice (for example, Eiríkr vs. Eirik or Eric; Guðríðr vs. Gudrid). With a few exceptions, the present book spells medieval Norse personal names and place names in the Anglicized or "normalized" manner, omitting whenever possible the acute accent. (Although helpful in indicating a long vowel, in Old Norse and modern Icelandic this same diacritical mark is also used to indicate a different sound to the vowel altogether and thus requires the reader to know the pronunciation rules.) The names of modern Icelandic authors will nevertheless observe all diacritical marks to aid name recognition for bibliographical purposes.

In the Index, medieval Norse names will be listed alphabetically by first names followed by the patronymic (for example, Leif Eiriksson), but post-medieval Nordic authors—including Icelanders—will be listed under their last name both here and in the Bibliography. Please note that the latter contains only the works I have actually cited in my text; it does not include background reading.

In the vast literature that now exists concerning the Vínland Map, there is considerable variation in the spelling of personal names, literary titles, and place names. In direct quotes, the writer's own preference will be observed, but I have otherwise made an effort to impose some uniformity. In particular, the reader needs to be forewarned that except when quoting other writers, I use the form "Vínland" to indicate the long vowel sound. Scholarly battles have been fought over less!

Maps, Myths, and Men

CHAPTER I

An American Place Named Vínland

America and the Medieval Norse

The very mention of Vínland evokes an old and enduring controversy in which the powers of mythmaking are discernible and in which there is not always sufficient distinction between myth and established fact.

An unabating and sometimes intemperate scholarly discussion about the Norse "discovery" of America has been well nourished by discrepancies in two early-thirteenth-century Icelandic accounts—the "Saga of the Greenlanders" and the "Saga of Eirik the Red." These works are known by the joint name of the "Vínland Sagas" because they contain the most extensive written details available about the voyages that the Norse made to North America around AD 1000.[1] Although several particulars in the two sagas are verifiable through other written sources and by means of modern archaeology, these tales are not dependable as historical sources. Both sagas contain obvious interpolations reflecting the fact that these stories were not written down until a couple of centuries after the events they commemorate, and there are many observations that seem opaque to the modern mind. In addition, comparing the two accounts reveals a number of contradictory passages.

The two works nevertheless speak with one voice on some key issues. Both sagas agree that Eirik "the Red" Thorvaldsson, generally thought to have been a feisty Norwegian-turned-Icelander, changed his homestead one last time by spearheading the Norse colonization of Greenland at the end of the tenth century and that his son Leif followed in his enterprising father's footsteps a few years later by investigating a coast even farther west. The "Vínland Sagas" also agree on the names assigned to the three regions that the Norse explored while sailing down the eastern Canadian coast after they had crossed the Davis Strait from Greenland. That novel shore was eventually linked with the New World and essentially appeared as a northern part of the continent named "America" on the 1507 world map by the German cartographer Martin Waldseemüller.

The medieval Norse carried no such mental baggage when they named various stretches of that coast, however, and while it was certainly "new" to them, they had ample reason to know that it was already home to other peoples.

From north to south, the Norse designated segments of that unfamiliar coast as *Helluland* (Slab Land), *Markland* (Forest Land), and *Vínland* (Wine Land). The first two names refer to general and recognizable coastal areas. Although the demarcation between a barren "Slab Land" and a tree-covered "Forest Land" leaves little doubt about the travelers' general progress down the Baffin and Newfoundland coasts, it is of little consequence to the ongoing discussion of early American exploration. These two northerly Norse landfalls are usually of subordinate concern to modern scholars, and they receive only perfunctory treatment in the two "Vínland Sagas."

With regard to Vínland, however, there has long been keen interest on both sides of the Atlantic in exactly where Leif Eiriksson decided "Forest Land" became "Wine Land" and in how far south in America the Norse ventured altogether. Among educated people there was considerable fascination with these problems as early as around 1590, when a young Icelandic scholar named Sigurd Stefansson combined saga descriptions with recent cartographical representations of the New World and drew a speculative map (to be discussed in later chapters) delineating a peninsular Vínland. His work was long regarded as the earliest extant map that in any way reflected the Norse discovery of America.

That situation changed on October 11, 1965, when Yale University Press published a large and handsome volume, entitled *The Vinland Map and the Tartar Relation*, in conjunction with an announcement by Yale University Library that it had acquired a manuscript world map dating from around 1440 and showing the part of North America that the Norse had named Vínland. Neither the mapmaker's identity nor the map's provenance could be ascertained, but the map's bold depiction of the Norse discovery of America was enough to draw worldwide attention. The Yale University Press volume explaining the significance of the map was widely distributed and subsequently became as much a focus of scholarly and pseudoscholarly discussion as the Vínland Map itself.

The Vinland Map and the Tartar Relation

During the seven years it had taken to prepare *The Vinland Map and the Tartar Relation*, the book project was kept just as secret as the existence of the actual map. This secrecy prevented the three authors from freely consulting other scholars when addressing such widely different subjects as codicological problems, the map's place in the cartographical record, and the map's value to the history of the Norse in America. Once the book had been published, however, a number of scholars willingly expressed their opinions about its authors' statements.

The book was the work of two British scholars and one American: R. A. Skelton (superintendent of maps in the British Museum), George D. Painter (assistant keeper in charge of incunabula in the British Museum's Department of Printed Books), and Thomas E. Marston (curator of medieval and Renaissance manuscripts at Yale). Their primary purpose was to demonstrate that the newly acquired Yale map indeed dated from about 1440 and that it was a legitimate cartographical representation of the Norse discovery in North America, based on knowledge handed down through several centuries. Their secondary purpose was to comment on a text manuscript named *Hystoria Tartarorum*, or the "Tartar Relation."

When Yale acquired the Vínland Map, the "Tartar Relation" was joined with the map in a fairly recent binding. A brief text, it is a partial recounting of the otherwise well-known story of John de Plano Carpini's papal mission to the Mongols in 1245–47. It was notably different from the two accounts that Carpini himself had written on his return home (*Hystoria Mongalorum*), therefore a separate section in the Yale book was well warranted.

Along with the Vínland Map and the "Tartar Relation" Yale had also acquired an incomplete four-book portion of Vincent of Beauvais's *Speculum Historiale*. These *Speculum* fragments were in a mid-fifteenth-century binding now generally believed to have also contained the "Tartar Relation" because both of the textual manuscripts employed similar mixed parchment-and-paper quires and the paper used for both texts carries the same watermark. The 1965 Yale volume thus concerns three manuscripts, not just two. The book's authors considered the three items closely related and sometimes referred to them collectively as "the manuscript."

The Vínland Map

A small black-and-white map executed on parchment, the Vínland Map depicts in the far northwestern Atlantic a large island, identified by two Latin legends next to it as *Vinilanda Insula* (see Figure 1). This island gave the map both its name and its hold upon the public imagination. Translated into English, the shorter map legend reads: "Island of Vínland discovered by Bjarni and Leif in company." The longer one is probably the map's most frequently debated feature and deservedly so: It contains a series of riddles that will be fully analyzed in Chapter 8 in conjunction with a new translation of the Latin text. The Yale book's translation of the full text here reads:

> By God's will, after a long voyage from the island of Greenland to the
> south toward the most distant remaining parts of the western ocean sea,
> sailing southward amidst the ice, the companions Bjarni [*byarnus*] and
> Leif Eiriksson [*leiphus erissonius*] discovered a new land, extremely fer-
> tile and even having vines, the which island they named Vínland. Eric
> [*Henricus*] legate of the Apostolic See and bishop of Greenland and
> the neighboring regions, arrived in this truly vast and very rich land,
> in the name of Almighty God, in the last year of our most blessed father
> Pascal, remained a long time in both summer and winter, and later re-
> turned northeastward toward Greenland and then proceeded in most
> humble obedience to the will of his superiors.[2]

The only "Bjarni" mentioned in the "Saga of Eirik the Red" is a man named Bjarni Grimolfsson. There is no mention at all in that tale of the man whom the "Saga of the Greenlanders" credits with the first glimpse of America, namely Bjarni Herjolfsson, a man so devoted to his father that he sailed to Greenland to find him and on his voyage glimpsed the American coast before he made his way back to Greenland and located his father's new farm.

In somewhat dissimilar ways, the authors of *The Vinland Map and the Tartar Relation* acknowledged that the longer Vínland legend poses the problem of identifying Leif's companion. For his own part, Skelton observed that the two "Vínland Sagas" differ concerning who "discovered" Vínland, and he noted that the "Saga of the Greenlanders" gives the honor of first sighting to Bjarni Herjolfsson. Leif Eiriksson is then credited with following up on the information with a properly organized expedition where Bjarni was not present. Skelton wrote: "None of the Icelandic accounts of Leif's voyage of discovery states that Bjarni accompanied him." The English scholar therefore reasoned that either this legend on the Vínland Map brought significant new historical information with regard to that point, or else "the cartographer, or the author of his source for this matter, has confused the two voyages, that of Bjarni in 985 or 986 and that of Leif in 1002." He also suggested the possibil-

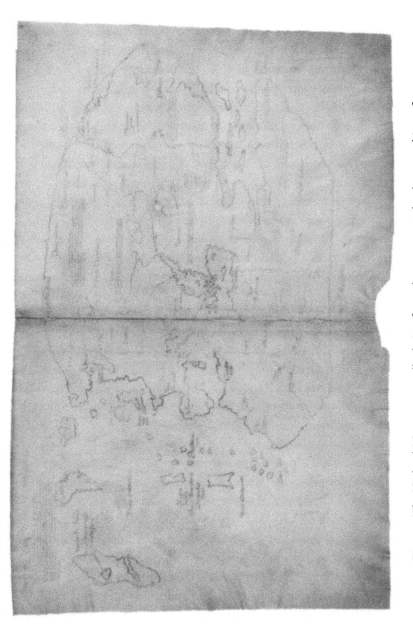

Figure 1. The Vinland Map, purportedly dating from about AD 1440, has been a subject of contention since 1965, when Yale University Library announced that it owned the map. Source: Beinecke Rare Book and Manuscript Library, Yale University. Reproduced with permission.

ity that Bjarni Herjolfsson had been confused with Bjarni Grimolfsson, the man "who accompanied the Icelander Karlsefni to Vínland ca. 1020."[3]

Painter regarded the map's delineation of Vínland as "a generalized and degenerate simplification of the saga narratives," but he believed that the map legends themselves provided "genuinely new evidence of the Norse discoveries" and possibly reflected historical fact. As for the long legend's reference to Bishop Eirik, Painter stated unequivocally: "This sober and weighty statement, both as a whole and in detail, seems hardly open to adverse criticism. . . . When seen in its historical context it is both confirmed and illuminated." According to Painter, a part of this historical context would have been the existence of "Vínland settlements . . . adapted from the Greenland model," for the souls of whose inhabitants Eirik would supposedly have been responsible as the Greenland bishop. Painter was also persuaded that the Vínland Map is a more reliable authority than the *Icelandic Annals* in the matter of dating Bishop Eirik's voyage to Vínland. Summing up his confidence in the information about the Norse that the map provides, he wrote: "The bare words of the VM caption concerning Bishop Eirik, we may reasonably consider, are authentic and true."[4]

Painter assumed that in Vínland, Bishop Eirik would have been responsible for installing priests, consecrating churches, and providing "the indispensable sacraments of the Roman Church." Painter thought the bishop might also have wanted to supervise in person the collection of tithes from what the longer map legend calls "this most wealthy country." Painter wrote: "We have studied the possibility that he undertook for reasons both religious and commercial the conversion of the fur-trading Skraelings, perhaps through native interpreters educated from childhood . . . by the settlers."[5]

Skelton tentatively allowed that the reference in the *Icelandic Annals* to Bishop Eirik's Vínland voyage "has been interpreted by some modern historians as evidence of the survival of a Norse colony in America into this period." His personal view, however, was that Bishop Eirik had likely been appointed for very specific duties outside the formal scope of church organization. Skelton addressed the discrepancy between the dates provided by the Icelandic sources and the longer "Island of Vínland" map legend. He noted that although "no original record of Bishop Eirik's ordination is known," he calculated that if Bishop Eirik [Gnupsson] went to Vínland in the summer before Pope Pascal II died in January of 1118, the date for that voyage would have been 1117, which conflicts with the date of 1121 given in the *Icelandic Annals*. Either

the bishop made two voyages, Skelton observed, or else the map legend cor-
rects the date that the *Annals* provide.[6]

The *Icelandic Annals* are indeed the only sources available for consultation
here. According to its notation in the *Lögmanns-annáll*, the Icelander Eirik
Gnupsson *upsi* (nose-drip or pollock) left Iceland in 1112 to serve as Greenland's first bishop. Six different annals have a listing for 1121 with a version of
the statement "Eirikr Grænlendinga byskup leitade Vínlands" or "Eirikr
byskup af Grónlanndi fór at leita Vínlanndz"—each instance signifying that
Bishop Eirik went in search of Vínland. No news of Bishop Eirik was recorded
after that year, but three years later, in 1124, the Norwegian priest Arnald was
consecrated bishop of Greenland.[7] Evidently, Eirik Gnupsson had not
resumed his episcopal duties in Greenland. The very lack of further documentation here has led to many conjectures about the bishop's fate, making
the allusion in the Vínland Map legend significant.

Much speculation has centered upon the interpretation of the Old Norse
verb *leita* (look for), which all six annal entries employ. Because Painter and
Skelton thought that a closer definition of *leita* might suggest the purpose of
the Greenland bishop's expedition and also indicate how much realistic knowledge the bishop had of the route on which he embarked, they had to grapple
with this linguistic problem, in a language unfamiliar to them and with the aid
of secondary sources published in English.

According to Skelton, "The best philological opinion, supported by the
Icelandic scholarship of Storm, Reeves, and Hermannsson, holds that the verb
leita can, in this connection, only have the meaning 'to search for something
undetermined, or lost.' " In that case, he wrote, "there could hardly have been
a Norse colony surviving in Vinland" and Bishop Eirik's motive for his voyage
"must have been the evangelization of the heathen." In Skelton's common-
sensical view, the longer Vínland legend on the Vínland Map "lends unmistakable support" to such an interpretation, although there is no telling where
the map's compiler had obtained his information.[8]

Painter did not question the notion that the map legend alluded to Bishop
Eirik's supposed missionary brief, but he doubted the validity of Skelton's suggestion that the Greenland bishop's aim had been to convert the heathen
Skrælings (the term covered Amerindians as well as Dorset and Thule Eskimos) living in the Vínland region. "A purely altruistic missionary journey to
convert distant savages dwelling out of all contact with European civilization
or commerce is not only inconceivable in a twelfth-century context but man-

ifestly impracticable owing to language difficulties," Painter wrote. In his view, the only reason for Bishop Eirik's journey would have been "the contemporary existence of Norse settlers in Vínland." Not only did the longer map legend overrule the *Icelandic Annals* regarding the date for Bishop Eirik's voyage, but it settled the discussion about the annalists' use of the verb *leita*, Painter argued. He admitted that this word would normally "indicate a search for something lost or unlocated," which would explain why these annal entries have so often been taken to mean that the location, or even the existence, of Vínland was uncertain and also to signify that Bishop Eirik never returned from his search. However, Painter felt certain that given the information provided by the map legend, the present case called for a different interpretation. "We now know that he both arrived and returned; and the doubtful words mean here, as occasionally elsewhere, simply 'set out for,' as Gathorne-Hardy [1921] had already maintained."[9] In Painter's view, therefore, Bishop Eirik was not only convinced of Vínland's existence but knew how to sail there and back.

Painter's reasoning inevitably gives rise to the question of whether the Vínland Map in any way reflects that geographical knowledge along with its relatively conventional representation of the non-Norse world.

Sources for the Vínland Map

The Vínland Map is a world map and an unusual one at that. Skelton alluded to both of these aspects of the work while explaining one of the map's many oddities, namely its essentially (but not entirely) ellipsoid shape. He noted that "the representation of Europe, Africa, and Asia . . . plainly derives from a circular or oval prototype." If that prototype had in fact been circular, he wrote, the shape of both Africa and Asia had been "flattened" into an oval framework "by vertical compression rather than lateral extension."[10] He went to considerable lengths to trace the map's possible cartographic ancestry and to provide a list of the most important world maps that have survived from the fourteenth and fifteenth centuries. In addition, he suggested that the maker of the Vínland Map might also have used noncartographic sources: "Whether and to what extent the author of the Vínland Map made use of textual information for certain parts of his map, and what its character may have been, will emerge from the detailed analysis in the following chapters."[11]

While Skelton noted many marked similarities between the Vínland Map and the world map in Andrea Bianco's 1436 atlas, he made it clear that Bianco's map did not provide a direct precedent for the Vínland Map's version of the Far East. Nor did any other extant map show anything resembling the Vínland Map's *Insule Sub aquilone zamogedorum*, the *Postreme Insule*, and a third, unnamed island off the remote eastern coast. Skelton therefore thought that the "prototype is, in this region . . . adapted to admit a new geographical concept which . . . can be considered a gloss on the Tartar Relation."[12] Because this far eastern region also includes the anomalous *Magnum mare Tartarorum* (Great Tartar Sea), he observed that "the name and delineation probably embody the mapmaker's interpretation of what he had read or been told of the Caspian Sea."[13]

In support of his argument that the *Magnum mare Tartarorum* (located between those three puzzling large islands farthest east and "the encircling ocean") most likely represented the mapmaker's own impressions gained from the "Tartar Relation" account, Skelton observed that Carpini had been "the first traveler to demonstrate . . . that Eurasia extended much further to the east than European geographers and mapmakers supposed." The English map scholar nevertheless thought it unlikely that the maker of the Vínland Map had seen an actual cartographic prototype illustrating the observations made during the Carpini journey, because "Carpini's report left no mark on fourteenth-century cartography." In Skelton's view, therefore, the Vínland Map is also unique in being the first map to provide information about the Carpini journey in cartographic form.[14]

Painter's view was that the "Tartar Relation" was "an independent primary source concerning the Carpini Mission." He was therefore reluctant to agree with Skelton's notion that the *Magnum mare Tartarorum* was merely "a product of the VM compiler's fancy, influenced by his textual sources" and without any graphic basis in the map model he had used. For his own part, Painter considered it quite possible that the friars on the 1245–47 mission to the Mongols had personally "believed that the Caspian [in other words, not the Black Sea] was a gulf of the northern ocean"—the implication being that they must have made a graphic sketch, now lost, of their geographical concepts. In addition, Painter argued that other versions of the Carpini report besides the "Tartar Relation" had influenced the map's delineations of the Far East.[15]

"Nevertheless," Painter noted, "the Tartar Relation remains highly important and interesting in its own right, as an independent primary source on the Carpini Mission to Central Asia in 1245–47, and the history and folklore of the Mongols at the zenith of their conquests." He also believed the "Tartar Relation" text to be "of vital significance to the Vinland Map," because it was one of the chief sources for the place names and legends appearing in the Asian section. He thought it proper "to value the Tartar Relation predominantly for the light it can throw on the Vínland Map, and on the intentions, resources, and psychology of the Vinland Map compiler."[16]

Skelton was as aware as Painter that only the Asian part of the Vínland Map reflected the "Tartar Relation" in any way—there was no trace of the text's influence farther west. His search for cartographical antecedents also failed to turn up extant cartographical prototypes for the map's depiction of the western Atlantic, where the map shows the British Isles, and where three islands—*isolanda Ibernica*, *Gr, and *Vinilanda Insula*—represent Iceland, Greenland, and "Wine Land." Although he cited a few near-precedents that might have led the author of the Vínland Map to name the island *isolanda Ibernica* (Irish Island)—a name for Iceland known from no extant written or cartographic source—Skelton appears to have been personally unconvinced by the possibilities he noted.[17]

He dealt more firmly with other aspects of these North Atlantic islands. He thought that because they are "outside the general oval framework of the map," they probably had not been included on the circular or elliptical prototype that he assumed had been followed for Africa, Europe, and Asia. Given the lack of extant prototypes for the northwestern islands shown, Skelton reasoned that the Vínland Map must be seen as "the oldest map of the North Atlantic Ocean in existence" and therefore unique in that respect as well.[18] He was nevertheless ready to entertain the idea that one or more prototypes had once existed:

> In view of the novel elements in the northwestern part of the map, we must reckon with the possibility—but no more—that [the Vínland Map's] author found this version of the British Isles on a map of the North Atlantic which may have served him as a model for this part of his work and from which may stem not only his representations of Iceland, Greenland, and Vinland, but also his revisions of Scandinavia and Great Britain and of the islands between.[19]

Although "the maps drawn in Iceland and Denmark from the close of the sixteenth century and during the seventeenth were the first to incorporate geographical information from the ancient Icelandic records," Skelton thought that, on the one hand, there might have been "ancient prototypes" for the Stefansson map, the original version of which he dated to 1570–90, as well as for the Gudbrand Thorlaksson map of the North (1606) and the Hans Poulson Resen map of the North (1605), all three of which were reproduced in the Yale book. On the other hand, in Skelton's view the circa 1424–27 map and description of the North produced by the Dane Claudius Clavus was of no importance as an antecedent to the Vínland Map.[20]

All three maps indicate Greenland as a peninsula, whereas Iceland (called by its usual name) appears everywhere as an island, therefore Skelton needed to explain why the Vínland Map shows not only Iceland but both Greenland and Vínland as islands before he could argue that the Vínland Map contains an element of actual Norse experience in its depictions of the northwestern Atlantic.

He attributed both Vínland's island status and its disproportionate size on the Yale map to the difficulties any mapmaker faces when giving graphic expression to written and oral sources without recourse to sketches made from experience and without any personal memory of the coast(s) under consideration. To a late-medieval cartographer, the outlines and dimensions of any trans-Atlantic coast could have been only dimly imagined, in Skelton's view.[21] Noting that a medieval Icelandic geographical treatise refers to both Helluland and Markland as islands while treating Vínland as a peninsula, he added that "none of the other Norse sources referring to Vínland, from the earliest in the *Íslendingabók* of Ari Frode (circa 1122–24), contains any indication that Vinland was thought to be an island."[22]

The fact that both Helluland and Markland are missing on the Vínland Map further suggested to Skelton that the mapmaker had not availed himself of a graphic model for this region but had been forced to rely on textual accounts of the Norse voyages. Even so, he had lacked information about landfalls other than the one in Vínland. The relative size as well as the delineation of Vínland on the Vínland Map seemed immaterial to Skelton because these characteristics revealed no cartographic precedents. More important, in his view, was the island's approximately correct position in the western Atlantic, indicating at least some sort of surviving knowledge. "If Iceland and Greenland are depicted from experience, the outline of Vinland must have been constructed from written or oral report," Skelton wrote.[23]

Skelton reminded his readers that Adam of Bremen (writing about 1075) had referred to Iceland, Greenland, and Vínland as islands. Judging from what he himself saw as the relative accuracy of the Vínland Map's Greenland delineation and orientation, he thought it quite likely that in the course of a period of exceptionally mild climate during the colony's establishment phase, the Norse had explored the Greenland coasts about as far north as seventy-five degrees northern latitude; indeed, they might even have circumnavigated their country.[24] He concluded his long analysis of the Vínland Map with the observation that this map "is the only surviving graphic record of the western voyages of the Norsemen to contain any element of experience."[25]

Skelton was convinced that "information about the western lands discovered and partly settled by the Norsemen must have reached southern Europe" due to the "regular communication between Rome and the episcopal sees of Iceland and Greenland: Scandinavian churchmen came to Rome and attended the ecumenical councils, and Papal legates went to Scandinavia; pilgrims from the north visited Italy on their way to and from the Holy Land."[26] It also seemed to him that the elusive mid-fourteenth-century work *Inventio Fortunata* (of which no copies are now extant, and of which we know only fragments through second- and thirdhand sources) must have strongly influenced medieval perceptions in Europe of the northern world known to the Norse Greenlanders.[27]

In short, Skelton believed that in the mid-fifteenth century there would still have been information available about not only Iceland and Greenland, but also about the landfalls that the Norse had made in North America. The likely center for such information would have been Iceland, and dissemination of such knowledge to other parts of Europe would have been facilitated by Iceland's trade with England in the fifteenth century. The English in their turn had enjoyed wide trade connections with the Iberian countries and with the rest of the European continent. To Skelton's mind, such a communications network would explain why the Vínland Map, despite its failure to add to our knowledge of "occasional communication with America," nevertheless "reflects the strong probability that in medieval Iceland the historical evidence of the Norse discovery of America was sustained by graphic as well as written memorials which have not survived."[28]

Painter was similarly conflicted when judging the amount of realistic knowledge available to the author of the Yale map. While he regarded the historical information contained in the two Vínland legends as authentic, he believed that "neither the Vínland Map, nor its prototype as far as we can visualize it, throws any light on the actual location of the Norse discoveries." In his view, the Vínland Map "manifestly bears no cartographic link with real experience"; it merely uses sketchy saga information to indicate landfalls in Helluland, Markland, Vínland, "including, as it seems, Keelness [Old Norse: Kjalarness]." Painter saw the map's "Island of Vínland" as an illustration of a substantial coastal stretch of the American mainland and found such strikingly similar antecedents for the first three landfalls in the Stefansson and Resen maps that he argued a common source for all three maps. "The Vinland Map and the maps of Stefansson and Resen may be held to derive independently from lost maps of the same family, and all three may be used for a reconstruction of the archetype," he wrote. In his view, the author of the Vínland Map had nevertheless departed from this unknown archetype in a number of ways.[29]

Skelton had no trouble accepting that the Stefansson and Resen maps (as well as the one drawn by Gudbrand Thorlaksson in the same period) "were the first to incorporate geographical information from the ancient Icelandic records." He was more tentative, however, when assessing the Stefansson and Resen maps as guides to what, if any, cartographical evidence had been available to postmedieval Icelandic intellectuals like Björn Jónsson of Skardsá (1574–1656) and Sigurd Stefansson or to the Danish theologian Hans Poulson Resen. "Whether, among the records which they rummaged and brought to light, the Icelanders found any early maps is uncertain," Skelton wrote. "No such maps have survived, and the only evidence that they may have existed is to be sought in the maps drawn at this late period in Iceland; to this evidence we may now add the Vinland Map."[30]

No statement of faith in the map's antecedents or authenticity could substitute for a traceable history for the map and its sister manuscripts prior to their sale in 1957, but Skelton's overall analysis of the Vínland Map led Yale's map librarian, Alexander Vietor, to state: "The Vinland Map contains the earliest known and indisputable cartographic representation of any part of the Americas, and includes a delineation of Greenland so strikingly accurate that it may well have been derived from experience. If, as Mr. Skelton supposes, this map originated in the North, and probably in Iceland, it represents the only surviving medieval example of Norse cartography."[31]

Guaranteeing Authenticity

Alexander Vietor's foreword to *The Vinland Map and the Tartar Relation* also demonstrates a clear understanding of the problems likely to arise in the

absence of proper provenance information for such high-profile and potentially controversial antiquarian items as the Vínland Map and its companion
manuscripts. He nevertheless stated his personal conviction that the map and
its sister texts are authentic:

> The arresting character of the documents naturally calls into question
> their genuineness. In the absence of an unbroken record of their history,
> there can be no absolute and unassailable demonstration that they are
> not counterfeit. Nevertheless, analysis of content and form in the histor-
> ical framework may create—and in this case, we believe, has created—
> a presumption of authenticity so strong as to be difficult, if not impossi-
> ble, to challenge.[32]

At least outwardly satisfied that the Vínland Map must be a genuine mid-
fifteenth-century artifact, just like its two companion texts, Vietor called the
map an important addition to Yale's collections and noted: "In some great
matters of history . . . the discovery of a single new document may significantly alter the accepted pattern; and its publication becomes an imperative
responsibility."[33]

In the Yale volume, the responsibility for explaining the complicated recent
history of the closely guarded manuscripts fell to Thomas E. Marston. He
summarized this information in a 1966 article he wrote for a Canadian journal and began by noting that "in October 1957 the antiquarian bookseller,
Laurence Witten, of New Haven, showed to my colleague, Alexander O.
Vietor and myself a slim volume containing an unknown account of John de
Plano Carpini's mission to the Mongols in 1245–47 and a map of the world
showing Iceland, Greenland and Vínland." A few months later (in April of
1958), Marston reported, he had obtained through his New Haven dealer a
portion of the *Speculum Historiale* that he had chanced to spot in a London
antiquarian catalog. When Witten shortly afterward compared the Vincent of
Beauvais fragments with the volume he had shown to Vietor and Marston, the
results were electrifying. Marston's *Speculum* portion "had suddenly become a
precious piece of historical evidence" because "the Vincent matched the map
and the Tartar Relation, the paper was the same, the wormholes followed the
same pattern and it was apparent that the map had been bound first in the volume, followed by the Vincent manuscript and that the Tartar Relation had
been bound in at the end of the volume."[34] Marston also described his first
major decision following the discovery that his and Witten's purchases were

related: "As the sum of money was inconsequential, I gave it [the Vincent fragments] to Mrs. Witten, who then owned the map and the Tartar Relation in hopes that this generosity would enable the Yale Library to control its sale if Mrs. Witten decided to sell it. This hope was fully realized."[35]

Thirteen printed pages were made to suffice for Marston's account in the 1965 book of how the three manuscripts had found their way to the Yale University Library and of the criteria that had been applied to establish their authenticity. Because Skelton's and Painter's analyses provided the textual bulk of *The Vinland Map and the Tartar Relation,* it is easy to overlook both the information those thirteen pages contain and the significant part that Marston played in the New Haven events that led up to Yale's 1965 announcement about the map and the book.

In Marston's opinion, scientific testing of the ink would be useless because the ink used in the map and its companion manuscripts was medieval and would therefore have been made of either iron salts or oak galls or a combination of both. "This type of ink does not lend itself to modern spectroscopic tests effective in determining the relationship of one ink to another of chemically known composition," he wrote. "The only kind of test that would yield valid results would require the scraping away of the amount of writing necessary to produce enough material to work on."[36]

Marston also provided several details about his and Witten's reliance on the two manuscript texts to authenticate the map and to carry its known antiquarian history back as far as the rather unusual circumstances permitted. He noted the visual appearance of all three manuscripts, and he commented on the paleography as well as on the two bindings. Because it seemed to him that all the physical evidence, including the paper and the binding, pointed to the Upper Rhineland, he suggested that the likely origin for the map and its companions would have been the Swiss town of Basel and that their creation had been prompted by the Council of Basel (1431 to 1449).[37] Agreeing with this theory, Skelton wrote: "In such a large gathering, and among the large staff of secretaries employed by it, it is not difficult to envisage circumstances in which maps of Scandinavian and of Venetian origin or authorship may have come together under the eyes of a single scribe or in the possession—perhaps only temporary—of a single scriptorium."[38]

Skelton also commented on the Vínland Map's general visual appearance. He judged its parchment to be "identical in texture, color, and thickness" with a conjugate pair of parchment leaves in the "Tartar Relation" and described the ink used for the outlines and lettering on the map as "a somewhat diluted brownish ink flecked with black." There was little doubt in his mind that "the map and the manuscript were juxtaposed within their binding from a very early date." He believed that the map had been drawn "immediately after the copying of the texts was completed," and in the same workshop or scriptorium; and that the map had been intended as an illustration to the two texts.[39] Painter (who also provided an annotated translation of the Latin text of the "Tartar Relation") envisioned a series of possibly inaccurate copyings from multivolume, complete editions of the works, which had eventually reached Yale, and he provided his own reconstruction of the likely derivation of Yale's three newly acquired manuscripts. He cautioned that the compiler of the Vínland Map "must not be identified with the scribe of the surviving exemplar of VM, which is itself a copy, perhaps at several removes, from the lost original. It is possible . . . that the compiler may have worked, perhaps several decades before, in the same scriptorium, which may well have specialized in the multiplication of manuscripts of the *Speculum Historiale* augmented with TR and VM."[40]

Showing the Map to a Wider World

Skelton and Painter helped prepare the press release intended for the journalists who were invited to view the Vínland Map and its companions when they were put on display at the British Museum on January 19, 1967. Their statement noted that all three documents, which "came from a library in Europe," had been "purchased by an American collector in 1958" and had been given to Yale University Library in 1964. The press release also called attention to the "vigorous discussion" that had arisen with the publication of the Yale University Press volume devoted to these three items. The novel aspects of the map made for "obvious difficulties in adjusting it to the accepted pattern of intellectual and cartographic history," and there were many unanswered questions about its sources and origins. "The date ascribed to it, and even its authenticity, have been challenged."[41] For the benefit of the general public visiting the exhibition, Painter and Skelton also prepared several pages of background information with synopses of a number of the main points made in the 1965 Yale volume.

The exhibition statement noted: "If, in the map, Greenland is largely fact, Vinland is a notion. Its outline, divided into three sections by deep inlets, suggests the three coasts on which (as recorded in the Icelandic sagas) landfalls were made by Norse seamen; those of Helluland, Markland and Vinland." Nevertheless, "the outlines of Iceland (wholly) and of Greenland (in part) appear to contain an element of graphic records derived—doubtless at several removes—from observation." It was the opinion of Skelton and Painter that the elements of Greenland's depiction reflecting experience could not have reached either Iceland or Europe later than in the middle of the fourteenth century, when "regular communication between Norway and the settlements in Greenland had practically ceased." Iceland was altogether in a different position and would have been a logical intermediary for providing other Europeans with information about medieval Greenland. "In the fifteenth century, Iceland was still densely settled, and there was trade with England and Flanders," the two men noted.[42]

Father Time and Daughter Truth

When the Yale book was reviewed in the *Times Literary Supplement* just a few weeks after its release in October of 1965, the anonymous reviewer was aware that a heated discussion had already developed and therefore cautioned that while there was great need for skepticism, one must not dismiss what is unique (for example, the depiction of Vínland) just because it is unique.[43]

Despite the time and care that both authors and publishers had lavished on the book, contrary voices had indeed been heard from the moment *The Vinland Map and the Tartar Relation* and the map itself became public knowledge. While scholarly opinions are unlikely to be unanimous at the best of times, and interpretations are always vulnerable to change, in the case of the Vínland Map the increasing clamor represented more than scholarly scuffles. The discussion was widely acknowledged to concern both the authenticity of the artifact and the credibility of the statements made in *The Vinland Map and the Tartar Relation.*

Alexander O. Vietor had anticipated such a reaction and cautioned in his foreword to the Yale book: "The present publication of these remarkable documents is designed to be a preliminary work; completeness or finality is not claimed for the commentaries, which are to be considered a springboard for further investigation."[44] Subsequent correspondence from Vietor's hand makes it clear that he retained an open and inquiring attitude toward the Vínland Map. It is in tribute to Vietor's sensible approach that the next eight chapters will submit both the Vínland Map and *The Vinland Map and the Tartar Relation* to further investigation.

The decades-long debate about the Vínland Map and the Yale book has brought into focus a number of different issues—codicological, antiquarian, chemical, and cartographical, to name but a few—that will receive scrutiny in the present book. I will begin by reviewing the known history of the medieval Norse in the North Atlantic as it affected their tenure in Greenland over half a millennium because the linchpin in the public's fascination with the Vínland Map has been the perception that Vínland represents the culmination of medieval Norse exploration beyond Greenland.

CHAPTER 2

The Norse in and near North America

A Flawed Source of Information

Much remains to be learned about the medieval Norse Atlantic voyages and colonization, but enough information was available even before 1965 to show not only what is unlikely to have happened during these undertakings, but also much of what in fact did happen. The omission of this knowledge in the first edition of *The Vinland Map and the Tartar Relation* is unfortunate. The failure to incorporate updated knowledge in the second edition (1995) is inexplicable.

Nevertheless, there is no disputing the profound impact of *The Vinland Map and the Tartar Relation* on the international reading public interested in the medieval Norse—an impact that was further aided by the relative ease with which works in English are disseminated and understood. Publication in a major language subtly confers greater status on a work than if it had been published in one of the "lesser" languages, and this kind of validation becomes especially problematic if accompanied by the prestige of two such world-renowned institutions as Yale University and the British Museum.

Institutional approval was more apparent than real in the case of *The Vinland Map and the Tartar Relation*, but the mere appearance of solid academic connections helped to ensure almost four decades of widespread misinformation about the medieval Norse. Many subsequent authors have trusted the book's self-proclaimed authoritativeness and have cited its essays in countless footnotes, thus securing a long secondary life for the book. Its lasting impact is a major reason to examine it closely.

All three of the book's authors were institutionally well connected and of blameless reputation. However, in this project they were required to tackle a number of questions about the Norse that had never been addressed before, and their position was made more difficult by their lack of the language background necessary to accessing Nordic primary sources. Instead, they had to depend on secondary sources in English, many of which predated their own work by four decades or more. The three men were naturally also hampered by the secrecy clause that had been imposed on them when they began their work on the book, which had prevented consultation with more than a few trusted colleagues far from the cutting edge of Norse research. In consequence, the authors' knowledge concerning the medieval Norse was both superficial and outdated.

The Icelandic map scholar Haraldur Sigurðsson (who also found plenty of cartographical evidence arguing against a 1440 date for the Vínland Map) reserved his harshest comments for the Yale authors' ignorance concerning the Norse:

> In their study of the text of the Vínland Map it is everywhere apparent that the editors are lacking in knowledge of the ancient Icelandic sources. They seem to have been unable to utilize the results of Nordic scholarship except in so far as they are available in English, French or German. Their work was carried on in an atmosphere of mystery and secretiveness which precluded the assistance of specially qualified linguists and historians. As a result the editors' conclusions are at times either baseless or demonstrably wrong.[1]

Painter's and Skelton's interpretation of the longer "Island of Vínland" map legend is central to their thesis about the map and reveals the nature of some of their problems. One difficulty becomes apparent in the two men's attempts to interpret Bishop Eirik's motives and expectations when he set out for Vínland. Dealing with this particular riddle required an understanding of the Old Norse word *leita* (look for), which is as enigmatic in Old Norse as in modern English. The phrase "I'm looking for my dog" suggests that the speaker has some idea of where to look, but it precludes any precision.

Skelton's and Painter's focus on a word that neither of them understood was counterproductive, as were Skelton's efforts to interpret medieval Norse course directions for sailing between Iceland and Greenland. Some of those directions survive to this day in late-medieval manuscripts, but they are so vague that they would have been of little use to people who did not already have practical experience with those waters. Skelton nevertheless hoped that they might pinpoint for him the "landfalls" that would have been possible during the various climate shifts he believed had occurred. For example, he considered several possible locations for a particular place called Hvarf in some of those sailing directions.[2] However, the word *hvarf* in Old Norse simply meant "turning point" and furthermore was not unique to Greenland; it could signify any obvious feature ashore that indicated to knowledgeable sailors that it was time to change course direction. To determine a specific location of that description in Greenland would at the very least have required corroborative evidence.

Skelton's assumption that these old sailing directions contained precise verbal transmissions of Norse geographical knowledge took him beyond attempting to locate Hvarf in Greenland; it also led him to grapple with the term translated as "a day's sailing." Again, he looked for precision where none had ever existed. Doubtless, this loose term had some significance for the medieval Norse, but it does not furnish "precise data on the relative position of, and distance between, the lands and islands of the Norwegian Sea and the North Atlantic."[3] Although the phrase has occurred in northern literature since the ninth-century account of northern voyaging that Ohthere the Norwegian gave King Alfred during a sojourn in England, "a day's sailing" is so enigmatic that it has been the subject of much debate right up to the present time.[4]

In fact, it is hard to think of any aspect of Old Norse life, culture, and achievement on which there is general agreement. Scholars don't seem able even to make up their minds about what to call these particular medieval denizens of the Far North.

Who Were the Norse?

There is no shortage of works featuring the medieval Norse. All too often, however, these writings describe the brawny exploits of piratical Vikings and only occasionally address ordinary life in the Nordic countries during the Middle Ages. Beginning in the late eighth century, European monks who had fallen victim to Viking raiders wrote accounts of the Norse that were as biased and dramatic as the heroic varnish applied by Victorians besotted with the Icelandic sagas. Those early accounts elicited both sympathy for the victims and exhortations from the church hierarchy about these "pagans who came by sea."[5] More recently, celebrations of what has variously been called the "Viking Millennium" and the "Viking Discovery of America" have again capitalized on the image of daring, violent seafarers streaming out of the Far North, apparently unstoppable until confronted with American natives.

The Vikings were Norse, but not all Norse were Vikings. Historically speaking, there was a Viking Age, spanning roughly from the end of the eight century until about 1050–1100. That period constitutes only a segment of the Middle Ages, however, especially as the term applies to the Nordic countries, where medieval conditions lasted technologically, culturally, and economically until at least 1500. By that time, people farther south were enjoying both the fruits of the Renaissance and the excitement over the European rediscovery of America, some five centuries after the Norse had first gone there.

While the Norse command of the sea enabled them to terrorize in ever widening sweeps away from their Scandinavian homelands, most of them did not make their living from pillage but from farming as they knew it and from trade. Both activities involved ships, but not every shipowner had piratical aspirations. It is also important to acknowledge that the Norse populations included women and children, who are not known to have engaged actively in Viking raids, but to have been aboard those ships only when the intention was to settle in a new place.

The broader term *Norse* also needs definition. Eastward expeditions across the Baltic Sea and deep into Russia were usually made by the eastern Norse— that is, primarily by Swedish and Finnish people who had no known role in the Vínland voyages and who therefore fall outside the realm of this study. Westward enterprises mostly involved people from Norway, especially western Norway, and Denmark. They were the active players in this story.

Given that the lives of Norse coastal populations revolved around ships and boats, it is not surprising that archaeological ship finds in both Norway and Denmark represent designs for everyday use as well as for warfare, and that they show an evolution over more than two millennia. The forerunners of the flexible, clinker-built Viking ships existed by around AD 300 at the latest, and although the Norse use of sails in oceangoing ships is generally thought to have begun only about AD 700, propulsion by means of a sail would have been known to them long before that time. The problem would have been how to design a rigging that could withstand the stresses and strains of a sail big enough to propel a large vessel forward and to allow the crew sufficient control over the ship even with a huge canvas. Recent Norwegian research indicates that at least two centuries before Vikings in square-rigged sailing ships descended on Lindisfarne and other hapless British and continental locations, Norsemen in large, oceangoing *rowing* vessels had made peaceful trading voyages to the continent and, quite likely, to the British Isles, adding to both their store of exotic goods and skill in navigation.[6]

By about AD 1000, the western Norse—Vikings and others—had established English, Irish, and Scottish colonies that included the Isle of Man, the Hebrides, the Orkneys, and Shetland. In addition, they had made themselves at home in the Faeroes, and they had created viable new settlements as far away as Iceland and Greenland. Archaeological excavations in all of these places give ample evidence of artisanal skills, trade, and settlement of families living peacefully off the land and sea rather than subsisting on stolen goods and extortion.

Among those who first ventured farther into the northwestern Atlantic were many who had spent a generation or two in the British Isles, including a number of people of Celtic ancestry.[7] Not all were willing passengers. Some were slaves (the Norse commonly used and traded in slaves, especially during the pre-Christian period), and others were wives and children who probably had not been consulted about their residential preferences. Regardless of ancestry or social status, however, they had to adjust to the new realities awaiting them as Icelanders or Norse Greenlanders. They could rely only on the ancient skills known to the coastal farmers of the Far North and on the resources that the northern seas provide. Without those skills and resources, they would not have been able to settle successfully in Iceland and Greenland, and they would never have made it all the way to North America.

Voyaging to New Lands

The image of medieval men, women, children, and animals—crowding into open ships and crossing storm-tossed seas in order to build new lives in Iceland and Greenland—stretches the imaginations of modern urban dwellers. The travelers themselves would probably have stared in disbelief if told that their stoic endurance would go down in history as heroism, when in truth they were surviving as best they could by means of the ancient skills known to their kind because a growing scarcity of good land back home—preferably unencumbered by heavy-fisted, tax-hungry rulers—had set them looking for farm sites far away from their place of birth.

It is no coincidence that these North European sailors gained mastery over their part of the Atlantic long before the southern section of that ocean was considered fully navigable. Slowly but surely they had come to understand the prevailing winds and currents in their share of the ocean—conditions that did not include the equivalent of the dreaded "doldrums" farther south. It also helped their navigation that the North Atlantic is not an immense, unbroken expanse of water like that traversed by Christopher Columbus and his men many centuries later, but features a sweep of islands and archipelagoes all the way across to North America.

Good ships, finely honed sailing skills, and just plain luck played as big a part in the outcome of a voyage as the actual distances to be covered, as did sensible provisions (see Figure 2). Despite their "island hopping," the Norse were dependent on their ship-board supplies when they ventured far into the North Atlantic well before AD 1000. They carried water in well-coopered barrels, and they relied on food stores that could keep for many weeks at sea if necessary. The unsalted, wind-dried cod known as stockfish was, and still is, a specialty of the Far North with no equal back then as a source of durable, high-quality protein. Besides its excellent keeping qualities, it does not produce the thirst left by heavily salted foods. Nor does it require cooking in order to be digestible—even ashore the Norse often ate it uncooked, pounded into thin strips, and spread with butter or other fat. In short, stockfish was the ideal fare for a long journey on the ancient highway of the sea. A sufficient supply would also have sustained colonists during their first winter in a previously unpopulated land.

The Norse no doubt felt at home in their wide, watery world. The Danish forensic anthropologist Niels Lynnerup was surely right in his recent observation that to the Norse, "Greenland was probably an extension of inhabitable lands and fjords stretching from Norway over the Shetlands, Orkneys, Faeroes and Iceland, all the way to Labrador and Newfoundland."[8] Modern scholars nevertheless tend to assume that in the Middle Ages, the Norse Greenland colony was both geographically and conceptually remote to most people, including to the Norse elsewhere. Thus it has long been taken for granted that the Norwegian mid-thirteenth-century work *The King's Mirror* reflected reality when it claimed that men who braved the dangers of the voyage to Greenland did so to satisfy their curiosity, to win fame, and to gain wealth through a trade from which a good profit might be expected in a place that "lies so distant from other countries that men seldom visit it."[9]

Conveniently overlooked are the work's lavish descriptions of the many impediments to safe and profitable travel in the seas around Greenland, including huge monsters and horrendous ice conditions. While these descrip-

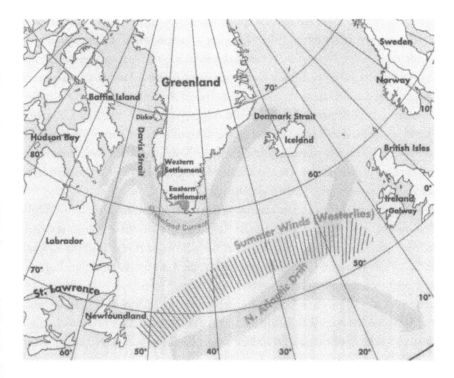

Figure 2. The North Atlantic, with prevailing currents and wind patterns during the sailing season. Copyright David O. Seaver.

tions in *The King's Mirror* might indeed make it seem reasonable that men would seldom go to Greenland, they are not a guide to how actual Greenland-farers approached their undertakings, especially when the reader of these stories recognizes them as fantasies so often found in other medieval literature intended to inspire awe concerning the outer limits of the world known to European savants.

Far North Was Far Away

In the unlikely event that fifteenth-century continental European scholars wrestled with the geography of the Far North, they would have found little in the delineations of the Vínland Map to sustain them. In reality, medieval cartographers were even less concerned with Greenland than with Norway, to which they gave little thought except as a presence far north in the ocean and chiefly known as a source of stockfish. For example, the Catalan map of 1375 (which predated Norway's loss of independence to Denmark through the Kalmar Treaty of 1397) depicts the kingdom of Norway simply as a large rectangle edged and bisected by mountain chains. A similar rectangle represents Norway on the Mecia de Viladestes chart (1413), but this work includes a new detail in the northwestern Atlantic in the form of a whaling scene off the coast of Iceland. Such peripheral treatment of the North persisted for a long time, omitting the American coasts investigated and exploited by the Norse inhabitants of a faraway place called Greenland.

The reason for this cartographic disinterest is not hard to find. While Iceland was visible in European trade from early on (its most unique resource being sulfur, and its most plentiful ones fish and wool cloth), nothing beyond Iceland had an acknowledged economic impact on pre-Columbian Europe, not even in the British Isles. Certainly, the Norse Greenlanders exported such commonly used goods as falcons, hides, wool cloth, eiderdown, blubber, walrus ivory, and various furs, but those wares were sold through Norwegian markets and were indistinguishable from other northern goods, including many from Iceland.

Had Greenland and Vínland been known as sources of gold, silk, or spices, European scholars from the eleventh century onward would quite likely have fitted both of those remote areas into their mapmaking. Similarly, if either Greenland or Vínland had been perceived as having a particular religious significance, both places might well have appeared on maps conceptually similar to those that show an Earthly Paradise in the middle of Asia. However, at that time Greenland and North America clearly did not represent either a celestial or mercantile paradise, and it is equally obvious from the cartographical record that the Norse themselves did little to call attention to the remote regions they themselves knew and used.

No Help from the Norse

Neither in the early eleventh century, nor at any other time prior to the mid-fifteenth century, when the Vínland Map was supposedly drawn, are the Norse known to have communicated to others the kind of information about North Atlantic regions that is featured in the Yale map's delineations. Nor does the map provide other plausible links between the pragmatic sailing knowledge of the medieval Norse and the geographical ideas taking shape in Europe in the fourteenth and fifteenth centuries, when portolan charts were beginning to develop into useful tools for those who navigated in the Mediterranean.

Maps are abstractions intended to place a given location in a larger context on a greatly reduced scale. However, there is no evidence at all that the medieval Norse made such abstractions; in fact, they did not even have a word for "map" or "chart." They relied mostly on experienced pilots, a wealth of sailing lore, and practical skills acquired at sea. Visual instructions to travelers would have been concrete and closely targeted to specific physical recognition marks on land or at sea.[10] The prominent and well-traveled Icelander Sturla Thordarson (d. 1284), who wrote down the earliest extant version of the *Book of Settlements*, clearly took this method of orientation for granted in the story of Örlyg Hrappsson, who had supposedly been fostered by the holy (and apocryphal) Hebridean bishop Patrick. The bishop told his foster son that on reaching Iceland, where Örlyg intended to settle, he should claim land where he could see two mountains from the sea, each with an adjoining valley. After a rough crossing and a winter spent in northwestern Iceland, Örlyg sailed south and west around the Snæfell Peninsula, where he spotted two mountains with adjoining valleys as he came up the fjord south of the Snæfell glacier. He knew then that he had reached his destination.[11]

Confident of their ability to go wherever they needed to go, the Norse would have seen no benefit in sharing their geographical knowledge with European cartographers whose maps would in any event have been of no use to ocean navigators like themselves. Medieval Icelandic treatises on geography reveal that while the learned Icelanders who wrote them were steeped in the theories of their continental colleagues, they rarely saw the need to brandish the practical sailing knowledge that the Norse had acquired (see Chapter 7).

Many Icelanders, including the famous Haukr Erlendsson (d. 1324), who prided himself on being a direct descendant of Thorfinn Karlsefni of Vínland fame, repeatedly traveled to various parts of the long Norwegian coast and knew that region well. The Vínland Map gives no evidence of such Icelandic knowledge, nor would one guess from this map that fur-trading Norwegians had sailed past the North Cape and across the southern Barents Sea on their way to Biarmaland (Russia, in the White Sea region),[12] starting long before the birth of Eirik the Red and lasting until the early thirteenth century. Although the Yale map supposedly demonstrates the Norsemen's direct knowledge of northern regions so remote that Adam of Bremen could only dimly imagine them, its delineations give no hint of knowledge thus gained. All told, one must look in vain for evidence in the Vínland Map of any parts of the Far North that were well known to the Norse.

Eirik the Red, Mariner and Merchant

The first European colonizer of Greenland, Eirik "the Red" Thorvaldsson, is generally believed to have gone with his father from southwestern Norway to Iceland after the two men had broken the law of their native land.[13] While the epithet "the Red" no doubt referred to the color of his hair, it could have signified a volatile temper, for the saga literature, which presents him as a forceful man with a gift for both friendship and leadership, also notes that his career in Iceland was punctuated by further violence. The first chapter of "Saga of the Greenlanders" (and chapter 89 in the *Book of Settlements*) tells about his being outlawed for murder (probably about AD 981–82) and his decision to spend the three years of his outlawry sailing westward from Iceland in search of some skerries that his relative Gunnbjörn Ulfsson had spotted earlier. These skerries have gone down in history as "Gunnbjarnarskerries" and are vaguely defined by modern scholars as located somewhere off the Ammassalik region in southeastern Greenland. The Canadian scientist Waldemar Lehn recently demonstrated that the "skerries" Gunnbjörn had spotted were almost certainly a mirage of the Greenland coast, projected toward Iceland and "arising specifically from optical ducting under a sharp temperature inversion."[14]

It is clear that Eirik explored more than a mirage, however, because he kept going until he reached a huge and solid landmass that he subsequently named Greenland in order to lure other colonists to the green pastures at the heads of deep fjords indenting the southwest coast. He knew that his fellow Norse would not settle anywhere without their cattle, sheep, and goats, the mainstays of traditional Norse stock farming that supplied not only leather and raw materials for clothing, but also the occasional meat dish as well as milk and milk products.

Eirik's three-year reconnaissance in Greenland enabled him to tempt his fellow settlers with more than a promise of fat cattle. Twenty-five ships loaded with people and their belongings set out for Greenland the summer after he had reported his discoveries back home in Iceland. Although only fourteen ships reached their destination, they were enough to start the Eastern Settlement, the main colony in the southwest, while "others went to the Western

Settlement" and set up a small community there as well, according to the saga description.[15] It has recently been demonstrated scientifically that both of the Greenland Norse settlements, located about four hundred miles apart in southwestern Greenland, were indeed populated around AD 1000.[16] Modern archaeological analyses also agree with the saga indications that during Eirik's first Greenland venture, he had explored at least as far as the inner part of the present Nuuk region, and that he had immediately staked out a family claim there to what was most likely Sandnes, always the best and most strategic farm site in that part.

Eirik had evidently realized that the northernmost area he chose for settlement possessed certain obvious economic advantages over the main settlement farther south because no shortage of land down in the Eastern Settlement demanded a satellite colony that early. The northernmost and smaller of the two Norse Greenland colonies, which the Norse called the Western Settlement due to the westward trend of the Greenland coast, was marginal for stock farming despite the pastures and sheltered farm sites found in the inner fjord areas (see Figure 3). Although the uplands were as rich in game as the surrounding waters were full of fish and seals, more important still was the settlement's location halfway between the main Norse colony in the south and Disko Island in the north.

Disko Bay was the center for the northern hunting grounds exploited by both Arctic natives and by the Norse, who called the region Norðrseta. The Western Settlement would have represented an important head start on the northern spring and summer hunt, and the first European to take systematic advantage of this fact appears to have been Eirik the Red. He came from an old trading culture and knew that if he and his fellow settlers wanted to import goods to their distant new colony, they must have the means with which to pay. An established market had long existed in Europe for such Arctic goods as blubber from sea mammals, walrus hides, narwhal horns, polar bear skins, and other furs, eiderdown, gyrfalcons, and above all for walrus tusks. Prized all over Northern Europe as a substitute for elephant ivory and actually preferred to the latter by many artisans elsewhere, the tusks were nonperishable and easy to ship and rewarded the hunter well for his trouble.[17]

The proximity of such valuable export goods constituted a good enough reason for Eirik to urge a settlement up north right away and to make a family claim to its most advantageous site. The "Saga of Eirik the Red" says that Eirik's youngest son, Thorstein, who is unlikely to have been offered second-

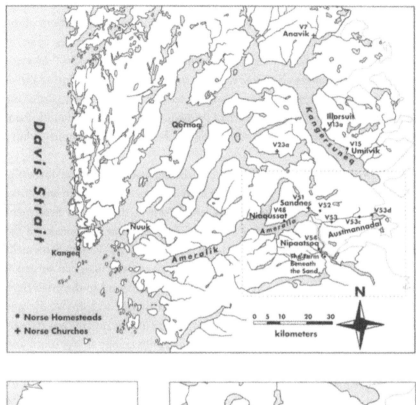

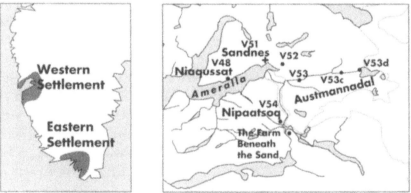

Figure 3. The locations of the Western and Eastern Settlements of the medieval Norse colony in Greenland. Copyright David O. Seaver.

best, owned half of a farm in Lysufjord (now Ameralla) in the Western Settlement. The strategic importance of the Sandnes site as an entrepôt in deliberate expeditions to explore the economic potential of the land eventually sighted in the west is evident from the two "Vínland Sagas." Indeed, the very existence of the Western Settlement helped the Norse find their way to the American continent shortly after their arrival in Greenland because they drew upon navigational knowledge obtained through the Arctic hunts that must have been under way shortly thereafter.

Norðrseta: The Northern Hunting Grounds

The name Norðrseta appears to have included both the Canadian Lancaster Sound area and the West Greenland coast at least up to about seventy-three degrees north. Judging from the recent archaeological record, it probably also extended to almost eighty-three degrees north in the Smith Sound-Kane Basin region. Here, in 1979 and again in 1995, the Danish-Canadian archaeologist Peter Schledermann and his colleague Karen McCullough examined the plateau on Washington Irving Island where the British explorer George S. Nares and his men had found two well-built cairns, thickly encrusted with lichen, when they went ashore in 1875. Unfortunately, Nares had ordered the cairns torn down and used the rocks from one of them to build a cairn of his own, leaving the second cairn as rubble. However, by combining the surviving physical evidence with the documentary record and a careful drawing done by a member of the Nares expedition, the two Canadian scholars became convinced that these cairns were the work of medieval Norse travelers, of whom there are other distinct reminders in the same High Arctic area, usually—but not invariably—discovered during excavations of medieval Dorset and Thule occupation sites.[18]

A touching reminder remains of the Norse Greenlanders' Arctic voyages: a small, beautifully incised rune stone found in connection with three cairns on the island of Kingittorssuaq in the Upernavik region, directly opposite the entrance to Lancaster Sound at almost seventy-three degrees north.[19] The rune stone's message is from three young men who said they had carved the runes and raised a cairn over their message on Rogation Day (either April 25 or one of the three days before Ascension Day). The text is still clearly legible, but the year is opaque. The inscription is believed to refer to sometime in the mid-thirteenth century.[20]

The island of Kingittorsuaq is surrounded by powerful currents and innumerable skerries, both of which make for dangerous sailing. However, this part of Norðrseta is so rich in animal resources that since time immemorial it has also been vital to Arctic natives as a source of meat and blubber as well as of eiderdown, narwhal horns, polar bear skins, and other valuable commodities. If the three Kingittorssuaq cairns were not simply marking the achievement of safe arrival at that particular location, the mission of those three young men who carved the runes may well have been to build the cairns as guides for other Norse who found it worth the risk to sail into those roiling waters.

Because the written evidence for voyages to the Far North in Greenland begins only with the late-twelfth-century work *Historia Norvegiæ*, the received wisdom has been that the Norse colonists waited some generations before engaging in far northern hunts up along their west coast, at which time they were supposedly motivated by the need for tithe goods that arose after Greenland got its first official bishop. Tithing cannot have been the primary impetus behind the Norse Greenlanders' systematic search for marketable goods, however, because it was in consequence of their demonstrable access to walrus ivory and other valuable export goods that they obtained their own episcopal see and the services of the Norwegian cleric Arnald. The prominent Greenlander Einar Sokkason had brought walrus tusks and a live polar bear to Norway to impress King Sigurd and his church officials with the Greenlanders' ability to pay for an episcopal establishment.[21]

Bishop Arnald was consecrated by Archbishop Asser in Lund, Sweden, in 1124. On his way out to his new diocese he wintered in Iceland. The *Icelandic Annals* note it as an unusual event because there were three bishops present at the Althing (General Assembly) in the summer of 1126.[22] There is no annal entry concerning Arnald's actual arrival in Greenland, but it is safe to assume that he completed his voyage to his new diocese because there was no reason not to do so at a time when the Greenland colony had proved itself viable and while the Roman Church was still in an expansionist missionary mode. In fact, about that same time (1122–23) there was a flurry of fake letters claiming retroactively that various archbishops of Hamburg had been given specific authority over Greenland. The short "Tale of the Greenlanders" (*Grænlendinga þáttr*), which the modern Icelandic scholar Ólafur Halldórsson judges to be a late-twelfth-century account based on good sources, is the only written account of Arnald's time in Greenland.[23]

The importance of the northern hunting grounds would no doubt have grown as the result of a greater need for export goods that arose when the Greenlanders finally got a regular bishop and became part of the organized Roman Church.[24] The Greenland Church reached its organizational zenith during the thirteenth and early fourteenth centuries; most Norse finds in the High Arctic have so far been relegated to the thirteenth century. It was also in the early to mid-thirteenth century that the three Norse Greenland hunters carved their small rune stone on Kingittorsuaq Island.[25]

Bishop Eirik of Vínland's notoriety *preceded* Bishop Arnald, who was by all accounts the first properly constituted representative of the organized Roman Church in Greenland. George Painter thus had no historical basis for his assumption that in Vínland, Bishop Eirik would have been responsible for installing priests, consecrating churches, and providing "the indispensable sacraments of the Roman Church," much less for supervising the collection of tithes from that new land. Furthermore, whatever else may have happened to Bishop Eirik on his western expedition, it is unlikely that he "undertook for reasons both religious and commercial the conversion of the fur-trading Skraelings, perhaps through native interpreters educated from childhood . . . by the settlers."[26]

Norse Relations with Arctic Natives

By "fur-trading Skraelings" Painter meant Amerindians, but the term also applied to the Arctic peoples with whom the Norse are known to have interacted.

Since 1977, "Inuit" has been the preferred name for the modern indigenous people of Eastern Arctic Canada and Greenland, but scholars still often refer to the pre-1500 Dorset and Thule peoples collectively as Eskimos, a term whose exact origin is still disputed. This usage is intended to distinguish those peoples from the native North Americans to whom the first Renaissance explorers from Europe referred as "Indians." However, until the eighteenth century, the term *Eskimo* was also used to refer to the native North Americans (Amerindians) in the region abutting Thule territory.[27] The European fishermen and whalers who descended on northeastern America after 1500 were thus no more discerning than the Norse, who referred to the two Eskimo peoples and the Amerindians as Skrælingar—inferior and puny sorts. Regardless of how the Norse spoke among themselves about their nearest neighbors, however, they were clearly used to encountering these strangers on either side of the Davis Strait.

The Palæo-Eskimo culture known as the Dorset culture preceded the Neo-

Eskimo Thule culture in Greenland, so the Dorset people are likely to have been the first Arctic natives with whom the Norse made contact during their northern hunting forays. The opportunity and timing of Norse contact with both Eskimo cultures is the subject of much debate to this day, however, because the dates for Dorset and Thule tenure in various locations are not yet fixed. As the Canadian archaeologist Robert McGhee recently explained, problems with radiocarbon dating and its interpretation make it particularly difficult to date early medieval remains at those high latitudes.[28] Problems with dating also make it harder to assess both the variables in Norse relations with the two Arctic peoples and the dynamics that governed the Dorset and Thule inhabitants, on both sides of the Davis Strait, in their relations with each other.

Much of the evidence about northern forays by the Greenland Norse comes from various tiny carvings fashioned by Arctic natives and clearly intended to represent Europeans as well as from a wealth of Norse artifacts found very far north in medieval Dorset and Thule Eskimo ruins in both Greenland and Arctic Canada. Quite recently, archaeologists found part of a European cast-metal pot all the way up in Smith Sound in a probable Dorset site dating from about the end of the thirteenth century.[29]

Peter Schledermann and his scientific team discovered more than fifty items of Norse origin in late-twelfth- or early-thirteenth-century Thule ruins off the east coast of Ellesmere Island. Among these articles were a carpenter's plane (with the blade missing) and several metal objects, such as ship rivets and pieces of chain mail. Some of this loot may have come from a pilfered shipwreck since it is unlikely that a live Norseman would have handed over his carpenter's plane if it was in good working condition, but Schledermann's overall judgment is that the circumstances in which the objects were found demonstrate face-to-face encounters between the Thule and Norse cultures. His team's discovery of chain mail also raises some interesting questions about the type of travelers who had braved these waters because chain mail was an expensive possession and would have been an unwieldy garment for fishermen and hunters going about their usual business.[30]

In none of the many instances of Norse objects found at Thule and Dorset sites can one be certain that a direct exchange of goods with the Norse had occurred, but the presence of Eskimo artifacts embedded in Norse Greenland farm ruins certainly suggests actual contact, as do the portrait carvings already mentioned. While one must also allow for traditional gift giving when objects changed hands, the beam of a small, folding bronze balance scale of the type used by Norse traders, which Patricia Sutherland found at a Thule site on northwestern Ellesmere Island, in her judgment quite likely implies trade between the Norse and the Arctic natives.[31] For such a relatively peaceful activity to have taken place, relations between the two trading parties must have been reasonably amicable, and the Norse would obviously have had to travel in far northern waters to engage in those exchanges.

From Arctic Greenland to Arctic North America

Observations made by the Norse colonists while hunting in northern seas would soon have suggested to them that a coast existed even farther west. Hunters would have had to steer generally west to remain in open water while pursuing the walrus, their prize game, because these huge animals must haul up out of the water to rest and therefore follow the ice as it recedes north (hugging the Canadian coast) in the summer season, to where the Davis Strait narrows (before widening again into Baffin Bay), trapping the drift ice. Under those circumstances, some of the Norse hunters would eventually have seen the distant glaciers of Baffin Island from out at sea. *Hillingar*—inverted reflections similar to those that very likely accounted for the so-called Gunnbjarnarskerries—are also known from that region and would have constituted additional portents of nearby land. Experienced seafarers would not have taken long to link that other coast with Bjarni Herjolfsson's tale, told in the "Saga of the Greenlanders."

According to this story, the summer after Eirik the Red and his first settlers had colonized Greenland (about AD 990), Bjarni returned to Iceland from Norway and learned that his father had emigrated with Eirik. Bjarni's subsequent pursuit of his father ended successfully, but before he spotted Herjolf's new farm, he had drifted way off course from the southwestern part of Greenland for which he had been told to aim. While sailing north again to regain the proper latitude, he observed a long, green, forested coast that gradually changed to a landscape of bare rocks and snow. Most of that barren stretch is now known as Baffin Island.

The "Saga of the Greenlanders" next relates that Bjarni reported these sightings after his safe arrival in Greenland. From such a story, those of his fellow Norse who had already become aware of the snowy cliffs across the water in the northwest could reasonably expect to find forests in that western land if they sailed far enough south. If Bjarni's tale actually represented news and was not just the saga narrator's conflation of several chance sightings by previous Norse sailors, the information must have been welcome indeed because Greenland lacked proper forests. Both driftwood and the native trees of Greenland—birch, willow, and mountain ash—had their uses, but they could not yield the sinewy heartwood planks needed to construct the ships that played such an important part in all medieval Norse societies. Greenland also lacked the bog iron necessary for the production of ship rivets. The Norse Greenlanders' hope of finding resources so vital to their domestic economy would have been a powerful incentive for sending that first deliberate expedition across the water.

The Vínland Voyages

The two "Vínland Sagas" differ considerably in their accounts of those first voyages undertaken to explore the resources of an unfamiliar western land, but both sagas demonstrate that the initiative and leadership for the expeditions rested with Eirik the Red and his family, as was right and proper. Like their contemporaries in Iceland, the Norse Greenlanders lived in a hierarchical society dominated by the chieftains, and Eirik was chief among all men there. The captains on the voyages commemorated by the "Vínland Sagas" were Eirik the Red's sons and other members of his immediate circle, including the renowned Icelander Thorfinn Karlsefni ("Makings-of-a-Man") Thordarson, who had married the widow of Thorstein Eiriksson.

One of the many troubling aspects of the Vínland Map is that it defines Vínland but overlooks the immensely long coastlines on both sides of the Davis Strait, which the Norse had already explored by the time they discovered grapes. The debate about the Vínland Map's depiction of Greenland as an island has also consistently ignored how the Norse perceived that country, just as the decades-long discussion about the map's "Island of Vínland" fails to take into account the meaning of the Norse designation *Vínland*. When the Norse told about their early experience in North America, they indicated that even those first voyages did not climax with the discovery of an island but involved going down a very long coast, presumably of a mainland, to which they gave successive names that reflected what they had observed ashore.

When discussing these millennium-old ventures, scholars still use the names that the Norse assigned to the three main American areas they investigated. The rock slabs and glaciers of Baffin Island were the most conspicuous features of the region they named *Helluland,* and which would also have included Cape Chidley and other treeless areas immediately south of the Hudson Strait. The designation *Markland,* which refers to the North American forest belt, signals that the Norse had come far enough south to find trees, a very desirable commodity indeed. Unfortunately for precision seekers, this forest belt has an undulating northern perimeter and continues both west and south for a very long way, varying only in the mix of tree species, so it is impossible to define either the Norse boundaries of Helluland and Markland or where that eminently useful Markland began to include the luxuries of Vínland, with its implied promise of grapes. The presence of grapes was merely the most remarkable new feature in a landscape that still featured trees.

Each name reflected the explorers' assessment of a given region's economic potential and demonstrates that those well-organized expeditions sought to profit from New World resources. Further support for this interpretation comes from details such as the "Saga of the Greenlanders" description of the Skrælings' eagerness to barter for cloth, which was a reliable Norse export staple.[32] While this particular detail may have been added later by the person who first wrote down the saga after two centuries of oral transmission, there is no mistaking the writer's assumption that this far-flung western voyage was a commercial venture.

The saga does not indicate where this supposed barter episode took place, however. Nor is it clear exactly where Eirik's son Leif decided that "Forest Land" became "Wine Land," because a member of his party had excitedly reported his discovery of "wine berries" (Old Norse: *vínber*). Despite this lack of precision, it is still widely and mistakenly assumed that Vínland ought to be definable in terms of modern place names and recognizable from the descriptions in the two "Vínland Sagas." Neither is the case.

With perseverance and luck, archaeologists may discover further evidence of how far south the Norse traveled in America, but efforts to determine the exact location of Vínland will remain counterproductive because they ignore fundamental aspects of the Norse naming practice to which the designations Helluland, Markland, and Vínland were no exception. During their expansion into the northwestern Atlantic, the medieval Norse assigned place names to reflect a remarkable feature of a general region only, without spatial definition and without excluding other observable features.

Iceland, which certainly offers its denizens much besides ice, is said to have been circumnavigated and defined as an island by Gardar Svavarsson before the Norse decided to settle there, but the descriptive name that has endured for the whole country was originally assigned to just one part of it by the disgruntled Norwegian traveler Floki Vilgerdarson, who spent a thoroughly disagreeable winter there in the late ninth century.[33] He had little or no concept of what the rest of the country might be like. In a similar manner, Eirik the Red named his own fledgling colony Greenland without knowing either the shape or the size of what turned out to be the world's biggest island. All that mattered to him and his followers was that the areas where they settled were green enough to support livestock, and that the adjacent coastal waters could provide additional food and trade goods.

The "Vínland Sagas" suggest that the Norse appreciated sheltered conditions and therefore had a predilection for investigating bays, fjords, and other inlets. When Eirik the Red explored Greenland, for example, he did not see anything of promise to settlers until he had ventured far enough into those deep fjords to spot green hillsides and quivering birches. Although sailing into those long, unknown inlets was an act of faith, it reflected a sure sense that the farther into a fjord or bay one goes, the more benign the landscape is likely to be. Eirik's decision to overwinter on an island is another example of cautious deliberation. The Norse used the same sensible approach when they explored North America in search of the timber they eventually found in Markland.

Wood analyses performed on ten ship's parts found in Norse ruins at both of the medieval Greenland settlements indicated six samples of larch, which did not at that time grow in Greenland, Iceland, or Norway. Poul Nørlund had also found larch used in a coffin when he excavated the churchyard at Herjolfsnes in 1921, in an area that contained mostly graves dating from the fourteenth century onward.[34] Larch is native only to North America and part of Siberia and is common in the Labrador region called Markland where the Norse were still sailing in 1347.

L'Anse aux Meadows

Attempts to answer the question of exactly where the Norse went on any of their American ventures are hampered by two factors peculiarly frustrating to modern archaeologists. One is that the Labrador coast covers an immense area; the other is that after so many centuries, evidence of short-term stays by a very small number of people is hard to detect even if left undisturbed by European settlers during the so-called contact period in North America, which began about 1500.

Some generalizations are nevertheless possible. Norse objects found at American sites suggest both that later voyages from Greenland were oriented toward quite northern resources and that they were seasonal and involved small crews, who brought little more from home than what they needed for the task ahead and evidently saw no need to construct real houses. The "Norse longhouse" foundations that the Canadian archaeologist Thomas Lee thought he had found in the Ungava Bay region, and the subject of much discussion, have been shown to be remains of Dorset structures.[35]

The Norse ruin site at L'Anse aux Meadows on Newfoundland's Northern Peninsula so far constitutes the only unassailable evidence of Norse dwellings in America. They were discovered by the Norwegian explorer Helge Ingstad after an intense and systematic search of the general area most likely explored by the Norse. Subsequent professional investigations of this location, led by Ingstad's wife, the archaeologist, Anne Stine Ingstad, were still incomplete in 1964 when the general American public first learned about the Ingstads' discovery, but there was already decisive evidence that this was a genuine Norse site at which women had been present. A small soapstone spindle whorl was the proof.[36] The sagas were thus on firm ground when they referred to female Norse participants in these early western ventures. Scientific evidence about the general composition of the crews using the place also confirms other aspects of the saga literature.

The houses at L'Anse aux Meadows are now widely believed to represent Leif Eiriksson's well-chosen wintering camp. However, it is clear that Vínland cannot be equated with Newfoundland, although this grapeless island should no doubt be included in the general Vínland designation. All one can say with reasonable certainty is that the Norse quite likely explored at least parts of Nova Scotia because Vínland must have included an area on the south side of the St. Lawrence, where both wild grapes and the American butternut tree (*Juglans cinerea*) grew and still grow.[37] Fruits and wood (the latter worked with metal tools) of butternut have been found in the thin Norse culture layer excavated at L'Anse aux Meadows, which is datable to about AD 1000. However, while this discovery supports the mention of grapes in connection with Vínland, it still does not define the location or extent of Vínland.[38]

Regardless of which Vínland saga one reads, one finds a sizeable contingent of Icelanders involved in those earliest ventures under the leadership of their chieftain Thorfinn Karlsefni. Recent tests involving ten jasper fire-starter fragments found at L'Anse aux Meadows similarly indicate a comparatively large Icelandic presence and thus tie in with the Icelandic saga writers' focus on their fellow countrymen. Such "fire stones" were considered personal equipment and had a rather short working life, which would suggest that any fragment located far from the stone's point of origin had recently accompanied its owner to the place where it was found. With his team, Kevin Smith at the Buffalo Museum of Science compared the distinctive "fingerprints" of these jasper fragments to one another and to jasper samples from Norway, Iceland, Greenland, Newfoundland, New Brunswick, and Nova Scotia, as well as from Maine, and down the eastern U.S. seaboard, including the Great Lakes drainage.[39]

Both Greenlandic and Icelandic jaspers were found among the ten samples studied. Greenlandic jasper, from the outer coast of the Western Settlement region, was found only in and around Hall F at L'Anse aux Meadows. This structure appears to have been the most hierarchically important building at the site, and the presence of Greenlandic "fire stones" there is a reminder of the Greenlandic overlordship in these American undertakings. Icelandic jasper turned up in and around all of the dwellings. The predominance of Icelandic jasper thus suggests that there were Icelanders in every house while a comparatively small number of Greenlanders shared Hall F with their Icelandic cousins.[40]

Birgitta Wallace, who (on behalf of Parks Canada) took over for Anne Stine Ingstad as leader of the L'Anse aux Meadows excavations, confirmed her predecessor's judgment that the thinness of the Norse culture layer there suggests a quite brief period of use—a decade or two at most. Calling the site the "gateway" to Vínland—thus merely a part of the region given that name—Wallace notes that during the site's short-term use, it appears to have functioned as a strategically placed transshipment station for American goods intended for Greenland-based trade. The structures on the site suggest the presence of three or four chieftains in charge of large crews during ship repairs, overwintering, exploration, and resource exploitation.[41]

Various saga details indicate that Wallace is also right in her estimate of the number of chieftains involved. In addition, the surviving literature supports the archaeological evidence that actual Norse tenure was of rather short duration in the region so tantalizingly named Vínland.

Grapes and Grain

Long before the Ingstads' discovery on Newfoundland's decidedly grapeless, but definitely green and grassy Northern Peninsula, the discussion about the true location of Vínland included a linguistic argument, which claimed that the prefix "*Vin-*" in this name actually has a short vowel and thus means "grassy field," corresponding to the suffix "*-vin*" in Bjørgvin (Bergen), for example. However, linguistic scholars have demonstrated that even as a suffix, this particular usage of "*vin*" had ceased well before the colonization of Iceland and Greenland.[42] It is conspicuously infrequent, not to say absent, in Norse-inspired place names reaching from the Scottish Isles and the Faeroes to Iceland and Greenland. If Vinland in the sense of "Green-Meadow-Land" had still been viable nomenclature at the time of Eirik the Red, signifying excellent pasturage, Eirik would surely have applied it to Greenland, which he reportedly named because he wanted people to believe in the country's farming opportunities.

It is doubtful that in sailing west from Greenland, with its sufficient pastures, the Norse would have become unduly excited by meadows on the American side. Furthermore, the Norse knew very well what kind of berry produced wine because they had been trading with and on the European continent for several centuries by AD 1000. Marauding Vikings who maintained wintering places in France and on the Iberian Peninsula are unlikely to have been slow learners in matters of food and drink, and the Norwegians who stayed at home would have enjoyed early imports of wine, raisins, and even fresh grapes from no farther away than Germany.

While it is reasonable to assume that the Icelandic saga writers passed along much concrete information that had survived oral transmission, it would be a mistake to think that all descriptive details in the "Vínland Sagas" (including those pertaining to landscapes and locations) are of factual value in the form they have reached us. For example, when describing the particular wonders of Vínland, the "Saga of Eirik the Red" notes that "self-sown wheat" also grew there. That is an embellishment, some two centuries after the event, of the nonspecific "unsown crops" mentioned about 1075 by Adam of Bremen, who may well have heard about the wild rice known to have been a feature of the St. Lawrence region both then and now.[43]

There is nevertheless a rational explanation for this literary mutation of Vínland crops. When the Norse first explored America, there were already a number of Christians in both Iceland and Greenland, but neither country was officially Christian. By the thirteenth century, when the two sagas were written, the Roman Church was long established in Iceland as well as in Greenland, and wine and wheat were known as the two ingredients essential to the Eucharist. Pope Gregory IX had made that abundantly clear to the Norwegian archbishop in 1237.[44] Both wine and wheat had to be imported into Iceland, so a place where both commodities supposedly grew wild for the taking would have been considered a uniquely blessed land—a kind of Paradise. Not unexpectedly, it is evident from the surviving sources that nobody attempted to alleviate Icelandic sacramental needs with American imports.

As realistic and shrewd traders, both Icelanders and Greenlanders would have known how to maximize their profits by avoiding middlemen as much as possible, by selling their wares in Europe through established outlets for traditional northern products, and by ensuring that the distances connecting them to European trade remained manageable. European merchants were already dealing in grapes, raisins, and other exotica obtained from reasonably reliable suppliers and would not have waited anxiously for shipments from Vínland via Greenland and Norway, however plump the Vínland grapes may have been at the time of harvest.

Although the wild grapes of Vínland proved worthy of notice in the subsequent literature, and although the presence of green meadows would always have been welcome to stock farmers, the forests of Markland would have been far more important than either grass or grapes to the Icelanders and Greenlanders who first reached America in the early eleventh century. After weighing the luxury produce of Vínland against the lack of welcome they had experienced among the natives in that region, the Greenland Norse evidently decided that there was no profit in future voyages taking them several hundred miles beyond what was necessary for their own needs, where materials for shipbuilding took precedence.

Abandoning Vínland

Besides the saga writers' conversion of Vínland crops into sacramental wheat and wine available for the taking, there are other literary indications that Vínland had already by the thirteenth century achieved a mythical status in Iceland, divorced from factual geographical knowledge. When learned medieval Icelanders wrote about distant western lands (of whose actual existence they were far more aware than scholars on the continent), some of their stories did not involve Greenland at all and were so fanciful that one must look for the influence of continental geographical tradition and Irish legends.[45]

There are already mythlike overtones to the report that Bishop Eirik had to "search" for Vínland in the early twelfth century. The descending veil of unreality is also visible in the *Book of Settlements*, the first known written version of which goes back to just before 1300, although it is said to have been at least partly compiled by Ari Thorgilsson the Learned (1068–1148). This work tells about Ari, the son of Mar Atlason, who reportedly drifted off to *Hvítramannaland* (White Men's Country), located west in the ocean near "Vínland the Good" and said to be six days' sailing from Ireland.[46] In this instance, "Vínland the Good" was made to fit with theoretical notions of geography, while the White Men's Country probably has more in common with Irish tales than with actual Norse peregrinations at any time in history.

The voyage of Gudleif Gudlaugsson from Straumfjord, related in the *Eyrbyggja saga* (probably composed around the middle of the thirteenth century), is even vaguer about a presumed trans-Atlantic destination. Gudleif was overtaken by a gale on his way to Ireland and drifted out to sea with his companions, supposedly sometime late in Saint Olaf's reign, which ended in 1030. After the ship had been driven off to the west and then southwest, "well out of sight of land," land finally came into view. The travelers were greeted ashore by an old man who refused to tell them either his own name or the name of the country they had reached. According to subsequent conjecture back in Iceland, he had doubtless been Björn from Breiðavík in Iceland, forced by Snorri the Priest (d. 1031) to leave home after having compromised Snorri's sister.[47]

These apocryphal travel tales should not obscure the fact that the medieval Icelanders knew very well that there was plenty of real land to the west of them besides Greenland. Along with similar stories, they most likely reflect a pervasive notion among the Icelanders that there was enough unexplored territory out there to serve as background for any number of tales. The anonymous author of *Eyrbyggja saga* was no stranger to either the Greenland colony or the Vínland adventures of Thorfinn Karlsefni and his men. The writer would have known that those who explored that far western land in the early eleventh century had returned home with stories of a very long coast indeed.

Even if only Norse Greenlanders, without the assistance of Icelanders, found it worth their while to cross the Davis Strait after the so-called Vínland voyages, Icelanders and Greenlanders maintained a close association during those earliest voyages, and cultural and familial bonds endured between the two Norse outposts. This connection remained sturdy for a long time, not only because of continued direct voyages between Iceland and Greenland, but because of a wide-reaching North Atlantic network among the medieval Norse generally.

The nature and duration of this network runs counter to Skelton's belief that residual information about the Norse in Greenland and North America would necessarily have come either through the fifteenth-century Anglo-Icelandic trade nexus or through the channels he presumed had existed within the Roman Church. Although modern archaeological excavations demonstrate that the Norse in both of the Greenland settlements kept in touch with each other to the last and retained contact with the other societies around the North Atlantic rim well into the fifteenth century, Skelton (like the author of the Vínland Map) appears to have been unaware of this continuing Icelandic access to the Greenlanders' knowledge of their own country and of the lands in the west. His failure to allow for communications between his own country and Greenland is easier to understand, because current knowledge about this subject is the result of archaeological work done after 1965.

Several versions of the coat of arms (circa 1330) used by the Scottish Campbell clan, found at Nipaatsoq, far inland from the present Greenland capital of Nuuk, constitute archaeological evidence of contact between the British Isles and the Western Settlement (see Figure 4).[48] In the Eastern Settlement there are also signs of a connection with the British Isles. For example, a late-medieval manufactured table knife, discovered in a late stratum at the episcopal site of Gardar, has a counterpart found in London. A pendant of English-type pewter turned up at Hvalsey, a large farm site that still has substantial remains of a Norse stone church and that modern scholars think was an important trading center throughout the duration of the colony. From the shore of the Greenland colony's southernmost trading port, at Herjolfsnes, comes a crucifix made of jet, suggesting an origin from the area around Whitby. Particularly intriguing are four pieces of semimanufactured iron that the Danish archaeologist C. L. Vebæk discovered in the uppermost stratum of a late-period Norse farm ruin quite far inland in the Vatnahverfi region (see Figure 5). These pieces would meet the description of the small iron pieces called "osmunds" that the fifteenth-century English used to barter for codfish in Iceland.[49] The English obtained their good-quality iron chiefly from Sweden (technically the home of

Figure 4. The coat of arms (circa 1330) of the Scottish Campbell clan. Sample found in a Norse ruin at Nipaatsoq in the Western Settlement. The original is at the Greenland National Museum and Archives in Nuuk. Reproduced with kind permission.

osmund iron), Normandy, and Spain.[50] One of the four pieces found in Greenland was recently analyzed by the Danish scientist Vagn Fabritius Buchwald, who judged it to have been produced in Sweden and noted that the undulations would be due to pitting from corrosion.[51] Buchwald did not examine the other three iron pieces shown in Figure 5.

Figure 5. Four pieces of semimanufactured iron found at Ø71 in the Eastern Settlement by C. L. Vebæk. Photo and permission to reproduce provided by C. L. Vebæk before his death.

There is no telling who had brought fifteenth-century Rhenish stoneware to the Norse Greenlanders, of which fragments have been found at both Hvalsey and Herjolfsnes.[52] Nor is there as yet a satisfactory explanation for the stylish fifteenth-century costumes made of homespun Greenland wool in which Norse Greenlanders had been wrapped for burial at Herjolfsnes. Some of these garments appear to postdate the period of 1406–10, when contact between Greenland and Norway was last recorded.[53] Such objects show that loss of contact with Norway beginning in the last quarter of the fourteenth century cannot be interpreted either as the start of complete isolation for the Norse Greenlanders or, by extension, as a major cause of their colony's ultimate disappearance.

Together with the sparse documentary material available, the archaeological evidence from Greenland suggests wide North Atlantic contacts as well as a viable Norse Greenland community well into the fifteenth century. This should come as no great surprise. The fact that the Norse Greenlanders were engaged for almost half a millennium in trade and travel indicates both that they had goods to trade abroad and that they still had ships, despite the lack of forests in their own country. These wider connections indicate that in the Greenland colony's fifteenth-century "final phase," the Greenlanders were affected both by their continued European contact and their proximity to North America.

Continued American Connections

As practical people needing the newly discovered American resources, the Norse Greenlanders were unlikely to give up on North America almost as soon as they had ascertained its economic promise. They had encountered Markland considerably north of the L'Anse aux Meadows site, so they knew from their earliest crossings that they could find both lumber and iron (and top off their profits with luxurious North American furs) in places much closer to home than the St. Lawrence region. Furthermore, there is solid evidence at L'Anse aux Meadows of Norse iron extraction from the local bog iron, which means that they possessed the necessary basic technology to exploit any iron resources they found. Modern investigators will have to determine whether the seemingly mediocre quality of the smelting results at L'Anse aux Meadows was due to inexperience or to the available resources.

In addition to the wood analyses of ship remains, some items that indicate protracted Norse contact with North America have recently turned up in a late-occupancy stratum at a Western Settlement site abandoned in the mid-fourteenth century (possibly later) and now dubbed "The Farm Beneath the Sand." Archaeologists have discovered bison hairs and fur fibers from brown or black bear, neither of which animal would have lived in Greenland. Textile samples from the site showed not only that the women on this farm had used whatever raw materials were available, but also that their weaving and spinning skills were similar to those of their contemporaries elsewhere in the Far North. In addition, they had possessed the expertise and self-confidence to make their own technical innovations and to develop a distinctive style. Among the plethora of artifacts found at this well-preserved site was a length of expertly spun yarn containing fur from Arctic hare as well as goat hairs.[54] This item was soon to prove another important link in the story of medieval Norse voyages between Greenland and North America.

The Canadian archaeologist Patricia Sutherland was among those present when the various textile discoveries were made at "The Farm Beneath the Sand." When she recently examined several artifacts from the Pond Inlet area in northern Baffin Island that Father Guy Marie de Rousselière had found years ago, at a site previously occupied by Dorset Palæo-Eskimos, she recognized a three-meter strand of expertly spun yarn as possible additional evidence of continued Greenland Norse contact with the Canadian side. An English textile specialist confirmed that this yarn, which also contained fur from Arctic hare, was identical in its distinctive spinning technique to the specimen from "The Farm Beneath the Sand." Other items from the Pond Inlet site included pieces of pine with holes made by iron nails. These pieces have been radiocarbon dated to the late thirteenth or early fourteenth century, like the strand of Norse yarn. Sutherland is currently analyzing more evidence of a similar nature from northern Labrador and southern Baffin Island sites.[55]

One cannot assume that Norse yarn found on the American side had simply been brought across by males. The discovery of the Norse spindle whorl that demonstrated the Norse connection at L'Anse aux Meadows provided ample proof that women had been present there and prepared to spin yarn from any available fibers. Sutherland's interpretations also fit a number of other archaeological finds often—but not exclusively—associated with medieval ruins left by the Dorset people, who preceded and to some extent overlapped with the Thule culture. Sutherland stresses that although just a few medieval Arctic native sites have so far been excavated and analyzed, the actual proportion of sites (relative to the large number of such dwelling sites estimated to have existed) containing evidence of Norse contact is already so high that one may reasonably expect further evidence of Norse interaction with native peoples along the extensive Canadian coast.[56]

There is also other proof that voyages from Greenland to the Canadian shores had continued. For example, an arrowhead excavated in the Christian churchyard at Sandnes, always the principal farm of the Western Settlement, is from a kind of chert (a flintlike quartz) often associated with Ramah Bay on the outer side of the northern Labrador coast but also found in significant quantities in the Ungava Bay region.[57] The weapon is made in a style commonly used by the North American natives in southern Labrador and Newfoundland between 1000 and 1500. Because the arrowhead was found in conjunction with a Christian churchyard, it evidently arrived in Greenland after the Vínland voyages because Greenland was not yet a Christian country at the time of the enterprises described in the "Saga of Eirik the Red" and the "Saga of the Greenlanders."[58]

A number of other finds on the American side bear further witness to subsequent crossings from Norse Greenland. Excavations of a twelfth-century Amerindian site on the Maine coast have yielded both Dorset Palæo-Eskimo artifacts and a Norwegian coin from the period 1065–80. The coin is generally believed to have been obtained by Dorset people trading with the Norse and then re-traded with the native North Americans farther south. However, in a recent detailed investigation, the veteran archaeologist Edmund Carpenter cast serious doubts on this interpretation.[59] In some of the Dorset sites along the coasts of Hudson Bay and Hudson Strait, archaeologists have found small fragments of smelted metal that most likely also indicate contact with the Norse. Especially interesting is the amulet made from European-derived copper, which the American archaeologist William Fitzhugh found during excavations led by Elmer Harp at a late-Dorset site along the Hudson Bay that has been radiocarbon-dated to between 1095 and 1315.[60]

Another copper piece was excavated by the French archaeologist Patrick Plumet on the northwestern coast of Ungava Bay, in a Dorset context associated with the eleventh to twelfth centuries. Because the composition of the metal is similar to that of the amulet found by Fitzhugh, Plumet's piece may also be assumed to have been brought by the Norse. In addition, Plumet found a small figurine roughly carved in wood and possibly representing a Norse person. Although the figurine was located in a Thule—rather than Dorset—context, it may not be significantly more recent than Plumet's copper piece because the Thule people arrived early enough in this area to over-lap with the Dorset inhabitants who constructed the much-debated long-houses found in the region.[61]

Particularly noteworthy in connection with continued Norse voyages across the Davis Strait is a small carving of driftwood found by the Canadian archae-ologist Deborah Sabo in 1972 at a thirteenth- or fourteenth-century Thule site located by Lake Harbour on the south coast of Baffin Island (see Figure 6). Beyond agreeing that the figurine represents a European, scholarly opinion differs sharply on what the carving represents, but the person's sex has always been assumed to be male.[62] However, I find good reason to believe that the figurine represents a human female, possibly pregnant under loosely fitted clothing which had been split to facilitate walking. The only European woman likely to have been spotted by a medieval Thule artist near any part of Baffin Island would have been Norse. The possibility is not far-fetched, given the other evidence of continued Norse Greenlanders' forays to this region.

Only the Dorset Palæo-Eskimos, Thule Neo-Eskimos, or Greenland Norse could possibly be credited with having produced two carefully, though dis-similarly, arranged accumulations of walrus mandibles (with the teeth ex-tracted) found on Willows Island, off the south coast of Baffin Island. Neither the Dorset nor the Thule people are known for ritual assemblages of walrus mandibles on either the Canadian or the Greenlandic side, but an arrange-ment of more than twenty walrus mandibles with the teeth extracted has been found in Greenland and explicitly associated with the Norse. The mandibles had been carefully buried outside the cathedral wall at Gardar, in soil that the Norse had brought in to provide sufficient fill for a graveyard.[63] There is thus no doubt about who had placed the walrus jaws there with such deliberation. The recent discovery of methodically arranged ox skulls on an early North Iceland farm adds to the possibility that the Willows Island assemblages are attributable to the Norse Greenlanders.[64]

Investigations of Baffin Island sites associated with Martin Frobisher's failed search during 1576–78 for the Northwest Passage and gold have revealed several crude iron blooms of a medieval type in addition to the walrus mandibles just mentioned. Radiocarbon dating performed on a couple of these blooms falls within the time of Norse tenure in Greenland, while an analysis of charcoal fragments in the blooms indicates spruce or larch, birch, and alder—wood species that the Norse would have been likely to use if smelting bog iron in the southern Ungava Bay region or elsewhere in the forested parts of Labrador.[65]

Figure 6. A small carving of driftwood found by the Canadian archaeologist
Deborah Sabo in 1972 at a medieval Thule site on the south coast of Baffin Island.
Photograph reproduced by permission of the Canadian Museum of Civilization
(negative no. 91-72).

It is regrettable that nobody has yet tested these blooms for possible chemical compatibility with the Labrador Iron Trough (which runs northward as far as Ungava Bay) and compared them with samples of worked iron from Norse Greenland farmsteads, where slag from reworked blooms is common, but where no primary smelting of bog iron appears to have taken place.[66] Vagn Fabritius Buchwald's recent painstaking work on medieval iron samples from Greenland does not compare either the iron or the slag samples he analyzed with compositional readings from the American side, even when his results were as anomalous to his data base as those that he obtained on a corroded iron nail found at Nipaatsoq in the Western Settlement.[67]

The lack of smelting pits on Norse Greenland farms is to be expected because the Norse would not have found bog iron within their reach in Greenland. The southwestern corner of Ungava Bay would have been the closest place where they could have obtained not only iron and the green wood required for their traditional method of iron extraction, but also lumber for ship construction, without the expense of Norwegian middlemen. In fact, they may well have resorted to building ships on the American side rather than freighting logs or boards.

Given the number of Norse artifacts that have turned up in the Ungava Bay–Hudson Bay region, Ungava Bay may have been a likely location for Norse ship construction. Other factors besides the availability of raw materials are liable to have made that region more attractive than the sheltered, forested areas farther down the Labrador coast, such as Hamilton Inlet. The trees farther south were certainly bigger, but the Norse did not need huge trees for their centrally cut heartwood planks and may well have preferred to deal with less massive specimens. This argument receives some support from a surviving fragment of the *Inventio Fortunata*—a lost work from about 1360. The fragment reveals that an English Minorite voyaging to Greenland and beyond saw evidence of felled timber and earlier ship construction in a far northern area where "Pygmies" (presumably Arctic natives) had been spotted on a promontory that the ship had passed shortly before.[68] That description suggests the southern tip of Baffin Island, which has many medieval ruin sites associated with Arctic natives.

Despite the notoriously treacherous waters of Ungava Bay and the Hudson Strait, the Norse may well have preferred to rely on their superb seamanship to being grossly outnumbered in engagements with hostile Amerindians. Although Werce encounters with native North Americans farther south (described in the two "Vínland Sagas") ended reasonably well for the Norse, these confrontations were reportedly the reason they pulled up stakes and returned to Greenland. Such a negative experience would quite likely have been balanced against the conditions in areas occupied by Arctic natives, whose hostility does not appear to have been a pressing problem, especially where the Dorset were involved. An additional reason for caution on later voyages would have been that Norse Greenland crewmembers were so few in number that they would have been especially vulnerable to attack. The voyage for lumber that took place in 1347 reportedly involved only seventeen or eighteen men.

The Literary Aftermath

The lack of saga accounts of subsequent voyages between Greenland and North America has led to a persistent postmedieval belief that during their initial forays, the Norse became so thoroughly disillusioned by their experience with Native North Americans that they never returned to any part of that newfound land. Examination of the impetus behind the "Vínland Sagas" allows one to discover why the Greenlanders' later American voyages passed without comment, although knowledge about subsequent crossings by the Norse Greenlanders must necessarily have reached the Icelanders through the continued contact between Iceland and Greenland during the more than two centuries that had passed between the actual Vínland voyages and the penning of the sagas.

The plain fact is that what the Greenlanders subsequently undertook in this respect was of no concern to saga writers commemorating voyages that to a large extent had involved their fellow Icelanders. When other Icelandic sources occasionally mentioned later westward crossings from Greenland, the reason was always that Iceland had somehow been involved. For example, when several Icelandic annals noted that Bishop Eirik Gnupsson "of Greenland" went in search of Vínland, the reason for this attention was that Bishop Eirik hailed from Iceland.[69] Three *Icelandic Annals* entries concerning the small ship— which in 1347 drifted off course on its way back to Greenland from a voyage to Markland—simply reflected the fact that the anchorless ship had ended up in Iceland.[70] It is also notable that in recording this episode, the annal writers did not explain that Markland was the forested western region to which the Greenlanders were still sailing to obtain lumber. Presumably, their fellow Icelanders were already well aware of the circumstances.

Disputed American Destinations

Recent centuries have produced their own myths about the Norse voyages to America. On both sides of the Atlantic, at one end of the belief spectrum are those who are convinced that the Vínland voyages represented a brief and finite fling, while at the other end there are people who think that there had been an enduring, widespread, and pervasive Norse presence on the American continent. Their conviction persists despite the fact that the L'Anse aux Meadows site so far remains the only evidence of Norse houses in North America, and despite many indications that there were comparatively few Norse Greenlanders available for travel at the best of times.

Nobody is certain how many Norse Greenlanders there were at any time during the existence of the two settlements, but most modern scholars concerned with the problem estimate between three thousand and five thousand at the peak of the curve. This is a far lower number than the population envisioned by nineteenth- and early-twentieth-century enthusiasts, whose intellectual footprints have proved resistant to erosion. Current believers in a pervasive Norse presence in North America are inclined to accept the views of the Norwegian writer J. Kristian Tornøe, who in 1964 and 1965 produced two books on the Norse and the Vínland voyages. Remarking in 1965 that no people were as well traveled as the Greenland Norse, Tornøe affirmed that they numbered about 37,333 souls about AD 1250.[71] Both of his books were written and published in English, which accounts for their influence. Their interpretations and supposed evidence certainly demand caution. Although the author repeatedly refers to medieval documents, he never actually consulted the *Diplomatarium Norvegicum* and other primary sources but relied instead on secondary works. One such writer was Hjalmar Holand, the first champion of the so-called Kensington Rune Stone, to whose opinions Tornøe added his own.

Besides the Kensington Rune Stone, a number of large and small objects found in continental North America have been used as evidence of how far afield the Norse went, in what numbers, and for how long a period in history.[72] However, Norse mooring holes found in Minnesota have proved as disappointing in this respect as swords, drinking horns, and an assortment of big and little rocks bearing the marks of human hands, including the Dighton Rock, whose inscriptions have been identified as Amerindian petroglyphs.[73] Some believers in a large Norse presence in America have linked another big rock (found at Westford, Massachusetts, and said by some to reveal the portrait of a medieval knight) with "Prince" Henry Sinclair of Orkney as well as with the Venetian Nicolò Zeno the Younger's 1558 publication of material containing supposedly firsthand medieval experience with the more remote sections of the North Atlantic. Fortunately, recent work by the Shetland archivist Brian Smith has put the Sinclair story into a factual perspective, and more than a century ago an American scholar showed quite satisfactorily that the Zeni map and letters are spurious.[74]

By far the sturdiest American objects supposedly reflecting medieval Norse workmanship are the Kensington Rune Stone and the Newport Tower. The Kensington Rune Stone, unearthed by a Swedish American farmer in 1898 in Kensington, Minnesota, did not at first dazzle the world with its tale carved in stone and carefully dated to 1362. According to this story, a group of Norwegians and Swedes had explored westward from Vínland and found ten of their men "dead and red with blood" on their return trip to their ship. In 1908, however, the self-styled historian Hjalmar Holand turned the rock into the centerpiece of a fanciful tale about the Norse in America in which he argued, among other things, that the Newport Tower had been built as the headquarters of a royal Norwegian expedition datable to 1355–64.[75]

The Danish scholar C. C. Rafn had been the first to call the Newport Tower a Norse church. It has subsequently been proved beyond a doubt that it was built in the late seventeenth century as a windmill on Governor Benedict Arnold's Rhode Island estate.[76] And yet the Rafn story endures among cult historians, as does the insistence that the "royal expedition" involved with both the tower and the stone can be traced to a supposed expedition to America by one of King Magnus's trusted men named Paul Knutsson. One need only consult the *Diplomatarium Norvegicum* to find that the supposed royal order to Paul, dated late in 1354, exists only in a dubious sixteenth-century copy. It mentions Greenland only, and the text has been misinterpreted as showing concern for the Greenlanders' Christian faith.[77]

Generations of seasoned experts in runology, archaeology, linguistics, and history have therefore judged the Kensington Rune Stone to be a deliberate hoax.[78] Common sense supports their arguments. For one thing, in Norse Greenland, where manpower was scarce and the struggle for survival great, the inhabitants could not have afforded to send people far away from the safety of shore and ships into the American interior, where the risks would have been great and the prospect of a reasonable economic return exceedingly small. For another thing, it is unlikely that any such group of people would have wasted precious time carving an elaborate story into a stone slab while supposedly fleeing from hostile North American natives.

The continuing fascination with the exact location of Vínland is the chief reason why also the *inland* reach of the Norse in America has attracted theories for which nobody as yet has found acceptable evidence. Others argue for an impressive southern reach that locates Vínland somewhere between Cape Cod and the Long Island Sound. Some modern writers believe that this southern hypothesis began in the early eighteenth century with the Icelandic Lawman Páll Vídalín (1667–1727), and that his arguments were supported by Bishop Finnur Jónsson (1704–89).[79] However, these two men merely continued the geographical speculations that were already evident in the maps drawn in about 1590 and 1605 and attributed to Sigurd Stefansson and Hans Poulson Resen, respectively (see Figures 7 and 8). The impetus for these maps came from repeated Danish efforts to reassert authority over the Norse Greenlanders (of whose continued existence the Danish authorities felt certain) as well as over the three American regions mentioned in the Vínland Sagas. In those dimly remembered places, the Danish reasoning went, there might still be descendants of the Norse who could legitimate the Danish king's claim to a slice of the New World with its post-Columbian promise.[80] The king's argument for a claim to the formerly Norwegian Vínland and Greenland was simple: Danish hegemony over Norway and its colonies had been affirmed by the Kalmar Union of 1397 .

A lengthy 1608 doggerel poem by Claus Christophersen Lyschander illustrates his Danish contemporaries' beliefs about Norse ventures westward from Greenland and contains much of the apocryphal history of the Norse that is still encountered today. Even more important, his work demonstrates that the Danes knew the chief requirement for claiming a portion of America. This prerequisite was spelled out in the 1493–94 Treaty of Tordesillas, which noted that primary possession by a Christian prince was necessary for a proper claim.[81] With that in mind, Lyschander stressed that the Greenland colony had enjoyed Christian roots from the very beginning—roots that had supposedly been made more secure still by Bishop Eirik Gnupsson and by the twelfth-century Danish archbishop said to have supervised this early piety.

Especially significant in the present context are these lines from Lyschander's poem: "Og Eirik paa Grønland lagde haand oppaae / Plantet paa Vínland baade Folk og Troe / Som er der endnu ved lige" (And Eirik [the Red] laid his hand on

Figure 7. Manuscript copy (1669) made by the Icelandic bishop Thord Thorlaksson of a map attributed to Sigurd Stefansson. The original, drawn about 1590, no longer exists. Manuscript Department of the Royal Library, Copenhagen. Reproduced with kind permission.

Greenland and planted both people and the Faith in Vínland, present there to this day).[82] It is unclear whether Lyschander considered Eirik the Red a Christian prince or merely the pious and legitimate representative of the Norwegian crown whose rights had been subsumed by the Danes, but his main point is obvious: In Lyschander's view, Vínland had first been discovered and settled by the Norse,

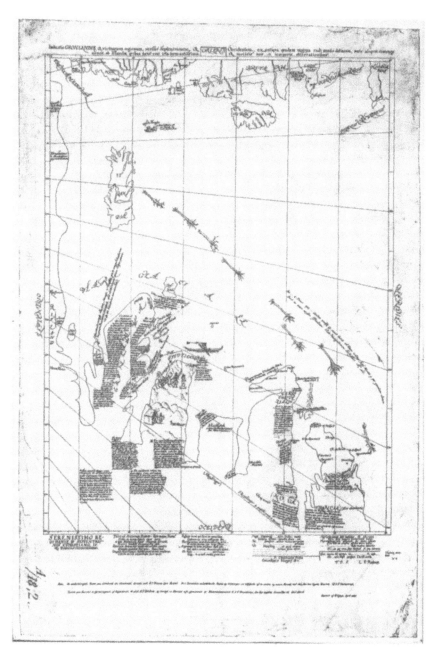

Figure 8. Map attributed to the Danish theologian Hans Poulson Resen, completed in 1605. Manuscript Department of the Royal Library in Copenhagen. Copy reproduced with kind permission.

good Christians all. By extension, therefore, the Danish king should be able to claim a stretch of New World territory where Norse descendants presumably still lived. Resen's map, which indicates the desire to have these territories be as large as possible, shows that this thinking was well established at least three years before Lyschander wrote his *Chronicle of Greenland.*

Stefansson's and Resen's efforts to reconcile Danish ambitions with saga descriptions and the slowly emerging cartography of North America were to some degree complicated by Nicolò Zeno the Younger's 1558 fictitious cartographical and verbal accounts of the North Atlantic region, but neither man let Zeno interfere unduly with his own agenda. Resen in particular located Vínland relatively far south along the still poorly explored northeastern shore of America and, for good measure, tossed in the supposed land of Norumbega, thus becoming the first Nordic cartographer actively (and mistakenly) associating this name with the Norse.

Sensibly, Skelton did not bring into his discussion about the Norse the imaginary wonderland of Norumbega, which reached its mythical bloom after Giacomo Gastaldi had placed "Nurumberg" in New France on his 1548 map of North America, evidently in homage to the German city of Nuremberg.[83] The Norse-in-Norumbega notion (arguing that "Norumbega" was a variant of "Norway") did not originate with either Gastaldi or Resen, however. The assertion was made in the 1570s on maps by the famous Dutch cartographer Ortelius.[84] By that time, fair-skinned North American natives had been portrayed on mid-sixteenth-century Dieppe maps illustrating French discoveries in the "Norumbega" region, resulting in images that would have provided the Danish authorities with ample fuel for a belief in the genetic influence of Norse "Norumbegans."[85]

Neither the seventeenth nor the eighteenth centuries gave scholars archaeological evidence for Norse activities on the American side. Useful postmedieval information about Norse farm sites in Greenland did not start trickling in until the Norwegian Lutheran pastor Hans Egede went to Greenland in 1721 to make good Protestant Christians of the Norse still assumed to be minding their own business there.

Sustaining Life in Norse Greenland

To argue that the Norse Greenlanders found Vínland far to the south of the St. Lawrence estuary, one would have to ignore not only the modern archae ological record on both sides of the Davis Strait, but all other existing information about the medieval economy of the Far North. It borders on cultural chauvinism if those of us living in a temperate climate assume that because northern regions are cold, the Norse Greenlanders would naturally have made their way quite far south once they reached America. This is akin to saying that traditional Inuit hunters would obviously be much happier raising vegetables in Massachusetts than catching seals in Baffin Island. In every way, the Norse Greenlanders' entire culture rested on traditions that relied on the resources found in far northern regions. Everything else, grapes included, was secondary to the serious business of sustaining life and trade by well-tested methods.

While the Norse Greenlanders evidently spared no effort in securing wood and iron for their domestic economy and Arctic goods for their foreign trade, the greater part of their daily endeavors would have been concentrated in or near their settlements and focused on gathering enough food to see their livestock and themselves through the many months of winter. Fortunately, their domestic animals, cattle included, were hardy creatures and able to survive on such hay stretchers as seaweed, dried heather and leaves, and fish scraps. Neither the human nor the animal diet in Norse Greenland would have suited modern Western notions, but the fare was varied and wholesome enough to keep the population in robust health to the very end of the colony. It featured roots, berries, and herbs of many kinds, seaweed and shellfish, dairy products, and meat from both terrestrial and marine mammals. Last, but certainly not least, humans and animals alike would have relied on fish.[86]

The Norse dependence on fish is widely underappreciated by modern scholars. Medieval Icelandic writers knew how important fishing was to survival. Relating the unfortunate experience of the presettlement traveler Floki the Norwegian, the *Book of Settlements* blamed Floki and his men for failing to secure hay for their cattle because they had been too absorbed in harvesting the abundant fish in the fjord. Another story in the same work tells about an early Icelandic settler named Asolf, a good Christian in an as-yet-heathen land, who had to move three times because heathen neighbors were envious of the fact that no matter where he settled down and built houses, his farm creek was always unaccountably full of fish. He went down in history as "the holiest of men."[87]

As Mark Kurlansky noted in his recent study of cod and cod fishing, the range of medieval Norse exploration and colonization in the North Atlantic equals exactly the range of the Atlantic cod.[88] Indeed, the medieval Norse, in Greenland or anywhere else, would not have survived their extensive ocean voyages, nor the rigors of long northern winters, without the ability to fish and to preserve their catch. The conditions for turning codfish into stockfish would have been as available to the Norse in Greenland as to their Icelandic neighbors. The preparation of stockfish simply requires a cool, bright, windy climate coupled with experience and skilled hands.

A passage in "The Tale of the Greenlanders" also suggests that the necessary skills were a part of the maritime culture that the Norse in Greenland shared with their Icelandic cousins. In this story, the temper and sagacity of Arnald (the first official Greenland bishop) were repeatedly tested after a Norse Greenlander named Sigurd Njalsson and his companions had come across a well-equipped Norwegian shipwreck and several bodies during a hunting and fishing expedition to the uninhabited east coast. The ship's owner was evidently a man named Arnbjörn. When Arnbjörn's Norwegian heirs showed up to make their claim, a feud ensued, and it became clear that the restoration of peace depended on the departure of the Norwegians. To augment their food supply for the return voyage, one of the Norwegians suggested a visit to a man named Thorarin, known for his plentiful food stores. When they descended on Thorarin's farm, they uncovered a large underground storage chamber containing not only large quantities of meat and butter, but also "lots of dried fish."[89]

The surviving medieval literature concerning Iceland and Norway has many other casual references to fishing, but it tells as little about its practical details as it does about dairying and other daily chores. However, there is no mistaking the disapproval with which the author of the "Saga of Eirik the Red" describes the happy-go-lucky ways of Karlsefni's party during their stay in beautiful Straumfjord, another hotly disputed North American location. There was tall grass everywhere for the livestock that the Norse had brought with them, but as far as human needs were concerned, the fat of the land apparently was thin: "They stayed there that winter, which turned out to be a very severe one; they had made no provision for it during the summer, and now they ran short of food and the hunting failed."[90]

This passage suggests that the would-be settlers had neglected the basic precaution of stocking up on fish for the winter months while they explored a region whose climate they had misjudged—presumably because they were unaccustomed to the summer lushness of large stretches of Labrador, which also deceived many a European explorer centuries later. They knew that they were at a latitude well south of Greenland, which makes a misjudgment all the more understandable. Had the explorers worried about winter provisions in time, however, they would have found plenty of cod and other fish along the American coast they investigated during their Vínland voyages.

Among the several species of edible fish available back home in Greenland were three kinds of cod, which is very lean and therefore the most suitable fish for drying. Most desirable is the Atlantic cod, *Gadus morhua*. The livers from any kind of cod, along with Greenland shark livers and fat from marine animal blubber, would have been useful to the Norse as food, fuel, and a source of light.[91] The comparative lack of codfish crania and backbones in Norse Greenland middens, as well as of fish hooks and sinkers, has nevertheless led some scientists to speculate that the Norse Greenlanders never relied much on the fish swimming along their coasts.[92] It is particularly interesting in this context that a new study at the University of Aarhus in Denmark, which involved twenty-seven human bone samples representing Norse Greenlanders throughout the better part of their colonial tenure, revealed increasing reliance on marine foods from early on.[93]

A commonsense approach is called for both in this matter and with regard to dairying in Norse Greenland, a community known to have kept and valued cattle. Well before the first barrels containing milk residue were discovered in Eastern Settlement ruins, and despite the continued lack of any butter or cheese remains found in Norse Greenland archaeological sites, the processing of dairy products in Norse Greenland was taken for granted by scholars from early on. Even the most deskbound Nordic sages of the nineteenth and twentieth centuries (who would also have eaten fish several days a week as a matter of course) knew that their own culture still valued butter, cheese, and other milk products, so they assumed that in Greenland as elsewhere, the evidence— perishable at best—would have been consumed or exported.

It is quite possible that large-scale fishing and fish drying took place away from the main Greenland settlements, closer to the outer coast and to the spring migrations of cod, and in a location with optimum drying conditions. The so-called Middle Settlement in southwestern Greenland (now generally considered the northernmost extension of the Eastern Settlement) may well have been optimal for the cool and windy conditions required for drying, especially if the spring season was likely to be sunny as well as windy and relatively dry. Furthermore, during the "spring" months of May and June, drift ice blocks the entrances to the Eastern Settlement fjords, which would have prevented the Norse in the inner fjords from reaching the cod fishing banks just off the outer coast, where the cod may arrive as early as March and is most plentiful during May, June, and July.[94]

According to Georg Nyegaard, the zoo-archaeologist who heads the Qaqortoq Museum in southwestern Greenland, the climate out by the Middle Settlement features cooler summers and milder winters than does the main Norse settlement region farther inland.[95] However, little archaeological information is available about the sites in this outer area, except that the ruins appear somewhat indistinct, which is at least partly due to the climatic conditions here, and that the area has so far yielded no indication of a local church, unlike the more heavily populated inner part of the Eastern Settlement where there were several churches of varying size.[96] No further investigation of the Middle Settlement is planned at this time.[97]

Everyday Life

Norse men and women arranged their lives in Greenland in a manner that had deep roots in an inherited culture that served them well. It has nevertheless been suggested that they should have "adapted" to their new country by copying Eskimo hunting methods, clothing, and social customs.[98] Any maladaptation theory begs the question of how the Norse managed to survive in Greenland for so many centuries. It also makes one wonder why the Norse would have been unprepared for life in an environment that was not appreciably more hostile than in the countries they had left behind, and where they had learned vital physical and social survival skills. Moreover, if the Greenland Norse had found their cultural habits unequal to the sub-Arctic and Arctic aspects of their new homeland, they would scarcely have survived hunting in far northern regions where many a modern explorer has come to grief.

In traditional medieval societies, men and women usually had well-defined occupations. Any profound change in how a Greenland Norse woman spent her time would have been accompanied by the disappearance of the domestic animals that provided most of the raw materials for her traditional labors and would have resulted in similar dislocations in male occupations. Discarding fundamental aspects of one's own culture hardly qualifies as adaptation, nor was it necessary to survival in this case. The Norse Greenlanders endured by adapting their practices to Greenlandic conditions when necessary but without discarding their own culture.

Exploiting both the marine and terrestrial food resources would have made for a harsh existence from the very beginning of the Norse colonization of Greenland, so it is hardly surprising that Niels Lynnerup's recent forensic studies of Greenland Norse skeletal material showed people of both sexes who had been well muscled from hard labor. Lynnerup also found evidence of bones that had healed after fractures from either accidents or violence, and he confirmed that many Norse Greenlanders appear to have suffered from arthritis as well as from other common diseases. There was much evidence of persistent middle ear infections, but there were no signs of malnutrition, nor of genetic deterioration.[99] The Greenland graveyards do not reveal, however, how many people drowned or otherwise disappeared while away from home in the course of their work.

A harsh life kills individuals, but it is unlikely to exterminate an entire population, otherwise we would not still have Icelanders, Faeroese, and Norwegians. Yet the Norse Greenlanders vanished after about half a millennium's reliance on food resources that in some ways were superior to those enjoyed by the Icelanders, who had no native large land animals and who repeatedly suffered famine because of unique environmental problems due to their island's volcanic activities. They were also far closer than the Greenlanders to European epidemic disease pools, and they were no more proof than the Greenlanders against the temperature fluctuations that were frequent in that part of the world.

How Cold Was It?

Contrary to widespread belief, the overall climate conditions in the eastern North American and West Greenlandic latitudes about the year 1000 appear to have been rather similar to those of 2000. Several experts on the climate history of the north have concluded that terms such as "The Medieval Warm Period" and "The Little Ice Age" ought to be discarded in favor of a much more nuanced view of climate oscillations in the last thousand years. Benign weather conditions were interrupted by periods of cold and stormy weather, and even periods showing a long-term downward trend in the mean temperature were interrupted by years of noticeable warming. Additional caution is warranted because long-term temperature trends discerned in one part of the world are not applicable to other regions without corroborative evidence and because the considerable short-term variations observed during longer periods of warming or cooling were often quite local.[100] Accounts of Arctic exploration during the past couple of centuries, for example, indicate that no expedition could rely on what others had experienced just a few years earlier when attempting to determine which parts of the Davis Strait and its auxiliary waterways would be open or frozen at a particular time of year.

Despite the lack of unanimity among modern climate historians about these and many other details, it is evident that the difference between late-tenth-century and early-twentieth-century mean temperatures on land and sea in the North Atlantic region would not have produced the dramatic contrasts argued by Skelton in 1965:

> In determining the extent of Norse navigation we shall be misled if
> we suppose it to have been controlled by a climatic situation identical
> with that of the present. It is clear that, during the Viking age, a milder
> climate allowed the Norse voyagers to use sailing routes, and to carry
> out explorations in high latitudes, that would be impossible in the ice
> conditions of the later Middle Ages or of today. Modern climatologists
> are agreed in regarding the period between about AD 950 and 1200 as a
> "climatic optimum" with unmistakable evidence of being warmer than
> now in Iceland and Greenland, presumably implying higher ocean tem-
> peratures in the northern Atlantic, and much less extensive ice in the
> Arctic seas.[101]

Even for the 1960s, this was a high-handed interpretation of the opinions expressed by the climatological scholars whose research Skelton thought "generally substantiate[d] the theory of cyclic changes in climate developed by Otto Pettersen over a half century ago."[102] There is now growing evidence that one must return to the time before the last great Ice Age to find Greenland without belts of ice blocking long stretches of its coast in summer as well as in winter.

Skelton certainly did not intend to belittle Norse accomplishment in navigating far northern waters, although that interpretation becomes inevitable if one claims that a considerably warmer climate had prevailed at the time of the Vínland voyages. He merely wished to provide an argument for early Norse explorations far up the Greenland coasts and for Norse knowledge of their country's island status. He also wanted to relate a perceived warm early period to the other "outlines and features in the [Vínland] map with the coasts known to have been discovered or frequented by the Norse."[103]

Among modern scholars there is a more restrained view of a "Medieval

Warm Period" compared with a "Little Ice Age" envisioned as a pervasive chilling, perhaps beginning before 1300, that supposedly played a decisive role in the end of the Western Settlement about 1350–1400 and of the Eastern Settlement by 1450–1500. The problem with this reasoning is that it ignores the reality that the oft-tested Icelanders have survived to this day, and also that there is no modern evidence for a pervasive and continuous cooling trend sufficient to force an end to Norse tenure in Greenland. To the extent that considerably colder weather eventually became a reality in Northern Europe (lasting until the early twentieth century), at least in Iceland it began only in the late seventeenth century, with a milder period occurring in the 1760s and 1770s.[104] To be sure, in northern latitudes even fairly small temperature swings may have a considerable impact, but it is well to heed the modern Icelandic historian Gísli Gunnarsson, who warns against a simplistic approach to the environmental and economic consequences of erratic weather.[105]

This is not the place to hone the finer points of northern climate research, however, but to note that the Norse had never found navigation in Greenlandic and Canadian waters to be anything less than a battle with Mother Nature. Nor did they ever experience the coasts of either place in a way radically different from the sixteenth- and seventeenth-century European explorers who reported back to the cartographers trying to envision the outlines of Arctic coasts.

Did Hard Times Become Harder in Greenland?

Any attempt to unravel the Norse Greenlanders' ultimate fate must first acknowledge the many gaps in our knowledge. For example, scholars do not know how many Norse Greenlanders remained in the colony toward the end, nor is there a single instance of either documentary or archaeological evidence supporting the frequently made claim that the Eastern Settlement was essentially defunct as early as 1450. There are in fact indications that the end came several decades later, but there is no firm evidence either way. Arguing for either end of the time spectrum demands caution, especially if one relies on Norse Greenland information alone.[106]

While it remains unclear what happened during the last century or so of Norse tenure in Greenland, there must have been complex reasons for the Norse Greenlanders' eventual disappearance. It is also evident that except for a few possible stragglers, the Norse were gone from the Eastern Settlement by about 1500 at the latest and about a century earlier from the Western Settlement.

The fact that the inhabitants maintained contact with the outside world right into the colony's last phase suggests that they still had the vigor and the means to go elsewhere. But what prompted such a community of hardy, independent farmers to give up their land? While the currently available archaeological material indicates neither the circumstances nor the timing of the Norse Greenlanders' decision to close down their two communities, it does show their final departure in each case to have been as deliberate and orderly as their arrival some five centuries earlier.[107] Not only did they leave their farms voluntarily, therefore, but the dearth of artifacts in the ruins of both farms and churches suggests a community decision to go elsewhere and to bring their valuables.

There is no shortage of archaeological material related to the approximate last phase of each of the two settlements, but one problem is that radiocarbon dating cannot by itself calculate dates very closely. A second problem is that many Norse Greenland sites, including graveyards, have not yet been investigated, or else they were excavated so long ago that modern archaeological methods were not brought to bear. A third problem is that in southwestern Greenland the sea level has risen several meters in the last five centuries, with the consequence that parts of the graveyards at Herjolfsnes in the Eastern Settlement and at Sandnes in the Western Settlement have been washed out to sea. Usually, the most recent burials were the most distant from the church, so the loss of those outer sections prevents certainty about when the last burials at Herjolfsnes and Sandnes took place.

What we do know is that in all the graves that have been examined, the bodies had been healthy enough in life and had been buried in a Christian fashion when dead. The archaeological record and the sparse written sources argue against a single, cataclysmic reason for the Norse Greenlanders' departure and against adversities such as pervasive Eskimo hostility, foreign marauders, starvation, pestilence, and deleterious inbreeding. As noted above, evidence is also completely lacking for the claims that the Greenland Norse fatally failed to "adapt" to their situation when they did not emulate the lifestyle of Arctic natives and that they did not adjust their other cultural practices in order to ensure social and economic survival.[108] Nor does any evidence support the theory that the Norse gave up their Greenland farms in order to return "home" to Iceland and/or Norway.[109]

One may as well argue that in an economic downturn, "old families" in today's Boston would consider going "back" to England, which the Pilgrim Fathers had left in 1620. There are actually several strong arguments against an eastbound exodus of the Norse Greenlanders. For one thing, in the fifteenth century neither Norway nor Iceland was a congenial place, economically and politically, for landless immigrants who lacked powerful connections. For another thing, the history of medieval Norse colonization in the North Atlantic shows that the settlers in each place soon thought of themselves as belonging to their new home and not to their former one, although the cultural affinity among these widespread Norse communities remained. Third, not a single extant document suggests that those who had inherited large numbers of farms after the Black Death in Iceland (1402–4) turned property over to outsiders, or that contact between Iceland and Greenland had endured past the first few decades of the fifteenth century. Last, but certainly not least, either in Iceland or in Norway, a determined and final eastward migration from Norse Greenland couldn't have escaped the notice of Dano-Norwegian royal officials, who were numerous and obtrusive in both countries by the second half of the fifteenth century.

It is in fact quite clear that no word had reached Danish, Norwegian, or Icelandic officials that the Norse Greenland colony had ceased to exist. About 1514, the Norwegian archbishop Erik Valkendorf (a Dane by birth and allegiance) planned an expedition to Greenland in the full expectation that the Norse would be reclaimable for church and crown after a hiatus of more than a century. He thought that this connection would be immensely lucrative because he believed Greenland to be part of a northern land mass connected to the New World and its reported riches.[110] One can only speculate about what Stefansson's map (Figure 7) might have looked like if Valkendorf's plans had been realized. As it was, the archbishop fell out of favor with King Christian II of Denmark before the voyage could take place.

Continued ignorance about the Norse Greenland situation prompted further attempts (1568–81 and 1605–7) by the Danish crown to reconnect with the Norse Greenland settlements, presumably in the hope of learning from their occupants just where to find their Norse cousins in North America. As already noted, the maps by Stefansson, Resen, and Thorlaksson grew directly out of these attempts and thus had their roots in the same informational void that made the Danish kings unable to advise their expedition leaders about just where to go in Greenland. Skelton thus had no reason for conjecturing that those three maps had been based on "ancient prototypes," much less that they reflected any other verbal information from the Middle Ages than that which is known to every reader of the sagas.[111]

Far from displaying ancient knowledge, the Stefansson, Resen, and Thorlaksson maps reflect the informational vacuum that began in earnest when Greenland lost its last official contact with crown and church in Norway toward the end of the fourteenth century, after the long decline of a connection that had always been tenuous at best. Nor was there any substitute source of information; in no way does the written record support Painter's and Skelton's claims that Rome was a storage and clearinghouse for knowledge about the Far North—including Greenland—of the kind supposedly reflected in the Vínland Map (see Chapter 8).[112]

A plethora of medieval documents actually points in the opposite direction by showing that the Roman Church was the first European institution to sever its ties with Norse Greenland. The documents make it painfully clear that concern for the inhabitants of that country might as well have involved people who lived on the moon.[113] Throughout the Middle Ages, continental European churchmen remained so ignorant about northern geography and conditions that as late as 1464, the Roman Curia issued a receipt to the Norwegian bishop Alf of Stavanger—"in Ireland."[114]

If ecclesiastical and royal oversight with Greenland had ever been of any consequence, it would have always been hampered by the huge distances involved. It suffered further in consequence of the Black Death that struck Norway in 1349 and the Kalmar Union of 1397, which resulted in Norway's loss of independence to Denmark (which lasted until 1814) and directly impacted the economic and political situation in both Norway and its former colonies. The Greenland Church, formally subjected to the archbishop of Nidaros in Norway, was increasingly buffeted by the domestic political winds around the archbishop as well as the power struggle between distant Rome and Avignon during the Great Schism that began in 1378. The last resident bishop of Gardar, Bishop Alf, died in Greenland at about that time and was never physically replaced. By then the Greenlanders would have had good coping mechanisms in place, however, because when Alf was consecrated to the Gardar seat in 1365, the country had been without a resident bishop for nineteen years and had experienced many a long hiatus before that.[115]

Bishop Alf's appointment appears to have been the direct result of the account that the Bergen bishop's representative, a man named Ivar Bardarson, gave when he returned from a long stay in Greenland for the purpose of allocating parish boundaries. His report indicated that the Greenlanders in the Eastern Settlement were in sufficiently good economic shape to pay their tithes. Ivar's judgment about the Western Settlement is equally interesting. In the form his report has come down to us (for example, as part of Archbishop Valkendorf's preparations for his aborted sixteenth-century Greenland voyage), Ivar claimed to have gone up to the Western Settlement with an armed party to defend the local Norse against the "heathens" (presumably Thule Eskimos, unless the reference was to the "Karelians" then believed to have land access from the northeast), and there he had found the place deserted of living creatures except some abandoned animals.[116]

There is much to say about Ivar's "Description of Greenland," but two observations will suffice here. One is that Ivar's statements about parish boundaries have often been misinterpreted as descriptions of church *ownership* of land and hence of the Greenlanders' profound economic subjection to the church. In fact, however, Ivar merely described the cure of souls "belonging" to a particular parish.[117] The definition of the church as the Greenlanders' all-powerful landlord began as the work of nineteenth-century scholars who had conscientiously read the "Description," but who had different assumptions from contemporary scholars about unquestioning acceptance of church authority.[118] Without reading the text in question, some more recent authors have perpetuated the notion that the Greenlanders were disastrously subjugated to their church—an interpretation for which there is no evidence in Ivar's report or anywhere else.

Modern investigations of Western Settlement sites, including of "The Farm Beneath the Sand," suggest that deteriorating environmental and economic conditions contributed to that settlement's abandonment by about 1400 at the latest.[119] For reasons best known to the Norse Greenlanders and to Ivar himself, the Western Settlement was apparently stricken from the church ledgers in the mid-fourteenth century. While Ivar's account of the Western Settlement's deplorable state in the mid-fourteenth century probably was self-serving, he must have had some cause to rule out its people as possible tithe payers; the most obvious reason would have been if the inhabitants were now refusing to provide the church with walrus ivory for profitable resale in Europe. Resentment against church levies had been running high for some time already both in Greenland and elsewhere in the North.

Assessment of the reasons for this resentment would take the reader too far afield here. The concern must remain with the practical implications for the inhabitants of both the Western and the Eastern Settlements when their formal connection with the Roman Church ceased in the last quarter of the fourteenth century, and when Queen Margrethe's heir, King Eirik of Pommerania, made it abundantly clear early in the fifteenth century that his concerns were not for the well-being of either Norway or Norway's Atlantic satellites.

The inevitable consequence of such developments was a major shift in the Norse Greenlander's traditional trade connections. This changed situation also meant that direct and current information in Norway about Norse Greenland slowed to a mere trickle and soon ceased altogether. Other countries did not take up the documentary slack—not even Iceland, where the last annals entry about Greenland is dated to 1410.

It was thus a case of pure fiction when the authors of *The Vinland Map and the Tartar Relation* claimed that important ecclesiastical information channels about Norse Greenland were still in existence about 1440.

Tusks, Tithes, and Other Troubles

The last document noting Norwegian import of Greenland walrus ivory intended as payment of church taxes is dated to the year 1327.[120] Around that same time, there were unmistakable signs of popular resistance to church taxes in both Norway and Sweden following some years of very bad harvests that had affected large parts of Europe. The Norse Greenlanders, however, had never raised grain either for domestic needs or for use in trade and in payment of taxes. The reason for their rebellion must therefore have been uniquely their own and unrelated to the temporary climate oscillations in Europe; when more clement weather returned to Europe, the export of Greenland walrus ivory to Norwegian church authorities evidently did not resume in sufficient quantities to produce a written record.

Even allowing for the major disruptions caused by the outbreak of the Black Death in Norway in 1349, it is highly unlikely that if shipments of Greenland walrus ivory had continued, the Norwegian church authorities would have failed to convert the tusks into silver through foreign (usually Flanders) merchants—a process that also left records. It is equally unlikely that continental merchants had become unable to make a profit through reselling walrus ivory. At any time, the product would have been welcomed by medieval European craftsmen who had only a vague idea of the routes by which such material reached them and an even vaguer idea of the creatures to whom the tusks had belonged. Well into the sixteenth century, most continental Europeans had no idea of what either walrus or narwhal in fact looked like.

Historically, the disruption of an established trade route inevitably leads to a diminished flow of information—a flow that from the northern regions had never been torrential. For example, on his *Carta marina navigatoria* (1516), the German cartographer Martin Waldseemüller drew an elephant-like creature accompanied by a legend explaining that the *morsus* (walrus) congregated in northern Norway. He also explained that a *morsus* has two long and quadrangular teeth.[121] As for narwhals, their spiral tusks were widely thought of as unicorn horns imbued with medicinal and magical powers, not only in Europe, but also in the Near and Middle East, where walrus tusks were also uniquely valued.[122]

There are several indications that by about the middle of the fourteenth century, the Norse Greenlanders were no longer collecting walrus ivory in the earlier quantities. The American scientist Thomas McGovern, an expert on bones found in Norse Greenland middens, has observed that late-phase middens appear to contain relatively fewer walrus elements than earlier ones.[123] Danish art historian Else Roesdahl provides another angle on reductions in walrus ivory imports in her detailed study of medieval ivory objects in various European museums. She found that a shift from walrus to elephant ivory occurred in Europe in the mid-fourteenth century and concluded from her data that at this early date African elephant ivory had already become so competitive in price and availability that it displaced walrus tusks in the European market. This, in turn, would have caused a serious economic downturn in the Western Settlement.[124]

Roesdahl's study is a useful piece in the incomplete puzzle of Norse Greenland's economic history, both because it documents that something must have been happening to European supplies of walrus ivory in the fourteenth century and because it illustrates a cause-and-effect economic link between faraway Greenland and mainstream Europe. Accepted knowledge about the African ivory trade with Europe in the Middle Ages does not support her conclusion about competition from elephant ivory, however. Nor does it allow for the fact that walrus ivory from northern sources remained prized in Muslim countries long after the last Norse cooking fire had died out in Greenland. Those Muslim countries included Egypt, where access to

African ivory would have been comparatively easy throughout the entire medieval period.

By AD 1000—just as the Greenland Norse had begun to exploit their access to walrus ivory—camel caravans were bringing riches from the western Sudan to eastern Africa and also to North African ports. Elephant ivory had long been so highly valued that by 500 BC there were no wild elephants left in the Middle East, and by the end of the fourth century AD African elephants had been hunted to extinction north of the spreading Sahara desert. As early as AD 77, Pliny complained that "large elephant teeth . . . are now rarely found except in India, the demand of luxury having exhausted all those in our part of the world."[125] When Muslim Arabs became entrenched in North Africa in the seventh and eighth centuries, they soon established trade with the peoples south of the Sahara in order to obtain gold, ivory (particularly from the African bush elephant), and other valuable goods. There are two important reasons why this development would not have interfered with the Western European market for walrus ivory until the very end of the fifteenth century, thus making it doubtful that the Western Settlement inhabitants' loss of a market for their walrus ivory compelled them to close down their small community in the fourteenth century.

One reason was the huge expense of camel caravans, which involved many middlemen and immense distances as well as horrendous conditions for both man and beast. Although precious in its own right, walrus ivory arriving mostly by water transport would have been measurably cheaper than its African competitor. The second reason why elephant ivory could not compete easily in the Far North was that the Muslims monopolized foreign trade in African goods—whether gold, ivory, or slaves—so that the Europeans were completely dependent on Muslim goodwill for the small quantities of expensive African ivory that Christian-owned galleys brought north across the Mediterranean. Portuguese circumvention of the Muslim control of trade with the African interior was accomplished through systematic exploration and by setting up strongholds along the African west coast, and it was not a reality until about 1500, when gold, ivory, spices, and slaves could be loaded directly from the equatorial Guinea coast onto European ships.[126] If African elephant ivory was nevertheless slowly making its way to European craftsmen in the fourteenth century, it must have been filling the void when walrus ivory was no longer coming south through the usual Norway-Flanders channels.[127]

It would be a mistake to think that the Flanders market was the main clearinghouse for all Arctic marine ivory. After tracing the trade routes that enabled the Bulgars on the Black Sea to become middlemen for walrus and narwhal tusks from the Far North, Richard Ettinghausen noted that while little or nothing is known about the actual starting points of these routes, it is clear that marine ivory and precious furs followed the same trade routes south from the Barents Sea region and the Baltic.[128] Merchants dealing in these goods would have known where to pick up their own segment of the trade route. If a significant segment of such a route disappeared for any reason, the effect would certainly have been felt by the original suppliers of furs and marine ivories for that particular route. More subtle, but equally important, would have been the consequences to general communications.

Whether the Norse Greenlanders stopped exporting walrus tusks because they objected to paying church taxes, preferred to expend their energy in other ways, or reacted to a shift in trade routes due to Dano-Norwegian royal policies, one must be cautious about assigning a cause for the end of the Western Settlement. Various other theories about the reasons of the community's demise have also been put forward, including the possibility that colder weather constrained northern hunting and made stock farming in that northernmost settlement too difficult.

Stock farming appears to have been secondary to the Western Settlement's economic structure from the beginning, however. Increased ice in the Davis Strait and Baffin Bay would presumably have resulted in a more southerly summer ice edge, thus the Norse would not have had to go as far north as before to catch walrus. However, it is probably well to focus more on the reality that inclement weather was a periodic and local occurrence in both settlements, and that no scientific study has fixed climate fluctuations as the direct cause of extreme difficulty among the Norse Greenlanders in either community. Nevertheless, if northern hunting (apparently the backbone of the Western Settlement's existence) suffered a substantial reduction for whatever reason, the lack of such activity might have made the settlement superfluous to the general Norse Greenland economy.

Long- or short-term weather changes may have had a number of indirect effects. For example, if the Thule culture's advance toward the south was closely linked to a more southerly range of walrus and other marine game, Thule hunters may have encountered closer competition with the Norse. Thule-Norse rivalry on the rich fishing banks along the outer Nuuk region coast may also have been a problem for Western Settlement denizens. Hans Christian Gulløv has shown that the Thule people gained their footing in Northern Greenland about 1200 and steadily made their way down the island's west coast during the thirteenth and fourteenth centuries.[129] More mobile than the Dorset people whom they displaced or absorbed, they appear to have been more aggressive as well, and they may conceivably have been less willing than the Dorset to share their hunting and fishing grounds.

These problems all have potentially wide ramifications, but I am more concerned here with the possible long-term effects on the Eastern Settlement after the Western Settlement was depopulated and could no longer serve as a viable way station for voyages to obtain American raw materials. Especially after about 1420, when the English had made the situation in the North Atlantic unsafe for ships belonging to other countries, Norse travel in Greenlandic waters may well have been made difficult by the increasing presence of English ships on a relentless quest for cod and other fish and fish products.[130]

It was no coincidence that just when Dano-Norwegian officials of church and crown had completely lost interest in Norse Greenland, the latter worked its way into the consciousness of European mapmakers along with an increasing curiosity about how other trans-Atlantic areas might be constituted.

The Many Names of a Much Loved Child

The Norwegian proverb "a much loved child has many names" certainly seems applicable to America, where, beginning with the Columbian voyage of 1492, American locales were given European names.[131] On both pre- and post-Columbian maps, the Norse regional names Helluland, Markland, and Vínland are of course conspicuously absent, and scholars will probably never know the full array of names that indigenous Americans applied to the places they knew. Long before Columbus first encountered those native names, however, European mapmakers had come up with some new names of their own for dimly imagined western regions.

A large, oblong island enigmatically named Antilia made its debut in the middle of the Atlantic Ocean on the 1424 nautical chart by Zuane Pizzigano of Venice.[132] Since nobody as yet suspected that an entire huge continent and another ocean interfered with direct access to the eastern coast of a vast Asian landmass, islands with names such as "Island of Seven Cities" or "Isle of Brazil" also crop up in the northwestern Atlantic, both on maps and in texts that allude to Portuguese and English probes in that general area.[133] The part that English maritime information played in Atlantic cartography by that time is certainly evident in a Catalan chart from about 1480.[134] It shows an elliptical *Illa de brazil* nestled just south of an elongated, but equally stylized *Illa verde* (Green Island). Both were placed well to the west of Iceland—an island to which many English navigators knew the route as well as they knew their home waters. The archaeological evidence found in Greenland for English connections suggests that there were English seamen who knew where Greenland was in relation to Iceland. At least some of these men would also have been aware that the "Isle of Brazil" (by 1480, or earlier, this was evidently the English synonym for the Newfoundland fishing banks) lay southwest of Greenland at about fifty-three degrees north, approximately the latitude of Galway Bay in Ireland.[135]

Early English familiarity with the Davis Strait region is graphically demonstrated by German cartographer Johannes Ruysch's world map of 1507, which was included with the edition of Ptolemy's *Geography* published in Rome the following year (see Figure 9). The editor, Marcus Beneventanus, wrote in his preface that Ruysch, sailing on board an English ship (probably about 1502–4), had followed the fifty-third parallel and then gone "somewhat northwardly" until he reached the new lands in the west. On his map, Ruysch showed this "new land" (here named *Terra Nova*) as modestly sized compared with the huge Greenland promontory looming to the northeast. Particularly revealing is the name that one of the states of this map gives to what was clearly the lower part of the Davis Strait: *Sinus Gruenlanteus*—the Bay of Greenland. In other words, *Greenland* was the most familiar element here.[136]

Skelton did not know about the archaeological discoveries in Greenland indicating English contact because they were mostly made after his death, but it is surprising that this expert on early printed maps neglected to check the various states of the Ruysch map.[137] Nor does he appear to have consulted Beneventanus's preface to the 1508 Rome Ptolemy edition, where he would have found another English link. Instead, the only English influences that Skelton found in the Ruysch map (besides a tenuous connection with the world picture that John Cabot appears to have had in his head in 1497) came from the lost English work *Inventio Fortunata*, which Skelton thought had served as Ruysch's "authority for the representation of the Arctic." Aside from these connections, Skelton noted "the striking similarity between the representation of Greenland and 'Terra Nova' in Ruysch's world map of 1507 and

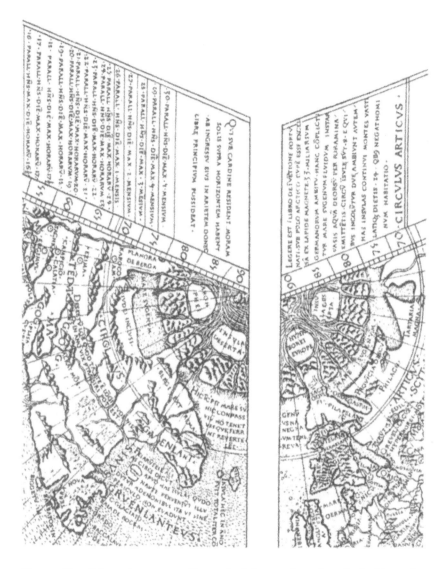

Figure 9. Detail from the 1507 world map by Johannes Ruysch with the "Bay of Greenland." Source: Bjørnbo, "Cartographia Groenlandica," p. 187, reproduced by permission of Dansk Polarcenter, Copenhagen, publisher of *Meddelelser om Grønland.*

that of Greenland and Vínland by Stefansson, ca. 1590."[138] It was not Skelton's intention to say that Stefansson must have seen the Ruysch map (which the young Copenhagen-educated Icelander probably had done), but to stress his conviction that Stefansson had supposedly been privy to medieval information that, by an extension of Skelton's argument, had reached both the author of the *Inventio Fortunata* and Johannes Ruysch.

According to Skelton, the Vínland Map's author had also used information from the specifically Anglo-Icelandic trade nexus when he formed his idea of the northwestern Atlantic. However, neither the Yale map's teasing representation of proto-America nor the analyses provided in *The Vinland Map and the Tartar Relation* give any hint of understanding that the silver that first impressed fifteenth-century Europeans in North America glittered off the backs of the coveted *Gadus morhua*.

About 1440, when the Vínland Map supposedly was drawn, cod was king in the North Atlantic, and the English led the royal progress. This situation had begun decades before Cabot and his men pulled up cod with their baskets somewhere off Newfoundland and long before the Portuguese gave yet another name to this region: the Baccalaos Island(s).

The Cod Wars Begin

English fishermen and fish merchants were important middlemen in what became a relentless pursuit of cod and cod products for both domestic and foreign markets. Fish liver oil and stockfish were as essential to the fifteenth-century English as they were to the Norse, and they were reliable staples for foreign trade. Oil was used everywhere for food as well as for heat and light, and fish was in demand as an important source of protein all over Europe when populations began to recover from the Black Death. Eventually, the demand for both of these commodities is very likely to have involved the Norse Greenlanders as English ships probed the waters to the west of Iceland.

Increasing English activities in Iceland after about 1400 set in motion important changes in Iceland's export economy and foreign relations (including with the Dano-Norwegian authorities and the German Hanse) as well as in the country's domestic economy and social structure. Personal wealth, tithes, and taxes were soon counted in loads of stockfish, while butter and other agricultural products became increasingly scarce as labor was deflected from farming to fishing.[139] Soon, the competition for both fresh and dried cod became so fierce in Iceland that violence involving English fishermen and merchants began to erupt in 1419. Although growing numbers of English ships were still leaving for Iceland with osmund iron and a variety of manufactured trade goods that they hoped to exchange for stockfish, competition on the fishing banks and increasingly onerous laws intended to protect the Dano-Norwegian crown's trading privileges drove English fishermen to push farther west in their search for new sources of fish. English ships also took to intercepting foreign vessels on the Iceland approaches—a task made easier by the maritime developments that gave the English supremacy of the seas in the North Atlantic at that time.[140]

During this earliest development of a cod war that still erupts from time to time, the Icelandic chieftain magistrates and other officials with whom the English cod merchants had the closest contact included several of the men whose voyage to Norway in 1410 went down in history as the last recorded voyage from Norse Greenland. One of these men, Thorstein Olafsson from North Iceland, had taken advantage of his four-year stay in the Eastern Settlement to get married in Hvalsey Church in 1408, his bride being the wealthy Icelandic heiress Sigrid Björnsdaughter. A letter that the foresighted Thorstein had secured from the Gardar *officialis* made it clear that conditions in the Eastern Settlement were normal—most likely at least as good as in Iceland, where the Black Death had recently wreaked havoc.[141]

When the highborn young Icelanders sailed from Greenland after their four-year sojourn, they thus knew that the Eastern Settlement was in fine shape when they left it, and they were obviously well aware of the potential profits from Greenlandic produce and trade goods because they headed straight for Norway, rather than for home, with their laden ship. Walrus tusks would still have been desirable to Europeans, and so would narwhal horns, hides, and lustrous furs. Fish and fish products may also have been taken on board in Greenland but are more likely to have figured in the men's relations with the English after they returned to Iceland.

As observed earlier, it is a matter of archaeological record that long after the Greenlanders' rupture with Norway, the Eastern Settlement had foreign visitors throughout a good part of the fifteenth century; some of the artifacts that the visitors left behind point to England. It would be odd indeed if these foreigners did not turn out to have been English. Greenland is Iceland's nearest neighbor and constitutes a prominent presence between that island and North America, the Englishmen's next recorded stop. Contact between the British

Isles and Norse Greenland went back a long way.[142] Thorstein and his Icelandic friends would also have had excellent Greenlandic connections by the time they returned to their native land where, as chieftains or chieftains' sons, they soon became involved with the English fish merchants. Any English fish merchant frustrated with the stockfish trade in Iceland and Norway would have paid attention if reminded that the Greenlanders also practiced the art of fish drying.

The lack of documentation for English activities in Greenland means little. At the time in question, fishing and the fish trade were notoriously under-reported, especially if tax avoidance was an issue. Fifteenth-century English (particularly Bristol) records of licenses and customs supposedly involving the Iceland codfish trade are so spotty and vague that much of the imported stockfish could have come from any northern region able to produce it.

Did a New Beginning Become an End?

Incomplete though it is, the available evidence strongly suggests that the Eastern Settlement not only was in good shape when Thorstein Olafsson and his companions left Greenland in 1410, but also that the inhabitants subsequently enjoyed a boost in prosperity that could have come only from foreign trade. At three of the four major trading centers in the Eastern Settlement—Hvalsey, Herjolfsnes, and Gardar—such important status symbols as festal halls appear to have been built early in the fifteenth century, well after official connections with Norway had been severed.[143]

The fact that the Norse Greenlanders continued to enjoy foreign trade in the fifteenth century, without relying on Norway, sends a strong message that they had been able to adapt to the changes taking place in the general North Atlantic economy at that time. To a considerable extent, those changes revolved around the trade in fresh and cured fish, a business that the English continued to dominate in the northwestern Atlantic for many decades, despite the increasing encouragement that the Dano-Norwegian authorities gave to Hanseatic merchants. If one accepts that the Norse Greenlanders' foreign contacts in the fifteenth century were in fact the English, and also that this contact to a large degree would have involved the sale of fish and fish products, it becomes necessary to take a fresh look at some recent scientific information about Norse Greenland on which different suppositions have so far been brought to bear.

In 1921, Poul Nørlund excavated Herjolfsnes graves—mostly from the fourteenth century and later—but found nothing to suggest a society in social or economic decline. Equally interesting is his observation that the climate in those parts did not cool significantly until after the Middle Ages because the masses of roots invading the shrouds showed that the ground had been warm enough to allow significant growth during subsequent summers, whereas in 1921 it was still very cold, even in summer.[144] Because some, although by no means all, of the recent climatological research nevertheless suggests that cold and/or erratic weather affected the Eastern Settlement during the period immediately prior to its desertion, several scholars have suggested that a worsening climate had been the reason why the home fields and pastures in the Eastern Settlement—by about 1450 or somewhat later—received less care than before and reverted to wild meadows.[145]

There is no arguing with the evidence assembled in the Eastern Settlement by the paleo-botanical expert Bent Fredskild, but interpreting such data in cause-and-effect terms calls for some basic caveats. For one thing, the lack of precise datings associated with the last phase of Norse habitation prevents certainty about the date of closure of the Eastern Settlement and about the relationship between the climate and the various other clues to the Norse Greenlanders' situation after the mid-fifteenth century. Other considerations, applicable to the entire period of Norse tenure in both settlements, relate directly to agricultural practices that the Norse Greenlanders shared with the medieval Icelanders.

It is generally accepted that in the sub-Arctic, the slow regeneration of plant cover removed through human or animal agency will be further slowed by a longtime reduction in the annual mean temperature of as little as one degree as well as by prolonged grazing. However, as the Icelandic biologist Ingvi Thorsteinsson recently pointed out, land deterioration in southwest Greenland in the Middle Ages was not nearly as severe as in Iceland, "which experienced similar effects of human habitation and cooling climate." He also noted that while soil erosion has been demonstrated in some areas in southwest Greenland, the physical properties of the soils in the region make it unlikely that large areas were thus damaged. Undisturbed areas in the former Eastern Settlement are not only green but also have a rich natural vegetation that amounts to "grazing lands of the highest quality."[146]

High-quality grazing lands had tempted Eirik the Red and his fellow Norse to settle in Greenland with their livestock. Cows require better summer pastures than either sheep or goats and will survive a sub-Arctic winter only with proper shelter and sufficient hay and other fodder. In return for such time-consuming care, cows produce more human food relative to grazing acreage than do sheep. In a thought-provoking essay discussing these equations, the modern Icelandic historian Axel Kristinsson points out that Iceland's pastoralist farmers have always lived with a situation where labor invested in keeping cows could outweigh the disadvantages of a property smaller than the large area needed for sheep farming. However, so long as there is plenty of search-and-destroy pasture, sheep (and goats) can cope with far more spartan conditions than their bovine competition can handle, which means less work for the farmer who is not required to fertilize his haying fields or gather both hay and other winter fodder.[147] Under certain circumstances, this situation would obviously provide important advantages for a sheep farmer.

There is no reason to suppose that the Norse Greenland farmers were less flexible than their Icelandic cousins or less able to create a balance between their needs and natural resources. If fertilizing and harvesting their home fields for the sake of their cows required a disproportionate amount of effort toward the end of their tenure, neglect would soon have been reflected in the manner suggested by Fredskild's pollen analyses. The available data do not prove that the Norse reduced their flocks of sheep while simultaneously neglecting their home fields. Cows were expendable, but sheep were not. The Norse Greenlanders may well have encouraged these tough animals to keep producing meat, milk, and wool with minimum supervision while roaming the hills because human labor was needed elsewhere.

Whether due to a spell of colder, damper weather or for other reasons, home fields falling into disuse sometime around the middle of the fifteenth century would at the very least signal a changing domestic economy. Corroborative evidence for such a change exists in skeletal and midden studies of Norse Greenland material, which in some locations has revealed a substantially increased reliance on marine food resources during the final occupation phase in the Eastern Settlement. The midden evidence consists primarily of an increased proportion of seal bones to other mammal bones.[148]

However, this evidence does not proclaim that the Norse Greenlanders, increasingly unable to feed themselves and their cattle, had killed off their animals, let their home fields go untended, and relied on seals in a desperate attempt to stay alive. Instead, there is a strong possibility that just like the Icelandic economy by this time, the Greenlandic one had become focused on supplying the English with stockfish and fish liver oil, and that this effort had siphoned labor away from the farms and into the fishing boats—as in Iceland during the same period.

Although the number of Norse Greenlanders involved in such economic changes remains unknown, it is safe to say that it would have been a fraction of the fifty thousand or so inhabitants of Iceland at that time. The quantities of stockfish and train oil that the Norse Greenlanders would have been capable of producing may nevertheless have been significant enough to warrant the attention of the occasional English trader eager to circumvent Dano-Norwegian taxes, thus providing the Eastern Settlement with sporadic ship arrivals much as in earlier times. The signs of economic upswing in the first part of the fifteenth century, coupled with the objects of foreign origin found in late-phase Norse farm ruins, suggest much the same story.

Greenland archaeology provides only a part of the tale, however. English and Icelandic records offer suggestions about what happened in consequence of the English exploitation of North Atlantic resources that eventually involved the fecund North American fishing banks. This transition period in the English cod fishing business affected English sailings to Iceland in the last two decades of the fifteenth century and would also have concerned Greenlanders, just when their own community appears to have been going through yet another transition from a modestly self-sufficient, fish-exporting community to a landscape where smoke no longer rose above turf-covered Norse roofs. The first signs of such economic change, more ominous this time, would have been fewer ship arrivals once the English were able to meet their needs more easily elsewhere.

While stockfish remained an eminently desirable cargo for English cod merchants, there was always a demand for fresh and salted fish as well. These commodities had the additional advantage that the crew could claim to have been fishing in "home waters," so that nobody could accuse them of having violated the taxes and restrictions that applied to stockfish. There were also other good reasons for the English to seek new opportunities for their fishermen away from Norway and Iceland, where the trade in stockfish was increasingly and jealously guarded, and where competition on the fishing banks continued to be fierce.

During the last couple of decades in the fifteenth century, Dano-Norwegian crown representatives and Hanse merchants made the English increasingly unwelcome in both Iceland and Norway. Fortunately for the

English, by 1480 at the latest, Bristol men in search of less troublesome fishing opportunities had learned how to navigate directly from western Ireland to the Newfoundland-Labrador banks ("the Isle of Brazil") without using the familiar outward route by way of Iceland and/or Greenland.[149] Now they could salt down quantities of fresh American cod and other fish before heading home along the fifty-third parallel, as Ruysch described doing on his voyage aboard an English fishing vessel shortly after 1500. Not only did the shorter route make it less likely that a cargo would spoil before it reached the home markets, but also as medieval economic historians like Maryanne Kowaleski have demonstrated, the second half of the fifteenth century saw big advances in the art of salting and curing fish just when English fishermen went ever farther into the Atlantic to catch their prey.[150]

The English nevertheless continued to buy stockfish from both Iceland and Norway during the later part of the fifteenth century. This caused considerable friction between them and the Germans in both places and produced at least a hint of documentary evidence for English voyages to Greenland in the late fifteenth century. On a visit to Copenhagen in the mid-seventeenth century, the Frenchman Isaac de la Peyrère learned from the Danish savant Ole Worm about an old Danish document (since lost) concerning an event in Bergen in 1484, when enraged Germans had killed a party of sailors bragging about the valuable wares they had obtained in Greenland. The Frenchman discounted the tale on the grounds that the Norwegians had long since stopped sailing to Greenland.[151] However, there is surviving documentary evidence of bad German-English relations in Bergen in both 1475 and 1476.[152] Any truth in Ole Worm's tale of confrontation just a few years later is therefore likely to have concerned English sailors rather than Norwegian ones, in which case the story indicates that some Englishmen had continued to trade with Norse Greenland until at least 1480.

With the growing English recourse to American fish, Greenlandic trade with the English would have begun to fall off at a time when, in addition to adjusting to new economic pressures, the Norse Greenlanders may also have suffered another period of inclement weather that made terrestrial food resources scarcer for both them and their animals. The Norse Greenlanders had gone through bad patches before, just like the Icelanders, and both they and their livestock had recovered, but if they were faced with converging economic hardships that now included the threat of virtual isolation from foreign trade, at a time when they no longer had oceangoing ships of their own after decades of isolation from Markland, they may have accepted an offer to relocate as skilled fishermen-farmers in a sheltered area along the Newfoundland/ Labrador coast, far enough north and east to avoid clashes with the Spanish over the 1494 Tordesillas line intended to forestall Spanish-Portuguese arguments over the right to newly discovered territory. The Cantino map of 1502, the earliest extant map to draw this line bisecting the Atlantic, makes it clear that after the Corte Real voyages, the Portuguese regarded as their territory not only southern Greenland, but also an imprecisely defined and imperfectly explored part of eastern Canada.[153]

If the Greenland Norse made the momentous decision to relocate farther westward, as their ancestors had done five centuries earlier, it would again have been to a land of whose existence they already knew. This time, however, the likely lure would have come from an English or Anglo-Portuguese enterprise hoping to use the Norse Greenlanders' skills in fishing and preserving cod, at a permanent Canadian fishing station where the presence of women and children would have ensured a reasonably normal and stable community.

Despite the shortage of documents concerning North Atlantic trade, fishing, and exploration in the years just before and after 1500, there is written evidence of joint English-Portuguese exploitation of New World resources in the Davis Strait region. Up until about 1500, neither England nor Portugal had a surplus population for colonization, and Greenland had the additional advantage of being close to the American northeastern coast. The most compelling reason for wanting Norse Greenlanders, however, would have been that making stockfish was a skill not traditionally acquired by people from milder climates because the process requires the cold, dry air of the Far North.[154]

Chances are that any such enterprise early in the "European contact period" would have foundered too quickly to leave obvious traces on the Canadian side. The sparse extant information about the earliest Renaissance colonization attempts along the Newfoundland/Labrador coasts certainly suggests that they ended in disaster. In the mid-sixteenth century, Francisco López de Gómara pointed out the dangers of such northern voyages, most of which had left no records. He wrote: "Many undertook to continue and complete the discoveries initiated by Christopher Columbus. . . . But as most of those who made discoveries were ruined thereby, there is no recollection left by any of them so far as I know, particularly those who steered northward, coasting the Bacallaos region and Labrador."[155]

The use of emigration to settle a new fishing station may seem far-fetched, but establishing year-round stations in North America was in fact a high priority among Europeans in the early sixteenth century. Furthermore, just over a century later, Nordic people were courted as immigrants to America on account of specifically northern skills. In the 1620s, for example, while the Plymouth Pilgrims were settling New England, modest numbers of Norwegians and Swedes skilled in shipbuilding and tar burning were recruited by the Dutch in New Amsterdam—now New York City.[156]

The above suggestion for what may have happened to the Eastern Settlement residents, sometime around 1500, is a theory only, just like every other explanation so far offered for the Norse Greenlanders' disappearance. It is nevertheless a theory that agrees with present knowledge about the Norse colonies in Greenland and Iceland and ties in with information about voyages in the North Atlantic and to eastern Canada during the early Renaissance.

Much is yet to be discovered, and some details will probably remain obscure despite infrared probes, underwater archaeology, and other impressive technological gains. There is sufficient knowledge to say that neither the Vínland Map nor *The Vínland Map and the Tartar Relation* reflects the history of the Norse in Greenland and North America. Both the map and the book express the mistaken notion that for only a brief and definable time in history did the Norse make their daring voyages to North America, before they retired for good to the safety of Greenland and Iceland where no Skrælings threatened.

George D. Painter's introductory essay to the second edition (1995) of *The Vínland Map and the Tartar Relation* reflected this attitude anew when he called the map a "major and authentic message from the middle ages on a hitherto unknown moment in the history of the world and American discovery."[157] Had any late-medieval cartographer been able to show the actual Norse experience with the North American east coast—from their first organized voyages about AD 1000 and for centuries more—the result would have looked nothing like the Vínland Map. Sadly, Painter's statement is representative of the nineteenth- and early-twentieth-century thinking that continues to influence the history of Norse voyages to America and to this day dominates the discussion about the Vínland Map.

CHAPTER 3

The Black Hole of Provenance

A Child of Unknown Parentage

The provenance of the Vínland Map and its companion manuscripts resembles a cosmic black hole—pregnant with the possibility of creation but invisible to the ordinary human eye.

In cataloguing medieval codices at Yale's Beinecke Library, Barbara Shailor weighed her words carefully when she stated that the volume with the Vínland Map "was acquired from a private collection in Europe by L. C. Witten, who subsequently determined that the Vinland Map and the *Hystoria Tartarorum* were once bound together with another manuscript then in the possession of Thomas E. Marston."[1]

Shailor did not specify what sort of "private collection" was involved (a notable stalling point with Witten), but she put the reader on notice that the primary responsibility for claiming that there is a close relationship between the map and not only one, but two companion manuscripts, rested with Laurence C. Witten II (1926–95), the New Haven antiquarian book dealer and Yale alumnus who brokered the deal that eventually resulted in Yale's ownership. He also played a key part in the developments leading to the 1965 publication of *The Vinland Map and the Tartar Relation* and stayed so closely involved with this process that when Marston was injured by a car while the book was in the final stages of preparation, Witten copyedited and proofread Marston's contribution, which he said he "certainly did not alter . . . very much."[2]

Witten's continued commitment might seem reasonable in an antiquarian book dealer handling such an unusual item as the Vínland Map, but it was not so reasonable in this case. A graduate of the Yale School of Music, Witten lacked the specialist historical, literary, cartographical, and paleographical knowledge necessary to evaluate these manuscript items. He nevertheless

87

made his judgment calls on the map, on its relationship to the two accompanying manuscript texts (the *Hystoria Tartarorum,* or "Tartar Relation," and four books of the *Speculum Historiale* by Vincent of Beauvais), and on the relationship of the two manuscript texts to one another.

It would be both unwise and unfair, however, to assume that Witten or any other named person was the primary source of the mycelium of deception, which in this instance spread beneath the surface of a respectable antiquarian trade. Whether Witten made his earliest decisions alone once he had purchased the volume with the map, or whether he was urged along by others similarly lacking in expertise, he did have associates from the very beginning of the Vínland Map enterprise, but not all of their names are necessarily known.

The comparatively voluble Witten nevertheless remains the first and best candle in the black void from which Yale's cartographic star emerged, especially because his accounts often contradict each other and thus inadvertently reveal the complexity of the maneuvers preceding Yale's fanfare announcement in 1965. In one respect Witten's accounts never wavered, however: He made it very clear that the central figure in his own purchase of the volume containing the Vínland Map and the "Tartar Relation" was a colorful Italian antiquarian dealer named Enzo Ferrajoli de Ry, domiciled in Barcelona with his Spanish wife Margarita. Witten subsequently revealed that Ferrajoli had also been directly involved in marketing the *Speculum* fragments that Marston bought just a few months later. The same few locations and people are in fact linked in varying constellations throughout the known early saga of the Vínland Map, and Witten associated with all of them.

Ferrajoli often left his home in Barcelona to search for books throughout Western Europe and was, in Witten's words, "a knowledgeable *courtier,* or 'runner,' of rare books and manuscripts." Although Witten first traded with Ferrajoli in 1957, when he was just six years into his own career as an antiquarian book dealer, the well-established Swiss dealer Nicolas Rauch had evidently introduced him to Ferrajoli a couple of years earlier. Witten's later and evidently more memorable encounter with him took place in Geneva, Switzerland, in 1957, in the shop belonging to their mutual friend Rauch, another key figure in the Vínland Map transactions. Rauch's Geneva shop "had a special importance in the antiquarian book world, because in Switzerland Rauch was in the ideal position to make banking arrangements for dealers and private clients in other European countries," according to Witten.[3]

During the period when Witten was first confronted with the Vínland

Map, Ferrajoli's frequent visits to Switzerland involved not only antiquarian deals but also acting as a courier between his native Italy and the former Italian queen, now safely exiled in Switzerland.[4] Switzerland had managed to stay neutral during World War II, its bank accounts remaining the very model of discretion and thus especially useful to anyone desiring anonymity. After the war, the country retained the advantages of its banking system, its neutral stance, and its strategic location relative to several European countries.

The first published account of Witten's 1957 Geneva meeting with Ferrajoli and Rauch, and of their subsequent business transactions, did not come from Witten himself, but from a brief description in the 1965 edition of *The Vinland Map and the Tartar Relation*, where Thomas E. Marston wrote about his own introduction to the map and its companion manuscript:

> In October 1957 the antiquarian bookseller Laurence Witten, of New Haven, showed to my colleague Alexander O. Vietor and myself a slim volume, bound in recent calf, which contained a map of the world, including Iceland, Greenland, and Vinland, and a hitherto unknown account of the mission of John de Plano Carpini to the Mongols in 1245–47. Mr. Witten told us that he had acquired it from a private collection in Europe.[5]

Early Misgivings About the "Private Collection"

Almost two years before Marston published his account of Witten's introduction of the Vínland Map to his two friends at Yale, the English geographer and cartographic historian E. G. R. Taylor wrote down her own recollections of the provenance of the Vínland Map volume, which differed somewhat from Marston's. She noted that in the summer of 1962, Marston's coauthor Skelton, who was then working on *The Vinland Map and the Tartar Relation*, had in confidence shown her photographs and blueprints of the map, which was said to have been discovered when an unnamed Spanish library was dispersing its collection. Taylor also observed that because early maps and atlases—especially those dealing with America—were now changing hands at high prices, forgery had become so profitable that a buyer should insist on being informed of an item's provenance and history.[6]

Curators and other scholars charged with authenticating an unusual or controversial item normally do not consider "a private collection" or "an unnamed Spanish library" sufficient provenance. Witten was therefore asked to address the problem directly when Wilcomb E. Washburn (1915–97), director of the Smithsonian Institution's Department of American Studies, invited an assortment of scholars to Washington, D.C., on November 15 and 16, 1966, to discuss the many questions that had arisen after the Vínland Map and the Yale book were made public the previous autumn.

Witten, the first presenter at the symposium, said Ferrajoli had arranged for him to see the owner's library with the volume containing the Vínland Map and the "Tartar Relation," and he had bought both that volume and several other things on the spot. During the discussion afterward, he stated:

> I think that Messrs. Marston and Vietor and the purchaser of the manuscript know that the Vinland Map came from a private library of fairly large dimensions. It had in it a rather large number of fifteenth- and sixteenth-century printed books and a rather large number of manuscripts. . . . While I do not know this to be a fact, I have the impression that other booksellers visited and bought from this library.[7]

Witten also quoted the owner of the library, which still contained both volumes in 1957, as having said that he did not know the origin of the volumes, but that he thought they had been in his library for two or more generations.

These detailed statements give the impression that Witten described a firsthand encounter with the Vínland Map volume's owner, but he consistently declined to reveal the name of the private collector whom Ferrajoli had represented in this case. At the 1966 conference, Witten claimed that the owner "did not wish it known that he had such valuable things . . . in his possession because he would be taxed on them."[8]

On March 6, 1966, the *Sunday Times* (London) had published a lengthy article entitled "Is the Vinland Map a forgery?" In a telephone interview, Thomas Marston, Witten's closest contact at Yale in these dealings, had reportedly said that there was no prospect that the map's provenance could be investigated further, adding: "I understood that the man it came from couldn't remember where he got it." When Witten was similarly questioned about the map's provenance, he had replied that he could not trace it past the owner he bought it from. "That aspect is a blind alley," he assured his interviewer.[9] Marston and Witten made their newspaper statements eight months before Witten told those who attended the Smithsonian conference about the "private library" he had personally been privileged to visit.

In an account that Witten published many years later, he wrote that the Vínland Map volume had been among several items that Ferrajoli was offering for sale through Rauch. There was no further mention of Witten's visit to the volume's previous home in the "private library." Nor was there any more talk of a specifically Spanish provenance. In fact, Witten repeatedly claimed that he never did learn where his friend Ferrajoli had obtained the volume containing the Vínland Map and the "Tartar Relation" because Ferrajoli insisted that he had promised not to divulge the previous owner's identity. Witten observed that this was in any case a period when buyers of rare books and manuscripts did not inquire deeply into an item's provenance.[10]

Ferrajoli's reported evasiveness on this issue makes an interesting contrast to the quite detailed information Witten possessed about Ferrajoli's private life, which he also reveals in this article, and with which Ferrajoli himself must have supplied him.[11]

The Spanish Connection

A letter of May 8, 1974, from Alexander Vietor at Yale to the well-known English map scholar Eila Campbell makes it abundantly clear that the "private library" had been a deliberate obfuscation on Witten's part. Despite the latter's statements at the Smithsonian in 1966, he never did see the private library and its owner, Vietor wrote, adding that he believed Witten had bought the map from Ferrajoli in Geneva and that it had come from Madrid.[12] Barely three weeks later, on May 28, Vietor wrote to Helen Wallis (in charge of the Map Room in the British Library since Skelton's retirement in 1967), telling her that Witten had suggested that the Vínland Map came from the Luís Fortuny library in Madrid. Vietor did not know how much to read into this, however, since it was clear that Witten had not personally gone to Fortuny's.[13]

Vietor's second letter shows that the possible connection between Luís Fortuny and the Vínland Map volume was known to Vietor at least as early as 1974 and that Witten had been the source of this suggestion. Witten himself made no secret of his suspicions, which he claimed dated back to 1963, when he had gone to Spain to visit Ferrajoli, who was newly out of prison after having been convicted of shady book transactions and who had introduced Witten to "a distinguished man of about fifty, Don Luís Fortuny." Witten "suddenly felt that this man Fortuny was the source of the Vínland Map" and challenged Ferrajoli on the matter but was reportedly made none the wiser.

After Ferrajoli's death from a heart attack not long after the 1966 Washington conference, Witten—who was still convinced that Fortuny "had played a major role in getting the manuscripts from wherever they had been sleeping"—gave Fortuny's name and address to both Marston and Vietor and urged them to get in touch with this Spanish dealer if they so wished.[14]

The possible involvement of Luís Fortuny was thus old news when Wilcomb Washburn wrote his prefatory essay for a second edition (1995) of *The Vinland Map and the Tartar Relation*. In that piece, Washburn mentioned neither Witten nor Vietor in this connection at all but instead claimed joint credit with Ardell Abrahamson for the Fortuny "discovery."[15] Abrahamson's investigations have remained unpublished and therefore unavailable for critical, scholarly review. Washburn's secondhand account of Abrahamson's work (which was evidently undertaken in the early 1990s) also included several unsubstantiated statements designed to make it appear that the Vínland Map had once belonged to Christopher Columbus. Soon after the publication of Washburn's essay, Abrahamson repeated these ideas to a reporter back home in Minnesota: "A very good case can be made that this was the very map used by Columbus to persuade the king and queen of Spain to send him on his voyage, and is thus a pivotal document in world history."[16]

Although biased in favor of the supposed Columbus link, some of the information in Washburn's 1995 piece concerning Ferrajoli's Spanish connections seems to have a basis in reality. Washburn noted, for example, that a description appeared in Rauch's Geneva catalogue number 19 (October 1957) of the 1507 Rome Ptolemy that Witten claimed (in 1966) to have bought from "the private library." In addition, Abrahamson reportedly had traced connections between Ferrajoli and a man named Luís Barba, the proprietor of the antiquariat Pro Libris in Barcelona, who in turn was closely connected both to Ferrajoli's wife Margarita and to the antiquarian dealer Luís Fortuny Biéto.[17]

Whatever its antiquarian point of origin, the Vínland Map was evidently well traveled by the time it came to rest in New Haven. As noted above, Vietor believed that the volume had in fact been in Madrid before it came to Geneva, and Skelton had told E. G. R. Taylor that it came from a Spanish library. In late 1966, at the Smithsonian conference, Witten mentioned that sometime in the spring or summer of 1957, before he himself had even seen the volume with the Vínland Map, Ferrajoli had shown both that volume and several others to booksellers in Geneva, Paris, and London.[18]

Considering that Ferrajoli made his home in Spain and ran a regular antiquarian business in Barcelona, a Spanish detour is a distinct possibility that obviously would not have precluded other stops along the way. One such stop is suggested by a memorandum that Eila Campbell wrote to herself on August 15, 1974. She noted that it might be worth interviewing Carla Marzoli in Milan because Marzoli had told her shortly after Skelton's death in 1970 that Italian booksellers would have nothing to do with the Vínland Map; they were not sure of its authenticity and had not been told about its provenance. In Campbell's judgment, it would therefore appear that an attempt had been made to introduce the map to Italian booksellers before it was brought to England.[19]

An English Sojourn

Shortly before the Vínland Map volume reached England, it had visited Paris, where it apparently met with little interest. Its career in London also turned out to be rather short and unsatisfactory. At the 1966 Smithsonian conference, Witten described the English event:

> Most keenly interested was a London bookseller, J. I. Davis, proprietor
> of Davis and Orioli, Ltd., who persuaded Ferrajoli to go with him
> to the British Museum to have the Vinland Map looked at by distin-
> guished members of the museum staff. The V.M. and the T.R. were
> taken to the museum, where they were seen by R. A. Skelton and
> George D. Painter (possibly by others, too). I do not know precisely
> what was said at this time, but the V.M. and the T.R. were returned,
> Davis could not make up his mind to buy them, and Ferrajoli continued
> on his travels. What I have related so far is well-supported hearsay.[20]

Whether "hearsay" or a convenient invention, this statement is at variance with a more elaborate version that Witten himself supplied some years later, and neither version is well enough supported to mesh with the few extant documents describing an event that barely caused a ripple at the British Museum at the time. Nor are Witten's statements compatible with the recollections of some of the people involved when the map was rejected as suspect following a brief look by British Museum manuscript experts.

There is sufficient documentary evidence to show that the map volume's chief contact at the British Museum, although brief, had been with the Department of Printed Books, whose principal keeper in 1957 was F. C. Francis. The Department of Manuscripts had been involved for just a few minutes.[21] The brevity and informality of the inspection in the latter department are clear from a 1966 letter written in connection with an impending London exhibition of the Vínland Map and the two textual manuscripts associated with it. Theodore C. Skeat, at that time the keeper of manuscripts in the British Museum, cast his mind back to his assistant keeper days of 1957 and noted tersely: "So far as I am concerned, the position is that although this is technically manuscript material, it was never deposited in my Department, and all the research and subsequent publication has been carried out by Skelton and Painter without any reference to me."[22]

Both in 1957 and 1967, Raleigh Ashlin Skelton ("Peter" to his friends) was under the authority of the Department of Printed Books, whose principal keeper when the 1967 exhibition was being arranged was A. H. Chaplin. Replying to Skeat's letter, Chaplin suggested that Skeat should get Skelton and Painter to tell him what they knew about this whole story.[23]

Considering that Skelton and his colleague Painter had evidently chaperoned the Vínland Map volume during its visit to the British Museum in 1957 and had also worked together on the secretly prepared 1965 book about the map and the "Tartar Relation," one might reasonably suppose that both men had eventually learned all about Witten's part in the map's saga, and both of them would remember the circumstances under which the map volume had been brought to their attention in London in 1957. However, this supposition is tested by the variant of the provenance story that Painter gave shortly after his retirement from what had just become The British Library.

At a meeting with Painter and Derek Weber (editor of the *Geographical Magazine*) on September 23, 1974, Eila Campbell asked Painter about the map's 1957 appearance in London. Painter replied that in 1957, the map was thought to have been acquired in Spain during the sale of ecclesiastical manuscripts— possibly in Zaragoza—but its origin had not been "firmly established." Because Skelton had been absent on leave when the map reached London, it had been brought to Painter by Davis of Davis and Orioli—not as an item offered for sale, but simply as an interesting discovery being "floated" by a dealer. According to Painter, he had been interested in the map, but at no time had he seriously thought of buying it for the British Museum. Instead, he observed that it had all along been expected that the map would end up in the United States.[24]

Painter's account is notable for several reasons. It leaves Skelton out of the early picture altogether; it runs counter to repeated assurances by Witten that the volume with the map was in no way connected with the Zaragoza cathedral library; it implies that a U.S. purchaser had essentially been the target all along; and it suggests that had Painter wished to do so, he would have had the authority to purchase a manuscript map for the museum. However, Painter's responsibilities involved early printed books, so he would have had no authority to purchase a manuscript map for the museum. The final say in such a matter would have rested with the keeper of manuscripts, who in 1957 was Bertram Schofield. The hierarchical and formal nature of the British Museum's administrative and curatorial structure would similarly have affected Skelton, who, like Painter, in 1957 was subject to the authority of the principal keeper of the Department of Printed Books.[25]

Witten had not been present during the 1957 British Museum interlude. His version of that event was published many years later, but while his account then was no doubt colored by the passage of time as well as by the secondhand nature of his information, there would have been little reason for him simply to invent the story he appended after noting that the London antiquarian dealer Davis had taken the "extraordinary manuscript" on approval and had contacted Skelton for an "expert approval." Witten wrote: "Without telling Davis, Skelton in turn showed the volume to his colleague George D. Painter. . . . (This transpired years later when Painter told me, with no attempt to conceal his amusement, that he and Skelton had surreptitiously taken a tracing of the map, in violation of all promises made to Davis.)"[26]

There is no uncertainty about the Vínland Map's having made a brief appearance in the Map Room in 1957. Helen Wallis, who at that time was Skelton's assistant superintendent, glimpsed the map and immediately suspected its authenticity on cartographical grounds, but her opinion was not asked at that time.[27] The minutes of a meeting she attended in London in June of 1975 provide further details about her own involvement in this event. The minutes state that she reported having been in the Map Room at the British Museum when George Painter brought the map in to show to Peter Skelton on a Saturday afternoon in 1957. Because Skelton was absent at that moment, she was the first cartographic expert there who saw it, but she did so only briefly.[28]

Wallis headed a symposium in February of 1974 at the Royal Geographical Society. Her published report leaves no doubt of Skelton's involvement. Wallis based her account on her intimate knowledge of the British Museum as well as on her personal experience with the 1957 showing of the map when she noted: "In London, escorted by the London dealer Joseph Irving Davis of Davis and Orioli Limited, Ferrajoli brought [the map] into the British Museum, where it was briefly examined by George Painter, Assistant Keeper in charge of incunabula in the Department of Printed Books, Dr. Skelton, Super-intendent of the Map Room, and Dr. Schofield, Keeper of Manuscripts. I also had a glimpse of it."[29]

Bertram Schofield clearly did not sense any ambivalence in Skelton's de-meanor in 1957 because he noted in 1974 that Skelton had been very anxious for the Department of Manuscripts to purchase the map. Cyril E. Wright, who had also been present in the Department of Manuscripts when the map was brought there in 1957, offered his own 1974 recollection of that moment. He told of having seen the map for less than an hour on the day it was shown to Theodore Skeat, and he definitely recalled that the Department of Manuscripts as such had been kept entirely out of the picture in 1957 and that the Map Room had taken a very proprietary view of the item. He could not remember, however, whether Skelton had actually said at that time that the Vínland Map was genuine, or whether he made that claim only after the map had been acquired by Yale, at which time his views naturally became well known.[30]

Skeat stated his views of this 1957 event in 1966 and reiterated them in 1974. It was his opinion that for the Vínland Map and "Tartar Relation" volume to receive serious consideration, it would have had to be deposited formally in the Department of Manuscripts, which was never done.[31] The principal keeper of printed books, A. H. Chaplin, observed in his turn that the Yale manuscripts in question were never deposited or kept in his department in connection with the 1967 exhibition at the British Museum, although he recalled that one of those manuscripts had been brought there some years earlier by a bookseller (actually the London dealer Irving Davis) who had showed it to George Painter. According to Chaplin, the volume had also been shown to Skeat's predecessor Schofield.[32]

When the map was brought into the Department of Manuscripts in 1957, it was in fact rejected by Schofield—a reaction that he subsequently did not disguise from his family. He found the map suspect because it lacked proper provenance, and as an experienced paleographer he thought the handwriting in the map legends had too strong a nineteenth-century flavor.[33] His was a very astute observation.

The Map's Provenance No Clearer by 1974

The 1974 symposium organized by Helen Wallis was an important event in the ongoing discussion about the Vínland Map. The main impetus for this undertaking was a recent announcement by the noted Chicago chemists Walter and Lucy McCrone that they had discovered a modern element in the Vínland Map's ink. They reported personally on their research at the Royal Geographical Society symposium.

It was in large part left to Wallis to answer the public questions that inevitably resurfaced about the map's provenance and about the reported English rejection of the manuscript volume. Skelton had died after a 1970 car accident, and the two antiquarian dealers Davis and Ferrajoli were also dead by the time the McCrones' news broke. When *The Observer* (London) took up these matters on January 27, 1974, Wallis told the reporter that the volume had indeed been shown to museum experts in 1957, and that Skelton "began with doubts, but then decided [the map] was authentic." She also recollected that the item had at one time been in the hands of the Hampstead booksellers Davis and Orioli, but she was uncertain whether the firm had ever actually acquired it.[34]

The Observer reporter was unable to contact Marston, who was on holiday in the Caribbean just then. If Painter was approached, no response was reported. The newspaper did question Witten, who expressed amazement and disbelief at the McCrones' disclosure. He confirmed that he had bought the map volume from Ferrajoli for "only" thirty-five hundred dollars but maintained that Ferrajoli's involvement with the theft of manuscripts from the Zaragoza cathedral library had no bearing on the authenticity of the map because it had never been a part of the La Seo collection. The article also noted: "Mr. Witten says that it was his understanding that Ferrajoli had not owned the manuscript for long, but had bought it from a Spaniard who said that it had been in his family for some time."[35]

Although three published accounts (including Witten's in 1966) indicate that Ferrajoli was personally involved at every stage of the Vínland Map dealings, it is unclear whether he had actually been present during the map's whirlwind tour inside the British Museum.[36] On balance, however, it seems likely that he was in London at that time. Just what happened between the time the museum showed its disinterest in purchasing the map and the time the map found its current home at Yale is as uncertain as whether Witten had been involved even before his well-publicized Geneva meeting with Ferrajoli and Rauch. Witten's own later admission—that he had met with Davis in Milan a day or two after he had decided to purchase the volume containing the Vínland Map—nevertheless suggests such an early involvement. "Davis rue-

fully congratulated me on buying the map volume," Witten reported in
1989.[37] Considering Davis's reported lack of success in unhanding the map volume up to that point, any ruefulness on his part over the sale to Witten is hard
to fathom.

Regardless of who the key players were in those convoluted, unsuccessful,
and possibly half-hearted attempts to sell the map and its companion manuscript in Europe in 1957, the sellers' chief obstacle was the lack of proper
provenance for the volume—a problem that did not go away with Witten's inconsistent stories about his first encounters with the other dealers involved.[38]

A Muddied Pond

Witten said that the reason he did not insist on "pedigrees" for the Vínland
Map and many other items he purchased in Europe during the same period
was that conditions in postwar Europe were such that people made whatever
profit they could, with few questions asked.[39] Indeed, much more recent news
stories involving auction houses and museums have amply demonstrated that
profits are still being made from heirlooms and other personal belongings
stolen or confiscated from Jews and others unfortunate enough to run afoul of
Nazi authorities or from items that had been taken as "souvenirs" by occupation soldiers at the end of World War II.

In this context, the Vínland Map and its companion manuscripts appeared
on the antiquarian market soon after 1955. That was the year the Allied
authorities handed over to the Germans and the Austrians the task of reunit-
ing Nazi loot with former owners. Oversight with looted property now
became even more lax in a still chaotic postwar Europe, with the result that
antiquarian items from any source could change hands and cross borders with
greater ease. For Ferrajoli personally, his professional life had probably also
become somewhat simplified in 1955 when Spain was finally admitted to the
United Nations.[40]

In the second half of the 1950s, the stolen codices from the Zaragoza cathedral library (which had been photographed in situ by the Leonine Commission as recently as 1954) appeared on the European antiquarian market,
leading to Ferrajoli's imprisonment. Ferrajoli was not the only dealer involved,
however. Several of these volumes, with the marks of former ownership
removed or defaced, passed through the hands of three or four of the people
most directly involved in the Vínland Map transactions, including Witten's.[41]

There is nevertheless reason to believe Witten's heated denials that the Vínland Map volume had come from the Biblioteca Capitular de la Seo because the volume's likely previous homes do not appear to have included this library. However, Witten's and his colleagues' involvement with the Zaragoza codices and similar deals suggests that they were not too particular about the sources of their merchandise.

Reflecting many years later on his Geneva experience, Witten wrote: "Whatever the Vinland Map and the Tartar Relation may ultimately prove to be, I fell under their spell in 1957. . . . In the end I was able to buy it from Ferrajoli with the blessing of Nicolas Rauch."[42] By his own account, the thirty-five hundred dollars that he paid for the volume containing the Vínland Map was an amount reportedly agreed upon in advance between Ferrajoli and the person on whose behalf Ferrajoli was acting. At the Smithsonian conference in 1966, Witten called this sum "too little for a conspiracy and too much for a really accidental find." Moments later, he described it as "an acceptable going price in 1957 for a fifteenth-century world map which is very far from beautiful," and he agreed with John Parker, who observed: "As to the price, Mr. Witten, I think you got the greatest bargain in the world." More than thirty years later, Witten claimed that thirty-five hundred dollars had been a "considerable" amount for him, especially given the dubious provenance of the material.[43]

He was certainly well aware of prices and trends operating in the antiquarian world by 1966. Five years earlier he had made a point of noting the purchase sum of about $182,000 for a thirteenth-century English "Apocalypse" codex with eighty-two miniatures (two to a leaf), or $2,250 per picture. Perhaps reflecting on his recent advantageous resale of the Vínland Map volume, he observed: "Many American institutions have been quite avidly acquiring manuscripts which are interesting primarily for their contents. . . . Marston at Yale has built up a very fine collection and has more recently turned to medieval texts."[44]

A Companion to the Vínland Map Volume

The price tag for the Vínland Map volume did not remain "reasonable" for long. A second volume surfaced, containing a manuscript that appeared to be another ancient companion to the map. Although this second volume, which contained four books of the *Speculum Historiale* by Vincent of Beauvais in a dilapidated old binding, earned the London dealer Irving Davis a mere seventy-five pounds sterling (according to Witten's statement during the Smithsonian conference), the two volumes together reportedly fetched about one million dollars when resold. Paul Saenger gives this resale figure as three hundred thousand dollars, but the one-million-dollar figure was reiterated in early 1996 by Wilcomb Washburn when he launched a fresh attempt to have the map declared authentic a short time before his death in 1997.[45]

The price increments cited here for the Vínland Map reflect only published figures. When the map's current curator at Yale's Beinecke Library was asked to confirm the various sales figures, he replied that he was unable to do so on the basis of the available records.[46]

In Shailor's 1987 catalog descriptions of the Vínland Map and its companion manuscripts, she cautiously noted that the two volumes were presented to the Beinecke Library by an "anonymous donor" in 1965.[47] The publishers' preface to the 1995 edition of *The Vinland Map and the Tartar Relation* finally confirmed the persistent rumor that this anonymous donor was Paul Mellon, a loyal and wealthy Yale alumnus who became widely known for his quiet and generous philanthropy and who, until his death in early 1999, usually kept a low profile in his numerous benefactions on both sides of the Atlantic. His gift of the three manuscripts to his alma mater is not nearly as odd as the tale of how the two volumes that he purchased in 1959, ostensibly from Witten's wife, had been reunited in the first place and priced so high that Yale could not acquire them out of regular funds but had to seek out "a friend of Yale University."[48]

The story of the map's escalating price tag does not end with Mellon's purchase and subsequent presentation of both volumes to Yale. One might compare the Yale map's stated value at any time since 1957 with the seven-million-pound ($12,250,000) valuation placed on the magnificent, huge, and colorful world map belonging to Hereford Cathedral, dating from about 1290 and boasting a provenance as solid as the Vínland Map's is flimsy. The Hereford map was put up for sale at Sotheby's of London late in 1988. The following year, after national and international protest, it was withdrawn from sale and saved for the British nation when, in November of 1989, the Hereford dean and chapter accepted two million pounds (about 3.5 million dollars) to keep this historic and artistic treasure in trust.[49] The Hereford *mappamundi* transaction happened exactly thirty inflationary years after Mellon had reportedly paid about one million dollars for a small, undistinguished, black-and-white parchment map of dubious provenance. To this day, no manuscript map, however rare, has been marketed for anything like twenty-four to twenty-five million dollars for which the Yale map became insured.

Given Paul Mellon's known interest in British culture and his support of various English cultural institutions, he is unlikely to have been in the dark about the Hereford map quandary and its eventual resolution because these developments were watched by international dealers and buyers alike. Nor is it likely that Mellon missed the considerable publicity generated on both sides of the Atlantic by the McCrones' 1974 report that the presence of modern, industrially modified anatase in the Vínland Map's ink argued strongly against the map's being an authentic mid-fifteenth-century creation. There is no public record of Mellon's own reaction to this revelation. He made clear the reason for his silence just a few months before his death when, in the course of preparing the present book, I asked if he had any further information concerning his involvement with the Vínland Map. He was too ill to be interviewed, but he responded through his personal secretary, Aliene M. Laws, who wrote, "He has nothing to say about the Vínland Map; he considers that completely a Yale matter."[50]

In the normal course of events, the difference between what Witten and Marston paid for the two volumes and the price at which the volumes were offered for resale to Mellon would have included a dealer's profit. However, normal business practice does not sufficiently explain the astounding price increase effected by the time Mellon entered the scene. More to the point are the admissions that Witten made to the director of the Yale University Library in 1974, after the McCrones had announced their scientific evidence for the map's modern manufacture. When pressed again to reveal the origins of the Vínland Map volume, Witten said that he had told a lie in claiming that he had actually visited the source library. He also explained that he could not undo the trade and return Mellon's purchase sum because much of the money had gone to the Internal Revenue Service as well as to Rauch and Ferrajoli. At the time he purchased the volume, he had "paid Rauch an immediate commission on [his] purchase and promised to pay more substantial sums to him and Ferrajoli if the manuscripts were later authenticated and resold." One finds another allusion to this arrangement in Witten's observation, made in a different context, that "Cora Witten paid the obligations agreed to at the time of her purchase of the manuscripts."[51] Not surprisingly, Paul Saenger thought that these contingency arrangements cast serious doubts on Witten's and

Marston's accounts of each volume's serendipitous appearance in the European antiquarian market and of their chance reunion in New Haven. He was also disturbed by a number of other transactions involving the close cooperation of Witten and Marston. The two men were evidently good friends through many dealings at both the private and official level—the former due to Marston's interests as a private collector, the latter occasioned by Marston's position at Yale. These transactions, which began well before the Vínland Map volume appeared, reached their zenith in 1958, just before Mellon was persuaded to buy both volumes related to the Vínland Map. With the help of Shailor's detailed catalogue information about Marston's manuscript purchases, Saenger demonstrated that Marston and Witten had repeatedly bounced items back and forth between them in order to drive up the price paid by a third party.[52]

Regardless of what went on behind the scenes, the fact remains that the asking price for the two Vínland Map volumes at the time of resale bore little relationship to the initial joint purchase sum for the two items. Furthermore, the appearance of the second manuscript volume did nothing to clear up the provenance problem still dogging the volume containing the map. Although the two volumes had ostensibly made their way to Yale along quite separate paths, they actually involved exactly the same dealers, and questions about their point of origin dead-ended in the same way.

At the 1966 Smithsonian conference, Witten spoke of his and Marston's joint efforts to establish the source of the *Speculum* volume. These had begun in the spring of 1958, when Marston bought the *Speculum* fragments, and had continued into the autumn of 1959, when the sale to Mellon took place. During that year and a half, the two friends had reportedly learned that Ferrajoli had also bought the *Speculum* volume when he first saw the volume with the map and the "Tartar Relation," and that he had obtained both items from the same library. "Neither he nor the former owner connected them in any way," according to Witten. This oversight is difficult to credit in such a seasoned dealer as Ferrajoli but not nearly as hard as explaining how Witten could fail to see that this statement was at odds with his own claim at the same conference that he had personally visited the "private library" from which the map volume came. In any case, Witten assured his 1966 audience that prior to his own first encounter with the Vínland Map volume, nobody else had seen any connection among the three manuscript items. During the several months preceding Witten's encounter with the map volume (but supposedly not with the *Speculum* volume) Ferrajoli had shown both volumes to dealers in Geneva,

Paris, and London. Unaware of the potentially profitable relationship between the two volumes in his possession, he had shown the *Speculum* to those other dealers—presumably people at least as knowledgeable as himself—"very casually, as a mere trifle." Witten added that J. I. Davis had subsequently bought the *Speculum* fragment from Ferrajoli.[53]

Marston's account in *The Vinland Map and the Tartar Relation* began with a description of how he had acquired the volume with the Vincent of Beauvais fragments after receiving an advance copy of a new sales catalogue from "a London bookseller." This was in fact the advance proofs of catalogue number 159 from Davis and Orioli, a name that presumably was printed on the copy Marston received. In his 1965 essay, however, he merely noted that he placed an order through his tried-and-true local dealer C. A. Stonehill, Inc., for two items that had caught his eye. One was "a manuscript of a portion of Vincent of Beauvais's *Speculum Historiale* at a very modest price" and the other "a manuscript of Bruni's translation of Plutarch's lives of Cicero and Demosthenes."[54]

When Saenger combined his own knowledge of the Newberry Library holdings with Shailor's catalogue details concerning Marston's purchases, he discovered not only that Witten had been professionally involved in deals connected to the Bruni translation, but also that Marston's report of even this seemingly simple, two-item transaction was distorted. Somewhat wryly, Saenger also commented that the final copy of catalogue number 159 from Davis and Orioli did not arrive at the Newberry until February of 1959—several months after Marston had made his fortuitous purchase and also five months after the same firm's subsequent catalogue (number 160) had arrived at the Newberry.[55]

At the 1966 Smithsonian conference, John Parker went to the heart of the antiquarian problem by observing that "Yale probably knows more than it tells," giving as an example that Yale did not at first identify the London bookseller from whose advance catalogue Marston had ordered the volume with four books of the *Speculum Historiale*. Referring to the connection between the two booksellers Davis and Ferrajoli, which Witten had just revealed, Parker wondered if Marston had made any effort to trace, through Davis and Orioli, the provenance of the *Speculum Historiale* fragments he reportedly had bought from Davis for seventy-five pounds in 1958. Marston replied merely that he had bought the volume through Mr. Barry of C. A. Stonehill because his relationship with Davis was not good.[56] This would surely have been a good time to mention that he and Witten knew that Ferrajoli had been Davis's source for both volumes, but Marston said nothing of the kind.

Davis, it will be remembered, was the dealer who had tried to persuade the British Museum to buy the Vínland Map volume for which Witten himself had paid Ferrajoli a modest finder's fee, as he reminded his 1966 listeners.[57] It is also clear from Witten's own statements that Davis had obtained directly from Ferrajoli the *Speculum* fragments that Marston subsequently bought. Quite apart from the question of whether the sale had technically taken place through Stonehill, rather than through Davis and Orioli, Saenger found reason to doubt Marston's seemingly innocuous account of his Vincent of Beauvais purchase and to be skeptical generally about Marston's information concerning where he had bought his manuscript items, many of which he had then resold to Yale. Various items in the latter category were scrutinized by Barbara Shailor, who observed:

> Unfortunately, Thomas Marston's zeal in collecting manuscripts far exceeded his interest in keeping records about the items he purchased. The files in the Beinecke Library contain very little information beyond that recorded in the Faye and Bond *Supplement*. For those manuscripts not listed in F & B, there is even less information. Marston often jotted down notes, in pencil . . . on the front pastedown or flyleaf of a volume. He did not usually indicate the source of his information, much of which we have not been able to verify.[58]

There is another reason to question Marston's account of how he had obtained the *Speculum* volume without suspecting a possible connection between the two items: By his own admission, when he bought the *Speculum* fragments, he was already familiar with the Vínland Map volume. In October of 1957 (well before he supposedly discovered the Vincent of Beauvais item in the Davis and Orioli catalogue by pure chance in April 1958), he and Vietor had inspected the volume containing the Vínland Map and the "Tartar Relation."[59] This chronology agrees with Witten's account of showing this volume to both Marston and Vietor (in his own office) shortly after he had returned from Europe with the map volume. Witten said that he had already become convinced of the map's authenticity at that time, but that he had been unable to demonstrate it. He had therefore withdrawn the volume from his stock and given it to his wife.[60]

Evidently, neither Witten nor Marston, who later pronounced with such assurance on the connection between the map volume and the binding with the *Speculum Historiale* fragments, had yet acquired sufficient expertise to retain in their heads the characteristics of the map volume, although both claimed to have been struck by the volume's principal features at that early time. Reflecting later on the aftermath to Marston's new purchase that heady April of 1958, Witten said: "As far as I was concerned, the Vinland Map was authenticated then and there beyond all reasonable shadow of doubt. It had stood at or near the beginning of a volume containing the map, the *Speculum*, and the Tartar Relation in that order, and the covers of the original binding were still within the *Speculum* volume."[61]

Cora Witten was soon to find herself the owner of not just one but two old volumes. Years later, Witten claimed that he and his wife had been "stunned" when she received the *Speculum* volume as an outright gift from Marston, who had decided against simply selling it to her. "He felt he had no right as a curator at Yale to sell this manuscript given its extraordinary special circumstances, and that anyway he did not know how to set a price."[62] Marston amplified this by saying that once he and Witten had decided that the volume with the Vínland Map and the "Tartar Relation" had originally been joined with the *Speculum Historiale*, he felt strongly that the two volumes "had to come under one ownership as soon as possible." After some reflection, he therefore gave his newly acquired *Speculum* volume to Mrs. Witten so that if she should decide to sell the map volume, Yale University might have some influence over its disposition.[63]

Unfortunately, it does not follow from Marston's reasoning why possession of the additional volume might make it easier for Yale to influence Mrs. Witten if she decided to sell her volume with the map. If anything, Marston foiled his reported wish to help Yale when he placed the second volume into Mrs. Witten's hands, for by this time her husband and he had concluded that together, the two textual manuscripts authenticated the map as a unique midfifteenth-century creation, for which a huge sum was soon to be asked.

Where Did the Profits Go?

Witten noted that additional checking on the map and its companion texts seemed necessary, but a year later, in the spring of 1959, "Mrs. Witten and I were ready to offer the manuscripts to Yale University, as we had promised." The sale to Mellon took place in August 1959, accompanied by Witten's personal guarantee of the manuscripts' authenticity. Concerning Mrs. Witten's part in this transaction, Witten said in 1966: "It seems necessary that I state categorically that all the proceeds of the sale in their entirety were paid to Mrs. Witten and that her financial records will show no payment of any kind to Mr. Ferrajoli or to Mr. Davis or any 'straw man' intermediary." As noted earlier, he wrote years later that "Cora Witten paid the obligations agreed to at the time of her purchase of the manuscript."[64]

While this last statement agrees with Witten's 1974 admission that both Rauch and Ferrajoli had retained a financial interest in the map volume that had subsequently been honored, it is distinctly at odds with claims that Mrs. Witten had received her two volumes as gifts. It also raises questions about another statement that Witten made in a very different quarter in 1974, in connection with the Royal Geographical Society's Vínland Map symposium where the McCrones had discussed the modern nature of the map's ink. According to a report in the *Sunday Times*, "Mr. Witten still does not think it is a forgery. He says that he has visited the Smithsonian Institute [*sic*], the Washington museum, and given all details of his financial transactions to refute the 'rumours' of passing off a fake as genuine."[65]

The Smithsonian Institution has never had a financial or curatorial interest in the Vínland Map. If Witten nevertheless did feel the need to explain himself in that quarter, it would most likely have been to Wilcomb Washburn, who was the most interested party there. In any case, the situation must have been considered urgent if Witten came down from New Haven to settle the matter.

Interestingly, 1974 was also the publication year of a handsome little volume entitled *The Beinecke Rare Book and Manuscript Library*. It celebrated the first ten years of Yale's new library dedicated to the university's remarkable collection of rare items, which had been inaugurated before the Vínland Map officially joined its collections. The publication highlights a number of the Beinecke's most prized possessions and expresses gratitude to high-profile donors such as Paul and Mary Mellon, but it is completely silent on the subject of the Vínland Map and its companions.[66] The original design for the upstairs entrance hall at the Beinecke features two bronze-and-glass cases, one displaying a beautiful first edition copy of the Gutenberg Bible, the other housing Yale's prized Audubon Elephant Folio; no third display case for the Vínland Map was added subsequently, despite the 1967 assurance by Yale's university librarian that the map was even more valuable than Yale's original Gutenberg Bible.

Despite the Vínland Map's murky provenance, Marston and Witten decided on a price so steep that only someone as wealthy as Paul Mellon could be expected to purchase the map and its companion manuscripts. Marston and Witten had arrived at their original "authentication" of the map chiefly by means of what Painter later referred to as "the dear little worms' serrated tooth marks."[67]

CHAPTER 4

Creating Matter from Wormholes

The Joy of Discovery

Marston and Witten told similar stories about their comparison of the two volumes that seemingly provided the reassurance about the map's authenticity that had so far been denied it by the map volume's lack of provenance.

When Thomas Marston had received the fragments of the *Speculum Historiale* and another manuscript that he had ordered through Stonehill from "a new catalogue of a London bookseller," he invited Witten to come and have a look at his new acquisitions. Witten then asked if he might borrow the *Speculum* item for a few days. Very excited by what he then discovered, he soon got in touch with Marston by telephone to tell him that "the Vincent manuscript was the key to the puzzle of the map and the Tartar Relation."[1]

Quite apart from the matching watermarks in the paper used in both text manuscripts and the supposedly identical handwriting in all three documents, the wormholes reportedly matched up in such a way that they inextricably linked the map with the two text manuscripts as well as with the old binding still enclosing the *Speculum* fragments (see Figure 10). Witten's own written account had not yet appeared when *The Vinland Map and the Tartar Relation* was published, however, and Marston's preliminary description in the book of the "three manuscript works . . . found in two separate volumes" was as brief as the rest of his analyses. He nevertheless assured his readers that his sketchy description would be followed by an examination of the relationship between the two volumes.[2] Marston's statement thus primed the reader to accept that there was a meaningful relationship.

While the two textual portions do indeed appear related and datable to about the mid-fifteenth century, this is the only significant judgment by the original commentators that has withstood later scrutiny. On its own,

Contained:

1. The 'Vinland Map'—parchment bifolium patched at the fold

2. The *Tartar Relation* (takes up first ten leaves of a 16-leaf paper-and-parchment quire)

   Note: The worm holes in the VM and the TR are mismatched.

Contained:

Books XXI–XXIV (variant: XX–XXIII) of the *Speculum Historiale* by Vincent of Beauvais. Written on fifteen quires @ 16 leaves (= 32 pp), as is the *Tartar Relation*. The quires are consecutively signed 'e' through 't'. There is no mention of a title page for this volume, still in the original binding.

Figure 10. The three manuscripts in the two volumes acquired by Yale. Copyright David O. Seaver.

Marston's account does not provide evidence for any of the other assertions made by either the authors of *The Vinland Map and the Tartar Relation* or by Witten. For example, neither the relatively uncontested dating of the text manuscripts in their present form, nor the many indications of their intended internal relationship exclusive of the map, can explain the version of the "Tartar Relation" that Witten bought together with the map and the fact that it has no parallel elsewhere in the well-known bibliographical history of works accounting for papal embassies to the Mongols in the period 1245–47.

General Description of the Two Volumes

As described in *The Vinland Map and the Tartar Relation*, the first Vínland Map volume to appear on the modern antiquarian scene contained "a parchment bifolium with a map of the world (VM) drawn on the inner double-opening and otherwise blank except for a brief inscription . . . on the recto of the first leaf." Bound with the map was the "Tartar Relation," a previously unknown written version of John de Plano Carpini's 1245–47 mission to the Mongols. This textual manuscript consisted of just one quire (preassembled pages) of sixteen leaves, "in which the outer and inner sheets [leaves 1, 8, 9, 16] are of parchment and the remainder of paper, the text being written, two columns to the page, on the first eleven leaves, with the remaining five leaves blank but ruled." The map and the "Tartar Relation" were joined in "a comparatively recent binding of gilt calf over pasteboard with decorated endpapers."[3]

The two items were still bound together when exhibited at the British Museum in 1967, but they have since been separated.[4] Before both of the Yale manuscript volumes left the museum, T. C. Skeat took one last look at them and wrote to Skelton: "If you stand the MSS upright and look at the top edges, you can see the ends of three well-marked vertical creases. Those in the Tartar Relation and the Speculum match so exactly as almost to prove, in themselves, that the two MSS had been bound together for a long period. I could detect no similar creases in the Vinland Map."[5]

Both text manuscripts still show the creases that Skeat noticed. If the map ever displayed even the suggestion of a crease, it was gone when I first saw the map in 1990 and has certainly not had a chance to develop under the Beinecke's careful custodianship. A visitor to the Beinecke today will find the map protected by a transparent casing and filed flat inside a sturdy cardboard casing, while the "Tartar Relation" retains the relatively modern binding in which Witten had bought it.

The actual contents of the fragmentary *Speculum* volume are presumably unchanged from when Marston bought the item, but several alterations have been inflicted upon the binding (repeated codicological interference is in fact much more evident in this second volume than in the first one). Inside the dilapidated binding remain only what Marston identified as Books XXI–XXIV of the *Speculum Historiale* by Vincent of Beauvais. The Yale fragments are numbered according to a thirty-two-book numeration system that assigns the status of "Book I" to the preface rather than following the thirty-one-book numeration system with an unnumbered preface originally used by Vincent of Beauvais and by the Douai edition of 1624.

George Painter agreed with Marston that both the map and its two sister manuscripts had been done by the same scribe around 1440. Like Marston, he also believed that the map had earlier been bound in front of the *Speculum* segments, which were then followed by the single quire containing the "Tartar Relation." In addition, Painter developed a complicated theory of the stages through which both map and texts had passed before they reached their current form. In his vision, "the remote but exciting possibility remains that the present publication may lead to the discovery of a hitherto unnoticed three-volume *Speculum Historiale* manuscript complete with the original Vinland Map and an earlier Tartar Relation."[6] A couple of years later, Painter reminded the British Museum's keeper of manuscripts that in *The Vinland Map and the Tartar Relation* he had argued that the Yale volume is the fourth volume of a five-volume *Speculum Historiale* copied from a four-volume set that was itself copied from a three-volume set, all of which sets had been complete and had included the "Tartar Relation" as well as the Vínland Map. Painter noted somewhat sourly that nobody seemed to have paid attention to this argument, which—if correct—would mean that the map could not be a later addition.[7]

Witten supported the views of both Painter and Marston concerning the original sequence of the map and the two text manuscripts. It had required the reunion of all three manuscripts to accomplish this crystal clarity, however, and this development had taken time. According to Witten, therefore, the chief reason Ferrajoli and his colleagues had met with buyers' resistance to the Vínland Map and the "Tartar Relation" in 1957 was that the original constellation had at that time been disrupted. The separation of the three works from

Contained:

1. The 'Vinland Map'—parchment bifolium patched at the fold

2. Books XX–XXIV (variant: XIX–XXIII) of the *Speculum Historiale* by Vincent of Beauvais; Book XX supposedly accounting for quires 'a' through 'd'.

Figure 11. T. E. Marston's concept of the "original" volume acquired by Yale. Copyright David O. Seaver.

each other had left the wormholes so mismatched as to make potential customers uncomfortable.[8]

For reasons also related to matching up the wormholes, Marston, too, envisioned an earlier, pre-worm volume in which the Vínland Map had been placed first, followed by five books of the *Speculum* and by the "Tartar Relation" (see Figure 11). Marston furthermore based his conclusions on the numbering commonly used by medieval scribes when they preassembled portions of parchment or paper or of both media combined. These assemblies—called quires—often carried letter signatures, starting with "a" and continuing through the alphabet for as many quires as a scribe thought he might need. In Marston's reasoning, the quire signatures of the surviving *Speculum* portions indicated that a preceding book had fallen out before the rebinding took place (see Figure 11).[9]

Although there are no discernible letter signatures on the single quire of sixteen leaves that accommodates the "Tartar Relation," there is reason to believe that this text as well had been part of a unified volume from early on in its history, most likely from the very beginning.[10] The old binding of the Yale volume containing Books XXI–XXIV of the *Speculum* has a new spine, cut just wide enough to accommodate the fifteen quires (with a missing first leaf) used by these four books. Measured at the spine, the contents of the mended binding take up about 4.5 centimeters. The single quire used for the "Tartar Relation," which has been leading a separate existence since 1957 at the latest, has had a chance to expand and now measures somewhat over 3 millimeters at the spine. An original volume with a wider spine would theoretically have been able to accommodate a few more quires, each barely over 3 millimeters in thickness, but extra bulk would have left the codex more prone to the separation that evidently took place.

Scholars still do not know when and why the volume first fell apart, nor is it possible to prove exactly what it had contained at that time. Matters are complicated further by the fact that the volume has been damaged not just once, but several times.

Scrutiny by Experts

Marston and Painter had no evidence for their assumptions about how the quires had been used up, so their views on this matter did not go unchallenged for long. When the medievalist and map scholar P. D. A. Harvey had examined both volumes in connection with their exhibition at the British Museum in 1967, he cautioned against drawing hasty conclusions about the composition of the "original" volume and the stages through which its components had passed. He wrote:

> I see no correspondence in staining between the last leaves of the SH and the first of TR. A brown "rust" stain on SH f.239b (shows through to a), top left, has no corresponding stain on the first leaf of TR. The brown foxing near the bottom (binding edge), very marked on the first few paper leaves of TR, has nothing corresponding in the last paper leaves of SH, though the intervening parchment leaves might prevent direct transfer.[11]

Harvey's observations suggest that in the original volume, one more quire had preceded the "Tartar Relation." His comments also fit with indications that there had been several stages of ownership. For example, it is obvious that the running titles and book numbers at the top of the pages in the *Speculum* books were added later, although not necessarily much later. They were put in by a different hand and in a brownish ink that is quite different from the black ink of the main text. A 1985 chemical analysis of both text manuscripts, which included a sample of the ink used in the *Speculum* chapter headings, revealed compositional data that were substantially different from those in the main text of both works.[12]

It is probable that these additions were made by a private owner and not by an institutional custodian because the same brownish ink was used in occasional marginalia. The most striking one shows a hand with a ruff at the wrist and with a long, elegant finger pointing to the bottom left column of f.59 *verso*. On f.69 *recto*, where some of the brownish ink has been spilled or streaked, even a copious involuntary application of the ink has the same color as in the writing.[13]

The signatures on the quires in the *Speculum* volume struck Harvey as being of an even later date than these additions, but probably not later than the sixteenth century. They were written with a thin, scratchy pen and quite inexpertly, he thought, and gave as an example that the signature "m iij" had been written so that the same stroke connected the last stroke of the "m" and the first "i."[14]

In addition to observing that there are "remains of leaf signatures" in the "Tartar Relation," Barbara Shailor confirmed Marston's claim that all fifteen quires in the surviving *Speculum* portions in the Yale manuscript have letter signatures, the last quire signed "t." Because the first quire is signed "e," both Marston and Painter assumed that the scribe had used up quires "a" through "d" on a Book XX (Douai XIX), which had since become lost. Marston inadvertently provided an alternative explanation for the numbering, however, when he noted that the scribe seemed to have worried about his paper supply—at times there were forty-eight lines to a page rather than the usual thirty-eight to forty. This leaves the possibility that the scribe had found it necessary to use quires left over by a colleague or from another job of his own.[15] Neil Ker, a paleographic expert invited to examine the Vínland Map and its two sister manuscripts during their short 1967 stay at the British Museum, reported that he saw no need to presume that the *Speculum* volume was missing quires "a–d" at the beginning. Those four quires might well have been used in a separate volume, he noted.[16]

The historian David B. Quinn also valued his opportunity to examine both of the Yale volumes at the British Museum in 1967 because it enabled him "to remove a number of misconceptions caused by Mr. Marston's inadequate description of the manuscripts." For example, Quinn rejected Marston's suggestion that the map belongs with the conjugate leaves l_1 and l_{16} in the *Speculum* volume.[17] Marston, who had claimed that there should be "a conjugate leaf of similar thickness and pliability [to the Vínland Map parchment] in the manuscript," thought he had found such similarities in the first and last leaves of quire "l." Skelton had made the same claim.[18] Agreeing with Quinn, Harvey said that there seemed to be no particular similarity between the map parchment and the parchment used in the conjugate leaves l_1 and l_{16}. Although this particular bifolium is thinner than the other parchment leaves in the *Speculum*, it is much softer than the fabric of the map, he observed.[19]

To my own eye, the parchment of the "Tartar Relation" seems marginally thicker and less pliable than that found in the *Speculum* volume. Furthermore, while the *Speculum* parchment appears quite uniform in both quality and thickness, one half of each bifolium in the parchment used for the "Tartar Relation" single quire is thicker and somewhat less pliable than the other half. Another suggestion of parsimony in preparing the "Tartar Relation" (which was also less elaborately penned) was the use of an obviously flawed skin for the inside bifolium in the quire. Here, in almost the center of the right page (f.9), there is a fairly large hole that is definitely not caused by a worm, but by an inherent weakness in the skin. The flaw does not interfere with the text, however, because the person who assembled the quire trimmed and arranged the parchment to make the hole fit the space separating the two columns.

Although the parchment used in the Vínland Map has a similar flaw, also unnoticed by Marston, it bears no other visual or tactile resemblance to the parchment in either the *Speculum* or the "Tartar Relation." Like so many other confident statements made in *The Vinland Map and the Tartar Relation*, Marston's description of the three manuscripts' fabric conflicts with easily observable reality.

Concerning the dimensions of the various pages, Marston claimed that "the leaves containing VM, Speculum, and TR are all of the same size (285 x 210 mm), except that the parchment leaves are sometimes of a very slightly differing size because parchment contracts and expands at a different rate."[20] For my own part, I found the map parchment to be fractionally smaller than the other parchment leaves, just enough to make me wonder about shrinkage for a different reason, such as dampness from cleaning.

When Barbara Shailor examined Beinecke's MS 350A (the library's joint designation for the map and the "Tartar Relation") and MS 350 (the *Speculum* fragments) for her catalogue, she recorded folio sizes for the two volumes that differ slightly from Marston's. For the Vínland Map volume, she gave the following figures: 285 by 212 millimeters (text: 206 by 150); for the *Speculum* volume, 281 by 210 millimeters (text: 205 by 150). Shailor described other aspects of the *Speculum* volume in much the same way as Marston, however. She noted that the binding contained Vincent of Beauvais's Books XXI–XXIV (numbered XX–XXIII in the Douai edition of 1624), with an imperfect and probably missing beginning to the text, and that the manuscript had parchment inner and outer bifolios (folios i + 239 + ii), as did MS 350A.

Shailor also accepted Marston's judgment concerning an inherent relationship between the two text manuscripts and noted that the surviving *Speculum* parts had previously been bound together with Beinecke MS 350A.[21] For the latter, she recorded parchment inner and outer bifolios in this sequence: folios i (paper) + 2 (Vínland Map) + 16 + i (paper)—the paper at the beginning and end clearly representing part of the recent binding procedure. Thus she did not contest outright Marston's description of the map's parchment as a bifolium. Whether the map was in fact drawn on a continuous sheet of parchment, and not on two leaves patched together, remains a contentious topic.

Who Ordered the "Improvements"?

Although Witten and the three authors of *The Vinland Map and the Tartar Relation* made no secret of the poor workmanship involved in the blatantly obvious "repairs" done to both the old volume and the new, they did not criticize the judgment of those who had sanctioned such unskilled work. Skelton merely commented: "As Mr. Witten reasonably surmises, these repairs 'were doubtless carried out at the time of the binding repair and separation of the map and Tartar relation [*sic*] from the Vincent of Beauvais.' "[22]

Witten is on record as believing that either Ferrajoli or Davis had ordered the repairs and rebindings, presumably shortly before the two volumes were sent out on the antiquarian market in 1957.[23] If this is so, and if Skelton is correct in his summary of other statements that Witten made in 1958 and 1961, Witten must have had reason to think also that the separation of the manuscripts had taken place while they were in the care of Ferrajoli and/or Davis. A couple of questions arise in consequence. One is why such experienced dealers, already in possession of all three manuscript portions, marketed them as two separate volumes and left their reunion in New Haven to a seemingly miraculous chance. The other question is why the portions were "mended" and rebound in such a peculiar manner after the separation.

The Bindings

Witten and Marston repeatedly assured the public that the volumes' former owner(s), including Ferrajoli, had seen no connection between the two text manuscripts; that was why the two volumes had been marketed separately. However, such reasoning does not explain why the map—which shows "Vínland" so prominently that any reasonably well-read modern person would have found it hard to ignore—was placed with the "Tartar Relation" between such undistinguished and recent covers. If the same person(s) simultaneously owned the map and its two companion manuscripts prior to marketing them, and if the owner(s) ordered the work that was done on them, it would surely have made better sense to indicate the venerable age of the startlingly unusual map and its companion by providing them with the old binding. Instead, the *Speculum* fragments, subsequently valued at a mere seventy-five pounds sterling, received this clumsily executed benefaction.

Despite the crude work done by the "restorers," the outside covers of both bindings appear to have been left essentially in peace. A picture of each binding appears as plates I and II in *The Vinland Map and the Tartar Relation*. According to Painter, plate I represents the *Speculum* cover as it was prior to the volume's being taken apart in New Haven sometime before the autumn of 1966. The picture apparently shows what had originally been the back cover, which at some later date had been switched to the front because it was in better condition than the original front cover, now cracked.[24] In the volume's present form at the Beinecke, the badly cracked cover is at the back.

At the 1966 conference, where Marston claimed that Yale had tried assiduously to trace the fifteenth-century binding containing the *Speculum* fragments, John Parker observed that the newer binding containing the Vínland Map and the "Tartar Relation" seemed more important to him than the old one. More specifically, he noted: "My examination of the binding on the Vinland Map-Tartar Relation manuscript leads me to believe that it is a Spanish polished calf binding, more likely of the twentieth than the nineteenth century."[25] Parker's expert opinion here is particularly significant in the light of Ferrajoli's Spanish home base. In longer retrospect, however, both bindings must be regarded as potential keys to the map's provenance and early marketing history, so it is unfortunate that both bindings suffered interference during the known antiquarian saga of these volumes, including after they had reached New Haven.

Witten's various statements suggest that the rebinding and related work done prior to the 1957 sale had taken place quite recently, and Marston agreed with this assessment. When A. D. Baynes-Cope (the principal scientific officer at the British Museum Research Laboratory) examined the bindings in 1967, he noticed what looked to him like a monofilament made of modern plastic, possibly poly-(vinyl chloride), in the spine of the *Speculum* volume. It was not possible to obtain a sample for chemical analysis at that time, but Baynes-Cope observed that if his visual impression should be confirmed, it would indicate work that postdated World War II.[26] The pink and green plastic stitching is still there, visible at both the top and the bottom of the modern spine.

Witten was in "little doubt" that the Vínland Map volume's blind- and gold-tooled, heavy tan calf binding "was made between 1900 and 1957," while Shailor estimated it to be of the nineteenth or twentieth century. These guidelines provide an approximate *terminus post quem* without indicating when the rebinding actually took place. Concerning the *Speculum* fragments in their old covers, Shailor reported that the entire binding ("covered in brown leather blind-tooled with concentric frames, the center panel filled in with small, square bird tools") was tooled upside down, with impressions of the tools going through to the wood. She also noted that the binding had four fastenings, originally with clasps on the upper board, and that the volume had been restored, in the process of which end bands had been added.[27]

While Marston considered the *Speculum* binding typical of German work from the mid-fifteenth century, he also thought he had found signs of Italian stylistic influences. In addition, he noted: "A cursory examination shows that the volume has been subjected to a complete modern rebacking and a slight restoration of the covers using a leather which does not match the original backing at all; this work is of very rough and inartistic nature."[28] He thought that this haphazard approach, which also appeared to be responsible for the upside-down placement of the sides, could most likely be explained by the already damaged nature of the contents.

Witten was of the same opinion and pronounced the new back strip, hinges, and endpapers "a very poor and cheap piece of work in which the sides of the binding were carelessly reversed so that the tooling is now upside down." Believing that the work had been done at the direction of either Ferrajoli or Davis, he added: "It is even possible that parts of the missing four quires of the *Speculum* still remained at the time Ferrajoli and Davis had the volume but that these defective fragments were deliberately suppressed to give the volume a more or less perfect beginning; this is, of course, mere speculation on my part."[29]

Neither Marston nor Witten speculated about whether the repairs done on the *Speculum* volume had been undertaken by the same person responsible for three instances of repairs done to the bottom of a leaf, where the lower margin had been trimmed right up to the bottom of the first line of text and replaced with a strip of blank paper or parchment as appropriate. Marston merely noted two of those repairs in passing.[30] His breezy treatment of these repairs is as troubling as the repairs themselves.

The three lower-edge replacements were in fact very skillfully done. T. C. Skeat, whose eye for such details had been sharpened through many years of experience with papyrus texts, judged these repairs to be of a modern date when he discovered them during his Department of Manuscripts examination of the *Speculum* volume in 1967. He commented that "the manuscript had been subjected to some very sophisticated treatment before being put on the market," and he puzzled over the reason for this treatment until he found what appeared to be the remains of a roundish library stamp in the bottom line of the text, where it could not be easily excised.[31]

In none of the three lower-margin strip repairs are there any neighboring indications of damage to the fabric, which is in excellent condition throughout the four *Speculum* portions. A need to get rid of an owner's mark of any kind is the most likely reason for such interference with a medieval manuscript. The suspicion in this case grows stronger when coupled with the obvious manipulations of the *Speculum* binding's pastedowns, where one might also expect to find the mark of one or more former owners.

The first excision is on paper, on the folio marked "26" in pencil. The repair is well executed with old paper of roughly the same general character and thickness as in the original. This paper is furthermore so similar to the endpapers in the modern binding holding the Vínland Map and "Tartar Relation" that a scientific comparison might be in order. The second replacement of a lower margin is on the leaf marked "79," also professionally done with parchment of matching thickness and pliability, although the bottom line of writing on the *recto* became somewhat fuzzy in the gluing process. The third excision is similarly on parchment, on the leaf marked "233." Here, one finds the reddish-purple smudge of ink in the bottom line that Skeat mentioned. A curved line of the colored ink, about 1.5 centimeters long, runs through to the verso side of the folio and is clearly unrelated to the touches of red ink in the text.

The Handwriting

Barbara Shailor judged the "defective fragments" of the *Speculum* to have been written in the middle of the fifteenth century, "as indicated by the overall appearance of the codex and the design of the watermarks [Briquet's "Spectacle Bull," or "Tête de boeuf" 15056], either in Germany or perhaps in Basel where the document once serving as pastedowns was presumably written." She described both of the text manuscripts as "written by a single scribe in a well-formed running hand with *bâtarde* shading," while a "somewhat later hand" had added running titles in the upper margin in italic script. She firmly observed that the same scribe had not been at work on the Vínland Map and, like Harvey, she found some slight stylistic differences between the two text items. She observed that the writing in the *Speculum* fragments has flourishes in the upper and lower margins that are often decorated with red. Red is also used elsewhere (for example, in some initials), while in the "Tartar Relation" only the incipit and the explicit are in red.[32]

Several other experienced paleographers have agreed with Shailor that Witten, Marston, Skelton, and Painter were wrong to claim that the hand responsible for the two text manuscripts had also been at work on the map. During Washburn's 1966 symposium, Melvin H. Jackson, an associate curator at the Smithsonian's Museum of History and Technology, said he believed that there was "much to be desired in the evidence concerning the handwriting in *all* parts of the codex."[33]

Well before the British Museum's 1967 exhibition, doubts had surfaced among British scholars about the quality of the paleographical and codicological work done preparatory to the publication of *The Vinland Map and the Tartar Relation*. One may be reasonably certain that the museum's principal keeper of printed books did not intend it as a compliment when he wrote, late in 1966, that all the work that Skelton and Painter published in the Yale book had been done while the manuscript was in the United States, and that he understood the paleographical study to have been entirely the work of people at Yale.[34] The only person "at Yale" to pronounce on these matters in *The Vinland Map and the Tartar Relation* was Thomas Marston.

A few months before the book came out, Marston had recovered sufficiently from his traffic accident to present his views in the journal *The Cartographer*, where he repeated his conviction that the hand was the same (an "Oberrheinische Bastarda") in all three manuscripts, and that surviving manuscript samples from elsewhere suggested that the Yale items under discussion had been written between 1395 and 1450. He then added a brand new explanation for why there are also easily discernible differences in the handwriting of these manuscripts. According to Marston's 1966 article, the "Tartar Relation" had been written very hastily, whereas the map had been prepared very carefully and the Vincent had been written with deliberation. His main point was that all three items had been copied by a single individual who wanted these works for his own enjoyment and who probably had not been a professional scribe. The 1965 Yale volume, however, featured no such theory about the relationship between private enjoyment and the miscellany of writing styles.[35]

Subsequent to examining the three Yale manuscripts at the British Museum in 1967, Neil Ker commented that he saw no reason whatever for supposing that the hand of the map was the same as that of the *Speculum* and the "Tartar Relation." He considered the writing on the map to be the work of a later and much more skilled hand; it was also different from the text manuscripts because it was not a typical German hand.[36] Skeat was no less decided in his own opinion that "the writing on the Map has no resemblance to the writing of either the *Tartar Relation* or the *Speculum*."[37] George Painter felt that in the light of the observations made by Ker and other English scholars, he ought to have another look at the manuscripts while they were available in London. His comments afterward to the keeper of manuscripts show that he did not consider his own paleographical expertise inferior to that of his fellow scholars.[38]

Witten claimed to have had second thoughts about some of the writing in the two manuscript volumes. At the Smithsonian in the autumn of 1966, he wondered aloud if Marston had not "gone a little far" when he insisted that the hand was "Upper Rhine bastarda," since that type of cursive writing had been in general use in Europe for a long time, up until about 1500. The scribe involved here might have been Flemish, for example. Marston stoutly countered that he had used the term "Upper Rhine bastarda" because that was the name given it by German paleographers many years earlier. It was in any event almost indistinguishable from "northern European bastard."[39]

To my own eye, the hand in the two text manuscripts appears similar enough to be either the same or belonging to scribes trained in much the same school. Whether or not the scribe was the same in both cases, the texts evidently represented different assignments in which the "Tartar Relation" had received a somewhat more perfunctory treatment. Skeat was of a similar opinion when he wrote:

> The *Tartar Relation* and the *Speculum* are in different, though very similar hands. The hand of the *Speculum* is the better of the two, being even and regular, with the slope of the letters carefully maintained. The hand of the *Tartar Relation* is a rougher version of the same basic type, the individual letters varying in slope and often in size. An objective test is provided by the capital letter Q which is formed in quite different ways in the two MSS.[40]

Independently of Skeat, Paul Harvey wrote that "there seems no great certainty in taking [the *Speculum* and the "Tartar Relation"] to be by the same writer. Note that TR wholly lacks the use of red in capitals and titles, and the lengthening of ascenders in the top line which occurs through SH."[41]

A Widening Inquiry

It is certain that the Yale University Library received Harvey's comments in the summer of 1967 because Skeat forwarded Harvey's notes to Alexander Vietor on July 14, and a scribbled message from Vietor a month later assured Skeat of the letter's safe arrival. He had received the mailing while on vacation and said he was delighted with Harvey's interesting analysis, which he would discuss with colleagues on his return to New Haven in September.[42]

The overall documentary evidence suggests that Vietor (who died in 1981) always wanted to learn as much as possible about the Vínland Map and its companion manuscripts, so there is good reason to believe that he did discuss with his colleagues not only Harvey's comments, but also the many other observations that Skeat had collected and passed on to Skelton for subsequent transfer to Yale, starting as early as February 17, 1967.[43]

The transfers were made in good faith and in keeping with the explicit agreements that Skelton had recorded after his meeting with John H. Ottemiller of the Yale University Library on September 16, 1966. The parties had agreed that, subject to being kept in the picture, Yale would give officers of the British Museum discretion to allow "competent persons" to study the documents. Furthermore, the Research Laboratory at the museum would be allowed to perform noninvasive tests. Skelton's memorandum specifically stated that the Yale University Library did not intend in any way to prevent publication of the findings of qualified scholars after they had examined the documents. On the contrary, Yale hoped to see as much freedom of publication as possible.[44] The British Museum kept its part of the bargain, but at Yale these promises were honored in the breach rather than in the observance, starting with the failure to make public the various 1967 misgivings about the paleographical judgments made by the authors of the Yale book.

Neither Marston nor Witten had the necessary expertise to pronounce on paleographic matters, as Paul Saenger pointed out when he reviewed the 1995 edition of *The Vinland Map and the Tartar Relation*. He called Marston's 1965 one-page essay on the paleography "amateurish" and censured the 1995 edition for "its failure to address the palaeographical and codicological problems posed since the Vínland Map's initial discovery in 1958." Recommending Shailor's detailed 1987 comments in these critical areas, which Witten had ignored in his 1989 essay, Saenger further castigated the second edition of the Yale book: "Yale University Press and the Yale Library from 1965 to this day have not actively elicited the judgment of senior palaeographers on the map's authenticity. Where palaeographers working outside the inner circle at Yale have run counter to the accepted theses, they are ignored in this volume."[45] The persistent failure to deal with these problems is indeed puzzling. For one thing, Yale obviously has long had expert paleographers available. For another, Skelton had made further paleographical study a central argument in his June 1966 plea, written at Yale's urging, that the British Museum consent to an exhibition of the map and its companion texts. Subsequent correspondence shows that in the view of the British Museum curators, there was certainly a need for expert paleographical and codicological evaluations as well as for scientific study of a kind that had clearly not been undertaken by Yale up to that point.[46] Furthermore, as already noted, the museum had received clear indications from Yale that the university would welcome any new scholarly comments, whether or not they were critical of the views expressed in the 1965 volume.[47]

Watermarks

At the Smithsonian conference, Boleslaw B. Szcesniak, already doubting the authenticity of the map and its relationship to the two other manuscripts for other reasons, declared that the map and the "Tartar Relation" were the work of different hands. In addition, he warned against dating *any* manuscript by its paleographic characteristics because such a judgment might be off by as much as a century. Nor were watermarks in the paper necessarily conclusive for establishing the date when the "Tartar Relation" or any other manuscript had actually been written.[48]

His warning is likely to have resonated with those of his colleagues who shared his feeling that Witten and Marston had been unguarded in using the watermarks and the wormholes as their principal arguments for the map's authenticity. Marston, who had found the old *Speculum* binding on the whole "decidedly Germanic," reported that the watermarks in the paper of both volumes indicated a Germanic source, traceable to a Rhine Valley mill at either Freiburg or Basel and with characteristics suggesting a manufacturing date of about 1440.[49]

At the Smithsonian in 1966, Witten reported that while studying the map volume he had recently bought in Europe, he had personally made the watermark identification in 1957, "identifying the paper in the Tartar Relation through Briquet's *Les Filigranes.*" After Marston had shown him his own newly arrived *Speculum* volume in the spring of 1958, Witten was equally confident about the paper identification he made in that connection. He said he remembered remarking to Marston on the fact that the paper had a bull's-head mark, and that he had stopped at the library on his way home to look up the watermark in Briquet. Back home, he had then compared the number he had written down with the one he had noted for the "Tartar Relation" several months earlier. This comparison revealed that the number was identical in both cases, namely Briquet's "Spectacle Bull" 15056.[50]

An examination of the two text manuscripts does reveal similar watermarks throughout both. Marston's own account and his support of Witten's initial watermark identification nevertheless suggest a worryingly casual approach to the Briquet association because both Marston's and Witten's stories indicate that the *Speculum* identification had been made from memory only. Witten had consulted Briquet before he took Marston's volume home for closer comparison with the "Tartar Relation" he already possessed.[51] If his visual memory was so exact that he avoided being sidetracked by Briquet's sketch 11046, for example, one may wonder why he had not recognized the similarities in the two volumes' watermarks before he left Marston's office that memorable day.

In various forms, the bull's-head watermark had been very common in Italy, France, and Germany for a long period, according to the Swiss expert C. M. Briquet. Its use dated back to before 1321 and stretched almost until the end of the sixteenth century.[52] Briquet's sketches indicate that the variant found in the two Yale volumes clusters around the 1430s and 1440s, and Paul Harvey saw no reason in 1967 to question the Yale volume's identification relative to the visual information provided by Briquet.[53] However, as Szcesniak remarked at the Washington symposium, even a correct identification of the "Spectacle Bull" watermark was not necessarily conclusive for establishing the date of origin of the "Tartar Relation" because many sixteenth-century manuscripts had been made on paper produced during the preceding century.[54]

There is more involved here, however, than assessing the time lag between the date a batch of paper left the paper mill and the date it was used. A string of questions arises in connection with a 1962 letter that the American expert Allan Stevenson wrote to Marston and that was reported in full in *The Vinland Map and the Tartar Relation*. It supposedly endorsed the watermark identification for the Vínland Map's sister manuscripts and, consequently, the authors' judgments about when and where the manuscripts had first seen the light of day. Marston amplified these claims in June 1966, assuring his Canadian audience that:

> Help [with the dating] came from an unexpected source, the paper. . . . Mr. Allan Stevenson, an authority on watermarks, was in London. The Vincent manuscript was sent to him together with photographs of the watermarks in the Tartar Relation. Both had previously been identified with Briquet's mark number 15056. On examining them Mr. Stevenson concluded that the paper had been made about 1440 at a mill near Basle by one Heinrich Halbisen.[55]

Actually, Stevenson never said any such thing, but instead went out of his way to be noncommittal. There is good reason to wonder why all three of the Yale book's authors found it so easy to overlook the reservations that he expressed in the letter Marston cited, especially since Marston's coauthor Painter was in close communication with Stevenson during this period. Stevenson's letter was datelined "British Museum 19 October 1962."

Just at that time, this well-respected American bibliographer was finishing up two years of research at the British Museum on the *Missale speciale*, a work written and used especially in the Upper Rhine region. The museum had a version of it printed on bull's-head paper. Stevenson's easy communication with Painter while in London is obvious from comments in the book that resulted from his British Museum research, and for which Painter read the galleys.[56] While Stevenson's presence in London and his specialized knowledge made it logical to involve him when *The Vinland Map and the Tartar Relation* was in the early stages of preparation, such an involvement ran contrary to the need for secrecy, however—a need of which Stevenson had clearly been informed.

A close reading of the published letter, coupled with some familiarity with the limitations of Briquet's information, will suggest that Stevenson's letter does not warrant Marston's triumphant tone. It was with considerable circumspection that Stevenson wrote: "The lucky thing is that L [mould-side left] can be identified with Briquet 15056. Ordinarily Briquet's tracings are insufficiently accurate or detailed for absolute identification." Stevenson thought that the identification with Briquet 15056 seemed 99 percent sure, but he warned Marston that Briquet's dating (1441) was for a single sample and did not allow for earlier and later states of the same use of the mould. It therefore represented only an approximate date.[57]

A year before his careful statements to Marston, Stevenson had published a work in which he noted that bibliographers sometimes "deceive themselves into supposing that an ability to spot a similar watermark within the four volumes of Briquet's *Les Filigranes* is quite enough to know about that watermark and the paper that it identifies."[58] His professional opinion was made even clearer in the book he subsequently published on the project that had occasioned his stay at the British Museum: "There is no need, here or hereafter, to claim overmuch for paper evidence. . . . Paper is cursed with ambiguities of provenance, dispersion, and use." In Stevenson's view, one must look for corroborating evidence.[59]

In that later (1967) publication, Stevenson also wrote that he regarded Briquet's work as great, but flawed, because the author merely noted the earliest known example of a type or species of mark without being able to demonstrate the earliest possible date of manufacture, and also because Briquet used the word *identique* too loosely. "The only thing that 'the same paper' can properly mean . . . is paper from the same mould or pair of moulds. . . . Nevertheless even the two members of a pair invariably differ in some detail of design, curve, or measurement—as well as in the manner and position in which their wires have been sewn to the mould." In Stevenson's study of the early printed version of the *Missale speciale*, he had observed that while all of this work's four books were on Missal Cross paper, they had been variously printed in Strasbourg, Basel, Speyer, and Mainz. He had found nothing in this work to show exactly where the paper had been manufactured, nor how long the paper had stayed at the mill before being shipped out, or where and for how long it had been warehoused prior to use. Inevitably, there was also the question of how long paper with the "same" mark had remained in use.[60]

Because intermediary dealers often stored and widely disseminated handmade papers, Stevenson warned that further uncertainty arises about when and where scribes or printers finally used their material. He went on to note that the demand for large paper runs increased dramatically with the advent of printing, and that demand also grew as a result of the needs generated by the 1431–49 Council of Basel. As an aside, he noted that official 1443 documents from the alternative council (in Florence, not in Constance as he seems to have believed) indicated the Ravensburg mill as their paper source. There is a note of exasperation when he admonishes anew: "It is mischievous and unscholarly to treat paper evidence as if it must be a cureall or else a quackery. . . . We should avoid those frustrated 'authorities' who have made no serious attempt to study the nature and incidence of watermarks. . . . For as yet there have been few notable proofs through watermark evidence."[61]

Nowhere in Stevenson's entire book did he claim credit for confirming the bull's-head watermarks in the two Yale manuscript volumes, although by 1967 he would have been able to read about the certainty with which Witten and Marston, using him as their authority, had assigned the Briquet sketch number to the paper used in both works. Perhaps seeing just how his own careful wording had been twisted to serve Marston's purpose was the reason he did not mention *The Vinland Map and the Tartar Relation*.

Stevenson's letter to Marston also reveals other details about the handling of the Vinland Map book project. For one thing, the confidential nature of the request for his help is made clear: "I am proud to have been let in on a piece of the mystery concerning the Map." For another thing, it is evident that one or both of Marston's English coauthors (or else Marston himself) had hinted to Stevenson that a date of circa 1440 and a Basel paper mill would fit nicely with other claims to be made in the projected book because Stevenson wrote at the close of his letter that a Colmar (in the Alsace) origin for Briquet's number 15056 sample dated 1441 would fit with manufacture at either Freiburg or Basel, and that "of the three sources around 1440, Piedmont, Freiburg, Basel, the chances seem but slightly to favor Basel."[62]

Further particulars about the paper source surfaced in London in the summer of 1990, when the Vínland Map took part in another British Museum exhibition called "Fake? The Art of Deception." The publicity information noted: "The style of the watermarks suggests that the paper was manufactured at Casella in Piedmont, near Turin, as was other paper found in the same account book in the Colmar archives. Paper from this source was regularly exported over the Alps and down the Rhine."[63]

The Rhineland was the favored focus from the start of the Vínland Map's public career. Summing up for the Yale volume his own version of the early history of the *Speculum* manuscript, Marston wrote that "all evidence points to the Upper Rhineland as the source of origin of the manuscript, paper, binding, and paleography." Only slightly less confidently, he added: "To pinpoint the source of origin is highly speculative, but there seems to be sufficient evidence to point to the Swiss town of Basle. This was the center of an important church council, which lasted from 1431 to 1449." After pronouncing the council "important in intellectual history," Marston gathered the Vínland Map volume to the *Speculum* bosom and asked rhetorically: "Where else could such a product as this be prepared, combining an East European account of a mission to the Mongols with the medieval historical text and a map (as Mr. Skelton shows) of Northern European origin? Basle certainly seems the most logical and sensible conclusion."[64]

Because Marston failed to reveal the "sufficient evidence" in 1965, his readers had no way to judge at that time how logical and sensible this conclusion might be. Skelton proved somewhat more generous with hypothetical details in his own essay, but he was equally sparing of proof when he described his personal deductions regarding the Basel connection:

> The period to which paleographical examination ascribes the execution (in their surviving form) of the Vinland Map and its associated texts is nearly spanned by the Council of Basle (1431–49). The delegates who attended this council came from northern and eastern, as well as southern, Europe. . . . In such a gathering . . . it is not difficult to envisage circumstances in which maps of Scandinavian and of Venetian origin or authorship may have come together under the eyes of a single scribe or into the possession . . . of a single scriptorium.[65]

The third and last reference to the Council of Basel in the Yale book is also from Skelton's pen and likewise notable for a priori reasoning taking the place of evidence. Giving it as his opinion that the author of the Vínland Map had "fused two geographical traditions," Skelton added: "Various considerations suggest that he may have found occasion to do so in the ambience of the Council of Basle, during the second quarter of the fifteenth century."[66]

Although "sufficient evidence" and "various considerations" pointing to Basel clearly existed in both Marston's and Skelton's minds prior to 1965 and had been communicated to Stevenson along with a request for his opinion, the time had evidently not been considered ripe for revealing the grounds for these considerations. The public had to wait another year to appreciate the authors' perspicacity in linking these manuscripts to the Church Council of Basel. When the revelation was made, it was purportedly news to everyone involved, from Witten on down.

In retrospect, it appears to have been just another carefully staged move in the effort to equip the Vínland Map with authentication by proxy.

The *Speculum* Pastedowns and the Council of Basel

In a sea of elaborate and conflicting statements from many sides, Barbara Shailor's 1987 description of the *Speculum* manuscript binding is a welcome island of simplicity. She writes: "On the glue left from the original paste-downs, now wanting, are the offset impressions from a single, heavily anno-tated manuscript document that was cut in half vertically; dated 1437 from the Council of Basel."[67]

George Painter's introductory article to the 1995 edition of *The Vínland Map and the Tartar Relation,* in which he commented on two discoveries "made when the *Speculum* binding was repaired and restored at Yale," provided a bit of background for this subset of the Vínland Map saga. These efforts were a part of the "preparation for exhibition in Washington . . . in conjunction with the Vínland Map Conference chaired by Wilcomb E. Washburn . . . and for further exhibition and examination in London at the British Museum in January and February 1967." According to Painter, these undertakings were necessary because "toward the end of the nineteenth century the . . . *Speculum* had been patched and rebacked. . . . The detached upper and lower covers . . . were then carelessly replaced upside-down and in reverse, and new modern paper pastedowns were supplied on the inner boards." Luckily, the Yale 1966 restoration saw "the misplaced covers . . . reinstated in their correct medieval position," and when the modern paper pastedowns were removed from their inner faces, the mirror image appeared of "two halves of a parchment document, since lost, which had served as a binder's waste pastedown in the original binding of c. 1440."[68]

These offset impressions, which in the volume's present state appear upside down, were the ones to which Shailor referred. The document used for the old pastedowns was unquestionably associated with a minor decision made at the Council of Basel, and it carried the explicit date of 1437. This next convenient miracle in the saga of the Vínland Map deserves a closer look, especially because the discovery was made after the authors of the Yale book had so confidently pointed to an association with Basel around 1440 without providing any explicit evidence.

As noted earlier, Painter differed from Witten in his opinion of when the clumsy repairs to the *Speculum* volume had taken place. His 1995 account of the process by which the Basel pastedowns were revealed also varied significantly from the version that Witten had provided in 1989. After reminiscing about his discovery of the relationship between the Vínland Map volume and the one containing the *Speculum* fragments, Witten had written:

> Additional corroboration was found during the studies at Yale that led to the publication of the map in 1965. The modern endpapers of the Vincent were lifted from the binding boards to make it possible to read any original pastedown or offset material that might still remain underneath. Luckily, enough offset writing remained on the boards to connect the offsets directly to the Council of Basel and yield a date, 1437. Both place and date closely matched those of the paper of the Tartar Relation and the *Speculum*, shown by Allen Stevenson to have been made at a specific mill in Basel in 1440–41. It was also found that the covers of the modern binding had been reversed by the modern repairer.[69]

Misrepresenting Stevenson's contribution to the watermark discussion, just as Marston had done on two earlier occasions, Witten thus gave it as a foregone conclusion that the information revealed by the pastedown offsets must constitute solid evidence about the date and origin of the two volumes because it "confirmed" what the watermark had supposedly already indicated.

In a remark made at Washburn's 1966 symposium, Vietor had taken a more measured and pragmatic approach to these problems: "I think the disclosure that we did find in the binding the offset of a document that was directly connected with the Council of Basel is of interest," he observed, "although it does not prove anything more than that the materials for the binder were at hand and date back to the Council of Basel." The supposed significance of the Basel connection implied by the offset document's text was nevertheless emphasized at the Smithsonian symposium and soon became set in mental concrete. During the 1966 discussion of the efforts made to trace the old binding containing the *Speculum* fragments, Marston assured his audience that "the offset of the document from the Council of Basel which we discovered in the binding shows that it was made in Basel."[70]

When the Smithsonian conference's *Proceedings* were published in 1971, the pictures of the pastedowns carried this caption: "Writing found under the pastedowns of the Vincent of Beauvais manuscript binding. The name of Bartholomaeus Poigncare, who was appointed a notary to the Council of Basel on 16 September 1435 and who resigned in February 1439, appears in the text."[71] Washburn's introduction to the volume furthermore reiterated Marston's assurances about when the offsets had been discovered. He wrote:

> Thomas Marston, curator of Medieval and Renaissance literature at Yale University Library, revealed that shortly before the conference the offset of a document from the Council of Basel had been discovered in the cover of the Vincent of Beauvais volume in which, according to the theory developed in the VM&TR, the map and the Tartar Relation had originally been bound. This discovery provided additional support for the deduction of the authors that the map was a product of the place and the period of the Council of Basel.[72]

Both Witten and Painter had claimed that the removal of the pastedowns was done at Yale. Witten nevertheless differed not only from Painter, but also from Washburn and Marston, because he observed that the steps leading to these "discoveries" had been undertaken before the map and the book were made public in 1965, rather than in 1966 for the supposed purpose of making the volumes more presentable for exhibition in Washington and London. Given two such substantially different versions of a seemingly simple chain of events, there is a good possibility of a third version closer to the truth. As the situation stands now, the variants provided by Witten, Marston, Washburn, and Painter mesh poorly with the realities of the time frame and fail to reflect reality as far as Yale's facilities for such undertakings are concerned.

Neither before nor after 1965 was Yale University institutionally responsible for any part of an operation involving the pastedowns. The Beinecke Library (in existence since October of 1963) has no record of any such activity under that library's own auspices, which at the very least means that the work was performed before the Vínland Map volumes were given into the Beinecke's care.[73] We cannot be certain whether an earlier sanction at the university library level merely failed to be included in the records that followed the manuscripts to the Beinecke, or whether the operation on the *Speculum* binding was performed either by Witten alone or by Witten and Marston together, but the latter option emerges as the more likely one.

The exhibition at the British Museum, which Marston, Witten, and Washburn claimed had given the impetus for the work done on the old binding, had first been broached as a possibility on June 9, 1966, and was being tentatively considered at the end of that same year. That the exhibition would take place at all was not settled until two months later, at which time the opening was quickly scheduled for January 1967. Throughout these negotiations Skelton acted as the liaison between Yale and the museum, somewhat irregularly in terms of museum practice. It is not apparent that he was aware of an intention to exhibit the Vínland Map during Washburn's symposium at the Smithsonian in November 1966, which he was planning to attend.[74] He also seems to have had little say in setting the time for the British Museum exhibition.

Early in the 1966 negotiations at the museum, Skelton wrote to Robert A. Wilson, the principal keeper of printed books, stating that he believed any time from autumn to spring would be acceptable to Yale. As far as Skelton was concerned, there would be an advantage to having the map in London that coming autumn because it might then be possible for him to escort it when he returned from the United States in November, thereby reducing the cost of the insurance premium by about one-half. Reporting on August 3 that arrangements with Yale were now under way, Skelton expressed the hope that Yale University Librarian James Tanis would allow a few simple, noninvasive laboratory tests while the volumes were in London. If Skelton were to bring them back with him in mid-November, there would also be time for paleographical and other studies before the volumes went on exhibit. Not until December 1 did the new principal keeper of printed books, A. H. Chaplin, write to the museum's director and state that he had just talked with Skelton about the Vínland Map, which Skelton had not brought back with him from the United States after all because the map had been placed on display at the Smithsonian

Institution.[75] In other words, Skelton had already returned from the Washington symposium when he talked with his new superior.

It is conceivable that Skelton had been apprised of the pastedown "revelations" long before he went to Washington, and that he had merely kept his cards close to his chest, but the surviving correspondence indicates that at least two reluctant department heads had had to be persuaded of the need to exhibit the map at the British Museum, which means that Skelton would have been unable to predict that the exhibition in London would actually take place. Furthermore, it is doubtful that he would have agreed to an imminent dismantling of the *Speculum* volume in New Haven if he had known such a procedure would be part of the preparations for exhibition; various letters suggest that he did not have much faith in Yale's ability to undertake scientific examinations of the kind that the British Museum Research Laboratory was well equipped to handle.[76]

Given the various changes made in the exhibition plans for the map, Skelton thought that a laboratory examination in London might well be done after the manuscripts had been exhibited in Amsterdam in April 1967, and he told Skeat that while formal permission must of course be obtained from Yale, Tanis had already indicated informally his approval of such scientific investigations. Skelton particularly wanted the scientists at his own institution to take apart the volume with the Vínland Map and the "Tartar Relation" in order to assess, among other things, whether the map had been drawn on a continuous sheet of parchment. T. C. Skeat, as keeper of the museum's Department of Manuscripts, was not about to give his approval to such a scheme, however. He felt strongly that any dismantling should be done by and at Yale so that neither his own department nor the museum generally could be held responsible for any real or imagined damage done in the process. Skeat noted: "Examining the manuscripts at a later stage, i.e. after removal from the binding, is an altogether different proposition. There is a world of difference between looking at a manuscript and pulling it to pieces!"[77]

Skelton nevertheless continued to press his argument. He thought each stage in such a dismantling might provide an opportunity for close examination and analysis and thus yield additional information about the history and origin of the documents. As far as he was concerned, the museum's own laboratory was surely the right place for such work. In any event, the binding was neither rare nor valuable, he observed.[78]

James Tanis, John Ottemiller, and Alexander Vietor at the Yale University

Library also wanted the British Museum to proceed under the guidance of its Department of Manuscripts and its Research Laboratory. Their only proviso was that the museum should preserve and return to Yale every bit of paper and other material that the dismembering of the map volume might loosen. Any such residue, together with the map and its companion manuscript, could then travel back to New Haven when the Beinecke's librarian, Herman W. Liebert, returned home from London. Ottemiller asked the director of the British Museum to regard his and his colleagues' letter as authorization to proceed, and he made it clear that Yale would accept full responsibility for having the volume taken apart at the museum's laboratory, which also in their view was uniquely well equipped to handle the procedure. Yale would in no way hold the museum responsible for mistakes that might occur, including the possible loss of evidence during the destruction process and the subsequent examination.[79]

Although Skelton wanted these analyses done under circumstances that the librarians at Yale freely admitted that they were unable to provide, they were not performed. Well before the "destruction" discussion about the Vínland Map volume even took place, however the medieval *Speculum* binding had already been dismantled "at Yale" and the pastedowns unceremoniously removed, with no qualms whatever and with no attempt at either analysis or preservation of the material. The process ought reasonably to have included examining or saving the glue that had been used for the modern pastedowns without making the offsets illegible.

These actions in New Haven give rise to further questions. Who ordered the old *Speculum* volume to be taken apart? And was Witten right in ascribing the motivation and timing of this operation to a wish to see what was under the modern pastedowns *before* the 1965 book went to press?

If Witten's 1989 statements about the situation are accurate, he was actively involved when the pastedowns were removed. The lack of any records of this activity at the Beinecke after its opening further suggests that the removal took place prior to 1963, while the Yale book was still under preparation and secrecy was of the essence. The secrecy clause makes it unlikely that the library's bindery facilities were used in the absence of a proper scientific laboratory for such work at Yale. In all probability, Marston and Witten saw to the whole operation themselves. It is equally probable that at least one of them knew ahead of time what the removal of the modern pastedowns would reveal, so that the text in *The Vinland Map and the Tartar Relation* could be properly seeded with astute surmises about the Council of Basel connection.

It is also likely that the original pastedowns were still in place when Ferrajoli and/or Davis had the various "repairs" done, and that these old pastedowns were removed at that time because they contained at least one owner's mark, just like the bottom strips that were replaced on some of the pages. Similar vandalism had befallen a late-thirteenth-century codex that Witten purchased from Ferrajoli in 1959 (through Nicolas Rauch) and sold to Marston in the same year. Interestingly, this was one of the manuscripts stolen from the Zaragoza cathedral library after it had been photographed in 1954 by the Leonine Commission, at which time the nineteenth-century bookplates that Barbara Shailor found when she examined the volume at Yale had not yet been present in the codex. Shailor also found other clear evidence of tampering. Among the evidence of former ownership that had subsequently been removed were an inscription and marginal notes in a fifteenth-century hand; an inscription on an original front flyleaf recording the donation of the codex to the Library of the Santa Iglesia del Pilar and the 1477 death of the donor Petrus de Montflorit; and a modern book label with the Zaragoza cathedral library's registration number for the codex.[80]

Such heavy-handed treatment contrasts sharply with the history of a number of volumes that Marston had purchased before the Zaragoza thefts and before the general ease with which questionable antiquarian items were marketed for several years after the mid-1950s. For example, there were no attempts to conceal the provenance of a number of books that Marston had purchased during the period 1948–49, including from Stonehill.[81]

If Ferrajoli decided to remove the traces of former ownership from the *Speculum* volume, the question then becomes a matter of how much Witten had seen or been told at the time he purchased, from the same source, his Vínland Map volume in a nondescript binding. One would also like to know at which point Marston learned that removing the modern pastedowns in his *Speculum* volume might produce a result so agreeable not only to Witten and himself, but also to his fellow authors of *The Vinland Map and the Tartar Relation*, who pronounced with such certainty on the connection of the map and its two sister manuscripts with the Council of Basel.

Why the Council of Basel?

Neither at the 1966 Smithsonian symposium nor at any time since has anyone actually questioned the assertions made in the Yale book that the Council of

Basel would have provided a logical nurturing ground for the text manuscripts as well as for the map—claims that are not backed up by internal evidence or by the historical knowledge available then and now.

Marston could not imagine where else "such a product as this [could] be prepared," while Skelton said he was convinced by the paleography that the map and texts overlapped with the council, and that such a gathering of people from all over Europe provided the right "circumstances in which maps of Scandinavian and of Venetian origin or authorship may have come together" to fuse two geographical traditions. Painter made a similar assessment in 1995, as already noted. However, the vast literature on this church council does not support the authors' statements either with regard to the event as a whole or concerning the supposed participation from the Far North of people qualified to provide inspiration for a map alluding to the Norse discovery of America more than four centuries earlier. The Church Council of Basel might have indeed affected the saga of the Vínland Map and the "Tartar Relation," but what actually took place at that council had little to do with the views expressed by the three Yale authors.

The Council of Basel's predecessor, the Council of Constance, had passed a 1417 decree that required a meeting of general church councils at stated intervals. Although the long schism in the papacy was ostensibly healed with the election of Martin V in November of 1417, the troubles in the Church were far from over, as became evident rather quickly. The council that Martin V convoked in Pavia in 1423 was soon transferred to Siena and ended there in 1424, after the delegates had agreed that the next general council, due to begin on March 8, 1431, should be in the Swiss city of Basel. The new council got off to an uncertain start, however, because Martin V died a couple of weeks before it was to open and was succeeded by Eugene. Pope Eugene IV approved of Pope Martin V's choice of Cardinal Julian Cesarini as president for the new council, but he could not control the political maneuvers that were soon to split the council and thwart its intention to deal with such festering problems as the Czech Hussites and the relationship between Byzantium and Rome.[82]

Despite these early hurdles, the Council of Basel formally opened on July 23, 1431. After six years of bickering, Pope Eugene IV and his followers broke with the council. By June 1436, there was no pretense of reconciliation on the part of Eugene, who had already tried to dissolve the council several times. His first attempt came during the period from July 1431 to December 1433, when he complained of poor attendance at the council. When the Council of Basel eventually declared Eugene a heretic and deposed him in 1439, he and his adherents set up a council of their own at Ferrara, which was later transferred to Florence.[83]

The authors of *The Vinland Map and the Tartar Relation* thus stretched their point considerably when they claimed that the Council of Basel lasted from 1431 to 1449. Rather than facilitating eighteen years of courteous exchanges about everything from exploration and cartography to spiritual concerns and practical needs, the council was clearly contentious and divided from the start and soon became split. What remained of it in Basel under the council's new pope, Felix V, began to dissolve in 1443, the year of the council's last general session.[84] Other incontestable facts about this gathering challenge the notion that at any time during its turbulent existence could the Council of Basel have provided factual and intellectual inspiration for the Vínland Map through information about the Far North in general and about the Norwegian Atlantic colonies in particular.

Norway and Iceland, normally considered key countries involved in Leif Eiriksson's voyage to Vínland, were not a presence at the Council of Basel. We do not know if Eugene's decree about attendance at Basel even reached Norway in 1433. For all practical purposes the Icelandic Church, which was in a chaotic state, was also left out of the loop. Gobelinus Bolant, the "bishop of Børglum" who was also another titular bishop of Gardar in Greenland, had supposedly been invited to Basel as a representative of Denmark, but that claim has no basis in reality. Gobelinus never went near either Børglum or Gardar, and at his incorporation in Basel in May 1432 he was listed as a suffragan to the bishops of Liège and Utrecht. Nor did the Danes and the Swedes leave much of an imprint on the proceedings. Like Norway and its former colony of Iceland, Sweden was subject to the rule of Eirik of Pommerania, whose aunt, Queen Margrethe of Denmark, had formally united all three Nordic countries at Kalmar in 1397. True to form, Eirik simply appointed the Swedish bishop Nikolaus Ragvaldi of Wäxjö and the Danish bishop Ulrik Stygge of Århus to represent his three kingdoms at Basel.[85]

On March 15, 1534, Bishop Nikolaus and Bishop Ulrik finally presented their credentials to the Council of Basel. Two written sources record the number of Danish delegates as two, while one other source (often repeated in posterity) says that the Danish king sent four ambassadors with a fine escort and many horses. This last source also gave a lavish description of the Danish king as one "on whose kingdom the sun never sets" (Rex Datie cuius regni non est finis).[86]

By the time the two Nordic ambassadors arrived with their comparatively modest retinues, there were already widespread misgivings about King Eirik back home. These included complaints about his lack of regard for Norwegian and Icelandic needs and worries about his constant involvement in costly wars. Widespread riots broke out in Sweden the following autumn (1435) and gave the king other things to think about than the affairs of a council that had never held his interest. His troubles at home culminated with his having to flee from Sweden in 1436 and to relinquish his home base in Denmark in 1438. After that, he lost interest in the council altogether, with the sun setting rather closer to his person than to infinity.[87]

King Eirik's disastrous economic policies had made it difficult to meet the costs of maintaining his ambassadors in Basel and of their travels over such long distances. The Norwegians in particular were unwilling to pay for keeping Bishop Nikolaus at Basel, although he was supposedly representing Norway. At the beginning of 1437, two Norwegian priests were sent to Basel directly from the Norwegian Church, ostensibly to voice Norway's opinion in the council's negotiations concerning the Greek Orthodox Church, but their chief task was to explain that the Norwegian Church was unable or unwilling to pay any more extra taxes for the maintenance of King Eirik's representatives. Nikolaus, the Danish king's remaining ambassador to the council, left Basel in June 1436 (but continued to demand payment even after he had returned home in 1437), and no Nordic representatives were sent to the breakaway council in Ferrara. Because King Eirik's rival and successor, Christopher of Bavaria, evidently favored Pope Felix V, there was a lively correspondence between Basel and Copenhagen during 1440 and 1441 concerning indulgences, but that was all. It is not known if the Norwegian authorities ever gave formal recognition to Felix.[88]

Recent information from Greenland was not likely to surface at the Council of Basel. The council was in its second year when Pope Eugene IV appointed Bartholomeus de St. Ypolito as the next bishop of "Grenelandia" after a certain Bishop Nikolaus, who had just died, and he provided the new "bishop" with six official letters, including one addressed to the "city and diocese of Greenland."[89] For almost two generations no resident bishop had been appointed in Greenland, while pro forma appointments such as that of

Gobelinus Bolant had become increasingly frequent. By the 1430s, few if any Norwegian and Icelandic churchmen thought about Greenland's position in the church hierarchy, much less about the voyages that had taken place far to the west of Greenland centuries earlier. Contributing to cartographical knowledge of these voyages would have been equally distant from the minds of these northern churchmen even if they had been chosen to breathe the heady cosmopolitan air of the church council.

The international squabbles and the meager Nordic attendance at the Council of Basel combine to invalidate Skelton's and Marston's assurances that at Basel, northern and continental information had melded and provided the impetus for the Vínland Map and, presumably, also for its sister manuscripts. The two men's reasoning in this respect is as unsatisfactory as the tale of the pastedown removal that supposedly confirmed Basel as the venue for this scribal undertaking about 1440.

Wormholes

Like a fine Swiss cheese, the Vínland Map was declared genuine by virtue of its holes. Fortunately for Witten and all three Yale authors, they had already played their trump card of "matching wormholes" when the pastedown information was made public as the next step in a series of carefully calculated revelations. Unfortunately for further scholarly inquiry, the disappearance of the modern pastedowns removed from the *Speculum* binding means that they cannot be examined for chemical details or for codicological evidence such as wormholes.

Marston and Witten agreed in their stories about the moment when it became clear to them that the wormholes in the volume with the map and the "Tartar Relation" matched those in the fragments of the *Speculum Historiale*. When Marston's *Speculum* volume was compared with the volume containing the Vínland Map and the "Tartar Relation"—already given to Mrs. Witten— Witten's expert eye reportedly discerned that the wormholes in all three manuscripts matched in a way that proved the map to have been an integral part of the volume before the worms went to work. Recalling that magic instant for the Washington symposium in 1966, Witten said: "As far as I was concerned, the Vinland Map was authenticated then and there beyond all reasonable shadow of doubt. It had stood at or near the beginning of a volume containing the map, the *Speculum*, and the Tartar Relation in that order, and the covers of the original binding were still within the *Speculum* volume." Ergo, Witten argued, since the two texts had separately been judged to be of the mid-fifteenth century, the map must be of a similar age and therefore authentic. Marston had agreed, and thus the two volumes had reached the next stage of their progress toward the Yale University Library.[90]

Painter was still convinced in 1995 that this evidence for the map's authenticity was unassailable. After describing various stages of "repairs" done before the two volumes reached New Haven, he addressed the exciting results of the interference with the *Speculum* volume:

> Lo and behold! When the true lower board was restored to its rightful position, its inner wormholes were found to coincide with those in TR; and . . . the worming inside the true upper board matched the worming in the map. There could hardly be a more striking and unpredictable new proof of the map's genuineness, of its coexistence in one binding with its companion documents from the c. 1440 beginning, and of the nonexistence of a forger who would deliberately conceal this vital evidence under the pastedown, and also disunite the map and TR from the *Speculum*, so successfully that their crucial relationship would remain forgotten and unknown for half a century.[91]

According to Painter, the *Speculum* volume had been taken apart at Yale after the publication of the book he had helped write, but prior to the Vínland Map's exhibition at the Smithsonian in November 1966. He also claimed that before the *Speculum* binding was taken apart, nobody involved with the map and its sister manuscripts had known about either the pastedown offsets or the matching wormholes in the cover. They had been able to make their sage judgments without the aid of these otherwise important revelations. His arguments involving the sequence of events here rest on his belief that the approximate date of the recent binding of the map and the "Tartar Relation" must also be the date when the various egregious "repairs" had taken place. If Witten's statements about these particular matters are true, they invalidate every one of Painter's arguments, so it is significant that Witten has not contradicted himself on the issues discussed here.

Witten was probably better informed than Painter about the codicological changes made in 1957 as well as about activities in New Haven both before and after 1965 because none of the three authors of the Yale book had dealt with Ferrajoli, Davis, and Rauch in 1957, only Witten and his European antiquarian colleagues. Nor does A. D. Baynes-Cope's observation about the post–World War II filament showing in the spine of the old *Speculum* binding invalidate Witten's claim that the main codicological changes and "repairs" had taken place in 1957, the year the Vínland Map made its antiquarian debut. Furthermore, Witten stayed in close proximity to Yale throughout the entire post-1957 period in question, whereas Painter and Skelton appear to have had insufficient contact with the American side during the preparation of *The Vinland Map and the Tartar Relation.*

Witten claimed in 1989 that "the only portion of [the 1965 book] I saw before publication was Tom Marston's history and technical documentation." That portion he must have known quite well, however, because he did the final work on it during Marston's recovery from his accident. Witten also continued to have close dealings with Marston in other matters and worked hand-in-glove with him for long enough to join in the public excitement over the Basel-document offsets. It is thus very likely that he was kept well informed throughout of the activities at the Yale end involving the three manuscripts—activities that he said he found easy to keep secret. He is also believable when describing how little contact he had had with Skelton and Painter because this reflected the realities of the prepublication period. Nor did Marston communicate unnecessarily with his two English coauthors, judging from both the published and the unpublished material available.[92]

So much avowed amazement on both sides of the Atlantic at the fortuitous matching of watermarks and wormholes begs the question of why Marston and Witten claimed to have been completely blindsided by the extraordinary coincidences they described, especially given their high regard for their own discernment and visual acuity in handling manuscripts and incunabula. One may also wonder why Painter and Skelton chose to believe the claim of their two American colleagues that matching wormholes must inevitably lay to rest any suspicions previously engendered in curatorial minds by mismatched wormholes.

Years of employment at the British Museum should have provided both Painter and Skelton with enough experience to suspect that the trajectories of the wormholes in the two Vínland Map volumes might simply provide wiggle room for the proverbial red herring. For example, among the British Museum manuscript maps (now in The British Library after its separation from the museum in 1973) is the item classified as Add. Ms. 31316, a volume of maps provisionally ascribed to Grazioso Benincasa. Both as superintendent of the Map Room and as a scholar with a keen interest in exploration, Skelton would undoubtedly have known this early-sixteenth-century atlas containing vellum maps mounted on wooden boards and manifestly rebound at a later date. The trajectories of the wormholes found there are peculiar, to say the least, but obviously not peculiar enough to have raised doubts about the authenticity of the maps contained in the volume.

When Neil Ker examined the two Vínland Map–related volumes in 1967, he thought that Marston had been correct in suggesting that the boards on the *Speculum* volume's old cover had been the wrong way up and back to front. When turning the boards the other way around, the pastedowns would no longer be upside down and the position of the wormholes showing inside the present upper cover would indeed coincide with the wormholes on the "Tartar Relation." To Ker, it also seemed that leaves 14 and 15 of the "Tartar Relation" were upside down as well. He did not make an issue of the wormholes taken as evidence of authenticity, however.[93]

My own perusal of the wormhole trajectories has left me with more uncertainties than answers. I would like to know why the map, which has a total of nine wormholes on its two folios, is significantly more worm-eaten than either of the two text manuscripts, particularly the multiquire *Speculum* portion. I also question Witten's and Marston's vision of the manuscripts' past internal relationship as well as their assumption that the wormholes in the three manuscripts occurred at about the same time and while the three manuscripts were in their "original" position. Some holes on the map's parchment match up reasonably well with its supposed neighbors, but others are not so easily accounted for. I also need an explanation for why the wormholes in the old wooden covers bear such a cursory relationship to the holes in either the map or the two text volumes, regardless of how the boards are positioned.

I found one wormhole on the "Tartar Relation"—more or less in the center of the page—running right through its single quire and continuing forward into the *Speculum* portion. Perfectly round and with a seemingly unchanging diameter, this hole has been said to represent the trajectory of a determined worm that ate right through the entire rear half of the *Speculum* at a remarkably straight angle. It is the only hole shared by the "Tartar Relation" and the *Speculum* portions, and it appears related to the two mid-page holes on the Vínland Map (see Chapter 6). The only other wormhole found in the "Tartar Relation" is smaller and starts at f.7 *recto*, ending with the rear folio (f.16). At the front end of the surviving *Speculum* fragments, the first three leaves have holes that match three pairs in the Vínland Map. Two of these matching holes continue through f.6 in the *Speculum*, while only the last one goes through to f.13.

An eloquent description of bookworm accomplishments reached George Painter in 1974 all the way from Uganda. B. W. Langlands, professor of geography at Makerere University in Kampala, said he knew more about the subject of bookworms than he cared to know because the creatures were rapidly consuming his book collections. He saw little point in using wormholes as evidence of anything other than unwelcome damage because in his experience a worm could eat its way through a good few hundred pages in a year. If a forger wished to establish an affinity between the Vínland Map, the *Speculum*, and the "Tartar Relation," he might just as well put a worm to work and not bother with making a hatpin hole. In Langland's judgment, wormholes did not establish a common age for the Vínland Map and the two text manuscripts but suggested only that *at one time* the various items had been together. Another aspect of the wormholes in the Vínland Map also bothered him, namely that in his own experience it was very unusual for the worms to eat in the *center* of the page—they seemed to move in from the spine, from the corners of the cover, or from the bottom edge, and occasionally from the top edge. In the few cases where the worms among his own books had been active in the middle of a page, he had always found activity around the edges as well.[94]

At the time this letter was written, the results of the McCrones' ink analyses were already turning the public discussion away from watermarks and wormholes and back to other physical aspects of the manuscripts. By then, however, the assertion that the wormholes determined the authenticity of the map had been given plenty of time to sink in, and remarkably little protest has focused on this issue since then. Instead, both defendants and detractors of the Vínland Map have long since convinced themselves that the entire problem will be solved just as soon as there is scientific agreement on the composition of the map's ink.

CHAPTER 5

A Star Is Born

The Vínland Map Reaches Yale

In the publishers' preface to the second edition (1995) of *The Vinland Map and the Tartar Relation,* John G. Ryden, director of Yale University Press, and his predecessor, Chester Kerr, sketched the sequence of events after Marston and Witten had convinced others at Yale that the Vínland Map is both genuine and indisputably tied to the two text manuscripts. Ryden's and Kerr's story suggests that Witten's personal assurances to Paul Mellon in 1958 about the map's authenticity had not been sufficient. When Yale turned to this generous benefactor, Mellon had reportedly said "that he would be glad to buy the map but that he would not donate it . . . to the library until it had been authenticated; he would loan it to the library for examination by suitable experts." With the help of Yale's map librarian, Alexander O. Vietor, the library then "selected . . . three highly qualified authorities" to undertake this examination, namely Raleigh Ashton Skelton, George D. Painter, and Thomas E. Marston. "In 1964, after seven years of scrutiny, they pronounced the map authentic. The owner then donated it to the library, and Yale University Press undertook its publication in an edition prepared by Skelton, Painter, and Marston."[1]

Witten evidently did not mind this initial caution on the part of the person who "ultimately made the courageous decision to acquire [the map]." According to Witten, with Yale's support he and Marston had in fact urged the purchaser to have the manuscript thoroughly studied by independent experts. The map's existence should be announced only when these studies had been completed. In Witten's recollections, this was the actual route to selecting Skelton and Painter to work on the map and the "Tartar Relation," while Marston "undertook the technical study of the manuscripts and their relationships."[2]

The Big Secret

The secrecy to which everyone connected with the project had been sworn kept the three authors from sufficient consultation with specialists in other fields, as noted earlier. It also prevented a well-informed, independent peer review of the finished manuscript prior to publication. At best an unusual step for a reputable university press to take, in this case it was a regrettable one. Knowledgeable consultants would have found much to worry about in a work that had as its sole object to reassure the public about the authenticity of an otherwise completely unknown map, even if they had not known that the book's authors had in fact rejected confidentially made cautions.

At Washburn's 1966 conference, Vietor explained the need for secrecy while the book was under preparation. He said that the volume had been financed by "the owner" (that is, Paul Mellon), who wanted no newspaper publicity ahead of time. Vietor therefore surmised that a dread of publicity might also have been the reason why "the owner" donated the two manuscript volumes to Yale in late 1964, after realizing the great amount of public interest the map was likely to generate. Because of the secrecy required, "we were not so open in consultations around the world as we might have been," Vietor confessed. "But I must say that Mr. Skelton, for his part, did on his own consult a number of authorities who were asked to keep the matter confidential."[3]

Stevenson's hesitant 1962 letter about the watermarks, discussed in Chapter 4, demonstrates that others besides Skelton had occasionally breached this secrecy. So do the 1966 recollections of the cartographic scholar Armando Cortesão. While in London in 1959, Cortesão had been "confidentially told of the discovery of a small map, probably of the early fifteenth century, in which America was represented for . . . the first time." On his way from Ottawa to Washington in 1961, he had stopped in New Haven to visit his friend Alexander Vietor for a couple of days, and at a lunch with Vietor and Witten he had been shown the map "in confidence." Later, when he arrived in Washington, someone mentioned the map to him there.[4] That "someone" was most likely Washburn, who was interested in old maps, and who in subsequent decades more than once demonstrated his determination to have the Vínland Map considered authentic.

Cortesão noted that soon after his Washington visit, "everybody" was talking about the map until the discussion climaxed with the publication of the book in 1965. His remarks at the Smithsonian conference also revealed that he was far from convinced personally that the Vínland Map is authentic. He declared: "I cannot say that I am absolutely sure that the VM is not a modern fake and that we are not involved in, or rather the victims of, a nasty swindle."[5]

It is a reasonable guess that Cortesão had voiced similar sentiments in London and New Haven before 1965. If so, the subsequent Yale book shows no evidence that the authors had been worried by his doubts. Nor had Skelton been deflected from his path by the criticism he received from E. G. R. Taylor after he had given her—also in confidence—photographs and blueprints of the unnamed map on which he was working in the summer of 1962 (see Chapter 3). Taylor's opinion about the map had not been solicited at the time, but from then on she was uneasy about what she had seen and eventually considered the matter more closely. By the following summer, she had concluded that the map was a forgery. Never one to mince her words, she confronted Skelton with her views about the map and about its lack of fit with the record of fifteenth-century manuscript maps, which she knew far better than he. Skelton politely dismissed both her arguments and her suggestion that he "see a doctor."[6]

Taylor's promise to Skelton that she would keep the matter confidential prevented her from publishing her views until after Skelton and his coauthors had brought out their book. Her article "The Vinland Map" was finally published in 1974 through the efforts of her longtime associate Michael Richey at the Royal Institute of Navigation. He had already provided an inkling of her views in January 1966 when he reviewed *The Vinland Map and the Tartar Relation* and summarized both his own and Taylor's misgivings about the map. He wrote in conclusion: "This very brief account of Professor Taylor's examination of the Vínland map (which she has only seen in reproduction) suggests at least that judgment on its authenticity should be suspended until further information is available." Years later, Richey also contributed his personal recollections of Taylor's passionate involvement with the Vínland Map.[7]

It is not unusual for scholars to solicit or provide information with the tacit understanding that it is uncouth to make professional hay from a meadow that a colleague had discovered first. *The Vinland Map and the Tartar Relation* is worrying because its three authors paid no heed to the misgivings of the senior scholars whose reactions they had actively sought, and who were far better qualified than themselves to judge if they were dealing with a genuine manuscript map showing the world known to at least one mid-fifteenth-century European cartographer.

The Big Names

The Yale book's unwavering focus on proving the authenticity of the Vínland Map was naturally a good reason for disregarding negative comments. It is nevertheless puzzling that Skelton, Marston, and Painter, men of good standing in their respective fields, committed themselves to a biased approach that was unscholarly at best and made worse by the general observance of secrecy. At least one of the three men appears to have had second thoughts about the restrictions imposed during the preparation of the book, however, and about the way in which they had carried out their task. Letters written by Skelton show that up until his untimely death in 1970, he actively sought new avenues of inquiry about the Vínland Map and its related manuscripts.

Skelton's letters reflect a reserved and methodical person intent on doing well in his profession, which he certainly did. Born in 1906, he was still in his midtwenties when he became an assistant keeper of printed books at the British Museum. This position, which he held from 1931 to 1939, encouraged him to develop an interest in exploration and early printed maps. When he returned from his service as a Royal Artillery officer in World War II, he resumed work at the museum, this time in the Map Room, of which he became superintendent after the death of Edward Lynam in 1950. He held that position until his retirement in March 1967, being made deputy keeper in 1953 and steadily adding to his reputation both as an able administrator and as an expert on early printed maps.[8] He had an international reputation as a map scholar by 1957 and was a logical person to turn to for an important book project in the field. However, he had little or no expertise in the three areas with which his work on the Yale book was directly concerned, namely manuscript maps, the history of the Norse and their Atlantic voyages, and parsing cosmographical concepts in late-medieval Europe, particularly in the Far North.

Skelton's colleague in the museum's Department of Printed Books, George D. Painter (born 1914), lacked expertise in the same three areas, but he also had areas of strength that were different from Skelton's. He became well known for his work as an incunabulist and added to his reputation by producing a scholarly work on Caxton; he was also a published poet as well as a biographer of Marcel Proust.[9] Later commentators have voiced serious misgivings about his work on Proust, however, listing several intellectual shortcomings that appear again in *The Vinland Map and the Tartar Relation*. A recent London review compared Painter's book with a new Proust biography and noted: "An undercurrent running through the [new] book is a criticism of George Painter's landmark biography (1959) of Proust, which took considerable liberty with the facts." Another critic wrote: "[Jean-Yves Tadié's] *Marcel Proust*, published in France in 1996, is a stern antidote to the deliberately credulous account by George D. Painter (two volumes, 1959 and 1965)."[10]

In reciting Painter's numerous and lasting accomplishments, a recent history of the British Museum's library does not mention the lengthy essays he contributed to both the first and the second edition of *The Vinland Map and the Tartar Relation*.[11] Painter retired in 1973, shortly after manuscripts as well as printed books and maps had been separated from the British Museum collections to form The British Library. Twenty-two years later, he restated publicly his faith in the Vínland Map's authenticity.

Thomas E. Marston (1904–1984), a man only two years older than Skelton and, like his coauthors, a well-regarded library curator, was the third person chosen to write the Yale book about the Vínland Map and its closest textual companion. A couple of years after obtaining his bachelor's degree from Yale in 1927, he entered the university's graduate program in order to study Egyptology and ancient history, but his interests appear to have changed, because both his master's and doctorate degrees (the latter in 1939) were from Harvard and focused on European history. He served in World War II and also took part in the Korean War, eventually becoming a colonel in the U.S. Army Intelligence. Returning to Yale after his military service, he became a library curator, first of classics and then of medieval and Renaissance literature, which was the post he still held when he retired in 1973. Throughout this time, his interests as a private collector ranged widely from fifteenth- and sixteenth-century printed books to medieval and Renaissance Western manuscripts, especially fifteenth-century Italian manuscripts in Latin and Italian.[12] Nothing in Marston's records as a private collector indicates an interest in maps for their own sake, however.

Despite the broad spectrum of Marston's skills and interests, they did not qualify him to judge the Vínland Map and its two related manuscripts. His linguistic and intellectual interests were focused on southern Europe rather than on the Germanic countries, and like Skelton and Painter he lacked curatorial expertise with manuscript maps as well as useful knowledge about the medieval Norse. Last, but not least: In the eyes of qualified experts, his treatment of the paleographical and codicological aspects of the two Vínland Map volumes was superficial.

In the overall Vínland Map enterprise, Marston was chiefly noteworthy as the liaison between Witten and Yale even before *The Vinland Map and the Tartar Relation* had reached the planning stage. In this regard, the part he played was crucial, although he kept a relatively low profile during the events that followed immediately upon the book's publication. His main contribution to the Vínland Map volume was his account of the *Speculum Historiale* fragments, which he had purchased for his own collection, and which was a virtual stepchild compared with its glamorous siblings—the Vínland Map and the "Tartar Relation."

The Big Launch

"Now, there arose a loud and somewhat terrifying advertising chatter where drums were played with such enthusiasm that it seemed as if someone had returned from the first journey to the moon."[13] Although the Icelandic cartographic scholar Haraldur Sigurðsson surely spoke for many when he thus described Yale's announcement, on October 11, 1965, of the Vínland Map's existence and of the monograph prepared for the occasion, there has been surprisingly little scrutiny of the procedures associated with the event itself. Few people know, therefore, that Yale's official U.S. announcement had been preceded by prelaunch activity. On Friday, October 8, a gala event had been arranged in Oslo at the Norwegian Academy of Sciences, where Helge and Anne Stine Ingstad were among the honored guests especially invited to hear a presentation by Chester Kerr, the then director of Yale University Press. According to the Norwegian press, Kerr had just flown in to tell this select assembly about the Vínland Map now in Yale's possession and about the scholarly volume soon to be released in the United States.[14]

Kerr gave a lengthy description of the map and backed it up with handouts that provided the Norwegian press corps with a tasteful account of how Yale had acquired the map and its sister manuscripts. The printed information included an assurance by the Yale University librarian, James R. Tanis, that he considered the map even more valuable than Yale's precious copy of the original Gutenberg Bible.[15] The Norwegians also learned that Yale regarded Kerr's presence in Oslo as a "courtesy visit" to the homeland of Eirik the Red. Given that Iceland is the home of the "Vínland Sagas" as well as the birthplace of Eirik's explorer son Leif, a similar visit to Reykjavík would presumably have been in order, but the only courtesy extended to the Icelanders was having the

London office of Yale University Press inform the local representative for the newspaper *Morgunblaðið* of the news on the same day that the announcement was being made at the Norwegian Academy of Sciences.[16]

This difference in the American treatment of the two countries had nothing to do with the national affiliation of either Leif or his father and everything to do with the nationality of Helge and Anne Stine Ingstad, who had recently discovered the genuine Norse ruins at L'Anse aux Meadows. While their discovery promised renewed respectability to believers in early Norse sailings to America (a respectability that arguments for the Kensington Rune Stone, the Newport Tower, and other "Norse" mementos had long denied it), the new archaeological evidence also menaced the perceived importance of Yale's recent map acquisition. The very existence of the Newfoundland site threatened to make the Vínland Map superfluous as "evidence" for the Norse discovery of America. Confirmation of the Norse ruins in Newfoundland had already become public knowledge in the United States in November 1964, when the *National Geographic* featured an article by Ingstad in which he described the archaeological site that he and his wife were still in the process of excavating with their team, and where the discovery of an unmistakably Norse spindle whorl had constituted the first of several items providing certain evidence for the site's nature.[17] At that point, the timing of Yale's announcement became critical.

Modern Norwegians have no direct historical investment in the Vínland voyages beyond the traditional linking of Eirik the Red with the southwestern coast of Norway, but they have always considered Norse enterprise around the Atlantic perimeter an important part of their cultural heritage. It was their own abiding interest in this heritage that made Helge and Anne Stine Ingstad undertake the work that culminated in the 1960 discovery at L'Anse aux Meadows. Once that find had been made internationally known, it became a matter of national pride for the Norwegians that two people from their own country had found concrete evidence for the daring medieval expeditions reported by the Icelandic sagas.

Of all the people in the world in October of 1965, the Ingstads were the most likely to be heard if they expressed doubts about the Vínland Map, which would have been the likely result if the couple had simply been left to read in their morning paper about Yale's thrilling new possession. Yale's publicity strategists apparently decided to take the Ingstads and the rest of the Norwegians by surprise and to overwhelm them with supposed corroborative information before any questions could be asked. The Ingstads' reaction to Yale's announcement would be just as significant to other Norwegians as to the Yale planners, although for rather different reasons—the Norwegians might easily resent any apparent upstaging of the Ingstads' recent discovery if their own proprietary pride in far-flung Norse exploration suffered in consequence. Both flattery and reassurance were therefore included with Yale's bombshell announcement in Oslo.

The difference between Norwegian and Icelandic newspaper accounts in the weeks immediately following Yale's announcement demonstrates that the Yale strategy of sending a special emissary, before the momentous news was made public in the United States, worked as planned.[18] In Iceland, public reception of the Vínland Map news was considerably frostier. Free to react without the public relations bombardment to which the Norwegians were subjected, Icelandic scholars were quick to note that the map's claim to being evidence for the Vínland voyages was neither here nor there, since their own sagas had already made it clear that the medieval Norse had reached North America. As for the various assertions made in the Yale book, the Icelanders took a wait-and-see approach.

It helped Yale's planners in 1965 that Helge Ingstad showed himself much less preoccupied with being upstaged than with absorbing the new information in his customary measured way. When the reporter for *Aftenposten* came up to him after Kerr's presentation and asked what he thought about the news, Ingstad merely said that it had come as a complete surprise, and that while the map certainly was interesting, he considered it premature to judge it before he had been able to acquaint himself with the background material. Then he added: "The value in this presentation of the map comes from the fact that an institution like Yale stands behind it, together with such authorities as one of the world's most highly regarded cartographic scholars, R. A. Skelton at the British Museum. I am given to understand that their final report is the product of many years of research and many investigations."[19]

Thus confronted with a hitherto unknown map and with a book that no outsider had yet been given an opportunity to examine, neither Ingstad nor anyone else subjected to Yale's preemptive publicity could possibly know that the book's sole purpose had been to promote the map as genuine. Nor was it possible, either then or later, to discern from the promotional literature that all the references to the three authors' affiliation with world-famous institutions were meaningless in this particular context. Neither before nor after the 1965 publication of *The Vinland Map and the Tartar Relation* did the British Museum and Yale University act as institutional umbrellas, nor did the Smithsonian Institution stand behind Wilcomb Washburn when he spearheaded the 1995 edition of the book. To this day, every high-profile claim that the map is authentic has been the work of a few individuals who have made sure that their respectable institutional ties were noted.

Having successfully completed his task, Kerr hurried back to the United States to be on hand for the flawlessly executed launch there on the day before Columbus Day in 1965. Given what we know about the Oslo interlude, the timing of that launch cannot be explained on the grounds of insufficient preparation, but practical considerations must nevertheless have suggested the timing of the news release back home.

Yale University Press had little wiggle room for a sufficient splash in mid-October, for in 1965 President Lyndon B. Johnson had just declared that October 9 was to be Leif Eiriksson Day, and Columbus Day fell on its customary date of October 12. In the words of the plainspoken Vietor, Yale University Press "does not like to lose money on books."[20] It is nevertheless difficult to imagine that the publishers would have lost money by waiting a few days longer with their announcement. Such a delay would certainly have given a large number of Italian Americans less reason to complain about deliberate cultural slamming.

The news about the Vínland Map made the front page of the *New York Times*, of the London *Times*, and of countless other newspapers around the world, many of which had clearly been primed with press releases well ahead of time. The *New York Times* of October 11 had a front-page headline ("1440 Map Depicts the New World") and an inside article. The New York *Herald Tribune* also had both front-page news and a story inside, entitled "New Evidence: Vikings Did Beat Columbus." *Time* magazine (presumably after receiving a prepublication copy of the Yale book) reviewed it on October 15 under the title "Map of History," while *Newsweek* presented the Yale volume on October 18 with the words "Seeing America First."

The Big Discussion

Immediately after Yale's announcement, it became abundantly clear that not everybody was impressed by the map and the book. Charles Swithinbank of the Scott Polar Research Institute at Cambridge University promptly responded to one of the most controversial claims made in the Yale book, namely that the Vínland Map shows Greenland as an island of recognizable shape because the Norse had circumnavigated Greenland early in their colonization period. In a terse letter to the London *Times*, Swithinbank wrote: "Peary never circumnavigated Greenland. Curiously enough, though Asia and the Americas were long since circumnavigated, there is still no recorded circumnavigation of Greenland by a surface vessel."[21]

The reaction of the Italian American community was considerably more emotional. In a pamphlet entitled *The Vinland Map and the New Controversy over the Discovery of America*, published by the Instituto Italiano di Cultura in New York, Italy's foreign minister Amintore Fanfani took issue with both the timing and the substance of Yale's announcement. Calling Yale's timing "aggressive," he was adamant that Columbus had not had any predecessors in his trans-Atlantic feat; the Norse had merely gone to a northerly part of America, perhaps as far as to Hudson Bay, where they thought they had arrived at "Thule" and therefore did not bother to go any farther. The news of Fanfani's outburst traveled fast. Three days later, on December 14, the Oslo correspondent for the *New York Times* reported that Helge Ingstad took exception to the Italian foreign minister's pronouncements.[22]

Farther north still, in Reykjavík, Yale's announcement provoked the acerbic comments of Haraldur Sigurdsson, who took exception to everything connected with Yale's treatment of "a rather defective map of the world . . . which the sponsors considered to be from the middle of the fifteenth century." The Icelandic scholar thought it was too bad that the three authors "did not seek competent advice in areas where they clearly did not have sufficient knowledge." Several years later, he was still unconvinced about the merits of this "simple and rather unimportant world map of doubtful origin and uncertain date and of the manner of its publication, which was attended by much to-do and publicity." Both in 1965 and in 1971, he noted several details that demonstrated the map's post-Columbian perceptions of the world.[23]

By mid-December of 1965, the gloves had long since come off in England as well. From the start, one of the most outspoken English critics was G. R. Crone, librarian and map curator at the Royal Geographical Society. His earliest published comment came in a letter to the London *Times* on October 14, 1965, under the title of "The Vinland Map: Questions to be Answered." He had much to say about the cartographical aspects of the map. For example, in his opinion, Vínland on the Yale map was simply the same island as the one that the Cantino chart of 1502 labels "Terra del Rey de Portuguall." Responding to Crone four days later in the *Times*, Skelton allowed that Portuguese charts certainly deserved study in conjunction with the Vínland Map, but he made it clear that he otherwise disagreed with Crone's cartographical observations.[24]

Unfazed, Crone published a scathing review in the *Geographical Journal* in the spring of 1966, stating his opinions in great detail and synopsizing what he perceived to be Skelton's views. His London colleague promptly rose to the bait with a letter dated April 24, 1966. The two men also carried on an increasingly ill-tempered correspondence in the pages of the *Encounter* during that month of April. A comprehensive summary of their cartographical discussion would be a digression here, but it is worth noting that in Skelton's *Geographical Journal* response, he firmly echoed Vietor's advice and observed that the Yale monograph "was designed as a preliminary presentation, leaving the door open—and (as far as possible) supplying the materials—for further and alternative interpretation or 'speculation.' "[25]

The reason for Skelton's growing exasperation with Crone is easy to understand; by the spring of 1966 a number of other scholarly reviewers had also expressed doubts about the book as well as about the Vínland Map itself. Wasting no time, the American historian Samuel Eliot Morison had bluntly noted his views on November 7 in the *New York Times Book Review*: "It all boils down to what we knew before."[26] Just three weeks later, a *Times Literary Supplement* reviewer (writing anonymously as was the custom at that time) suggested somewhat more evenhandedly that while skepticism was certainly in order, one could not dismiss the uniqueness of the map's Vínland just because it was unique. Nevertheless, besides pointing out that this anomalous map had no known antecedent or descendant—in fact, no close relatives of any kind—the reviewer posed a few polite questions about other "puzzling" aspects of "this handsome and distinguished book." He or she took the precaution of adding: "While a tinge of regret may be felt at the absence from the team of a professed devil's advocate, the impressively restrained persuasiveness with which the genuineness of the map is presented invites admiration."[27]

Nobody has ever questioned the handsomeness of the Yale volume, and not all the reviewers have doubted the quality of the book's contents or the authenticity of the map. One of the more generous commentators was Wilcomb Washburn, who wrote about the Yale book for the *American Historical Review* in April 1966 and reiterated his views at a conference in France that same summer. He found the discussion around the map and the Yale book especially interesting because the controversy demonstrated the great importance that people attach to a map—a judgment with which it is hard to quibble.

Other remarks that Washburn made in the months leading up to his 1966 Smithsonian conference suggest that he was in fact prepared to argue for the Vínland Map's authenticity as a circa 1440 product. At the same time, he did his best to appear independent and neutral by disputing minor points made in the Yale book, such as that Skelton had overlooked the similarities between the Vínland Map and the 1448 map by Andreas Walsperger. Washburn also thought that Skelton had generally failed to take into account the transitional period in cartography that had followed upon the reintroduction of Ptolemy's ideas in the first half of the fifteenth century. "It was precisely during the time when the Vinland map was made, the second quarter of the fifteenth century, that the monks in Vienna and at Klosterneuburg began to create a scientific projection, making use of astronomical tables and other means," he advised.[28]

Washburn's evident acceptance of the claim that the Vínland Map had been made about 1440—a belief that is fundamental to any verdict of authenticity—was no doubt the reason he worked so hard to bring out a second edition of the Yale book in 1995. Like the first edition, the second one had been prepared in secrecy; its aim was to affirm the authenticity of the map, and it was launched with as much fanfare and carefully planned media attention as its predecessor. The "new" version was in fact unchanged from the first one except for the publisher's introduction and four essays added as frontal matter. One of those four was Washburn's own piece; another was Witten's article, which had been published elsewhere six years earlier and thus hardly qualified as new evidence.

In their note from the publisher in the new edition, Kerr and Ryden expressed the hope that this 1995 version would rehabilitate "one of history's most important cartographical finds." There seems to have been some ambivalence on Mr. Ryden's part, however, because on March 23, 1996, the *Star Tribune* of Minneapolis, quoted him as saying that "the cumulative weight of the evidence is that the map is authentic. But I don't mind that some mystery remains. It's sexier that way."[29] In addition, Kerr and Ryden noted Washburn's 1966 Smithsonian conference, which they saw as evidence of the interest generated from the start by the Vínland Map. They cited several examples of the original edition's immediate success, such as the front-page story in the *New York Times*, the book's distribution through the Book-of-the-Month Club and the History Book Club, and the "leading attention paid to the book in

American Heritage magazine."[30] These examples may safely be regarded as evidence of successful publicity by a major university press that is rarely ignored in the first place. It also becomes evident that before the Yale news broke, the Vínland Map's unofficial support group numbered quite a few people in strategic positions, who had planted the seeds of approval in various places including in *American Heritage*.

The October issue of the *American Heritage* magazine touting the Yale book was published almost simultaneously with Yale's October 11 announcement. Indeed, the attention that the magazine accorded both the map and the monograph was the result of advance footwork, just like the other cases of instant approval cited by Kerr and Ryden. The issue featured not only an editorial introduction, but also substantial articles written by Skelton and Painter, while a boxed notice called attention to the recent Yale publication, concluding with the words: "We wish to thank Mr. Vietor and Chester Kerr, director of the Yale University Press, for making our presentation possible."[31] This remark openly acknowledges the careful planning that had gone into the magazine's presentation of Yale's news, and it also shows close cooperation between the Yale University Library and the Yale University Press during the creation of the 1965 book. The magazine's editorial acknowledgment is equally interesting for what it left out, namely that Chester Kerr's wife, Joan Paterson Kerr, was one of the magazine's associate editors at that time.

Despite these early accolades on the American side, the tide of doubt and skepticism was rising rapidly on Skelton's home shore. Further acrimonious exchanges between Crone and Skelton occurred in consequence of the hostile review of the book that Crone had recently published in the *Encounter*, and on February 24, 1966, there was a private meeting of the Society of Antiquaries at Burlington House, which was chaired by the distinguished paleographer Francis Wormald, and which did not augur well for the promoters of the Vínland Map. After Skelton had presented a paper to the group, the consensus of the discussion that followed was that much work remained to be done before Skelton's premises about the map could be accepted.[32]

The *Sunday Times* reported on the situation in early March. The chief trigger for this decision seems to have been the recent revelation that E. G. R. Taylor's warnings to Skelton about the map had been deliberately ignored. The report noted that: "Professor Taylor was shown a reproduction of the map some four years ago, when Skelton was working on it. She told the Yale team she did not believe it was a genuine fifteenth-century product. They decided, however, that her criticisms did not affect the authenticity. Professor Taylor then prepared a long critique of the map, to be published after the Yale book came out."[33] The newspaper went on to note that Taylor had become too ill to see to the publication of her piece and had turned it over to her literary collaborator Michael Richey, who had now seen to the publication of a brief, nonillustrated outline of her paper.[34]

Taylor had suffered a stroke and was almost blind by the time she was free to publish her thoughts without breach of confidentiality. That was why she let Richey show the *Sunday Times* her complete paper, together with some of the drawings with which she had accompanied her cartographical arguments. Richey said he hoped to publish her paper in full later, perhaps after her full recovery.[35] She died later in 1966, but in 1974 Richey kept his promise of making her arguments better known, including her belief that the map's shape had essentially been dictated by a modern elliptical projection known as the Aitoff projection. Another close associate of hers, Eila Campbell, published both her mentor's and her own views concerning a map that, as she sternly noted, continued to suffer from its lack of provenance.[36]

The provenance issue reared its head again in 1972, when the *Times Literary Supplement* published a review of Washburn's 1966 conference *Proceedings*, which had finally appeared in a volume with a dedication to Skelton. The anonymous reviewer observed that at the time of the Smithsonian symposium, the Vínland Map had not passed the stringent tests necessary to make up for its lack of proper provenance. "Until the truth, whatever it may be, is established beyond a reasonable doubt, progress towards a better understanding of fifteenth-century geographical concepts is bound in the prevailing uncertainty to be impeded."[37]

Dissidents Need Not Apply

Whatever Wilcomb Washburn's motives may have been when he called the panel of scholars together in November 1966 and while putting together the results of their discussions, his efforts were a worthwhile endeavor. Despite transparently manipulative editing, his *Proceedings* remains the best collective record of early scholarly opinions in the Vínland Map debate. A number of questions nevertheless remain about Washburn's participation in the discussions about the Vínland Map, particularly with his masterminding of the second edition of *The Vinland Map and the Tartar Relation*.

The launch of this new edition was the occasion for a symposium in early February of 1996. Held in New Haven, it had been arranged by Washburn, who also presided over it in his capacity as "Director, American Studies Program, Smithsonian Institution," as he styled himself at the end of the essay he wrote for the new edition. His position at the Smithsonian had evidently changed since he held his 1966 Vínland Map conference in Washington, D.C., because the list of participants at the 1966 conference described Washburn as "Chairman, Department of American Studies, Smithsonian Institution."[38] More important than this subtle distinction between two professional titles, however, is the change that appears to have taken place in Washburn's approach to the Vínland Map discussion.

In sharp contrast to the broad scholarly spectrum of Washburn's 1966 conference at the Smithsonian, the New Haven symposium fell far short of being an impartial scholarly inquiry. Only people who believed in the map's authenticity were invited to participate in a gathering to which Washburn referred in a television interview as a new "Vínland Map conference."[39]

Known skeptics like myself were subsequently—and publicly—reported to have "declined" an invitation to take part, but such invitations were in fact never issued, except for two that were given insultingly late. One last-minute invitation involved Walter McCrone, who with his wife Lucy had reported in 1974 on their discovery of modern anatase molecules in the map's ink. The second tardy invitation concerned Kenneth M. Towe, the senior research geologist at the Smithsonian who had confirmed the McCrones' data. Both scientists were told that there would be only an "informal discussion" about the map's authenticity, and that there were no new data to consider. They were not informed that the affair was intended to publicize a second edition of the Yale book containing new material. Because McCrone had got wind of the situation by chance less than a month before the symposium, he came prepared with a printed handout stating his position. Shortly after the completion of the event, Towe wrote a long letter to Washburn and expressed his disapproval of the tactics employed in order to claim that the map had now been "vindicated."[40]

The Cost of Public Stargazing

During Washburn's 1996 New Haven event, the Vínland Map was brought in under armed guard for a brief appearance before being returned to its vault. The science editor of the *New York Times* learned from a representative of Yale

University Press that this elaborate precaution was necessary because of the twenty-five-million-dollar insurance valuation placed on the map. According to Washburn, however, the insurance was set at a "mere" twenty-four million dollars.[41] Any sum of such a magnitude seemed to call for an explanation, therefore I wrote to Yale University Press asking if this insurance had been arranged by the Press specifically for the occasion, or whether the valuation represented the sum for which the Beinecke Library routinely insured the map for its collections. I was advised to redirect my inquiry to the map's custodians at the Beinecke Library, but when I acted on that advice, I learned that this was a question best answered by the Press.[42]

This inflated insurance valuation, which in no way reflects a formal judgment made by independent assessors, is grotesque in the light of the ten million dollars that the Library of Congress in the summer of 2001 agreed to pay Count Johannes Waldburg-Wolfegg of Wolfegg Castle for an indisputable treasure, namely the only existing original print (probably done about 1515) of the 1507 world map by Martin Waldseemüller.[43] A large, elaborate work, this is the map that gave the American continent its name. There is absolutely no doubt about its authenticity, provenance, or startling novelty in its depiction of the ocean to the west of the American continent, separating it from the Asian coast.

To find an explanation for the supposed valuation of the Vínland Map at two and a half times the price paid for the Wolfegg treasure only six years later, one must go back to the series of carefully calculated escalations that began when the map was to be exhibited in several European capitals, starting its tour in early 1967 at the British Museum. In the summer of 1966, Skelton had brought up the issues of security and insurance soon after he approached his superiors at the museum about exhibiting the Vínland Map and its companion manuscripts. Writing to the principal keeper of printed books, he said that he assumed that correspondence between the director's office and Yale would deal with these sensitive subjects. Somewhat testily, the principal keeper replied that he had as yet had no direct communication from the museum's director about this exhibition—an event, moreover, that had been proposed by Skelton at Yale's urging rather than through the usual channels. He also asked Skelton what kind of special protection he had in mind, because the museum did not normally insure material lent to it for exhibition. Such questions came under the coverage of Treasury indemnity.[44]

Subsequent correspondence shows that soon afterward, the museum director's advice was sought concerning both insurance in transit and security and indemnity while the manuscript items were in the museum's care. Extra warding would be essential, in the opinion of the principal keeper of printed books, who asked the director for further guidance regarding any security particulars that Yale's university librarian might request. These requirements were evidently not simple, because the director decided that he had better see to them himself. When Skelton met with John H. Ottemiller from Yale in mid-September, the two men formally agreed that administrative arrangements involving transportation, security, insurance, and publicity would be made in correspondence between the director of the British Museum and the librarian of Yale. Yale would arrange to transport the documents to England sometime before January 4, 1967.[45]

When the museum's director, F. C. Francis, wrote to James Tanis in late October, he said in conclusion that they would have to reach a mutual agreement about indemnification against loss or damage during transport, and that he would appreciate Tanis's letting him know what he considered an appropriate valuation in this case.[46] This point had still not been answered by December 1, however. The available records do not reveal the size of the evaluation eventually fixed upon, but an agreement was obviously reached. Meticulously recording what took place on his watch as principal keeper of manuscripts, T. C. Skeat noted in a memorandum to himself that the Vínland Map was to arrive in London on Friday, December 30, at 9:50 PM. There was to be absolutely no publicity prior to that date—a condition that was clearly related to Skeat's terse statement: "*No* insurance, but indemnity to be given."[47]

Memoranda written by Skelton confirm the care with which the museum intended to handle the Yale items. Skeat was to meet the courier at the London airport on the evening of December 30, after which the documents would pass through Customs with no delay and be immediately deposited in the Department of Manuscripts. The courier on this leg of the trip was the director of Yale University Press, Chester Kerr, arriving on British Overseas Air Corporation flight 510. When Skeat took delivery of the manuscripts, he signed two receipts for them and also gave Kerr a copy of a letter signed by the director of the museum that noted the terms of the indemnity. Kerr and Skeat immediately went to the museum's Department of Manuscripts, where the precious parcel was unwrapped in the presence of Skeat, Kerr, and the director, before being placed in a safe.[48]

The London exhibition ran from January 20 until February 17. Tanis was

Figure 12. Opening of the Oslo exhibition of the Vínland Map on February 22, 1967. Left to right: King Olav V, Harald Tveterås, James Tanis, Chester Kerr, Mrs. Joan Paterson Kerr, R. A. Skelton, and Mrs. Skelton. Photo: *Aftenposten*, Oslo, February 23, 1967, p. 14. Source: Scanpix. Reproduced with permission.

to be the Yale representative responsible for seeing the manuscripts safely on to their next stop in Oslo. Skelton told Skeat that there would be no need to go out to the London airport on February 21 unless he wanted to because the manuscripts would be accompanied to Norway by both Tanis and himself. Besides, the museum would provide not only transport, but also a body-guard—evidently not an unusual arrangement in such cases.[49]

Photographs published after the map's arrival in Norway give good evidence of the success of this Anglo-American cooperation (see Figure 12). They also demonstrate that Yale University Press and Yale University Library were still working closely together to promote both the Vínland Map and the 1965 book. Among those greeted by King Olav V at the opening celebrations in Oslo were Tanis and Skelton together with Mrs. Skelton, as well as Kerr and his wife Joan.[50]

The exhibition in Oslo was due to start on February 22 and scheduled to run for about three weeks, but the date of the map's actual arrival was kept secret, just as it had been in London. Like their British colleagues, Norwegian curators and museum specialists had received Yale's demands regarding security and insurance, but in keeping with Norwegian practice at that time the negotiation process in Oslo was essentially public. Already on January 14, *Aftenposten* had reported that those responsible for Yale's treasures while they were in the custody of the Oslo University Library had insured the map and text manuscripts with Lloyds of London for thirty million Norwegian *kroner*.[51] That was the equivalent of more than four million dollars according to the prevailing exchange rate, and it represented an immense sum in pre-oil-era Norway as well as in terms of the international antiquarian market at that time.[52]

To understand why the Norwegians were willing to treat the Vínland Map as a unique cartographical item deserving both a hefty valuation and round-the-clock guard, one needs to look no further than to Kerr's successful visit to Oslo in October 1965, followed up by the delegation of foreign luminaries in February 1967. The Norwegians' acceptance of Yale's terms set the chief precedent for future inflated claims about the map's market value.

As soon as the exhibition closed in Norway, its American components were put on a plane bound for Reykjavík in Iceland, where they arrived on March 14, just a day before the next scheduled event in the public life of the Vínland Map. A picture taken right after the map had been placed in its display case in Reykjavík shows five well-known Icelanders and not a single American. Evidently, nobody from the Yale University Library or Press had felt it necessary to supervise the map's transfer to this small island nation that had given birth to the "Vínland Sagas," or to be on hand for the exhibition's opening. Instead, a high-ranking Icelandic official had gone to Oslo to pick up the map and its companion manuscripts for the display that was to run until March 30. While the Vínland Map was in the custody of the National Museum of Iceland, it was insured for forty-three million Icelandic *kronur* (about one million dollars), according to the newspaper *Morgunblaðið*. The article added that this sum had "not been confirmed," which suggests both that the reporter had considered even that sum unusual enough to warrant an inquiry and that, as in London, an agreement about the insurance had been reached through discreet, high-level negotiations with people at Yale.[53]

When the exhibition reached Copenhagen on April 1, 1967, it was opened by the minister of cultural affairs "before a large audience of experts and other guests" that included the American ambassador but no emissaries from Yale.[54] The Danes had insured the three manuscripts for eight million Danish *kroner*. Although this was still a large sum, it actually represented stubborn Danish resistance to Yale's demands. The Dutch were apparently similarly disinclined to be impressed by Yale's treasures. Before the University Library in Amsterdam agreed to the arrangements necessary to holding an exhibition there, a letter from Tanis told the Dutch that they must insure the map for U.S. $755,000 during the exhibition, and that Yale would cover insurance during transport.[55]

Although the Vínland Map has never told the world anything about the Norse that the world did not already know, the item still carries such a high insurance tag that the Smithsonian Institution could not afford to display the original when its high-profile exhibition "Vikings: The North Atlantic Saga" opened in Washington, D.C., in April 2000.[56]

CHAPTER 6

Portrait of the Vínland Map

A Map with No Equal

The present condition of the Vínland Map, which is notable for having been constructed with inferior materials, is a source of continued controversy. As many readers will know, innumerable opinions about the composition of the ink have been published in venues of miscellaneous scholarly quality and have commanded varying degrees of publicity.[1] Those interested in this large literature—as well as in works on many other aspects of the map—will find it helpful to consult the updated Vínland Map bibliography recently published in the journal *Pre-Columbiana*.[2] To conserve space and preserve reader sanity, the discussion here will consider only the main features of reports by recognized, unbiased, scientific authorities who have conducted actual laboratory investigations.

Even the staunchest admirers of the Vínland Map have never called it beautiful, but few would deny that the map has several unique features. One characteristic that immediately catches the eye is the map's asymmetrical design. Defenders and detractors alike furthermore acknowledge that the map is sui generis in that its overall message has no known cartographical precedents or descendants. Skelton, too, admitted that when depicting the western Atlantic, the map is "in isolation outside the main stream of cartographic evolution." He nevertheless argued that it has precursors in other respects.[3]

Thomas Goldstein grappled with the map's mixed visual messages when he remarked during the 1966 Smithsonian symposium:

> There is little doubt that the map is undistinguished in its cartographic technique, so that it would be futile to look for its authors among a major mapmaking school. Instead, overall conception as well as the inclusion of Vínland would seem to suggest an authorship distinguished

by a remarkable grasp of geographic theory and by the broad scope in the use of geographic sources which permitted the inclusion of a portion of the New World.[4]

Immediate Visual Appearance

Drawn and lettered in unevenly faded ink, the Vínland Map's design covers most of a double-paged parchment measuring 27.8 x 41 centimeters (about 11 x 16 inches), with a bottom margin (4.0–4.5 centimeters) about twice the width of the upper one, and with rather narrow side margins.[5]

The bottom margin of the map is damaged on both sides of a crudely made center strip, but no attempt has been made to repair the damage that Skelton described as "cut away from the foot of the vellum, in the center."[6] There is no way to tell when the damage occurred, but magnification times ten reveals a torn (or rotted) edge, not a deliberately cut one as suggested by Skelton's statement.[7] The only deliberateness here involved the center strip, which was cleanly trimmed to fit the curving edge above the gap left by the worn-away parchment.

Both editions of *The Vinland Map and the Tartar Relation* were formatted to the actual dimensions of the map and its companion manuscripts and provided two full-scale reproductions of the map. One map image is unmarked, while the other one has red key numbers coordinating each of sixty-seven map legends with translations and explications. Washburn's conference *Proceedings* similarly features a photograph of the map, reproducing the deceptively clear image used in the 1965 Yale volume. During the 1966 conference, Vietor admitted that the reproduction of the map was not very close to the tone of the original, and he said that he and Yale University Press took responsibility for allowing the publication of an image enhanced by using a very high contrast film to bring out the legends and map outlines.[8] It was surely a good decision, however, because readers of the book would otherwise have had little to work with.

In an essay written for the 1995 edition of *The Vinland Map and the Tartar Relation*, the research team headed by Thomas A. Cahill of the Crocker Laboratory at the University of California at Davis, described the "natural color" of the map as a "faded beige."[9] In its report to Yale University Library in 1985, the team also included physical details about the parchment, which the investigators had found to be of variable thickness and density of fibers—qualities that were especially obvious under transmitted light. The research team further noted the somewhat soiled outer edges and the holes in the map, the latter patched with parchment that was visually different from the main fabric and of a color described as "off-white to yellowish-white in natural light."[10]

Neither Yale's photographic reproductions, nor the pictures taken under various kinds of light at the British Museum Research Laboratory and at the University of California at Davis, can substitute for observing the condition of both the parchment and the ink in the original map. Nor do these photographs take the place of the painstaking reports made by specialists who have investigated the map's physical and chemical properties.

As Skelton had hoped, the 1967 British Museum exhibition provided an opportunity for scientists at the museum's Research Laboratory to examine the map and its two text companions—an investigation performed after Yale's announcement about its new treasure had already been given time to burrow into the public consciousness. The time allotted for the investigation at the museum turned out to be frustratingly short, however, and the technical tools available were limited compared with those at the disposal of scientists some years later.[11] Despite such hurdles, during this first specialist investigation of the three manuscripts Baynes-Cope and A. E. Werner recorded several significant observations that have stood the test of time but are little known even today because the two scientists were prevented by Yale's confidentiality requirement from reporting publicly on the results of their examination.

The results of the laboratory's investigations were sent off to Yale in late 1968, and a signed copy of the report was deposited with the British Museum authorities. This copy formed the basis for the statements that Baynes-Cope finally was at liberty to make in 1974 during the Royal Geographical Society symposium chaired by Helen Wallis.[12] Their carefully phrased message (never published by Yale) was that after examining both the fragmented *Speculum* volume and the Vínland Map and "Tartar Relation" volume, and after focusing on several particulars of the Vínland Map, both scientists doubted the authenticity of the map, although they were willing to accept that the parchment used most likely came from the same source as the two text manuscripts.[13]

The two British Museum investigators openly regretted that not only insufficient time, but also fear of causing damage to the map, had made it impossible to go beyond simply observing that as far as the map's fabric was concerned, "the map is drawn on a single sheet of parchment folded down the centre. This sheet is in fact mounted on a guard strip at the fold, since it is torn and almost completely separated into two halves."[14] Baynes-Cope noted that if the two halves were in fact joined naturally, it was by only a single fiber that he was afraid to touch even with the point of a needle. He therefore doubted that the piece had originally been a proper bifolium. He was also alert to other aspects of the map's center join, such as the absence of sewing holes on the guard strip (possibly an indication of extreme dilapidation at the fold prior to application of the strip) and the excellent bonding of the strip provided by a glue that so far has not been chemically analyzed.[15]

The two British scientists were not the only ones at that time to worry about whether the map's two parchment halves had originally been continuous or consisted of two discrete halves. T. C. Skeat, who saw the Vínland Map when it was shown to him and his British Museum colleagues in 1957 and who examined it again during the exhibition ten years later, was keenly aware of this intrinsic problem with the fabric of the map. He informed Skelton that he remained "unconvinced that the two halves of the Map are actually continuous at any point" and added:

> Certainly for the greater part of the central fold the two halves are separate, and are only held together by the strip of vellum at the back.
> If the piece of vellum were in two halves *before* the map was drawn, this would be almost fatal to its authenticity, since it is inconceivable that the scribe could not have found a single sheet of vellum large enough for his purpose.[16]

Skelton was unlikely to miss the significance of Skeat's comment because he had written in his own published description of the map: "Along the central fold the vellum had cracked and fractured; this had been repaired by a strip of later vellum pasted along the back."[17]

Creating a "bifold" from reasonably matched, but discrete, halves would have been relatively simple by means of the center strip.[18] However, if such a makeshift measure had been necessary to create a large enough surface for the map at the time when the two text manuscripts were also in preparation, one may justifiably ask with Baynes-Cope why the mapmaker had not simply availed himself of a fresh paper bifolium from the supply available at that time.[19] The mapmaker chose not to do so, however, but instead used parchment contemporaneous with that in the *Speculum* fragments and the "Tartar

Relation" and most likely coming from the same original volume. The mid-fifteenth-century date of the parchment has recently been scientifically confirmed through research by Douglas J. Donahue, Jacqueline S. Olin, and Garman Harbottle.[20]

Although doubtful, it is not impossible that the map's parchment was once a proper bifolium. An examination of the center join with a loupe at a magnification times ten shows clearly that the edges of the parchment have separated, but without considerably greater magnification or a DNA test of both halves it is impossible to determine whether the fabric ever was a continuous sheet of parchment. It is nevertheless obvious that the two halves were either partly or completely separated at the time the map was drawn because no lettering, only a few simple outlines, straddle the repaired center line.

There are no easy answers to either the bifolium problem or to another question that arises during a simple visual examination, namely whether the center guard strip is older than the patches behind ten holes in the map. Possibly due to a thicker application of glue, the strip seems slightly yellower than the small, square patches, and the center at the guard strip is certainly dirtier from trapped ink particles than the smaller "repairs." The strip is similar to the patches, however, in that it is unchamfered and so unworkmanlike that it is tempting to assume that both the strip and the patches are the work of the same amateurish hand, but the possibility remains that the patches, which serve no practical function, were applied to detract attention from the guard strip (which does serve a vital function), thus making it seem as if the strip and the patches were contemporaneous with each other.

These and other lingering concerns caused Baynes-Cope to ask bluntly at Helen Wallis's Vínland Map symposium: "What explanation is there for the appearance of a sheet of parchment upon which the map is drawn being different from that of the parchment of the related documents?"[21]

The Map Parchment and Its Flaws

The tradition of using animal skins as a writing surface is an ancient one. The quality of that surface depends partly on the specific animal and partly on the skills and methods employed to achieve the finished product, and it therefore varies considerably. The words *parchment* and *vellum* are often used interchangeably. Although *vellum* is often used to indicate the superior quality of a product derived from the whole thickness of a calf's skin (or skins from lambs or kids), in common usage it may refer to what would otherwise be called *parchment*—the skins of animals such as sheep, goats, cattle, or deer, from which the outer layer has been removed.[22] In the case of the Vínland Map, the species of animal used for the map has not been determined, but the quality of the fabric was clearly second-rate from the start.

Marston chose to overlook several important details when he described the parchment used in both of the volumes associated with the Vínland Map. Instead, he made a point of noting that the material showed signs of deriving from sheep or goats and that it would therefore be incorrect to call it *vellum*. He judged the parchment used in the two text manuscripts to be "definitely of second quality, perhaps the best [the scribe] could afford," but he neglected to single out the map parchment as being in exceptionally bad shape compared with that in the companion texts.[23] The poor quality of the map's fabric has nevertheless struck many another observer, including the several scientists asked to examine the Vínland Map.

While the parchment sheets in both of the text manuscripts are still cream-colored and pleasantly supple, the same cannot be said for the map's parchment; it clearly underwent fairly traumatic treatment at one point. Whether or not preexisting ink lines were the reason for the map parchment's crude "cleaning," it seems doubtful that the fabric would have survived the treatment if the skin had been as thin as that used in the *Speculum* books (rather than resembling two thicker parchment folios in the "Tartar Relation"). Regardless of the nature of the cleaning treatment, its consequences are evident in the map parchment's strangely pale color, uneven surface texture, and odd stiffness. When the map is held up against the light, its flimsy fabric has innumerable random pinprick holes (suggesting hair follicles) in addition to the patched wormholes. Pumicing, followed by wiping the surface with a damp cloth or rinsing it with water, would have been one way to produce such a fragile effect as well as a slight shrinking and hardening of the skin. Another and equally simple method would have been the use of scouring powder and water.

The "bloom" has so clearly left this piece of prepared animal hide that it is easy to understand why Werner and Baynes-Cope used the term *washed-out* to describe an appearance that suggested to them a process involving water. They surmised that this same treatment might be responsible for the absence of color in the wormhole linings (the wormholes in the *Speculum* had showed orange, fluorescent linings).[24] Their suspicion that the parchment had been cleaned in an unorthodox manner increased when they viewed the map surface under ultraviolet light and found that it fluoresced differently from the parchment in the "Tartar Relation." A tiny fragment of parchment scraped from the bottom of the map was not sufficient to draw any conclusions about possible residues of chemical bleaching agents, however.[25]

Later, Cahill and his Davis team likewise found that the parchment fluoresced blue under long-wave ultraviolet light, with the fluorescence appearing to be fairly uniform across the map except for the ink lines and the various repairs.[26] The primary goal of both the 1974 analyses by the McCrones and the 1985 investigations at the University of California at Davis was to determine the chemical composition of the map's ink, therefore neither group actively addressed the question of what lines, if any, might have been removed from the parchment surface before the Vínland Map was drawn. The possibility of a palimpsest (a residual former image on the parchment) has not been scientifically investigated since 1967, when Werner and Baynes-Cope used ultraviolet light and photography under various light conditions to reveal residual ink lines or traces of metal-point drafting if such were present. They concluded that there was no evidence of a palimpsest on the map parchment.[27]

Despite the manipulations of the map's parchment, there are good reasons for supposing that it came from the same early volume as the two text manuscripts. There are also indications that, as either a bifolium or two disparate halves, it came from the particular supply used in the "Tartar Relation" section of that volume. One indication of this relationship is that one-half of this text's parchment sheets appears somewhat coarser than any of the parchment leaves employed in the *Speculum* books. Another sign is a discovery that Cahill and his associates made while investigating the three manuscripts in 1985, namely that although the parchment in the two text manuscripts had similar general profiles, the "Tartar Relation" parchment showed a calcium level reminiscent of the Vínland Map, while the *Speculum* parchments (folios 219 and 222) had twice the calcium levels of the map parchment.[28]

Equally suggestive of a common source is a natural flaw in the map's fabric that is very similar to the one found in f.9 of the "Tartar Relation" (see Chapter 4). In the upper middle of the map's right-hand side (f.2 *recto*), there is a hole only slightly smaller than the one in the "Tartar Relation" manuscript. Although tilted in the opposite direction, the hole on the map has a similar shape to that found in the text manuscript; it constitutes the middle hole in a cluster of three patched penetrations. The map design could easily have accommodated this flaw by placing the ink line a fraction to the right of its present path, but no attempt was made to circumvent this original defect in the fabric, as the "Tartar Relation" scribe had done. A strong impression therefore lingers that in order to construct the map, someone had made do with materials that were limited by more than economic concerns.

No ink shows on the patch glued behind this comparatively large hole on the map. Perhaps when the map was drawn, something was placed underneath the hole to allow the ink line to continue without interruption because it runs right up to the edges of the hole, and there is no sign of interrupted pressure on the pen as the line disappears and is picked up again. If anything, the line is particularly thick right there.

Skelton appears to have noticed neither the nature nor the large size of that particular hole on the map. He merely observed that "a square patch of vellum has been pasted on the back of the sheet underlying each of the ten small holes." He was more precise when he wrote in his general physical description of the map: "The [map's] vellum appears to be identical in texture, color, and thickness with a conjugate part of vellum leaves (l1, l16) used in the [*Speculum*] text."[29] P. D. A. Harvey did not agree with this assessment after examining the three manuscripts at the British Museum. While he had found the parchment in the *Speculum* l1 and l16 to be slightly thinner than other parchment leaves in the same manuscript, with a transparency reminding him somewhat of the map's fabric, he thought that the *Speculum* bifolium in question was too soft to be like the parchment used for the map. Harvey continued: "The parchment of the VM, on the other hand, seems less unlike that of TR, though somewhat thinner."[30]

David B. Quinn, who similarly rejected Marston's suggestion that the map belongs with the conjugate leaves l1 and l16 in the *Speculum* volume, based his judgment on "the evident difference in 'feel' and colour between the Vinland Map and both the Tartar Relation and the Vincent de Beauvais." He was also troubled by the considerable soiling on the map and by the indications of an attempted cleaning, which might well be responsible for the washed-out appearance of the map's parchment.[31] "The impression is of a pale, brownish-grey surface, quite distinct from the fresh, creamy surface of the parchment leaves elsewhere," Quinn wrote. He concluded his report by expressing the hope that the museum's laboratory experts would be able to examine not only the treatment of the parchment, but also several other questionable aspects of the map's physical properties.[32]

Like Harvey and Quinn, Neil Ker did not find any particular similarity between the map's parchment and the conjugate leaves l1 and l16 in the *Speculum*. He also expressed surprise at the faded and indistinct appearance of the map when seen in reality, compared with the photographs of it—he thought that the map's background color seemed oddly white and quite unlike medieval parchment altogether. He was even less happy with the paleographical comments provided by the authors of *The Vinland Map and the Tartar Relation*.[33]

The Handwriting

It has already been noted that the principal keeper of printed books at the British Museum took a dim view of the American paleographical investigations supposedly done in preparation for the 1965 Yale book.[34] Other experts were also quick to disagree with the position that Witten and the authors of *The Vinland Map and the Tartar Relation* had taken with regard to the handwriting on the map—a position that Marston summarized by stating that the scribal hand in the map was "apparently" the same as that used in the two text manuscripts, namely an "Upper Rhineland bastard (or cursive) book hand."[35]

The paleographical protests began in earnest at the Smithsonian symposium in the fall of 1966. Boleslaw B. Szcesniak declared that the map and the "Tartar Relation" were not the work of the same hand, and Melvin H. Jackson thought that while the "Tartar Relation" and the *Speculum* were clearly the work of a professional scribe, the writing on the map was "sprawling, frameless . . . [and] at variance with the medieval sense of form and propriety."[36] In London a year later, Ker noted without hesitation that he saw no reason at all for supposing that the hand of the map was the same as the hand of *Speculum* fragments and of the "Tartar Relation."[37] T. C. Skeat was equally decided in his opinion: "The writing on the Map has no resemblance to the writing of either the *Tartar Relation* or the *Speculum*."[38] Barbara Shailor, too, was convinced that a different scribe had been at work on the Vínland Map.

It is obvious even to a nonspecialist that the writing on the map bears little resemblance to the script used in the two text manuscripts, and that there are two different styles of writing just on the map alone. There is no reason to suppose one person incapable of creating both kinds of writing used in the map legends, however, since the professional lettering of an architect or graphic designer, for example, may be exquisite even if the everyday handwriting of the same person is close to illegible.

In the Vínland Map, the tiny lettering in the longer map legends constitutes an orderly, formal script, while some of the place names and shorter legends use larger, quite inconsistently shaped letters varying in slant from 90 to about 105 degrees. This informal writing was done without a line guide and has a tendency to waver at the bottom, whereas the minute, disciplined script follows ruled lines spaced exactly two millimeters apart.[39] Such a decidedly metric measurement is unusual enough in a purported fifteenth-century manuscript to raise a red flag (see Chapter 9).

In both the formal and informal script there are inexplicable variations and uncertainties in the formation of the letters, especially of some of the capital letters. Michele Brown, curator of medieval manuscripts in The British Library's Department of Manuscripts, noted furthermore that she was troubled by inconsistencies in the orthography of the map legends as well as by frequent use of alternative letterforms (for example, the use of "ae" as well as "æ") and by a general infrequency of abbreviations (for example, "et" rather than "&"), which she found surprising in such a work.[40] The American medievalist F. Donald Logan harbors similar misgivings about the letterforms used in the map. He is particularly bothered by the use of both "ae" and "æ" in the legend *Magnæ Insulæ Beati Brandani Branziliæ Dictae*.[41]

Before exploring other contentious issues, such as the map's wormholes with their repairs and the various scientific analyses done on the map's ink, it may be useful to examine a couple of additional details whose problematic relationship to the map has also been much discussed over the years, and which are related to the paleographical issues just discussed.

Delineacio prima pars . . .

Two separate short texts deserve joint consideration here, although just one of them comes from the map. The other is from the last *Speculum* book among Yale's fragments, which concludes with the words: "Explicit tercia pars speculi hist(orialis)" (Here ends the third part of the *Speculum Historiale*).

As far as I am aware, nobody has questioned either the transcription or the translation that Marston provided of this explicit in 1965, and there seems to be no reason to doubt that this line dates to about the mid-fifteenth century, just like the rest of the *Speculum* manuscript. Harvey, for example, observed that the hand in this *Speculum* colophon "is clearly of a piece with the text."[42] Plenty of questions arise from Painter's interpretation of the significance of this colophon, however, when he states: "Here, beyond doubt, is the explanation of the title of the Vinland Map. The Map was originally drawn to illustrate a three-volume manuscript of the *Speculum*, and the title means, simply, that the Map is a "delineation" illustrating the whole work."[43] Knowledgeable scholars have expressed serious doubts about Painter's transcription and translation of what he calls "the title of the Vinland Map," which refers to a one-line inscription in the upper right corner of the outside front of the folded map (f.1 *recto*), otherwise as blank as the folded parchment's outside back (f.2 *verso*).

This front inscription (reproduced in *The Vinland Map and the Tartar Relation*) has baffled both defenders and detractors of the map. For one thing, as the historian L.-A. Vigneras has noted, it does not inspire faith in a fifteenth-century origin for this line that the word *delineatio* (alternatively *delineacio*) is used to denote "map" because this usage had disappeared in the Middle Ages and was not revived by cartographers until the second half of the sixteenth century. Fifteenth-century Ptolemy manuscripts and incunabula employed terms such as *descriptio, figura, imago, pintura, tabula*—never *delineatio*.[44] For another thing, Harvey was clearly correct in his 1967 observation that the handwriting here is very different from the writing on the map proper as well as from that employed in the *Speculum* right through to the colophon.[45]

It does not help matters that as the inscription now stands, it appears to refer explicitly to the map inside and to link it to the *Speculum* manuscript because the problem all along has been the legitimacy of the map and its relationship to the two text manuscripts. Moreover, there is no assurance that the line has not been tampered with. Indeed, one might reasonably ask whether the inscription is bogus from start to finish. The line is written in brownish ink, with the first few words appearing somewhat fainter than the rest, so that when the map is held up against the light, the ink in the first few words does not seem to have soaked well into the parchment. The color of the ink appears similar to that used by the later hand that added the chapter headings and marginalia to the *Speculum*. Although the writing style of the map's "title" gives the impression of being from the same later period, there are enough problems associated with this short inscription to warrant doubts about both the time it was written (in whole or in part) and the reason why it was written.

Marston admitted that the line had caused him some problems at first. He reported that in late 1957, after he and Vietor had examined the volume with the Vínland Map and the "Tartar Relation" that Witten had just brought back from Europe, they had found the notation on the front of the map as "disconcerting" as the mismatched wormholes that had not yet been explained through the fortuitous arrival of the *Speculum* fragments. When those doubts had been cleared away, however, Marston became the first to publish a transcription of "the title of the Vinland Map." He also translated it as "Delineation of the first part, the second part (and) the third part of the Speculum."[46]

When Witten wrote about this anomalous inscription in his 1989 essay, he was evidently too ill to act on several corrections that Barbara Shailor had published meanwhile. Noting in his essay that he had not been able to read the line properly himself at first and therefore had gladly deferred to Marston's superior knowledge of Latin, he still used Marston's original transcription except for expanding it to read: "delineatio primae partis. secundae partis. tertiae partis. spec(u)li." Essentially also using Marston's translation of this phrase, Witten agreed with his friend that it "makes a direct connection between *Speculum* and the contents of the Vinland Map."[47]

According to Shailor, however, this line on the map's outside actually reads: "Delineacio prima pars secunda pars tertia partis [?] speculi."[48] Harvey's 1967 notes also refer without hesitation to "*delineacio . . . speculi.*"[49] As Saenger has observed, the phrase was not only mistranscribed and mispunctuated in the 1965 Yale volume, but also mistranslated "to sustain a purported relationship between the map and the text of the *Speculum* with which it had supposedly been originally bound." Supporting Shailor's corrected version, Saenger found indications of an ungrammatical "modern confabulation" that may have been added by a dealer wishing to relate the map more closely to the colophon in the *Speculum* remains.[50]

The significance of this inscription naturally depends on whether one interprets it as a real or a bogus bindery instruction, but it seems that Saenger had good reason to suspect a "modern confabulation." Other scholars with a good knowledge of Latin agree with his and Shailor's critiques of the transcription and translation provided in the Yale volume.

Logan noted that to be grammatically correct, the last part of the inscription, "*tertia partis speculi,*" would have had to read "*tercie partis speculi.*" In that case, the whole line might conceivably be seen as constituting a brief table of contents for a binder, listing the map (the *delineacio*) as the first item, followed by the first and second parts of the third part of the *Speculum Historiale*. Literal interpretation is further complicated, however, by the fact that another of the abbreviations used in the original allows for two different transcriptions—"*tercia partis*" or "*tercia parte.*" The former would have to be emended as noted above, while the latter version merely constitutes a mixture of Italian and Latin.[51]

If the unsteady grammar in this line is simply due to a bilingual slip, it is worth recalling that Ferrajoli was a native Italian. In the same context, the "Tartar Relation" (which never mentions a map) most likely had been part of an original volume housing several books of the *Speculum,* and Witten had indicated that Ferrajoli possessed both the map and the two text sections when he initiated the various "repairs" that resulted in two volumes, rather than one, being offered for sale in 1957. In other words, any relationship of the map to both text manuscripts must have been well known to Ferrajoli at that time.

If "the title of the Vinland Map" were a genuine bindery reminder from the time when the old binding held not only a map, but also both the *Speculum* books and the "Tartar Relation," the instruction should have included the "Tartar Relation." The fact that it did not suggests that at the start of the Vínland Map's antiquarian career, it was considered expedient to equip the map with an enigmatic reference to the *Speculum* volume that would surface in the fullness of time and "authenticate" the volume with the map and its "Tartar Relation" companion. If that plan succeeded, the inscription on the map's front would demonstrate the work's authenticity by indicating close ties among all three manuscript items even if the matching wormholes had failed to accomplish this. Additional reassurance would presumably have come from the fact that the "Tartar Relation" is the main source of the names and captions in the map's Asiatic regions, as Skelton made clear in his legend explications and as Helen Wallis observed in 1974.[52]

If we are dealing here with an inscription in which only *delineacio* constitutes a recent addition, the remainder of the line presumably refers to "the first and second parts of the third part" of the *Speculum Historiale*. This brings us back to the *Speculum* colophon's baffling reference to "the third part," which suggests that the original volume may have contained only a select portion of the *Speculum*.

Not all medieval manuscript copies of the Vincent work were complete versions, and (as the Douai edition demonstrates) there was no uniformity in either the numbering of the books or in how the basic "parts" of the larger work were perceived. By dividing the *Speculum* into biblical and temporal history, a subdivision of the latter allows for calling Yale's last fragment, Book XXIV (or Book XXIII in the Douai edition), "the end of the third part of the *Speculum*."[53]

Using "the title of the Vinland Map" to construct a link to the genuine colophon text might at least be considered a logical approach, even if the intention was to deceive. By contrast, Painter's reasoning about the connection between the outside map inscription and the *Speculum* colophon is as illogical as his belief in an original three-volume work containing the complete *Speculum Historiale*. It was Vincent's very last book (hypothetically Book XXXII in Yale's enumeration), which would have contained a synopsis of Carpini's version of the papal mission to the Tartars, but that was obviously missing from the Yale volume. In the fragmentary Yale volume, the explicit announcing "the end of the third part" occurs several books short of the actual last book of Vincent's work and thus has no possible connection with the end of a complete version of the *Speculum*.

Any Vínland Map allusions to the mid-thirteenth-century account of the Carpini mission to the Mongols must either have come from the particular "Tartar Relation" version with which the map was bound at the time of sale or else from Vincent's own synopsis in the final book of a complete *Speculum Historiale*. There is no reason to believe that this synopsis was ever a part of Yale's incomplete manuscript in the old covers, however, or that it had anything to do with the *Speculum* colophon announcing the "end of the third part." If the mapmaker's source of information was neither the Vincent synopsis nor a separate account of the journey to the Mongols, any allusions on the Vínland Map to the latter enterprise must necessarily have reflected the mapmaker's own ideas.

In short, the attempt to link the three items sold in 1957 through the map's "title" is as suspect as the efforts to link the three manuscripts by means of wormholes.

The Wormholes on the Map

The worms chewing their way through the map and its two companion manuscripts neglected to leave a hole in the contentious inscription on the map's outside, but there is otherwise ample evidence of "the dear little worms' serrated tooth marks."[54]

In addition to the larger hole caused by the flaw in the skin, there are nine other holes on the map. All ten holes have been patched. Of the nine holes that look as though they might have been made by worms, four holes on the left folio match four perforations on the right. The holes of one of those pairs, in the center of each page, are round, perfectly matched, and positioned similarly to the "Tartar Relation" wormhole running in a straight trajectory right through the quire and continuing forward into the *Speculum* portion. It is the only trajectory shared by the "Tartar Relation," the *Speculum* portions, and the Vínland Map.

A ninth hole, off the southeast coast of the *Vinilanda Insula* looks convincingly like the work of a worm, but it has no equivalent on the right side of the map. However, if the map is placed upside down in relation to the text of the *Speculum,* so that the map overlies the current back cover of the old volume, there is a match on the inside cover both for that hole and for the map's holes on *Rex Noruicorum* (f.1 *verso*) and in the middle of the six-line legend just below *Thule ultima* (f.2 *recto*). That is the very pair of holes that lacks a match in the front of the *Speculum,* unlike the three pairs of matched holes discussed in Chapter 4.

These anomalies may argue against contemporaneity among all of the wormholes, and they do little for the "original" codicological sequence favored by Witten and the authors of *The Vinland Map and the Tartar Relation.* Skelton was nevertheless of the opinion that the map's physical association with the *Speculum* manuscript was "demonstrated beyond question by three pairs of wormholes which penetrate its two leaves and are in precise register with those in the opening text leaves of the *Speculum.*" In addition, he noted that a fourth pair of holes, located on the second (right-hand) leaf of the map, has no match in the *Speculum* leaves. He was somewhat less precise regarding stains, observing only that "the brown stain around one pair of wormholes is repeated in a few leaves of the text."[55]

Ker was considerably more blunt in his 1967 judgment. He had reservations about the positions of the wormholes generally and especially about the relationship of these holes to the old binding containing the *Speculum* portions. After his own examination of the volumes he commented that he still failed to make sense of the wormholes on the present lower cover compared with those on the map and at the beginning of the *Speculum.*[56] In their confidential report to Yale that same year, Werner and Baynes-Cope also expressed misgivings about the wormholes, and they were sharply critical of the crude patches affixed to the back of the map, observing that "such repairs are not regarded as normal practice and have not been done on the wormholes on any page of the Tartar Relation or the Speculum Historiale." [57]

Marston's approach to both the patching and the locations of the holes was insouciant. He stated:

> VM and TR are both slightly wormeaten, but the wormholes through VM, which have been repaired with small squares of parchment, do not match in position or in number those of TR, which are unrepaired. . . . While the wormholes in VM do not match those of TR in number or position, those of VM do precisely match those at the beginning of *Speculum*, and the worming in TR precisely matches that it the final leaves of the *Speculum*. [58]

In Skelton's brief 1965 description of the patched holes, he seemed no more bothered than Marston by the botched repairs. [59] He was furthermore convinced that whoever drew the map had worked *before* the worms were active—an opinion he reiterated at the Smithsonian symposium in 1966 during a discussion of these special wormholes in Yale's custody, saying: "The wormholes penetrate the legends of the map." During the same conference session, Marston urged caution in applying any sort of visual test here, because the uneven cure of the vellum had meant that in some places the ink would not take. Witten added his voice to Skelton's, however, and said that "microscopic analysis" showed that the wormholes occurred *after* the map was made, since there are sharp breaks in the ink. When Vietor addressed the issue, he noted matter of factly that the wormholes were uneven in size and had teeth marks, and that they diminished in size farther in. Two of the other scholars present simply dismissed the usefulness of wormholes as evidence. According to the Smithsonian's Melvin Jackson, the "worm borings" could have taken place at any time during the volume's existence, and the medievalist Robert S. Lopez noted that not only is it easy to create wormholes with a hot wire or by introducing live worms, but also in this case the wormholes did not make up for the map's unsatisfactory cartographical pedigree. [60]

Little had escaped T. C. Skeat when he cast his sharp eye over the Yale treasures in 1967. He still remembered his personal concerns about the wormholes a couple of years later, when he wrote to the keeper of the British Museum Research Laboratory to thank him for his and Baynes-Cope's report on their scientific investigations of the Vínland Map. Skeat observed:

I wonder whether you still have copies of the ultraviolet and infrared photos which were taken in the Museum? I am interested in one particular wormhole, viz. that in the middle of Siberia, about halfway between the legends "Thule ultima" and "Imperium Tartarorum". Between these there are six lines of very small writing, in the third line of which the wormhole occurs. The original text at this point apparently read "zamogedos et indos" but owing to the wormhole the final "s" of "zamogedos" and almost the whole of the following "et" have been lost. The strange thing is, however, that in a photograph I have here there seem to be faint but distinct traces of the lost letters *on the piece of parchment patching the wormhole.* If any of your photographs show any trace of this curious phenomenon, I should be glad to know.[61]

Werner replied that in examining the negatives and prints of the map in his possession, he had found no evidence of the lost letters "s" and "et." However, in two of the negatives (the ortho and blue sensitive films) he had noticed what looked like a faint "28" showing on the wormhole patch. This possible trace of writing had appeared dark in the negative in contrast with the white of the ink, the difference being especially noticeable in the negative taken with a blue sensitive film. In Werner's opinion, this left the possibility that the figures 28 had been done in a bluish ink. If that turned out to be the case, it would corroborate the assumption that the wormholes had been patched fairly recently, but he did not care to speculate on what seemed to represent lettering of some kind, except to note that the figures could be seen on the negative but were hardly visible in the prints.[62]

Enclosing negatives as well as prints for Skeat's further perusal, Werner suggested a meeting to discuss the problem and to examine the photograph that Skeat already had in his files. An addendum in Skeat's handwriting shows that Skeat discussed the matter with Baynes-Cope instead when the latter brought Werner's letter and the photos from the laboratory to the Department of Manuscripts. Skeat thought that the points he had raised with Werner showed most clearly in the photo he already possessed, so after his discussion with Baynes-Cope he concluded that "no further investigation of the point could be made without direct inspection of the original."[63]

Skeat's 1967 photograph, which is still in his file, does suggest faint lettering inside the wormhole, toward the right. Half of the "s" in the actual legend line to the left of the wormhole is missing, while to the right of the hole, a suggestion of the "t" in "et" is visible, mostly as a horizontal stroke. An examination of the original by bright daylight, augmented by a handheld spotlight and with the aid of magnification by ten, similarly suggests lettering in the hole but yields no conclusive evidence. There is so little black pigment left generally in the map's ink that several letters have now essentially vanished where the written line in question continues to the right of the wormhole.

At present, one section of the edge of this particular hole is dark enough to suggest the possibility that black ink particles were trapped there after falling off the map. In any event, the location of this black trace indicates that it is not likely to have come from a line deliberately inked across an existing hole. Thus Skelton and Witten would have been at least partly right when they claimed, at the 1966 symposium, that the worms had been at work after the map was made. The two men nevertheless overstated their case because this is the only map legend penetrated by a wormhole. It should also be noted that this hole constitutes one half of a map pair and has no match in the *Speculum Historiale* front folios.

Finding out which holes show trapped black ink particles and how the particles are dispersed is obviously a problem that only a targeted scientific investigation can resolve. Because there is no evidence of the map's ink on the front of any of the wormhole patches, one can at least assume that these patches were applied after the map was drawn and the legends written, but at this late date it will likely remain unknown why the holes in the map were patched in the first place, especially since no such "repairs" were undertaken on the "Tartar Relation" before it was bound together with the Vínland Map in a relatively modern cover.

Also elusive is a rational explanation for why the few people who were privy to the activities involving the map between 1957 and 1965 spoke and wrote as if no investigative stone had been left unturned, when in fact these same people had consistently failed to invite professional scientific analyses of the three manuscript items. At the 1966 Smithsonian symposium, Witten concurred with Skelton's opinion that the map had been drawn before the worms were active, and he then stated that a "microscopic analysis" had indeed indicated that the wormholes occurred after the map was made. This was presumably the "analysis" to which Marston had referred a couple of months earlier, when he said in a BBC radio program:

> [The] only test given to the map was a microscopic analysis of the content of the ink to make sure that the inks were all the same. No other

tests were given. Actually, when this thing first came up, I consulted a friend of mine in the FBI, which has the problem—is faced with the problem of dealing with forgeries, and he was convinced that any testing that might be done would prove practically nothing. The one possible test is the carbon fourteen test, and that for age, and the results of that are so indefinite as to time that they would be of little use to us.[64]

Marston's statements in his 1966 Canadian article make it quite clear that he had little use for laboratory analyses. Neither the parchment nor the ink would be of any help in dating the map, he wrote. In his opinion, there were at least three reasons why it would be useless to analyze the map's ink. One reason was that iron-gall ink was used throughout the entire Middle Ages; another was that until a couple of centuries ago such inks were homemade and therefore of mixed quality; a third reason was that while professional scriptoria managed to have some control over their ink quality, the scribe working on his own did not.[65] This last referred, of course, to Marston's groundless conclusion that the scribe responsible for the Vínland Map and both of its sister texts had been a nonprofessional working for himself.

To learn more about what Witten regarded as adequate scientific analysis one need look no further than to an article that he wrote around the time the map and the book were first announced in 1965, and in which he claimed that the fortuitous reunion of the two separate manuscript volumes had occasioned a period of intensive work for him personally. "It took me about a year to write my long description of the material. During that year I applied every test of its authenticity which I could devise, short of reducing the whole thing to ashes for Carbon 14 dating."[66]

Those given to worrying will find no reassurance in Witten's and Marston's writing that the two men knew any more about testing inks than they did about radiocarbon dating. This would not have mattered, however, had they sought the assistance of experts.

European Medieval Ink

The highly qualified scientists who have examined the composition of the Vínland Map ink agree on two crucial points, namely that the writing medium found on the map is quite unlike the ink in the two associated text manuscripts, and that its composition is different from that of any other known medieval ink. In other words, the ink in the Vínland Map is completely anomalous.

There has been no lack of theories about how the ink could have been made. The most common ink in medieval Europe was "iron-gall" (actually iron-gallo-tannate) ink. This was also the only widely used ink produced by chemical reaction. Iron inks are known to have been employed since 1130, but the underlying process had already been discovered at the time of Pliny; he knew that if paper had been treated with copperas (ferrous sulfate), an infusion of nut galls could blacken it.[67]

Iron inks are still produced commercially, but they have become modified to suit modern purposes. Those in need of a medieval-style iron-gall ink today will therefore have to clear space on the kitchen counter and make their own from the large variety of recipes that still exist for combining oak galls or gall nuts with ferrous sulfate, water, and gum arabic.[68] Aside from oak galls, sources of tannin such as bark, walnuts, and acorns also served for the iron-gall ink used by medieval scribes. Gum arabic is soluble in water, and adding it to ink suspends the pigment particles, which are insoluble. The inclusion of gum arabic also modifies the viscosity (hence the flow) of the ink and helps bind it to the writing surface. If too much is added, however, the ink becomes inflexible when dried, and it may crack and peel off.[69] The viscosity considered optimal for quill pens was deemed too thick for a good flow when steel nibs came into use, so the gum arabic used as a stabilizer was replaced with sulfuric acid, which exacerbated the causticity of the older style iron-gall ink.[70]

The chemical reaction between iron sulfate and the tannic acid inside the gall nuts will (with the addition of gum arabic) produce a purple-gray ink that turns lustrous black in application, but it is not problem free. Iron-gall ink is described as encaustic because it does not remain on the surface, as carbon black ink does, but etches the writing into the surface of the fabric used. An improperly made medium could thus be quite destructive. It was another drawback that with time, this type of ink was likely to produce the effect seen in both of the Vínland Map's sister manuscripts, where two delicately rust-colored panels on every page frame the still-dark writing.[71] The complete absence in the Vínland Map of this type of browning is one of many indications that the ink used was not of a medieval iron-gall type.

Regular carbon black ink was an even older common type of black writing medium than iron-gall ink. In fact, one way to ensure a lasting black color in iron-gall ink was to add carbon (lamp) black, as there is reason to believe was done in the case of both the Lindisfarne Gospels and the Hereford *mappa-mundi*.[72] Carbon black ink is simple to make from carbon mixed with mucilage (gum or animal glue) dissolved in water. The carbon particles can be obtained by burning bones, ivory, or various seeds or fruit stones. The easiest method involves collecting lamp black by holding a lighted candle under an inverted bowl. When mixed in a little warm gum-water, this soot produces a black ink that—unlike iron-gall ink—cannot turn brown with age.[73] However, while carbon ink is regarded as permanent, "some examples of documents and drawings have been found in which the binder has failed to hold the ink particles firmly to the paper or parchment."[74] A nineteenth-century essay on India ink (which is carbon based) warns against using glue as a binder, because "it cracks and shrinks in drying, as gum arabic does not, and it does not easily dissolve in cold water, as gum arabic does. India ink, made entirely with glue in place of gum arabic, is decidedly objectionable, being too hard."[75]

Another fairly old type of ink, called bistre, is an aqueous extract made with soot deposited by wood fires; it was used primarily from the fourteenth to the nineteenth centuries. Experts at the Courtauld Gallery in London note that such ink has a warm-brown color when first applied, and that the shade of brown will vary with the type of wood burned. In addition, "bistre lines and washes are usually more transparent than iron-gall ink."[76] Most popular was the variety made with soot from beech wood. The soot was dissolved in hot water and cold filtered to produce an ink that varied from "dark blackish-brown to brownish-saffron yellow to cool greenish-brown," and of a slightly resinous nature that made it somewhat difficult to mix with other inks. On its own, bistre produces excellent artistic effects, but it is also considered somewhat impermanent. As with other carbon inks, gum arabic might be added to bistre to improve its viscosity, but too much gum would cause cracking.[77]

Other kinds of inks, made from local ingredients, were also used. The Romans, for example, used sepia, the dark, semitransparent ink produced by cuttlefish. Coloring agents obtained from other animals as well as from plants and minerals included alizarin, indigo, pokeberries, and the brilliant red of cochineal. Like their continental cousins, the Icelanders used ink made with soot, but they also knew that a certain berry juice made a beautiful, purple-black ink, and they made extracts of golden willow or bearberry, both of which contained natural tannins that would darken on oxidation.[78]

Like its venerable ancestors, the modern commercial substance known as India ink is still basically a mixture of carbon and binders. Also called Chinese ink, it was invented in China and Egypt about 2500 BC for the purposes of writing and drawing with a brush. Over its long existence, the medium has been adjusted to accommodate different writing surfaces and application tools, and modern chemistry has provided both waterproof and water soluble versions, either of which may be diluted with water while in their liquid state.[79] The artists' arsenal was further enhanced after 1900, when dye bases for inks were being made in all colors.[80]

Shellac is a commonly used binder in India ink. It dissolves in alcohol (the more readily if a base such as borax or ammonia is added), and the solution is capable of sinking into the writing surface. As shellac hardens, however, it becomes increasingly polymerized and insoluble.[81] If applied to parchment, waterproof India ink (which uses shellac and borax) may lose its flexibility after a while and fall off the writing surface, unlike a good grade of traditional iron-gall ink.[82] Another problem with carbon ink is that a poor-quality product may contain a high proportion of tarry material, which produces a brown, rather than black, color. With a high tar content, the ink might in fact become quite pale, especially under poor storage conditions. It is not always easy, therefore, to distinguish between aged carbon ink and iron-gall ink—one cannot go by color alone. Although most iron-gall inks turn brown as they age, some very old iron-gall ink may still be black, and even carbon-based ink may show traces of iron when tested.[83]

While iron is a major component of some inks, it tends to be present in at least minor concentrations in most inks, especially if the ink was prepared in an iron pot. Consequently, the presence of iron is not by itself sufficient to determine the type of ink involved. Modern ink specialists such as Jan Burandt therefore recommend that more than one analytical technique be used to determine an ink's composition, so that the results obtained by one method may be weighed against those from others.[84]

Expert investigators of the Vínland Map ink have invariably shared Burandt's belief. Others have obviously not been as scientific in their approach. Considered jointly, the statements made by Witten and Painter indicate that the reported "microscopic analysis" of the ink had been undertaken by Witten, who was hardly an expert on such procedures, and who had no proper laboratory at his disposal. It is therefore fortunate that during the years that have passed since Witten "applied every test of its authenticity which [he] could devise," several well-equipped and qualified scientists have analyzed the Vínland Map ink.

The Vínland Map Ink Debate

Despite the scientific consensus about the anomalous nature of the map's ink, the conclusions of the individual scientists involved have failed to settle the authenticity debate so far. As one journalist put it: "It is relatively easy to prove a fraudulent work as a fraud, but it is often virtually impossible to prove authenticity."[85]

Skelton let the London press know right away in 1967 that British Museum scientists would examine the Yale manuscripts while they were in London for the museum's exhibition. The *Times* noted on January 20:

> Results of tests conducted in London on the controversial Vinland Map, which goes on exhibition to the public at the British Museum today, are to be sent to America where the findings will be published. . . . Minute samples of the vellum have been microscopically examined by infrared light and photographed in the British Museum laboratory. Mr. R. A. Skelton . . . said the laboratory would send reports to Yale University, the owners, so that an independent judgment on its age could be formed.[86]

The article was presumably still quoting Skelton when it also reported that Yale had undertaken to publish the results of the tests "whether favourable or unfavourable."

About two weeks after the exhibition opened, *The Observer* published an article headlined "Vinland Map ink puzzles experts." The text noted that tests carried out at the British Museum had "shown that the ink on the map is different from the ink on the two written documents that go with it. Unlike the ink on the documents, the ink on the map itself shows no traces of iron in its composition. This will strengthen the doubts of those who question the map's authenticity." *The Observer* journalist had also obtained the reaction of George Painter, who said: "This discovery is odd, but not suspicious." He still believed the map to be genuine and suggested that scribes may have used special ink on medieval maps. To this, the journalist commented: "The Museum laboratory is checking contemporary maps to see if this was so. Mr. R. A.

Skelton, Superintendent of the Map Room . . . said further tests might show that the base of the ink was lamp black, burnt bone, or dried blood."[87]

Although Skelton was no doubt aware of the laboratory's confidentiality agreement with Yale, the remarks that he made to Norwegian journalists during an Oslo press conference seem needlessly disingenuous considering the information he had already given the London press. The newspaper *Aftenposten* reported that Skelton had reiterated his belief in the map's authenticity while stressing that until the expert investigations at the British Museum were completed, he did not wish to enter into details.[88] Skelton completely avoided mentioning that he had already known for three weeks about the two Research Laboratory scientists' discovery communicated to the British Museum curators concerned with the manuscripts on loan from Yale.[89]

Almost thirty years later, the two English scientists still vividly recalled that disturbing event in their laboratory. Their message was brief and straightforward: "Our examination, under low-power microscopy and by ultraviolet illumination, established that the appearance of the ink was so anomalous as to raise serious doubts about the authenticity of the map."[90] At a magnification by about ten, the ink had revealed "a peculiar structure unlike that of the accompanying textual documents or of the ink which has been found on other manuscripts of the period or on a number of drawings of the same reputed locality and date which were examined." Even to the naked eye, the ink did not exhibit the visual characteristics of a faded iron-gall ink, the two men observed. "Instead it consists of a palish brown colour that has been absorbed into the parchment accompanied by numerous darker particles having a greyish almost metallic lustre; also in many areas these dark particles are outside the brownish contour and lie directly on the parchment." Werner and Baynes-Cope also noted that "the ink in the areas of fine writing on the map had a pale-brownish colour only and none of the dark particles were present."[91]

Further evidence that the ink is not of the iron-gall type was obtained through infrared photography, which produced a reaction inconsistent with iron-gall ink. Even more interesting was the behavior of the ink under ultraviolet light. As Baynes-Cope explained at the 1974 Royal Geographical Society symposium:

> Iron compounds quench the fluorescence induced in the background by ultraviolet light and for this reason, faded iron gallo-tannate ink, yellowish brown by daylight, will appear black against a bluish or yellowish

fluorescent background under this form of lighting. The inks used in
both the "Tartar Relation" and the *Speculum Historiale* showed this phenomenon whereas the ink used for the outline of the map itself and for
the text on the leaf did not show this phenomenon.[92]

Baynes-Cope and Werner considered possible medieval alternatives, such as
sepia ink, but found that the appearance of the map's ink was not consistent
with such an explanation.[93] Looking to the future, it seemed to both scientists
in 1967 that the use of a microanalytical technique would be particularly useful in analyzing the black particles in the ink. They concluded that although
"the results obtained by this limited examination do not provide definite evidence that can be regarded as bearing on the authenticity of the map," they
had established the abnormal character of the ink as well as the unusual
appearance of the parchment, both independently of and compared with the
two text manuscripts.[94]

While the map was in the British Museum Research Laboratory, the
museum's photographer took several pictures under various lighting conditions. Before handing the prints over to Baynes-Cope, the photographer—a
man of long professional experience—said very firmly: "You do realize, don't
you, Sir, that this ink cannot be iron gall."[95]

In the first picture, which used Kodak Commercial orthotype "B" lights, the
ink looks quite faint overall, but some of the map's outlines show up much more
clearly in some places (for example, the west coasts of Greenland and the Iberian
Peninsula with France) than in others. In a second photograph, taken with a
blue sensitive film under normal type "B" lights, the map's delineations show up
better. In both photographs, the wormholes appear as faint, dark circles.

In a third photograph, the outlines are darker overall than in the first two
pictures. The ink lines that appear darker in the two former images are relatively darker here as well. Unlike photographs one and two, however, the third
one shows the small script very faintly. There is also a reflective sheen in the
parchment background, especially in the northwestern Atlantic. A fourth
image closely resembles the first of the series, taken with Kodak Commercial
orthotype "B" lights.[96]

A little more than a year before the Vínland Map paid this first visit to a
proper laboratory, Vietor had attempted to explain the map's faint and uneven
ink lines. He observed that it looked to him as if the scribe had used a very
dilute ink, which would have made it easier for him to write small, and that

"in some places it looks as if he just ran dry or did not start off very well."[97] There can be no question that Vietor subsequently read the British Museum's laboratory report, which was completed and sent to Yale in early 1968, for in the spring of 1974 he wrote to Eila Campbell that there was no reason to be disturbed by the anomalies revealed in 1967–68 British Museum tests; there were all sorts of inks made in the Middle Ages. Besides, cleaning agents used on the parchment might account for the odd fluorescences.[98]

The judicious tone of Vietor's letter suggests that at the time these results were first communicated, there had been a consensus among those at Yale directly concerned with the map that the preliminary scientific discoveries were not sufficient to condemn the map. This judgment was theirs to make, but the fact remains that Yale and the British Museum had agreed that the laboratory's findings would be disclosed regardless of their nature.

Given the unsettling nature of those first scientific observations made in London, one might have expected Yale to press for immediate further investigations into the chemical composition of the map's ink, but the year was 1971 when Vietor asked Walter and Lucy McCrone to undertake such a study. According to Vietor (who had made other efforts meanwhile to obtain firm data), the idea had been his own and not prompted by the results obtained at the British Museum Research Laboratory. He had personally chosen the McCrone Research Institute in Chicago as the only firm able to perform such tests. The McCrones did not feel that they had the right technology until at least a year later, however, at which time they collected twenty-nine ink samples from the map, seven from the "Tartar Relation," and eighteen from the *Speculum Historiale* fragments.[99]

After the pinprick-sized samples had been individually collected under magnification by forty, they were examined by polarized light microscopy, by both X-ray and electron diffraction, by scanning as well as transmission electron microscopy, or with electron and ion microprobes. A large number of photographs were also taken during the examination process. The final results were then coordinated with each other and with the samples' positions on the manuscripts.[100] Two reports sent to Yale, as well as subsequent scientific articles, provided the details of the McCrones' methods and interpretations. Here, I will focus only on the issues at the heart of the scientific debate that began when the first McCrone report was made public in 1974.

Like their two British Museum colleagues before them, the McCrones

found that conventional iron-gall inks had been used in the two text manuscripts but not in the map. In addition, they discovered that the anomalous ink
in the map contained pigment particles of anatase having a characteristic crystalline appearance. Their smooth shape and narrow range of particle size were
intended for dispersal in paints and inks and could only be achieved through
a modern process involving precipitation followed by calcination at a very high
temperature and a milling step to break up aggregates. Quite reasonably, the
McCrones argued that this evidence for industrially modified anatase in the
ink condemned the map as a modern fake. Furthermore, the anatase appeared
to be present only in the yellowing ink line and not in the crumbling line of
darker pigment. The dark line in fact had a completely different compositional
profile and appeared to the McCrones to have been applied separately on top
of the yellowish line in order to simulate aging iron-gall ink. Any such inten-
tional simulation would obviously be a sign of attempted deception, constituting further evidence of the map's fraudulent nature.[101]

In 1991, Walter McCrone visited the Beinecke Library and obtained additional samples from the yellow ink line embedded in the map's parchment.
The results of his subsequent compositional analysis were very similar to those
that he had obtained two decades earlier. Significantly, he found titanium
white pigments throughout and at all levels of the yellow ink film. This time
he also analyzed the ink's medium or binder, which turned out not to be gum
arabic, but a form of collagen or animal glue (easily made from parchment
scraps, for example), inexpertly mixed with various pigments.[102] "The fact
that the particles in the film are not well dispersed proves a lack of proper
mixing and this is characteristic of 'homemade' (noncommercial) inks," he
concluded.[103]

McCrone remained convinced that the ink had been applied in two operations with the intent to deceive, and he surmised that the yellow color might
be due partly to oxidized iron in an impure early anatase and partly to the
addition of a bit of finely divided yellow ocher (traces of which were found in
the ink) to achieve the proper degree of staining.[104]

Seen both with the naked eye and at magnification by ten, the existing pattern of the remaining black particles indicates, in my own view, that the inking was done just once. One would do better to focus on the McCrones'
well-founded suggestion that the mapmaker used a makeshift medium, mixed
from incompatible elements that did not adhere properly to the parchment

and to each other and that in disintegrating produced the effect now visible on the map.

Later chemical investigations have raised questions about the key observations made in both London and Chicago concerning the map's ink, but not one subsequent study has changed the minds of people familiar with the many troubling aspects of the map. No minor objections can detract from the most significant discoveries made by the McCrones, which fully demonstrated both the recent date of the map's ink and the fact that Werner and Baynes-Cope had correctly identified the medium as carbon based and unrelated to any other known medieval ink, including that used in the two text manuscripts.

At first, it seemed as if the McCrones' ink analyses had settled the issue about the Vínland Map's authenticity. Soon after the new scientific results had become known in London, Roy Perrott wrote in the *Sunday Times*:

> Support for [the map] was dwindling fast last week even at Yale University. . . . Yale's librarian, Mr. Rutherford Rogers, says that the report of the ink analysis from the laboratories who have re-examined it seemed "overwhelming evidence" that the Vinland map was a forgery. . . . A systematic search for fifteenth-century manuscripts from the Upper Rhine which did not use iron compounds of some kind in their ink has proved fruitless . . . and this was one of the factors which finally persuaded Yale library, egged on by the always-skeptical History Department, to hand the map and manuscripts over to McCrone.[105]

George Painter, now retired from his British Museum post, was not persuaded by the McCrones' study. Some months after their announcement about their discoveries concerning the composition of the map's ink, he stated unequivocally that he was probably the last surviving person who believed that the Vínland Map was not a forgery, and that as far as he was concerned, no new ink testing would be of any use—he was completely firm in his convictions. Indeed, twenty years later he still had not changed his mind. He wrote in his introductory essay to the second edition of *The Vinland Map and the Tartar Relation*: "It is not surprising that no valid argument has ever been discovered, or ever will be, against the genuineness of the Vinland Map. It is logically impossible, even for the most persistent of scholars, to find reliable evidence against a true proposition." Driving home his point, he called the McCrones' position on the ink absurd, pointless, incredible, and preposterous and instead directed his readers to likely occurrences of titanium in nature.[106]

Painter's reference to natural occurrences of titanium reflects a point made
in the first scientific inquiry into the McCrones' conclusions, which was undertaken by Jacqueline S. Olin at the Smithsonian Institution's Conservation
Analytical Laboratory. Having found several inconsistencies in the McCrones'
report, she decided to question their claim that the anatase in the ink is a modern, industrially modified product and hence incontrovertible evidence of forgery. Her study over several months reflected her wish to account for the
presence of both anatase and iron in the ink, although her scientific predecessors had found the amount of iron too small to indicate iron-gall ink. Because
titanium frequently occurs with iron in nature, the anatase in the Vínland
Map ink, in her opinion, might have resulted from a natural process. "Green
vitriol could contain anatase if it were produced from an ore which contained
ilmenite," she argued. Wilcomb Washburn used Olin's ideas in the second edition of *The Vinland Map and the Tartar Relation,* just as Painter had done,
because her argument against a modern industrial process fit his contention
that the ink was likely to be medieval. Washburn took from her thesis only
what served his own purpose, however. To follow Olin's arguments properly,
the interested reader must go to the complete version of her article, which was
published only recently.[107]

Kenneth M. Towe, who was in charge of the Smithsonian's Electron
Microscope Laboratory at the time Olin completed her study, disagreed with
her hypothesis after he had studied her data and done further checking on his
own. He noted in particular that Olin's arguments did not allow for the fact
that naturally occurring anatase crystals lack the unique structure of the industrially modified anatase that McCrone had found in the map's ink. He
acknowledged, however, that she had correctly identified several discrepancies
in the McCrones' report. To resolve the several questions raised, he eventually
contacted the McCrone Research Laboratory and asked to review their analytical records of the Yale ink study. Walter and Lucy McCrone made all their
data, including their photographic records, available to him when he visited
their laboratory in Chicago. As Towe reported to Yale in 1982, he found several discrepancies between the actual evidence obtained by the McCrone scientists and the manner in which the results had been reported, but he saw no
reason to disagree with the basic conclusions presented in the McCrones' second report (1975) to Yale. In his view, the Chicago scientists had fully demonstrated that the anatase in the Vínland Map is not a ground, natural anatase.
In Towe's opinion, "No hypothesis using either a ground mineral anatase or a

precipitated, but uncalcined anatase can be readily used to explain the VM anatase."[108]

Towe also accepted Walter McCrone's conclusion that the map had seen two applications of ink rather than just one. During his personal examination of the map at the Beinecke he had found a complete lack of register between the yellow and the black lines in a segment of the English west coast. In addition, he thought that McCrone must be correct about the reason for the yellowish color of the faint "primary" ink line since "these early anatase pigments were often yellowish-brown in color because of associated iron oxides which the technology of the day had been unable to remove." He made this observation after he had taken the precaution of meeting with representatives of the Titanium Pigments Division of NL Industries.[109]

This firm has been a major player in the production of anatase pigments from American ore since 1916. Its industrial experts would certainly know the properties of their own early product, but their information does not automatically apply here. In the present context, any speculation about discoloration resulting from oxidized iron in an impure product rests on the untested assumption that the industrial-grade anatase predated the time when a reasonably pure product had been achieved. The Vinland Map was made in Europe, where the method for producing pigment-grade anatase for the paint industry, using Norwegian ore, had been perfected at about the same time as in the United States. These observations do not obscure the far more important issue here, namely that the proven presence of modern, industrial-grade anatase crystals in the ink line demonstrates a twentieth-century date for the map.

Some years after the McCrones' study, Thomas A. Cahill and Bruce H. Kusko reported directly to Yale on the analyses that they and their team at the Crocker Nuclear Laboratory had performed on the three Yale manuscripts on January 30 and 31, 1985. Their investigation of the Vinland Map included photography by transmitted and ultraviolet light, thirty-two colored microphotographs, and 159 PIXE (Particle Induced X-Ray Emission) analyses of parchment and ink. Also, forty-five analyses were made of the parchment, papers, and inks of the "Tartar Relation" and the *Speculum Historiale*.[110] The results of their investigations by means of PIXE revealed variations in the composition of various parts of the map's parchment as well as marked variations in the composition of the ink lines. In addition, as noted above, Cahill and his team reported that "the parchments of the three documents showed some variations one from the other." The ink lines of the map's delineations and legends were described as being 0.1 to 1.6 millimeters wide and varying in color from yellowish-brown to black, "usually without sharp discontinuities evident to the eye."

Cahill and his associates reported that their analysis of the ink in the body of the two text manuscripts (by the same methods as those used on the Vínland Map) had revealed levels of iron, copper, and sulfur ten to twenty times greater than those found in the map's ink. They also noted that titanium "above the minimum detectable limit" had not been found in the parchment of either of these texts. The Davis team nevertheless recorded titanium as the most frequently occurring element in the map's *ink* (found 65 percent of the time), while zinc and iron came next, each with a 35-percent occurrence rate. In their view, there did not "appear to be a good correlation among these three elements for the body of the VM ink," while the presence or absence of titanium seemed to them unrelated to the color of the ink. After examining each area of small lettering on the map, they noted that "all of the legends have a chemical profile similar to that of the main body [that is, outlines and legends in larger lettering] of the VM ink."[111] In other words, the same kind of ink was used throughout.

Particularly significant to the present discussion is the fact that Cahill and his team agreed with their scientific predecessors that the inks used in the "Tartar Relation" and the *Speculum* fragments are similar to each other but radically different from the ink in the Vínland Map.[112] The Cahill team's essay "Compositional and Structural Studies of the Vínland Map and Tartar Relation" in the second edition of *The Vinland Map and the Tartar Relation* nevertheless encouraged supporters of the map's claim to authenticity, despite the fact that the Davis team's summary of their 1985 analyses was far from coming down firmly on the side of authenticity. Cahill and his team wrote in conclusion: "We must . . . restate our original caveat that 'while our work argues strongly against the specific McCrone Associates proof that the map is fraudulent, we do not claim therefore that the map is authentic. Such a judgment must be based on all available evidence, cartographic and historical as well as compositional.'"[113]

This disclaimer had first appeared in the report that Cahill and his team filed with Yale in 1985 after examining the ink and the parchment of the three manuscripts by methods so different from those employed by the McCrones that a point-by-point comparison is meaningless. It is nevertheless possible to compare the general results and conclusions of their inquiry with those obtained in other studies, so long as the Davis team's scientific reports (both published and unpublished) are the texts consulted, not the version provided for the 1995 Yale book.

Like the previous Vínland Map investigators, the Davis scientists described the degradation of the map's ink. According to Cahill and his team, this process had resulted in the brownish-yellow line that had bonded with the parchment (briefly fading away in some sections of the map delineations and varying in intensity elsewhere), and in the dark line that had remained on the surface and was now flaking off. Cahill and his colleagues differed from earlier investigators by deciding that the yellow lines were always *within* the width of the remaining black lines wherever the latter were still observable, the only exception being the location on what they interpreted as the Welsh coast, where both McCrone and Towe had found the lack of overlap that convinced them that the map had seen two applications of ink. The Davis scientists argued that this discrepancy—the only such on the entire map—might well be due to "a short retracing of that line after re-dipping a pen that had run dry."[114]

After Helen Wallis, as the head of The British Library Map Library, had received a copy of Cahill's 1985 report to Yale, she asked both Baynes-Cope and the McCrones for their professional comments on these latest test results. In Baynes-Cope's opinion, a major problem with the new study was one that Cahill himself had mentioned in his report, namely that the technique used by the Davis team was not sensitive to elements lighter than sodium in the periodic table and therefore did not register them. Nor could the PIXE method reveal the structure of the titanium compound(s) they detected. "In short," Baynes-Cope concluded, "the new examination helps very little." He also reviewed the main arguments from the Chicago study, noting that "the McCrones showed that the globules in the 'ink' matched in chemical composition, crystalline nature, shape and range of particle size the commercially produced anatase titanium dioxide paint pigment, and only that." The McCrone Laboratory had obtained its evidence by scanning electron microscopy capable of showing the surfaces of objects in great detail and by transmission electron microscopy, which looks through object to show details that light cannot resolve due to its long wavelength.[115]

Walter McCrone had not yet seen the Cahill report when Wallis asked him to comment. He therefore suggested that she might want to have Kenneth

Towe review the results of this new study and said he would depend on Towe's conclusions whether or not they agreed with his own. While he regretted the errors that Towe had found in the 1973 Chicago ink analysis as well as the time constraints that had led to carelessness, McCrone restated his conviction that the size and shape of the anatase pigment particles in the yellow ink line were possible only with post-1916 technology.[116]

The 1987 publication in *Analytical Chemistry* of Cahill and his team's 1985 Vínland Map ink study reignited the authenticity debate. McCrone responded by demonstrating that his scientific arguments had not been disproved, while Laurence Witten told the *New York Times* that he thought he had been "partly vindicated" by the Davis study. The newspaper also solicited a reaction from Ralph Franklin, the director of the Beinecke Library, who was cautious in assessing the California laboratory's PIXE data. Concerning the map, Franklin said: "We do not designate it as authentic, but it remains a very interesting document."[117]

Because Cahill, too, had found titanium on the map, the subsequent scientific discussion essentially narrowed down to the kind of titanium, where on the map it could be found, and in what relative quantities—questions that McCrone addressed again some years after he had read Cahill's report. He considered the PIXE instrument used by the Davis group inappropriate to an analysis of the Vínland Map, especially because PIXE could not detect the type of titanium dioxide compounds involved. The instrument was unable to discern individual particles in the Davis samples and assumed instead that "every sample is a homogeneous mix of atoms." In McCrone's view, that was why Cahill's team had failed to come to grips with his own earlier observation concerning the unmistakably modern form of the anatase crystals. In addition, Cahill's study had calculated the percentage of titanium present (0.0062 percent) on the basis of parchment and ink lines in combination, an approach that McCrone considered meaningless because the titanium could be found only in the ink line. "There is no anatase in other clean areas of the map or in the two associated documents other than slight traces." If the map's parchment surface was left out of the calculation, Cahill's 0.0062-percent titanium would in fact correspond to the average of 13 percent that McCrone had figured on the basis of eleven ink samples.[118]

McCrone's observations regarding the anatase crystals had still not been disproved when the second edition of *The Vinland Map and the Tartar Relation* was launched in early February 1996, nor have they been refuted since that time. Yale University Press therefore overstated the publisher's case in advertising the 1995 edition to History Book Club members thus: "Recently the Map has been rehabilitated, for reappraisals of both scientific and humanist evidence have established its authenticity." Neither the new essays by Cahill and by Painter, nor Wilcomb Washburn's own synopsis of scientific and other developments up to that point, sustained such an optimistic view, nor did they give Washburn any reason to tell the science editor of the *New York Times*: "I think the evidence is clearly on the side of authenticity."[119]

The new essays in the 1995 edition of *The Vinland Map and the Tartar Relation* added misinformation to other areas besides the scientific one. Paul Saenger took issue with what he saw as a particularly objectionable aspect of the approach taken in this new book: "By continuing a now decades-old attempt to narrow the discussion to the issue of ink, ignoring profound palaeographic, codicological, philological and historical contradictions, the new edition of this volume does a disservice to Yale University Press, to the Beinecke Library's excellent collections, and to scholarship."[120]

Shortly after the publication of the second edition of *The Vinland Map and the Tartar Relation,* Washburn received a strongly worded letter that Kenneth Towe wrote after he and McCrone had attended the New Haven launch and that left little room for the sanguine interpretations that had just been dispensed to the public. Towe summarized the issues involved in the scientific discussion about the Vínland Map ink and noted that he had also engaged Cahill in a discussion about some of these problems during the New Haven event.

Like Baynes-Cope and McCrone before him, Towe observed that Cahill's methods had produced an elemental analysis incapable of discerning "either the mineralogical identity or the crystallographic perfection of any substance simply from the presence of the elements found in an ink." He also pointed out that a mineralogical analysis is very different from a chemical one, and that using anatase as a synonym for the element titanium, as Washburn had repeatedly done, is grossly misleading. Well-crystallized anatase is not as common a material as the element titanium. Of the three mineral polymorphs containing titanium dioxide—anatase, rutile, and brookite—anatase is in fact the least common. Besides reiterating that "the presence of well-crystallized anatase . . . is central to the [McCrone] forgery conclusion and not the presence of the element titanium," Towe reminded Washburn of the unassailable early conclusions drawn by Baynes-Cope and Werner at the British Museum.

He also reviewed the research done by Olin, the Davis team, and Ardell Abrahamson (who had contacted Towe directly about the anatase issue) before concluding: "If, in fact, the Vínland Map is a genuine 15th century document, the details of its provenance notwithstanding, the scientific evidence has yet to be presented that can overturn the simple McCrone observation that well-crystallized anatase (free of clay minerals) is present in the ink."[121]

Just before Walter McCrone died on July 10, 2002, two British scientists published a study in *Analytical Chemistry* that supported every major point made by Werner, Baynes-Cope, McCrone, and Towe. The new article, entitled "Analysis of Pigmentary Materials of the Vinland Map and Tartar Relation by Raman Microprobe Spectroscopy," reported that Katherine L. Brown and Robin J. H. Clark at the Christopher Ingold Laboratories at University College, London, had applied state-of-the-art scientific technology to the map and one of its sister manuscripts. They had then discovered that while the ink in the map delineations is the same as that used in the map legends, it has nothing in common with the ink used in the "Tartar Relation." The latter was clearly a conventional iron-gall ink applied several centuries ago, with vermilion providing the red color used in the rubricating. The black pigment in the Vínland Map decidedly comes from carbon, and what little is left of it lies on top of a yellow line containing anatase and organic binders—possibly gelatin, as McCrone had suggested. Only the yellow line contains anatase, a relatively rare form of titanium dioxide. Anatase occurs nowhere else on the map and has never been found in medieval manuscripts. Furthermore, the anatase crystals observed in the matrix of the Vínland Map ink are of the modern, industrially modified variety not commercially available until about 1923. In the authors' view, therefore, the map is a modern artifact made by someone who tried to emulate the yellowing lines that medieval iron-gall ink would have caused over time.[122]

Modern Anatase

The importance attached to the titanium dioxide crystals embedded in the map's ink calls for some additional details about modern anatase before the remaining three chapters take the discussion of the Vínland Map out of the laboratory and into the realms of history and cartography.

Scientists familiar with the crystalline structure of the titanium dioxide that McCrone found in the Vínland Map agree with him that it was a modified anatase developed specifically for the modern paint industry. McCrone knew that he was dealing with a titanium dioxide because anatase (and also rutile) crystals have a very high refractive index, and he was able to observe this quality very clearly in the crystals found in the yellowing ink line. Furthermore, when viewed through an electron microscope these crystals were such tiny, smooth globules and had such a narrow range of particle size that they could not possibly represent crushed crystals (that is, ground mineral anatase) but had to be the result of the complicated modern process involving chemical precipitation followed by calcination at very high temperatures.[123] Kenneth Towe has provided an additional reason why the titanium dioxide in the Vínland Map ink could not be crystals of a naturally occurring anatase, namely that sedimentary occurrences of anatase are always accompanied by—and subordinate to—clay minerals that have not turned up in the map's ink.[124]

Accepting these criteria leads to such further questions as where the crystals had been manufactured, when they might have found their way into the matrix of the Vínland Map ink, and where and how the anatase had become available to the mapmaker. This last question is best left for the discussion in Chapter 9, but answers to the first two belong here because they are inextricably linked with the documentable story of industrial-grade pigment anatase.

The crystals found embedded in the map's ink might theoretically antedate by a few years the 1916 patenting of pigment-grade anatase, when full-scale industrial production of the modified crystals began simultaneously in Norway and in the United States.[125] The history of the manufacture and use of industrial-grade pigment anatase nevertheless indicates that McCrone was correct in fixing on about 1920 as the earliest time that this substance would have been generally available. One may narrow the time frame for the Vínland Map's creation further by noting that the map made its antiquarian debut in 1957.

The history of the Vínland Map and its two related manuscripts, to the degree it is known, demonstrates their European origin. Assigning a European origin to the anatase found on the Vínland Map cannot rely on scientific analyses alone but must also depend on historical information about the refining methods that produce industrial-grade anatase. Although the visual distinctions among the different TiO_2 polymorphs (anatase, rutile, brookite) are clear to a specialist, an analysis designed to identify the geographical origins of a particular Fe(Ti) oxide mineral ore would be a daunting task, observes the Canadian geologist J. Victor Owen. "These oxide minerals are so common, tend to have such predictable compositions, and are so commonly found together in the same geological settings, that it would be virtually impossible to distinguish North American specimens from Scandinavian ones, even if one resorted to extremely detailed investigation of their trace element contents."[126]

Prior to 1939, any industrially modified titanium dioxide pigments would definitely have been based on anatase and not on titanium dioxide in the form of rutile because the method for extracting pigment-grade anatase from rock ilmenite was fully patented in 1916 (after earlier preliminary patenting in Norway), whereas a reliable process for industrially modified rutile pigments was not available until about 1939.[127] In the context of the Vínland Map discussion, it is also important to note that the use of pigment-enhancing anatase in paints was, from the start, closely paralleled by a similar development in manufactured inks. Torstein Bryn, the official historian of Jotun, Norway's largest producer of paints, notes that these two branches of the industry depend on much the same chemistry and technology.[128]

Elemental titanium, abundant in nature, has a scientific history that goes back to 1791, when the English clergyman and amateur mineralogist William Gregor found a mineral that he dubbed menachanite. Four years later, the German Martin H. Klaproth discovered that this mineral contained a hitherto unknown chemical element, which he named titanium. Although he was unable to extract the element in its pure form, he managed to produce titanium dioxide (TiO_2), little suspecting its future role as a bone of scholarly contention.[129] Farther north still, in Norway, there are such abundant occurrences of rock ilmenite ($FeTiO_3$) that Norwegian mines still supply (through the mining company Titania A/S) all the ilmenite ore used in European plants producing titanium dioxide in the form of pigment-grade anatase.

Titania A/S was established in 1902 and expanded its operations in step with the 1916 start of anatase manufacture at Titan Company (now called Kronos Titan A/S) in the town of Fredrikstad. Simultaneously, the U.S.-based National Lead Company in northern New York State began a similar production based on North American ilmenite.[130] Full-scale production in both countries may be dated to about 1918. Both factories depended on methods developed in a race between American and Norwegian scientists to extract and modify the anatase, using sulfate and high-temperature (at least eight hundred degrees Celsius) calcination to convert the decidedly black ilmenite into a white titanium dioxide pigment.[131] In Norway, the sulfate method (still widely used in the production of anatase) was in large part the brainchild of the Nor-wegian scientist Gustav Jebsen, who was trained as an engineer in Germany and also earned a Swiss doctorate. Under the auspices of the Norwegian com-pany Elektrokemisk, in 1904 Jebsen and his fellow countryman Peder Farup developed the innovation that led to the essentially white titanium-based pig-ment and, subsequently, to the founding of Titan Company in Fredrikstad.[132]

Titan Company was a success from the start, no doubt as a result of care-ful technical and marketing research. While the factory was still in the plan-ning stage, Norwegian experts sent a representative to Vienna in the summer of 1910 to obtain the latest technical information on testing and comparing pigments in paints, and a series of experiments began later that same year in Norway. Judging from the preliminary results, the quality and shades of the colors containing titanium varied considerably, so work continued on improv-ing the pigments, with laboratory samples sent off to paint factories both at home and abroad. When encouraging reports came back about the good cov-erage and depth provided by colors made with anatase, and about how easily this new pigment mixed with linseed oil, its economic prospects were as bright as the paints it enhanced. The tiny anatase globules created opaqueness, but not discernible color, and they added a hard finish, easy spreadability, and depth of color for the tints used. In varnish (to which it would have been added in a weaker suspension), the anatase added some opacity to an other-wise rather transparent medium.[133]

The early competition between Norway and the United States in the man-ufacture of anatase soon gave way to significant industrial cooperation. Kronos Titan in Norway and the Titanium Pigment Company, Inc., in Maine entered into an agreement in 1921 to share their information and experience within this manufacturing sector. The Norwegian sulfate method for producing anatase was the basis for the production at a new factory in St. Louis, Mis-souri, in 1923, while Kronos Titan in Norway began production of mixed pig-ments according to American methods.[134] A watershed in the paint industry came in the late 1920s, when good ready-mixed paints were becoming avail-able to consumers who until then had relied on professional painters to mix what they needed from linseed oil and other kinds of oil, varnish, turpentine, and dry pigments.[135]

Truls Tandberg, a former chief executive officer of Kronos Titan in Fredrik-stad, notes that a sister factory in Levenkussen, Germany (still one of the six Kronos plants worldwide), was in full operation from at least 1927, producing anatase pigments from Norwegian ore for use by German companies, many of which are still making well-known brands of paints and inks. The tinting material came in the form of pastes that, in addition to the anatase (titanium dioxide), contained barium sulfate, calcium sulfate, zinc oxide, and sometimes ocher (iron oxide—Fe2O3) or other tinting agents.[136] These staple chemicals are familiar from the list of substances detected by the McCrones, Towe, and Cahill.

German experts have observed that both anatase and rutile have a very slight yellowish cast (anatase rather less so), and also that while anatase pigment in powder form does appear blindingly white to the naked eye, titanium dioxide was not in itself considered a pigment.[137] Kenneth Towe notes that a brochure from the American manufacturer NL Industries describes selling a product "of an inferior grade" up until 1925, at which time an improved Titanox-A was placed on the market. The improved product was 99 percent titanium and 1 percent impurities.[138] This sequence parallels the product development in Norway, where considerable impurities in the earlier industrial anatase made it appear slightly yellower than the more recent anatase, which is perfectly white even to the naked eye.

Erik Lund, a chemical engineer long familiar with the processes used at Kronos Titan A/S, found evidence in a 1920 publication that at that time the factory used barium in the production of titanium dioxide. The reason was that during the application of high heat to remove the last remnants of sulfuric acid in the precipitated and washed titanium hydrate, it was difficult to avoid using such high temperatures in the ovens that the quality of the finished product might suffer, so before the hydrate was fed into the ovens, barium carbonate was added to neutralize the acid, and this formed a barium sulfate. Cautioning that there is no way of knowing how much barium was added at this point in the process, Lund suggests that it may have constituted a substantial portion of the resulting finished product.[139]

Lund also notes that the Norwegian plant's most important commercial product in the early years was a "paste," or thick paint, which the 1920 publication described as follows:

> The superheated product is pulverized in a mill by means of forced air separation, down to a fineness of below 0.05% residue on a mesh of 5000 per square centimeter. This pulverized product is used to produce the paste which is now being marketed. The product is mixed with

linseed oil and also a small addition of zinc white, for reasons we shall return to later. The mass is then intensely manipulated in centrifugal mixers and subsequently on the usual grinding mills. After this mixing, the process is considered complete.[140]

The so-called mixing-pigments and pastes, which in addition to TiO_2 also contained zinc oxide (ZnO) and considerable amounts of extenders, were produced and marketed right up to the 1960s, according to Lund.

With great generosity, people associated with Kronos Titan in Fredrikstad not only provided me with information about their early Norwegian anatase production, but also sent me two laboratory samples each of their anatase produced in 1923 and 1968.[141] All four samples were subsequently sent out for independent testing. When J. Victor Owen checked both sample pairs, his X-ray diffraction (XRD) data indicated that the 1923 sample contained 42–43 percent anatase (by weight), and 57–58 percent (by weight) of the mineral barite, otherwise known as barium sulfate. The 1968 product was found to be essentially pure anatase.[142]

After examining the first two pairs (1923 and 1968) of anatase samples by transmission electron microscopy, Peter Buseck and Li Jia at Arizona State University noted that both samples represented fine-grained crystals in the range of tens of nanometers. It also seemed to them that the two samples differed somewhat in their grain-size distributions, but they cautioned that this was a preliminary observation only.[143] Erik Lund confirmed that changes in calcination procedures between 1923 and 1968 might account for the difference in particle size, but he noted that there were also day-to-day variations that cannot be accounted for at this late date. Moreover, in their dry state, these primary particles tend to agglomerate during storage, so that proper dispersal of these composite units in a binder requires the application of physical energy.[144]

Even kitchen table experiments with the physical behavior of pigment-grade anatase demonstrate the product's unique and baffling properties, some of which have a direct bearing on the ink mixture likely to have been used in the Vínland Map (see Chapter 9).

A tiny amount of anatase suspended in water instantly produces opacity, and if some of that milky fluid is drizzled on construction paper with a bit of salad oil added on top, the anatase-water mix forms a film that causes the oil to slide off to the sides, forming darker lines, with enough of the oil remaining on top to lock in the anatase particles when the droplets dry. When a water-based anatase suspension is allowed to dry on paper without any such additive, a fine white powder forms on top and may easily be rubbed off. Even the slightest coating of anatase on a fingertip repels soot from a candlewick, while getting the same white powder off dark clothing is a frustrating task. In short, the industrially modified anatase particles bond to a surface under some circumstances but not others, and they readily disperse in, and combine with, some substances but not others.

It appears that mixing a high-quality, durable ink containing pigment-grade anatase would pose quite a challenge to a nonspecialist. This challenge was not met in the Vínland Map.

CHAPTER 7

The Vínland Map as a Cartographic Image

A Flat Earth—or a Globe?

The author of the Vínland Map demonstrated his cartographical knowledge in a variety of ways. Equally important to identifying its author and to a proper reading of the map are the many indications that while drawing an ostensibly late-medieval map, the mapmaker presupposed mental attitudes that not only accepted the rotundity of the earth but also that imagined the land masses distributed fairly evenly around the globe.

Prior to the fifteenth century most, but not all, European world maps derived from two basic schematic representations that did not attempt to incorporate geographical information as we understand it today, and whose treatment of distances and directions somewhat resembled modern underground system diagrams. One major map model was a zonal or climatic map with north at the top (see Figure 13); the other was a tripartite T-O map, usually with east at the top (see Figure 14). The latter was known to the Europeans from at least the seventh century onward, but probably much earlier. The "O" is the ocean that surrounds the continents of Asia, Europe, and Africa, while the base of the "T" is the Mediterranean, separating Europe from Africa. The two halves of the crossbar represent the rivers Tanais (Don) and Nile laid end to end.[1]

The fact that medieval maps were handily contained within a flat circle certainly did not mean that their authors thought of the earth as a flat disk, but rather that the known, inhabited (or habitable) part of the world, which was all one needed to represent, essentially took up only half of the planet's circumference. While such circular maps eventually inspired the mistaken notion that throughout the better part of the Middle Ages, even learned people on the continent had believed that the earth was flat, the modern scholar O. A. W.

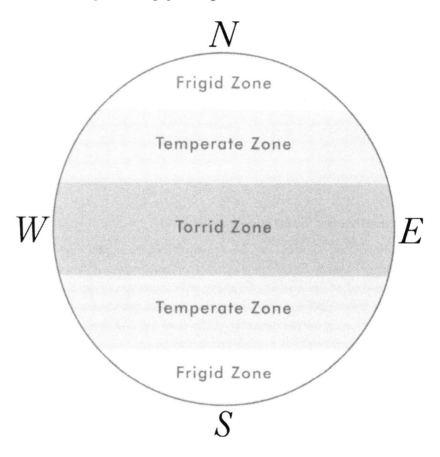

Figure 13. A zonal or climatic map with north at the top. Copyright David O. Seaver.

Dilke notes succinctly: "The spherical world of the Greeks (and the Romans, for that matter) was never forgotten."[2] The author of the Vínland Map was ahead of his contemporaries in understanding this important concept and in his general ability to interpret both early- and late-medieval thought because he had the double advantage of being thoroughly grounded in early cosmography as well as the writings of the church fathers.

Whether one credits Pythagoras (fl. 530 BC) or Parmenides (fl. circa 530 BC) with figuring out that a spherical earth existed within a spherical universe, few are likely to discount the importance of Herodotus (circa 489–425 BC) in driv-

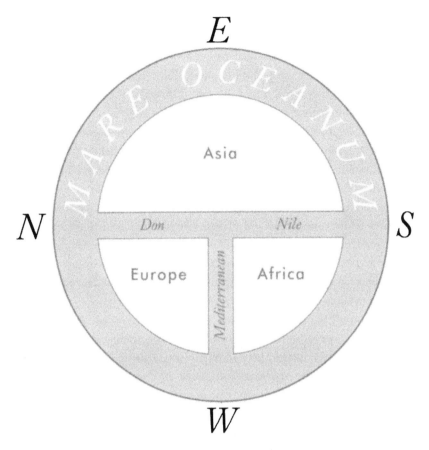

Figure 14. An example of a T-O map with east is at the top. Copyright David O. Seaver.

ing home the idea. Far from fading away with the heyday of Greek and Roman intellectual hegemony, this concept of *orbis terrarum*, an orb-shaped earth, survived intact into the Middle Ages, espoused by Isidore of Seville and successive scholars intent on describing the earth and its place in the universe. The idea that medieval people were taught to believe in a flat earth is a modern myth suggesting that regressive thought in such matters had been started by reactionary teaching on the part of the church fathers—the majority of whom (most notably Saint Augustine) in fact believed in a spherical earth. Some of the notions about flat-earthers have their roots in misinterpretations of certain medieval texts, or else they stem from an inability to separate divergent minority opinions from commonly held ideas.[3]

Northern medieval sources in Latin as well as in Old and Middle Norse make their underlying geographical perceptions just as clear as southern sources do, but they often pose linguistic difficulties for modern scholars. Interpreting either northern or southern medieval sources also means being aware of the degree to which modern geographical knowledge has influenced scholars' own attitudes. For example, we know for a fact that the Americas lie between Eastern Asia and Western Europe, but to an educated pre-Columbian European, whether continental or Norse, the Atlantic Ocean by any name and width would have been the physical feature dividing the west coasts of Europe and Africa from eastern Asia and Africa. Everywhere within the continental European sphere of learning the world was perceived as a globe in the Middle Ages, only with a missing American continent and thus without a Pacific Ocean, while pure speculation had to make do for the earth's southern and northern extremes.

Early printed maps on which Skelton was an expert, antedate the 1492 Columbian voyage by some decades, so he was no stranger to late-medieval cosmology or indeed to any aspect of the history of cartography. It is therefore surprising that he misinterpreted both Adam of Bremen and later medieval northern sources when these sources described the positions of Iceland, Greenland, and Vínland relative to Norway.[4] It is clear from his references that he relied on work by the Danish cartographic historian Axel Anton Bjørnbo (d. 1911) in these matters, but that does not explain his failure to realize that Bjørnbo, a child of his own time, had reached his conclusions in the firm belief that his medieval sources from Adam of Bremen's time onward had imagined the earth as flat.

Was Skelton a Reluctant Commentator?

The chief responsibility for commenting on cartographical issues in *The Vínland Map and the Tartar Relation* rested with R. A. Skelton. (George Painter's observations about such matters were essentially comments to Skelton's lengthy analysis of the Vínland Map.) This arrangement was entirely fitting because Skelton was the only one of the book's three authors with any real knowledge of cartographical history and with a substantial reputation for scholarship in this field.

Once the Yale book was out, it was only to be expected that Skelton's work would encounter close scrutiny from such colleagues in the map field as G. R. Crone at the Royal Geographical Society, who had wasted no time in raking him over the coals. Another early critic was the Smithsonian Institution's map expert Melvin H. Jackson, who had helped Washburn put on a special display of the Vínland Map in time for the 1966 Smithsonian conference, and who also contributed to the symposium's discussion of the map. On the latter occasion, he aired his doubts about the authenticity of the map, which he thought looked wrong for the period it was supposed to represent, and he took issue both with Skelton's statement that "the representation of Europe, Africa, and Asia . . . plainly derives from a circular or oval prototype" and with his claim that the shape of both Africa and Asia had been "flattened" into an oval.[5] Jackson observed bluntly that the ellipsoid shape was not used during the Middle Ages, and that he suspected the map to have been made later than the date assigned to the two sister manuscripts.[6]

Jackson was probably better prepared than most to voice his misgivings about the book at the Smithsonian symposium. More than half a year earlier, he had reviewed *The Vinland Map and the Tartar Relation* for an important Canadian cartographical journal. He began his review wryly by noting that "some objections have been raised that the manner of releasing this publication somewhat resembled the launching of a new commercial product," but his critique of Skelton's work for this "sumptuous volume" was anything but flippant. He was clearly troubled when he wrote:

> R. A. Skelton, also of the British Museum, supplies an essay on the background of the Vinland Map, the state of the contemporary cartography and an elaborate attempt to rationalize the revolutionary implications contained in the map, as well as account for some of its troublesome anomalies. This reviewer, at least, had a distinct impression that Mr. Skelton was not happy in his work.[7]

After perusing Skelton's contribution to the Yale volume, scholars familiar with his work both before and after 1965 on cartography and exploration are likely to agree with Jackson's assessment. Skelton was such a careful scholar that everyone involved in the Yale book project (including Skelton himself) would have had reason to assume that he would give a creditable analysis of the Vínland Map. It is my personal belief that he would have done so if he had not been obliged to write a study that never once questioned the authenticity of the map, and if he had been given sufficient time and freedom to consult as widely as his instincts clearly inclined him to do.

The plethora of evasions and unconvincing arguments that Skelton's analysis of the Vinland Map contains leaves the impression of someone who felt that he must soldier on despite increasing doubts about the task given him. Such an interpretation is surely supported by his irritable reactions to those of his London peers who were so quick to suggest that in *The Vinland Map and the Tartar Relation* he had compromised his scholarly reputation, and it would explain the speed with which he afterward joined Vietor's call for further research on the map and its text companion.

Many Cartographical Traditions—and None

The Vinland Map's delineations and textual references are so enigmatic and anomalous that much of the discussion since 1965 has concerned not only individual cartographic oddities but also the mixture of cosmographic concepts governing the map.

The map was clearly intended as a *mappamundi*—the term used for manuscript maps representing the late-medieval concept of the world before the westward voyages of Christopher Columbus had taken place. The map shows no obstacles to east-west circumnavigation of the globe and depicts open seas in every compass direction. Especially notable is the fact that the waters from Western Europe to Eastern Asia are broken into manageable widths by means of a number of islands, including the Island of Vinland.

Showing north at the top, the map roughly delineates Europe, Africa, and Asia and adds both named and unnamed islands with a fairly lavish hand. If one disregards these islands and the fragmentation of the East Asian coast, the map does essentially fill the bill as a *mappamundi* from the mid-fifteenth century, when some cartographers were making conscious efforts to discard medieval map models without being laced into a corset of Ptolemaic coordinates. In a synopsis of this transformation period, Leo Bagrow wrote that when Petrus Vesconte in the early fourteenth century drew the first recognizably representational map of the world, he had no imitators for a good while, unless one counts the contemporaneous world map in the so-called Medicean Sea-Atlas. Not until the middle of the fifteenth century do a number of world maps presage the end of medieval geography, examples being the so-called Borgia map (about 1450); two Genovese maps from about 1447 and 1557 respectively; the Leardo maps from 1442, 1448, and 1453; the Catalan map at Modena (about 1456); and—most famously—the Fra Mauro map of 1458.[8]

After the first quarter of the fourteenth century there had been cartographic indications of islands at the western edge of the Atlantic, as previously noted. Stylized and speculative, with names such as Antilia, Brazil, and the Seven Cities, these islands were placed at a latitude commensurate with the classical thinking on which medieval European cosmographers relied as they cast their eye westward to what they conceived of as the east coast of Asia. It is probably no coincidence that the Vínland Map, which is generally sparing with chorographic details and place names, indicates several rivers and names the five major cities in the greater Mediterranean region— Alexandria, Cairo, Mecca, Jerusalem, and Rome. Aside from this feature, a relatively large proportion of the sixty-two geographical names provided in the shorter legends are located in Asia, as Skelton noted in his general description of the map.[9]

The map's supply of islands is not unusual in itself, but the names, shapes, and locations of those islands have certainly provided tinder for discussions. For example, one would never know from the Vínland Map that even in the early eleventh century, the Icelanders had been aware of their island's latitudinal position relative to Norway and southern Greenland. By contrast, the map's outlines of Greenland are uncannily prescient considering that the piecemeal circumnavigation of that country was not completed until the early twentieth century, when the country's island status was confirmed at last. It is also typical of the mapmaker's penchant for anachronisms that the map's treatment of "Thule" might either derive from antiquity or else represent cutting-edge thinking at the time when late-medieval cartographers began to consider latitudinal and longitudinal grids, and when scholars such as Pierre d'Ailly (d. 1425) speculated on the nature of the habitable earth. In that connection, this passage from D'Ailly's is worth noting:

> According to Aristotle and Averroes . . . beyond the Tropic of Capricorn there is an earthly paradise. But we have not found any such country. But far north . . . where the day is only six hours long, and the extreme point of the earth, happy people live who do not die except from satiety with life, at which point they throw themselves from rocks into the sea. In Europe they are called the *Hyperborei* and in Asia the *Arumphei*. . . . Regarding the line which bounds the climates on the west there are few or no habitants except perhaps some little islands, since there is a great

sea there which is called the ocean. . . . Regarding the line which bounds
the climates on the north, there is many a habitation beyond it, as for
example Anglia, Scotia, Dacia, Norwegia, and many other countries,
the ultimate of them being according to some authorities Tyle [Thule].[10]

The Vínland Map makes no attempt to show latitudes or longitudes, but at the
apex of the long, curved line delimiting the farthest north of the Eurasian continent is the legend *Thule ultima*. This small outcropping corresponds to a latitudinal position somewhat north of Iceland, but one can only guess at this
northernmost point's latitude in actual degrees. While Iceland is called *isolanda
Ibernica* on the Vínland Map, on a number of early maps Iceland is indicated
as an island named *Thule*, *Tile*, or *Tyle*. Is the *Thule ultima* on the Vínland
Map—shown neither as an island nor at an imagined meridian approximately
equidistant between Alexandria and the Fortunate Isles (Canaries)—intended
to represent Ptolemy's *Thule* at sixty-three degrees north?[11] Or is it supposed to
reflect the *Thule ultima* of Eratosthenes (about 275–194 BC), who calculated the
distance north along the Alexandrian meridian and arrived at a latitude of sixty-
six degrees north?[12]

The ideas that Eratosthenes harbored concerning the extremes of the habitable world were perpetuated by Strabo (about 60 BC–circa AD 25), another
of Ptolemy's predecessors, whose *Geographika* has survived almost in its
entirety. Strabo also thought that the function of geography was to interpret
only the inhabited part of the world, which would exclude both the equatorial zone and anything beyond the reportedly wretched conditions found in a
northern and remote island called Ireland, and he certainly did not believe
that there was an island of Thule where people could actually live.[13]

For reasons linked to the discussion in Chapter 9, the map's author combined the main strands of mid-fifteenth and early-sixteenth-century geographical thought with Adam of Bremen's description of the Norse discoveries
involving three islands in the northwestern Atlantic. The map is oriented to
reflect Adam's underlying concept of north as "up," and it is possible to recognize several of his other geographical ideas described in the *History of the
Archbishops of Hamburg-Bremen*, which he had completed about 1075, but
which he kept revising until his death sometime before 1085.

Because the eleventh-century German ecclesiastic wrote that after successfully colonizing the islands of Iceland and Greenland, the Norse had recently
also discovered an island even farther out in the ocean that they called Vínland,

he became the earliest historian to report on an enterprise that Painter described as "a moment in the history of the world and American discovery."[14]

Adam of Bremen

When Archbishop Adalbert of Hamburg-Bremen received his pallium in 1044, Pope Benedict IX had specifically granted him authority over the northern countries: Denmark, Sweden, Norway, Iceland, and all the "adjoining" islands.[15] In consequence, one of Adam's goals was to account for the success of Christian missions in the Far North. He also went to considerable trouble to describe various geographical and other circumstances related to the Baltic, North Sea, and North Atlantic regions, drawing upon a wide variety of information from classical writers, from later sources such as Orosius and Bede and from contemporary accounts. Concerning the "ancients," he tartly observed that they "were sometimes not above adorning what they learned from travelers, merchants, sailors, and adventurers who themselves were not above adorning what they related." In assessing his contemporary sources, he gave special credit to King Svein Estrithson of Denmark and to other "trustworthy Danes" for information about the Baltic and Nordic countries, including Iceland, Greenland, and Vínland.[16]

Adam affirmed that Norway was the world's "farthest country" ("Nortmannia . . . ultima orbis provintia est")—indeed the northernmost country where human habitation was at all possible. Beyond it, one would find "nothing but ocean, terrible to look upon and limitless, encircling the whole world" (Post Nortmanniam, quae est ultima aquilonis provintia, nihi invenies habitacionis humanae nisi terribilem visu et infinitum occeanum, qui totum mundum amplectitur). Although this concept of the Far North was already some centuries old when Adam repeated it, he showed by his choice of words that he accepted the notion of an encircling ocean. His assumption of a globe-shaped world, an *orbis terrarum*, is also apparent in his explanation for the occurrence of night and day, which he ascribed to the rotundity of the earth ("Nam propter rotunditatem orbis terrarum necesse est, ut solis circuitus accedens alibi diem exhibeat, alibi recedens, noctem relinquat").[17]

Adam's concept of the earth's shape is central to understanding both his own geographical notions and those of the medieval Norse. Many of his ideas were echoed a century later in the work *Historia Norvegiæ* (about 1170), which also attempted to make northern lore about sea and land fit with contemporary geographical theories from elsewhere. If one separates Adam's acceptance of the earth's rotundity from his reliance on geographical and anthropological myths, it becomes possible to follow his thinking as he struggled to imagine some of the northern places of which he had heard tell, but for whose locations he had neither graphic nor literary precedents.

Book I of Adam's four-book work is in large part concerned with the early Christian missionaries and their uphill work among the savage inhabitants of the Far North—Swedes, Danes, and Norwegians. Book II devotes much attention to the Danish struggle to dominate England, in descriptions that let the reader glimpse a safely deskbound and urban Bremen cleric as Adam relates that "the British Ocean" (the North Sea) is "very large and exceedingly dangerous," and that crossing this sea from Denmark to England would take three days "with a southeast wind blowing," according to what sailors had told him. After recounting several plausible and implausible historical events in Denmark and Norway, Book III approaches the subject closest to Adam's heart, namely the central role of the Bremen archbishopric in placing the Far North under the influence and administration of the Roman Church. He wrote proudly: "Bremen was, like Rome, known far and wide and was devoutly sought from all parts of the world, especially by all the peoples of the north. Among those who came the longest distances were the Icelanders, the Greenlanders, and legates of the Orkney Islanders. They begged that he send preachers thither, which he also did."[18]

With evident relish, Adam described the barbarous nature of northern peoples, from whom further trouble must be expected, before he closed Book III by observing that the time had come "to describe the location of Denmark and the nature of the countries beyond Denmark." Book IV is therefore devoted to his personal concept of the North.

Adam wrote that the Baltic Sea is "also named the Barbarian Sea or the Scythian Lake, from the barbarous peoples whose land it washes." According to him, it "stretches from the Western Ocean towards the east" and also "extends a long distance through the Scythian regions even to Greece." He noted that "the Western Ocean apparently is the one which the Romans . . . called the British Ocean" and repeated his warning that this sea (the North Sea) "is of immense breadth, terrible and dangerous."[19] The western part of that perilous body of water "encompasses Britain to which is now given the name England." Because he thought of north as "up," he used the term "on the left" in noting that west of England again "there is Hibernia, the fatherland of the Scots, which now is called Ireland." North of England, the British Ocean "flows by the Orkney Islands and then encircles the earth in boundless expanses." To the east of the British Ocean lie Denmark and the mouth of the Baltic, and beyond Denmark, northeast of England, "there are the crags of Norway, and farther on the islands of Iceland and Greenland. There ends the ocean called dark."[20]

Adam was on reasonably firm ground when describing areas fairly near to home, such as the areas close to the entrance to the Baltic. Letting his mind travel east from Norway, he observed that Scania belonged to the Danes, and that north of there one would find the Goths. Clearly beyond his ken after that, he described a northern version of the imagined female preserves that have been a literary staple since antiquity by noting that beyond the Goths, the Swedes ruled over a spacious region extending to the land of women [usque ad terram feminarum]." One of Adam's informants had also told him that among the many Baltic islands there was a large island called Estland. "This island is said, indeed, to be very near the island of women." Adam drove home his titillating message a few paragraphs later: "Round about the shore of the Baltic Sea, it is said, live the Amazons in what is now called the land of women" (Item circa haec littora Baltici maris ferunt esse Amazonas, quod nunc terra feminarum dicitur). Adam was disinclined to believe that these women conceived by sipping water, however. He preferred such practical explanations as that "they are made pregnant by the merchants who pass that way, or by the men whom they hold captive in their midst, or by various monsters, which are not rare there."[21]

Past this exciting Amazonian territory in the Baltic region, "as far as Russia," the Wizzi, Mirri, Lami, Scuto, and Turci are said to live. Having by now moved conceptually to the distant and unknown northeast, Adam returned to more westerly regions: "In going beyond the islands of the Danes there opens up another world in the direction of Sweden and Norway, which are the two most extensive kingdoms of the north and until now nearly unknown to our parts."[22]

With its rough mountains and far northern location, Norway topped Adam's list as "the most unproductive of all countries, suited only for herds." Having at least escaped being "softened by overindulgence in fruits," the country's inhabitants numbered many brave fighters, who were often forced by their poverty to take up piracy abroad. "In this way they bear up under the unfruitfulness of their own country." To this generous explanation for Viking raids, Adam added: "Since accepting Christianity, however, imbued with better teachings, they have already learned to love the truth and peace and to be content with their poverty—indeed, to disperse what they have gathered, not as before to gather what has been dispersed." According to Adam, Norway had at last become a Christian country, except for the Lapps, and so had all the islands in the sea off Norway, such as the Orkneys, which similarly came under the ecclesiastical umbrella of the archbishopric of Hamburg-Bremen.[23]

Adam went on to observe that far off in the ocean, remote from all the other islands, lies the barely known island of Thule (*Insula thyle*). It is quite clear that he did not intend this Thule to be synonymous with Iceland because he explained that the Thule that Pytheas of Marseilles had reported as lying six days' sailing north of Britain "is now called Iceland." As Adam described it, this other Thule—that is, Iceland—was very large, with many people who supported their frugal lives by raising cattle. They were uniquely blessed, not only because they were content to be poor, but also "because all have now adopted Christianity." To Adam's mind, this event was so special that after the Bremen archbishop had consecrated Isleif Gizurarson in 1055 as the first native bishop of Iceland, Bishop Isleif had received letters to be transmitted "to the people of Iceland and Greenland" (Per quiem transmisit archiepiscopus suos apices populo Islandorum et Gronlandorum). Evidently anticipating some incredulity among his readers, Adam added: "Disregarding the fabulous, these facts about Iceland and the farthest Thule we learned are true."[24]

Adam's statements affect the Vínland Map discussion in two important ways. One is that he provided the seeds for later claims that a steady stream of solicitous pastoral letters had been issued by continental church authorities to subjects in the misty north.[25] The other point to remember is that Adam thought in terms of *two* islands called Thule—one reachable (Iceland) and one as good as inaccessible, located somewhere in the remote northern seas between the eastern and western coasts of the known lands of the *orbis terrarum*. The Vínland Map has *Thule ultima* as its most northerly point and teasingly displays it as a triangular point (a peninsula?) connected to the Eurasian terra firma. It is thus equidistant from both continental coasts and presumably far less accessible than the islands depicted in the extreme east and the extreme west on the map.

The Vínland Map represents Adam's view of the Far North, a medieval world picture in which not only a recognizable Iceland, but also the locations of Greenland and Vínland are found far north in the Great Ocean, just not to

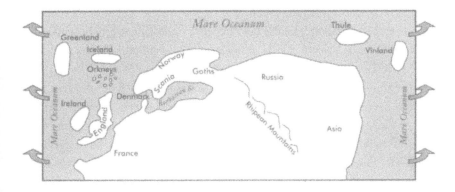

Figure 15. The geographical pattern that Adam of Bremen envisioned in northern latitudes. Copyright David O. Seaver.

the very farthest north. That position is reserved for *Thule ultima*. There exists an authentic cartographic representation of the distinction made between a known Iceland and a conceptual *Thule*. Called the Cotton Map and owned by the British Library, this anonymous work from about the first half of the eleventh century shows a large island named *Island* north of "*gothia*" and a "*Tylen. I.*" in the farthest northwest.[26]

The geographical pattern that Adam envisioned in these northern latitudes takes on firmer contours in this passage (see Figure 15):

> In the ocean there are very many other islands of which not the least
> is Greenland, situated far out in the ocean opposite the mountains
> of Sweden and the Rhiphaean range. To this island they say it is from
> five to seven days' sail from the coast of Norway, the same as to Iceland.
> The people there are green from the salt water, whence, too, that region
> gets its name. The people live in the same manner as the Icelanders
> except that they are fiercer and trouble seafarers by their piratical attacks.
> Report has it that Christianity of late has also winged its way to them.[27]

The fact that despite their uncouth demeanor, the Greenlander had converted to Christianity, naturally was credited to the early and encompassing influence of the Roman Church, but Adam's placement of Greenland relative to Sweden and the imaginary "Rhiphaean Mountains" is more relevant to the present discussion. In Adam's perception, this daunting mountain chain lay to the *east* of Sweden and prevented knowledge of the regions still farther east.[28]

Adam's trusty Danish informant had told him about yet another island in that ocean. "It is called Vínland because vines producing excellent wine grow wild there," Adam wrote. "That unsown crops also abound on that island we have ascertained not from fabulous reports but from the trustworthy relations of the Danes." Many commentators on the Vínland Map have observed similarities between this glowing description of Vínland and a segment of the longer Vínland legend on the map. Much less frequently observed is the need for caution when interpreting another Latin passage in Adam's description of Vínland: "Praeterea unam adhuc insulam recitavit a multis in eo repertam oceano, quae dicitur Winland, eo quod ibi vites sponte nascantur, vinum optimum ferentes." Some nineteenth-century translators and also the modern (1961) German scholar Werner Trillmich have correctly translated these words to mean that the island of Vínland was *discovered by many*—an interpretation that connects with the Vínland Map's claim that Vínland was discovered by more than one person, in this case by Leif and Bjarni together.[29]

Adam's reference to Greenland as an island has also been at the core of the Vínland Map debate from the start. This discussion tends to ignore certain details, such as the fact that in the Middle Ages, the stretch of northwestern Norway still known as Hålogaland was also widely thought to be an island, or that Adam himself referred to Estonia as a Baltic island. However, Greenland soon came to be regarded as either an island or a peninsula by those who thought to describe it at all. For example, the *Historia Norvegiæ*, written by a Norwegian cleric a century or so after Adam penned his *History*, envisioned Greenland as the westernmost part of a large northern landmass to which it was connected by a hazily imagined land bridge, and another Norwegian work, *The King's Mirror* (about 1250) likewise considered it possible that Greenland was part of a mainland. Neither work mentioned Vínland.[30]

Adam's trustworthy Danes appear to have had more influence with him than with their fellow countryman Saxo Grammaticus of Archbishop Absalon's circle. Having blended myths with national pride to create an account of glorious feats by Danes (and occasionally by Icelanders), Saxo finished writing his *Danish Chronicle* in 1204. In one place, he tells about three ships that were sailing north along the Norwegian coast when they ran into a fierce headwind outside Hålogaland and endured many hardships before a favorable wind brought them to Biarmaland. In this vaguely perceived White Sea region, Saxo's sailors found snow and ice in a place that was just as cold in summer as in winter but nevertheless was home to many men and boasted great rivers and deep forests. Saxo's geographical knowledge, which simply reflected old, conventional ideas about the Far North, had no impact on cartography before the time of Sigurd Stefansson (see Chapters 1 and 2), who had been educated in Copenhagen and who clearly had used Saxo as one of his sources when he drew the circa 1590 map that is his only known cartographical effort. Saxo mentions neither Vínland nor Greenland, however. In fact, there is no further mention of Vínland in the Nordic literature until the works by later medieval Icelandic scholars who shared the main features of Adam's mental image of their northern world. Skelton's remark that the Vínland Map "vividly suggests" a passage from Saxo is thus meaningless. In addition, contrary to Skelton's belief, Saxo's work had remained obscure until it was printed—the first edition (in the original Latin) came out in Paris in 1514.[31]

Drawing heavily upon the Danish scholar Axel Anton Bjørnbo's reconstruction of how Adam had perceived the Far North, Skelton observed that Adam's geographical concepts were derived from "authority, tradition, and legendary lore," and that the contemporaneous description of Vínland that Adam related fit his other cosmographical notions as a matter of course. In Skelton's opinion, Adam's placement of the three islands Greenland, Vínland, and Iceland lingered on "in the geographical views held in southern Europe as late as the fifteenth century; incorporated in the tract *Inventio Fortunata* . . . it was adopted into Renaissance world maps; and so it passed, in the sixteenth century, into the main stream of European cartography."[32] Skelton's opinions now linger in the mainstream of current thought regarding these topics. It is unfortunate, therefore, that he lacked a clear concept of these medieval views of northern geography.

Inventio Fortunata

A manuscript map from 1580, bearing the name of the Elizabethan polymath John Dee, is one of the map treasures at the British Library with which Skelton would certainly have been familiar. It incorporates startlingly accurate information derived from Martin Frobisher's 1576–78 voyages to Baffin Island and also reflects the influence of Gerhard Mercator, whose 1569 world map Frobisher had studied while preparing his search for a Northwest Passage to the riches of Cathay. During Dee's own intense involvement with this project, he had consulted his old friend Mercator, and it is to a badly fire-damaged reworking of a 1577 letter from Mercator to Dee that we owe the only surviving fragments of the *Inventio Fortunata* (about 1360). Scholars are in E. G. R. Taylor's debt for her reconstruction and translation (with commentaries) of Mercator's original letter with Dee's notations.[33]

Mercator had not obtained his own information through direct access to an *Inventio* manuscript, but by reading a work written (probably about 1364) in the "Belgic tongue" by one Jacobus Cnoyen of Herzogenbusch. To Mercator's account of Cnoyen's report, Dee then added his own reflections, which are also synopsized on the back of his 1580 map in fulsome assurances to Queen Elizabeth I of her ancient rights to many northern regions in consequence of earlier English discovery and-or subjugation of these regions. Dee's close friend Richard Hakluyt subsequently published Dee's encomium in his famous work *Principall Navigations of the English Nation*. He had evidently not seen Mercator's original letter, however, given his unquestioning acceptance of Dee's judgment that a mathematician named Nicholas of Lynn was identical with the "Oxford friar" who had voyaged to the Far North in 1360 and written the *Inventio Fortunata* to tell about his experiences. Hakluyt also published the full text of the lengthy reference to the *Inventio Fortunata* on Mercator's 1569 world map, in both Latin and English.[34]

Having written elsewhere about several aspects of the *Inventio Fortunata*, I will comment here only on Skelton's concerns with the geographical ideas supposedly contained in this work, which he thought had also influenced the Vínland Map.[35] Skelton's focus on the *Inventio* is likely to have been further stimulated by his joint work with David B. Quinn on Richard Hakluyt's *Principall Navigations* in a facsimile edition that was published the same year as *The Vinland Map and the Tartar Relation*.[36] However that may be, Skelton called the *Inventio* "the principal vehicle by which the medieval Scandinavian view of the North was incorporated into European geography and cartography of the Renaissance." The first part of this statement is wrong. The second part is correct only when allowing for the very good possibility that all of the direct cartographical references to the *Inventio* that Skelton mentioned (the 1492 globe by Martin Behaim, the 1507–8 world map by Johannes Ruysch, and Mercator's 1569 world map) in fact reflected the derivative work by Jacobus Cnoyen of Herzogenbusch, whose "Belgic tongue" all three of these cartographers would have been able to read. The known textual (noncartographical) references to the *Inventio* that Skelton noted relate to Christopher Columbus and indicate only that a firsthand description of travels in the Far North must once have existed, and that Columbus understandably was interested in learning more about it.[37]

In Skelton's view, the Norwegian explorer Fridtjof Nansen had been justified in stressing the influence that the fourteenth-century *Inventio* had exercised on fifteenth-century thinking, as exemplified by the work of the Danish cartographer Claudius Clavus, by Martin Behaim's 1492 globe, and by "the papal letter of 1448."[38] There are many problems with Skelton's easy acceptance of these examples. To begin with, the Claudius Clavus and Behaim cartographical depictions of the Far North don't have much in common. Furthermore, the Claudius Clavus map does not reflect the *Inventio Fortunata's* indications that the voyage being described had aimed north into the Davis Strait from southwestern Greenland, where the Norse still lived, and where the Gardar *officialis* Ivar Bardarson most likely was the priest with whom the English Minorite is said to have exchanged an astrolabe for a Bible. Besides coming equipped with an astrolabe, the Minorite had carried the conventional wisdom of his time concerning far-northern latitudes and conformed to these notions when he described the icy, roiling, "indrawing" seas and the magnetic mountain he had encountered. One would be as hard put to locate these physical features in the work of Claudius Clavus as in "the papal letter of 1448." In that letter, sent in the name of Pope Nicholas V to the carefully unnamed Icelandic bishops of Skalholt and Holar to express concern about the inhabitants of the "island of Greenland," the papal proxy merely described that country as "situated We are told at the extreme limits of the Ocean."[39]

Skelton frequently cited Nansen's 1911 work *In Northern Mists* in the mistaken belief that Nansen was reliable as an historian as well as knowledgeable about early maps. Nansen was an eminent explorer and scientist and a brilliant writer, but he replaced historical methodology with personal opinions, and he judged old maps with a man of action's common sense mixed with impatience. Fortunately, he realized that interpreting early maps called for expertise and therefore relied heavily on Bjørnbo, who practically to his death provided Nansen with expert advice in this difficult area.

Bjørnbo's help was only perfunctorily acknowledged in Nansen's introduction, but the correspondence between the two men, still preserved at the Norwegian National Library in Oslo and at the Royal Library in Copenhagen, reveals Nansen's limited understanding of old maps. For example, when he first contacted Bjørnbo in February of 1910, the Danish scholar's response shows that Nansen had asked him for cartographical illustrations of the north predating the late-ninth-century Norwegian voyage of Ohthere.[40]

Skelton, too, had a deservedly high regard for Bjørnbo's learning and relied on his work much as Nansen had done, but it was bound to cause problems that Nansen's and Bjørnbo's ideas were already several decades old in 1965 and, on crucial points concerning the history of the Norse in Greenland and North America, promoted opinions that by Skelton's time had been refuted. However, that history was not Skelton's strong point, as one sees from his statement about the supposedly ipso facto influences on both Jacobus Cnoyen and the original author of the *Inventio*:

> [Cnoyen's] geography of the north, like that of the *Inventio* which he quotes, is in close accord with that of the old Scandinavian geographical treatises of the thirteenth century, notably the *Historia Norvegiae* (ca. 1200) and the *King's Mirror* (ca. 1250). It was surely in Norway that the author of the *Inventio,* and Cnoyen also, picked up their concepts of islands in the north (including "Grocland" divided by channels, or "indrawing seas", which poured into the polar ocean.[41]

Skelton went on to argue that the northern "whirlpool" (in the *Inventio* said to be caused by the turbulent "indrawing seas"), which several medieval Latin writers mentioned, "strongly recalls the *Ginnungagap* of Norse lore." Elsewhere, he referred to *Ginnungagap* as "the great abyss which in [Norse] mythology formed the bounds of the ocean and the world" and related these medieval constructs to "seventeenth-century geographies and maps composed in Iceland," which located *Ginnungagap* between Greenland and Vínland.[42]

Contrary to Skelton's claims, Norse knowledge did not appreciably affect the cosmographical thinking of scholars farther south. If it did, its influence was slight compared with that exercised by the great Ptolemy.

The Influence of Claudius Ptolemæus

Unknown or poorly known regions accounted for much guesswork in pre-Columbian cartography, so the maker of the Vínland Map had a wide choice in reflecting the cartographic theory and practice that followed the reintroduction to Europe of the *Geographia* by Ptolemy (Claudius Ptolemæus), who lived and worked in Alexandria about AD 90–168.[43]

In 1397, with the fall of Byzantium threatening, the Byzantine scholar

Emanuel Chrysolaras brought to Florence a Greek manuscript copy from about 1300 of Ptolemy's mid-second-century treatise. The modern Ptolemaic scholar Marica Milanesi suggests that this act was the premeditated and inevitable result of the resurgence in mathematical and astronomical learning that was already well under way.[44] A Latin translation of Ptolemy's text, begun by Chrysolaras, was completed by his pupil Jacobus Angelus by about 1409, and shortly afterward two Florentines, Francesco di Lappacino and Domenigo di Beninsigni, translated the maps.[45]

Many scholars believe that Ptolemy did not illustrate his own work with maps and observe that the cartographical works accompanying the earliest surviving Greek copies of the *Geographia* were simply based on the mathematical coordinates that Ptolemy had calculated through astronomical observations made from his home in Alexandria and noted in his original text. The later editions of Ptolemy, which did feature maps, were substantially different from each other and fall into two main categories: version A, which includes twenty-six maps with Book VIII of the *Geographia*; and version B, in which sixty-four maps are distributed throughout the text.[46]

The Vínland Map reflects an important feature of Ptolemy's focus by giving the Mediterranean region a central position. With its many references to the travels undertaken by Christian emissaries, the Yale map also obeys Ptolemy's observation in Book I, chapter 1, of the *Geographia*: "We consider it fitting at the outset to put forth that which is the first essential, namely a reference to the history of travel, and to the great store of knowledge obtained from the reports of those who have diligently explored certain regions."[47] Indeed, within the first few decades of the *Geographia*'s reintroduction, European geographers would have been as aware of the teachings of Ptolemy as of contemporary reflections on the new travelers' tales that trickled in and were added to ancient lore. There was little potential for cosmographical conflict here because "Ptolemy was one of the few ancient geographers willing to admit that the theoretically habitable land mass of the world extended indefinitely beyond the limits of knowledge of his time."[48]

The Vínland Map nevertheless deviates from Ptolemy's ideas in significant ways. For example, it shows Scotland in line with the north-south axis of England (rather than skewed strongly to the east, as on all fifteenth-century purely Ptolemaic maps), and its depiction of the Indian Ocean reflects ideas that had just become current when Andrea Bianco drew his 1436 world map.[49]

Ptolemy had envisioned Africa extending eastward to become an "unknown land which encloses the Indian sea and which encompasses Ethiopia south of Libya."[50] Although the Vínland Map shows Africa reaching far enough eastward to encompass Ethiopia and more, the Indian Ocean (*mare Indicum*) is open to the south as well as to the east, rather than closed off by an "unknown land."

Evidently forgetting about Adam of Bremen, Skelton observed at the 1966 Smithsonian symposium that the map's showing north as "up" is one of many indications that the Vínland Map to a large degree reflects Ptolemy's theories.[51] Thomas Goldstein agreed that Skelton had reason to note Ptolemaic influences in the map, but he believed that, taken as a whole, the map conflicted with Ptolemy's two-part division of the earth (half continuous landmass, half continuous ocean), and he suggested that the map conformed instead to the global concept that Strabo had expressed in his *Geographika*. Strabo implied that the entire ocean is potentially navigable; that the *oikoumene* extends over the entire globe; and that the ocean might even contain major inhabited land formations not yet known to the Greco-Roman world. As far as Goldstein was concerned, the general global concept of the Vínland Map was readily explained by Georgius Gemistus Pletho's introduction to the West of Strabo's views, which had taken place at the Council of Basel's offshoot, the 1439–40 Council of Florence.[52]

The timing involved here is a major impediment to accepting Goldstein's belief that "one should . . . think of these Florentine discussions not only as the first substantial introduction of Strabo to the west, but as a reconstruction and reintegration of the two leading geographic theories of the ancient world."[53] According to Marica Milanesi, Strabo's work, which had been brought to Italy in the late 1420s, was not translated from the Greek until 1459, and even then it did not have anything like the immediate and universal impact of Ptolemy's *Geographia*.[54]

During the discussion that followed Goldstein's comments in Washington, Marston said that he did not dispute that such an exchange of information could have taken place during the Council of Florence, but he was not about to give up on Basel's claim to having provided the impetus for the Vínland Map. If something was known at the Council of Florence, it was also known at Basel within six months, Marston argued, "and it is perfectly possible that the scribe may have gone to Florence or the information have come to Basel." Goldstein was not easily deflected from his path, however. "If I managed to shake some of the authors out of their fairly firm though tentatively expressed conviction that the map must have been done at Basel, I am happy."[55]

Pletho's supposed distribution of Strabonian concepts at the Council of Florence was not the only reason why Goldstein assumed that the Vínland Map reflected information obtained through conciliar exchanges in 1439–40. Pletho's many important contacts included the Florentine cosmographer and physician Paolo Toscanelli, who was also present at the Council of Florence and who later convinced not only himself, but also Christopher Columbus, that the "Ocean Sea" was narrower than other scholars had imagined it, and who thus encouraged the explorer's plans for sailing westward to reach "Cathay." At Florence, Goldstein argued, Toscanelli had shown Pletho a map of the North by an unnamed cartographer, most likely the second map (about 1427–30) made by Claudius Clavus Swart. What is usually thought of as his second map of the North has been lost for so long that its creation and contents are known to us only from the so-called Vienna texts. Even more famous for having gone missing is the map that Toscanelli reportedly sent to Christopher Columbus before 1481, after he had first sent a copy to the Portuguese king. Although nobody now knows exactly what that map looked like, Goldstein maintained that the description Toscanelli provided in a letter to the king gave much the same picture as the Vínland Map. He said that he would not go so far as to suggest that the Vínland Map actually is the lost Toscanelli chart, however.[56]

Skelton expressed himself rather more soberly in *The Vinland Map and the Tartar Relation*, where he noted that a reconstruction of Toscanelli's chart should also include two surviving cartographic works that contain his ideas, namely a circa 1490 manuscript world map belonging to Yale, made by Henricus Martellus Germanus, and Martin Behaim's 1492 globe.[57] Together with another manuscript world map (now in The British Library) from about 1490 by Henricus Martellus, these two works replace Ptolemy's notion of an enclosed Indian Ocean with a more realistic view of Africa and India, in Skelton's opinion.[58] It is hard to see a pressing resemblance in those two maps to the Vínland Map, however, and Skelton sensibly refrained from belaboring the point in relation to the lost Toscanelli work.

It is nevertheless safe to assume that the Toscanelli chart was a Ptolemaic world map representing informed thinking in the third quarter of the fifteenth century, by which time familiarity with the African west coast had grown considerably as a consequence of Portuguese probes. With regard to the Far

North, however, there had been no revolutionary expansion of knowledge since the midcentury, despite the cartographic introduction of Greenland for which Claudius Clavus had been responsible, and which in various subsequent cartographic manifestations bore little resemblance to northern reality.

Claudius Clavus Niger

Our only graphic information about how Claudius Clavus (active about 1410–30) perceived the regions north of his homeland derives from a copy of the first map that he is known to have drawn, which is still in Nancy, France. It was found with a Latin translation of Ptolemy's *Geographia* completed in 1427, which had been the property of Cardinal Guillaume Fillastre (d. 1428). This manuscript contained an addendum describing the North and was accompanied by a map attributed to "Claudius Clauus Cymbricus." Further information about Claudius Clavus's perceptions of the Far North is contained in the two "Vienna texts" that Bjørnbo discovered in 1900. These, too, were copies of earlier works. Bjørnbo estimated that the copies had been made at the beginning or middle of the sixteenth century.[59]

Known to his fellow Danes as Claus Claussøn Swart (the Black) and to some of his continental colleagues as Nicolaus Gothus, this fifteenth-century cartographer does indeed deserve credit for introducing Greenland into formal European cartography—probably during a sojourn in Rome. He represented Greenland as a giant peninsula running approximately north-south and located to the west of Norway, and he showed it connected to the Eurasian landmass as it arched westward above Iceland and the "frozen sea," with Iceland positioned between the two countries (see Figure 16). Claudius Clavus's vision of the northern world did not include any kind of land farther west. He was evidently able to amaze his continental peers just by placing Greenland on the map.

Skelton considered it "unnecessary, and probably unsafe, to postulate the influence of Claudius Clavus . . . on Bianco's representation of the North, although this is chronologically possible," but he did not explain why Bianco would also have been immune to the supposed wealth of information about the North available throughout the Middle Ages and mostly attributed to the communications network of the Roman Church. Nor did Skelton appear to fear self-contradiction when he observed that in the third decade of the fifteenth century, the Italians (of whom even the peripatetic Bianco was surely

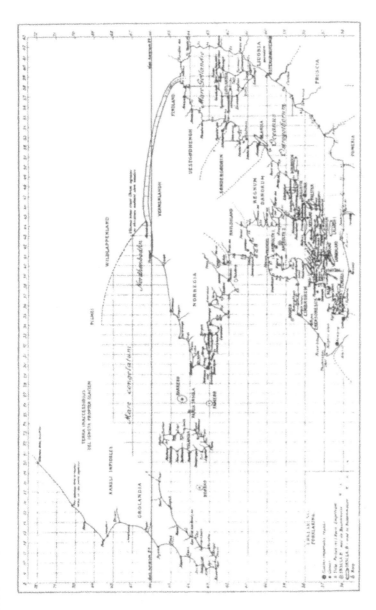

Figure 16. The second (circa 1427–30) Claudius Clavus map, reconstructed by A. A. Bjørnbo from the so-called Vienna texts. Source: Bjørnbo, "Cartographia Groenlandica," reproduced with permission of Dansk Polarcenter, Copenhagen, publisher of *Meddelelser om Grønland.*

one) were made aware through Claudius Clavus of "the image of the Atlantic lands conceived by the Scandinavian cartographers."[60]

No pre-Columbian cartographer depicted anything that could reasonably be interpreted as reflecting direct experience with any part of North America. Critics of the Vínland Map have focused on this simple historical reality ever since the autumn of 1965, when G. R. Crone noted that the "Island of Vínland" depicted on the Yale map was merely the same island that had been depicted for the very first time on the "Cantino" chart of 1502, where it was called "Terra del Rey de Portugall" in honor of the Corte-Real voyages.[61] True to the Mediterranean focus of their Greco-Roman heritage, medieval European cartographers had failed to include not only the North American littoral known to the Norse, but also Greenland, and few had shown any interest in the Eurasian Far North except as lands of myths, frigid mists, and fish. Fish put Norway on the circa 1414 world map by the Venetian Albertin de Virga, for example, where "Norueca" is written plainly in three places to signify the three Norwegian towns known abroad through the fish trade.[62]

Maps made in Northern Europe did somewhat better in representing areas closer to home. For example, a late-twelfth-century Henry of Mainz *mappamundi*, which P. D. A. Harvey notes is the earliest of a group (all with English associations) that includes the Hereford and Ebstorf maps, has a distinct *Islād* directly north of a peninsula representing Scandinavia. Even so, nothing on this map suggests a concern with Greenland and coasts beyond it.[63] This omission of any land or islands beyond Iceland is certainly interesting when one recalls that just a century earlier, Adam of Bremen had included both Greenland and Vínland in his description of the northern world.

Adam's view of Greenland and Vínland, which he described as islands, obviously had not registered with Claudius Clavus, who omitted Vínland altogether and gave Greenland a massive peninsular form. For a long time after the second half of the fifteenth century, Ptolemaic maps incorporated Claudius Clavus's concept of a peninsular Greenland, sometimes as an extrusion at the northwestern edge of the Eurasian continent and sometimes as a peninsula running east-west above Norway. Neither variety is reflected in the Vínland Map.

Although the Vínland Map shows no overt cartographical influence by Claudius Clavus, there are two good reasons (besides the fact that he drew Greenland as a peninsula rather than as an island) to include him in the general discussion about the map. One reason is that Axel Anton Bjørnbo and

Carl S. Petersen claimed in 1904 that their eponymous hero had visited the remaining Norse in Greenland; a belief that Bjørnbo restated somewhat more obliquely in his "Cartographia Groenlandica," published posthumously in 1912.[64] The second reason is that Bjørnbo lived long enough to learn that Nansen completely dismissed the idea that Claudius Clavus had ever been to Greenland, but not long enough to tell the author of the Vinland Map, with whom he corresponded, how he intended to phrase his partial change of mind in this matter.

Skelton was aware of the controversy between Nansen and Bjørnbo concerning the supposed Greenland sojourn by Claudius Clavus and made it clear that on this issue he sided with Nansen, who claimed that he had brought Bjørnbo around to his way of thinking in the end.[65] The situation between the two men was not quite that simple, however.

When Nansen first approached Bjørnbo for help with the cartographical analyses in his forthcoming book, he had let the Danish scholar know right away that in his own opinion, Claudius Clavus had not been to Greenland or Norway. Bjørnbo demurred but admitted that Nansen had planted seeds of genuine doubt in his mind. At increasing cost to his own strength, he patiently commented on the pages Nansen sent him, at one point advising Nansen against tiring the general public with too much specialized information. In a letter dated February 15, 1911, Nansen regretted that Bjørnbo's health was "not good."[66] Bjørnbo died on October 6 that same year, before he had completed his own book and without fully admitting to having changed his mind on the Clavus-in-Greenland issue.

The anonymous preface to Bjørnbo's "Cartographia Groenlandica" states that barring the addition of some texts to the planned map illustrations, the pages that had been finished under the author's own supervision had been left untouched except when something had decidedly needed correction. Bjørnbo had also left behind a draft to an introduction in which he referred to his recent exchange of opinions and information with Nansen. Because their correspondence had taken place in a spirit of loyalty and confidence, Bjørnbo wrote, he considered it distasteful to disagree in print about the interpretation of important points. The anonymous preface writer resumes at this point, noting that Bjørnbo had intended to reprint sheets 7–8 because Nansen had just claimed, in his *In Northern Mists*, that Bjørnbo had agreed that Clavus could not ever have been to Greenland. In the main text to his book, Bjørnbo enigmatically observed that since the earliest (Nancy) map appears to show that

Clavus was unfamiliar with the Greenland west coast and evidently placed the Eastern Settlement on the east coast, right below the Polar Circle, one might safely assume that Clavus had not personally visited the country when he made his *first* map of Greenland.[67]

Bjørnbo then went on to state that while he was not persuaded of Nansen's views, this disagreement about the circa 1427 map was relatively unimportant because in his own view the cartographical information found in the Vienna texts, substituting for the second (lost) Clavus map, showed that before creating his later work Clavus had indeed been to Greenland. Furthermore, Bjørnbo had no doubt that both the earlier and the later work had been based on the Norse discoveries on the far side of the Atlantic. Little suspecting the use that others would make of his beliefs later, he wrote that firsthand observations by Norse seafarers had given rise to a uniquely Norwegian-Icelandic worldview.[68]

This singular Nordic worldview would, by Bjørnbo's definition, have encompassed not only Greenland, but also America—the land that the Norse had found on the other side of the Atlantic five centuries before Columbus reached the Caribbean and four centuries before Claudius Clavus called attention to populated regions beyond the common European sphere of interest. The problem with Bjørnbo's definition is that he misunderstood medieval Nordic ideas about northern geography and was misled by late-medieval and early-Renaissance cartographic renditions of massive northern continents.

Leading up to Circa 1440: The European View

From *Thule ultima* at the apex of the Eurasian landmass to a truncated Africa ending just south of the latitude of modern Senegal, the Vínland Map's north-to-south coverage combines with the long east-west extension of the Eurasian continent to suggest the Ptolemaic influence that had already become evident when Cardinal Guillaume Fillastre included the Claudius Clavus view of the North with his 1427 manuscripts of the *Geographia*. This influence dominated scholarly thought throughout the fifteenth century right up until the time Columbus sailed west to discover a workable route to the riches of Cathay. According to these ideas, a ship that succeeded in sailing west from Europe across the *Mare Oceanum* was bound to reach the east coast of Asia on the other side.

Even when sixteenth-century explorers and cartographers had accepted that the earth's circumference must accommodate the newly discovered American lands in the West, it took many more decades to acknowledge that those poorly surveyed new regions were unconnected to Asia in the extreme north and belonged instead to a separate New World continent. Nor was the existence of the Americas the only adjustment that post-Columbian cartographers had to make; they also had to grapple with the great unknowns of the Arctic and sub-Arctic regions.

Although Skelton, Painter, Marston, and Goldstein all claimed that learned exchanges during the Church Councils of Basel and Florence had imparted major new perceptions of the Far North, there is no cartographic or documentary evidence for their position. Around 1440, essentially everything north of Denmark's Jutland Skaw, east of the Caspian Sea, and south of Cape Verde and the Sahara would still have been as hazy to European cartographers as the southwestern reaches of the Ocean Sea were to practical navigators. Change was slow in coming, and when it did come, in the last quarter of the fifteenth century, it took the form of two different adaptations of Claudius Clavus's work as far as the northwest was concerned. These adaptations were made by Donnus Nicolaus Germanus (starting in the 1460s) and Henricus Martellus Germanus (fl. 1480–1496), whose geographical ideas had been shaped not only by Ptolemy and other classical luminaries, but also by such learned Europeans of their own century as Cardinal Fillastre's friend Pierre d'Ailly.[69]

Cardinal d'Ailly, who died in 1425, is generally believed to have written his famous work *Imago Mundi* around 1410, shortly after Ptolemy's *Geographia* had made its appearance in Latin. His cosmographical ideas were still very much current in 1436 when Andrea Bianco drew his world map with so many acknowledged similarities to the Vínland Map. It is a further testimony to the enduring influence of D'Ailly that Christopher Columbus owned a copy of the *Imago Mundi* that he carefully annotated. D'Ailly drew on both Ptolemaic and Aristotelian concepts when he wrote:

> The end of the habitable earth on the east and the end of the habitable earth on the west are "moderately close"; and in between is a small sea as to its breadth, although over the land there is a larger area that extends over half of the earth's circumference. Therefore if the climates extend to the end of the west as the authors say, and do not reach farther than over half of the earth's circumference, then it follows according to Averroes

that the climates do not stretch to the end of the west, and that there are vaster habitations still beyond, i.e. outside the climates. Wherefore it follows by necessity that the climates or at least some of them are of greater length than the astrologers suppose.[70]

In 1440, any European cosmographer worth his gown would have known D'Ailly's views and have understood them to mean that the east-west extent of the earth's continental mass had to include habitable regions beyond the mere half of the earth's circumference that were generally reckoned within the "climates"—that is, within the latitudinal belts where conditions allowed for human life. Without recourse to modern globes and maps, learned men were forced to think in terms of geographical abstractions and would have had no problem grasping what D'Ailly meant by another passage, which probably was music to the ear of Christopher Columbus:

But the true east and west are under the equinoctial circle and, in dividing the earth, ought to be taken within the farthest points of the earth where the sea which is called the ocean disappears. This is the most distant habitable part of Ulterior Spain on the West and the most distant part of Ulterior India on the East. So the east of the earth is said to be the first part of the habitable land toward the east of the equator, or the east of the first horizon of the habitable earth on the equator. The west is assumed on the opposite side.[71]

Besides affording us an early-fifteenth-century, post-Ptolemaic view of how east meets west on the unseen half of an imagined globe, D'Ailly also guides us through other geographical concepts that were common to his time and are found again on the Vínland Map, such as an open Indian Ocean replacing the original Ptolemaic sea enclosed by the joining of the Asian and African continents. D'Ailly laid this imagined enclosure at the feet of the "ancients" who had included "Oriental Ethiopia" as a part of India. In his own view, India and the other Asian regions together made up one-third of the earth's landmass, and the ocean constituted Asia's southern boundary. To the east, "sunrise" marked the border; to the west, the demarcation was "Our Ocean" (the Mediterranean), while to the north, Asia was enclosed by "Lake Maeotis" (the Sea of Azov) and the Tanais River (the Don). Noting again that Asia was "surrounded on three sides by the ocean" as it stretched across the entire eastern region, D'Ailly spelled out how he envisioned Asia's southern limits: "I say then that the southern frontier of India thrusts toward the Tropic of Capricorn hard by the region of Pattala and neighboring land which a great arm of the oceanic sea surrounds as it runs down from the ocean which lies between India and Lower Spain, or Africa."[72]

The Vínland Map shows the *mare Indicum* running south along the coast of a northeastern extension of Africa, and then one's eye is taken sharply west to follow the African coast along the *Sinus Ethiopicus*. In an unbroken stretch of sea, this "Bay of Ethiopia" joins the *Mare Occeanum* [*sic*] as it heads north again up the west coast of Africa, having the *Beate Insule fortune* to the left. The map does not otherwise reflect D'Ailly's ideas any more slavishly than it obeys other medieval sources. This is only to be expected in a map so clearly intended to tease and confuse by including identifiable fragments of information without making it possible to place the work within known and definable ancestral possibilities.

A case in point here is the Vínland Map's treatment of Norway, Sweden, and Denmark. The name *Dacia* for Denmark would not be unusual in a map from the early fifteenth century (Pierre d'Ailly used it, for example), and representing Denmark as a peninsula reaching north toward the entrance to the Baltic essentially reflects reality, but placing Sweden—*Rex Suedorum*—south of the Baltic is hardly realistic even if Bianco's map showed the same peculiarity, as Skelton noted.[73] Even more peculiar is the Vínland Map's depiction of Norway—*Rex Noruicorum*—as a sizable peninsula overarching the Baltic and continuing west for a considerable distance toward Iceland. This is at odds with the political reality in the Nordic countries as it must have been known to educated Europeans by the time the Council of Basel took place. With the Kalmar Union of 1397, Norway had lost its autonomy to Denmark, first through the actions of Queen Margrethe and even more decisively thanks to King Erik of Pommerania. The generous representation of Norway on a map that features a relatively small Denmark seems intended as a reminder of Norway's importance as the "mother country" when the Norse voyaged all the way to America in the eleventh century.

Despite the Vínland Map's many anomalies, there is nothing naive or random about either the map's legends or its deceptively simple delineations that superficially conform to the conventions operating about 1440–50. Even the seemingly awkward, off-center design fits with the map's basic purpose—a purpose that the defenders of the map consistently overlook when they accept it as a legitimate offspring of mid-fifteenth-century thought.

A Subtle Composite

The patchwork nature of the map worried many scholars after 1965, but such misgivings seem not to have afflicted the authors of *The Vinland Map and the Tartar Relation* when they began their task of convincing the public that the Vínland Map represents the missing informational link between the Norse arrival in America and post-Columbian awareness of the New World. On the contrary, they made a considerable effort to sketch plausible routes by which such information might have reached a mid-fifteenth-century continental mapmaker and made him as well informed about the eleventh-century Norse as about the geographical influences of his own time.

An astute map scholar, Skelton had detected the footprints of others besides Ptolemy and Strabo in the map's representation of the world known to Renaissance cosmographers, and he was certainly aware that the American continent did not intrude on cartography until after 1500. However, he seems to have lacked an intuitive understanding of the geographical concepts that prevailed in the first half of the fifteenth century (which the Vínland Map's author exploited), because he missed the significance of the two large islands shown in the extreme northeast, named *Insule Sub aquilone zamogedorum* and *Postreme Insule*. His mental eye did not travel around "behind the map" from the farthest east to the extreme west, therefore he failed to connect those two islands with the three islands in the northwestern Atlantic described as *Vinilanda/Vimlanda Insula*, *Gronelāda*, and *isolanda Ibernica*. Together, those five islands help convey the map's central message, but Skelton missed its significance, quite possibly because he had become too troubled and discouraged by the analytical maze in which he was trapped.

As noted earlier, Marston, Skelton, and Painter believed that the Council of Basel was a likely venue for obtaining valuable information about Greenland and Vínland, but by no means the only place. Skelton in particular believed that on the long road to mid-fifteenth-century enlightenment about Norse voyages to North America, there had been purely cartographical stages that had since become lost. While he acknowledged that the western part of the Vínland Map has "no extant antecedent," he considered it "not at all improbable" that there had once been a map of Scandinavian origin showing the Scandinavian peninsula, Iceland, and Greenland.[74] Skelton's faith in cartographic precedents is particularly evident when he comments more generally on the northwestern Atlantic portion, where there is a complete lack of similarity to Andrea Bianco's 1436 world map despite the many indisputable Bianco parallels elsewhere on the map. He wrote:

> In view of the novel elements in the northwest part of the map, we must reckon with the possibility—but no more—that its author found this version of the British Isles in a map of the North Atlantic which may have served him as a model for this part of his work and from which may stem not only his representations of Iceland, Greenland, and Vinland, but also his revisions of Scandinavia and Great Britain and the islands in between.[75]

It is not just the actual statement here that reveals a blind spot, but Skelton's footnote explaining that the Vínland Map's representation of Great Britain has a parallel in the circa 1490 work by Henricus Martellus Germanus. If Skelton had allowed that the Vínland Map might be a modern work rather than a precursor to late-fifteenth-century mapping of the North, he might have seen the Henricus Martellus evocation as perhaps a shade too tidy.

Skelton naturally saw that the map contained a series of chronological as well as cartographical conundrums, and he commented extensively on many of the riddles he encountered, not the least of which was the anomalous *Magnum mare Tartarorum* (Great Tartar Sea) shown in the northeastern section of the map. He observed that both the name and the delineation here probably represented what the mapmaker had "read or been told of the Caspian Sea." Noting that the *Magnum mare Tartarorum* was neither named nor implied in the Vínland Map's companion piece, the "Tartar Relation," Skelton thought that this feature on the map reflected the geographical uncertainties that had plagued Carpini and other mid-thirteenth-century emissaries to the Mongols and had resulted in such precursive names as *Magnum Mare* and *Mare maius* applied to the Black Sea. He therefore surmised that when the Carpini mission had come as far as to the Caspian Sea, they thought that they had reached an inlet of the ocean lapping against the far Asian shore.[76]

Skelton's reasoning prompts the question of why a mid-fifteenth-century mapmaker, intent on placing earlier medieval travels into the context of more recent knowledge, in this instance would eschew the geographical views that had resulted from Marco Polo's accounts of Asia, for example—an influence that Bianco's map certainly shows.[77] However, in the case of the *Magnum mare Tartarorum* the anachronism (one of several in the Vínland Map) actually heads in the opposite chronological direction. As far as anyone can tell, the first time a "Tartar Sea" in that region appears on an undoubtedly genuine map is in Tommaso Porcacchi's 1572 world map (a stubby sausage shape representing a compressed globe), where the maritime feature is called *Mare di Tartaria.*[78] Porcacchi's map, which shows East Asia separated from the North American west coast by only a narrow strait, locates the *Mare di Tartaria* in northeastern Asia and indicates that this sea would (if east met west here) funnel into the strait running south between Asia's eastern littoral and the North American west coast. The *Magnum mare Tartarorum* on the Vínland Map appears off the northeastern coast of Asia just as in Porcacchi's map, but running along the west coasts of three large islands to the east before joining the *mare Indicum.*

The *Magnum mare Tartarorum* is only one of several cartographic "firsts" on the Vínland Map; Vínland is certainly another, while in Skelton's opinion the map is also the earliest to provide information in cartographic form about the Carpini journey.[79] This conviction is of course closely linked with an acceptance of the map as a genuine late-medieval work, and this combination so obstructed Skelton's view that even as he recorded the mapmaker's unique textual and graphic references to the Norse, the nature and intention of the map's allusions eluded him. He did not understand the world of the medieval Norse and therefore missed the false notes of the Vínland Map that resulted from the mapmaker's even more idiosyncratic notions about the Norse and their geographical perceptions.

Northern Geographical Conventions

Literacy has a long tradition in the Far North. The use of runes reaches back into prehistoric times, and the introduction of Christianity about AD 1000 brought the Roman alphabet and formal learning, including theology, cosmology, and numeracy, in its wake. However, while the incorporation of continental ideas is a striking feature in northern written sources from the medieval period, there is little to suggest that continental savants accepted more than cursory instruction from visiting Nordic colleagues. Contrary to the beliefs of Skelton and his coauthors, it was the Norse who did most of the absorption.

A strong appetite for foreign learning set its stamp on Norse culture in the eleventh and twelfth centuries despite the considerable traveling distances involved. Foreign missionaries constituted one agency for information in the earliest days, but more important in the long run was the impact back home when Norwegians and Icelanders returned from foreign study or from pilgrimages abroad. The first native bishop of Iceland, Isleif Gizurarson, was educated in Germany, and so was his son. Two twelfth-century Icelandic bishops studied in England, while the first bishop of Holar in Northern Iceland, Jón Ogmundsson (1106–1121), and Iceland's first historian, Sæmund Sigfusson (1056–1133), both went to France to acquire learning.[80] Norwegian churchmen similarly had educational roots on the continent as well as in the British Isles. Through them and others like them, however, new ideas filtered and even reached Greenland.

It is therefore no surprise that the Norse knew about the cosmographical ideas penned in the early twelfth century by the prolific continental scholar Honorius Augustodinensus. His encyclopedic work *Elucidarius*, originally written in Latin, was translated into both Old Icelandic and Swedish. When a late-twelfth-century German version appeared entitled *Lucidarius*, it was also translated into a number of North European languages, including Danish and Icelandic. The work was a compendium of biblical and general knowledge intended for the general public, and it was widely read all over Europe for a long time.[81]

The Old Icelandic *Elucidarius* was evidently one of the earliest European vernacular versions of this work; the oldest extant Icelandic manuscript is dated to about 1200 and is thought to be a copy of a copy of the original translation. When Honorius's work was first made available in Iceland, literate people there were already familiar with such encyclopedic literature as the works of the Venerable Bede (673–736) and Isidore of Seville (about 560–636). Both the early- and late-twelfth-century versions of the *Elucidarius* would have provided descriptions of the earth and its place in the universe, ideas that Honorius also expressed in his *De imagine mundi*. Didactic in style, the *Elucidarius* (later: *Lucidarius*) has the master twice tell his disciple that the universe is shaped like an egg, the earth representing the round yolk suspended in the egg white by means of divine power. Buoyed by the masses of water surrounding it, the earth floats rather high up in its suspended state, but an abundance of water also flows *through* the earth in several deep *tracones*—an explanation for tides and general water circulation. Because of the earth's orb shape, the sun barely reaches the "outer edges" (the extreme north and south), which therefore are far too cold for human habitation. Only a third of the world—the temperate middle zones—is populated. People in those favored zones are otherwise said to live everywhere on the globe, distributed so that some people have their feet facing south and others have their feet directly opposite.[82]

The Norse may simply have shrugged their shoulders on reading this dismissal of the colder zone that they themselves inhabited, but it is more likely that they defined themselves as living in the "temperate" zone, and that they allowed for plenty of Arctic wastes farther north.

The anonymous Norwegian creator of the *Historia Norvegiæ* certainly believed in a dangerous and frigid North and took a rotund earth for granted as easily as Honorius did and as Adam of Bremen had done even earlier.[83] Recounting a tale of sailors whom wind and fog had caused to stray on their eastbound voyage home to Norway from Iceland, the *Historia Norvegiæ* noted that the men had "for certain" found a land with giants as well as the home of maidens who became pregnant from drinking water. The reader also learns that Greenland, which Icelanders had settled and strengthened with the Catholic faith, was separated by icebergs from the lands (presumably islands) of giants and maidens. Despite these sops to conventional beliefs, other parts of the work suggest that the author drew on reports based on actual experience, such as when he wrote that north of the Norse settlements in Greenland there were some small men whom the Norse called Skrælings, and who used walrus ivory and stone instead of iron for weapons and knives.[84]

The author clearly envisioned Iceland as lying so far south that someone who drifted off while heading either east or west from that island might credibly round the southern tip of Greenland. In the narrative just mentioned, the original eastbound voyage had met a terrible fate indeed because the sailors had found themselves in chilly, monster-infested seas *northwest* of the Greenland settlements. There is a clear influence from conventional European ideas here, not only in the allusion to monsters but also in the work's description of Greenland as the *westernmost point of Europe*, reaching almost to "the African islands where the Great Ocean floods in." The homes of the giants and maidens encountered by the hapless Norwegian crew were supposedly located between Greenland and Biarmaland—the White Sea region of northern Russia. As the author imagined the land areas in those far northern seas, Greenland represented the extreme west and Biarmaland the extreme east, separated by a relatively narrow, dangerous ocean containing the islands of the maids and the giants (see Figure 17).[85]

Historia Norvegiæ does not mention Vínland or otherwise allude to the eleventh-century Norse voyages that Adam had described about a century earlier, but that does not mean that the Norwegian cleric had never heard of the Norse discoveries to the southwest of Greenland. What is important in the present context is that the work's reference to "the African islands" moves it a

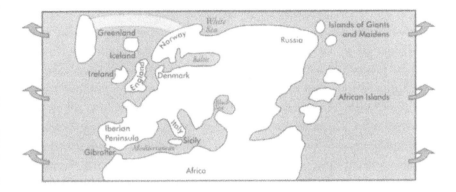

Figure 17. The geographical concepts evident in the *Historia Norvegiæ*. The work mentions neither Helluland, Markland, nor Vínland. Giants and maidens were supposedly located between Greenland and Biarmaland (the White Sea region of northern Russia). Copyright David O. Seaver.

century closer to the world picture found in a later Icelandic geographical treatise. Also, by moving the islands of giants and maidens to the icy seas northwest of Greenland, rather than giving them a Baltic reference point as Adam had done, the writer gives an unabashedly Nordic twist to the tale.

The land or island of women, maidenly or otherwise, became as much a movable feast in medieval and early Renaissance cartography as *Thule* and the "Magnetic Island" of ancient lore, and the situation was not helped by the semantic confusion arising from the late-ninth-century Anglo-Saxon version of Orosius's history of the world (a work that Adam also used, although probably in the original Latin). As noted in Chapter 2, the Anglo-Saxon king Alfred had received a visit from a North Norwegian chieftain named Ohthere, who described his voyage around the North Cape and into the White Sea region. In the tale that the enterprising Ohthere told the king, he said (accurately enough) that Sweden was touched on the north side by the Land of the Kvens—rendered as *Cwena land* in the Anglo-Saxon version. In Richard Hakluyt's sixteenth-century English translation of this passage, the name became "Queeneland," because the translator had obviously confused *cwena* (belonging to the Kvens—an ethnic group living just northeast of the innermost Bothnian Bay) with the Old English *cwene* (woman). There would have been a similar potential for confusion among the Norse, because "the Land of Women" would have been *Kvennaland* in Old Norse.[86]

The Vínland Map chastely avoids such all-female preserves, but it is attuned to other Nordic geographical perceptions. Any person who regarded the world as orb-shaped would also understand that in the Far North, the distance between extremes of east and west, on both land and sea, would be considerably foreshortened compared with farther south. Such a perception allows for the way the *Historia Norvegiæ* described Biarmaland, Greenland, and the sea that separated them. The same concept is used in the Vínland Map's representation of proto-America, or Vínland, which the Norse had reached by a manageable voyage westward from Greenland, and from which comparatively short hops would take one to the *Postreme Insule* first and to the Asian mainland second.

In *The King's Mirror*, a didactic work from about 1260, the shape of the earth is likened to an apple rather than to an egg as the anonymous author emulates not only his Norwegian predecessor's belief in a round earth, but also his fondness for monsters, mermaids, and mermen in the distant Greenland seas. In this work, a Norwegian father imparts to his son knowledge that he considers useful to a merchant and man of the world. He explains why there are variations in seasons and hours of daylight; he gives the reasons for cold and warm regions; and he tells his son that the earth's circle is round as a ball ("Nú skaltu á thví marka, at böllóttr er Jarðarhringr"). He then instructs the young man to light a taper representing the sun and to suspend an apple between the taper and the wall because that will enable him to observe that the apple's back side remains in the shadow, and that the fruit's bulk prevents the taper's light from reaching the wall. Furthermore, the exercise will show that the middle of the apple's front half, having the shortest distance to the taper's flame, will get the most heat and light, and the northernmost and southern-most points will receive the least.[87]

When the son expresses a wish to know in which part of the world Greenland is located, it becomes clear that the father envisions both an east-west (equatorial) circuit around the globe and a north-south one running through both poles. He explains that he cannot fully answer the young man's question, because he has not found anyone familiar with the entire globe ("ek hefi engan thann funnit, er kannat hafi allar kringlur heimsins"), but it had in any event been reliably reported that Greenland lies at the northern edge of the habitable world (or the edge of the world's landmass). Beyond Greenland, the father could imagine no further land, only the vast ocean that encircles the world. Another passage in the same work distinguishes clearly between the *kringla* (double loop/circuit) concept and the notion of just a single encirclement of the earth:

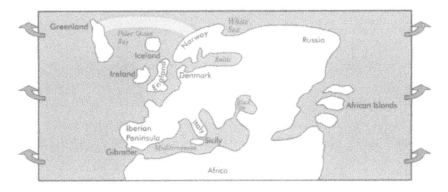

Figure 18. The geographical concepts described in *The King's Mirror*, whose anonymous author was uncertain whether Greenland was an island or part of a mainland. Copyright David O. Seaver.

"It seems to me most likely that the hot region runs east-west, with a curved ring of burning heat swung around the entire thickest part of the earth-ball" (Thá thykkir mér that líkast, at hinn heiti vegr liggr ór austri ok í vestr, með bjúgum hring brennanda vegarm unkringðum öllum jarðar böllum). Moreover, learned men had said that the empty ocean cuts down into a deep strait by Greenland and separates it from the entire land (that is, from the large Eurasian landmass) with fjords and bays, before running into the loop around the world.[88]

This description, illustrated in Figure 18, is very similar to the ideas found in Figure 17. The underlying assumption here clearly implies access by sea to both eastern and western Greenland. The author of *The King's Mirror* nevertheless appears to have been of two minds about such a version of northern cosmography, for elsewhere in the book the father expresses uncertainty about whether Greenland should be considered an island or whether it might be part of a mainland. As an argument for the latter, he notes that the presence there of many animals normally found only on a mainland suggests mainland status for Greenland as well.[89] In that case, the linkage would have been to the northwestern Eurasian continent. Claudius Clavus acted on similar assumptions some 160 years later when he drew his map linking Greenland to the northwestern European landmass and indicated that beyond Greenland, there would be only water until one reached the east Asian littoral.

A fourteenth-century Icelandic geographical text (of which several versions exist) makes it clear that the geographical conventions of northern medieval

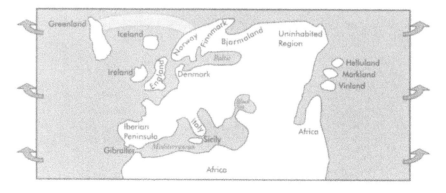

Figure 19. The geographical conventions of northern medieval scholars assumed that the world was a globe. The fourteenth-century Icelandic text *Leidarvísir ok borgaskipan* assigns Helluland, Markland, and Vínland to the "other" side of the only known ocean. Copyright David O. Seaver.

scholars continued to be based on the assumption that the world was a globe, but it adds some interesting details (see Figure 19). Unlike the *Historia Norvegiæ*, which mentioned neither Helluland, Markland, nor Vínland, this treatise, *Leiðarvísir ok borgaskipan* (Itinerarium and list of towns), fits all three of these Norse discoveries on the "other" side of the ocean into the existing conceptual framework using three known continents. It also places the Nordic and Baltic countries in a recognizable relationship to each other before explaining that Finnmark lies north of Norway. From Finnmark the land stretches northward and eastward to reach Biarmaland, which pays tribute to the king of Garðaríki. (Novgorod and the surrounding region). From Biarmaland the land continues eastward to the uninhabited regions (*óbygðir*) in the north, toward Greenland ("*viðtekri Grenland* [*sic*]")—a phrase implying proximity to Greenland but not physical connection. It is south of Greenland that one will find Helluland, followed by Markland, and from there it is not far to Vínland, "which some think extends from Africa, and if so, the Great Ocean [*úthaf*] comes in between Vínland and Markland."[90]

Because the medieval Norse accepted that the world was spherical, they could envision an Outer Ocean running above and below the habitable world as well as between the eastern and western extremes of that world—in other words as *also* forming a large north-south body of water that they knew people had crossed when sailing west to reach Greenland, Helluland, Markland,

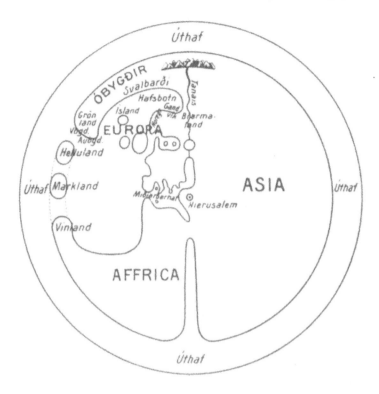

Figure 20. A misleading reconstruction of the Nordic world view by the Danish cartographic historian A. A. Bjørnbo, who believed that medieval people thought of the world as encompassed within a flat disk. Source: Bjørnbo, "Cartographia Groenlandica," p. 82, reproduced by permission of Dansk Polarcenter, Copenhagen, publisher of *Meddelelser om Grønland.*

and Vínland. It is even more important to a proper understanding of the Norse geographical perception in the *Leiðarvísir ok borgaskipan* to realize that the promontory or island constituting Vínland was envisioned as reaching northward from the *eastern* shore of Africa, not from the west as imagined by Bjørnbo (see Figure 20). As far as Bjørnbo was concerned, conflicts between northern experience and cartographic statements of imagined geography had arisen as soon as circular world maps began to rely on the descriptions of northern countries provided by Adam of Bremen in the last quarter of the eleventh century.[91] The problem was not with medieval mapmakers, however, but with Bjørnbo's interpretation of how medieval northerners envisioned Earth and its place in the universe.

Skelton, who never questioned Bjørnbo's interpretation, thought that the views just described were incorporated "in the geographical views held in southern Europe as late as the fifteenth century," just as he believed that medieval northern views of this kind had made their way into the *Inventio Fortunata* and subsequently into "the main stream of European cartography" in the sixteenth century.[92] Rekindled interest in the *Inventio* in the late fifteenth and early sixteenth centuries certainly affected how the Arctic regions were depicted on Renaissance maps, but these cartographic representations bear no relationship to what northerners themselves believed during all the centuries when they did not make maps themselves.

The Vínland Map reflects medieval Nordic beliefs in one important respect, however: It depicts a rotund world where variously named ocean segments flow so freely into one another that a ship might go wherever good or bad luck would take it.

Snorri Sturluson's Universe

The famous Icelandic author Snorri Sturluson (1179–1241) took a keen interest in the physical world. In this he was a product of his time, both in terms of the information available to him and because his curiosity was in tune with the resurgent interest in cosmography and cartography between about 1100 and 1200, which, according to David Woodward, left as its "main legacy . . . the expounding of the principles of empirical science." As an example of this development, Woodward points to the Franciscan Order, which was founded in 1209 and nurtured scientific scholars such as Roger Bacon and William of Occam.[93] The order's stress on learning about the natural world also produced travelers like Friar John de Plano Carpini, who with his fellow Franciscan Benedict the Pole braved the long journey to the Tartars in 1245–47 and later accounted in his *Hystoria Mongalorum* for the area they had traveled through.

As already noted, a more sophisticated approach to northern geography than Adam of Bremen's is already discernible in the *Historia Norvegiæ* and *The King's Mirror,* and a well-educated thirteenth-century Icelandic chieftain might reasonably have wanted to augment conventional learning with contemporary, firsthand observations. However, the well-traveled Snorri never presented either his personal travel experience or his secondhand knowledge in graphic form. Although one finds an echo of the early T-O maps in Snorri's description of a tripartite inhabited earth, like the rest of his European contemporaries he would have seen those formal representations of the habitable world as diagrams with no bearing on actual travelers' practical knowledge or needs. Like his learned colleagues elsewhere, he would also have known that the earth is round. However, he would not have needed an intellectual construct to tell him that he lived on a globe with the sun as its source of light and heat, for he had lived near the sea all his life; he had sailed abroad on vast expanses of sea where the curvature of the earth is easily visible; and he made his home on an island where even ashore the sky is an immense and beautiful cupola.

Snorri assumed a world in which an *Úthaf* (Outer Ocean) not only separated Eastern Asia from Western Europe, but flowed over the top and bottom of the globe in much the same manner as that envisioned by the authors of the *Historia Norvegiæ* and *The King's Mirror*.[94]

While a voyage on a steady course either eastward or westward would eventually close an imaginary loop, it would be a far more dangerous proposition to attempt closing the north-south loop by sailing "over the top," where fog, ice, and rushing currents would warn a sailor that he was approaching the region where reality and myth blended in the supposed *Ginnungagap,* which Skelton thought was such an important feature of early Norse geographical thinking. Given what scholars know about medieval Norse voyages across the Atlantic and far into the Arctic, it is very unlikely that real-life Norse sailors feared voyaging so far west or north that they reached a void, whether it was called the *Ginnungagap* or something else. Their worries would have been reserved for the demonstrable and ever-present dangers posed by the winds, waves, and penetrating cold of the icebound North—dangers that had been familiar to sailors from the time ships were first used in the North. That would reach far back into time indeed.

One of Snorri's well-known works is a compilation of royal sagas often called *Heimskringla,* because the first saga opens with the words "*Kringla heimsins.*" The phrase is usually translated as "The Earth's Circle" accompanied by the mistaken belief that Snorri thought that earth was a disk on which a circle marked the perimeter. The Old Norse word *heimr* fortunately offers no difficulties; it denotes "home," "earth," and "world" and essentially describes where humans may or do in fact live. Snorri's thinking about the shape of that "home" is a different matter, and the key word here is *kringla. Kringle* in modern Norwegian usage refers to any double-looped bakery item in the shape

Americans call a pretzel. To understand what sort of "double loop" Snorri had in mind while using the word *kringla*, one needs to look no further than to his predecessors Adam of Bremen and the Norwegian author of *Historia Norvegiæ* or to *The King's Mirror*. "*Kringla heimsins*" is simply medieval Icelandic for "*orbis terrarum.*"

Snorri suggested elsewhere that the pagan Norse had envisioned a universe of orbs within orbs. There was an inner circle or orb, *Miðgarðr* (inner yard), where humans and gods lived, and an outer region appropriately named *Útgarðr* (outer yard), which was reserved for giants and other unfriendly non-humans. Additionally, *Miðgarðr* distinguished between the lower space occupied by mortals and the upper region allotted to the gods. Although the latter were unpredictable, especially when angered, the humans evidently found it reassuring to have the gods as immediate neighbors in their universe.

Miðgarðr and *Útgarðr* were separated from each other by a body of water where the huge *Miðgarðr* serpent lived and discouraged unwise attempts to cross the boundaries between humans and gods. The Danish scholar Kirsten Hastrup describes the essence of this thinking: "The opposition between the 'inside' and 'outside' in the Nordic cosmography . . . mirrored an opposition between the familiar and the dangerous at a whole series of levels. The closer a person was to the center of the world, the less dangerous it was."[95] In that respect, the Norse would not have been unlike Aristotle (384–322 BC), who thought that outside the familiar and relatively manageable Mediterranean, a hostile ocean stretched westward from the Pillars of Hercules (the Strait of Gibraltar) to the east coast of India, and who considered sailing in that direction far more hazardous even than exploring the vastness of Asia's terra firma to the east.[96]

Modern understanding of pre-Christian Norse cosmography is far from perfect, however, because Snorri's representations are unreliable; he was a Christian whose artistic and antiquarian interests both needed to be satisfied. In his retelling of the heathen past, he used ideas and images from the Bible and added them, along with notions of his own, to the lore and thinking common to his own day. Anthony Faulkes, a modern commentator, notes as an example that in Snorri's version of the end of the world, the Christian Doomsday blended with Ragnarök (fall of the gods).[97] Fusing one's sources in this manner was common practice at that time, but the results require caution in a modern reader.

Much of what we think we know about heathen Norse cosmography comes from *Völuspá* (The sybil's prophecy), a late-tenth or early-eleventh-century poem consisting of a series of myths. *Völuspá* begins by describing the creation of the world and of the men and the gods who inhabited it. The poem ends by prophesying a cataclysmic battle of the gods (Ragnarök) and the destruction of the world, followed by a new beginning.[98] In the third verse we find the first mention of the *Ginnungagap*, which carried the seeds of the creation of heaven and earth. This verse ends: "gap var ginnunga /en gras hvergi."[99] The precise meaning of *"ginnunga"* has been greatly debated, but the two lines may be tentatively translated as "the void /gaping mouth was delusionary /deceptive (or, pregnant with magic power) /and of grass there was none."[100]

Regardless of how the stanza is interpreted, it is important to realize that whatever metaphysical importance the heathen Norse may have attached to this image, it had only a superficial bearing on the geographical imaginings of such Christian writers as Adam of Bremen and the authors of *Historia Norvegiæ* and *The King's Mirror*, as well as of Snorri himself. When Snorri compiled the work known as the *Prose Edda*, or *Snorra Edda*, he deftly wove several stanzas of *Völuspá* into his own version of the pre-Christian Norse concept of the world's creation.[101] He presented these pagan myths in the sections of his *Edda* that are usually called *Gylfaginning* and *Skáldskaparmál*, with *Gylfaginning* in particular detailing the cosmology that accompanied the myths.[102] Even before the world of gods and men took shape, there had existed a tricky and nebulous void called *Ginnungagap*, which in *Gylfaginning* (the tricking of Gylfi) is located between the hot "end of the world" called *Muspellsheimr* and the coldest, farthest north known as *Niflheimr*.[103]

Ginnungagap was thus originally part of a supposedly heathen Norse story about the creation and appears subsequently to have become transmuted into a consciousness that mysterious, cosmic hazards might still be lurking in the distant northern seas whose actual dangers Norse sailors knew all too well. Never bothering with maps, the medieval Norse did not nail down any kind of *Ginnungagap* as a cartographic feature, however. That development comes much later and proves that mythmaking has remained alive and well right down to modern times.

Ginnungagap and the Birth of a Cartographic Myth

Skelton never claimed to have read Snorri's works, much less the *Historia Norvegiæ* and *The King's Mirror*.[104] Instead, he relied on the interpretations that

Nansen and Bjørnbo had provided about northern geographical concepts. Among the personal ideas that he added to the discussion, the most important one in the present context was his belief that the "indrawing seas" described in the Cnoyen version of the *Inventio Fortunata* (and subsequently featured by Mercator in 1569) had been inspired by the Norse *Ginnungagap*. Having no idea of the earlier history of this concept, he observed that the *Ginnungagap* is shown clearly named and with an indication of a whirlpool on a 1606 Icelandic map by the Icelandic bishop Gudbrand Thorlaksson.[105]

Bishop Gudbrand imagined the *Ginnungagap* as a strait separating southern Greenland from *Estoteland*—the latter located at approximately the latitude of Galway Bay in Ireland and obviously inspired by the fictitious North Atlantic region introduced in the spurious 1558 Zeno map, from which Mercator had also borrowed in 1569 (see Figure 21). Because Mercator's map had indicated a substantial littoral to the west and southwest across from a large, peninsular Greenland, Skelton stated categorically that Bishop Gudbrand's *Ginnungagap* "plainly represents Davis Strait" and that the piece of land to the south of that strait must consequently be "Baffin Land." Skelton also noted in his essay that the bishop had struggled "to reconcile the geography of the old Norse world, which he had studied in the ancient records of his country, with that of more recent European mapmakers and explorers."[106] Actually, Bishop Gudbrand revealed in a number of places that his map contains little realistic information from any period.

The texts to the letter keys on Bishop Gudbrand's map are an excellent guide to his conclusions about the *Ginnungagap* and many other features, but Skelton simply ignored much of this crucial information, such as the text accompanying the three letter keys "H" (running along the west Greenland shore), which says: "H.H.H. The west side of Greenland, uninhabited and unknown to the Ancients [in other words, the Old Norse]." Given that both of the Norse Greenland settlements had been on the western side, it is clear that the bishop's information here was so shaky that it could not possibly have links to medieval knowledge. Similar geographical uncertainties appear in the text to keys "I" (at the entrance to *Ginnungagap)* and "L" (in the middle of the strait), but Skelton overlooked the latter (which refers to "an ocean abyss which the Ancients believed was the cause of high and low tide") and merely provided the untranslated Latin text to the former. According to Bishop Gudbrand, the letter key "I" denotes "the strait between the extreme part of Greenland to the south and another continent, which the Moderns call

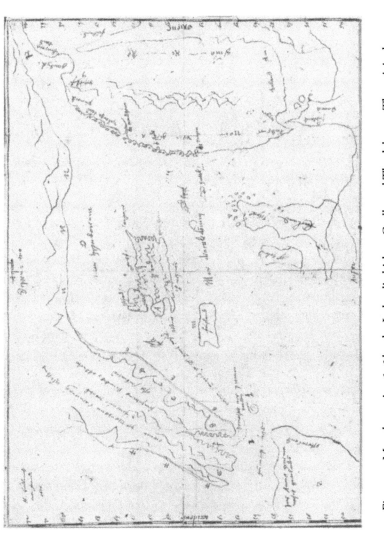

Figure 21. Map drawn in 1606 by the Icelandic bishop Gudbrand Thorlaksson. The original still exists, carrying an inscription by Hans Poulson Resen (see Fig. 8) noting that "Thorlacius" made this map in his own hand. Manuscript Department of the Royal Library in Copenhagen. Reproduced with permission.

America; through this strait the Ancients had run in former times when they found Vínland. The Ancients called this strait *Ginnungagap*."[107]

In Skelton's opinion, Bishop Gudbrand's map was closely related to the works made around the same time by Sigurd Stefansson and Hans Poulson Resen (see Figures 7 and 8, pages 57–58), and he believed that the title text on Resen's map suggested that an ancient map prototype showing the Norse discovery of America had still existed in 1605. In a detailed, published study, Peter C. Hogg of The British Library's Scandinavian Section dealt a quiet scholarly blow to this mistaken and commonly held belief concerning a key passage in the Resen map's long Latin title:

> Indicatio Gronlandiæ & vicinarum regionum, versus septentrionum, & occidentem, ex antiqua quadam mappa rudi modo delineata, ante aliquot centenos annos, ab Islandis qvibus tunc erat ista terra notissima & nauticis in tempore observationibus.[108]

The crucial phrase here is "ante aliquot centenos annos." Hogg notes that this would indeed mean "some centuries ago" if *centeni* were understood in a distributive sense ("by the hundred"). However, in classical Latin (Vergil and earlier) it has also been used as a cardinal number for "one hundred." In medieval Latin, *centeni* was not used in this way, but Resen, a highly educated man, adhered to classical Latin usage. Hence, his reference would indicate a prototype made shortly after 1500, which is certainly possible. Hogg has shown that the forerunner to the circa 1590 map by Stefansson may well have been a sketch prepared for Archbishop Valkendorf's projected voyage to Greenland in 1514.[109]

These demonstrably post-Columbian map efforts do not support either Painter's or Skelton's suppositions that cartographical antecedents with or without a *Ginnungagap* had once existed for the northwestern Atlantic regions pictured in the Vínland Map.

Neither Resen nor Stefansson used the name *Ginnungagap*. Stefansson's map (Figure 7) shows that instead of any kind of troublesome *Ginnungagap* of ancient lore, he envisioned comparatively sheltered coasting along the American shore after crossing from a peninsular Greenland reached by a westward voyage from Iceland. The legend accompanying the letter key B on this map reads: "Next to [Skrælingeland] lies Vínland, which was called 'the Good' because it was so fertile, and because of its abundance of other useful things. Our countrymen thought that this would terminate to the south in the great, savage ocean, but I can tell from the recent stories that either a fjord or a sound separates it from America."[110]

The striking outlines of the Stefansson map served as the prototype for the so-called Hungarian Vínland Map—a crude fake that surfaced in Hungary after World War II and that was subsequently brought to the attention of Helge Ingstad while he was working on his first book about the L'Anse aux Meadows site. In good faith, Ingstad published the Hungarian map in his 1965 *Vesterveg til Vínland* (Westward to Vínland), but when Hogg studied it at The British Library later, he found solid literary evidence on the map itself that the work is a modern fake.[111]

The two or three different kinds of writing on the Resen map are uncannily reminiscent of the Vínland Map's mixture of informal and formal scripts, the latter in carefully ruled longer legends on both maps. The Resen map was not reproduced or widely known until K. J. V. Steenstrup arranged for it to be copied and published in 1886.[112] At that time, however, Steenstrup's efforts helped shape the perceptions of scholars during a key period in Nordic studies generally and in the story of the Vínland Map particularly.

By the late 1880s, serious scholarly interest in the Norse discovery of America and in Norse Greenland was reaching a high pitch on both sides of the Atlantic. The four hundredth anniversary of the first Columbian voyage across the Atlantic was approaching, and escalating national pride in both Denmark and Norway was not calculated to douse the heat. One of the most productive and highly regarded researchers in the Norse field was the Norwegian historian Gustav Storm, who before his death in 1903 had published a number of books and articles focused on Norse history in general and on Iceland, Greenland, and Vínland in particular. He was also fascinated by early maps and geographical treatises and wrote no fewer than four articles on Claudius Clavus.[113] Probably the most influential historian in his field at the time, his advice and opinions were widely sought. The bibliography in *The Vinland Map and the Tartar Relation* lists his 1889 work *Studies on the Vineland Voyages*, and Skelton frequently referred in his text to Storm's opinions about the *Ginnungagap* and the Stefansson, Resen, and Thorlaksson maps, among many other matters.

Together, Bjørnbo, Nansen, and Storm were the most internationally visible Nordic exponents of the notions about medieval Norse geographical concepts that prevailed during the years just before and after 1900, and to this day, they are cited with some regularity as if their information and conclusions still measure up. Although representative of early twentieth-century thinking, many of their concepts were already outdated when Skelton wrote his analysis for *The Vinland Map and the Tartar Relation*. Some of these ideas stand out clearly in Storm's article "Ginnungagap i Mytologien og i Geografien" (*Ginnungagap* in Mythology and Geography), published in 1890, a year after his book on "Vineland" had appeared. In this article, Storm commented on a possibly fourteenth-century scholium added to a fifteenth-century Danish manuscript copy of Adam of Bremen's history of the Bremen archbishops, which told a story involving two men named Olyden Helgessøn and Gunnar Raasvein. Storm observed that the men appear to have once existed, but that their harrowing experiences on a northern voyage stretch credulity. Upon reaching the northern end of the world, the two men had been forced to turn around or else face dropping off into the terrible void called *Ginnungagap*. Storm continued: "Underlying this story is clearly the assumption that the inhabited earth was a flat disc, surrounded by the ocean; when sailing far north, one will ultimately reach the place where the ocean comes to an end and one risks falling into the abyss."[114]

According to Storm, in the eleventh century (and probably also later) this abyss was thought to lie to the north of Norway. That indicated to him that people at the time were not familiar with the most northern reaches of that ocean or indeed knew much about the far northern regions generally. In conclusion, Storm observed that this was precisely the view of the cosmos found in the ancient poem *Völuspá* and in Snorri Sturluson's *Edda*. Storm also regarded Adam as a fellow believer in both a flat earth and a vast abyss at the "end" of the northern ocean.[115] The medieval sources to which Storm referred can be interpreted in this manner only by someone already convinced—as Storm and Bjørnbo certainly were—that medieval people thought of the world as flat.

Nobody has ever questioned Storm's familiarity with the Norse literature, however, so it is worth reviewing his comments about the metamorphosis that the concept of *Ginnungagap* appears to have undergone over time. He observed that in *Völuspá*, the earliest source, *Ginnungagap* began as the original matter from which the world was made. Ymir's body arose from this matter and was then spread about to create the visible world. Snorri's *Gylfaginning* had retained this concept of *Ginnungagap* as the mystical cosmic void where ice and frost control the north and burning fires rule in the south, but by the later Middle Ages *Ginnungagap* shows up as a geographical name and has been moved "farther west."[116]

The westward movement Storm noted here refers to a description found in Björn Jónsson of Skardsá's *Greenland Annals*, a work from the first part of the seventeenth century. Here, Björn presents an idiosyncratic version of a lost geographical treatise, known as *Gripla* and assumed to have had its origins in the fourteenth century. In its surviving form, the description says that Helluland is now called Skrælingeland. South of this lies Vínland the Good, "which some men believe is connected to Africa; the *Ginnungagap* lies between Vínland and Greenland, it comes out of the ocean which is called *Mare oceanum* and which encircles the whole world." As Storm also observed, southwest of Greenland is essentially where one finds the *Ginnungagap* on the 1606 Gudbrand Thorlaksson map.[117]

Navigating by the Vínland Map

Even allowing for a relatively slow dissemination of knowledge prior to the introduction of printing, the dramatic descriptions of the northern seas provided by Adam, Snorri, and other medieval northern sources evidently did not impress other learned Europeans enough to result in cartographic speculations involving Vínland. Nor was there any attempt to show Greenland until after the influence of Claudius Clavus had made itself felt.

The Vínland Map eschews the peninsular shape that Clavus had given to Greenland, but it pays full attention to all of the three islands that Adam had described as lying in the most distant part of the habitable north. A skipper plotting his course by the Vínland Map could expect that sailing west in the northern part of the *Mare Occeanum* should get him to Iceland, Greenland, and Vínland, in that order, and that by going beyond Vínland he would eventually reach one or the other of the two northeastern islands that this map calls *Postreme Insule* (the outermost islands) and *Insule Sub aquilone zamogedorum* (the islands below the dark and frigid north, associated with the Samoyeds). Neither island, or group of islands, is found on any other map. In fact, they baffled Skelton so much that he passed hastily over them both.[118]

Should a navigator subsequently venture south and descend from the *Magnum mare Tartarorum* into the *mare Indicum*, he would encounter several more islands, all of them unnamed on the Vínland Map and not accounted for by other medieval maps. Medieval and early Renaissance cartography was otherwise generous with islands everywhere, including in the Atlantic. It was known quite early that the islands of Shetland, Orkney, and the Hebrides were numerous. The Faeroes as well as the Isle of Man were also frequently accounted for in some way, as were islands of dubious reality or featuring a confusing variety of names. The author of the Vínland Map took full advantage of the resulting cartographic confusion when he placed a number of big and little islands in the *Mare Occeanum*, most of them south of England.

Only three archipelagoes in the southern half of the Atlantic are named on the Yale map. The northernmost designation is *Desiderate insule*, which Skelton identified as the Azores and the Madeira group, but with this rider: "The general name *Desiderate insule* given in the VM to these islands is not found in any other map." That is not the only problem here, however. As Skelton pointed out, the name *Insule Fortunate Sancti Brandani* and other variants of a name associated with Saint Brendan (d. 576) have also been applied to islands in this general area, some of them also involving references to the *Insulæ Fortunatæ*. The latter name is now widely accepted as antiquity's name for the Canaries, and this is the interpretation given to the Vínland Map's *Beate Insule fortune* group located south of the *Desiderate insule*. The stage is set for further confusion west of the *Beate Insule fortune* and *Desiderate insule* archipelagoes, where we find *Magnæ Insulæ Beati Brandani Branziliæ dictae*.[119]

As the Portuguese cartographic historian Armando Cortesão has noted, islands reflecting the legend of Saint Brendan and his voyage with seventeen other monks were featured in many maps from the thirteenth through the fifteenth centuries, appearing for the first time off the northwest coast of Africa on the circa 1270 Ebstorf map. Skelton observed for his own part that the "VM is the earliest known map to move the name further out into the ocean and apply it to the Antillia group." He then endeavored to align it with, for example, the *Antília* on the 1424 Pizzigano chart and with the ubiquitous "Isle of Brazil," both of which geographical concepts have frequently been discussed in terms of growing European curiosity and information about lands to the west.[120]

By moving the reference to Saint Brendan far west into the southern half of the *Mare Occeanum*, the mapmaker put down another peripheral marker for the early influence of Christian missionaries. With references to Prester John in the far southeast, to mid-thirteenth-century papal emissaries to the Mongols in northeastern Asia, and to Bishop Eirik's activities in Greenland and Vínland in the extreme northwest, the map's intended purpose stands out with a sharpness that is in direct contrast to its deliberate cartographic obfuscations. The map's message is that by the mid-thirteenth century, Christian missionaries had spanned the entire inhabited world.

Comparing the Vínland Map's delineations with those found in authentic maps from the mid-fifteenth century and earlier suggests that the map's author created an idiosyncratic picture of the world that could nevertheless pass for a mid-fifteenth-century one. The same mixture of borrowing and invention is evident in the longer map legends, which form a textual narrative as strictly original as the graphic one, even in the areas that supposedly illustrate the regions traversed by thirteenth-century Franciscans and demonstrate beyond any doubt that the mapmaker possessed the "Tartar Relation" manuscript when he made the map.

CHAPTER 8

The Vínland Map as a Narrative

The Roman Church at the "End of the World"

Seven long legends constitute much of the Vínland Map's narrative, which in large part centers on the reach of the medieval Roman Church. The extant documentation that relates directly to the ecclesiastical administration of Norse Greenland begins with Pope Leo IX's bull of January 6, 1053, the first such document to refer to Greenland by name. The document trail ends with Pope Leo X's 1519 appointment of Vincent Petersson to the Gardar See, four years after King Christian II of Denmark-Norway had been granted an indulgence for Archbishop Valkendorf's projected voyage to reclaim the Norse Greenlanders for church and crown (see Chapter 2).[1] As a body, these documents mostly reflect administrative concerns, appointments, and directives, or they state measures that have been taken to collect taxes, borrow money, or grant dispensations to royalty and other prominent persons. They sometimes contain interesting hearsay, but there is so little reliable information about the Greenlanders that for particulars about their situation we must turn to annals and financial records, the latter kept mostly, but not exclusively, by the ecclesiastical authorities in Iceland and Norway. Local details reached continental church authorities chiefly when it was necessary to explain—not always truthfully—why tithes and Peter's Pence were slow to reach the papal coffers.

There are only occasional glimpses of information about the Norse Greenlanders themselves in church-generated documents pertaining to that Norse outpost, including in those written by the Norwegian archbishops and by the successive bishops of Bergen who had the ecclesiastical oversight with the Atlantic Norse colonies. These men's interest in Greenland waned as the income from that colony dwindled and eventually stopped. The circa 1360 "Description of Greenland" attributed to Ivar Bardarson (the Bergen bishop's *officialis* at Gardar) was merely an internal report to the church authorities in Bergen and Trondheim, not intended for Rome. It has nevertheless played a central part in the later search for knowledge about the Norse Greenlanders' elusive island society. The report contains a number of later interpolations, however, and therefore calls for circumspection.

The known documents concerning Rome's relations with the Far North demonstrate a mixture of bewilderment, ignorance, concern, and indifference that provides little support for claims that the medieval church harbored valuable information about Rome's provinces at "the end of the world," much less about places that presumably would have been thought farther away still, such as Vínland. The notion nevertheless persists that the church constituted a clearing house for reliable knowledge about all areas touched by the Christian faith. The author of the Vínland Map clearly shared that conviction. For example, the longer *Vinilanda Insula* legend presupposes written instructions from Rome when it notes that Bishop Eirik had "proceeded in most humble obedience to the will of his superiors." Other aspects of the map imply that with the knowledge and encouragement of the Vatican, Christian emissaries had spanned the entire world in a series of outreaches that were completed in the mid-thirteenth-century by Franciscan journeys to the Mongols.

Adam of Bremen's circa 1075 history of the Bremen archbishops was seminal to the idea that the central position of the Roman Church involved frequent and meaningful communications between the Far North and northern as well as southern continental Europe. Adam remarked that in 1055, the Bremen archbishop had given Bishop Isleif of Iceland letters for the Icelanders and Greenlanders, fueling the belief that the church was a repository for all kinds of information; that the Hamburg-Bremen archbishopric served as the main ecclesiastical link to the Far North; and that from the mid-eleventh century onward even the most distant communications were aided by letters. There is no independent record of the pastoral letters supposedly sent out with Bishop Isleif, however, and nowhere does the medieval Norse literature concerning early church organization in Iceland and Greenland imply that formal responsibility for Greenland was ever a part of Isleif's portfolio. In fact, the scant extant information about the twelfth-century Greenland bishops Eirik and Arnald suggests something quite different.

In Adam's estimation, Bremen did not take a back seat to the Eternal City as a center for church-related communications. Like Rome, his German hub of piety was "known far and wide and was devoutly sought from all parts of the world, especially by all the peoples of the north," with the Icelanders, Greenlanders, and Orkney islanders traveling the longest distances. These northern travelers seem to have left little useful knowledge in their wake, however. The papal proxy, writing in 1448 on behalf of Pope Nicholas V about "the island of Greenland," had trouble imagining a place "situated We are told at the extreme limits of the Ocean." Indeed, he acknowledged that "this island (which is said to be very extensive)" was quite beyond his ken as he confessed that "touched as We are . . . by the desires expressed by the indigenous people . . . of this island of Greenland, nevertheless We do not have at Our command sufficient information about the described situation."[2]

This 1448 letter suggests that very little information about the Far North had been made available to the Roman Curia since the 1433 episcopal appointment to Greenland.[3] Nor does the Vatican appear to have become more comfortable with northern geography by 1464, when the Norwegian bishop Alf of Stavanger was assumed to be domiciled in Ireland, or in 1492 when Pope Alexander VI confirmed Matthias (Mads) Knutsson as yet another bishop of Gardar "at the end of the world, situated in the country of Greenland" (in fine mundi sita in terra Gronlandie).[4]

However, Painter called the 1448 papal letter an "important brief," despite the fact that this cautiously formulated missive exudes ignorance about the Greenlanders' situation. To take an example, it notes the many disasters said to have befallen those luckless people but without depriving them of their "fervent piety." Those calamities supposedly included the destruction by barbaric pagans of all but nine churches saved by their inaccessibility.[5] Nine churches would actually have represented about two-thirds of the total number of such edifices in the Eastern Settlement. Moreover, for obvious reasons the known Greenland church sites are all in comparatively accessible locations.

Painter and Skelton evidently also found it reassuring that the 1448 letter several times described Greenland as an island. In addition, Skelton believed that both the 1448 letter and Pope Alexander VI's 1492 confirmation of the putative Bishop Matthias "betray information, doubtless from report by way of Iceland, about the state of Christians in Greenland."[6] In reality, the Icelandic Church was in such disarray throughout the better part of the fifteenth century that the Icelanders had more than enough with their own worries without concerning themselves with the Greenlanders' arrangements.

Overall, there is good reason to agree with L.-A. Vigneras when he comments that the fanciful book *La Salade* (circa 1440) probably reveals as much information concerning Greenland as any southern European text at that time was likely to have. The author began his geographical chapter on Greenland by describing the frozen seas in a region that contains an island named *Yslant* (Iceland), as well as the countries named *Gronelant* and *Unimarch* (Finnmark), where there are large numbers of completely white bears.[7]

Despite the lack of evidence that continental Europeans possessed useful information about the Far North through communications engendered by church business, the authors of *The Vinland Map and the Tartar Relation* argued throughout their book that ecclesiastical channels had provided much of the knowledge governing the map's depiction of the northwestern Atlantic. Skelton believed that besides the informational hub at the Council of Basel, there was not only "regular communication between Rome and the episcopal sees of Iceland and Greenland," but also Scandinavian clergy attended ecumenical councils in Rome, papal legates went to the Scandinavian countries, and Nordic pilgrims to or from the Holy Land traveled through Rome.[8] Painter's prefatory essay in the second edition of the book enlarged upon Skelton's optimistic scenario. "The Church of Rome maintained during four centuries a Greenland bishopric, on the beginning of which under Pope Pascal and Bishop Eirik Gnupsson the map gives us new information," Painter wrote.[9] Unfortunately, he overestimated by about a century and a half the period when the Roman Church could possibly have been considered actively concerned with Greenland, given that the first official Greenland bishop had been consecrated in 1124, while the very last resident bishop of Gardar died at his post, in administrative obscurity, around 1378.

It stands to reason that travel and other kinds of communication with the Far North were a part of church business in the Middle Ages, but those activities were necessarily on a modest scale because of the huge costs involved in sending messengers to and from those small and distant countries, and there is little justification for supposing that information traveled equally well in both directions. Furthermore, while an informal gossip network no doubt existed among medieval travelers—clerics as well as traders and fishermen— historians can examine only the information committed to writing, which in the case of Greenland was precious little and usually to be taken with a grain of salt. An example of the need for caution is the *Reisubók Bjarnar Jórsalafara* (The travel book of Bjarni the Jerusalem-farer) with its mostly apocryphal account of a 1380s sojourn in Greenland by the Icelandic chieftain Björn Einarsson, nicknamed "Jerusalem-farer" after a pilgrimage to the Holy Land.

This work exists only in a rather confused and idiosyncratic version found in the *Greenland Annals* that Björn Jónsson of Skardsá composed in Iceland in the seventeenth century.[10] The *Reisubók* is a worthy cousin to sightings of Prester John or the exploits of Baron von Münchausen.

The overall written record about Norse Greenland is indeed so sparse that one must ask why the idea still persists that the medieval Roman Church was an important link to the Norse Greenland colony. At least three answers come to mind. The first is that much of the information now available about Norse Greenland is quite recent; it takes time for new awareness to settle into the scholarly literature. The second reason is that when the Norse-in-America fervor was at its height in the nineteenth and early twentieth centuries, authors on both sides of the Atlantic reflected the contemporary respect for authority in general and for ecclesiastical authority in particular. A third reason is that many subsequent authors have merely passed on received wisdom without checking the available sources themselves.

A good example of the third approach is the historian Samuel Eliot Morison (1887–1976), who made no secret of the scholarly shortcuts he used when he addressed the subject of Vínland and Norse Greenland without reading the documentary and archaeological evidence available at the time. "The question of what became of the Norse Greenlanders is argued in all the general works, in varying degrees of acrimony; I have discussed it pleasantly and profitably with Dr. Helge Larsen of the National Museum, Copenhagen," he wrote. "Whilst not denying that the Eskimo may have moved in on Brattahlid when its survivors were too weak to resist, Dr. Larsen and I regard any such attack as a mere *coup de grâce* to a dying community, dying from isolation, and undernourishment." Concerning the 1448 letter written in Pope Nicholas V's name, Morison stated on his personal authority: "I have no doubt that it is a genuine papal brief, and the fact that it is addressed to an imposter does not discredit the information which the Pope doubtless received from other sources."[11]

A Haphazard Quest

The American scholar Arthur Middleton Reeves (1856–1891) learned German, Swedish, Icelandic, French, Italian, Danish, and Spanish to facilitate his work and surely earned the right to speak out on the issue of inadequate research. Shortly before his untimely death, he noted, for example, that of the approximately 250 years that had passed since the Norse discovery of America was first announced in print, the last fifty years had been particularly active as far as this topic was concerned. He linked this intensified activity to the interest engendered by C. C. Rafn's *Antiquitates Americanæ* (1837). As far as Reeves was concerned, it was unfortunate that Rafn's book had become the standard authority in the field because he thought that Rafn had been in too great a hurry to get his material out and in consequence had produced a number of "dubious theories." Reeves added: "Upon any other hypothesis than this it is difficult to account for the disposition American historians have shown to treat Icelandic discovery as possible, from conjectural causes, rather than as determined by the historical record preserved by the fellow-countrymen of the discoverers."[12] Similar comments might apply to some of Reeves's European contemporaries and near-contemporaries who, knowing none of the Nordic languages, availed themselves of Latin texts such as those published by C. C. Rafn and of completely secondary works of doubtful value.

One of the more outlandish believers in a strong church presence in both Norse Greenland and North America was the Frenchman Gabriel Gravier. The authors of *The Vinland Map and the Tartar Relation* had the good sense not to cite him, but his influence among his continental contemporaries was rather greater than merited. According to Gravier, the Norse had occupied the entire western side of Greenland and had been in possession of the eastern coast of North America until the fourteenth century. In addition, they had probably traversed all of North America. Their important discoveries were known in Europe, Gravier assured his readers. He also emphasized that the Greenland colonies had enjoyed their own bishops right up to 1537.[13]

Among somewhat later European writers, two in particular provided information about the Greenland bishops that other scholars relied on for a long time, and to which Skelton (apparently unaware of a more recent compilation in the *Diplomatarium Norvegicum*) turned in his discussion of Bishop Eirik. Skelton believed that if one allows for the possibility that Bishop Eirik undertook two voyages to Vínland rather than one, it is possible to reconcile the differences between two late-nineteenth-century authors' knowledge about Bishop Eirik and the information found in the *Icelandic Annals*. He suggested as an alternative that the Icelandic annalist might have entered the wrong year for the bishop's American voyage, for he believed that the Vínland Map version of Bishop Eirik's undertakings was the one carrying conviction.[14] The two scholars whose work he used as benchmarks here were the ecclesiastical historian Pius Bonifacius Gams and the Dalmatian Franciscan friar Luka Jelic (1863–1922).[15]

Luka Jelic

Very early in the post-1965 Vínland Map debate, Jelic became suspected of having created the map or at least its longer legends.[16] Jelic's Franciscan affiliation was a major reason for suspecting him of having authored or co-authored the Vínland Map because the map emphasizes the early reach of Rome's missionaries as much as Jelic's writings about the Norse had done, and because his religious order seemed to connect with a long legend just below *Thule ultima* on the map. Although there are several good reasons why Jelic cannot be accused of having had anything to do with the Vínland Map, he was at one time well known for his belief in a strong Roman Catholic influence among the medieval Norse in Greenland and America, and his name crops up in the Vínland Map discussion to this day.

Skelton was careful to note that the name *Thule ultima* does not appear in Bianco's 1436 world map, nor is it found in either the reports written by William of Rubruck and Carpini or in De Bridia's "Tartar Relation."[17] He and Painter were less careful when they transcribed, translated, and interpreted the Latin text of the legend below it. The Latin text reads as follows:

> Montes inferiores abrupti. In hanc terram primi fratres nostri ordinis iter faciendo ad Tartaros, Mongales, Zamogedos, Indos transiuerunt nobiscum—per obedienciam et subieccionem tam debitam quam deuotam Innocencio, sanctissimo patri nostro, pontifici maximo—per totum [possibly totam] occidentem et in reliqua parte usque ad mare occeanum orientale.[18]

F. Donald Logan's translation renders it as:

> Low, steep mountains. Into this land the first friars of our order traveled with us when journeying to the Tartars, Mongols, Samoyeds and Indians—through obedience and subjection, due as well as devout, to Innocent [IV], our most holy father, the supreme pontiff—through the entire west and in the remaining part as far as the eastern ocean sea.

Although the designation "the first friars of our order" has generally been interpreted as referring to Carpini's Franciscan Order (hence the suspicion cast on Jelic), the expression also contains a chronological conundrum involving the sources used in Yale's *Hystoria Tartarorum* text. The phrase "the eastern ocean sea" is unique to the Vínland Map, and the legend undoubtedly refers to the Carpini journey, but in ways that were not obvious to Skelton, Marston, and Painter. In Skelton's view, the phrase "appears to be abstracted from TR," which also used the same four ethnic designations as those that appear in the map legend. He also observed, quite accurately, that the "Tartar Relation" does not in fact mention Pope Innocent IV by name.[19]

To those who suspected Jelic of having had a hand in the matter, the legend's text appeared to echo an expression that he had used in a published article. However, the link to Jelic is again tenuous at best. Indeed, the Vínland Map does not reflect any of his ideas about the Greenland Norse. Like Tornøe years later, Jelic was convinced that there had been about ten thousand Christian Norse Greenlanders, enough to create one or more medieval American colonies in need of Christian missionaries. According to him, the American territories comprised not only Vínland, but also Helluland, Markland, and "Hvítramannaland" (the White Men's Country)—regions which, in his view, represented the entire North American east coast from Labrador to Florida. As satellites of the Norse Greenland colony, these areas had supposedly yielded to the civilizing influences of Christianity in the early eleventh century, and in the twelfth century the missionary efforts of Bishop Eirik Gnupsson (whom Jelic called Irish) had borne additional fruit among the native Americans. However, this rosy observation makes doubtful Jelic's claim that in 1418, the Norse Greenlanders had been invaded and enslaved by barbarians from the American continent. Jelic cited the 1448 papal letter as evidence that the Greenlanders had later freed themselves from this bondage and were now asking the pope for help to rebuild their ravaged land and churches—a request that Jelic said was renewed half a century later and resulted in the 1492 letter from Pope Alexander VI. Jelic was in fact the first to publish this 1492 letter, which he had discovered in the Vatican Archives while searching for documents concerning the Greenland Norse. He chose to interpret the letter's contents as a quick and loving response by Rome that had resulted in Bishop Matthias's posting to Greenland.[20]

Jelic's inability to read the Nordic sources was undoubtedly the reason why he did not know that the Curia's endorsement of the putative Bishop Matthias was one of many pro forma Gardar appointments. He was forced to rely on material such as Gravier's work, which he considered a superior work on pre-

Columbian Christianity in America. Confident of his own judgment, he did not hesitate to assert that the Greenlanders had no cattle, and that therefore the hides and other cattle products they used for paying their tithes must have come from America.[21] He furthermore implied that when the Norse had continued their sailing westward from Greenland, they had already known essentially where they were going because Europeans had believed from the time of Ptolemy that there was an immense continent on the other side of the Atlantic. Besides, Saint Brendan had actually explored the Atlantic, Jelic wrote, claiming that medieval maps provided ample evidence for those voyages. Two good examples, in his view, were the Hereford *mappamundi* and Martin Behaim's 1492 globe.[22]

Although the Vínland Map makes no claims for either the successes or the disasters that Jelic ascribed to the Greenland Norse, the map's generally shaky grasp of Norse history and culture might conceivably point to the Dalmatian friar as the author were it not for two excellent alibis. In the first place, he had shed his interest in the Norse by 1900 and was a respected specialist in canon law when he died in 1922, too early for him to have had easy access to any substance containing modern, industrially modified anatase crystals. In the second place, he had little knowledge of medieval maps, whereas the Vínland Map shows ample evidence of having been created by a master cartographic historian.

The Land "Our Brothers" Saw

Inland and straight east from the British Isles on the Vínland Map, in a general region that a modern person would consider part of central Russia (but which here is marked *Imperiu[m] Tartarorum*), a carefully lettered legend states that "the Russians have their empire adjoining on the east that of the Mongols and the Tartars of the Great Khan, to the north they have the frozen sea and a great river which passes through the midst of the mountains and the islands, debouching amongst the ice of the northern ocean."[23]

While reasonable in terms of the Mongols' westward reach both in the 1240s and two centuries later, the name for the wider region—*Imperiu[m] Tartarorum*—might seem to be in conflict with the map legend's definition of Russian territory. However, the geographical description here is so vague that it could have come from any medieval source. In conjunction with nearby features on the map, this short text merely constitutes another of the mapmaker's deliberate ambiguities and forces an investigator to consider all of the known thirteenth-century reports by Christian ambassadors to the Great Khan.

Immediately above this legend and contrasting with its carefully controlled script is the toponym *Tanais*, done in the larger, more informal lettering. *Tanais* is the ancient Latin name for the Russian river Don, which terminates at the northeastern end of the Sea of Azov. On the Vínland Map the name *Tanais* does not apply to a riparian feature, however. Instead, it suggests a general inland region with firmly drawn rivers to the east and the west and with equally well-defined inland seas, including a recognizable Sea of Azov immediately north of the Black Sea. Observing that the Vínland Map in fact shows no big river flowing into the Sea of Azov, Skelton noted that the "Tartar Relation" (which he regarded as the chief source for the legend) does not mention a "great river." He therefore reasoned that the map might instead reflect concepts similar to those evinced by William of Rubruck when he reported on the journey to the Mongols that he had undertaken with permission from the French king. Skelton nevertheless thought it unlikely that the Vínland Map was directly indebted to William's report.[24]

Friar William of Rubruck and his companion Bartolomeo of Cremona, Franciscans just like John de Plano Carpini, Benedict the Pole, and possibly a third companion (Ceslaus the Bohemian), spent the years 1453–55 on a journey of their own all the way to Karakorum.[25] Friar John's party, it will be remembered, had passed the years 1445–47 on their diplomatic mission to the Mongols on behalf of Pope Innocent IV, who had also sent Friar Ascelin, a Dominican, on a similar errand by a more southerly route. Ascelin was accompanied by three other brothers of his order, including a Friar Simon, who subsequently provided an account of their expedition.[26] Friars John and Benedict also reported on their experiences upon their return.[27]

These and other previous reports on eastern travel would have enabled Friar William to benefit from his predecessors' experiences and geographical descriptions of regions still poorly known to Western Europeans.[28] This advantage may explain why he felt confident that *Tanais* was another name for the Don, discharging into the Sea of Azov, while Friar Benedict in his dictated account had reported an encounter with the mighty Tartar prince Bati "on the great river Ethil, which the Russians call the Volga, and which is supposed to be the Tanais."[29]

266 The Vínland Map as a Narrative

Subsequent to Friar William's departure in search of the Mongol leaders, the final version of the last book in Vincent of Beauvais's *Speculum Historiale* appeared, providing information from both Friar John's and Friar Simon's accounts of their respective journeys.[30] Elsewhere, Marco Polo's return to Venice in 1271 gave rise to further tantalizing travel descriptions of China and the route thither, with additional information from European merchants and missionaries trickling in until 1363. At that time, a series of political, religious, and economic strictures, imposed by both Asian and European authorities, effectively put an end to European expeditions and thus to further knowledge brought home by western travelers.[31] Mediterranean merchants would still have heard stories about faraway Asian and African locations, but such piecemeal information would primarily have involved coastal regions.

As Richard Hakluyt indicated in his preface to the second edition (1598) of his *Principall Navigations*, one cannot assume that even information accumulated prior to 1363 was readily available to European scholars during the next couple of centuries. Hakluyt wrote that the journals of the two "Friers" John de Plano Carpini and William of Rubruck "are so rare, that Mercator and Ortelius (as their letters unto me do testifie) were many yeeres very inquisitive" about them. As a service to his two cartographer friends and to others, Hakluyt published these documents in Latin and English.[32]

Both Painter and Skelton surely knew that Hakluyt did not have to go very far afield to locate either text because two years before the Vínland Map and the "Tartar Relation" made their 1957 debut in the antiquarian market, Christopher Dawson had noted that while the longer version of Carpini's "History" survives in a number of manuscripts, the best one (used by Anastasius van den Wyngaert in 1929) is now at Corpus Christi College in Cambridge. This manuscript, which also contains one of the few surviving texts of William of Rubruck's *Itinerary*, originally belonged to St. Mary's Abbey at York.[33]

The cartographic and textual ambiguities with which the Vínland Map invests the Asian region traversed by the friars, and which it peppers with chronological enigmas, are in sharp contrast to the matter-of-fact style of the "Tartar Relation." (The contents of this Yale manuscript version also vary substantially from the two known Carpini accounts and from the synopsis that Vincent of Beauvais subsequently gave of the 1245–47 Mongol missions.) The map is nevertheless designed to reflect, in a credible manner, the geographical traditions that would have been plausible about 1440 for anyone depicting the regions connected in some fashion with the mid-thirteenth-century Carpini journey to the Tartars, and it draws on the "Tartar Relation" in such obvious ways that a reasonably attentive reader will assume that the two works belong together.

The 1245–47 Carpini Visit to the Mongols

Like so much else connected with the Vínland Map, both the authenticity and the significance of the "Tartar Relation" have been much debated. For example, at the 1974 Vínland Map symposium that Helen Wallis arranged at the Royal Geographical Society, Francis Maddison voiced skepticism concerning the antecedents of the short text manuscript with which the map had been bound at the time of Yale's acquisition.[34] While the mid-fifteenth-century date of this manuscript is now rarely contested, Maddison's questions about its contents and creation still warrant attention.

The author of the "Tartar Relation" identifies himself only as Friar C. de Bridia. We never learn his first name. George Painter, who concluded that De Bridia's *Hystoria Tartarorum* is an important independent source of information about the Carpini mission to Central Asia, noted, among other things, that its title differs from Carpini's *Historia Mongalorum quos nos Tartaros appellamus* (History of the Mongols whom we call Tartars).[35] Throughout his essay on the "Tartar Relation," Painter also recognized the textual differences among the various surviving accounts and quite rightly suggested that checking De Bridia's "Tartar Relation" against Friar Benedict's brief report might pay dividends. It is equally to his credit that his reproduction of the complete text in Latin and English employed italics for every passage in the "Tartar Relation" that does not have a match in Carpini's Latin text as provided by Wyngaert.[36]

Painter was justified in considering Yale's "Tartar Relation" an independent and authentic account related to the 1245–47 Carpini journey. However, his faith in the Vínland Map as an authentic expression of mid-fifteenth-century geographical knowledge blinded him to many important aspects of the map's textual companion, and he therefore did not suspect that Yale's *Hystoria Tartarorum* might originally have been written down for a different purpose than honoring the triumphant return of the Carpini party. Nor did he ask if someone about 1440 might have had a specific reason for wanting a copy of both this particular text and of selected portions of the *Speculum Historiale*. In Painter's view, the "Tartar Relation" version of the Carpini report was quite inferior to the latter and had survived only because it had at some point become linked with Vincent of Beauvais's substantial and popular work. "And the Vinland Map owes not only its survival, in the same way, to its incorporation in a *Speculum Historiale* manuscript," Painter wrote, "but even its actual creation, since it was produced as a cartographic illustration to the *Speculum Historiale* in association with TR."[37]

Just as Painter evidently saw no reason to seek other explanations for the existence of De Bridia's account of the friars' journey to the Tartars, he saw no need to elaborate on his assertion that De Bridia must have received much additional information from Friar Benedict the Pole, Carpini's companion. In Painter's opinion, De Bridia had largely based his account on Benedict's experiences and views, "except for the few unidentifiable details which could possibly have been derived from Carpini or Ceslaus." Aware that Friar Benedict had dictated a report of his own to a scribe in Cologne that had subsequently become an introduction to Carpini's report as it is now known, Painter claimed that "TR, in fact, is to Benedict's narrative of the journey what *Carpini*, chs. I–VIII, is to *Carpini*, ch. IX; and we may identify TR as representing the hitherto missing portion of Benedict's own complete account of the mission."[38]

Painter's hypothesis about Friar Benedict's pervasive influence conflicts in obvious ways with internal evidence in the "Tartar Relation" text. Moreover, the beginning of Benedict's own account stresses that he and Carpini had been partners in—and joint survivors of—a unique and dangerous enterprise, and that makes it difficult to suppose that he would have wanted an unknown person like De Bridia to serve as his mouthpiece concerning the high-profile journey from which he had just returned.[39]

We know nothing about Friar C. de Bridia except what he himself revealed in the *Hystoria Tartarorum*. From this account, we learn that he was a Minorite who had been asked by the local superior of his Franciscan Order, Friar Boguslaus, to write an account of what he, De Bridia, knew about the Tartars. Several of De Bridia's elaborations suggest that at the time he was handed his task, he already possessed background knowledge from personal experience and/or from the study of existing accounts. Friar Boguslaus, who had been appointed minister of the Franciscan Order's Bohemian and Polish province that same year (1247), had an especially good reason to request an updated report on the Tartars because they had recently martyred two friars from his province.[40] Prior knowledge of these dangerous neighbors would have been a good explanation for De Bridia's assignment when the Carpini party was passing through so opportunely. The modest friar nevertheless acknowledges his indebtedness to "the venerable friars of our order, namely Friar John [de Plano Carpini] . . . and his companions Friar Benedict the Pole and Friar Ceslaus the Bohemian."[41]

With their horses and other retinue, the three returning travelers had safely reached as far as Kiev in early May 1247. Both there and while proceeding through the rest of Russia as well as Poland and Bohemia, the weary ambassadors were warmly welcomed and provided with good food and a chance to talk repeatedly in public about their experiences. (Carpini apparently had mixed feelings about the latter aspect of their reception, for he concluded his own account by admonishing his readers not to add or cut out anything of what he himself has written because it is the only true and complete report.)[42] It is very probable that De Bridia was present at one or more oral reports because he completed his own narrative on July 30, 1247, whereas neither Benedict the Pole nor Carpini is credited with having produced written reports until after they had reached Cologne in late September of that year.[43]

Such a sequence of events would provide a reasonable explanation for two major peculiarities that Painter observed in De Bridia's text, namely its irregular Latin spelling and grammar and the fact that, despite a number of similarities to Carpini's well-known written report, the informational elements in the De Bridia account occur in a different order and are also phrased differently.[44] These features are just what one would expect if De Bridia had written his report for Friar Boguslaus based on notes from oral reports and conversations as well as on any previous, personal knowledge he may have had. Only during the final stage of composition would De Bridia have translated into Latin both his own thoughts and what he had learned from fellow Eastern European Minorites speaking to him in German, Polish, or Czech. His own knowledge of Latin grammar and spelling would then have been his only guide.

The scribe who eventually copied the report about 1440 appears to have been in something of a hurry, which may have caused him to add some spelling mistakes of his own. De Bridia's original report cannot be compared with other manuscript versions of the same text, however, because it is known to us only from Yale's copy.

Most experts now accept that the two text manuscripts associated with the Vínland Map are of a genuine mid-fifteenth-century date. It is evident from the delineations in the map that the Vínland Map's author had this period firmly in mind. Furthermore, some of the map legends reveal that he had the mid-fifteenth-century copy of the "Tartar Relation" in his possession when he drew the map, and that he had correctly identified both its date and its unique nature. Using the expression "brothers of our order" in the legend discussed above, he subtly planted the notion that the map had been made by a Franciscan brother from De Bridia's own province, working about two centuries after the original had been penned.

While the actual identity of the scribe who copied the De Bridia account will likely remain unknown, it should be possible to deduce approximately where he is likely to have found the original text from which he worked. Nor is it difficult to imagine what may have prompted someone in the 1440s to commission copies of both the De Bridia text and the *Speculum Historiale* account of thirteenth-century European threats by the Tartars; in the first half of the fifteenth century both secular and ecclesiastical noblemen and scholars in Eastern Europe had every reason to worry about further incursions by infidels from the East. For example, after a visit to the Levant, the French king's trusted man Gilles le Bouvier/Berry provided a precise description of the Turk invasion of Hungary about 1443.[45] This invasion could certainly not have taken the region by surprise, for Turkish incursions into Hungary had been going on for so long that they were on the Council of Basel's agenda in 1436.[46]

Fear of further Mongol attacks might easily have caused people with sufficient means to obtain copies of any available historical information about similar events in the past. The numerous copies of the *Speculum* would have made it relatively easy to obtain, but De Bridia's original manuscript probably existed only in the one Latin copy that he himself had prepared in 1247 for his superior in the Franciscan Order. The most likely reason the manuscript survived long enough to be copied about 1440 is that its home had remained a monastic library known to, and used by, a limited number of people in the Bohemian-Polish region—in other words De Bridia's account had remained in the order's provincial library when Friar Boguslaus left office (1251) as minister of the Franciscans' Bohemian and Polish province. The monastic library in which the scribe copied De Bridia's account (and possibly parts of the *Speculum*) may well have been destroyed shortly afterward because that was the fate of many religious establishments during the protracted Hussite wars and other turbulent events in that region.

Mounting Troubles

There are at least two good reasons to take a closer look here at some of the troubles that befell Eastern Europe in the first half of the fifteenth century. One is that the renewed threat of Mongol incursions into Eastern Europe is likely to have provided the impetus for copying the Beauvais and De Bridia reports on those terrifying people. The other is that growing discord at the Council of Basel in the period 1436–37, which directly involved representatives from the Bohemian and Moravian region, provides a reasonable explanation for why a discarded document from the council came to be used as pastedowns for the old binding in which Yale obtained the *Speculum* portions associated with the Vínland Map and De Bridia's "Tartar Relation." The two texts, it will be remembered, are generally believed to have originated in the Upper Rhine region, which would include not only Bavaria, but also Bohemia and Moravia, with Moravia being especially exposed to attack in the southeast where there was no mountain barrier.

At least technically, Bohemia remained an independent kingdom until 1526. Saxony is its neighbor in the northwest and Silesia in the northeast. To the southwest lies Bavaria, while Moravia (which for several centuries was a part of Bohemia until both came under Austrian rule in 1526) is to the southeast. Unstable political conditions and a somewhat incompatible ethnic mixture of Germans, Magyars, and Slavs are not the only problems with which this region has had to contend over the centuries. In the succinct phrase of one writer, "Bohemia is the ancient battlefield between Romanism and Protestantism." Moravians and Bohemians had made their growing concerns known at the Church Council of Constance, and 250 Bohemian and Moravian noblemen had united in protest in May 1415. Although King Sigismund of Hungary (who had become Roman emperor in November 1414) evidently recognized the political threat that this protest represented to himself and to his brother (King Venceslas of Bohemia), in the end he told Johannes Hus that he must either renounce his beliefs publicly or else face prosecution for heresy.[47]

The problem did not disappear when Hus was burned at the stake in 1415 following a decision made during the Council of Constance. Indeed, one of the main reasons for convoking the Council of Basel in 1431 was the continuing problem of the Hussite wars, and the unstable situation that soon developed at Basel owed much to the resistance to Roman Catholic authority that Hus and his Czech followers had represented for three decades. In the ebb and flow of the Hussite fortunes after 1415, betrayal had continued to alternate with compromise, nourishing an emotional climate in the Bohemian-Moravian region that owed its volatility not only to religious dissent, but also to a growing nationalism that resented German cultural and political dominance.

The effects of political and religious strife were felt not only at home in general, but also in the Franciscan Province's response to the contentiousness of the Council of Basel over the incendiary issue of rival popes. It had dire consequences for the Bohemian-Polish Province, where "schism and discord" was still producing strong factionalism in 1442–43.[48] At the Council of Basel, these problems had been festering since early 1433, as is clear from the adversarial questioning to which some of the Bohemian ecclesiastical representatives to the council were subjected.[49] It did not soothe the general turmoil that Bohemia just then was scourged by pestilence, at the same time as the Turks (at that time often considered synonymous with Tartars) were pushing into Hungary.[50]

Just prior to the council's opening, Pope Martin V had organized a 1431 crusade against the Hussites, but he died just before the council began, and Cardinal Julian Cesarini was asked to preside over the council as well as to lead the Hussite crusade. The crusade did not go well for the church, however, so the council invited the Bohemians to send delegates to Basel, supposedly to negotiate a peaceful solution. The result of these negotiations, the so-called Compacts, was announced on July 6, 1436. However, the Compacts proved a worthless compromise, because Pope Eugene IV refused to confirm them and King Sigismund began a fierce war against the Czech Hussites on their home turf, starting with an invasion of Prague in August 1436. In 1437, Eugene and his followers withdrew to their own Council at Ferrara after a showdown with the Council of Basel over how to deal with the Greek Orthodox Church.[51]

Cardinal Cesarini had remained as the council president until July 31, 1437, when the council summoned Pope Eugene IV to appear at Basel within sixty days to answer for his disobedience. When the dissident council left for Ferrara in September 1437 to join Eugene there, Cesarini went with them. In fact, during that whole summer of turmoil, very few delegates attended the Council of Basel.[52]

Pro-Hussite Bohemians and Moravians would have had little reason to keep going to Basel after 1437 because they would not have found any sympathy for their position there. Nor would they have followed Pope Eugene IV to Ferrara. However, lay and clerical moderates from the region would most likely have attended the Council at Ferrara if they were still sending delegates to the council at all, despite the pestilence that was widespread in their home area by that time. Either way, the year 1437 was a watershed for the council because such a large number of delegates, representing a wide spectrum of political and religious beliefs, left Basel.

The pastedowns in the original binding for Yale's *Speculum* and "Tartar Relation" texts were made from the two halves of a document dated 1437 and written at the Council of Basel. There must have been a reason for making out that receipt in 1437, but when the document subsequently was used as binder's waste, it was clearly seen as having no further value. It is therefore not unreasonable to suppose that sometime after 1437—a time so critical to the Bohemians and the Moravians—someone who had attended the Council of Basel had returned home with this trifling document in his possession. Nor does it seem unreasonable to suppose that about 1440, when the Bohemian-Moravian region was threatened by the Turks already menacing Hungary, someone saw to the creation of a volume that contained selected portions of the *Speculum* and the only known copy of C. de Bridia's *Hystoria Tartarorum*. What nobody bothered to do at that time, however, was draw a map that made much of the Norse discovery of Vínland but paid only perfunctory attention to the region that Carpini and his companions had traversed two centuries before.

Which Way to the Caspian Sea?

As suggested earlier, the Vínland Map's author had considerable latitude in depicting the Central Asian region through which the Carpini party journeyed. Consider, for example, the vague tone of Cardinal Pierre d'Ailly's observation in the early fifteenth century: "Modern travelers who have journeyed through the Scythian countries declare that the Caspian Sea occupies a vast region between the Hyrcanian and Caspian Mountains, having neither outlet nor inlet, but is formed by the confluence of very large rivers which collect into a sort of lake, whose shores are inhabited by the Caspians and Hyrcanians." The cardinal was considerably more precise with regard to the "Earthly Paradise" that was supposed to exist somewhere in Central Asia, beyond the Tropic of Capricorn. Despite the claims that both Aristotle and Averroes had made for its existence, "We have not found any such country," D'Ailly wrote.[53]

On the Vínland Map, the traditional "Earthly Paradise" with four rivers flowing from it (as first described in Genesis) is conspicuously absent. Skelton credited the map's author with refreshing originality here because this feature had stubbornly persisted in accounts of the Far East long after the travel accounts of Marco Polo and Friar Odorico da Pordenone had indicated that the region contained no such marvel.[54] Odorico, a Franciscan missionary, was not otherwise averse to telling a tall tale or two in 1330 when, on the orders of his provincial minister back in Padua, he told a scribe about his experiences in India and China.[55]

When L.-A. Vigneras commented on the omission of the "Earthly Paradise," he considered its absence "all the more startling if the author of the Vínland Map was a fifteenth-century churchman, as Messrs. Painter and Skelton believe him to be." In the same skeptical vein he noted that "if the author of the map meant it to be a visual illustration of the Carpini mission, his scheme did not work out. . . . The VM's truncated appearance shows a complete disregard for the two texts which have been connected with it: the Tartar Relation, and Vincent de Beauvais's *Speculum Historiale*, whose Book XXXII includes a condensed account of the Carpini mission."[56]

Those are just some of the oddities in Yale's unique map. Directly south of the Black Sea and Sea of Azov delineations, the Vínland Map shows a place named *Samaca*, which Skelton identified as "Shamaka" in the eastern Caucasus. He translated the three lines of neatly written legend below that name as follows: "The Nestorians pressed on assiduously to the land of Cathay. The remaining children of Israel, also admonished by God, crossed toward the mountains of Hemmodi, which they could not surmount." The mountains of Hemmodi are described a little farther to the east on the map, between the three lines of legend and the self-explanatory toponym *Terra Indica*, where a few short lines nestle between two rivers coming out of the only other lake shown in this work. The short text here reads: "Kemmodi/montes/Superiores/ Excels. siue/Nimsini." Neither the neatly written longer legend, nor the shorter one sandwiched between the rivers, has a counterpart in either the Carpini or the De Bridia accounts of the friars' Asian journey—they merely served the mapmaker's agenda. Skelton did not do much with these texts beyond pointing out that the *Nimsini* most likely refers to the Naiman tribe, and that *Kemmodi* is a corruption of *Hemmodi* and refers to the Himalayas.[57]

Nestorian Christians, Naimans (Naymans), and Samoyeds were some of the peoples who had been conquered by the Tartars, according to both

Carpini and De Bridia.[58] The Samoyeds enter into the decoding of other legends on the Vínland Map, and the references to Nestorians and Naimans are also significant because they suggest locations to the west of the Mongols' homeland and of the Himalayas' formidable barrier, which had prevented the early Nestorians and "the remaining children of Israel" from spreading the Christian message even farther east at that early time.

Another region conquered by the Tartars, the Karakhitai (Black Khitai), had originally been settled by fellow Mongols. Whereas De Bridia was clearly uncertain about the exact location of the Karakhitai region, the author of the Vínland Map did not have the same problem. He firmly drew a lake with two rivers running into it from what must necessarily be higher elevations in the *Terra Indica*—elsewhere known loosely as "the land of Cathay." A modern map shows the northernmost of two similar rivers draining into the Aral Sea as Syr Daria, fed from the mountains of Karakhitay, while the more southerly river, coming down from the mountains of Tibet, is named Amu Daria.

Other aquatic features on the Vínland Map are equally interesting. The map's creator chose to terminate the Asian continent just east of *Terra Indica*, where there is a large and continuous body of water named *mare Indicum* in the south and *Magnum mare Tartarorum* in the north. The sea alongside the strangely amputated East Asian shore has the name *mare Occeanum Orientale* (the *Eastern* Ocean Sea) on the segment located directly north of the *Magnum mare Tartarorum* but still inside the chain of large islands, just before joining the greater Ocean Sea above the *Insule Sub aquilone zamogedorum*. The name *mare Occeanum Orientale* directly repeats the reference found in the six-line legend below the name *Thule ultima* and above the toponym that declares the territory to be the *Imperiu[m] Tartarorum*. This legend (already partly analyzed in connection with Luka Jelic) ends with the reference to the "brothers of our order" who had gone "as far as the eastern ocean sea" (usque ad mare occeanum orientale). [59]

In order to gain room for the novel maritime feature *mare Occeanum Orientale* in addition to the large islands even farther east, the Vínland Map's author had to foreshorten the width of the Asian continent. This he could do in good conscience, because the map was not primarily intended to illustrate the immense distances traveled by Carpini and his brothers in Christ. Furthermore, Cardinal d'Ailly, with whose *Imago Mundi* the mapmaker would certainly have been familiar, could easily have provided a fifteenth-century excuse for conflating the Caspian and Aral seas (as Bianco also appears to have done), given the cardinal's vague reference to one large lake in this general area. In conjunction with the two neighboring rivers, the Vínland Map's placement of the conflated Caspian and Aral seas identified the approximate eastern longitude at this point. This feature also appears to have had another practical mission, in that the comparative realism of the two rivers is similar to the map's easily recognizable depiction of Greenland, with each feature marking the midpoint between the map's center and its eastern and western extremities.

Skelton saw these aspects of the map differently. Comparing the Vínland Map with the 1436 Bianco version of the region under discussion, he observed that the "general form of the Caspian Sea, as a rough oval, is similar in the two maps. The Aral Sea is not represented in either." At the same time, he noted some riparian features that are completely different in the two maps:

> The four streams issuing from Eden, shown by Bianco as the headwaters of two rivers flowing west and falling into the Caspian Sea from the northeast and south, have disappeared from the Vinland Map, in which we see only the two truncated rivers entering the Caspian from the east and south respectively. A third Asian river (representing the Volga and the Kama) is drawn in Bianco's map with a T-shaped course, rising from two headstreams and flowing south to a delta on the northwest Caspian. In the Vinland Map the double headstreams are absent, and the river is traced from the Caspian to the ocean in northeast Asia, where it is given the name *Tatartata fluvius*; this delineation is not parallelled [*sic*] in any surviving map and doubtless springs from the cartographer's misreading of the Tartar Relation.[60]

The Central Asian region on the Bianco map is in fact so markedly different from that shown in the Vínland Map that the former is unlikely to have constituted any kind of model for the latter in this regard. The *Tatartata fluvius*, which runs straight from the Asian north coast into the north shore of the conflated Caspian and Aral seas, may or may not be interpreted as the Volga flowing into the Caspian. Its presence is in any case sui generis, like so much else on the Vínland Map.

To understand Skelton's reading of these features in the Yale map, it is necessary to go back to his explanation for the anomalous *Magnum mare Tartarorum*—the "Great Tartar Sea," which he thought represented what the mapmaker had "read or been told of the Caspian Sea." While acknowledging that the "Tartar Relation" contained nothing to suggest a *Magnum mare Tartarorum*, Skelton thought that this aspect of the map reflected the geographical uncertainties from which Carpini and other mid-thirteenth-century emissaries to the Mongols had suffered, and which in his view made it reasonable to suppose that when the Carpini mission reached the Caspian Sea, it thought that it had found an inlet of the ocean lapping against the far Asian shore.[61] This conviction, coupled with his determined search for meaningful connections between the Vínland Map and the "Tartar Relation" as well as for genuine links with well-known fifteenth-century maps, made him miss the Vínland Map's narrative when his eye traveled eastward from Europe.

Room for Prester John

The east-west and north-south foreshortenings of the world as shown on the Vínland Map are symbolic as well as practical. Symbolically, the world had shrunk through the spreading of the Christian message. The practical advantage of these foreshortenings is equally plain because they allowed sufficient room, on a parchment of limited size, for a world image that incorporated the concept of a New World. The truncated Central Asia necessitated some further adjustments, however. Thus, while the Red Sea and Gulf of Aden are clearly drawn and identifiable by the cities of Jerusalem and Mecca, the Persian Gulf and the Gulf of Oman are missing.

It would not have been unusual about 1440 to show northeastern Africa more or less as it appears on the Vínland Map, where Africa reaches so far east that its north coast forms the southern coast of the *mare Indicum* without actually enclosing it. To the east, this extension also joined the *mare Indicum*, while its southern shore was bordered by the *Sinus Ethiopicus*—the Bay of Ethiopia. Inland, well to the east of the name *Ethiopi*, we find the toponym *Emibar superior*, which Skelton considered sufficiently like the Bianco map's *inperiu[m] emibar* to allow speculations about a "debased form in a common source" with the Vínland Map. It was in any case a corruption of Zanzibar, the Arab name for East Africa, he noted. The name written on the extreme tip of the extension, *Imperiu[m] Basora* (Basra), was also one which he had found in the Bianco map.[62]

Sandwiched between these two place names is another Latin legend consisting of three neatly written lines. In English translation the legend reads: "These are the populous lands of Prester John situated in the south near the southern gulf. Although of diverse languages it is said that they believe in one God and in our Lord Jesus Christ and have churches in which they can pray."

Skelton observed that in placing Prester John in northeastern Africa, "Bianco and the author of the VM" reflected current opinion in the early fifteenth century.[63]

The legend of Prester John is one of several moving targets on medieval maps. The myth began in early-twelfth-century Rome and received a powerful stimulus from the pre-1158 Chronicle of Bishop Otto von Freisingen as well as from a forged letter written some years later and said to have come from Prester John himself. Pope Alexander III, who hoped that this powerful Christian monarch would help to reconquer Jerusalem for Christendom, wrote to Prester John in 1177, but it remains unknown how far his messenger traveled. Prester John appears to have made his cartographic debut about 1307 on a chart by Giovanni da Carignano, who placed Prester John in Ethiopia. Only a short time later, a couple of world maps from about 1320 moved him to India. From then on until well into the sixteenth century, he turned up not only in India and China, but also in various regions of Africa, and was generally seen as a powerful bastion of Christianity in the midst of Islamic peoples such as the Tartars. Along with his equally apocryphal son David, he was featured in the accounts of both the Carpini and Ascelin missions to the Tartars.[64]

Nothing stood in the way of the medieval inventiveness lavished on Prester John's whereabouts because no search expedition, however determined, had ever found a trace of him. Furthermore, reasonably accurate European knowledge of both the African and Asian interiors was long in coming, as was a proper understanding of Africa's east coast and its adjoining waters. The author of the Vínland Map took full advantage of this confusion when he placed the reference to Prester John in a region that may be interpreted as northeastern Africa but reaches so far to the east of the Gulf of Aden that it could just as well be taken to represent some part of southern Asia. Further teasing occurs in the actual map legend with its strong echoes of the Carpini and De Bridia reports, both of which had located Prester John in Asia, as Skelton pointed out.[65]

In the midst of these conundrums, the legend's central message stands out clearly. Myth or man, Prester John represented the cherished and common medieval conviction that long before the Franciscan undertakings of the mid-thirteenth century, Christianity had marked its presence in a truly remote southeastern portion of the *oekumene*. This detail in the map's narrative lends significance to the next legend as we move our attention north along the coast of *Terra Indica*.

"A New Land"

Flanked by the Asian landmass as well as by the southernmost of three large and seemingly inexplicable islands, and appearing midway between the *Magnum mare Tartarorum* and the *mare Indicum* toponyms, there are four lines of neatly written text: "Tartar affirmant absq' dubio / noua terra in extremis mundi partibus / sit posita nec ultima terra nisis solummodo / mare occeanum inuenitur." Skelton's translation is straightforward enough: "The Tartars affirm beyond doubt that a new land is situated in the outermost part of the world, and beyond it no land is found but only the ocean sea."[66]

Trouble surfaces upon comparing this legend with a related passage in the "Tartar Relation." Following his own head and not Carpini's, De Bridia had written: "As the Tartars themselves told the friars, [the Narayrgen woman] . . . asserted without a shadow of a doubt that the aforesaid country is situated at the very end of the world [dicta terra in extremis mundi partibus sit posita], and beyond it no land is found, but only the ocean sea [nec ulterius terra nisi solummodo mare oceanum invenitur]."[67] Skelton was puzzled by what he considered the map's perversion of the "Tartar Relation," since De Bridia had used the term *dicta terra* in his account of what a Narayrgen woman had told her Tartar captors about her native land (information that the Tartars in turn had passed on to the Carpini party), while the author of the map legend had substituted the phrase *noua terra*. Skelton found it hard to tell whether the mapmaker might have had in mind the anomalous islands shown in the extreme east on the Vínland Map, or whether the expression might reflect information about real discoveries made or reported by the Mongols or the Chinese.[68]

By substituting *noua terra* for *dicta terra*, thus drastically altering the geographical concepts described in the "Tartar Relation," the author of the Vínland Map created another riddle. This small detail in the legend constitutes more than a tease, however. It is another important link in the map's narrative about the joining of the east to the west, geographically as well as in the name of Christ. Interpreting both the riddle and its message requires only the knowledge of medieval Norse history, which the map's author clearly possessed. As a child of his own time he would furthermore have been aware that a twentieth-century European scholar most likely would associate the expression *noua terra* with post-Columbian exploration and discovery.

According to Vigneras, medieval cartularies often used the expression *terra nova* to mean a landed property newly acquired or recently cleared for cultivation, but as a geographical term signifying "land to be discovered" or "land newly discovered" the concept was alien to the medieval mind. In the latter sense, the term *terra nova* was first found in a 1484 charter of João II, where the term was applied to land recently discovered in Equatorial Africa by Diogo Cam. Both the term and the notion behind it had subsequently fallen into disuse for some years, in Vigneras's view.[69] As is well known, however, the phrase was soon revived, as either *noua terra* or *terra noua* in conjunction with new discoveries in northeastern America.

Vigneras was evidently unaware that in the late thirteenth century, the Norse had coined the term *Nyjaland* (New land) to signify the discovery of a previously unknown coast. The Dano-Norwegian king Eirik "the Priest Hater" Magnusson sent a man named Hrolf (Landa-Rólfr) off to Iceland in 1289 "to search for *Nyjaland* (*at leita Nyjaland*)." Hrolf reportedly arrived in Iceland the following year and recruited men for his expedition, but when he died in 1295, he had evidently been unsuccessful in his mission since there is no further word of a discovery. There is reason to agree with the Icelandic scholar Hermann Pálsson's suggestion that the greedy and anticlerical king may have been the victim of a practical joke when word reached him that in 1285, two Icelandic brothers named Adalbrand (who died in 1286) and Thorvald Helgasynir, both of them priests, had spotted a new coast far to the west of Iceland while drifting off course on their way home from Norway. Their report has been linked to a 1285 notice in the *Skálholt* annals stating: "*Funduz Duneyjar* [Down Islands discovered]," but that makes little sense, given that one has to go ashore to discover vast quantities of down (presumably eiderdown), whereas the two priest brothers had reported spotting *Nyjaland* from out at sea.[70]

Many thirteenth-century Icelanders, especially long-distance seafarers like Adalbrand and Thorvald, would in any event have known about the coasts to the west of Iceland and Greenland to which the Norse had long since given specific names. However, stories about the *Duneyjar* and about *Nyjaland* were subsequently added to the other vaguely identified lands and islands that northern seafarers had spotted "in the west." By describing the Island of Vínland as *terram nouam uberrimam*, the author of the Vínland Map equated *terra noua* by any name with Vínland and placed it where it would have been located if the Narayrgen woman had in fact claimed that New Land lay beyond the end of the world as she knew it.

The term *noua terra* is not the only detail in this Vínland Map legend demanding attention. Equally significant is the fact that De Bridia's account uses the name *mare oceanum*, as does the map legend (except with the spelling *Occeanum*), and that this name also appears twice as a toponym on the *western* half of the map. In the latter case, it clearly signifies the Atlantic Ocean, the only "Ocean Sea" consistent with medieval cosmography. The map legend locates the *Mare Occeanum* "beyond" (east of) the *terra noua*. To the pre-Columbian European mind, this region would also represent the extreme western part of the Atlantic or *Mare Occeanum*.

Here again the mapmaker stressed the point, so central to the map's narrative, that the *Mare Occeanum* was the physical feature on the *orbis terrarum* that joined westernmost Europe to the coast across the ocean—and that coast belonged to America as represented by the Island of Vínland and by the *Postreme Insule*—a toponym that obviously refers to the "farthest" part of the world. To reach the *Insule Sub aquilone zamogedorum* (the island(s) under the dark cold north and associated with the Samoyeds) and the rest of the East Asian coast, involved navigating the *Magnum mare Tartarorum*. To a student of mid-fifteenth-century mapping, this feature might well heat up the perennial question of how soon Europeans knew or assumed that a Pacific Ocean existed.

Skelton appears to have been quite uncomfortable with these unorthodox features. With regard to the *Mare Occeanum* west of Europe, he commented only that the name was written twice, and that this ocean contains an unnamed island west of Ireland, which he suggested might represent the legendary Island of Brazil.[71] His search for links between the Vínland Map and the "Tartar Relation" had again limited his options because this approach made him look for similarities rather than for differences. That was probably why he did not see that the map's anomalous delineations along East Asia actually illustrate the map legend's twist to De Bridia's description of the world beyond the Narayrgen land conquered by the Tartars.

Presumably, the map legend's use of "new" signified land that someone had recently discovered, otherwise its existence would not have been known. "New land" (*terra noua*) is conceptually different from "unexplored territory" (*terra incognita*) because the former implies not only that the land in question has only recently been observed, but also that it is somehow physically separated from territory previously known to exist—a separation that is usually due to a body of water. In the Vínland Map, the Tartar dominion indeed ends abruptly with a large body of water, beyond which lie the islands representing the *noua terra*. On modern maps, this extended "new land" between the Atlantic and the Pacific is presented as the American continent and is still often referred to as the New World.

"Tartars, Mongols, Samoyeds, and Indians . . ."

North of the *Insule Sub aquilone zamogedorum* and just east of the extreme northeastern tip of the Eurasian landmass, a three-line legend stresses the remote location of the Vínland Map's northernmost "eastern" island. It also introduces the concept of sea ice, which medieval literary sources from Adam of Bremen onward had included in their accounts of far northern waters and which is repeated in the longer legend associated with the *Vinilanda Insula*. There, the discoverers of Vínland are said to have sailed "amidst the ice" (*inter glacies*).[72] Contributing significantly to the Vínland Map's narrative, the legend reads: "Lands not sufficiently explored [Terre non satis perscrutate]. They are placed among the northern ice and concealed by it." As Skelton rightly noted, this message is not in any way ascribable to the "Tartar Relation." Nor could Skelton associate it with accounts of northern people subjugated by the Mongols.[73]

Such a lack of connection is hardly surprising, given that the mapmaker was obeying his own agenda rather than De Bridia's and obviously had maritime, not terrestrial, expeditions in mind. The Mongols would have been faced with the cold and ice of high altitudes and of windswept northern steppes, not with "northern ice."

The long legend just below *Thule ultima* names the "Tartars, Mongols, Samoyeds, and Indians" as the tribes whom the "brothers of our order" encountered on their way to the Vínland Map's idiosyncratic "eastern ocean sea."[74] Vigneras, who noted that the Carpini, Benedict, and De Bridia accounts all mention the Samoyeds along with about forty other peoples conquered by the Mongols, tartly observed that the Vínland Map's author seems to have singled out the Samoyeds for special treatment because they were also assigned an island (or islands) of their own, marked on the map as *Insule Sub aquilone zamogedorum*.[75]

The Vínland Map's two references to the Samoyeds—in the legend on the northeastern mainland and in the toponym *Insule Sub aquilone zamogedorum* in the extreme east—essentially correspond to reality and suggest that the far northern *mare Occeanum Orientale* is intended to represent the Kara Sea around which the Samoyeds had their homes. As Vigneras explains, the Samoyeds still occupy their ancient territories on the Siberian mainland (on the shores of the Kara Sea and on the Yamal Peninsula) as well as on two large islands, namely in southern Novaya Zemlya and on Vaigats Island. Medieval maps do not refer to these people, however. As far as Vigneras was aware, Waldseemüller's 1516 *Carta marina* was the earliest map to mention the Samoyeds.[76]

Although the references to the Samoyeds on the Vínland Map thus seem to be somewhat precocious, they are in keeping with the author's penchant for "firsts." Regardless of whether the Vínland Map's emphasis on the Samoyeds is cartographically premature, however, its inclusion along with that of the proto-Pacific *Magnum mare Tartarorum* suggests that these details are important to the map's narrative. They are in fact central to its combined cartographic and textual message that by the mid-thirteenth century, Christians had reached the far corners of the inhabited world, and that emissaries of the Roman Church had spanned the *orbis terrarum* right across both segments of the *Mare Occeanum* as well as the *Magnum mare Tartarorum*.

Figure 22 shows the two halves of the Vínland Map fitted together in reverse order, revealing not only the geographical thrust of the map but also the inherent symmetry of the design conceived by its mischievous author. It now becomes clear that the northernmost insular delineation called *Insule Sub aquilone*—"the island(s) under the dark cold north"—is in fact located west-north-west of the *Vinilanda Insula*. That places it in the outermost cold regions beyond Vínland, toward where Adam of Bremen believed that the "second Thule" had its station. Had Skelton understood the Vínland Map as its author intended it to be read, he would have found ample explanation not only for the large islands east of the Great Tartar Sea, but also for the seemingly awkward, off-center design of the map, and for the longer legend describing the Island of Vínland. Instead, the *Insule Sub aquilone zamogedorum*

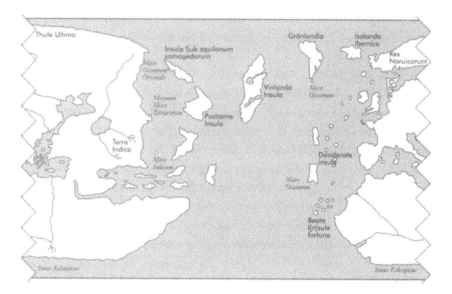

Figure 22. When fitted together in reverse order, the two halves of the Vínland Map form a symmetrical design and reveal the geographical notions behind the map. Copyright David O. Seaver.

and the *Postreme Insule* had him so baffled that he passed hastily over them both. Even worse, he altered the meaning of the longer legend by the *Vinilanda Insula* to fit his mistaken concept of the map's information.[77]

Translated correctly, this legend provides a crucial link in the map's narrative. It also demonstrates beyond any doubt that the map is a modern fake.

Adding to the Vínland Myth

On the Vínland Map, Vínland is depicted as a rather large island with two deep bays in its eastern coast, and it is accompanied by two legends that argue against any notion that the island's almost tripartite shape is intended to suggest Markland and Helluland in addition to Vínland. The shorter legend says: "Island of Vínland, discovered by Bjarni (*Byarno*) and Leif (*leipho*) together." Presumably in order to eliminate any doubt about what these delineations represent, the longer legend says that Bjarni and Leif together had discovered an extremely fertile new land (*terram nouam uberrimam*), "the which island they named Vínland" (quam Vinilanda[m] insula[m] appellauerunt).[78] In other words, Vínland in the far western ocean is conceptually linked with the "new land" that was to be found east of the *Magnum mare Tartarorum*.

The translation in *The Vinland Map and the Tartar Relation* of the longer Vínland legend reads:

> By God's will, after a long voyage from the island of Greenland to the south end of the most distant remaining parts of the western ocean sea, sailing southward amidst the ice, the companions Bjarni (*byarnus*) and Leif Eiriksson (*leiphus erissonius*) discovered a new land, extremely fertile and even having vines, the which island they named Vínland. Eric (*Henricus*), legate of the Apostolic See and bishop of Greenland and the neighboring regions, arrived in this truly vast and very rich land, in the name of Almighty God, in the last year of our most blessed father Pascal, remained a long time in both summer and winter, and later returned northeastward (*ad orientem hiemale[m]*) and then proceeded in most humble obedience to the will of his superiors.[79]

This legend's "sober and weighty statement" convinced Painter that "the bare words of the VM caption concerning Bishop Eirik, we may reasonably consider, are authentic and true."[80] The sobriety, weight, and authenticity of the two *Vinilanda Insula* legends become doubtful when subjected to closer scrutiny, however. Like the other legends in the Vínland Map, they are so enigmatic and calculated to stir debate that only someone wise to the relevant historical and cartographical bones of contention could have produced them. Nevertheless, despite the mapmaker's wide historical and cartographical knowledge and his obvious command of Latin, the two Vínland legends reveal a person with an insufficient knowledge of Old Norse culture and language.

As Peter Foote pointed out early in the discussion generated by the Yale book, the name Eirik (enjoyed by Leif's father as well as by the Greenland "missionary" bishop) is all right as far as it goes—Henricus was the usual medieval Latin form of Eirik in Scandinavia as well as on the European continent. Erissonius for Eiriksson is a pure invention, however. A medieval Nordic writer would have latinized this as either Erici or Erici filius, Foote argued. He therefore thought it likely that the map's author did not recognize Eiriksson as a patronymic at all.[81] Foote also observed that "Bjarni" is a weak masculine name that would normally have been latinized as a third declension noun, in this case as *Biarno*; the form *byarnus* found in the Vínland Map "would seem quite exceptional." He also commented on the map's repeated use of "*-landa*" as the latinization of the Norse suffix "*-land*" (for example,

Vínland). In medieval Scandinavia, he noted, the preferred literary latinization would most likely have been *-landia*, including for the map's designations *Isolanda* and *Ierlanda*.[82]

These linguistic stumbles tell quite a bit about the mapmaker. Equally revealing are the further contents of the longer legend, which show the author as someone who, despite his shortcomings, was sufficiently well acquainted with the literature concerning the Norse in Greenland and Vínland to draw upon conflicting opinions in riddle after riddle, such as the conundrum of precisely which Norsemen discovered America.

It is well to remember that before the late sixteenth or early seventeenth century, there was no interest outside of Scandinavia in the Icelandic saga texts and their tales of American discovery. Any non-Scandinavian crediting Bjarni and Leif with joint discovery would therefore have indulged in such musings well after the supposed mid-fifteenth-century date of the Vínland Map. Considerably more important is the fact that neither before nor after the mid-fifteenth century has any Scandinavian source placed Leif and Bjarni aboard the same ship. The notion that Leif Eiriksson and "Bjarni"—presumably Bjarni Herjolfsson—were together when they discovered Vínland runs counter to the saga information, which distinguishes sharply between the two men's voyages and accomplishments.

Who "Discovered" Vínland?

The only "Bjarni" mentioned in the "Saga of Eirik the Red" is a man named Bjarni Grimolfsson. There is no mention of Bjarni Herjolfsson, the devoted son who sailed to Greenland to be reunited with his father and who caught a glimpse of the North American coast while drifting off during his voyage. The "Saga of the Greenlanders" therefore credits Bjarni Herjolfsson with the first sighting of a new land west of Greenland before it reports on Leif Eiriksson's well-organized follow-up voyage of exploration, in which Bjarni did not take part.

Dealing with this problem in the longer Vínland legend, Skelton wrote: "If this be fact, it is unrecorded in any surviving textual source for the voyage and must derive from an oral or written tradition otherwise lost."[83] He was cautious about claiming that the Vínland Map sheds new historical light on this problem, but he suggested the possibility that Bjarni Herjolfsson had been confused with Bjarni Grimolfsson, "who accompanied the Icelander Karlsefni to Vinland ca. 1020." Alternatively, he proposed that "the cartographer, or the author of his source for this matter, has confused the two voyages, that of Bjarni in 985 or 986 and that of Leif in 1002."[84]

The information in this map legend is certainly both confused and confusing, but the confusion took place long after 1440 and began with a source that is both extant and identifiable. The first time Leif and Bjarni shared a ship was in 1765, when the German Moravian Brother David Crantz published his *Historie von Grönland*. It was chiefly intended as a report on the new German missions in Greenland, about which Crantz presumably knew something, although a contemporary of his, the Danish missionary H. C. Glahn, found him generally ill prepared also for this task.[85] He made that judgment even without addressing Crantz's perfunctory summary of Greenland's Norse period, which claims that after Bjarni Herjolfsson had reported drifting off to unknown lands in the west on his way to Greenland to join his father, Leif Eiriksson "fitted out a ship with 35 men, and went to sea with Biærn."[86]

On the European continent, Crantz's book quickly gained a wide audience because it was the only work available to non-Scandinavian readers concerning the recently (1721) recolonized Greenland. Soon translated into French and English, the work was still considered current in 1864 when Charles Francis Hall published his *Life with the Esquimaux* and provided his own account of the medieval Norse, in which he cited Crantz as the source for his story about "Bjorn's" discovery of "a new country covered with wood" in 1001. Hall added: "On his [Bjarni's] return, Leif fitted out a vessel, and with Bjorn as pilot, went in search of this new land."[87]

Crantz punctiliously attributed his own information about Bjarni and Leif to Paul Henry Mallet's *Introduction à l'histoire de Dannemarc*, a two-volume work published in 1755–56, and to Bishop Erik Pontoppidan's *Natural History of Norway*, published in Norwegian in 1752 and translated into English in 1755.[88] Both men had obtained their information from "Arngrim Jonas" [*sic*] and Thormodus Torfæus (1636–1719) and had confirmed it with Adam of Bremen, Crantz assured his readers. Unfortunately, he also took seriously Claus Christophersen Lyschander's 1608 poem concerning Norse ventures westward from Greenland, which claimed that the Christian conversion of the Greenlanders, including of Eirik the Red, was fully assured when Eirik of Gardar (another Henricus in the Vínland Map legend) became their bishop in 1114 and in 1124 planted the faith in Vínland before dying of "illness and suffering."[89]

Mallet had indeed noted his reliance on Arngrim Jónsson's *Gronlandia* (originally written in Latin about 1600) for information about Greenland, and on Torfæus's later works for knowledge about Vínland, but he had not processed this information in the way Crantz retold it. After giving Arngrim's version of the "Saga of the Greenlanders" and recounting the story of how Bjarni Herjolfsson had drifted within sight of unknown western coasts on his way to Greenland, Mallet had written: "The following summer, viz. in the year 1002," Bjarni went to Norway to see "count [Earl] Eric" and told about his sighting of the unknown land in the west. Evidently unimpressed, the earl had chided Bjarni for not being more curious. According to Mallet, Bjarni on his return to Greenland therefore "began to think seriously of exploring those lands with more attention. Leif, the son of that same Eric *rufus* who had discovered Greenland . . . , being desirous of rendering himself illustrious like his father, formed the design of going thither himself; and prevailing on his father Eric to accompany him they fitted out a vessel with five and thirty hands."[90] Still following the "Saga of the Greenlanders," Mallet then related that Eirik the Red had fallen off his horse on the way to the ship, and that the superstitious Leif had decided to set sail without his father. There certainly was no Bjarni said to be aboard.

Mallet had correctly understood Arngrim, whose work cannot be construed as that Bjarni and Leif sailed off together, and who nowhere suggested that Bjarni suffered from exploration fever. According to Arngrim, it was only Leif Eiriksson who, at his father's urging, had sailed with a ship and thirty-five men to the new lands that Bjarni had spotted, and that the Norse subsequently called Helluland, Markland, and Vínland.[91] Nor did Thormodus Torfæus say anything that resembled Crantz's version of the story.[92] An Icelander born, bred, and well educated in Copenhagen, Torfæus had no trouble reading his sources in both Latin and Old Norse. He conveyed the saga information just as scholars know it today. Considering that Crantz misread Mallet, it is not surprising that he got Pontoppidan wrong as well. The Norwegian bishop had also relied on Arngrim Jónsson in telling how Leif Eiriksson had sailed off on his quest with thirty-five men, not one of whom was Bjarni.[93]

Adam of Bremen does not even mention who discovered Vínland. His reference to its discovery is nevertheless significant to the discussion here, both because he called the place an island and because the best surviving Latin text of his work says that *many* had discovered this island (Preterea unam adhuc insulam recitavit a multis in eo repertam oceano, quae dicitur Winland).[94]

All told, the various sources so confidently cited by Crantz fail to corroborate the story of a joint voyage by Bjarni and Leif. Crantz's explicit statement about Bjarni and Leif therefore does not go back beyond 1765, which means that those two Vínland Map legends don't antedate 1765, either. If a mid-sixteenth-century claim were made for a map of North America showing Washington, D.C., this anachronism would be enough to condemn that map as a fake. It seems appropriate to apply a similar standard to the Vínland Map.

The author of the Vínland Map, familiar with the work of both Crantz and Adam, designed a conundrum that made full use of the latitude afforded him by the two men's statements regarding the discovery of Vínland. As with every other facet of the Vínland Map's narrative, the story of Leif and Bjarni has a double purpose. One is to tease, the other is to move the author's underlying message along. In this segment of his story, he made the reader both textually and graphically aware of Vínland's existence as well as of its strategic location.

In telling about Bishop Eirik, the map legend makes it clear that the Norse discovery of a *noua terra* in the form of an island called Vínland eventually came to include an unspecified stretch of mainland that Bishop Eirik had reportedly experienced as "truly vast and very rich." According to the internal logic of the Vínland Map, this mainland would be the map's carefully contrived proto-American *Postreme Insule* that separated the *Magnum mare Tartarorum* from the *Mare Occeanum*.

Missionary to the Samoyeds

After providing an account of Vínland's discovery that was bound to provoke just such a discussion as we have witnessed for decades, the Vínland Map's creator worked in a version of Bishop Eirik Gnupsson's tale that was clearly intended as another conundrum. The post-1965 literary record shows that he succeeded perhaps too well because the resulting clamor effectively obscured his other reason for telling the bishop's story in the way he did.

Painter assumed that in Vínland, Bishop Eirik would have had extensive organizational and religious responsibilities as a missionary bishop among the Norse. One of those responsibilities would have been the effective collection of tithes from the fertile and wealthy country described in the map legend; another would have been the conversion of North American natives whom Painter described as "the fur-trading Skrælings." His various assumptions here were as erroneous as his interpretation of a passage in the "Tartar Relation" that also bears directly on the meaning of the phrase *ad orientem hyemalem* in the longer Vínland legend. When Painter explained paragraph eleven in the "Tartar Relation," which said that Genghis Khan had sent his son Jochi "to the west against the Comans . . . and another with another son against Greater India to the northeast" (alterum vero cum alio filio contra Maiorem Indiam ad orientem hyemalem), Painter wrote: "The friars probably did not realize that Greater India (i.e. the main peninsula of India between the Indus and the Ganges) was southwest rather than southeast of Mongolia, but they can hardly have supposed it lay northward. 'Northeast' must be a mere slip, not an error." What Painter failed to reckon with was that De Bridia, the man telling this story and responsible for adding the phrase *ad orientem hyemalem* (which is not found in Carpini), was domiciled somewhere in the Bohemian-Silesian region and naturally used that as his reference point.[95] To him, "Greater India" would indeed have been to the northeast.

Skelton's approach to the longer Vínland legend was somewhat different from Painter's, but he shared the latter's confusion about directions. It is understandable that Skelton's sketchy knowledge about the Norse would prevent him from seeing the linguistic shortcomings that Foote, a noted Norse scholar, had no trouble spotting. More perplexing is Skelton's failure to see the Vínland Map as a depiction of the globe-encircling influence of the Roman Church and thus to understand the real significance of the Vínland legend and its supposed answer to the enduring historical riddle of what had happened to Bishop Eirik of Greenland.

Skelton thought that "two historical events are here described: first, a voyage of discovery by Bjarni [no patronymic] and Leif Eiriksson "southward" from Greenland to Vínland; and second, a visit to Vínland by Bishop Eirik [Gnupsson] in a specified year, viz. AD 1117, his stay in the country, and his return." This statement seems sober enough until it becomes obvious that Skelton had simply mistranslated the longer *Vinilanda Insula* legend at a crucial point to fit his own mistaken views. He claimed that Eirik "later returned northeastward toward Greenland and then proceeded in humble obedience to the will of his superiors" (postea versus Gronelanda[m] redit ad orientem hiemale[m]) and suggested that this might simply refer to Eirik's going "home to Europe."[96]

The proper translation of the phrase is: "later returned toward Greenland and then proceeded to the wintry east in obedience to his superiors."[97] This interpretation means that after sailing north from Vínland in the direction of Greenland, Bishop Eirik had continued his voyage by going east—in the Cabotian and Columbian sense of east, which meant continuing westward until reaching "the East" in the form of Asia. Figure 22 (page 284) shows that such a northwesterly course would have led the bishop to the *Insule Sub aquilone zamogedorum*, where he would have had an opportunity to preach the Christian message to the Samoyeds and other tribes that Carpini had associated with the easternmost Eurasian continent. Bishop Eirik's apocryphal final home, the *Insule Sub aquilone zamogedorum* is delineated to fit with the combined island-and-mainland status of the Samoyeds. It is also a reminder of Adam of Bremen's description of the "second Thule . . . situated far off in the midst of the ocean" and requiring only one more day's voyage to the permanently frozen sea.[98]

By stating that Bishop Eirik never returned to Greenland, the map legend implies that before he set out for Vínland, the bishop had received from his ecclesiastical superiors a communication concerning his next missionary undertaking. Identifying Eirik's "superiors" (Archbishop Asser of Lund? Pope Pascal II? Bishop Gizur of Skálholt?) would have been hard for both his contemporaries and modern scholars—but not as difficult as imagining any such communication at a time when the Gardar See did not yet exist in the church hierarchy.[99]

As a "floating" bishop in a remote location, Eirik would have been free to make his own decisions and accountable to no one in particular, which is the most likely reason why his career ends in a documentary void. The medieval Norse sources give no hint of what became of him after he had set out in search of Vínland (*att leita Vínlands*). Speculations about his fate have nevertheless surfaced as regularly as opinions about the location of Vínland and about Bishop Eirik's reasons for going there. About his earlier career, we know only what the *Icelandic Annals* tell us about the Icelander Eirik Gnupsson *upsi*. He evidently left Iceland in 1112 to serve as a bishop in Greenland, and there is no reason to suppose that he did not in fact go there. Perhaps the economic and community conditions under which he served were unsatisfactory enough to make a voyage to Vínland seem worth the trouble; it is also possible that by 1121 he had been pressured to undertake a voyage to save the souls of a few Norse Greenlanders encamped over there. It is impossible to determine either why he went or why he failed to return, but it is at least reasonable to assume that the Norse Greenlanders had given Eirik up for lost when, three years after his departure for Vínland, they went to such evident trouble to secure Bishop Arnald's appointment at Gardar.[100]

The Vínland Map's explanation for Bishop Eirik's disappearance is as ingenious as his missionary zeal would have been commendable had there been any truth to it. Alas, the reality is that even after 1124, when formal church affiliations began with Arnald the Norwegian, there is no evidence that the Norse Greenlanders made any effort to convert to Christianity the Dorset and Thule people they met, either at home or on the American side of the Davis Strait. Thus it is probably also safe to assume that Bishop Eirik did not aim to save either Skræling or Samoyed souls in either the Old World or the New.

The legend's conundrum continues with the oblique dating of Bishop Eirik's fateful voyage. According to the Vínland Map, Bishop Eirik went in search of Vínland "in the last year of our most blessed father Pascal." Historians know that Pope Pascal II died in January 1118 (which in the Julian calendar would still have been 1117), and that Eirik's voyage is dated to 1121 in the *Icelandic Annals*, but this detail in the legend was intended as another riddle and was most likely inspired by B. Kahle's 1905 German edition of the religious work *Hungrvaka* (The Appetizer). This made available to German speakers a work that uses the year of Pope Pascal II's death to "place" a Norse bishop, and that has an internal chronology placing everything seven years earlier than in fact was the case.[101] A reader might consider it arguable that after residing in Greenland from about 1110 or 1112, Bishop Eirik went to Vínland on a first and successful visit "in the last year of our most blessed father Pascal" (1116), "remained a long time in both summer and winter," and eventually— in 1121—"proceeded in most humble obedience to his superiors." However, "the last year of our most blessed father Pascal" should be neither 1116 nor 1121, but 1123, which is 1116 plus seven years.

The year 1123 was a wickedly clever target. It was the year Einar Sokkason— presumably convinced that their makeshift Bishop Eirik was gone for good— left Greenland to persuade the Norwegian authorities that the Greenlanders deserved a proper bishop. Equally important for someone aiming at a German audience would have been the fact that in Germany about 1122–23 there was a flurry of fake letters claiming retroactively that various archbishops of Hamburg had been given specific authority over Greenland.[102] When the Norwegian Arnald became the first properly constituted bishop of Greenland in 1124, he was actually consecrated by Archbishop Asser in Lund, Sweden.[103]

More important here, however, is the actual date, because prior to 1124 Greenland was not a part of the Roman Church administrative hierarchy. Unbe-
knownst to both the mapmaker and to Skelton, there would have been no
messages sent between Bishop Eirik and his "superiors."

When writing his history of the Hamburg-Bremen archbishops in the
eleventh century, Adam of Bremen stated that Vínland got its name "because
vines producing excellent wine grow wild there. That unsown crops also
abound on that island we have ascertained not from fabulous reports but from
the trustworthy relations of the Danes."[104] The map legend echoes this passage
when praising Vínland, which is said to be "extremely fertile and even having
vines." This fulsome description of Vínland also suggests that Bishop Eirik's
subsequent "humble obedience," if real, would have represented a considerable sacrifice, for the passage is as redolent of material comfort and economic
promise as the information that Bishop Eirik "arrived in this truly vast and
very rich land." The region populated by the Samoyeds was no doubt vast, but
before the discovery of northern oil and mineral resources, nobody would
have called their land "rich."

Further Ambiguities

To the west of Europe, the Vínland Map has many rogue apparitions besides
the "Island of Vínland" and the recognizable delineations of an insular Greenland. One example is the map's reference to the Saint Brendan legacy. In order
to mark the southwestern reach of early Christian influence, the map places
the *Magnæ Insulæ Beati Brandani Branziliæ dictae* west of the *Beate Insule fortune* and *Desiderate insule* archipelagoes and well south of the British Isles. Not
only did these archipelagoes have the potential for a contentious debate about
early cartographic references to "Antilia/Antillia" and "Brazil," but also chronological problems arose from the fact that the first appearance of an island
named *Deseada* or *Desiderata* was a consequence of the second (1493) voyage
of Christopher Columbus, as Vigneras observed.[105]

Immediately to the east of the *Desiderate insule* lies a recognizable Iberian
Peninsula with the name *Hispanoru[m] rex* written across it. There is no conflict here with early-fifteenth-century geographical concepts and nomenclature,
an example being Pierre d'Ailly's statement that "Spain was formerly named
'Iberia' from the river Iberus (Ebro), later and correctly Hispania, from His-
panus; also Hesperia from the westerly star Hesperus."[106] The map's teasing

nevertheless continues as our eye travels north. The outlines of England, Scotland, and Ireland are easily recognizable, which is only to be expected, because this region had been well known to continental Europeans since well before the Middle Ages, including by the Romans (who surely did not forget all about these places when they gave up their dominion over England in AD 410) and by Christian missionaries both during and after Roman times. However, the map uses the name *Anglia terra insula* for the southern half of what is clearly England and Scotland combined, while leaving Scotland unnamed and depicting it on a straight north-south axis with England, in defiance of the fifteenth-century Ptolemaic convention of pushing Scotland far to the east. The toponym *Ibernia* straddles an island immediately west of England that obviously represents Ireland. Directly north of this island is *Ierlanda insula*, which is evidently not intended to apply to Ireland, nor to the two smaller islands farther north. The latter are unnamed and left to us to imagine as perhaps representing the Shetlands and the Faeroes.

Naming England *Anglia terra insula* is as reasonable as using the name *Ibernia* for Ireland, although changes in early nomenclature have been as frequent here as elsewhere in the premodern world. Adam of Bremen, for example, indicated that in his own time there had been changes in the names used for the British Isles and Ireland, and he noted that west of England "there is Hibernia, the fatherland of the Scots, which now is called Ireland."[107] The Vínland Map's designation *Ibernia* for Ireland is therefore not at variance with Adam's concept. Instead, the name is significant because it also links Ireland to the delineation that equally obviously represents Iceland and here is called *isolanda Ibernica*.

Skelton was evidently puzzled both by the island's Irish namesake farther south and by the free-floating *Ierlanda insula* because he failed to come to grips with why the Vínland Map referred to Iceland as *isolanda Ibernica*. In an attempt to explain these mysteries in terms of fourteenth- and fifteenth-century cartography, he thought that he had found some similarity to the name *Herlant* used for Shetland in post-1466 maps derived from the work of Claudius Clavus.[108]

Like so many other details on the map, the names that link Ireland and Iceland are rooted in the wish to demonstrate the influence of the medieval Roman Church. The name *isolanda Ibernica* indicates that Irish monks had beaten the Norse to Iceland, as noted in the *Book of Settlement*'s perfunctory reference to the Irish hermit monks whom the Norse found when they first settled Iceland. The unusual toponym is also another piece in the puzzle of identifying the twentieth-century author of the Vínland Map.

The historical and cartographical erudition demonstrated in the map's innumerable riddles makes it likely that the map's learned creator also ventured into print in his or her own name and thus remains visible to us even now. Many other considerations help to narrow the quest further.

Searching for the Author

Sometime between 1923 and 1957, when the Vínland Map appeared on the antiquarian market, the person who made it had gained access to what appears to be the only extant copy of De Bridia's report. The map's author had considerable facility with Latin and was steeped in fifteenth-century maps and cosmography. Other interests clearly included the early diffusion of Roman Christianity and thirteenth-century papal missions to the Tartars. The author must furthermore have been sufficiently keen on the Norse discovery of Vínland to make its location and delineation the map's most memorable feature and to create so many riddles in the longer *Vinilanda Insula* legend.

In addition to Vínland, there are several other cartographic "first appearances" on the Vínland Map—for example, the Samoyeds, the *Magnum mare Tartarorum*, and the references to the Carpini journey—a characteristic that provides further insights into the mapmaker's preoccupations. De Bridia's report on the Tartars as well as the Yale copy of his account had been written somewhere in the Upper Rhine region, where the main language was and is German. The Crantz and the Kahle connections also suggest that the map's author was a German speaker.

Combining these criteria substantially limits the geographical and intellectual field of possible candidates. The search may be further narrowed by focusing on some inadvertent deficiencies that the Vínland Map reveals. Some of these shortcomings are obvious, such as the mauled and makeshift parchment, the inexpertly mixed and self-destructive ink, the inconsistencies in the lettering, and the consistent two-millimeter distance between the lines of the finely lettered legends. Other deficiencies are more subtle, but they nevertheless reveal that while the Vínland Map undoubtedly is the work of a scholar, it was made by someone who thought that he or she knew more about the

Norse than in fact was the case, and who was ignorant about medieval Norse naming practices. Last, but certainly not least, the author was ambivalent about how and whom to credit with the Norse "discovery" of America.

One or more of the map's singularities might separately reflect views held by a well-known scholar. However, within the period of 1923–57 there was only one person with an educated interest in the medieval Norse and their activities in Greenland and North America who was equally knowledgeable about medieval missionary activities to the far reaches of the known world, and who also was an expert on fifteenth-century maps and cosmography. That one person was known for his passionate interest in all three areas of research. He also understood—as Skelton and Painter evidently did not—the subtler ramifications of medieval geographical concepts. Dating all the way back to 1440, the only person in the world who could have made the Vínland Map is Father Josef Fischer, S.J., a German/Austrian contemporary of Luka Jelic.

Fischer was as proficient in Latin as Jelic, and just as ignorant about Old Norse culture, but unlike Jelic he was a true scholar of the history of cartography, particularly as it involved world maps of the fifteenth and early sixteenth centuries. His interest in the Norse discovery of America was kindled early in his professional life and never left him, and he would always have had the necessary skills to create a map as full of conundrums as the Vínland Map, but the opportunity and motive to do such a thing came his way quite late in life. His motive had nothing to do with money and much to do with conditions in Germany and Austria at a time when this pious and honorable scholar was ready to enjoy his well-earned retirement.

CHAPTER 9

The Vínland Map as a Human Creation

Father Josef (Joseph) Fischer, S.J. (1858–1944)

The decorative painter and gilder Gustav Fischer and his wife Elizabeth (the daughter of a farmer and miller named Kürten) were joined by an infant son, Josef, on March 19, 1858, in Quadrath, near Cologne. Gustav Fischer made certain his son received a good general education, but history and geography were the only subjects in which young Josef—an excellent gymnast—got decent grades upon graduating from the gymnasium. He nevertheless appears to have determined both his religious vocation and his intellectual interests at an early age, for he joined the Society of Jesus in the autumn of 1881 and had gained international recognition as an historian of geography and cartography while still in his early forties. Neither of his parents lived to see his success as a scholar, however. Gustav Fischer died in 1890 at the age of sixty-four, and Elizabeth Fischer breathed her last in January 1902, before the book detailing her son's first important cartographic discoveries had been released and while Father Fischer was still putting the finishing touches to the German original of his book on the Norse discovery of America.[1]

Following his novitiate, the young Jesuit student spent three years pursuing humanistic and philosophical subjects in The Netherlands, taking advantage of the study houses that his German province of the Jesuit order maintained abroad. He continued his theological studies at Ditton Hall in England in 1888 and was ordained to the priesthood on August 31, 1890, at which time he also began a probationary period as a teacher of geography and history at Stella Matutina in Austria, which drew Catholic students from both Germany and Austria. Stella Matutina became both his permanent employer and his home when he returned there in 1895 with the title of professor of geography, having devoted the years between 1891 and 1893 to further studies at the University of Vienna and in Innsbruck. While he expressed gratitude for the excellent grounding in historical methodology that he had received in Vienna from such famous scholars as Ludwig von Pastor, the Innsbruck geographer Franz Ritter von Wieser had the most enduring intellectual influence on his life.[2] His life and career were otherwise chiefly dominated by interlacing connections with Wolfegg Castle, the Society of Jesus, and Stella Matutina.

A venerable Catholic institution with roots going back to sixteenth-century Freiburg, Stella Matutina as a Jesuit boarding school had since 1856 been located in the Austrian town of Feldkirch, just across the border from Germany and within relatively short reach of the many public and private libraries that Fischer explored over the years. One of these libraries belonged to Wolfegg Castle, a beautiful Baroque castle in Baden-Württemburg, where Fischer made his first important map identifications, and to which he returned many times. The castle's noble owners had long been in the habit of sending their sons to be educated at Stella Matutina, therefore Fischer would have needed no further introduction when he contacted the Wolfegg librarian to ask if the castle collections might include a manuscript map showing Greenland as a European peninsula in the manner of the 1482 and 1486 Ulm editions of Ptolemy's *Geographia*.[3] His being a student of Professor von Wieser's was also a recommendation in itself.

The social and academic etiquette of Fischer's time and environment required public deference to Professor von Wieser even after the latter's death in 1923, regardless of the priest's private inclinations. Although the younger man politely disagreed with his mentor in the pages of the book he wrote about the Norse in America, his quibbles were always minor and subdued, but a letter that he wrote to the Princess Sophie at Wolfegg Castle suggests that he was already chafing under his relationship with Von Wieser in the spring of 1902. He confided to the princess that *Hofrat* von Wieser had been very nasty when they met after a talk that Fischer had recently had with a visiting American scholar.[4]

Nevertheless, from the time Fischer wrote his preface to a book on Norse discovery and cartography (1902) until he produced an autobiographical essay for the first volume of the international journal *Imago Mundi* (1935), he punctiliously noted his respect and gratitude to *Freiherr* and *Hofrat*, Professor Dr. von Wieser. Even so, his feelings may have appeared conflicted to close observers. Hugo Hassinger, professor of geography at the University of Vienna, wrote a memorial essay on Fischer a year after the priest's death in which he noted somewhat cryptically that while Fischer might not have been without the pride of discovery, he had otherwise remained a modest and helpful man. Although Fischer's junior by twenty years, Professor Hassinger clearly knew him and would also have been well acquainted with the local minefields that both of them had to negotiate throughout their careers.[5]

It was a token of continued esteem on Fischer's part when he dedicated his 1910 work on a circa 1490 German Ptolemaic planisphere to "*Hofrat* Prof. Dr. Franz R. v. Wieser."[6] Well aware of the rules that governed his life, he is unlikely to have been surprised that his mentor claimed (and received) equal credit for the discoveries that he himself had made at Wolfegg in 1901, especially since the association also benefited himself. It would have been a wonder, however, if he did not react privately, at least, to a public put-down that his professor administered in 1912, after the wealthy Viennese art collector Albert Figdor had approached Von Wieser with a request to determine the authenticity and relative importance of a manuscript world map purporting to be the work of one Albertin de Virga of Venice.

All that is known about the Venetian cartographer Albertin de Virga (active about 1409–14) is what can be learned from two maps that have survived into modern times. One is a 1409 sea chart featuring both the Mediterranean and the Black Sea, along with the eastern Atlantic shores up to the southern Baltic region and including the British Isles.[7] The other is the colorful world map (briefly mentioned in Chapter 7) that Figdor asked Von Wieser to analyze, but which can no longer be reproduced from the original because the map's current location is unknown.

Von Wieser confirmed the identity of the cartographer as well as the authenticity of the map that had been offered to Figdor. Although a fold in the map's parchment obscured the last digit(s) of the date, which should probably be interpreted as either 1411 or 1414, Von Wieser gave it as his opinion that the work most likely dated from about 1415 because such a date would accord with Claudius Clavus's representation of Northern Europe. Despite Von Wieser's fascination both with De Virga's representation of the North and with the medieval Danish mapmaker, he dismissed Fischer's recent (1911) work on Claudius Clavus when he published his analysis in 1912 with a footnote in which he brusquely refuted his former pupil's contention that Claudius Clavus had brought North America as well as Greenland into European cartography. He stated unequivocally that Fridtjof Nansen was right on this issue, while both A. A. Bjørnbo and Fischer were wrong—Claudius Clavus could not possibly have been to Greenland.[8]

While Von Wieser was correct in that respect, his own judgment was also seriously flawed, because he was certain that the large area on the De Virga map with the name *Norueca* also included part of Greenland's vast landmass. There was nevertheless no acceptable way for Fischer to gainsay Professor von Wieser outright. He had to bide his time before he could retaliate in any way, however subtle. We do not know if Von Wieser's blunt remark in 1912 may have contributed to his student's lack of publication in the Norse field between 1912 and 1932, nor do we know what Fischer's reaction was in 1925 when the Ferdinandeum Museum in Innsbruck published a volume commemorating the professor's death on April 8, 1923.

Several scholars from Fischer's own sphere had contributed to this volume, but his own name is not among them. The only clear references to him and his relationship with Von Wieser appear in remarks made by Eugen Oberhummer, a professor at the University of Vienna. "Suddenly, a happy find by his pupil Pater Josef Fischer, S.J., placed before him a great new task," Professor Oberhummer observed, adding that after personally ascertaining the identity of these maps, Von Wieser had acquainted the public with the importance of the Wolfegg discoveries, first with an article in *Petermanns Mitteilungen* in 1901 and subsequently in a book written jointly with Fischer and published in 1903 to great acclaim.[9]

Whatever slights Fischer may have encountered from status-conscious fellow academics during this period of his life, he clearly found encouragement elsewhere because his publications repeatedly demonstrated his pleasure in scholarly exchanges both at home and abroad, especially when these corroborated his own firmly held views.

Scholarly Connections

Fischer's scholarly correspondence provides sufficient evidence to connect him with the name *isolanda Ibernica* on the Vínland Map. During an exchange of letters with his Danish colleague A. A. Bjørnbo, Fischer wrote from Austria on January 3, 1911: "I am very glad that [Nansen] is bringing out the information about the ancient Irish. It has always been my view that the Irish who removed to Iceland also sought out the Westland [Greenland]. But I lacked convincing historical evidence."[10]

When Fischer made it clear that in his mind, Iceland and Ireland were inextricably connected through a pre-Norse outreach by Christian monks, he was already enjoying a growing reputation both at home and abroad as an historian of cartography who was especially concerned with the Norse discovery of America. His first monograph on this subject, *Die Entdeckungen der Normannen in Amerika: Unter besonderer Berücksichtigung der kartographischen Darstellungen* (1902), appeared in English just a year later, and it had soon been followed by several articles and lectures on related topics.[11]

Fischer's 1911 letter to Bjørnbo about the Irish was written on the eve of the publication of Nansen's *In Northern Mists*, while Bjørnbo was still struggling to provide the famous Norwegian with cartographic information and to finish his own crowning achievement, the "Cartographia Groenlandica." Meanwhile, Fischer had been engaged for some time on a work entitled "Claudius Clavus, the First Cartographer of America," published later in 1911.[12] He was well aware that this was a topic that Bjørnbo had covered in considerable detail in his and Carl S. Petersen's 1904 publication *Fyenboen Claudius Claussøn Swart (Claudius Clavus)*, because that work had been a major reason for the exchange of ideas between Bjørnbo and himself that started in May 1904 and ended with a postcard of May 10, 1911, sent from Fischer's home in Feldkirch.[13]

In his many messages to Bjørnbo, Fischer interspersed pedantic notes about early Ptolemaic maps—on which he considered himself more expert than Bjørnbo—with questions and comments that show genuine attention to Bjørnbo's research. He also made frequent references to his own consuming interest in the Atlantic explorations of the medieval Norse and kept Bjørnbo abreast of his publications. With his January 3 (1911) letter to his Danish friend, for example, he enclosed his latest article, entitled "Die älteste Karte vom Fürstentum Liechtenstein" (The oldest map of the principality of Liechtenstein) and told Bjørnbo that he was also sending along separately a copy of his Claudius Clavus book, which had just been published in the United States.[14]

Fischer's letters do not reveal whether he was aware of Bjørnbo's rapidly declining health, the poor state of which Nansen had noted in February 1911.[15] Nor is it known when Fischer learned about the Danish scholar's death on October 6 that same year. It must have been fairly soon after the event, however, because the anonymously written preface to Bjørnbo's posthumously published magnum opus singled out "the two famous Austrian geographic historians *Hofrat*, Prof. v. Wieser in Innsbruck and Prof. Jos. Fischer in Feldkirch" when it acknowledged assistance from "colleagues abroad" in ensuring that the standards intended by the author had been met.[16]

The preface writer also regretted that it was impossible at that time to recip-rocate the kindness shown by the two Austrian scholars.[17] This allusion to one-way communication suggests that neither then nor later did Fischer and his mentor learn just what information the "Cartographia Groenlandica" con-tained. While many of Bjørnbo's views would have been familiar to Fischer through their correspondence in German, he never did find out Bjørnbo's gen-eral intentions concerning Nansen's objection to the claim that Claudius Clavus had visited Greenland. He could not read what Bjørnbo had actually written about this matter shortly before his death. Like Professor von Wieser, Fischer was unable to read Danish.[18]

Bjørnbo had compromised with Nansen after a fashion, observing that it was of no particular significance that the first Clavus map, copied by or for Cardinal Fillastre about 1427 from a circa 1424 original, appeared to have been drawn without personal experience of Greenland. Far more important, in Bjørnbo's view, was the cartographical information found in the Vienna texts from which he himself had constructed a second Clavus map. He argued that these later texts showed that Clavus had undoubtedly visited Greenland imme-diately after producing his first map, and that in both cases the medieval Danish cartographer had obtained his remarkable geographical knowledge from reports of early Norse navigation in the western Atlantic.[19] When Bjørnbo expressed these views in the "Cartographia Groenlandica," he already knew that Nansen would not accept the Vienna texts as evidence that Clavus had vis-ited Greenland because the Norwegian explorer had told him in early 1910 that Clavus's later textual references to "Pygmies" and "Carelians" argued decisively against personal experience.[20]

The correspondence between Bjørnbo and Fischer shows that the two scholars discussed Nansen's objections and that both of them had found Nansen's arguments wanting. However, Fischer reserved the thrust of his own interpretation for his work on Claudius Clavus. Fischer stated categorically that Claudius Clavus had left Rome for Greenland in 1423–24 with the inten-tion of conducting a cartographical survey of Greenland in accordance with the Ptolemaic precepts he had learned during his long stay in Rome.[21]

Once made, Fischer's conclusions were not likely to shift, even when they were as axiomatic as the thinking revealed in the title to his treatise on Claudius Clavus. Whereas Bjørnbo had called Claudius Clavus "the first cartographer of the North," Fischer credited Claudius Clavus with being "the first cartographer of America." His explanation for the switch in definition was simple: "As early as the first quarter of the fifteenth century (in 1424) he charted and minutely described not only Northern Europe but also northern America, i.e. Greenland." Not only had the intrepid Dane personally explored up the Greenland coast as far as to seventy degrees ten seconds northern latitude after producing his first map, but "the result of this first scientific polar expedition was the far-famed map of Greenland, that for three centuries influenced the entire cartography of the North," Fischer wrote.[22] Given the knowledge that several other scholars already possessed, his claim that Claudius Clavus had been to Greenland was in fact untenable, but he never relinquished the convictions that had prompted his claim. As he told Bjørnbo in 1904, he had arrived at these views even before the two of them began their correspondence.[23] Indeed, his propensity for rigid and idiosyncratic thinking in this and several other areas was a flaw from which even his great erudition and undeviating honesty did not protect him.[24] It is also the very quality that gives the Vínland Map its unique flavor.

In addition to telling Fischer about the progress of his own research, Bjørnbo had acquainted him with some of his own and Nansen's exchanges of opinions, but he appears not to have imparted to Fischer that he and Nansen also had a difference of opinion concerning the Norwegian historian Gustav Storm. Bjørnbo told Nansen in the course of their correspondence that he admired Storm, but that he also thought that the Norwegian scholar often overlooked evidence in order to strengthen his own thesis.[25] This criticism was actually justified, but Fischer never wavered from his conviction that Storm's judgment was absolutely trustworthy. In his books about the Norse and Claudius Clavus, Fischer repeatedly referred not only to Bjørnbo's work, but also to that of Storm, from whom he had also received much personal help.

To a limited degree, Fischer also received assistance from the Icelandic scholar Finnur Jónsson. His own inability to read either the medieval or the modern Nordic languages, which obliged him to use a translator for any Nordic material put before him, had made him dependent on other people's guidance about both the Old Norse literature and the current philological, archaeological, and historical research on the medieval Norse.[26] After Storm's death in 1903, Fischer had still been able to count on Bjørnbo's support for several years more. The Danish scholar's death was certainly a blow to his foreign colleague, now left with nobody to advise him about the medieval Norse and to discuss with him the geographical information he was convinced that the Norse had been able to impart.

Fischer did not lack colleagues closer to home, of course. His "highly esteemed patron and master, Dr. von Wieser," who had been instrumental in starting him on a cartographic study focused on Norse discovery, was reportedly generous with the use of his private library as well as with his personal erudition.[27] Although this liberality would have been valuable in the fields of geography and cartography, it was not likely to broaden Fischer's knowledge about the medieval Norse, but his distinguished professor's social and professional contacts probably helped him when he asked advice from the three most highly regarded Nordic scholars with an interest in all aspects of Norse exploration as well as from intellectuals closer to home.

The head of the Vatican Library, Father Francesco Ehrle, was another important link in the scholarly information chain connecting Von Wieser, Fischer, Bjørnbo, and Storm. Like Fischer, Father Ehrle—"a great connoisseur of Antiquity"—enjoyed the trust and respect of the noble Catholic family at Wolfegg Castle, in whose magnificent collections he had been the first to identify a codex of antique drawings as the work of Amico Aspertini.[28] Bjørnbo, too, had benefited from Count Franz Waldburg zu Wolfegg's generosity with the use of his collections, although—as Count Franz's grandson remarked after Fischer's death—"the life of Prof. Josef Fischer was tied to that of Wolfegg Castle in Schwabia in a particular way."[29] In his work on Claudius Clavus, Bjørnbo made clear his own indebtedness to this continental web of support.[30]

When Fischer and Professor von Wieser arranged to have Bjørnbo's work published in German in 1909, in Von Wieser's hometown of Innsbruck, the Dane had further reason to be grateful for this close international network of scholars who shared his interests. The benefits were clearly mutual. Writing to Bjørnbo at the end of 1907 to wish him a Happy New Year, Fischer noted enthusiastically that he had now read the first thirty-two pages of what was to become *Der Däne Claudius Claussön Swart* (Claudius Clavus) *der älteste Kartograph des Nordens*, and had learned many things that had escaped him when he struggled through the Danish version.[31]

At the time the German edition of Bjørnbo's work was published, interest in the medieval Norse in general and in their "discovery of America" in particular was still at a fever pitch on both sides of the Atlantic. This enthusiasm had propelled Fischer to his own early fame and lasted long enough in his own case to inspire the map likely to be his most enduring legacy. Many years later, the translation of Bjørnbo's book on Claudius Clavus that Fischer had seen to its successful conclusion enabled Skelton to access the work when he was working on the Vínland Map. Although he was unable to read Bjørnbo's subsequent "Cartographia Groenlandica," he easily accepted Nansen's dismissal of the idea that Claudius Clavus had personal experience with Greenland, but he also noted enigmatically: "We cannot dismiss quite so lightly that there may be a link of some kind, perhaps in a common source, between Clavus' lost second map (the counterpart of the Vienna manuscript of his descriptive text) and the Vínland Map; and although such a connection, however weak, seems to us unlikely, it deserves mention for further investigation by any student who may think the exercise profitable."[32] As it turns out, the "common source" linking the Vínland Map to Bjørnbo's reconstruction of the second map made by Claudius Clavus would have been Father Josef Fischer, S.J., better and more creditably noted for having discovered the genuine, one-of-a-kind map that soon was dubbed the "baptismal certificate" of America.

America's "Baptismal Certificate" and Its 1516 Sibling

Von Wieser's and Fischer's joint treatise, *The Oldest Map with the Name America of the year 1507 and the Carta Marina of the year 1516 by M. Waldseemüller (Ilacomilus),* was dedicated to His Highness Prince Franz von Waldburg zu Wolfegg-Waldsee, at whose castle Fischer had made several important discoveries. The flourish of this dedication was in every way appropriate to the occasion, for prior to 1901 the 1520 world map drawn in Vienna by Peter Apianus had been considered the oldest surviving printed map showing the name "America."[33]

The Fischer-Von Wieser book is still familiar to historians of sixteenth-century cartography, but few readers are aware of the actual reason for Fischer's presence at Wolfegg, namely his intent search for cartographical evidence of the Norse discovery of America—a quest prompted by the treatise that Von Wieser had assigned him in 1894 as his final academic project. Fischer's stated motive influenced not only the views that he expressed in the book he wrote jointly with Von Wieser, but also the topics he pursued on his own during the rest of his long professional life. In his 1902 treatise on the Norse discovery of America, Fischer noted his Norse focus while at Wolfegg and provided a summary of those 1901 events in statements that contrast markedly with those made in the 1925 Von Wieser memorial volume, which claimed that as soon as Fischer had informed his professor of the interesting cartographical material he had found, Von Wieser had gone to Wolfegg and "immediately recognized the maps by Martin Waldseemüller he had so long been seeking."[34]

Fischer's own erudition and his outstanding visual memory had in fact enabled him to identify Waldseemüller's 1507 map on the basis of somewhat later copies and descriptions of the work. For his own part, he wrote:

> I must also thank Father H. Hafner, S.J., who kindly consented
> to search for Ptolemy MSS. in Wolfegg Castle, belonging to Prince
> Waldburg-Wolfegg, and was fortunate enough to discover a valuable
> MS. by Donnus Nicolaus Germanus, whose maps of Greenland . . .
> corresponded to those of the Ulm editions of Ptolemy of 1482 and
> 1486. I paid a visit to Wolfegg Castle to determine the relation between
> the Wolfegg MS. and the printed Ulm editions. I met with the best
> possible reception. I was able to identify the Wolfegg MS. as the proto-
> type of the Ulm editions. Last, but not least, came a most important
> discovery: the long lost large World Map and "Carta Marina" of the
> cartographer Martin Waldseemüller (Ilacomilus), 1507 and 1516, cov-
> ering some 24 large folio sheets. This lucky discovery was remarkable,
> if only for its bearing on the discoveries made by the Norse men . . .
> as well as on their relation to the later discoveries of Columbus and
> his successors.[35]

The Wolfegg manuscript by Donnus Nicolaus Germanus added considerably to Fischer's satisfaction with his discoveries because this gloriously colored manuscript turned out to be the prototype for the same cartographer's printed "maps of Greenland" in the 1482 and 1486 Ulm editions of Ptolemy's *Geographia*. However, Fischer's recital does not mention another discovery that he made at Wolfegg during that same period, namely the only surviving copy of the 1611 world map by the famous Flemish cartographer Jodocus Hondius. The map underwent extensive restoration in Rome before Fischer and Edward Luther Stevenson could publish it with a long commentary in 1907. While the two authors' text is irrelevant to the Vinland Map discussion, it should be noted that the 1611 map (the discovery of which he proudly recalled in 1935)[36] features a *Mare tartaricum* just east of *Nova Zemla* and above the rest of Asia.[37]

Both the "baptismal certificate" and the *Carta marina* were found bound into a volume carrying the ex libris of the German mathematician Johann Schöner (1477–1557) and containing, in addition to the Waldseemüller maps, the globe gores for Schöner's 1517 celestial globe and a print of the 1515 Stabius-Heinfogel star map drawn by Albrecht Dürer. When the codex was taken apart in order to reproduce the Waldseemüller maps, the actual binding was found to contain pieces of what Fischer identified as Schöner's 1515 globe gores.[38]

Setting aside the question of credit for discovering and evaluating the treasures at Wolfegg, both Von Wieser and his pupil had good reason to be pleased when the bilingual (English and German) edition of their joint work was published in Innsbruck in 1903 with support from the Imperial Academy in Vienna. Handsomely printed on thick paper and in large format, the book did justice both to the map reproductions and to the text. Although Fischer's *Entdeckungen* had come out the year before his and Von Wieser's joint work, a good deal of the attention that his own work received was due to the latter volume, in which Von Wieser stood behind his student's work and shared his own considerable reputation with him.[39]

The material so recently brought to light was indisputably significant to the history of cartography generally and to the history of early American mapping particularly. Most important to the Americanists was Fischer's discovery of the only extant copy of the 1507 Waldseemüller world map, where the name *America* had been coined for the occasion and prominently applied to the southern half of an unmistakable American continent.[40] There is no mystery about Waldseemüller's inspiration for giving the New World the name it has enjoyed ever since, because the map's companion text, the *Cosmographiae Introductio*, argued that America was a fitting name for the New World.[41] He also paid fulsome tribute on the map itself to the explorer Amerigo Vespucci (1454–1512). In Waldseemüller's equally rare 1516 *Carta marina*, which Fischer had also found at Wolfegg (and which up to that time had been known only from a reworking by Laurentius Fries), his enthusiasm for Vespucci had visibly waned, however. The name *America* is missing, and the appellation *parias* appears on the southern part of the new continent while the northern part is called *Terra de Cuva Asie Partis*.[42] Fischer and Von Wieser interpreted this nomenclature as post-Columbian influence while noting that the New World delineations were much the same on the 1516 and 1507 maps.[43]

In Fischer's judgment, Waldsemüller represented Northern Europe in his 1507 world map so strictly in accordance with traditional Ptolemaic concepts that he left out the peninsular Greenland that had already been introduced by Claudius Clavus and was prominent on both the anonymous "Cantino" map of 1502 and the circa 1505 work by Nicolaus de Canerio (Nicolò Caveri). Waldseemüller also drew India essentially according to Ptolemy in 1507, rather than using representations of the latest Portuguese discoveries in the East. For many other parts of the world, however, Fischer believed that the German cartographer had relied on the recent Portuguese information expressed in the "Cantino" and Canerio maps. He argued that the New World shown in both of those earlier works is similar to Waldseemüller's 1507 representations, with delineations of South America resembling those in Canerio's map so closely that Waldseemüller must surely have owned a copy of the Canerio chart.[44]

The similarities between Waldseemüller's American coastlines and those found in early post-Columbian charts in the Portuguese tradition are so widely discussed and accepted by modern cartographic historians that they need no further comment here.[45] Of more concern to the present discussion is Fischer's conviction that when Waldseemüller used Canerio's delineations in depicting the New World, he also reflected eight decades of a uniquely informed German cartography of the North sparked by Claudius Clavus.

Fischer's belief in this convergence of information is relevant to the Vínland Map discussion because several critics of the map have long suspected that both the depiction and the placement of Vínland derive from the brief tradition begun with the "Cantino" chart of 1502 and copied by Canerio about 1505 (see Chapters 5 and 7). Waldseemüller's 1507 "baptismal certificate" depicted a somewhat similar island in the far northwestern Atlantic, northeast of the continental New World and separated from it by a further expanse of ocean. In his 1516 *Carta marina,* Waldseemüller made his debt to Canerio more explicit in the shape of the island and by including a southern Greenland projecting downward from the upper edge of the map.

Both features had indeed been introduced in 1502 by the anonymous Portuguese author of the "Cantino" map, which paid homage to Gaspar Corte-Real by depicting a large island in the ocean southwest of a projecting Greenland. This island—unambiguously detached from the coasts in the southwest that represented the Columbian discoveries on behalf of Spain— has a much-indented eastern coastline, which the Tordesillas line separates from a forested area in the west. Portuguese flags decorate both this island and the large Greenland tongue reaching down from the northeast. Gaspar's 1501 voyage to North America is widely assumed to have included some part of the Labrador-Newfoundland-Nova Scotia region, which Gaspar called *Terra verde,*

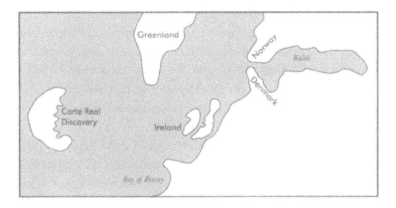

Figure 23. Several close descendants of the 1502 "Cantino" chart show an island with an indented east coast and in approximately the same position relative to a peninsular Greenland coming down from the icy wastes of northwestern Eurasia. Copyright David O. Seaver.

but which the 1502 chart labeled *Terra del Rey de portuguall.* It has represented a conundrum for exploration historians ever since.[46]

Several close descendants of the "Cantino" chart, including the Canerio map, show a similar island with an indented east coast and in approximately the same position relative to a peninsular Greenland coming down from the icy wastes of northwestern Eurasia (see Figure 23). Canerio did not name "his" island, but when Waldseemüller drew a similar island southwest of a pendent Greenland on his 1516 *Carta marina,* he labeled it *Terranova Coterati,* thus associating the New Land with the Portuguese and with the Corte-Real voyages. This 1516 work, in which Fischer saw evidence of access to northern German and possibly Nordic information about the Far North, is also the earliest map known to mention the Samoyeds who are alluded to twice on the supposedly mid-fifteenth-century Vínland Map.

The longer *Vinilanda Insula* legend links the "extremely fertile new land" that Leif and Bjarni discovered along with the island they named *Vínland* and with the mainland that Bishop Eirik had found when he proceeded "east" to the Samoyeds. *Vinilanda Insula* lies south and west of the island that represents Greenland, with the *Mare Occeanum* lapping at the shores of both. The southern half of Greenland has the same distinctive elongation as the peninsular versions in the "Cantino," Canerio, and 1516 Waldseemüller maps. The most likely explanation for these Vínland Map delineations is that the "Island of Vínland" is intended to conflate Portuguese *rediscovery* of a North American region with the original Norse discovery of the same region. In other words, this section of the Vínland Map supposedly demonstrates how residual Norse information might have been perceived by a particularly well-informed person of the mid-fifteenth century *before* the Portuguese had laid claim to North America.

Given Fischer's own scholarly convictions, neither the shape nor the placement of the *Vinilanda Insula* would have constituted a misrepresentation of the record he believed had once existed. He was certain of where Vínland had been. He was equally convinced that realistic information about the Norsemen's eleventh-century discovery had been available throughout the Middle Ages long before it was expressed cartographically by Claudius Clavus, and like Skelton he believed that earlier map sketches might once have existed.

A great many early maps are indeed known to have been lost. Although it is sometimes possible to retrace the information they contained, any "missing source" argument is still hazardous because a lost document is by its very definition incapable of verifying a theory. Fischer was prone to argue that almost by definition, cartographical discontinuity resulted from the loss of a map or maps that had once existed, and he always relished the challenge of identifying the sources used by early mapmakers, aiming for positive source identifications whenever possible. He concluded, for example, that when Waldseemüller delineated northern, eastern, and southern Asia, he had been influenced by several extant fifteenth-century cartographic works reflecting Marco Polo's descriptions of his journey in the late thirteenth century.[47]

At the time of Fischer's 1901 Wolfegg sojourn, his erudition was already as impressive as his ability to remember names, shapes, and spatial relationships, but his analysis of Waldseemüller's 1507 world map also showed a penchant for trusting a map's immediate visual appearance—a foible that continued to cloud his judgment throughout his career and eventually made him the unsuspecting purchaser of a modern fake purporting to be a Venetian map from 1519. He relied largely on cartographical and geographical details and on his ability to recognize both watermarks and various types of manuscript hands. These priorities are also reflected in his and Von Wieser's joint treatise on the Waldseemüller maps at Wolfegg and not invariably to the authors' credit. Their book had been out for more than a year before Fischer realized a crucial mistake in their analysis.

As the American typographical expert Elizabeth Harris has later demonstrated, Fischer and Von Wieser's analytical methods had caused them to make a mistake when dating the surviving Wolfegg copy of the printed 1507 world map. Because the two authors had perceived the black print of the woodcuts as lying on top of a quadratic network of degrees drawn in red ink, they were of the opinion that both the 1507 and the 1516 Waldseemüller maps represented prepublication proof sheets.[48] Harris's own detailed examination of the 1507 map (during its 1983 exhibition at the Smithsonian) led her to report that only the 1516 *Carta marina* has red lines covering the whole map; on the earlier map, only parts of the Old World have a red grid. More significant still is her observation that the red lines were in fact superimposed on the black print. Having them under the black lines would have been pointless as well as useless, Harris tartly noted. After studying the blocks, the paper, and the typeface, she concluded that Wolfegg's 1507 world map is not a first impression, but one made in 1515 or later together with the surviving copy of the *Carta marina*. She thought it regrettable that Fischer's erroneous judgment had subsequently led to much misdirected research and commentary on America's "baptismal certificate."[49]

Equally sad, however, is the fact that Fischer eventually reached the same conclusion and confronted his mentor with it in 1904. Von Wieser violently disagreed and let Fischer know his displeasure with such presumption.[50]

Despite this and other problems, the detail and sagacity of the two men's analysis of the Wolfegg material can still reward readers a century later. Of particular interest to the Vínland Map discussion are some of their observations concerning the 1516 *Carta marina navigatorio*. For example, they concluded that—as the title suggested—the map drew upon several maps based on information from recent Portuguese voyages, and Fischer found additional support for his belief that the circa 1505 Canerio chart had directly influenced the 1507 Waldseemüller world map, and because the *Carta marina* made the debt to Canerio even clearer, Fischer concurred with his mentor that Waldseemüller's 1516 work was "a printed edition of the Canerio chart; not indeed a slavish reprint, but an improved and, with regard to the interior of the continents, much enlarged edition."[51]

As noted, the similarities between the Canerio map and the *Carta marina* included not only the delineations of America and southern Africa but also extended to Greenland's depiction and to the island associated with the Corte-Real brothers. Furthermore, both maps finished at precisely the same eastern and western longitudes. With regard to Waldseemüller's depiction of Northern Europe, however, Fischer and Von Wieser believed that the mapmaker must have accessed a new source since 1507 because in the later map "Jutland and the whole Baltic territory agree in delineation and nomenclature neither with the world-map of 1507 nor with Canerio. Judging from the nomenclature this must have been a Low-German or northern map." The two scholars found the 1516 northern delineations somewhat uncertain, however, and noted that a framed legend placed in *Norbegia* (Norway) said that Waldseemüller hoped to draw a special map of this region later.[52]

The *Carta marina* had several such framed legends containing essential information. A legend in the lower left corner lists some of Waldseemüller's most important textual sources, among which are several names with strong links to the saga of the Vínland Map and its textual companions. One acknowledged source was the Franciscan friar Odorico da Pordenone, whose fourteenth-century account of his travels and missionary work in the Far East had reinforced Marco Polo's information that no "Earthly Paradise" could be found there. Waldseemüller also paid tribute to Cardinal Pierre d'Ailly, whose *Imago Mundi* Fischer and his mentor believed the cartographer had most likely used. Friar Ascelin, the Dominican who had led the mid-thirteenth-century papal mission taking the southerly route to Cathay, is similarly on Waldseemüller's list, and last, but certainly not least, "Joannis de Plano Carpio"—John de Plano Carpini—is included.[53]

Quite reasonably, Fischer and Von Wieser assumed that Waldseemüller had accessed the Ascelin and Carpini relations about the Tartars in the abridged version provided by the *Speculum Historiale*, which by Waldseemüller's time was available in print, as were the accounts by Friar Odorico and Cardinal d'Ailly.[54] Given the 1363 curtailments to European information about Central Asia and the Far East, it was equally reasonable to assume that even in the early sixteenth century, cartographers depicting those remote regions needed more information than had become available with Portuguese voyages after Vasco da Gama's 1497–99 expedition had rounded Cape Horn and reached India. Because this recent knowledge involved coastal regions only, scholars must still rely on firsthand narratives by thirteenth- and fourteenth-century churchmen and merchants for information about the vast interior.

When Fischer analyzed the two Waldseemüller maps, he already knew their cartographic and textual sources at least as well as the cartographer himself, and his subsequent publications indicate a lifetime spent in the further pursuit of fifteenth-century cartographic expressions of many remote regions, based on written sources such as the information gathered by emissaries of the Roman Church.

Of all distant places, none was closer to his heart than the medieval Norsemen's sphere of action. He firmly believed that "the discoveries made by the Norsemen in the eleventh, twelfth, and thirteenth centuries rendered it possible to draw a map of a part of America (Greenland), long before the time of Columbus, and a map so accurate . . . that a cartographer, to whom Nordenskiöld showed a copy, stoutly maintained it to be 'a forgery of the nineteenth century.'"[55] To this quiet, erudite priest who had never visited either Norway or Iceland, much less Greenland and North America, the Norse "discovery" of America was his first academic love, and it never lost its lure.

The Norse Discovery of America

As if to complete a symbolic circle, Fischer's 1902 monograph on what he considered cartographic evidence of the Norse voyages to Greenland and America was published in Martin Waldseemüller's birthplace of Freiburg in the Breisgau.

Many years later, Fischer shed further light on what his preoccupations had been while he worked on *Die Entdeckungen der Normannen in Amerika*. In an autobiographical essay, he listed four pieces that he had published during 1900–1901, and which he considered direct forerunners to his monograph on the Norse. One article queried the convention that "Pseudo-Donis" (Donnus Nicolaus Germanus) had been a Benedictine monk in Reichenbach. In his second piece, he demolished the notion that "Bishop John of Ireland" had been the first Christian martyr in America. His third article shows a direct focus on the Norse because it discusses a 1327 Latin work as a possible source of information about Norse colonization of mainland America. The fourth piece—again on "Pseudo-Donis"—brought the quartet full circle to his concern with cartographical issues.[56]

In his map analyses for the *Entdeckungen*, Fischer paid respectful attention to the work of predecessors, but it soon becomes clear that he trusted his own skills and visual perceptiveness more. For his general historical and textual interpretations of the Nordic sources he had nevertheless been forced to depend on secondhand analyses. Fortunately, his view of what constituted good scholarship was as uncompromising as his own ideas, and that aided him in the task of choosing and reconciling the works on which he openly relied. Explaining his approach, he noted:

> Where I formed my conclusions on the basis of the researches of G[ustav] Storm, A[rthur] M[iddleton] Reeves, D[aniel] Bruun, Jónsson Finnur [*sic*], Baron A. E. Nordenskiöld, etc., I have endeavoured to refer to the original authorities and to bring forward fresh arguments. It has also been my aim to make more accessible to general circles the discoveries of Scandinavian savants—discoveries not so widely known in Germany as they deserve.[57]

Underlying Fischer's decisive style are a number of preconceived notions about the medieval Norse. When he wrote about supposed cartographic manifestations of their voyages in Greenlandic and North American waters, his reasoning rested entirely on three axioms. The first relied on his faith in the influence and credibility of Claudius Clavus as the first realistic cartographer of the Norsemen's North Atlantic sphere. The second was based on his assumption that by definition, early maps showing Greenland also indicated America. The third axiom depended on his belief in an enduring verbal tradition that had begun when the first missionary bishops were sent out to Iceland, Greenland, and eventually North America.

From the start of his project, Fischer had been convinced that solid geographical knowledge about Greenland and North America had been a reality in the Middle Ages, and that studying the connection between Claudius Clavus and fifteenth-century German mapmakers would be productive. Professor von Wieser's 1894 suggestion that his star pupil undertake the study that culminated in the 1902 publication of *Entdeckungen* had essentially been a request to pursue a line of study that he himself had already drawn up and that had persuaded him that an early cartographic record of Norse discoveries had actually existed and warranted a further search.[58] In Norway, meanwhile, Gustav Storm had determined that the work of Claudius Clavus must have informed the northern delineations on late-fifteenth-century Ptolemaic maps.[59]

Fischer's Wolfegg research uncovered the Nicolaus Germanus manuscript (subsequently dated to October 4, 1468) that had inspired the maps of the North in the 1482 and 1486 Ulm editions of the *Geographia*.[60] Taken together with the Waldseemüller maps and other works that Fischer examined, he felt justified in claiming that he had found evidence of a proud fifteenth- and sixteenth-century German cartographic tradition, a prominent example being the Nuremberg globe that Martin Behaim had made in 1492. In addition, Fischer had concluded that Claudius Clavus "was the first scholar to add to Ptolemy's description of the world the discoveries of the Norsemen." Embracing Storm's opinions in this regard, he also shared the Norwegian historian's mistaken belief that the hostile "Karelians" threatening the Greenlanders from the North must have been Eskimos.[61] That was because those Arctic natives were not connected with Europe, but with Greenland and North America, so that as far as Fischer was concerned, Claudius Clavus had known that Greenland represented part of the Norse's further westward reach to America, instead of being the westernmost fixture on the familiar Eurasian continent.[62]

Assessing Claudius Clavus's impact on representations of the Far North in early editions of the *Geographia* involved analyzing why Nicolaus Germanus at first (in his Wolfegg manuscript) had mistakenly shown Greenland as a peninsula well to the north of Norway but had nevertheless soon been able to locate it in its true position west of Iceland. Fischer's 1902 conclusions, made before he had read Bjørnbo's report on the Claudius Clavus Vienna manuscripts, focused on three "editions" of the Ptolemy-related maps of the northern regions: "To the first edition belong the Rome editions of Ptolemy of 1478 and 1490, to the second the maps of the Canerio or Cantino-type, so far as it relates to Northern Europe and the peninsula of Greenland, and to the third the Ulm editions of 1482 and 1486." A visit to Nancy to check Cardinal Fillastre's 1427 codex convinced him that the cardinal's text had caused Nicolaus Germanus's initial confusion. Using "some other Norse sources," Fillastre had written down his text prior to seeing the first Claudius Clavus map and had evidently found it difficult to align the map with a description locating Greenland beyond Norway and Sweden and above a northern bay that is frozen during one-third of the year. Fischer's notions about the relationship between the text and the map in the Fillastre codex had changed somewhat by 1911, but he remained convinced that Claudius Clavus had at one point visited Greenland. In 1902, he was already certain that a map based on the cardinal's text "or similar Scandinavian authorities" must necessarily delineate Greenland to the north of Norway and east of Iceland. As evidence of the existence of "similar reports on the far north," Fischer referred to the "Genoa Mappemonde of 1447," which showed Greenland (*grinland*) north of the Scandinavian peninsula and east of the unnamed islands.[63]

With reasoning as convoluted as it was detailed, Fischer explained how these unspecified Nordic sources had caused Cardinal Fillastre to write that Greenland (*grolandia*) "points eastward toward the Island of Thule as does the whole northern region as far as to the terra incognita which Ptolemy never mentioned" and had brought about the misplacement of Greenland to the north of Norway. Then followed his observation that "Donnus Nicolaus made use of Scandinavian authorities." Only by inference does it become evident that Fischer simply assumed that Nicolaus Germanus's Nordic sources had been more recent and better informed than those used by Cardinal Fillastre.[64]

In Fischer's lengthy discussion of issues so central to his thesis, he repeatedly stressed the importance of the information that he thought Claudius Clavus had obtained through personal observations made in Greenland and that subsequently had been adopted by Nicolaus Germanus. Taking his axiomatic reasoning further, he suggested that a manuscript map by Nicolaus Germanus of the "second edition" Ptolemaic type may have influenced the 1502 "Cantino" map, whose Canerio offspring Martin Waldseemüller had subsequently used when making his *Carta marina*.[65] Fischer's later publications show that he did not change his views on any of these matters.

He also retained his perception that mapmakers at least from the time of Claudius Clavus had thought in terms of an *orbis terrarum* when they drew "correct" representations, which located Greenland west of Iceland and east of an isolated island representing the "first discovery" of northeastern America. In connection with the Vínland Map discussion, it is important to note that when he credited Claudius Clavus with thinking "in the round" in the early part of the fifteenth century, he was far in advance of not only Bjørnbo and other contemporary colleagues, but also of a generation or two of cartographic scholars yet to come. While he consistently misinterpreted medieval Norse geographical descriptions that he could not read, he understood correctly what he saw on the maps and globes he studied and therefore took for granted the capacity of a circa 1440 mapmaker to envision a voyage as going to the east if it went far enough west. One must also keep in mind Fischer's strongly held belief that the fifteenth and sixteenth centuries had seen several masters of cartography who were uniquely well informed about the Far North and the northwestern Atlantic region.

The Vínland Map is clearly intended to represent knowledge about the Norse in Greenland and North America after Claudius Clavus had left his imprint on continental European colleagues, especially on German mapmakers. The Yale map's globe-spanning image features the New World island that Fischer had traced from Waldseemüller back to Canerio, from Canerio to Cantino, from Cantino to Nicolaus Germanus, and from Nicolaus Germanus to Claudius Clavus. The question nevertheless arises of why a map that indicates global thinking as well as what Fischer called "the whole northern region as far as to the terra incognita which Ptolemy never mentioned," nevertheless leaves out both Markland and Helluland even as it displays the Cantino-Nicolaus Germanus-Waldseemüller island, here named *Vinilanda Insula*.

For his own part, Claudius Clavus had omitted not only Markland and Helluland, but also Vínland. Except in the minds of those who, like Fischer, defined the Danish cartographer's perception of Greenland as including a reference to Arctic America, Claudius Clavus did not even hint at any kind of American island or mainland known to the Norse.[66] Fischer had a confident explanation for the Dane's omission of the three American regions specifically named and explored by the Norse, however. He wrote:

> Greenland was for centuries a flourishing Norse colony, and the news
> of this discovery was handed on for generations through the Arctic
> maps of Claudius Clavus and his followers. Norsemen from Greenland
> discovered Helluland, Markland, and Wineland, but ceased to visit
> them towards the close of the fifteenth century, and it is therefore quite
> natural that Claudius Clavus omitted these countries from his map, and
> that thus they escaped the Ptolemy map of the world.[67]

Put differently, Fischer believed that the cartographical information provided by Claudius Clavus had been limited by the Danish mapmaker's strict scientific honesty, which had prevented a description of remote places he had been unable to survey personally. He nevertheless thought that the Dane's self-imposed limitations were regrettable because they had gotten in the way of wider knowledge about Norse voyages to Greenland and North America.

By the time Fischer published his first deliberations on the Norse voyages of discovery, he was certain that he knew where in North America "Wineland the Good" had been located. This designation could only refer to "the present Nova Scotia in conjunction with Cape Breton," he wrote. This was also the view of his Norwegian advisor Gustav Storm, who believed that Cape Breton should be equated with *Kjalarness* (Keelness), a promontory northeast of Vínland described in the "Saga of Eirik the Red."[68] The *Vinilanda Insula* on the Vínland map shows the actual Nova Scotia-Cape Breton constellation

Figure 24. The *Vinilanda insula* on the Vínland Map shows the actual Nova Scotia-Cape Breton constellation with the pseudorealism found in the island of *Gronelāda* delineation. Copyright David O. Seaver.

with the pseudorealism found in the *Gronelāda* delineation, while preserving the island's approximate "Cantino"-style shape and location (see Figure 24).

In contrast to this simple assertion, the question of who had actually discovered Vínland in the first place was as complicated in Fischer's mind as it is in the longer *Vinilanda Insula* legend on the Vínland Map. In the first place, Fischer knew from his own recent experience at Wolfegg that defining and attributing "discovery" (*Entdeckung*) was no simple matter when more than one person had demonstrably been involved. Secondly, during his academically formative years shortly before and after 1900, a fierce discussion had been raging about which "Vínland Saga" had the greater claim to historical authenticity—the "Saga of the Greenlanders" or the "Saga of Eirik the Red."

Fischer nevertheless felt equipped to address the Leif-or-Bjarni conundrum. He acknowledged that "the authorities differ entirely as to the name and person of the first discoverer, as to the time and circumstance of the discovery and subsequent exploration." As he understood Gustav Storm's explanation, the Icelandic priest Jón Thórdarson had been responsible for the story that Bjarni Herjolfsson chanced to discover new land west of Greenland. When Jón wrote down the saga of King Olaf in the *Flateyjarbók* in 1387, he borrowed material from the "Saga of Eirik the Red," but he unfortunately also knew of another account of the "voyage to Wineland." Attempting to merge this second account with the "Saga of Eirik the Red," which credits Leif Eiriksson with first discovery, Jón had painted himself into a corner in telling about Leif's return voyage from Norway to Greenland and therefore had found himself obliged to omit stating that "then Leif discovered Wineland the Good." Fischer added: "Only in this way could the priest ascribe the honour of the discovery of Wineland to his hero Bjarne, who was really only one of the band who accompanied Thorfinn Karlsefni on his later expedition."[69]

Like Reeves before him, Fischer was thus convinced that there had been only two voyages of American discovery—a chance one by Leif and a deliberate one by Karlsefni accompanied by Bjarni and others. It was only later that Karlsefni's "principal associates" became independent leaders of new expeditions (which did not qualify as discovery). Fischer would have found ample support for his position in Adam of Bremen's description of Vínland as an island "discovered by many." Previous chapters have noted Adam of Bremen's influence on the Vínland Map, such as the similarity between his description of Vínland and that found in the longer *Vinilanda Insula* legend. Given Fischer's implicit faith in the Bremen canon's information, these links are only to be expected. Fischer in fact regarded the Bremen churchman as the earliest and most trustworthy authority on the Norse voyages to America because Adam had written quite independently of the Icelandic manuscript literature, relying instead "immediately on contemporary Scandinavian traditions."[70]

Fischer was cautious enough in his book to follow Storm's and Reeves's interpretations of the older Nordic sources that he could not read, but his inability to access these sources directly prevented him from exercising similar caution in evaluating Crantz's statement that Leif and Bjarni had been on the same ship when they discovered Vínland together. To those German scholars throughout Fischer's lifetime who were interested in Norse Greenland, Crantz's work would have been as well known as Adam of Bremen's history of the Bremen archbishops and the "Vínland Sagas." Fischer's ambivalence about which of only two initial voyages to Vínland had accomplished the actual "discovery" gave him good reason to take note of David Crantz's *Historie von*

Grönland. Because he did not actually cite the work in his book on the Norse discovery of America, he could not include it with the short bibliography in the German edition, but he was sufficiently familiar with Crantz's work to approve its inclusion with the bibliography to the English translation of his *Entdeckungen.*[71]

Fischer's English translator, the superintendent of the Map Room at the British Museum, left his own marks on the book. In the expanded bibliography, he noted if a work was not available in the British Museum, and he occasionally editorialized in his actual translation, most notably with regard to Luka Jelic's research in the Vatican archives, which had led to the discovery of the 1492 papal letter about the Norse Greenlanders. In the English translation, Jelic is accused of enjoying a "cheap triumph," whereas Fischer had written no such thing despite being generally critical of Jelic's scholarship.[72] Although both the German and English bibliographies list the pertinent works by Jelic, the expanded English version is especially interesting because it reveals much about the many intellectual debts that Fischer only partially acknowledged in the preface and footnotes of his 1902 German book. Not surprisingly, several editions of Adam of Bremen's works are listed.

Adam had died about 1085 and therefore was unable to help Fischer with the vexing question of when the Norse voyages to America had ended, but Storm had researched this matter as well. Fischer accepted his conclusions with a statement that has an intriguing resonance in the longer Vínland Map legend next to *Vinilanda Insula.* "The history of Wineland ends with the probably ill-fated mission voyage of Bishop Eric in 1121," Fischer declared. Reasoning that the successful "plantation" reported in C. C. Lyschander's 1608 poem must therefore have been of fairly short duration, Fischer observed firmly: "Wineland, Markland, and Helluland, in short, the continent of America, were only occasionally visited, but were not colonised as intended." He therefore took sharp issue with C. C. Rafn, Luka Jelic, and other historians who believed that there had been a viable, populous, and enduring Norse colony in North America. At the same time, he stressed his agreement with Storm that there had been a religious impetus behind Bishop Eirik's 1121 venture. Storm had written: "Later critics have without exception regarded the voyage as a missionary undertaking; and this is no doubt the right construction." Concurring, Fischer observed: "He went in search of Wineland to preach the Gospel, but we do not even learn that he made a single convert, nor have we any grounds for theories on this point." He also echoed Storm when he emphasized that the *Icelandic Annals* merely stated that Bishop Eirik set out from Greenland; nothing was ever recorded about Bishop Eirik's subsequent fate.[73]

This intriguingly open-ended conclusion to the bishop's Vínland voyage paved the way for implying on the Vínland Map that Bishop Eirik had gone even farther afield, and so did Fischer's perception that Bishop Eirik's undertaking had been a natural extension of missionary efforts in Greenland. With a precision that no modern expert in the field would feel comfortable applying, Fischer wrote that Christianity had been introduced in Greenland during the winter of 1000–1001. He dated these efforts to the earliest days of the Greenland colony because he trusted the story (now known to be a later interpolation in the *Flateyjarbók* version of the "Saga of Eirik the Red"), which claimed that King Olaf Tryggvason of Norway had charged Leif Eiriksson with bringing Christianity to the Greenlanders. Although it had taken another century or so "before the Roman Catholic religion completely dominated the defiant and bloodthirsty Norsemen . . . the introduction of Christianity soon proved the best channel for a constant and assured intercourse with Christian Europe," Fischer observed, naming as an example Adam of Bremen's description (Book III) of "the visits of the Greenland envoys to Archbishop Adalbert of Bremen, when they come in search of missionaries." He implied that the 1112 appointment of "the first missionary bishop, Eric," had been the direct result of the Bremen archbishop's concern for Norse Greenlandic souls.[74]

Fischer firmly believed that long before Bishop Eirik's time, religiously motivated travelers would have informed both the Bremen archbishop and the church authorities in Rome about the earliest Norse voyages to America. For instance, the "Saga of the Greenlanders" reported that Karlsefni's widow Gudrid had gone on a pilgrimage to Rome in the early eleventh century. Observing that communications with the North would have been even more frequent in the twelfth century, Fischer reasoned that from such sources medieval cartographers must have "had opportunities of hearing full details of the discoveries of the Vikings in the west." Apparently unaware that Bishop Alf's demise in 1378 had put an end to resident bishops of Gardar, he thought that bishops had continued to occupy the Gardar See right up to the time of Claudius Clavus's supposed visit about 1427–30, making church communications with Greenland possible throughout that whole period.[75]

As a result of his unwarranted assumptions, Fischer felt certain that church-related communications with Greenland had produced a considerable written record, starting long before the 1448 and 1492 papal letters that he regarded as eminently trustworthy, and he expected future revelations from the same archival source. "As Greenland was converted to the Roman Catholic religion, it is possible that the most important records of Greenland may still be found in the archives of the Vatican," he wrote.[76] Employing a generous allowance for guesswork and suppositions, this view is still in vogue among defenders of the Vínland Map, and it is also reflected in the longer *Vinilanda Insula* legend on the map, which implies that Bishop Eirik had received one or more written communications from his ecclesiastical superiors.[77]

Father Fischer's faith in Bishop Eirik as a fully accredited representative of the Roman Church would have linked up seamlessly with his conviction that through the archbishops of Bremen, the German Church had been both a significant institutional player during the period in question and a recipient of vital information about the Norse in their Christian outposts.

By taking for granted a variety of oral and written sources of information, some running parallel to each other and some converging, Fischer easily persuaded himself that there were other early manifestations of Norse geographical knowledge besides those produced by Claudius Clavus. He cited N. A. E. Nordenskiöld's conviction that the *Insula Rovercha* on Andrea Bianco's 1436 map should be translated as "Walrus Island" and that it referred to Greenland. However, the *Rovercha*, shown west of Trondheim and close to the Norwegian coast, has the word *stocfis* next to it.[78] Its presence on the map obviously refers to the fisheries in the Lofoten Islands. Nordenskiöld also believed that the reference to white bears on the "Dulcert map of 1339" could just as easily point to Greenland as to the north of Norway where the legend is located. Indeed, as far as Fischer was concerned, Greenland was altogether so widely known in the colony's earliest times that "it is even shown as an island on a mediæval circular map which Professor von Wieser discovered, and of which he intends to write a detailed account." When evaluating some of the earliest maps showing islands marked *illa verde* (Green Island) and a neighboring *brazil* or *brazir*, Fischer trusted both in the fact that Markland meant "Forest Land" and in Storm's assertion that "Brazil" was used in Spanish maps to denote thickly wooded islands. It was but a short leap from these notions to a conclusion of his own, namely that the designation *novus cotus de brazir* ("the new coast of Brazil") on the 1367 Pizzigani map might perhaps be traced to "the publication of the latest accredited historical information about Markland in 1347." His remark reveals a naive notion of how medieval Norse information had been broadcast and is also a reminder of the importance he attached to cartograph-

ical "firsts" and to any cartographical version of "*nova*" that could be interpreted as a name indicating European exploration of North America.[79]

Concerning the *Nyjaland* that Adalbrand and Thorvald, "the sons of
Helgi," had discovered, Fischer thought that this 1285 discovery must relate to
"new land just opposite to Iceland, the Sandhill Islands," and noted that this
account is "as we read in the Icelandic annals."[80] Unfortunately, the annals do
not in fact say this. Although Fischer was dismissive of mere Icelanders like
Adalbrand and Thorvald, he was convinced that the Greenland Norse had
explored the east coast of Greenland during the eleventh, twelfth, and thirteenth centuries, reaching the Spitzbergen region as early as 1194. As evidence
of similar feats up along Greenland's west coast, he referred to the Kingittorssuaq Rune Stone (which he thought dated from about 1135) and to a 1266
voyage up to latitude seventy-five degrees and forty-five seconds north for
which "the priests in Greenland" had been responsible.[81] To his way of thinking, the Norse Greenlanders would practically have circumnavigated Greenland before the end of the thirteenth century and would thus have had a very
good notion of the country's shape and size.

Fischer believed that "all arguments hitherto brought forward in support of
a permanent colonization of Wineland by the Norseman have proved falla-
cious," but he cited the 1347 *Icelandic Annals* notice about the small Greenland
ship fetching up in Iceland after a voyage to Markland as evidence that the
Norse had continued with intermittent voyages to the North American *mainland*. By 1347, however, the purpose of such voyages would supposedly have
been to fish rather than to look for timber—this based on Fischer's a priori
reasoning about the threat that the encroaching Inuit supposedly posed to the
Norse Greenlanders' way of life at home. In addition, he argued that this 1347
voyage to Markland may have had some influence on the cartographical representation of America as it was known to the Norsemen. Helluland, too, had
continued to show up in northern geographical information, Fischer believed,
although not always in the same place. Confident that he knew just where in
North America the Norse had explored, not just with regard to Vínland, he
castigated C. C. Rafn for the latter's "gratuitous assumption" that there had
actually been *two* "Stone Lands" just so he could "place Wineland much further to the south."[82]

Evidently finding it easier to forgive early mapmakers who attempted to
illustrate the remote regions explored by the medieval Norse, Fischer took a
breezy approach to what might be called the "island problem" connected with

both verbal and graphic references to Norse discoveries and colonization in the northwestern Atlantic. The first Norse "pioneers" to cross the Davis Strait "had initially thought the new masses of land were islands," but that view changed later, he wrote. The cartographic representation of Greenland just "varies with the accounts—sometimes it is shown as an island, sometimes as a peninsula. This latter description merits most careful consideration, as in recent years it has received much attention from savants."[83]

He never questioned the geographical knowledge of the eleventh-century savant Adam of Bremen and believed that his fellow German churchman had been unjustly blamed for a "later addition" that said that "after Wineland there is no habitable land in that ocean, but all that emerges is icebound and wrapped in impenetrable mist." Fischer assured his readers that Adam's geographical knowledge otherwise agreed both with twelfth-century Icelandic accounts of the Far North and with the *Historia Norvegiæ*.[84] His own equation of Vínland with Nova Scotia-Cape Breton also agreed in both "the geographical position and horizontal form" with these same early descriptions, he declared. One need only "omit the learned conjecture as to the relation of Wineland with Africa" to see that these medieval Norse accounts also correspond "exactly" to the saga accounts of Greenland's relative position to the North American regions that the Norse had explored.[85]

Quite apart from the geographical knowledge that Fischer believed that the medieval Norse had contributed to the world of learning, "the expeditions of the hardy Norsemen undoubtedly had a moral influence, immediate or otherwise, on later explorers" such as Martin Frobisher and, very likely, Christopher Columbus.[86] There is no need here to discuss these speculations, but the core of his statement contains two more convictions that were always at the heart of his work. One was his belief that medieval and early Renaissance geography was based on an unbroken European chain of information reaching far back in time, its separate links restorable through patient research. The other was his equally unshakable certainty that human endeavors must exert some kind of a moral influence to be of lasting value.

Together with his devotion to the Catholic Church, these two precepts informed everything he wrote. While the Vínland Map reflects his lifelong zeal for discovering cartographic "firsts" and for solving pedantic riddles, far more significant is the map's stress on the continuity and complexity of medieval information and on the Roman Church's ability to transcend physical and cultural obstacles in order to take the Christian message around the world.

An Active Life

Without a doubt, Father Fischer brought his spiritual, moral, and intellectual convictions into the classroom every day of his teaching career, which began formally in 1895 when he was appointed professor of history and geography at Stella Matutina and lasted until he more or less retired at the age of seventy-one in 1929, although clearly remaining active in the institution's academic life well beyond that date.

A few years after Fischer's death, a former colleague wrote a commemorative essay for the Stella Matutina house organ in which he observed that teaching must have represented a great sacrifice for Fischer, who was first and foremost a scholar who had found himself unable to take the necessary time to write a doctoral dissertation, and who had had to wait until 1935 to be rewarded with an honorary doctorate. Furthermore, he had little natural aptitude for teaching and often had trouble maintaining discipline in his classroom, especially among the younger boys. However, those students who were able to benefit from his great learning reportedly remained grateful to him for the rest of their lives.[87]

Throughout the period 1895–1929, Fischer devoted himself to his teaching duties and had only limited time for travel and research. His accomplishments as a scholar during those years are therefore remarkable, and so is his productivity in retirement. His last projected work was an edition of the oldest maps of Abyssinia—a study that had been suggested to him by a friend some twenty years his junior, Achilli Ratti—better known as Pope Pius XI during his reign from 1921 to 1939.[88] Particularly before Ratti became a cardinal in 1921, Fischer would have had several opportunities to exchange ideas with this learned friend, who had been made chief librarian of the Ambrosian Library in Milan in 1907 and advanced from there to become prefect of the Vatican Library in 1914. Fischer's own account of this friendship indicates that the relationship had started with his first study trip to Italy in 1903–4.[89]

His communications to the princess at Wolfegg during that same period indicate that on that study trip to Italy, he had first spent some time in Rome before going on to Florence, where he would presumably have had the opportunity to see a 1447 *Planisfero Terrestre* that is unabashedly ellipsoid in shape.[90] While in Rome, he had been honored with a private audience with Pope Pius X, who had copies lying on his worktable of both *The Oldest Map with the Name America* and Father Fischer's monograph on the Norse. As Fischer reported to Princess Sophie, the Holy Father had expressed pleasure that these maps had been made by a prelate (Waldseemüller) "before the so-called Reformation." Adding to Fischer's own enjoyment of his Italian sojourn was its beneficial effect on his constitution, which apparently never was strong.[91]

As many an author can testify, a well-received book provides no excuse for resting on one's laurels but instead brings heightened public and personal expectations. Fischer sustained just this kind of pressure after the publication in 1902–3 of not just one, but two scholarly works bearing his name, preceded by four scholarly articles dealing with his principal research interests.[92] Back at Stella Matutina after his Italian study tour, Fischer wrote to Princess Sophie in the early spring of 1904 that he was receiving one invitation after another to attend the next (1906) Americanist conference in Washington, D.C. Such an undertaking would have been beyond Fischer's financial means, but at least he had the satisfaction of reporting to the princess later that summer that he had been at the Jesuit Congress in Friedrichshafen, where he had enjoyed a conversation with Princess Therese, and where the king had asked with whom the princess was talking.[93]

He had returned to Wolfegg Castle for more research in the summer of 1904 when he wrote a postcard to Bjørnbo apologizing for having been too busy to thank the Dane for his latest letter. He was still too busy for more than a postcard when he wrote to Bjørnbo again in October, this time from Feldkirch, where he had resumed his teaching duties.[94] One reason for his feeling under pressure would have been his participation in the fourteenth (1904) International Congress of Americanists held in Stuttgart, where he gave a paper on the cartography associated with the Norse discovery of America. His paper began by noting that the Norse discoveries of America had been the object of very enthusiastic and fruitful interest in the last twenty years and by lauding some of those who had helped pave the way to knowledge— Nordenskiöld, Von Wieser, Reeves, and Storm.[95] He also mentioned the work that Bjørnbo and Petersen had published on Claudius Clavus that same year, but that he had not himself been able to read properly. Emphasizing his belief that Claudius Clavus had personally visited Norse Greenland, he mostly repeated the arguments presented in his 1902 monograph.

His interests and beliefs showed no changes in the articles that he produced over the next few years. For American Jesuit colleagues he wrote a piece entitled "The Tithes for the Crusades in Greenland."[96] This was a subject about which he knew so little that when addressing it elsewhere during the same period, he claimed that both the written sources and modern archaeological studies "testify to extensive cattle breeding," therefore the Norse could easily pay their tithes in calfskins. He wrote that it was not surprising "that the crusade tax levied on the inhabitants of Greenland, who had no currency, consisted of cattle hides, sealskins, and the teeth of whales."[97] In several articles for *The Catholic Encyclopedia*—on subjects ranging from the pre-Columbian discovery of America and Claudius Clavus to Cardinal Fillastre and Nicolaus Germanus—he hammered home the conclusions he had reached while writing his thesis for Von Wieser. Wrapping up a long essay on the pre-Columbian discovery of America, he wrote confidently: "The recollection of Greenland was kept alive by charts and geographical descriptions even at the time when all communication with the Norse colonies had been broken off."[98]

Fischer had little reason to discard conclusions and theories that had already stood him in such good stead that he received a letter from President Theodore Roosevelt, who had recently been given a copy of *The Oldest Map with the Name America*. In his own hand, President Roosevelt had written: "I congratulate you on your wonderful work." Reporting this flattering news to Princess Sophie, Fischer noted that the president of Brazil had also received a copy of the book, and he suggested that perhaps the German emperor ought to have a presentation copy as well, in addition to the birthday gift that Fischer was sending him—a copy of the oldest world map with the name Berlin.[99]

The search for cartographical "firsts" was as much a constant in Fischer's life as his adherence to the cartographical theories he had developed early in his career. The immutability of those theories was not due to a shortage of new material, however. Throughout his professional life, he mined reports of both secular exploration and early Christian missionary activities for information that might have served medieval mapmakers, and he used every opportunity to study old maps in private as well as public libraries. Fresh back from Vienna in late September 1904, for example, he reported to Princess Sophie at Wolfegg that he had visited the library belonging to the prince of Luxembourg, and not only the Wolfegg collections, but also princely libraries in neighboring regions remained accessible to him for as long as he could travel around.[100]

While he continued his teaching, he was both supervising the German translation of Bjørnbo's Claudius Clavus work and working on his own treatise on the same topic. He nevertheless managed to squeeze in further research and some foreign travel. Together with Von Wieser, he attended the sixteenth International Congress of Americanists held in Vienna in December of 1908, and he told Bjørnbo that he would be in Italy during the 1909 winter semester.[101] The year 1909 also allowed him to spend some time at the British Museum, where his retentive mind and powers of detection again served him well, as demonstrated by the information that Sir George Frederic Warner (keeper of manuscripts 1904–11) dated October 1, 1909, and included with a rare volume in his collection: "The Rev. F. J. Fischer informs me that this is part of the Mount Athos Ms. published in facsimile by T [?] Langlois, Géographie de Ptolémée, etc., Paris, 1867."[102] The volume itself contained a map by Agothodaimon of Alexandria—a man of whom so little is actually known that he "could have lived any time between Ptolemy's lifetime and the thirteenth century," according to the modern scholar O. A. W. Dilke.[103]

Upon his return to Stella Matutina after his travels, Fischer was busier than ever, partly as a result of construction work at the school and partly in consequence of his indefatigable intellectual labor, which resulted in the 1910 publication of the Liechtenstein article he sent to Bjørnbo, and to the appearance that same year of a monograph about a map that he had found in the Vadiana in St. Gallen in 1902, which he had identified as the only surviving copy of a circa 1490 world map intended for a German edition of Ptolemy's *Geographia.* In this small book, which was dedicated to "*Hofrat* Prof. Dr. Franz R. v. Wieser," Fischer noted that the *Planiglobus* map (a circular map drawn like a globe) showed the creation of a specifically German cosmography based on sources besides Ptolemy and using numerous older and newer authors. In this pre-Columbian map, he had been particularly interested to find the large peninsula that reached outward and northward from Northern Europe, because at Wolfegg just a year earlier he had discovered this same peninsula, representing Norse Greenland (which Claudius Clavus had represented "so strikingly correctly") in the Ulm Ptolemy of 1482 and 1486.[104]

When Fischer finally published his reflections concerning the British Museum's Agothodaimon map in 1916, he also expressed other familiar and characteristic convictions. He was certain that maps by Ptolemy had survived, essentially unchanged, in an A-redaction containing twenty-six maps of separate countries or regions (*Länderkarten*) and a B-redaction with sixty-three local maps (*Provinzkärtchen*). Ptolemy's own world map, however, had in his view survived only in the form shown on the Agothodaimon map.[105] The problem with that last argument is that rather few scholars then or now have shared Fischer's certainty that Ptolemy had drawn maps of his own, instead of merely providing the coordinates and instructions for others to use when creating maps. The well-known cartographic scholar Leo Bagrow, who rarely minced his words, wrote about Fischer:

> We may certainly add that Fischer was firmly convinced that Ptolemy supplied his original work with maps which he had drawn himself. However, Fischer has not arrived at this opinion as a result of his work—this idea was the main incentive for this painstaking and long work. To Fischer, this idea grew into the assertion: Ptolemy has made maps. However, the author has not succeeded in finding a single direct evidence showing that anyone has ever seen Ptolemy's original maps.[106]

Another idiosyncrasy of Fischer's echoes directly in the Vínland Map, namely his obvious problem with foreign names. In his account of how he had identified the British Museum's Agothodaimon map, he referred to the keeper of manuscripts, Sir George Frederic Warner, as "Sir Warner" instead of as "Sir George," the correct short form in English usage.[107] While he was always punctilious about titles, he repeatedly demonstrated such a tin ear for non-German names that he never grasped the Old Norse and modern Icelandic tradition governing patronymics (which change with each generation) and tried as much as possible to avoid dealing with them. While he often recognized names with the suffix "-son" as surnames, he appears not to have understood how such last names were constructed and therefore felt uncomfortable using them. Throughout his book on the Norse discovery of America he referred to Leif Eiriksson as "Leif" or "Leif, a son of Eric the Red," and to Bjarni as "the son of Herjolf," and he never mentioned Bishop Eirik's parentage at all. Both his German and English bibliographies list the Icelandic scholar Finnur Jónsson as "Jónsson Finnur" without a comma, although Fischer referred correctly in his text to the medieval Icelandic historian Ari "the Learned" as Ari Thorgilsson. Fischer's handicap resulted in *byarnus* (no patronymic) and *leiphus erissonius* in the Vínland Map legend. It also explains why the same legend referred to Bishop Henricus without an attempt at a patronymic, because any kind of Latin version of "Gnupsson" would have been as big a challenge as finding a plausible Latin version of "Herjolfsson."

Before writing up his investigations of the Agothodaimon map in "Sir Warner's" manuscript collection, Fischer completed his "Claudius Clavus, the First Cartographer of America" as well as a piece describing a "globe goblet" at

Wolfegg, both works carrying a 1911 imprint.[108] These were followed in 1912 by two more publications, one concerning the first map with the name "Brazil" and the other the transmission of Ptolemaic manuscript maps.[109] As the threats of war drew closer, he managed to turn out two more articles that were still closely focused on his specialties.[110]

Scholars will probably never know the full extent of Fischer's published writing because Stella Matutina made its own printing and publishing arrangements right there in Feldkirch for items of local and in-house interest, of which Fischer was a loyal contributor. One such item from his hand was a handsomely printed pamphlet, with a colored map enclosure, entitled "Massenas Sturm auf Feldkirch 1799 März 23" (Massena's attack on Feldkirch 1799, March 23), which described a planned but failed attack on their town.[111] His painstaking account ends on such a reassuring note that one suspects he was addressing local worries about what might happen in the event of a new war; the pamphlet was written in 1913 and printed in 1914, the year that World War I broke out.

The title of a 1915 out-of-house publication from his hand, "Von alten Kriegskarten" (From old war maps), also suggests that this Jesuit scholar in a quiet Austrian valley was not immune to the political realities of his time.[112] A short history of Stella Matutina published in 1990 reinforces that impression. The only event it notes between 1912 and the spring of 1923 is Kaiser Wilhelm II's visit to campus on June 5, 1917, the last year of the war.[113] A Stella Matutina film to be made in 1938 was somewhat more informative, with scenes for the period 1914–18 that began with the departure of Stella Matutina pupils for the war and went on to record scenes of the first war-wounded returning home, of life at the front, and of small boys back in Feldkirch as they sat in a communal dining room, ready to partake of a scanty meal of polenta and very little bread.[114]

Fischer had become an Austrian citizen when he began teaching at Stella Matutina.[115] However, with intellectual and personal anchors in both Austria and Germany, he would have thought of himself as belonging to both countries, and as a teacher of both German and Austrian pupils, he would have felt the pain of seeing many of his students reach draft age while still in school. He left no personal record of how he experienced the years 1914–18, however, or of how he reacted to the aftermath of the 1919 treaties at Versailles (for Germany) and Saint-Germain (for Austria). These treaties marked the end of the Hapsburg Empire, leading to exile for Kaiser Wilhelm II, and ensured years of political and economic humiliation for both Austria and Germany. The economic consequences of the two treaties' injunction against any kind of political or economic union between Austria and Germany were especially hard on tiny Austria where Fischer lived and worked, so the practical and emotional impact on his life must have been considerable. Both Germany and Austria experienced disastrous postwar inflation until the League of Nations intervened in 1924, and the situation was not improved by widespread unemployment and by unstable conditions in many other parts of the globe. When the Spanish Influenza struck in 1918 and decimated populations around much of the world, it hit hardest among those who were already weakened by war and hunger.

It says a great deal about the strength of Father Fischer's religious faith as well as about his commitment to scholarship that those difficult years did not distract him entirely from his usual intellectual concerns. During the first war year he published a short commentary on the 1513 Strasbourg edition of Ptolemy's *Geographia*, to which Martin Waldseemüller had contributed both a beautiful world map showing Greenland as a long peninsula north of Norway and an equally striking map of the New World—works that gave Fischer occasion to reminisce about his important discovery of the mapmaker's 1507 and 1516 maps.[116] A work that Fischer brought out the following year (1915) indicated that his research focus had expanded to include late-fifteenth-century German travel information about Eastern Europe and Russia.[117] However, in two articles published in 1916 and 1917 he was still making good use of Waldseemüller's *Carta marina*. One article discussed the Russian czar (shown as "Kaiser" on the 1516 chart) and the other piece honored the four-hundredth anniversary of Catholic missions.[118] The latter work is significant to the discussion here because it reflects his enduring interest in the early missionary activities of his church and in the reports of churchmen who had traveled extensively for professional reasons. Another 1916 article, "Zwei verschollene Nürnberger Weltkarten" (Two missing world maps from Nuremberg), is equally interesting because it shows both his focus on the rich scholarly heritage of his home region and his lifelong interest in lost maps, which he frequently saw as "missing links" in continuous cartographical records he was convinced had once existed.[119]

He repeatedly felt challenged to investigate what such lost maps might have contained and, if possible, to reknit former paths of cartographic and textual information. He would not have seen the Vínland Map and its many cartographic "firsts" as a falsification of a once-existing record because he would have been confident that each feature had been based on precedents that were now lost. Furthermore, he considered neither the missing maps he took for granted, nor the maps still available for analysis, any less reliable if they represented reconstructions based on written sources rather than being copies of earlier graphic works.

As World War I ground on and Fischer continued his work on Waldsee-müller, in 1917 he also published the first of three articles on the Nuremberg physician and humanist scholar Hieronymus Münzer, who had a close connection with Feldkirch. According to Fischer himself, he had first become interested in Münzer after Professor von Wieser lectured on a letter that Münzer—unaware of the Christopher Columbus expedition—had written to João II of Portugal on July 14, 1493, advocating a westward voyage across the Atlantic in order to reach Cathay. Von Wieser had jokingly suggested that perhaps Münzer deserved the honor of being called the discoverer of America.[120]

There would have been much besides Münzer's thoughts concerning westward sailing to attract Fischer's attention to the learned Nuremberger. Münzer had contributed to the 1493 *Nuremberg Chronicle* a woodcut map of Germany, the Baltic, and southern Scandinavia based on the mid-fifteenth-century map that Cardinal Nicholas of Cusa (Cusanus) is known to have made before he died in 1465.[121] Fischer saw Münzer (who also had known Behaim) as a vital link in the German cartographical tradition, and it is clear from his article that during his research he had found many suggestive indications of how information had traveled in the fifteenth century, including Münzer's belief that the Duke of Muscovy had recently rediscovered Greenland.[122] His Münzer studies also brought him into contact with several private libraries in his region and are therefore central to determining the source of the Vínland Map parchment and parent volume.

Throughout this postwar period, Fischer's preoccupation with tracing Ptolemy's influence on early cartography ran parallel with his other research areas. He published no fewer than three papers on Ptolemaic maps in the period 1918–22.[123] After that, his interests took another turn with an article discussing whether the first missionary to "the Indian Islands" (that is, the New World) had been a Benedictine or a Franciscan.[124] Although his topic here concerned Columbian discovery rather than Norse, it suggests that he was again casting his eye westward to examine early church influence on poorly known regions far from Rome. His fascination with this topic was evidently well known to others in his circle because he wrote to his younger admirer Robert Haardt in 1936: "Concerning the spread of religion and of the missions, you would do best to turn to the 'Katholischen Missionen,' for example to G. Alfons Väth, S.J., in Bonn, Hofgartenstr. 9, and mention my name."[125]

It was not until 1932 that Fischer resumed an active interest in the Norse and their North Atlantic activities. Up to that time, his study of early German cartographic information channels had continued unabated alongside his patient work on a multivolume work devoted to early Greek Ptolemy manuscripts in the Vatican Library. A rather pedestrian article in 1928 was followed by three pieces that added more directly to his professional reputation.[126] The first concerned a Greek Ptolemy manuscript that he had found at the British Museum (now in the British Library), which he had originally intended for his encompassing study of the Vatican Library manuscript maps, but which he wrote up for a Stella Matutina seventy-fifth anniversary publication, and in which he again referred to Sir George Frederic Warner as "Sir Warner." The second article discussed a missing Nicholas of Cusa map, "the oldest map of Central Europe," and the third one dealt with the oldest state of the famous 1507–8 world map by Waldseemüller's contemporary colleague Johannes Ruysch, a native Dutchman who had spent most of his adult life in Germany.[127]

The Ruysch map delineates Greenland and the rest of the western Atlantic region in a manner startlingly different from Waldseemüller's world map of the same date. This difference is particularly noteworthy because Ruysch had personally visited the Newfoundland region sometime between 1502 and 1504.[128] However, while Ruysch thus made an important contribution to early German cartography, Fischer's 1931 article concentrated on the minutiae of three different stages of the 1507–8 map, not on its place in cartographic genealogy. His article that same year on Cardinal Nicholas of Cusa (Cusanus) is more important to the Vínland Map analysis because his study of Cusanus both directly and indirectly involved a number of the same elements as the "Tartar Relation" discussion. It is also interesting because of what it reveals about Fischer's complicated relationship with his mentor and because it suggests that he was capable of gentle mischievousness.

In a lecture on Cusanus that Von Wieser gave before a learned audience in 1905, he had compared the so-called Eichstädt map of the German region, which he dated to 1491, with what he considered traces of the lost Cusanus work in a Florentine, late-fifteenth-century Henricus Martellus Germanus version of Central Europe. He declared that Henricus Martellus had come closer than the 1491 work to the cardinal's original map. Only a couple of excerpted reports on Von Wieser's lecture were published, however, and the professor clearly never returned to the topic.[129] He subsequently asked Fischer to find the cardinal's original map, according to Fischer's own work on the topic, which he published many years after Von Wieser's death. In this article, Fischer observed that the Cusanus map has been handed down in two different rescensions— one going back to Donnus Nicolaus Germanus and one done by the somewhat younger, Florence-based Henricus Martellus Germanus. Recounting Von Wieser's work on Cusanus, he particularly noted that his mentor had called attention to the connection between the work of Claudius Clavus and the maps by Henricus Martellus Germanus that incorporated Greenland. Silkily, he added that his "esteemed teacher *Hofrat* Prof. Dr. Franz R. von Wieser" had not told him about discovering the Henricus Martellus Florentine manuscript until he, Fischer, had returned from his 1904 research trip to Florence and reported on the Henricus Martellus manuscript he had located at the Biblioteca Nazionale there. The subtext here is that only then had his mentor rushed to make public hay on his Florentine "discovery" years earlier.[130]

According to Fischer, he had decided soon after Von Wieser's death in 1923 to pursue the subject of his professor's 1905 lecture and provide his own evaluation of the Cusanus-influenced map that both he and Von Wieser had studied at the Biblioteca Nazionale in Florence, but other concerns had kept intervening for several years. While he acknowledged in his article that the original Cusanus map of Central Europe unfortunately was still as lost as the original Claudius Clavus works, it is evident that he took great satisfaction in noting the likely influences both on and by Cusanus and in tracing the connections between the Ptolemaic maps made by Henricus Martellus on the one hand and the influence of Claudius Clavus and Nicholas of Cusa on the other. Overall, his analysis was focused on finding evidence that Ptolemaic maps made sometime between 1480 and 1490 by Henricus Martellus Germanus had incorporated both Cusanus's lost image of Central Europe and the lost Claudius Clavus image of Greenland. He intended to say more about several of these details in his forthcoming magnum opus on the Codex Urbinas Graecus 82 in the Vatican Library, he noted.[131]

An eye-catching feature in the facsimile map that accompanied Fischer's Cusanus article is its *Mare Maior*, oriented north-south and doubtless representing the Black Sea. It runs most of the way up the eastern side of the map toward the northeastern corner, where a *Mare Tanai* borders a region named

Ruscia inferior sive alba. This feature spawns the question of how far east Cusanus had in fact traveled. The modern cartographic historian Robert Karrow has written a concise chapter on Cusanus. The cardinal, whose last name reflects that he had been born (circa 1401) in the German city of Cues (located on the Mosel River in the Rhineland and now called Bernkastel-Kues) does not seem to have spent much of his adult life there, especially not after 1425, when he began his diplomatic career as secretary to the archbishop of Trier. He took part in a papal mission as far as to Constantinople in 1437 and also negotiated on the pope's behalf with fractious German princes. Made a cardinal in 1448 and appointed papal legate for Germany in 1450, he continued his travels throughout Germany and the Low Countries, of which he evidently made some kind of scientific record.[132]

Karrow observes that Cusanus probably established many of his locations himself with the aid of an astrolabe and a *torquetum* (Turkish instrument) that he had acquired in 1444.[133] If Cusanus himself had drawn the *Mare Maior* on a map, it would not have been from personal experience and measurement, however, because his own travels would not have given him that opportunity. Throughout the fifteenth century, the region beyond the Black Sea would have remained little known to Europeans, and mapmakers would still have had to rely on older lore. For this and other reasons, the men with whom Cusanus exchanged information would therefore have had an important influence on his thinking in addition to his own travels, and Fischer, always a careful investigator, would have done his best to trace those sources.

At an early time, Cusanus had formed an enduring friendship with the Florentine polymath Paolo Toscanelli, whose optimistic views regarding the width of the Atlantic Ocean encouraged Columbus in his westward quest for Cathay, and whose ideas had influenced both the Henricus Martellus Germanus circa 1490 manuscript world map belonging to Yale and Martin Behaim's 1492 globe. This information chain would naturally have been of considerable interest to Fischer, but at least as important to his thinking and to the Vínland Map discussion would have been Cusanus's prominence in the Roman Church hierarchy. Cusanus was a member of the Council of Basel from its inception, when he was scarcely more than thirty years old, and served (unsuccessfully) as the advocate of Ulrich von Mandersland until 1435, after which he represented the German nation in the council's unproductive transactions with the Bohemians. When he abandoned the council in 1437 (actually leaving Basel in August 1436), it was in protest over the council's policies and its election of Pope Felix V. Pope Eugene IV rewarded Cusanus's orthodoxy and loyalty by making him his envoy to the empire from 1438 until 1447. A year later Cusanus, who had just become a cardinal, was asked to promote a crusade against the Turks as well as to reunite the Hussites with the church.[134]

Fischer was no doubt well acquainted with the history of Turkish threats to his general home region, familiar as he was with the *Speculum Historiale* and with the accounts of the mid-thirteenth-century embassies to the Tartars. His training would also have made him well informed about the Church Council of Basel. Convinced that church connections and communications were major sources of geographical information, he would have looked for the potential at Basel, during the council's early years, for learned exchanges between such people as Toscanelli and Cusanus. Given that in Fischer's 1902 book on the Norse he referred three times to Gustavo Uzielli's work on Toscanelli, he would also have been aware of Uzielli's assumption that from Cusanus, Toscanelli would have been given access to Alfred the Great's translation of Orosius with the king's own added descriptions of the voyages that Ohthere and Wulfstan had made to far northern regions.[135]

Two years after completing his Cusanus analysis, Fischer delivered on his promise to Edward Luther Stevenson that he would write a preface for Stevenson's translation of Ptolemy's *Geographia*. Until very recently, this translation was the only one available in English, so it is regrettable that it is reportedly full of errors. Two modern Ptolemy experts wrote: "Stevenson appears to have based his version primarily, if not exclusively, on the Renaissance Latin texts of the *Geography*, and very frequently misunderstood even them."[136] These commentators do not belittle Fischer's preface, however, which was written with his usual attention to detail. On the contrary, their own analyses bear out several of his views, the most important one of which was his conviction that Ptolemy's original manuscript to the *Geographia* must have included both regional maps and a world map, drawn according to his coordinates.[137] In their recent Ptolemy translation, J. Lennart Berggren and Alexander Jones wrote: "Although some scholars have gone so far as to doubt whether Ptolemy actually drew, or had drawn for him, the maps that he describes in his *Geography*, it seems hard to imagine how he could not have done so."[138]

Being entirely of the same opinion, Fischer developed his theories about Ptolemy's own maps further in his four-volume work published the same year as Stevenson's Ptolemy translation. He intended his *Claudii Ptolemaei*

Geographiae Codex Urbinas Graecus 82, undertaken at the request of Pope Pius XI, to be the crowning achievement of his scholarly career.[139] Alas, it also became ammunition for his severest critic in a devastating 1933 review. Had Fischer been alive today, however, he would have seen his well-thumbed work still occupying its space on the reference shelf at The British Library Map Library and still cited in modern scholarly treatises. In 1932, after more than three decades of diligent research and writing, Fischer had reached the height of his career, and his work was earning him honors both at home and abroad.

Public Recognition

In recognition of Fischer's contributions to the history of cartography, he became a member of the Academy of Sciences in Vienna (elected 1932, full member 1934) as well as of the Papal Archaeological Academy. In 1933 he received a silver medal from the Geographical Society in Berlin, sent to him by diplomatic post because he was unable to travel there.[140] The University at Innsbruck awarded him an honorary doctorate in 1935 on the fortieth anniversary of his admission to that university. That was also the year he was invited to contribute an autobiographical essay to the very first issue of the international journal *Imago Mundi*, founded by the formidable Leo Bagrow. Honorary memberships in the Royal Geographical Society (1925) and the American Geographical Society (1935) constituted further evidence of Fischer's international reputation.[141]

Fischer was pleased and grateful for each accolade, but no honor seems to have given him greater joy than the gold medal that he received in 1932 from Pope Pius XI upon the completion of his *Urbinus Graecus* work. Poor health had prevented him from personally delivering to Rome the two volumes of text and two volumes of map reproductions when they were first published and also from receiving his gold medal directly from the pope's hands. The medal was therefore brought back from Rome by the two emissaries who had delivered the books to the Vatican. Late in 1932, however, Fischer's nephew in Wiesbaden, Eduard Fischer, offered to accompany him to Rome. This nephew was a physician by profession and could look after his uncle during the journey, so the aging scholar accepted the offer. The two men arrived in Rome on November 25, 1932, for Father Fischer's fourth and last visit to the Eternal City. During their three-week stay, Fischer had two audiences with the Holy Father, and it is

clear from his subsequent account in the Stella Matutina house organ that both
he and his nephew had been treated with the greatest kindness and respect.[142]

When Fischer's eightieth birthday approached and congratulatory letters
came in from near and far, Pope Pius XI honored him again, this time with a
letter written on his behalf and signed by Cardinal Pacelli. At about the same
time in 1937, Kurt von Schuschnigg—who referred to himself as a grateful former pupil of Fischer's—also extended his warmest good wishes on stationery
from the office of the Bundeskanzler, the Austrian chancellor.[143] Chancellor
von Schuschnigg's letter was written twelve months before Hitler's annexation
of Austria, which Von Schuschnigg had struggled to prevent, but both
Germans and Austrians would already have been feeling the consequences of
Hitler's ascent to power in early 1933. Even before that time, the political and
economic turbulence in both Austria and Germany, which was propelling
Hitler forward, worried the administration and staff at Stella Matutina so
much that the institution's seventy-fifth anniversary in 1931 was seen as a welcome diversion indeed.[144]

And yet Fischer soldiered on, buoyed up as before by his faith and by his
intellectual curiosity, and now also by his acknowledged standing in the scholarly community.

Returning to the Norse

Twenty years after Professor von Wieser had published his findings on the
Albertin de Virga world map and rejected Fischer's views on Claudius Clavus
in the process, the De Virga map went missing after its current owner withdrew it just prior to an auction to be held by the prestigious firm of Gilhofer
and Ranschburg in Lucerne, Switzerland, in June 1932.[145] After Albert Figdor's
death in Vienna on January 22, 1927, his niece Margarete Becker-Walz, the
wife of a prominent Heidelberg lawyer, had become the heir to Figdor's splendid collections, which still included the De Virga map.[146] It was clearly she
who made the decision not to sell it after all at that auction; the only mystery
is why she made such a choice. There was no reason to doubt the map's
authenticity, nor were there any cartographical scholars in her family who
might have wanted to study it. Most likely, she had lately been told that it
would increase in value if a new study were to show features in the work that
nobody as yet had suspected.

The reserve price of nine thousand Swiss francs stated in the sales catalogue was high, but the De Virga map, listed as item number 56, was by no means the most expensive piece in an auction that, in addition to other items that had belonged to Figdor, featured treasures from the Tsarskoije-Selo Library of the last Russian czar and from the collections of Duke Albrecht of Sachsen-Teschen.[147] Item number 56 seems nevertheless to have been considered prime bait, because the auction catalogue began with an excellent photographic reproduction of the map, approximately half-sized, and it described the item in considerable detail, mostly quoting from Von Wieser's 1912 article.

It would have been impossible to miss this singular item for anyone connected with the auction house or having access to this auction catalogue. Fischer had a particularly close relationship with Gilhofer and Ranschburg in the 1931–33 period. This circumstance, which is likely to have played a key part in the Vínland Map story, furthermore suggests a possible connection between Fischer and the 1932 recall of the De Virga map.

While there is no reason to believe that the map ever got as far as to Stella Matutina, it may have been Fischer who persuaded the map's wealthy owner to allow time for a study similar to one that he had just completed on a volume of manuscript maps that Gilhofer and Ranschburg were about to offer at another one of their important auctions, and that he had written up in an article published in Switzerland in 1932. The article, which analyzed a manuscript copy made by one Georgius Schbab [Schwab] of an early edition of Ptolemy's *Geographia,* reveals the degree to which Fischer was at that very time enjoying the trust and respect of the exclusive Swiss-Austrian auction firm, because Gilhofer and Ranschburg had allowed him to keep the Schbab manuscript at Stella Matutina for the better part of a year before offering it at an auction in Lucerne, scheduled for June 25–26, 1934. Fischer made it clear that he appreciated the firm's trust in letting him have the Schbab maps available while he was completing his major work on the *Urbinas Graecus* maps at the Vatican. It is equally evident that he was fully informed about the upcoming auction because his article mentioned the pertinent auction catalogue in a footnote, and the auction catalogue in its turn referred to his Schbab article.[148]

It is thus as unlikely that Fischer was ignorant of the Gilhofer and Ranschburg 1932 offering of the De Virga map as that he had forgotten any detail of his mentor's 1912 article. His memory was still enviable, and in the German-speaking world his reputation as a cartographic historian was at such a height that he was one of the few cartographic historians in that part of Europe of sufficient stature to approach a wealthy person with such a request.

He would also have had a powerful double incentive regarding the De Virga map. In the first place, he was no longer in Von Wieser's shadow and could speak his own mind without fear of repercussions. In the second place, he had never lost his belief in medieval cartographic manifestations of the Norse discovery of America, and in the De Virga map he would have found much to sustain his wishful thinking. The map would have been particularly interesting to him because it predated the known works of Claudius Clavus, who reportedly had arrived in De Virga's Italian homeland in 1410.

Professor von Wieser, it will be remembered, had been certain that De Virga's huge *Norueca* in the northwest included part of Greenland's vast landmass. Fischer, who thought he had seen so many indications of Greenland and North America in other pre-Columbian maps, would certainly have found it tempting to analyze De Virga's map showing such a disproportionately large landmass featuring a crown and the name *Norueca* (Norway). The name recurs in three more places in the same region, probably to indicate the three Norwegian towns best known to Hanse fish merchants who interacted with Venetian fish merchants in the Baltic, while the generous indication of the country's size simply shows that Norway's rapidly diminishing autonomy and economic position was too recent for news of it to have reached Venice. De Virga had drawn the map at a time when Queen Margrethe of Denmark, Norway, and Sweden was not yet dead or had only recently died (1412), and when her chosen heir King Eirik of Pommerania had not yet made his disastrous policies felt.[149] To someone of Fischer's mindset, the size and diffuseness of *Norueca* would have suggested Norway's medieval expansion westward into the North Atlantic and all the way to a Greenland connected with America.

Many of Gilhofer and Ranschburg's records disappeared in the confusion of World War II, making it impossible either to ascertain the circumstances of the withdrawal of the De Virga map from the auction or to trace its current whereabouts. It is unfortunately easy to conjecture what may subsequently have happened to the map in post-1932 Germany, in an atmosphere of increasing political turbulence and as a result of savage anti-Semitism after Hitler's power grab. Margarete Becker-Walz's husband Ernst Walz was a defiant supporter of the Weimar Republic to the republic's bitter end, and as German Jews the couple would soon have experienced the further developments of a situation that had already been difficult for Margarete Becker-Walz when she became Figdor's heir. At that time, the Austrian authorities had at first refused to allow Figdor's collections out of the country.[150]

Auctioning off the map in neutral Switzerland would have been one thing, but sending the map from Heidelberg in Germany to Fischer in Austria would quickly have run into an unscalable bureaucratic wall. Furthermore, arrests of Jews, boycotts of Jewish businesses, and the dismissal of Jews from academic and other public positions had begun almost immediately after Hitler's assumption of power in January 1933. Recent newspaper stories about sales of art and manuscript treasures of questionable provenance have made it abundantly clear what happened to the property of Jews and others who fell afoul of the Nazis. After Germany's surrender in 1945, Nazi loot was found in makeshift storage all over the former Third Reich.[151] It remains to be seen whether the De Virga map is still at large or else destroyed.

No such uncertainties attach to the Schbab *Geographia* manuscript over which Fischer had been able to take his time in the safety of his Stella Matutina study, and which is of double significance to the Vínland Map discussion as evidence of his connection with the firm of Gilhofer and Ranschburg and as the direct cause of his revived interest in tracing Norse influence on early cartography—an interest that had lain dormant for twenty years. The Schbab manuscript also nourished his continued interest in the uniquely German cartographical tradition that he had been tracing backward and forward since his 1901 Waldseemüller discoveries at Wolfegg.

While he considered Schbab's world map very similar to the one found in Gregor Reisch's encyclopedic work *Margarita Philosophica* (first published in 1503), he was certain that an unnamed northern peninsula sticking out from the edge of one of the Schbab regional maps represented Greenland in a manner that differed markedly from the Ulm Ptolemy editions of 1482 and 1486 that the map otherwise resembled. Recalling his own past preoccupation with depictions of Greenland (and detailing his previous publications on the subject), Fischer confidently judged the Schbab map with Greenland to have been made after 1513, not only because it was so different from the Ulm (Nicolaus Germanus) world map, but also because it reflected some features found in the map that Waldseemüller had made for the 1513 Strasbourg edition of the *Geographia*. These features convinced him that Schbab's main source for this map had been the 1513 Strasbourg volume. Among the similarities between the Schbab map and the 1513 Waldseemüller map, Fischer mentioned the lack of any kind of Iceland west of Greenland. Both maps mentioned the Tartars— Schbab referred "in the high north" to *alaniscythe nunc tartari* (Scythian Alanis, now Tartars), and Waldseemüller had a similar reference east of his large Caspian Sea. Furthermore, the two maps gave similar treatments to the *Sinus Magnus* (Great Gulf).[152]

As a maritime feature in the far eastern *oekumene*, the concept of a *Sinus Magnus* goes all the way back to Ptolemy, therefore it is not in itself surprising to find it represented on Ptolemaic world maps made in the late fifteenth and early sixteenth centuries. O. A. W. Dilke notes that Ptolemy's *Sinus Magnus* has usually been assumed to refer to the Gulf of Tonkin (off the coast of Indochina), and he cautions that there is no reasonable argument for interpreting it as the Pacific—one must be very careful about arguing on the basis of early printed editions of Ptolemy.[153] By the same token, however, we do not know what Waldseemüller associated with this feature in 1513, and we can only guess what Fischer read into it while comparing the Schbab and Waldseemüller world maps. He was certainly familiar with Waldseemüller's 1507 *Cosmographiae Introductio*, which said:

> Now, however, the continents have been researched more comprehensively, and a fourth one has been discovered by Americus Vesputius (as can be heard subsequently), I would not know why anyone should object to naming this continent Amerigo or America, after its discoverer Americus, a man of great ingenuity and wit, as both Europe and Asia were given female names. Its location and the customs of its people can easily be gathered from the two journeys Americus made twice, as described in detail below.[154]

To this description one must add Fischer's own conviction that from Ptolemy's time to his own, people had been able to think globally. He was equally certain that the medieval Norse had conveyed information back to Europe about the existence of an American mainland, and that Claudius Clavus, "the first cartographer of America," had given concrete cartographical expression to that ancient Norse information. From such basic tenets it would not require much of an intellectual leap to reconcile Waldseemüller's 1513 delineation of the *Sinus Magnus* (which cuts deeply into East Asia on a north-south axis) with a proto-Pacific *Magnum mare Tartarorum*—another cartographical tease on the Vínland Map that also ties in with the enigmatic hint, on Waldseemüller's 1507 world map, that an ocean must be separating the American New World from Asia.

During his analysis of the Schbab codex, Fischer studied the watermarks in the paper used for the manuscript. He found them particularly interesting because one of those marks was so far unknown; it did not appear in Briquet's *Les Filigranes*, he observed.[155] In other words, Fischer was familiar with the same 1907 Briquet volumes that Laurence Witten consulted in 1957 and subsequently used to convince others that the *Speculum Historiale* fragments and the "Tartar Relation" had originally been parts of a codex using paper with a watermark corresponding to Briquet's sketch number 15056. Fischer would have had no more trouble than Witten in assigning the approximate date and regional origin of the bull's-head mark found in the Vínland Map's companion manuscripts because the likely possibilities in Briquet start with number 15046, which has the six-pronged "star" topping the midline above the head, and after number 15057 the differences are so marked that it would be hard to confuse them with the earlier ones.[156]

A Moravian Castle Library

All commercially manufactured paper in the mid-fifteenth century would have had a watermark, but nobody thought it necessary to note the mark(s) in the paper used in a comparatively insignificant volume that Gilhofer and Ranschburg were offering as item 292 in the same 1934 auction catalogue that described the Schbab codex as item 81 and featured selected items from Mikulov Castle in Brno (Nikolsburg Castle in Brünn) in Moravia (see Figure 25). When the bibliophile Beda Dudik had catalogued the collection in 1865, it had dazzled him with manuscripts dating from the fifteenth and fourteenth centuries or even earlier, including one from the twelfth or perhaps even the eleventh century that he identified as having once belonged to the library of Ferdinand Hoffmann (1540–1607), the Freiherr of Grünbüchel and Strechau, who had amassed a large number of the exquisite items offered during the Gilhofer and Ranschburg auction of Nikolsburg items.[157]

Among the many important articles from this splendid library, item 292 is a modest offering. It is described as a paper manuscript from the fifteenth century, bound in half-leather, which means that the binding was more recent than the manuscript.[158] There are no other details about the binding, however, nor about the size of the pages, but it was most likely a folio-sized volume, as was the original volume containing the "Tartar Relation" and Yale's *Speculum* selections. In the fifteenth century there were generally two sizes of paper used—small (folio size) and large, the latter roughly double the size of the former and only infrequently employed.[159]

The auction catalogue noted that item 292 was a fragment from the *Speculum Historiale* by Vincent of Beauvais ("Speculum historicum" by "Vicentius Bellovacensis"), taken from the part of the *Speculum* that contained references to King Alfred, Charlemagne, Emperor Otto, and so on. This small, rebound portion consisted of thirty-six leaves in generally good condition except for leaves 7 through 12, which had been damaged by a nail. The catalogue then went on to observe that the neatly written text employed two columns, and that the lettering was touched with red.[160] This description of the writing style and general layout of the *Speculum* fragment for sale in 1934 is certainly reminiscent of the two Vínland Map companion manuscripts, but neither feature would have been unique in that period. Other aspects of that Gilhofer and Ranschburg auction provide better reasons for connecting item 292 with Fischer and the codex containing the Vínland Map's sister manuscripts—and hence with the Vínland Map itself.

One important link to the Yale *Speculum* portions, to which I will return shortly, is the actual contents of the Nikolsburg fragment. Fischer's close connection with Gilhofer and Ranschburg during the period when the Nikolsburg library auctions were taking place is obviously another important aspect to consider, and so is his demonstrably close connection with the Nikolsburg library that was now being auctioned off in three different events. Two auctions had already taken place. The first had been in late November 1933 (again in neutral Switzerland, where buyers would have encountered few export or exchange obstacles) and the second in February and March of 1934, this time in Vienna.[161]

In the mixed paper-and-parchment quires of sixteen leaves each used for the Vínland Map's sister texts, the proportion of parchment to paper in the quires is 1:7. The Gilhofer and Ranschburg auction catalogue described item 292 as an all-paper manuscript totaling thirty-six leaves in good condition (as are the Vínland Map's companion manuscripts in their present form), except for the nail holes running through leaves 7 through 12. The sale description does not say how many pages had been left blank, but it is in any case unlikely that the unused part of a quire would have been cut away. The "Tartar Relation" scribe had left blank several pages of valuable writing surface, which demonstrates that even parsimony did not tempt him to break up a quire.

As noted in Chapter 4, quires of sixteen leaves (thirty-two pages) were somewhat less common than quires with eight leaves, but multiples of eight would be involved in either case. Three quires of eight leaves each would yield

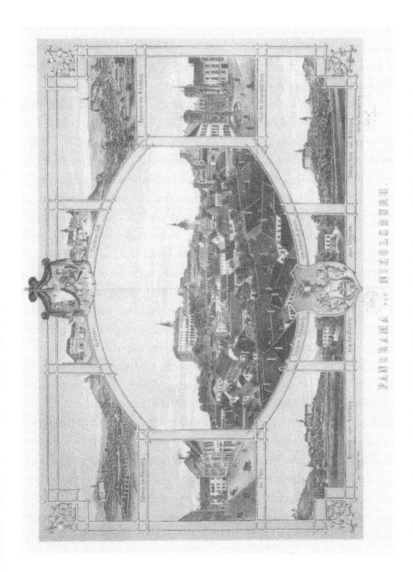

Figure 25. Panoramic view (1869) of Nikolsburg Castle, Brünn (Mikulov Castle, Brno), now in the Czech Republic. The castle was damaged in World War II and has since been restored. Source: The British Library (Maps 27515 (3), London). Reproduced with permission.

a total of twenty-four leaves, while four quires so constituted would provide thirty-two leaves—not thirty-six. Two quires of sixteen leaves each would similarly yield only thirty-two leaves. Unless item 292 had been missing some leaves at the time of its rebinding, one must therefore assume that the scribe had used three quires of twelve leaves each—which would probably also explain why leaves 7 through 12 (the entire second half of the first quire) had a hole from a nail going through the right half of a quire, which may have been left open at the time the damage occurred.

Quires of twelve leaves are certainly not a rarity. [162] They were used in a mid-fifteenth-century Nikolsburg manuscript that Beda Dudik recorded in 1865 while making his list of the manuscripts then in the castle library—a list that included neither the *Speculum* fragment offered as item 292 in 1934 nor any parent volume damaged from the loss of three twelve-leaf quires. In fact, a perusal of Dudik's whole list makes it clear that he took no interest in impaired or incomplete manuscripts. Among the codices that passed muster was one containing the *Biblia pauperum* (Poor man's Bible) in German, with the year 1456 inscribed at the end. Dudik described the work as neatly written on mixed paper and parchment quires. These were made up of twelve leaves, with parchment constituting the outer and inner sheets (leaves 1 and 12, 6 and 7). [163] In other words, their composition resembled the one used in the *Speculum* and "Tartar Relation" manuscripts from the same period and general region, except that the number of leaves involved was different. If parchment was not available to the scribe writing the portion of the *Speculum* being offered as item 292, it would have been easy to make up all-paper quires of twelve leaves each. Three such quires would produce thirty-six leaves.

Although an earlier owner had clearly considered this manuscript fragment worth rebinding, it was evidently uninteresting to twentieth-century collectors because it failed to sell at the auction. Despite my innumerable efforts to track it down, the present location of this *Speculum* fragment is unknown even to the firm of Gilhofer and Ranschburg, which now exists as two separate Swiss and Austrian entities, from both of which I received replies to my inquiries. [164] The bulk of the Nikolsburg library had already been purchased in 1931 by the textile magnate Josef Barton and is now state-owned property in the Archives of the Castle of Zamrsk in the Czech Republic. Only old and potentially valuable items were sold separately, either by private tender or at the Swiss and Austrian auctions of 1933 and 1934. [165] Because it contained just a single book from the *Speculum*, item 292 had only its age, its former noble home, and its association with Vincent of Beauvais to recommend it to a twentieth-century collector wealthy enough to contemplate buying Nikolsburg treasures. Those attractions evidently were not sufficient either to lure a buyer at the auction or to record the item's subsequent fate separately.

It is doubtful that just a single book of the *Speculum Historiale* would have had sufficient value even in the mid-fifteenth century for anyone to order a copy of that and nothing else. If joined to the "Tartar Relation" and the four *Speculum* books now in Yale's possession, however, the value and original purpose of item 292 would look very different.

According to the Gilhofer and Ranschburg catalogue, the *Speculum* fragment from Nikolsburg Castle concerned King Alfred, Charlemagne, and Emperor Otto, among others.[166] This description identifies it as the book that sequentially belongs immediately after the four books that Yale obtained in connection with the Vínland Map transactions. If one uses the Yale thirty-two-book numeration system for the *Speculum*, the Nikolsburg fragment would be Book XXV (following Books XXI–XXIV); if one uses the 1624 Douai edition's thirty-one-book numeration, it would have to represent Book XXIV (following Books XX–XXIII). This is the book that deals with Charlemagne, King Alfred, and King Henry I of England, King Louis the Pious of France, and the emperors Otto I, II, and III. In large part, this section concerns the threat to Christian Europe from the heathen peoples pressing in from the east. Together with the four preceding books, it would have formed a logical bridge to the subject of the "Tartar Relation." To a mid-fifteenth-century European in the Bohemian-Moravian region, where the Tartars were once again pressing against the borders, such a combination of historical information about the enemy would have made perfect sense.[167]

Chapter 6 discussed the reference to "the third part" in the *Speculum* colophon of Yale's Book XXIV and noted, among other things, that this concluding remark indicates that the original fifteenth-century volume had contained only a selection from the still-popular Beauvais work. The differences between the *Speculum* portions and the "Tartar Relation" in style and materials (see Chapters 4 and 6) also suggest that although joined in a common binding, these portions had constituted two different, but closely related, scribal projects. Such an arrangement would have been particularly likely if the person commissioning the work wanted the job completed in a rather short time. There is no reason why a Book XXV (Douai XXIV) might not have constituted a third part of such a project, undertaken by a scribe who had no parchment to hand when he made up his quires and who therefore resorted to quires of twelve paper leaves each.

It is ascertainable that item 292 at the 1934 Swiss auction represented all or part of Book XXV (Douai XXIV) of the *Speculum Historiale*, described as written in a manner similar to those in the Yale fragments. Most likely it dated from the first half of the fifteenth century, before the advent of printing in 1450 made such works as the complete *Speculum* widely available to the not-so-rich. The concern in Book XXV (Douai XXIV) with Christian kings and their handling of brutal infidels would have found an echo in the Bohemian-Moravian region in the 1430s and 1440s, where religious and political leaders alike were preoccupied with the continuing Hussite wars and with the Turks who had already made deadly incursions into Hungary. Anyone during that period, and in that general region, who was rich and interested enough to commission a copy of past works with a direct bearing on such problems, would probably not have settled for just that one book of the *Speculum*. It is just as unlikely that someone would have commissioned a combination of the four preceding Beauvais books and the "Tartar Relation" without the logical bridge that Book XV (Douai XXIV) provides.

None of these considerations actually proves that item 292 had originally been a part of the same project as the Vínland Map's sister manuscripts, but together they strongly suggest that this was the case. The rebound fragment's slightly different material composition may well have made it more prone than the other parts to fall out of the parent volume after much use or in consequence of rough treatment. Indeed, the history of the Nikolsburg Castle library had included crises of the kind that gives archivists nightmares.

When Dudik catalogued the collection's manuscripts in 1865, he also consulted previous catalogues of Nikolsburg items. One was the 1631 work of a Georg Dingenauer, S.J., the original of whose list of the Nikolsburg collection was still in the Brünn Landesarchiv in 1865 but had been made obsolete within a few years, thanks to the ravages of the Thirty Years' War (1618–48). The library collected by the castle's first owner, Cardinal Franz von Dietrichstein (d. 1636), was seized in 1645 by the Swedes, who had conquered the castle on April 7, and both books and manuscripts were crated and shipped back to Stockholm, where the Royal Library still has a list of the works from that booty. (Eventually, in 1855, some of the manuscripts that had remained in the Swedish queen's possession were donated to the Vatican Library.) As far as Dudik could tell, all of the cardinal's books had been taken away at that time. The end of the

Thirty Years' War and the return of Nikolsburg Castle to private owners did not signal the end to all local upheavals. When Johann Cajetan Neuhaus, a canon of Nikolsburg, made a catalogue of the more recent castle collections in 1814, his task was severely hampered by the fact that he had to perform it in the large horse stable because the large library room in the castle was serving as a hospital during the war with the French.[168]

Under any such turbulent circumstances, old and brittle volumes would have been especially likely to suffer harm, and such a huge collection moved from one location to another would have confronted its owner with a formidable task if one or more quires had fallen out of its binding and become separated from the rest of the contents. Rather than search for the damaged parent volume during a cleanup, a careful custodian would have been better off rebinding any reasonably valuable fragment, as seems to have been done with item 292.

As the two-volume Gilhofer and Ranschburg auction catalogue of the Dietrichstein family library at Nikolsburg indicated, the collection included valuable manuscripts with miniatures from the ninth through the fifteenth centuries. Many of them must therefore have been in earlier collections elsewhere, and they would have been subjected to many transfers and other potential perils during their existence. One therefore cannot take it for granted that all damaged volumes in the post-1648 Nikolsburg library had been in mint condition when they arrived there.

Perhaps as much as two-thirds of the Nikolsburg collection that Dudik catalogued, and that was still in the library when it was disbanded in 1931, constituted the private library of the Austrian bibliophile Ferdinand Hoffmann (1540–1607), Freiherr of Grünbüchel and Strechau. His father, Hans Hoffmann (circa 1480–1564) had owned more than half of Upper Styria (in upper and central Austria) by the time he died, and Ferdinand used much of his inherited wealth to add to the many valuable items that came into his possession by other means. When the well-known bibliophile E. P. Goldschmidt surveyed the Nikolsburg library in 1916, he estimated the Hoffmann-owned contribution to have been around ten thousand printed and manuscript volumes, for which several sources could be identified.[169]

A catalogue dating from 1515 lists the collection in a Styrian castle from Maximilian I's time and shows that an old family library must have been one source of Ferdinand Hoffmann's collection because the list included thirty-six works, mostly Latin classics, of which a Friedrich Hoffmann was said to be the

owner. Ferdinand Hoffmann's own most important acquisition was his purchase (date unknown) of some five hundred volumes that had constituted the
library of Hieronymus Holzschuher, since 1499 the husband of Hieronymus
Münzer's only child Dorothea. Hieronymus Holzschuher died in 1529, but his
library remained in Nuremberg until 1600. In accounting for how the Hoffmann library eventually came into the possession of the Dietrichstein family
and was transferred to Nikolsburg, Goldschmidt wrote that Prince Ferdinand
of Dietrichstein (the great-nephew of Cardinal Franz von Dietrichstein, whose
library had been taken to Sweden) was the guardian of Ferdinand von Hoffmann's last life heirs, Maria Elisabeth and Johanna—rich young women whom
Prince Ferdinand sensibly married off to two relatives. In gratitude for his
guardianship, his two former charges gave him the library that had belonged to
their great-grandfather. The collection came to Nikolsburg in 1669.[170]

The Gilhofer and Ranschburg auction catalogue of the Nikolsburg items
naturally reflects the interests that had been at work in collecting the early
items. These interests would presumably also have indicated the Dietrichstein
castle-owners' individual concerns, although the catalogue notes that most of
the 1933–34 sale items carry the ex libris of Ferdinand Hoffmann (which the
first catalogue volume reproduces), from whose home region of Styria the
mapmaker Schbab had also come, according to Fischer. Besides the Schbab
Ptolemy manuscript and the *Speculum* fragment already discussed, the collection contained other valuable early maps as well as a number of works on
Christian confrontations with pagans and on early travel. Listed among the
mid-fifteenth-century manuscripts are a paper transcript (1440) of the *Welt-
chronik ("Christherrechronik")* by the thirteenth-century poet Rudolf von Ems
and a German translation of Ordericus de Pordenone's *De mirabilibus oriental-
ium Tartarorum germanie* (Reise in die Tartarei), the latter bound in a sixteenth-
century half-leather cover although the manuscript itself is dated to about 1450.

Goldschmidt observed that Holzschuher's books, especially those acquired
in later years, have no owner's mark, so that conclusions about provenance
must sometimes be based solely on the bindings, each of which had the title
of the book carefully inscribed on the back in red ink. He also noted that
except for those books that were still in their original bindings, the volumes
that Hoffmann had owned had been bound in green leather with his coat of
arms on the cover. However, as the title of Goldschmidt's book suggests, he
was primarily interested in tracing the works that had once belonged to
Hieronymus Münzer. In the Nikolsburg library, he identified seven manu-

Figure 26. Stella Matutina's oval library stamp, done in purple-blue ink, would have been on every item Father Josef Fischer, S.J., acquired for his institution, including on items intended for his personal study. Source: The author's own collection.

scripts and 165 printed books that definitely had belonged to the famous Nuremberger. On the front cover of about half of those volumes, Münzer had written his name and the date when he purchased the work. All of Münzer's books had been bound in Nuremberg by the bookbinder who also worked for Hartmann Schedel, the publisher of the *Nuremberg Chronicle* (1493), with the commonest type of binding being brown calf with blind-tooled decorations.[171]

While Goldschmidt's general information concerning bindings, owners' marks, and other details certainly does not enable us to identify the binding that once held both of the Vínland Map's sister manuscripts, it does suggest why someone wanting to disguise the provenance of an old work would re-stitch and reback the volume as well as get rid of any pastedowns with revealing marks and notations. Replacing bottom strips on text pages falls into quite another category, however, because it suggests removal of an institutional stamp and not of the owner's mark from a private library.

Chapter 4 discussed the excision on the *Speculum* parchment leaf marked "233," where a reddish-purple, curved smudge of ink remains in the bottom line and shows through on the *verso*. As already noted, the color is unrelated to the touches of red used in the text. Anyone who has used benzene or a similar cleaning fluid to remove old-fashioned stamping ink knows the change from purple-blue to purple-red and the fruitlessness of any attempt to make the latter disappear. My copy of Fischer's publication "Massenas Sturm auf Feldkirch" carries the oval, purple-blue library stamp of Stella Matutina, which would have been on every item Fischer acquired for his institution, even if primarily intended for his own study (see Figure 26). Under the rules of his Jesuit Order, he would not have possessed private property as such.[172]

Just as there are weighty reasons to credit Fischer with creating the Vínland Map, there are good grounds for believing that he obtained the original

Speculum and "Tartar Relation" manuscripts in their disintegrating binding at the time when the Nikolsburg library was being dismantled and Gilhofer and Ranschburg had asked him to evaluate the Schbab manuscript from that collection. This Fischer had done in a manner that was certain to enhance the item's value at the auction. It would have been reasonable for either the auction house or the Dietrichstein heirs to offer him a chance to pick out—as a gift or for a reasonable price—one or more items too dilapidated to bring to auction but still of potential value to a scholar and teacher.

Only a unique combination of circumstances could have put the volume with the *Speculum* portions and the "Tartar Relation" into the hands of a poor, but honest scholar. It is hard to imagine an opportunity for such a transaction in Fischer's part of the world, during the pertinent time frame, other than the disbanding of the ancient Nikolsburg library. A broken binding, containing four books of the *Speculum Historiale* and what would have seemed to most observers an inferior version of the Carpini report, would not have been worthy of a high-profile Gilhofer and Ranschburg auction.

Prior to 1931, when the Dietrichsteins' Nikolsburg collection was still intact, it had held many attractions for Fischer. Hieronymus Münzer, for example, was of major interest to him because of the learned Nuremberger's intellectual connections, his forays into cartography, and his advocacy of a westward crossing to Cathay just when Columbus had proved that such an Atlantic voyage was feasible. It is therefore not surprising to learn from Goldschmidt's treatise on the Nikolsburg collections that Fischer was very familiar with the castle library. In fact, Goldschmidt's book is dedicated to Fischer and repeatedly refers to his publications and opinions regarding the history of German cartography.

When I visited Wolfegg Castle, I asked about Fischer's connection with Nikolsburg. Count Maximilian replied that his family would have given Fischer their personal recommendations to the Dietrichstein family, and that Fischer had probably used the Nikolsburg Castle library many times to search for items related to early cartography.[173] There, he would have found a wealth of material to aid him in his research because it contained old maps—the Schbab Ptolemy volume being just one example—as well as items concerned with early travels and missionary activity.

Like the noble family at Wolfegg, the Dietrichsteins were German Catholics. This was no problem in Württemberg at the time when Fischer was doing his Münzer research, but it was a growing liability in Moravia, where the

Nikolsburg family had come under increasing stress after World War I. When the heirs to the last Dietrichstein owner of this handsome castle disbanded the library in 1931 and called in the firm of Gilhofer and Ranschburg, it appears to have been a first move toward giving up the property itself, prompted by the double pressure of anti-German feelings in the new Czechoslovakian Republic and by the implementation of a Land Reform Act designed to curtail and redistribute the holdings of great German Catholic landowners like themselves. In the general economic crisis that enveloped both the United States and Europe after 1930, Czechoslovakia was particularly hard hit by unemployment due to curtailed exports and cuts in production, and the so-called Sudeten Germans found themselves the target of increasing anti-German sentiment on the part of Czechs and Slovaks alike. When Austria and Germany signed a Customs Union in March 1931, the small Czech Republic refused to join, fearing that once more it would be placed at a severe disadvantage.[174] Small wonder, then, that under such circumstances the Dietrichstein heirs decided to disband the collection in 1931 and let the firm of Gilhofer and Ranschburg sell the more important items during the same auction that featured the manuscript edition of the *Geographia* lent to Fischer, who must have received it for study in 1931— in other words rather early in a disposal process that would have begun with sorting out the most important items from thousands and thousands of volumes.[175]

Father Fischer's Choice

A Stella Matutina photograph of an aging Fischer shows him at his ample work-table surrounded by many large volumes and with bookcases in the background.[176] Regrettably, there is no record anywhere of what the Stella Matutina library contained when the Nazis took over the institution, but it is clear that it was very well stocked and that it catered as much as possible to Fischer's research and reference needs. Any identifiable mid-fifteenth-century manuscript, however dilapidated, would have been a nice addition to his beloved institution's library, but especially such a recognizably regional and Church-related work as the "Tartar Relation."

Thoroughly acquainted with both the *Speculum* and Carpini's *Historia Mongalorum*, which he would have been well able to read in Latin, Fischer would have wanted the "Tartar Relation" precisely because it differs from the standard version and because it had local value. He would not have had to read farther than paragraph eleven to see the author's Bohemian reference point in recounting the story of the Khan's son who went *ad orientem hyemalem* (the phrase must have struck Fischer forcefully, because it recurs in a different context in the longer legend about Vínland on the map), nor would it have taken long for someone of his experience to date the volume by the watermarks in the paper. The pastedowns would have provided further dating clues, whether they were still in place (with some of the writing showing through and still with an old owner's mark) or merely displaying the offset impressions described in Chapter 4. It is in any event beyond dispute that the Vínland Map is generally suitable to a circa 1440 codex and uses a number of expressions found only in De Bridia's account.

It is unlikely that any other motives besides investigating the "Tartar Relation" as a hitherto unknown aspect of the Carpini mission would have played a part in the research and collecting decisions that Fischer made before the end of 1932. Despite the increasingly alarming situation across the border in Germany, from which the Stella Matutina seventy-five-year anniversary celebrations had provided a distraction, he had little reason at that time to think that his own future or the future of his highly respected institution in the Austrian Vorarlberg region could be seriously threatened, especially because he had experienced so many political and economic anxieties, ever since World War I began, that such a state would eventually have seemed the normal order.

At the personal level, as 1932 drew to a close, Fischer could bask in the knowledge that he had completed his big Ptolemy study and had earned recognition from the pope as well as from other scholars. Now he was free to tackle other projects that had been pushed aside. He could not know that he was about to enter the worst period of his life.

Annus horribilis—1933

Confidence in the future is evident in Stella Matutina's expansion of its physical plant during the 1920s. This expansion was partly a response to the authorization that the German educational bureaucracy had given the school in 1924, allowing it as a foreign institution to grant the official German Abitur degree permitting entry to university level education. A new building for gymnastics and indoor games was inaugurated in 1929, and the following year saw the graduation of the first twenty German students who had benefited from the new arrangement. However, barely ten years after the German authorization had been given, it was withdrawn. The last German students graduated in 1934, subsequent to a notification in August 1933 that by the following April, Stella Matutina's large contingent of German students must be transferred to Saint Blaise in Switzerland if they wished to continue their education in a Jesuit school. An Austrian Jesuit school could no longer grant them valid diplomas.[177]

The reason for this sudden decision is not hard to find. After years of political turbulence in Germany and strained relations between Austria and Germany, the Germans had a new chancellor. Adolf Hitler had ascended to power at the start of 1933, riding the wave of general postwar discontent that had allowed his German National Socialist Party to flourish. Hitler and his party were both anti-Catholic and anti-Semitic. The modern German historian Christian Jansen believes that the Nazis could not have gained their footing without the nationalistic, antiliberal, and authoritarian style of the German leadership elite, which included university professors. The large majority of the German ruling elite consisted of Protestants, with Catholics and Jews decidedly in the minority.[178] Things did not bode well for institutions like Stella Matutina.

The withdrawal of German degree-granting status was only the first Nazi move against an Austrian school proud of having had eighty of its students enter the priesthood, among the 436 who had graduated in the period 1920–34.[179] Although direct action in Austria by German Nazis did not take place until Hitler invaded that country in 1938, Fischer and his Stella Matutina colleagues would have had early experience with the new Third Reich in a number of ways and would certainly have reacted to the arrests of German Catholic priests, which began almost immediately in 1933 and left little doubt by 1934 of what the future was likely to hold for defenders of the Roman faith.[180] For example, on April 23, 1935, the Bavarian Secret Police issued secret instructions to all police stations concerning the Jesuits, who were to be prevented from public assembly and to be carefully monitored in their private assemblies. In addition, together with all the other clergy the Jesuits were now forbidden to refer to others as "unchristian."[181]

For Fischer, one consequence of this development would have been an effective stop to his further publication with the German series *Stimmen der Zeit* (formerly *Stimmen aus Maria-Laach*), which had turned sharply political almost immediately. From the start of 1934, many articles in that old and respectable series were concerned with the impact of National Socialism and the authoritarian state on society and religion in general and on the Roman

Church in particular. In that first 1934 volume, Joseph Schröteler described Hitler's October 1933 Rückeberg speech as having revealed the nature of the upheavals that had just taken place, and he declared that the National Socialist Party was concerned neither with individuals nor with humanity.[182] Fischer is hardly likely to have disagreed with this description of the Nazis, but it was evidently not in his nature to be politically active. Nor would his school administration have encouraged him to become overtly involved after 1933 because the Jesuit Order had a long and strong tradition of avoiding needless confrontations.

The record of Fischer's publications after 1933 demonstrates that he responded to the new developments much as he had to World War I and the difficult period that followed—he continued to serve Stella Matutina and his church while seeking intermittent refuge in his learning. Although his response to the political realities of the day was so oblique that one might think he had simply ignored them, it is clear that he did not turn a blind eye, for after 1933 he wrote no more articles about medieval missionaries and other traveling emissaries of the Roman Church. In fact, he published nothing at all for several years, and when he finally resumed publication of any kind in 1939, he did not produce another word about the Norse, despite his revived enthusiasm for the subject while analyzing the Schbab manuscript.

The long reach of the medieval Roman Church would have been a politically sensitive topic, while any subject involving the medieval Norse would have been taboo for somewhat different reasons. Having grown up in German-occupied Norway, I still remember the revulsion with which all but the local Nazis reacted to the Third Reich glorification of the Teutonic (Aryan) people, through the concoction of an historical past in which Hitler and his culture bearers linked the Germans directly with the supposedly blond and brave Old Norse. In Norway or anywhere else, honest scholars like Fischer could not in conscience touch the subject of the Old Norse in public for many years to come because of Rosenberg, Reinerth, and other "scholars" who were twisting German prehistory in this manner. Adolf Rieth, a German museum expert who watched these developments at close hand, observed: "Research without prejudice was henceforward forbidden and naturally both the work and the nation suffered."[183]

Seven years passed before Fischer published anything after the 1932 launch of his grand work on the early Greek Ptolemy manuscripts in the Vatican. This long interval was due neither to a lack of uncontaminated subjects nor to an old man's need for rest, for while he had never been strong, his health had still allowed him to visit Rome in late 1932. Furthermore, between 1939 and 1942 he produced six more articles. Instead, the hiatus had complex, personal causes for which none of the honors still coming his way could compensate, and which must truly have made 1933 the pivot that tipped his life toward the shadows.

The first blow fell in early 1933, when his magnum opus on Ptolemy, the pride of his professional life, was prominently slaughtered. None other than Leo Bagrow reviewed the four new volumes briefly, but devastatingly, in the noted German journal *Petermanns geographische Mitteilungen*. After punctiliously describing the contents of the volumes and the vast amount of labor and erudition this long-awaited work represented, and before expressing regrets that such an expensively produced work would be available to only a few, Bagrow commented witheringly that Fischer was once more claiming that maps had been a significant part of the *Geographia* from the beginning—indeed, Fischer had argued that except for the world map, the maps handed down in early manuscripts conform closely to Ptolemy's text, and he believed that Ptolemy himself had drawn these maps.[184]

Bagrow's longtime London friend Dr. Loewenson described him as not always easy to deal with, being "masterful by disposition, and revealing not infrequently a peremptory temper and formidable obstinacy." The plainspoken Bagrow evidently had run-ins with most of his associates at one time or another, but these disagreements "were seldom lasting, for malice was foreign to him."[185] However that may have been, Bagrow made clear once more in the pages of *Imago Mundi*, published a couple of years after his first review, that he strongly disagreed with Fischer's views. In his opinion, Fischer had failed to deal with a number of problems and therefore had not convinced him of his thesis. Despite the shortcomings of Fischer's Ptolemy study, it was nevertheless a valuable reference tool, the reviewer noted, but in a tone so patronizing that it is not likely to have comforted the book's author.[186]

Judging from an account that Bagrow wrote right after he had heard about Fischer's death, he had been both surprised and disturbed to learn how upset his first (1933) review had made Fischer. In a preface to the English translation of his own treatise on Ptolemy, Bagrow wrote:

> I deeply deplore that Dr. Fischer did not have the opportunity of reading my present work. Dr. J. Fischer knew, however, my views on Ptolemy's *Geographia*. He had read my first review of his work, he wrote and told me how grieved he was when to see [*sic*] that so large a labor of his had not, despite all, proved anything. He had

nightmares; he suffered because he could not translate into German "*Parturiunt montes, nascetur ridiculus mus.*" To my sincere regret I received the following day, a letter from the academician Kubitschek, Vienna, who said that he shared my views and would write J. Fischer about it. Poor old man! I availed myself of the first opportunity to pay him a visit at Feldkirch and express my regret for the grief which I had caused him.[187]

It is difficult to understand what possible joy Fischer could have received from Bagrow's essay on Ptolemy (originally written in German in 1938), because it merely reiterated why Bagrow was right in his views and Fischer had been wrong.

W. Kubitschek's personal letter to Fischer, advising him that another negative review (and a long one at that) was coming, would have reached the aging scholar at Stella Matutina when he was still reeling from Bagrow's first volley and while he, like everyone else around him, had to grapple with the consequences of Nazi rule in Germany as well as with increasingly worrying developments in Austria.[188]

Outwardly, Stella Matutina nevertheless remained forward-looking and stubbornly dedicated to education and religion, as demonstrated by the fact that it renovated its school chapel in 1935 and expanded its educational curriculum in 1936.[189] By the same token, Fischer would have been occupied with many institutional concerns during the day. But he was no longer active day to day in the classroom, and it is evident that just after his enthusiastic involvement with the Schbab manuscript and the disposal of the Nikolsburg library, he entered a period of being unable to focus on research and writing.

Retirement

The redoubtable Eila Campbell was known for her sharp intuition. In 1974, she wrote presciently: "I wondered, as long ago as 1962 . . . if [the Vínland Map] had been compiled by an historian of cartography who during the World War II had taken refuge in a library and thus had time on his hands both to read the [Tartar Relation] (assuming he came across it) and to draw a map."[190]

Campbell died the day before I called our mutual friend Helen Wallis in 1994 to tell her that I had traced the 1765 source of the Vínland Map's reference to a joint American discovery by Leif and Bjarni. With a percipience equaling Campbell's, Wallis had suggested in 1990 that the Vínland Map might be a joke or a tease—the product of jeu d'ésprit.[191] Before Wallis died on February 7, 1995, she knew that I had probably found "an historian of cartography who during the World War II had . . . had time on his hands" to draw a playful map full of cartographical and textual enigmas, invented by a man who fully knew the joys and frustrations attendant on the discovery of a hitherto unknown map. I felt as certain then as I still do that this mapmaker was Father Josef Fischer, S.J.

Although Fischer's retirement gave him time on his hands for the first time in his adult life, the depressed spirits in which he appears to have entered his formal retirement would have made it difficult for him to use his free hours in the same way as before, and his depression would not have been improved by the restless nights that he described for Bagrow. While it is not for anyone to say whether making the Vínland Map put him on the road to recovery, it seems clear that it was during this period that motive and opportunity coalesced for him.

By this time in Fischer's life, he would have received any unauctionable items procured for Stella Matutina from the Nikolsburg library, and it is probable that one of those items would have been the broken-down binding with the *Speculum* portions and the "Tartar Relation." It seems certain that this old volume was the source of the map parchment. Once catalogued by the Stella Matutina library and provided with the school stamp, its next likely stop would have been Fischer's own desk so he could study the "Tartar Relation" as originally intended, before it had become risky to write about medieval papal missions.

Active minds faced with disturbed sleep tend to search for distraction of some kind, and there is little reason to believe that Fischer would have responded differently. Recent developments within his intellectual and linguistic sphere would furthermore have provided plenty of food for thought. In a recent book entitled *Maps and History: Constructing Images of the Past,* Jeremy Black noted: "Geopolitics in general became more important in the 1920s and 1930s and influenced Nazi ideas from early in the party's history. German geopolitics was to affect Nazi foreign policy." Black referred to separate works by H. Kot and David Murphy concerning "the degeneration of German geopolitical maps in the 1920s and early 1930s, as objective geographic standards and values were abandoned in favour of tendentious presentation in response to the aggressive and racist conservatism of geopolitical circles in this period."[192] Surveying the thrust of Nazi cartography after Hitler's rise to power in 1933, Mark Monmonier dryly remarked that "the Nazi ideologues who ruled Germany from 1933 to 1945 warrant special mention."[193]

Father Fischer spent a lifetime viewing history through maps. Nothing gave him greater pleasure than to parse an old map's texts and delineations or to imagine how an old text could have been translated cartographically. It is quite unthinkable that he would not have reacted to the Nazis' manipulations of history, geography, and cartography to create a falsified record of Germanic hegemony-by-ancient-rights and to glorify their supposedly Aryan past. It is just as unlikely that he would have been unaware of a book published in 1924 entitled *Die Entdeckung des Paradieses* (The discovery of paradise), in which Franz von Wenden insisted that Paradise, the Garden of Eden, had actually been in Germany, and that it was the Jews who had made the false claim that it was in Asia.[194]

Von Wenden's ideas would have seemed as outrageous to a pious and upright cartographic historian as a new edition (1931) of an historical atlas intended for school use. This work not only had a map showing the supposed territory of "Greater Germany's" linguistic and cultural influence (hence German by rights), but also it featured as its very first map a depiction of "Germany as the bulwark of European culture against the Asiatic hordes, the latter depicted in terms of Huns, Avars, Arabs, Magyars, Turks, Mongols, Jews, Czarist Russia, and Communism."[195] It added to the surrealness of the times that in other visual arts, the production of fake "Norse" artifacts of many kinds was a booming business.[196]

There is no telling just when Fischer decided quietly to counter such intellectual outrages and to while away difficult hours by depicting the early worldwide flow of Christian influence. I suggest, however, that the idea started with the availability of parchment suitable for a private exercise and slowly took shape in his head and heart while Nazi threats and propaganda continued their crescendo all around him, tainting the scholarly areas he held most dear.

Quite possibly, the parchment piece(s) used for the map represented parchment that had served to wrap the quires prior to binding, but they would in any case have been likely to be lying there loose already, because Fischer would not have vandalized intact manuscript quires. Loose parchment would have been more prone to soiling than the remaining intact quires of the old volume, which are still surprisingly clean. Only further scientific studies might determine whether it was necessary to piece together two parchment halves with the glued strip now holding the Vínland Map together—an unimportant detail compared with the creation of the actual map.

As discussed in Chapter 6, it is evident from the present state of the Vínland Map's parchment that it was subjected to a somewhat clumsy cleaning by a method that would have depended on the available remedies. The cleaning also appears to have involved a water rinse or wiping with a damp cloth at some point, as Baynes-Cope and Werner observed back in 1967. None of the various scientific investigators have found indications of a palimpsest on the map parchment, so it is probably safe to assume that removal of earlier ink was not necessary. It would certainly have been contrary to Fischer's nature and training to destroy any part of an old map or text, however fragmentary.

Drawing and lettering the map on the cleaned parchment would, like the preliminary cleaning, have involved simple aids and ingredients that were close at hand. Fischer's financial means were very limited, and any mechanical devices or other supplies that Stella Matutina provided would have been strictly targeted to his professional requirements. For his research, he would have needed a light table and a magnifier on a stand, and he would obviously have needed ink. According to the marvelously helpful Isolde Listmayer at the modern Stella Matutina Foundation, not only the school's pupils, but also Fischer and the other teachers used ordinary black or blue ink for writing. Black India ink, being more expensive, was reserved for drawing and decorative lettering, such as making library labels. One of the priests also used a distinctive purple ink for some archival labels, she noted.[197]

Once he had decided on a map design geared to the size of the parchment as well as to the global sweep intended, all Fischer had to do was draw the outlines with India ink on a paper pattern, place it on the surface of his light table, and clamp the parchment on top. When he turned on the light underneath the glass surface, the black outlines would show through the translucent parchment and could easily be traced with either a steel nib or a quill pen dipped in ink. But what kind of ink would he have used? In the absence of a telltale ink pot or other hard evidence representing the proverbial smoking gun, one must rely on the extant information about the components of the ink used, the parchment and the map's current condition, and Fischer and his world.

During Fischer's active years, sophisticated chemical ink analyses of the kind lavished on the Vínland Map were still a long way into the future, but

scholars familiar with medieval manuscripts had long been aware of the varying rates at which old ink deteriorated, as well as of the fact that carbon ink
had been used in the Middle Ages right along with iron-gall inks. As early
as 1898, Father Francesco Ehrle—head of the Vatican Library and Fischer's
friend—had called a conference in St. Gallen in Switzerland because he was
worried about the growing threat to old manuscripts from damage due to ink
corrosion. He wanted to encourage systematic scientific research that might
explain the causes of such destruction by degenerating ink.[198] Fischer would
very likely have followed developments in an area so close to his own concerns
and would also have had enough personal experience to know that color
alone does not give away an ink's age or composition.

Black India ink or even the thinner black ink provided by his school for
everyday use would nevertheless have seemed too black to convey an immediate impression of old ink when seen cheek by jowl with the "Tartar Relation"
and its genuinely aged iron-gall ink. Four of the scientific studies described in
Chapter 6 (by Baynes-Cope and Werner, Walter and Lucy McCrone, Kenneth
Towe, and Katherine Brown and Robin Clark) provide clues to the simple
ingredients that Fischer is likely to have used to make a brownish concoction
intended to simulate old ink.

The black pigment in the ink came mostly from carbon, while the yellow
line remaining on the parchment when the black fell away contains evidence
of modern, industrially modified anatase. In addition, both the McCrone and
the Brown-Clark study found traces of animal collagen in that yellow line.
Commercial India ink and some other black inks were (and are) carbon based,
readily available, and comparatively inexpensive. By the early 1930s, the
Germans were also making excellent colored inks in a variety of hues, bene-
fiting from advances in the production of color pastes with anatase to enhance
the brilliance of other pigments. Animal-based glue would have been just as
widely available, and it would have made good sense to add a few drops to a
water-based ink to make it flow better and adhere to the parchment surface—
and possibly also to control warring elements in the glue itself, if my own
experience is any guide.

A couple of years ago, already convinced by the existing scientific reports
that the black particles in the Vínland Map contained carbon, I experimented
with mixing two water-soluble inks. As soon as I added my Winsor and
Newton's plain, black India ink to a bottle of "Sunshine Yellow" ink by the
same manufacturer in order to darken it, the mixture curdled. It was possible

to stir it together and write with it, but it was clearly not a compatible mixture, and it soon started to separate again in the pot. During my equally informal test with early Norwegian anatase and soot (carbon), the anatase repelled the carbon (see Chapter 6). This suggested to me that the black particles may have separated out from the Vínland Map ink lines over time for the same reason, leaving on the parchment mostly the yellowish color containing the anatase crystals and traces of gelatin or animal glue.

The Brown-Clark study stated unequivocally that the ink is of the same composition throughout the map, in the delineations as well as in both styles of lettering. This again suggests that the makeshift ink had been made from standard, commercially available materials. However, I cannot agree with the explanation, in this latest study, as well as in the McCrone report, that the mapmaker had drawn the yellow line first in order to simulate oxidized iron-gall ink, and that he had topped it with black in a second application. If nothing else, the tiny size of the formal lettering in the longer map legends precludes such an approach. Consequently, if the ink in these legends is the same as that in the larger, informal writing and in the map outlines, all the inking must have been done in single applications.

That is not to say that all the work was done within a brief period. When I try to follow the hand that created the map, I see a project that gradually grew in complexity. First, the map's delineations had to be composed on paper before they were put down on parchment. The larger, informally scripted names and legends were probably added within a short time after the map outline, but the finely written legends seem to have been an afterthought and would in any event have been too time-consuming to be accomplished quickly. There is a complete absence of ruling by stylus or other means for those beautifully scripted lines of tiny letters. Penning them would have required exquisite control even with the aid of the line guide that had clearly been placed underneath—a process that would also have involved a light table allowing a paper line guide to show through to the parchment.

The lines in all of the delicately lettered map legends are exactly two millimeters apart. When Fischer wrote letters, he used an underlying line guide with a ten-millimeter spacing to control a tendency to wavering that is also a noticeable feature in the informal writing on the Vínland Map. A postcard from the Wolfegg Castle Archives shows what happened when he did not use a line guide (see Figure 27). It also demonstrates his ability to write tiny, perfectly shaped letters. Chapter 6 discussed such details in the Vínland Map writing as the inconsistencies in both the letters themselves and in the orthography. There are other notable irregularities as well. For example, while the informal writing on the Vínland Map definitely suggests right-handedness, it wobbles from a straight ninety-degree angle to a right slant of about 105 degrees. This kind of inconsistency easily occurs with attempts to disguise one's usual handwriting. When Fischer wrote letters, his writing slanted to the right at a rather uniform 117–18-degree angle.

Other features in the writing on the Vínland Map suggest Fischer's private writing more strongly. While the obvious dissimilarity between the informal and formal scripts on the map represents no more than the difference one may find between the formal script an architect employs on drawings and the writing that the same architect uses in personal letters and jotted notes, the marked inconsistencies in the larger, informal lettering are idiosyncratic. A handwriting sample from Fischer's correspondence with Bjørnbo shows a similar inconsistency, especially in the formation of capital letters (see Figure 28).[199] In this communication, which is datelined Feldkirch, May 25, 1904, there is a notable difference between the elaborate "F" in "Feldkirch" and the much plainer one found in the second line of the body of the letter, in the word *Funde*.

Fischer was forty-six years old when he wrote this letter to his Danish colleague, and his handwriting was well established. It remained remarkably unchanged over the years. As the sample indicates, it is a firm handwriting with determined down strokes and a horizontally looped and somewhat impatient "d" very similar to the one that occurs repeatedly on the Vínland Map. These features remained consistent in all of the Fischer letters I examined at Wolfegg Castle, the Royal Library in Copenhagen, and the Royal Geographical Society in London.[200] Equally idiosyncratic and recognizable (but not found in the Vínland Map) is the peculiar "flagged" capital "D" found in his letter to Bjørnbo. Frequently, Fischer used a short line above a letter to denote a missing "n" or "m." This mark is also used on the Vínland Map. Neither there nor in Fischer's private writing is it a consistent practice.

With a last elaborate map legend, Fischer completed a work that only a man with his vast erudition could have produced, and that quite clearly had a purpose besides occupying his mind and hands. He was getting on in years, and he had good reason to suppose that if and when the map was discovered at Stella Matutina after his death, it would eventually invite the scrutiny of Hitler's politically correct "scholars." These worthies would then have to decide

Figure 27. A postcard dated November 5, 1901, from Father Josef Fischer, S.J., to the princess of Waldburg-Wolfegg. The writing here shows a wavering tendency similar to that found in the informal writing on the Vínland Map. Note also the finely shaped small lettering at the bottom. Source: Wolfegg Castle Archives. Reproduced with permission.

whether to reject the map's depiction of the early and worldwide influence of the Roman Church, or to swallow that aspect of the work in order to crow over its equally clear depiction of American discovery by their "ancestors" the Norse. Did the Roman Church have the greatest claim to worldwide hegemony? Or might it perhaps be said that because the Norse had been defined as a part of that vast Germanic cultural dominion (in other words, the supposed basis for Hitler's Third Reich ambitions), North America belonged by ancient right to Greater Germany and its new order? Either way, Nazi investigators could be expected to fall victim to their own cultural and geopolitical propaganda. The map represents a carefully constructed dilemma worthy of its author, who had been schooled in logic as well as in moral philosophy. Not in his worst nightmares during that dark period in his life could Fischer have foreseen what actually happened when the map finally surfaced in public.

We must hope that the creator of that exquisite tease derived some cheer

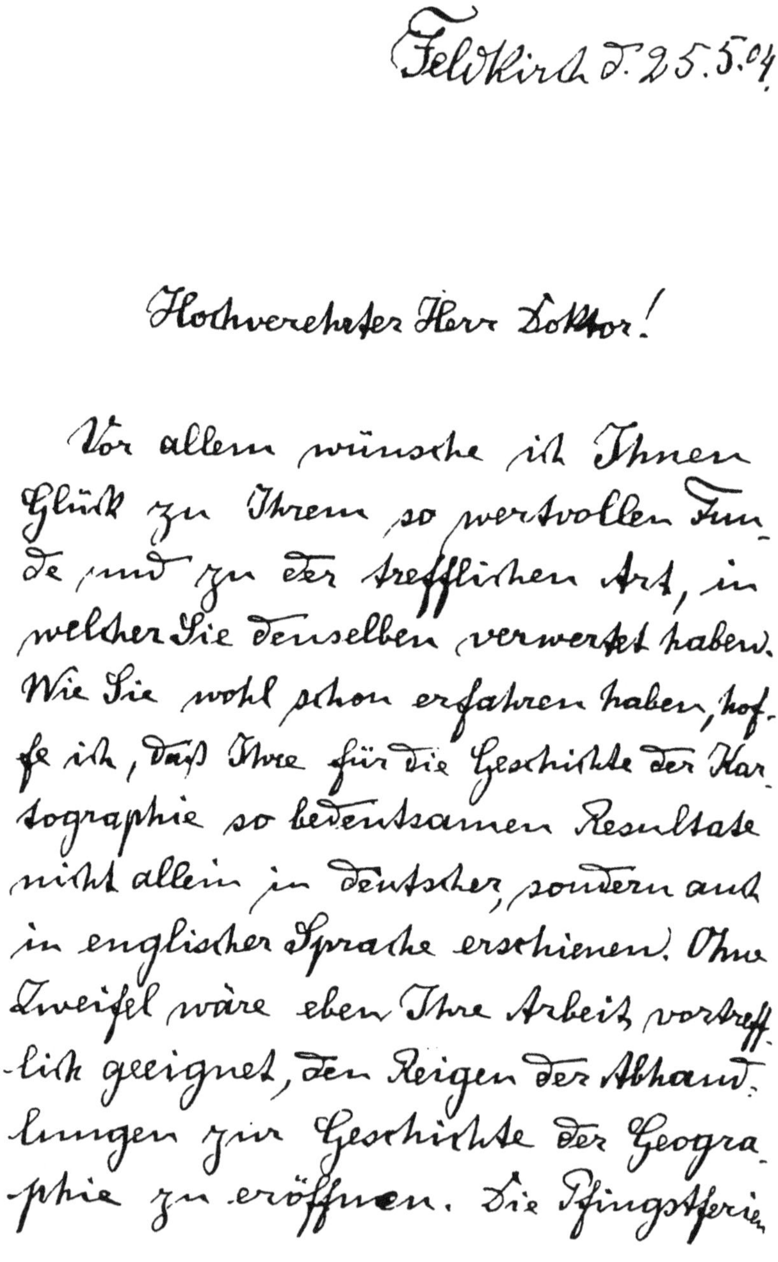

Feldkirch d. 25.5.04

Hochverehrter Herr Doktor!

Vor allem wünsche ich Ihnen Glück zu Ihrem so wertvollen Funde und zu der trefflichen Art, in welcher Sie denselben verwertet haben. Wie Sie wohl schon erfahren haben, hoffe ich, daß Ihre für die Geschichte der Kartographie so bedeutsamen Resultate nicht allein in deutscher, sondern auch in englischer Sprache erschienen. Ohne Zweifel wäre eben Ihre Arbeit vortrefflich geeignet, den Reigen der Abhandlungen zur Geschichte der Geographie zu eröffnen. Die Pfingstferien

Figure 28. A handwriting sample from Father Fischer's correspondence with A. A. Bjørnbo. It reveals considerable inconsistency in the forming of letters, especially capital letters. Source: The Royal Library, Copenhagen, Ny kgl. Samling 2508. 2°, folder 3. Reproduced with permission.

from it in the midst of a political situation that was steadily deteriorating. Fischer's former pupil, Chancellor von Schuschnigg, proved powerless against growing National Socialism within Austria and against the pressures that Hitler's Germany exerted across the border. The Anschluss (Hitler's annexation of Austria) in March 1938 marked the end of Austria's status as an independent republic, and the consequences for Stella Matutina were swift and devastating. During the night of March 11–12, 1938, members of the National Social-Democratic Party occupied Stella Matutina's buildings, and four days later seven hundred German soldiers began a ten-day encampment at the school and caused complete chaos.

By the end of June, all private schools had become subjected to public authority, and a month later, the old Stella Matutina building to the right of the River Ill was forcibly sold to the Germans for seven hundred thousand marks. This relentless chain of events, which followed a pattern recognizable to every nation or group of people who suffered Nazi subjugation, led to the closure of the school on September 29 that same year. One must try to imagine Father Fischer's feelings when he and his remaining Jesuit brothers left Stella Matutina for good on February 13, 1939, after a last High Mass and sacrament in the school chapel and following months of cunning and brutal intimidation.[201]

Fischer was eighty-one years old when he had to leave his home of forty years, taking only a few personal belongings with him to Ignatiushaus, the Jesuit house at Kaulbachstrsse 31a in Munich, where he found shelter for the next two years. The atmosphere there must have been conducive to the resumption of work on projects for which he had brought along notes, because an article discussing Abyssinia on the 1492 Behaim globe appeared in the spring of 1941 and was soon followed by two more on equally safe topics, namely on the eastern Mediterranean region around 1500 and on a world map supposedly from 1519 and made in Venice.[202]

The third article has links to the discussion here. Fischer noted that for many years, the Stella Matutina museum had exhibited a "Depiction of the World by Dolfin Bonaldus, Venice, 1519." Having personally acquired the map for his institution in the belief that it was genuine and that its representation of the New World was well worth studying, Fischer was now no longer entirely certain that the map was genuine, but he was clearly still hoping that it might be. Besides providing fresh evidence of his proneness to wishful thinking, his article demonstrates that he had not been able to take the map with him to

368 The Vinland Map as a Human Creation

Munich, although he was still trying to sort out the identity of "Bonaldus." He had in his possession only a photograph of the map. Equally revealing is the fact that he never mentioned why he no longer had access to the Stella Matutina collections that he had helped to build. All during the German occupation in Norway, one had to write in an equally bland style in order to get past the Nazi censors, but non-Nazi readers could read between the lines.

Fischer may have started work while still in Munich on these three articles, but work must have become increasingly difficult as World War II brought mounting difficulties for the civilian population. Jesuits in particular continued to be prime targets for Nazi spite, as was made clear in May 1941, when Gauleiter Wagner declared that he would have all of the Jesuits out of Bavaria in a few weeks.[203] This was no idle threat, for just a month earlier, the Gestapo had seized the Jesuit house in Munich that held the editorial office and press of the journal *Stimmen der Zeit*. All the inhabitants were kicked out, and everything in the house was confiscated.[204] Although the Ignatiushaus was spared a similar fate, Fischer had every reason to accept an invitation from Count Maximilian zu Waldburg Wolfegg to live at Wolfegg Castle, the place he appears to have treasured above all others outside of Stella Matutina. Again, he packed his few belongings and got on the train, a frail figure indeed, but still of sound mind.

Last Return to Wolfegg

The younger Count Maximilian told me in 1995 that by 1941, Wolfegg Castle was so full of refugees that Father Fischer had to lodge in its dining room. He also said very firmly that they already had a chaplain at the castle, so that Fischer's priesthood would not have been the actual reason for inviting him— although that may have been a convenient story to tell the Nazi authorities in Munich.

It nevertheless appears that Fischer's calling and piety provided spiritual comfort to his surroundings. The older Count Maximilian's son, Johannes zu Waldburg Wolfegg, wrote in his moving 1958 tribute to Fischer that he would never forget the thankful look his dying mother gave the old priest when he stepped into her death chamber and provided his own unique encouragement. "Many thought of him as a holy man," Count Johannes observed. He also described Fischer as so frail toward the end of his life that he had to be supported on both sides to make it to Holy Mass in the castle chapel. However,

Figure 29. Father Josef Fischer, S.J., photographed in 1937 by his younger friend and admirer Robert Haardt. Source: The Austrian National Library, Vienna. Reproduced with permission.

Fischer merely joked about his physical condition, the count wrote, giving as an example the old man's name for his aided walks to the chapel: "The Triple Alliance."[205]

The plethora of books and diaries describing the effects on Europe of World War II has long since made it clear to any thinking person that war, with its ever-present threat of imminent death, is an intensely personal experience that may change a person's entire outlook on life. Remarkably, Fischer's own personality appears to have remained scholarly, pious, and leavened with a certain kind of wry humor. One gets a good measure of the man by looking at what in fact was going on right around him. His younger friend and admirer, Robert Haardt, who visited Wolfegg in 1943 (a few years after he had taken a splendid picture of Fischer with a globe), confirmed Count Maximilian's description of the castle as overflowing with refugees, and so did a relative by marriage of the Waldburg family, a remarkable American woman who managed to keep a diary throughout those difficult years (see Figure 29).[206]

Countess Frederica zu Waldburg (née Marvin) lived with her husband Count Heinrich at Tiefenbach near Oberstdorf in Bavaria, on land that belonged to Wolfegg Castle. They were close enough to the castle for regular family visits that, as the war ground on, could no longer be undertaken by private motor car. They had to depend on an increasingly unreliable train. The pages of Countess Frederica's diaries reveal a growing struggle to obtain food in a society where, after a while, neither servants nor neighbors could be depended upon for loyalty if they stood more to gain by being informers to the Nazi authorities. Nevertheless, the countess carried on, working long hours to keep the house in order and her husband fed and contented.

Her nerves frayed by worry, overwork, and family demands, she began her diary for 1944 with a bitter remark about Nazi propaganda bluff. On January 2 she noted the ninth air raid on Berlin since November 18; the following day she observed that a bomb had fallen on their own village. As the Allied bombs fell ever closer, she tried to seek comfort in the remoteness of their own region "behind its rampart of mountains," but that protection soon proved inadequate. In broad daylight the Americans bombed Augsburg (to the north) on February 24 and 25. Heavy bombers flew overhead more and more frequently during that late and cold spring. On July 18 bombs fell in the immediate vicinity of Tiefenbach, and two American airmen were shot dead "in cold blood" in the aftermath of that raid. Under the date of October 20, the countess noted that her husband was nervous about leaving for a visit to Wolfegg because there seemed to be so many heavy bombers about. There had been continuous air raid warnings in Oberstdorf, she wrote; the telephone had been turned off; and the radio stations in Vienna, Stuttgart, and Munich had been silent all morning.[207]

Six days later, with the din of war all around him, but safe within the old castle's enclosed courtyard, Father Fischer died on October 26, 1944, as quietly as he had lived. In accordance with his last wish, he was buried in a grave that already held two of his Jesuit brothers. Father Eugen Mark, the Wolfegg archivist and Fischer's confessor, described the old scholar's death as a moving experience and wrote: "Er hat heilig gelebt und ist heilig gestorben" (He lived and died in a holy manner). When Robert Haardt wrote to Count Johannes and asked what had happened to the scholarly material Fischer had left behind, he learned that everything had been turned over to the Jesuit foundation at Pullach near Munich.[208]

A Map Without a Home

Father Hans Grünewald and Dr. Rita Haub at the Jesuit Provincial Archives in Munich confirm that they have the papers that Fischer possessed when he died at Wolfegg, together with some part of the geographical works that had belonged to the Stella Matutina library, and that had been turned over to the Munich collection at the beginning of the 1990s.[209] It appears that none of these papers and books, while potentially valuable to other scholars, is of any outstanding monetary value.

My experience with the many Jesuit archives and institutions in Austria, Germany, and Switzerland, during my search for information about Fischer and his books and paper, has been one of unfailing kindness and generosity. Everyone understood the nature of my quest because they were scholars them-selves and, perhaps more importantly, because they knew the duress under which people had lived during the Nazi régime. They were therefore able to accept that the Vínland Map represents a quiet and courageous act of sabo-tage. The legacy of shame belongs not to Fischer, but to those who profited from marketing the map in 1957 when it surfaced with no indications of its previous whereabouts, but under circumstances that strongly suggest that the old volume that had also contained the *Speculum Historiale* fragments and the "Tartar Relation" had been looted during the Hitler years.

Throughout the spring of 1939, more forcible sales of Stella Matutina real property had occurred, and the institution was gradually emptied of all people and objects associated with its educational and religious purpose. This process included moving books out of the library and from the studies formerly occu-pied by Father Fischer and his colleagues.[210] The books were temporarily stored in the large chapel before they were taken away for safekeeping in the country-side, at a house that the Jesuits owned in Garina near Feldkirch. When the books were finally brought back in the early 1950s, they were evidently again stored in the chapel before they could be properly arranged in the library. The chapel was reconsecrated in 1953 as a prelude to the resumption of teaching. Father Grünewald said that around that time, he had observed the books stacked in the chapel at a height of about one meter. He stressed that although the contents of the Stella Matutina library had not been confiscated by the occupying Nazis at the time of the Anschluss, the library had certainly been emptied later.[211]

Beginning with the dismantling in 1939 and for a period of twelve or thirteen years subsequently, the Stella Matutina collections may have been vulnerable to pilfering, however. As is known from innumerable postwar reports, and as many still remember from personal experience, pilfering was common all over Europe both during and shortly after the war and was a temptation to which soldiers were peculiarly, but not exclusively, prone. As hotel keepers, librarians, and museum curators know all too well, looters usually indulge for one of two reasons: they want an unusual souvenir for themselves, or they want something that they can sell for a good sum later. The old binding with the Vínland Map and its two sister manuscripts would probably have appealed on both counts.

At Stella Matutina, the Nazis were in charge until French forces advanced in 1945 and used some of the buildings for their own needs, while other buildings were used as school rooms for Feldkirch pupils.[212] The French soldiers are above suspicion in this case, however, because the books were still away at Garina. Furthermore, any war loot brought back to France—or to the United States, for that matter—would probably not have passed through Ferrajoli's hands before they fetched up in New Haven. Instead, the volume had reached Switzerland by 1957 at the latest. It is therefore far more likely that the pilferer had his home in the general region that included the parts of Austria and Germany with which Fischer had been most familiar. What we know about the behavior of the Gestapo, the SS, and other enforcers of Hitler's Third Reich dreams, taken together with eyewitness accounts by some of the priests when they reunited at their old school after the war, strongly suggests that the pilfering of valuables at Stella Matutina took place during the invasion of the school in March 1938.

This outrage took place at night as a surprise event involving a large number of soldiers and a clash with troops from Von Schuschnigg's Austrian Heimwehr (home defense) in the immediate vicinity. Through the pages of the priests' terse accounts of that night and the two or three days and nights following, one hears shrill whistles, shouts, and the heavy trampling of boots. One sees the frightened faces of young boys trying to grasp what was happening, while they watched the German soldiers devour the breakfast meant for themselves and were told that they could not leave the house. One imagines the tautly controlled faces of the priests who had to reassure their pupils, and who were not allowed to leave their own rooms without a military escort. Most important to the discussion here: One learns that from the very beginning of that dreadful night, the invaders conducted not just one house search (ostensibly for weapons), but repeated searches, one after another, every one without the presence of a member of Stella Matutina's staff, all of whom were under house arrest. These searches involved every room in every building, including the priests' own rooms.[213]

It would have been the work of a moment to make off with a book. Did one of the members of the SS or the Gestapo on the rampage in 1938—or perhaps after the priests had left—also steal the "Bonaldus" map that Fischer had acquired for the Stella Matutina museum, and that is evidence that looting took place at Stella Matutina? This map was offered at an auction to be held in 1984 by Christie's of London and was described in the auction catalogue as a "portolan chart of the world." There was also a note saying that manuscript maps from this period (1519) were extremely rare. David Woodward, who in 1994 published the information about the Christie's auction, noted that the catalogue did not mention Fischer's 1941 article on the Stella Matutina "Bonaldus" map. This seemed odd to Woodward because he had recognized the Christie's item as the map to which Fischer had referred in his publication and to which he had lost access when he moved to Munich. Equally peculiar was the withdrawal of the map before the sale. The catalogue did not say who the current owner was; the only explanation provided about the withdrawal was that the map was "incorrect," which may simply have been a euphemism for "fake." That possibility was certainly not far-fetched because Woodward had recently made a study of four similar maps at the Newberry Library and had concluded that these and similar maps, including Fischer's "Bonaldus," were fakes made at the end of the nineteenth century or the beginning of the twentieth.[214]

Woodward's account sheds light on Fischer's shortcomings as a collector and on Stella Matutina's vulnerability during the long night of Nazi dominance and war. It is also important to the saga of the Vínland Map for another reason. When Woodward wrote his article in 1994, the discussion about the Vínland Map had lasted for almost three decades with no end in sight, despite the accumulating evidence that the map is a fake. There is a clear echo of this discussion when Woodward writes: "At the very least, all the maps listed here and others of similar type and style must be carefully scrutinized before being used as scholarly evidence or being purchased on the antiquarian map market. Chemical analysis of the pigments might reveal industrial compounds not available before the nineteenth century."[215]

We may well wonder at the likely result had the Vínland Map been subjected to proper scrutiny while there was still time to prevent it from being evidence of anything other than a desperate time in history—a time that we ought never to forget.

REFERENCE MATTER

Notes

The following abbreviations appear throughout the notes:

ACE	*American Catholic Encyclopedia*
BL	The British Library
BLML	The British Library Map Library
BMMD	The British Museum Manuscript Division
DD	*Diplomatarium Danicum*
DI	*Diplomatarium Islandicum*
DN	*Diplomatarium Norvegicum*
GHM	*Grønlands Historiske Mindesmærker*
MoG	*Meddelelser om Grønland* (Copenhagen)
MoG: M&S	*Meddelelser om Grønland: Man and Society* (Copenhagen)
NNLO	The Norwegian National Library (Oslo)
RLC	The Royal Library (Copenhagen)

Chapter 1

1. See *The Vinland Sagas: The Norse Discovery of America,* trans. and ed. Magnús Magnússon and Hermann Pálsson (London: Penguin Books, 1965).

2. The English translations of both legends are provided in R. A. Skelton, Thomas E. Marston, and George D. Painter, *The Vinland Map and the Tartar Relation* (New Haven, Conn.: Yale University Press 1965), pp. 139–40.

3. Skelton et al., *Vinland Map*, pp. 139–40. Not one of the dates mentioned by Skelton is verifiable. He was following contemporary notions in English-language texts, however.

4. Ibid., pp. 255–62.

5. Ibid., p. 260.

6. Ibid., pp. 140–41, 223–26.

7. Gustav Storm, comp. and ed., *Islandske Annaler indtil 1578* (1888; repr.,

377

Oslo: Norsk Historisk Kjeldeskrifts-Institutt, 1977), pp. 19, 59, 112, 251–52, 320, 473. See also Kirsten A. Seaver, *The Frozen Echo: Greenland and the Exploration of North America ca. AD 1000–1500* (Stanford: Stanford University Press, 1996), pp. 32–33. Bishop Eirik's nickname, *upsi*, suggests a constant nose drip, reminding people around him of the pollock fish.

8. Skelton et al., *Vinland Map*, pp. 225–26.

9. Ibid., pp. 255– 60; quotes pp. 257, 260.

10. Ibid., p. 119.

11. Ibid., pp. 111–14, 124–27.

12. Ibid., pp. 119–20, 124–27, 153, and plate VI.

13. Ibid., pp. 136, 151–53.

14. Ibid., pp. 119–20, 149–50, 153, 155, 231.

15. Ibid., pp. 21, 248–49.

16. Ibid., p. 21.

17. Ibid., pp. 138–39.

18. Ibid., pp. 123 (quote), 167.

19. Ibid., pp. 116–17 (quote), 145.

20. Ibid., pp. 167, 177, 199–202, and plates XVII–XIX. These early maps of the North will be discussed in their historical context in Chapter 2 and in their geographical context in Chapter 7.

21. Ibid., pp. 209, 215.

22. Ibid. 139, 172–73, 195, 221, 239.

23. Ibid., p. 233.

24. Ibid., pp. 182–83, 189, 195.

25. Ibid., p. 239.

26. Ibid., quotes pp. 175–76. As his source for this judgment, Skelton cited Josef Fischer, *The Discoveries of the Norsemen in America* (London, 1903), pp. 101–4.

27. Skelton et al., *Vinland Map*, pp. 175, 179–82.

28. Ibid., pp. 178, 189, 192, 227, 235.

29. Ibid., pp. 250–54, 262; quote p. 262.

30. Ibid., pp. 192, 199.

31. Ibid., p. v.

32. Ibid., pp. v–vi.

33. Ibid., p. v.

34. Marston, "Vinland Map," pp. 1–5, quotes p. 1. See also Skelton et al., *Vinland Map*, p. 3.

35. Marston, "Vinland Map," pp. 1–5, quote pp. 1–2.

36. Skelton et al., *Vinland Map*, p. 11.

37. Ibid., pp. 16, 230. See also Marston, "Vinland Map," esp. p. 4.

38. Skelton et al., *Vinland Map*, p. 178.

39. Ibid., p. 109.

40. Ibid., p. 243.

41. BMMD, "Recurrent file—Vinland Map." Press Notice PG. NO. 403/3/67, GR. NO. 11/67.

42. Ibid. Printed information accompanying the exhibition of the Vínland Map and its companion texts at the British Museum, Jan. 20–Feb. 17, 1967.

43. *Times Literary Supplement,* Nov. 25, 1965, anonymous review of *The Vinland Map and the Tartar Relation,* in Brigid Allen, "The Papers of Eila Campbell (1915–1994)." The files on the Vínland Map: cat. no. II/3/1–12, BLML.

44. Skelton et al., *Vinland Map,* p. vi.

Chapter 2

1. Haraldur Sigurðsson, "The Vinland Map, its date and origin," typed text to offprint of *Thjóðviljinn,* Dec. 24, 1965, BLML, "The Papers of Eila Campbell"; Haraldur Sigurðsson, *Kortasaga Íslands,* vol. 1 (Reykjavík, 1971), pp. 261–62, quote from p. 262.

2. Skelton et al., *Vinland Map,* pp. 185–87.

3. Ibid., p. 169.

4. The most thoughtful discourse on this topic remains the study made by Roald Morcken: *Sjøfartshistoriske artikler gjennom 20 år* [Articles on maritime history through 20 years], with summaries in English (Bergen: privately published, 1983). A recent article on this topic by Sivert Fløttum (*Mariner's Mirror,* Nov. 2001) does nothing to solve the problem.

5. See, e.g., *DD* 1: 2–24, 29–31, 34, 36.

6. For an informed recent overview, see Arne Emil Christensen, "The Age of the Vikings," *Scientific American: Discovering Archaeology* 2, no. 4 (2000): 40–47. See also the newspaper *Nytt fra Norge* (Oslo) 44 (Jan. 13–19, 1998): 14; Bruce E. Gelsinger, *Icelandic Enterprise: Commerce and Economy in the Middle Ages* (Columbia, S.C.: University of South Carolina Press, 1981), esp. pp. 124–25; Christiane Villain-Gandossi, Salerno Bussutil, and Paul Adam, eds., *Medieval Ships and the Birth of Technological Societies,* vol. 1, *Northern Europe. European Coordination* (Malta: Centre for Research and Documentation in Social Sciences, Foundation for International Studies, 1989).

7. The Icelandic scholar Gísli Sigurðsson is one of several who have researched this topic. For a graphic view of Celtic settlers in Iceland, see Gísli Sigurðsson and Sigurjón Jóhannesson, *Vikings and the New World,* exh. cat. (Reykjavík: The Culture House, 2000), p. 13. For the latest in mitochondrial DNA studies intended to unravel the genetic heritage of modern Icelanders, see Agnar Helgason, Sigrún Sigurðardóttir, Jeffrey R. Gulcher, Ryk Ward, and Kári Stefánsson, "mtDNA and the Origin of the Icelanders: Deciphering Sig-

nals of Recent Population History," *American Journal of Human Genetics* 66 (2000): 999–1016.

8. Niels Lynnerup, "The Greenland Norse: A Biological-Anthropological Study," *Meddelelser om Grønland: Man and Society* (Copenhagen) 24 (1998): 128.

9. *The King's Mirror*, trans. Laurence Marcellus Larson (1917; repr., New York: Twayne, 1972), p. 142; *Konge-speilet. Speculum Regale. Konungs-skuggsjá*, ed. R. Keyser, P. A. Munch, and C. R. Unger (Christiania: Kongeligt Norsk Frederiks Universitet, 1848), p. 42.

10. See "Europas eldste sjømerker?" in Morcken, *Sjøfartshistoriske artikler*, pp. 67–108 passim.

11. *Landnámabók* [The book of settlements], trans. and ed. Hermann Páls-son and Paul Edwards (Winnipeg: University of Manitoba Icelandic Studies, vol. 1, 1972), ch. 15. As in the case of many early works for which we no longer have the original, there is some dispute over its actual author, but Ari "the Learned" Thorgilsson is frequently credited with its creation as well as with that of the *Íslendingabók* (The book of Icelanders).

12. For a recent discussion of what "Biarmaland" encompassed, see Tatjana N. Jackson, "*Biarmaland* between Norway and Old Rus," in Ingi Sigurðsson and Jón Skaptason, eds., *Aspects of Arctic and Sub-Arctic History: Proceedings of the International Congress on the History of the Arctic and Sub-Arctic Region, Reykjavík, 18–21 June 1998* (Reykjavík: University of Iceland Press, 2000), pp. 113–20.

13. The Icelandic scholar Ólafur Halldórsson does not share this view. He believes there is much to suggest that Eirik grew up in western Iceland. See Ólafur Halldórsson, *Grænland í miðaldaritum* (Reykjavík: Sögufélag, 1978), pp. 319–21.

14. Waldemar H. Lehn, "Skerrylike Mirages and the Discovery of Greenland," *Applied Optics* 39, no. 21 (2000): 3612–19; quote p. 3612.

15. *Vinland Sagas*, quote p. 52.

16. Claus Andreasen, "Nordbosager fra Vesterbygden på Grønland," *Hikuin* 6 (1980): 135–46, esp. pp. 135–36; Ingrid Sørensen, "Pollenunder-søgelser i møddingen på Niaqussat," *Grønland* 30 (1982): 296–304; Seaver, *Frozen Echo*, pp. 21–22.

17. A good source of information about the use of walrus ivory in the Near, Middle, and Far East in the Middle Ages is Richard Ettinghausen, *Studies in Muslim Iconography*, vol. 1, *The Unicorn*, Occasional Paper I: 3 (Washington, D.C.: Freer Gallery of Art, 1950), pp. 117–31.

18. Karen McCullough and Peter Schledermann, "Mystery Cairns on Washington Irving Island," *Polar Record* 35 (1999): 289–98.

19. [Rasmus Rask and Finn Magnusen], "Efterretning om en i Grønland funden Runesteen med dens Forklaring, forfattet af Professor Rask, og nogle

dertil hørende Oplysninger ved Professor F. Magnusen," *Antiqvariske Annaler* (Copenhagen) 4, part 2 (1827): 309–43, with an addendum containing a report by the missionary P. Kragh, July 1826, pp. 367–79.

20. Seaver, *Frozen Echo*, p. 37; Jette Arneborg, "Contact between Eskimos and Norsemen in Greenland," in Else Roesdahl and Preben Meulengracht Sørensen, eds., *Beretning fra tolvte tværfaglige vikingesymposium, Aarhus Universitet* (Aarhus: Aarhus Universitet, 1993), p. 28. Arneborg refers to a personal communication (1991) from Marie Stoklund for the dating of this rune stone.

21. "Grænlendinga tháttr," in Guðni Jónsson, ed., *Íslendinga sögur*, vol. 1 (Reykjavík: Íslendingasagnaútgafan, 1968), p. 395; Ólafur Halldórsson, *Grænland í miðdaldaritum* (Reykjavík: Sögufélag, 1978), pp. 103–16 (text), 401–5 (analysis); Seaver, *Frozen Echo*, p. 63.

22. *Islandske Annaler*, pp. 20, 59, 112, 113, 252, 320, 473; *DI* 1: 22. I will return later in this chapter and in Chapter 8 to the "floating" Bishop Eirik Gnupsson, who preceded Bishop Arnald.

23. *DD* 1: 28, 119, 280, 294; 2: 47; John Porter, trans., "The Tale of the Greenlanders (Grænlendinga tháttr)," in Víðar Hreinsson, gen. ed., *The Complete Sagas of Icelanders* (Reykjavík: Leifur Eiríksson Publishing, 1997), pp. 372–82; Ólafur Halldórsson, "Einars tháttr Sokkasonar," in Phillip Pulsiano and Kirsten Wolf, eds., *Medieval Scandinavia: An Encyclopedia* (New York and London: Garland Publishing, Inc., 1993), p. 160.

24. *DI* 1: 22.

25. Seaver, *Frozen Echo*, pp. 37, 61–66.

26. Skelton et al., *Vinland Map*, p. 260; Seaver, *Frozen Echo*, pp. 32–33, 63–65.

27. Patrick Plumet, "L'Esquimau: Essai de synthèse de la préhistoire de l'arctique esquimau," *Revista de Arqueología Americana* 10 (1996): 12–13. Note also the current practice of calling precontact (before 1500) Amerindians in this region "Recent Indians."

28. Robert McGhee, "Radiocarbon Dating and the Timing of the Thule Migration," in Martin Appelt, Joel Berglund, and Hans Christian Gulløv, eds., *Identities and Cultural Contacts in the Arctic* (Copenhagen: Danish Polar Center, 2000), pp. 181–91.

29. Jette Arneborg and Hans Christian Gulløv, eds., *Man, Culture and Environment in Ancient Greenland: Report on a Research Programme* (Copenhagen: The Danish National Museum and Danish Polar Center, 1998), pp. 151–71.

30. Peter Schledermann, "Norsemen in the High Arctic?" in Birthe L. Clausen, ed., *Viking Voyages to North America* (Roskilde, Denmark: The Viking Ship Museum, 1993), pp. 54–66, esp. p. 57; idem, "The Norse in the Arctic," *Scientific American Discovering Archaeology* 2, no. 4 (2000): 59; idem,

"Ellesmere," in William W. Fitzhugh and Elisabeth I. Ward, eds., *Vikings: The North Atlantic Saga* (Washington, D.C.: The Smithsonian Press, 2000), pp. 248–56; Karen McCullough and Peter Schledermann, "Mystery Cairns on Washington Irving Island," *Polar Record* 35 (1999): 289–98, esp. p. 293; Seaver, *Frozen Echo*, p. 42.

31. Patricia D. Sutherland and Robert McGhee, "Arktisk Kontakt," *Skalk* 3 (1983): 12–15; Patricia D. Sutherland, "The Norse and Native Norse Americans," in Fitzhugh and Ward, eds., *Vikings*, pp. 238–47, illus. p. 245.

32. Kirsten A. Seaver, "Land of Wine and Forests: The Norse in North America," *Mercator's World* 5, no. 1 (2000): 18–24; idem "Far and Yet Near: North America and Norse Greenland," *Viking Heritage Newsletter* (Visby, Sweden) 1, no. 1 (2000): 3–5, 23.

33. *Landnámabók*, chs. 4–5. This work, thought to have been originally undertaken by Ari "the Learned" Thorgilsson (circa 1067–1148), survives in later redactions, chief of which are those found in the *Sturlubók* and *Hauksbók* compendia. See Liv Kjørsvik Schei, trans., with an introduction by Hermann Pálsson, *Landnåmsboken* (Oslo: H. Aschenoug and Co., 1997); [Det Kongelige nordiske Oldskrift-Selskab], *Hauksbók, Udgiven efter De Arnamagnæiske Haandskrifter No. 371, 544 og 675, 40.* Copenhagen, 1892–96.

34. Erik Andersen and Claus Malmros, "Ship's Parts Found in the Viking Settlements in Greenland," in Clausen, *Viking Voyages*, pp. 118–22; Poul Nørlund, "Buried Norsemen at Herjolfsnes," *MoG* 67, no. 1 (1924): 60–71, 251. See also Seaver, *Frozen Echo*, pp. 28, 100.

35. Patrick Plumet, "Les maisons longues dorsétiennes de l'Ungava," in *Géographie Physique et Quaternaire* 36, no. 3 (1982): 253–89.

36. Helge Ingstad, "Vinland Ruins Prove Vikings Found the New World," *National Geographic Magazine* 126 (Nov. 1964): 708–35.

37. Additional arguments favoring a Nova Scotia destination may be found in Birgitta L. Wallace, "The Norse in the North Atlantic: The L'Anse aux Meadows Settlement in Newfoundland," in Sigurðsson and Skaptason, *Aspects of Arctic and Sub-Arctic History*, pp. 486–500.

38. Birgitta L. Wallace, "L'Anse aux Meadows, the Western Outpost," in Clausen, *Viking Voyages*, p. 39; idem, "The Viking Settlement at L'Anse aux Meadows," in Fitzhugh and Ward, *Vikings*, pp. 209–13.

39. Kevin P. Smith, e-mails to author, Sept.–Oct. 1999; see also Kevin P. Smith, "Who Lived at L'Anse aux Meadows?" in Fitzhugh and Ward, p. 217. Smith is currently the deputy director/chief curator for the Haffenreffer Museum of Anthropology, Brown University, in Providence, R.I.

40. Smith, e-mail; see also Smith, "Who Lived at L'Anse aux Meadows?" p. 217.

41. Birgitta L. Wallace, "The Vikings in North America: Myth and

Reality," in Ross Samson, ed., *Social Approaches to Viking Studies* (Glasgow: Cruithne Press, 1991), pp. 206–12; idem, "L'Anse aux Meadows, the Western Outpost," pp. 30–42; idem, "Norse Expansion into North America," Internet report for Canadian Heritage, Atlantic Region, 1996, http://www/heureka/fi/en/x/nxwallace.html (accessed Aug. 12, 2002).

42. Gísli Sigurðsson, "The Quest for Vínland in Saga Scholarship," in Fitzhugh and Ward, *Vikings*, pp. 233–34; also Professor Kari Ellen Gade, Indiana University, personal communication, Palo Alto, Calif., May 1998 and July 4, 1998.

43. Concerning "yet another island of the many found in that ocean," Adam wrote: "It is called Vinland because vines producing excellent wine grow wild there. That unsown crops also abound on that island we have ascertained not from fabulous reports but from the trustworthy relations of the Danes." Adamus Bremensis [Adam of Bremen], *History of the Archbishops of Hamburg-Bremen*, trans. with introd. and notes by Francis J. Tschahn (New York: Columbia University Press, 1959), Book IV, chs. 38–39, p. 219.

44. *DI* 1: 131. The pope warned Archbishop Sigurd of Nidaros that beer was not an acceptable substitute for wine. Celebration of the Eucharist required "panis de frumento et vini de uvis."

45. *Landnámabók*, p. 61n48. See also Kirsten A. Seaver, "How Strange Is a Stranger?" in Thomas H. B. Symons, ed., *Meta Incognita: A Discourse of Discovery. Martin Frobisher's Arctic Expeditions, 1576–1578* (Hull, Quebec: Canadian Museum of Civilization, Mercury Series, vol. 2, 1999), pp. 523–52, esp. p. 526.

46. *Landnámabók*, p. 61.

47. *Eyrbyggja saga*, trans. Hermann Pálsson and Paul Edwards (Edinburgh: Southside, 1972), pp. 152 (ch. 48), 193–96 (ch. 64). King Olaf Haraldsson, Norway's patron saint, died in AD 1030.

48. Claus Andreasen, "Nordbosager fra Vesterbygden på Grønland," *Hikuin* 6 (1980): 60–61, 81–82, 135–46; idem, "Nipaitsoq og Vesterbygden," *Grønland* 30 (1982): 177–88. See also Seaver, *Frozen Echo*, pp. 120–23.

49. C. L. Vebæk, "Vatnahverfi: An Inland District of the Eastern Settlement in Greenland," *MoG: M&S* 17 (1992): 85–86 (including fig. 119), 120; Seaver, *Frozen Echo*, pp. 227–53.

50. Eleanora Mary Carus Wilson, *The Overseas Trade of Bristol* (London: Merlin Press, 1967), pp. 171, 180.

51. Vagn Fabritius Buchwald, "Ancient Iron and Slags in Greenland," *MoG: M&S* 26 (2001): 35.

52. Nørlund, "Buried Norsemen," pp. 54, 221, 236, 254, 255, 267. See also Seaver, *Frozen Echo*, p. 235.

53. For a further discussion of this topic, see Seaver, *Frozen Echo*, ch. 7.

54. Arneborg and Gulløv, *Man, Culture and Environment.*

55. News release by the Canadian Museum of Civilization, Hull, Quebec, Dec. 1, 1999; Patricia Sutherland, e-mail to author, Dec. 12, 1999. See also Sutherland, "The Norse," esp. p. 241; Patricia Sutherland, "Strands of Culture Contact: Dorset-Norse Interactions in the Eastern Canadian Arctic," in M. Appelt, J. Berglund, and H. C. Gulløv, eds., *Identities and Cultural Contacts in the Arctic* (Copenhagen, 2000), pp. 159–69. I am very grateful to Sutherland for giving me the opportunity to examine these artifacts at the Museum of Civilization in October of 2001.

56. Sutherland, "Strands," esp. pp. 164–65.

57. For a description of this type of chert and of early techniques used to shape it, see Serge Lebel and Patrick Plumet, "Étude Technologique de l'Exploitation des Blocs et des Galets en Métabasalte par les Dorsétiens au Site Tuvaaluk (DIA.4, JfEI-4)," *Journal canadien d'archéologie* 15 (1991): 143–70.

58. Robert McGhee, "Contact Between Native North Americans and the Medieval Norse: A Review of the Evidence," *American Antiquity* 49 (1984): 13; Aage Roussell, "Sandnes and the Neighbouring Farms," with an appendix by Erik Moltke, "Greenland Runic Inscriptions 1." *MoG* 88 (2) (1936): 106–8; Jette Arneborg, personal communication, Mar. 21 and Apr. 26, 1993; William W. Fitzhugh, "A Review of Paleo-Eskimo Culture History in Southern Quebec—Labrador and Newfoundland," *Inuit Studies* 4, nos. 1–2 (1980): 29–30; idem, personal communication, May 25, 1996. See also Seaver, *Frozen Echo*, p. 26.

59. Kolbjørn Skaare, "En norsk penning fra 11. årh. funnet på kysten av Maine, U.S.A.," *Meddelelser fra Norsk Numismatisk Forening* no. 2 (May 1979): 2–17; I thank Kjell Karlsen for a copy. See also McGhee, "Contact," p. 28; Robert McGhee, "The Skraellings of *Vínland*," in Clausen, *Viking Voyages*, pp. 49–50; idem, "A New View of the Norse in the Arctic," *Scientific American: Discovering Archaeology* 2, no. 4 (2000): 58; Edmund Carpenter, *Norse Penny* (New York: The Rock Foundation, 2003).

60. Fitzhugh, "Review," p. 30; Elmer Harp, "A Late Dorset Copper Amulet from Southeastern Hudson Bay," *Folk* 16–17 (1975): 33–44.

61. Patrick Plumet, "Le Site de la Pointe aux Bélougas (Qilalugarsiuvik) et les maisons longues dorsétiennes," *Archéologie de l'Ungava* (Montréal) no. 18 (1985): 188–90, 195 (Plate 32; photos 79, 81–82), 357–58; Patrick Plumet, personal communication, Mar. 29, 2001.

62. George and Deborah Sabo, "A possible Thule Carving of a Viking from Baffin Island N.W.T.," *Canadian Journal of Archaeology* 2 (1978): 33–42; Seaver, *Frozen Echo*, pp. 39–40.

63. Poul Nørlund, "Norse Ruins at Gardar," *MoG* 76, no. 1 (1929): esp. p. 137.

64. A report on the Icelandic ox skulls was given in an address ("Settlement in Light of Recent Archaeological Investigations") by Orri Vésteinsson, Sept. 16, 2000, at the Viking Millennium International Symposium in St. John's, Newfoundland. For a general discussion of the walrus mandibles, see Kirsten A. Seaver, "Baffin Island Mandibles and Walrus Blooms," in Symons, *Meta Incognita* 2: 563–74.

65. William W. Fitzhugh and Jacqueline Olin, eds., *Archeology of the Frobisher Voyages* (Washington, D.C.: Smithsonian Institution Press, 1993).

66. Seaver, "Baffin Island," pp. 563–74. For a dissenting view, which does not take the pertinent Norse Greenland archaeological literature into consideration, see William W. Fitzhugh, "Iron Blooms, Elizabethans, and Politics: The Frobisher Project 1974–1995," *The Review of Archaeology* 17, no. 2 (1997): 12–21. This is a special issue, edited by Jeffrey P. Brain, and subtitled *Contributions to the Historical Archaeology of European Exploration and Colonization in North America.*

67. Buchwald, "Ancient Iron," pp. 44–47.

68. For a further discussion of the *Inventio Fortunata*, see Seaver, *Frozen Echo*, pp. 123–24, 132–37, 150, 262.

69. *Islandske Annaler*, pp. 19, 59, 112, 252, 320, 473. For Bishop Eirik's Icelandic genealogy, see *Landnámabók*, ch. 17.

70. *Islandske Annaler*, pp. 213, 353, 403.

71. J. Kr. Tornøe, *Columbus in the Arctic? and the Vineland Literature* (Oslo: Brøgger, 1965), pp. 52–53; idem, *Norsemen Before Columbus* (Oslo: Universitetsforlaget, 1964).

72. Connoisseurs of this imaginative literature know that it is vast. Newcomers to the field will find it well represented by, e.g., Frederick J. Pohl, *The Vikings on Cape Cod: Evidence from Archaeological Discovery* (Pictou, Nova Scotia: Pictou Advocate Press, 1957); O. G. Landsverk, *The Kensington Runestone: A Reappraisal of the Circumstances under which the Stone Was Discovered* (Glendale, Calif.: Church Press, 1961).

73. Erik Wahlgren, *The Vikings and America* (London, Thames and Hudson, 1986), ch. 6.

74. Brian Smith, "'Earl Henry Sinclair's Fictitious Trip to America,'" *New Orkney Antiquarian Journal* 2 (2000), prepublication typescript; idem, "The Not-So-Secret Scroll: Priceless Relic or Floorcloth?" *The Orcadian* Mar. 29, 2001, p. 18; may also be accessed on http://www.orkneyjar.com/history/historicalfigures/henrysinclair/kirkwallscroll2.htm. See also Frederic W. Lucas, *The Annals of the Voyages of the Brothers Nicolo and Antonio Zeno in the North Atlantic about the End of the Fourteenth Century and the Claim Founded thereon to a Venetian Discovery of America* (London: Henry Stevens and Son, 1898).

75. Hjalmar R. Holand, *Explorations in America Before Columbus* (New

York: Twayne Publ., 1956), esp. pp. 7–8. See also idem, *The Kensington Stone* (n.p.: privately printed, 1932).

76. For a recent summary, see Johannes Hertz, "The Newport Tower," in Fitzhugh and Ward, *Vikings*, p. 376.

77. *DN* 21: 83. See also Seaver, *Frozen Echo*, p. 103 and n41.

78. See, e.g., Theodore C. Blegen, *The Kensington Runestone: New Light on an Old Riddle* (St. Paul: Minnesota Historical Society, 1968).

79. Matti Enn Kaups, "Shifting Vinland—Tradition and Myth," *Terrae Incognitae* 2 (1970): 37.

80. Kirsten A. Seaver, "Renewing the Quest for Vínland: The Stefánsson, Resen and Thorláksson Maps," *Mercator's World* 5, no. 5 (2000): 42–49. Note that Norway and its former colonies had effectively been under Danish hegemony since 1397.

81. Richard Eden, *The First Three English Books on America [?1511–1555]*, ed. Edward Arber (Birmingham and Edinburgh: Turnbull and Spears, 1885), pp. 201–4 ("Of the Landes and Ilandes lately founde. Pope Alexander VI. Bull dividing the New World between the Spaniards and the Portuguese, 4 May 1493.").

82. Claus Christophersen Lyschander, *Den Grønlandske Chronica* (1608; repr., Copenhagen, 1726), pp. 14–16, 19–26, quote p. 19. In Lyschander's historical meanderings there is no mention of Columbian discovery in connection with 1492 (pp. 60–61).

83. Kirsten A. Seaver, "Norumbega and *Harmonia Mundi* in Sixteenth-Century Cartography," *Imago Mundi* 50 (1998): 34–58.

84. For an interesting older synopsis of this development, see Arthur Middleton Reeves, *The Finding of Wineland the Good: The History of the Icelandic Discovery of America* (London: Henry Frowde, 1890), pp. 94–95.

85. For a color reproduction of the "Vallard" chart, see Kenneth Nebenzahl, *Atlas of Columbus* (Chicago: Rand McNally and Company, 1990), plate 35; Le Testu's map of "New France" is reproduced in Michel Mollat du Jourdin and Monique de la Roncière, with Marie-Madeleine Azard, Isabelle Raynaud-Nguyen, and Marie-Antoinette Vannerau, *Sea Charts of the Early Explorers 13th to 17th Century*, trans. L. le R. Dethan (New York: Thames and Hudson, 1984), plate 49.

86. Seaver, *Frozen Echo*, pp. 21, 48–58 passim, 74, 120, 127, 162, 220–21, 241–42, 253.

87. *Landnámabók*, chs. 5, 24.

88. Inger Marie Holm Olsen, "The Helgøy Project: Evidence from Farm Mounds: Economy and Settlement Pattern, AD 1350–1600," *Norwegian Archaeological Review* 14 (1981): 96; Odd Vollan, "Torskefiske," *Kulturhistorisk leksikon for nordisk middelalder* 18 (1974): cols. 506–10; Mark Kurlansky, *Cod:*

A Biography of the Fish that Changed the World (New York: Penguin Books, 1997), pp. 19, 35, 243, 251.

89. "The Tale of the Greenlanders (Grænlendinga tháttr)," in Hreinsson, *Complete Sagas*, pp. 372–82, quote p. 381. See also the Icelandic/Old Norse text in Halldórsson, *Grænland*, pp. 105–16. Here (p. 114), "lots of dried fish" appears as *skreið mikla*—"lots of cod." In other words, the assumption is that if found in a storage room, the fish would have been dried.

90. *Vinland Sagas*, p. 95.

91. William G. Mattox, "Fishing in West Greenland, 1910–1966: The Development of a New Native Industry," *MoG* 197, no. 1 (1973): 18–20, 28–29, 32–33; Kurlansky, *Cod*, pp. 38, 41–43.

92. See, e.g., Thomas McGovern, "Bones, Buildings, and Boundaries: Palæoeconomic Approaches to Norse Greenland," in Christopher D. Morris and D. James Rackham, eds., *Norse and Later Settlement and Subsistence in the North Atlantic* (Glasgow: University of Glasgow, Department of Achaeology, 1992), pp. 193–230, esp. pp. 195–96; Thomas McGovern and G. F. Bigelow, "Archaezoology of the Norse Site Ø17a Narssaq District, Southwest Greenland," *Acta Borealia* 1 (1984): 85–101, esp. pp. 96–97. For a useful treatise on the commercial fish in Greenland waters, see Mattox, "Fishing." See also Seaver, *Frozen Echo*, pp. 54–60.

93. Poul-Erik Philbert, "Man er hvad man spiser," *Polarfronten* 2 (2002): 12–13.

94. Charles Drever, *Cod Fishing at Greenland. The White Fish Authority*, ca. 1972, typescript, British Library x.313/380, pp. 1–32. This summary of an English trawling skipper's experiences with the Greenland fishery gives a clear picture of the conditions along the outer coast of the former Eastern Settlement.

95. Georg Nyegaard, Qaqortoq Museum, e-mail to author, May 14, 2001, with permission to cite.

96. C. L. Vebæk, "The Church Topography of the Eastern Settlement and the Excavation of the Benedictine Convent at Narsarsuaq in the Uunartoq Fjord," *MoG: M&S* 14 (1991): 5–20; conversations with C. L. Vebæk and Jette Arneborg in Copenhagen on May 2, 1991, when Arneborg had recently been on reconnaissance in the Middle Settlement. She noted that the ruins there were in such a uniformly bad state that it was impossible to tell whether they were of a greater age—or had been abandoned earlier—than the rest of the Eastern Settlement farm sites.

97. Nyegaard, e-mail, May 14, 2001; May 26, 2002, with permission to cite. I am very grateful to Nyegaard for sharing his extensive local and professional knowledge.

98. See, e.g., Thomas McGovern, "The Economics of Extinction," in T. M. Wrigley, M. J. Ingram, and G. Farmer, eds., *Climate and History:*

Studies in Past Climates and their Impact on Man (Cambridge, England: Cambridge University Press, 1980), pp. 404–34, esp. pp. 404–29; see also Seaver, *Frozen Echo*, pp. 239–41.

99. Lynnerup, "Greenland Norse."

100. Stig Rosenørn, Jens Fabricius, Erik Buch, and Svend Aage Horsted, "Isvinter ved Vestgrønland: Klima, vestis, oceanografi og biologi," *Forskning i Grønland/Tusaat* 4, no. 2 (1981): 2–19; Willi Dansgaard, "Bringer luftforureningen torsken tilbage til Grønland?" *Forskning i Grønland/Tusaat* 8, no. 1 (1985): 24–25; Niels Reeh, "Indlandsisen på langsom skrump," *Polarfronten* 3 (2000): 4–5; A. E. J. Ogilvie and T. Jónsson, "'Litte Ice Age' Research: A Perspective from Iceland" *Climatic Change* 48 (2001): 1–46, special monograph issue, A. E. J. Ogilvie and T. Jónsson, gen. eds.; Ray Bradley, "1000 Years of Climate Change," *Science* 288 (2000): 1353–55; Poul-Erik Philbert, "Tryk på klimaet i Nordatlanteren," *Polarfronten* 1 (2001): 6–7; Neville Brown, *History and Climate Change: A Eurocentric Perspective* (London and New York: Routledge, 2001).

101. Skelton et al., *Vinland Map*, p. 185.

102. Ibid., p. 185.

103. Ibid., pp. 184–85.

104. A. E. J. Ogilvie, "Climatic Changes in Iceland AD c. 865 to 1598," in Gerald F. Bigelow, gen. ed., "The Norse of the North Atlantic," *Acta Archaeologica* 61 (1991): 233–51; Ogilvie and Jónsson, "'Little Ice Age,'" p. 22.

105. Gísli Gunnarsson, "Given Good Time, Legs Get Shorter in Cold Weather," in Sigurðsson and Skaptason, *Aspects*, pp. 593–602.

106. My own views here have not changed from those I expressed in, e.g., Seaver, *Frozen Echo*, chs. 6–8; and in Kirsten A. Seaver, "Norse Greenland on the Eve of Renaissance Exploration," in Anna Agnarsdóttir, ed., *Voyages and Exploration in the North Atlantic from the Middle Ages to the XVIIth Century* (Reykjavík: Institute of History, University of Iceland, 2000), pp. 29–44.

107. For an archaeologist's description of this orderly scene, it is hard to improve upon that of Joel Berglund, whose poetic sensitivity to his beloved Greenland scenes makes his professional prose as moving as it is succinct and informative. See Joel Berglund, "The Decline of the Norse Settlements in Greenland," *Arctic Anthropology* 23 (1986): 109–35, esp. pp. 111, 122.

108. See, e.g., McGovern, "Economics," pp. 404–29; Kirsten Hastrup, "Sæters in Iceland, 900–1600," *Acta Borealia*, 6 (1989): 72–85.

109. See, e.g., Lynnerup, "Greenland Norse," pp. 126–28.

110. Valkendorf's expedition (which never took place) received a papal indulgence on June 17, 1514. *DN* 17, nos. 1260, 1263.

111. K. J. V. Steenstrup, "Om Østerbygden," *MoG* 9 (1886): 1–53; Skelton et al., *Vinland Map*, pp. 201, 203. Skelton's statements in this connection

reveal that he never read K. J. V. Steenstrup's useful Danish dissertation on these maps—a circumstance that is particularly troubling because he referred to Steenstrup's work twice as if he had actually accessed it firsthand. In neither mention by Skelton is there any suggestion of a secondhand source, although he was obviously unable to access the original Danish text. Steenstrup's work is also listed in the Yale book's bibliography.

112. Skelton et al., *Vinland Map*, p. 175; Skelton et al., *Vinland Map* (1995 ed.), p. xiv.

113. The printed documents in the *Diplomatarium Norvegicum* (21 volumes) would be a good place for an interested reader to start.

114. *DN* 17: 1085, letter dated July 24, 1464.

115. Seaver, *Frozen Echo*, pp. 91–112.

116. Finnur Jónsson, *Det gamle Grønlands Beskrivelse* (Copenhagen: Levin and Munksgaard, 1930); idem, "Grønlands gamle Topografi efter Kilderne: Østerbygden og Vesterbygden," *MoG* 20 (1899).

117. See, e.g., McGovern, "Economics," pp. 406, 414–16. McGovern's viewpoint has been widely disseminated.

118. Seaver, *Frozen Echo*, ch. 4, esp. pp. 91–95.

119. Arneborg and Gulløv, *Man, Culture and Environment*; Claus Andreasen, "Nordbosager fra Vesterbygden på Grønland," *Hikuin* 6 (1980): 135–46; idem, "Nipaitsoq og Vesterbygden," *Grønland* 30 (1982): 177–88; Seaver, *Frozen Echo*, pp. 120–23; Inge Bødtker Enghoff, "Hunting, Fishing and Animal Husbandry at The Farm Beneath the Sand, Western Greenland," *MoG: M&S* 28 (2003).

120. Peter Andreas Munch, *Pavelige Nuntiers Regnskabe* (Oslo, 1864), pp. 25, 29. See also Seaver, *Frozen Echo*, pp. 80–82.

121. Kirsten A. Seaver, "'A Very Common and Usual Trade': The Relationship Between Cartographic Perceptions and Fishing in the Davis Strait, c. 1500–1550." *British Library Journal* (June 1996): 1–26. Also in Karen Severud Cook, ed., *Images and Icons of the New World: Essays on American Cartography* (London: British Library Publications, 1996), pp. 1–26.

122. Ettinghausen, *Studies*, pp. 117–18; Zygmunt Abramowitcz, "The Expressions 'Fish-Tooth' and "Lion-Fish" in Turkish and Persian," *Folia Orientalia* (Kraków; Académie Polonaise des sciences, Centre de Cracovie, Commission Orientaliste) 12 (1970): 25–32.

123. Thomas H. McGovern, Gerald F. Bigelow, Thomas Amorosi, James Woollett, and Sophia Perdikaris, "The zooarchaeology of Ø17a. In C. L. Vebæk, "Narsaq—A Norse *landnáma* farm," *MoG: M&S* 18 (1993): 58–74, esp. pp. 66–67.

124. Else Roesdahl, "L'ivoire de morse et les colonies norroises du Groenland," *Proxima Thule, revue d'études nordiques* 3 (spring 1998): 9–48.

125. Derek Wilson and Peter Ayerst, *White Gold: The Story of African Ivory* (London: Heinemann, 1970), Pliny quote p. 18.

126. Peter Russell, *Prince Henry 'The Navigator': A Life* (New Haven and London: Yale University Press, 2000), esp. ch. 10; Michael Vickers et al., *Ivory: An International History and Illustrated Survey* (New York: Abrams, 1987). There is also excellent information on http://uwacadweb.uwyo.edu/history3120/ivory/ivory.htm#introduction (accessed May 8, 2001). For a contemporary account of fifteenth-century voyaging down the African west coast, see, e.g., G. R. Crone, trans. and ed., *The Voyages of Cadamosto and Other Documents on Western Africa in the Second Half of the Fifteenth Century*, series 2, vol. 80 (London: Hakluyt Society, 1937).

127. Seaver, *Frozen Echo*, pp. 80–82.

128. Ettinghausen, *Studies*, pp. 117–31, passim.

129. Hans Christian Gulløv, "The Eskimo Culture in Greenland and the Medieval Norse," in Sigurðsson and Skaptason, *Aspects*, pp. 184–93.

130. This problem is discussed in Seaver, *Frozen Echo*, ch. 7.

131. In Norwegian: "Kjært barn har mange navn."

132. The Pizzigano chart belongs to the James Ford Bell Library in Minneapolis, Minnesota. I am very grateful to Carol Urness for giving me the opportunity to examine this glorious artifact in the original.

133. Seaver, *Frozen Echo*, chs. 9 and 10.

134. A section of this chart, which belongs to the Biblioteca Ambrosiana in Milan, appears in Seaver, *Frozen Echo*, p. 212.

135. This broad topic is discussed in detail in Seaver, *Frozen Echo*, chs. 7–10.

136. Claudius Ptolemaeus, *Geographia* (Rome, 1508), BLML, copies 1 and 2, press marks C.I.d.5 and .6; Henry Harrisse, *The Discovery of North America*, 2 vols. (London: H. Stevens, 1892), p. 304; Nils A. E. Nordenskiöld, *Facsimile Atlas to the Early History of Cartography* (New York: Kraus Reprint, 1961 [1889], plate 32 and text; Seaver, *Frozen Echo*, pp. 214–18, p. 363n103.

137. Joseph Fischer, "Das älteste Stadium der Weltkarte des Johannes Ruysch (1508)," in *Zeitschrift* (Bern; Schweizerisches Gutenbergmuseum) 17, no. 4 (1931): 180–81.

138. Skelton et al., *Vinland Map*, pp. 179 and n138, 17n243, 238.

139. See, e.g., *DI* 16, no. 8, and cargo lists in Carus-Wilson, *Overseas Trade*, pp. 252–53; Jón Th. Thor, "Fisheries in the Traditional Icelandic Society," in Sigurðsson and Skaptason, *Aspects*, pp. 611–17; Seaver, *Frozen Echo*, pp. 192–95.

140. Seaver, *Frozen Echo*, ch. 7.

141. *Islandske Annaler*, p. 289; *DI* 3, nos. 597, 632; 4, no. 376; C. C. Rafn

and Finn Magnusen, comps. and eds., *Grønlands Historiske Mindesmerker*, vol. 3 (Copenhagen: Det Kongelige Norske Oldtids-Selskab, 1845), pp. 145–59; Seaver, *Frozen Echo*, p. 89, chs. 6 and 7, appendices A and B.

142. Seaver, *Frozen Echo*, pp. 121–24, 131–37, 150.

143. Ibid., pp. 95, 153–54, 235, 250.

144. Nørlund, "Buried Norsemen," pp. 60–71, 237–45, 251.

145. Bent Fredskild, "Palaeobotanical Investigations of Some Peat Bog Deposits of Norse Age at Quagssiarssuk, South Greenland," *MoG* 204, no. 5 (1978): 1–41; idem, "Agriculture in a Marginal Area: South Greenland from the Norse Landnam (AD 985) to the Present (1985)" in Hilary H. Birks, H. J. B. Birks, Peter Emil Kaland, and Dagfinn Moe, eds., *The Cultural Landscape: Past, Present and Future* (Cambridge, England: Cambridge University Press, 1988), pp. 381–94; Kevin D. Pang, "Climatic Impact of the Mid-Fifteenth Century Cuwae Caldera Formation, as Reconstructed from Historical and Proxy Data," *Eos* 74 (1993): 106; Seaver, *Frozen Echo*, pp. 243–48.

146. Ingvi Thorsteinsson, "The Environmental Effects of Farming in South Greenland in the Middle Ages and the Twentieth Century," in Sigurðsson and Skaptason, *Aspects*, pp. 258–63.

147. Axel Kristinsson, "Productivity and Population in Pre-Industrial Iceland," in Sigurðsson and Skaptason, *Aspects*, pp. 270–78.

148. Jette Arneborg, Jan Heinemeier, Niels Lynnerup, Henrik L. Nielsen, Niels Rud, and Árny E. Sveinbjörnsdóttir, "Change of Diet of the Greenland Vikings Determined from Stable Carbon Isotope Analysis and 14C Dating of Their Bones," *Radiocarbon* 41, no. 2 (1999): 157–58; Thomas McGovern, "The Economics of Landnám. Animal Bone Evidence from Iceland and Greenland" (report, conference of The North Atlantic Saga, Reykjavík, Aug. 9–11, 1999).

149. Seaver, *Frozen Echo*, chs. 8–10.

150. Maryanne Kowaleski, "The Western Fisheries," in David J. Starkey, Chris Reid, and Neil Ashcroft, eds., *England's Sea Fisheries: The Commercial Sea Fisheries of England and Wales since 1300* (London: Chatham Publishing, 2000), pp. 23–29; idem, "The Expansion of the South-Western Fisheries in Late Medieval England," *Economic History Review* 53, no. 3 (2000): 429–54, esp. p. 450.

151. Finn Gad, *Grønlands historie*, vol. 1 (Copenhagen: Politiken, 1970), p. 223; J. Kisbye Møller, "Isaac de la Peyrère: Relation du Groenlande," *Grønland* 29 (1981): 168–84; [Henry Lintot and John Osborn, eds.], *A Collection of Voyages and Travels*, vol. 2 (London: Henry Lintot and John Osborn, 1744), pp. 363–406. See also Seaver, *Frozen Echo*, pp. 205–6, 251, 361n65.

152. *DI* 6, nos. 66, 67.

153. The beautiful Cantino map belongs to the Biblioteca Estense in Modena, Italy. A portion of it is depicted in black and white in Seaver, *Frozen Echo*, p. 278; see also pp. 277–80.

154. Seaver, *Frozen Echo*, ch. 10.

155. Francisco López de Gómara, *Historia de las Indias* (first published in Seville, 1553), as cited in Harrisse, *Discovery*, vol. 1, p. 131.

156. James M. Cornelius, *The Norwegian Americans* (New York: Chelsea House Publishers, 1989), pp. 31–32.

157. Skelton et al., *The Vinland Map* (1995), p. xvii.

Chapter 3

1. Barbara Shailor, *Catalogue of Medieval and Renaissance Manuscripts in the Beinecke Rare Book and Manuscript Library, Yale University*, vol. 2 (Binghamton, N.Y.: Medieval and Renaissance Texts and Studies, 1987), pp. 183–86.

2. Laurence C. Witten, "Vinland's Saga Recalled," in Skelton et al., *Vinland Map* (1995 ed.), p. li.

3. Wilcomb E. Washburn, ed., *Proceedings of the Vinland Map Conference* (Chicago: University of Chicago Press, 1971), p. 4; Witten, "Vinland's Saga," pp. xli–xlii.

4. Witten, "Vinland's Saga," p. xlii.

5. Skelton et al., *Vinland Map*, p. 3.

6. Typescript draft to an article by E. G. R. Taylor, "The Vinland Map," with a handwritten addendum by Eila Campbell: "Written in January 1964." BLML, "Papers of Eila Campbell." Campbell acted as E. G. R. Taylor's "academic aid" after Taylor's eyesight had been impaired by a stroke in June of 1963. Nothing in this draft, or in correspondence from the last period prior to her death in 1966, suggests that Taylor was intellectually unfit in the manner implied by George D. Painter in the 1995 edition of *The Vinland Map and the Tartar Relation*, pp. xiii–xiv.

7. Washburn, *Proceedings*, pp. 4, 8, 14 (quote).

8. Ibid., p. 12.

9. Clipping, "Is the Vinland Map a forgery?" *Sunday Times* (London), Mar. 6, 1966, p. 13., BLML, Helen Wallis files, "Vinland Map File/General."

10. Washburn, *Proceedings*, esp. p. 6; Roy Perrott, "The great map forgery," *Sunday Times* (London), Feb. 3, 1974, p. 1; Witten, "Vinland's Saga," pp. xli–lviii; Laurence C. Witten II, "Vrai ou fausse? La saga de la *Carte du Vinland*," *Bulletin du bibliophile* (Paris), no. 2 (1990): 286–313 passim.

11. Witten, "Vinland's Saga," pp. xlii–iii, liii–lviii.

12. Alexander Vietor to Eila Campbell, May 8, 1974, BLML, "Papers of Eila Campbell."

13. Vietor to Helen Wallis, May 28, 1974, BLML, Helen Wallis files, "Vinland Map File/Current."

14. Witten, "Vinland's Saga," pp. liv–lv, lviii.

15. Skelton et al., *Vinland Map* (1995 ed.), pp. ii–xxv.

16. *Star Tribune* (Minneapolis), Mar. 23, 1996.

17. Skelton et al., *Vinland Map* (1995 ed.), pp. xxii–xxv.

18. Washburn, *Proceedings*, p. 4.

19. BLML, "Papers of Eila Campbell."

20. Washburn, *Proceedings*, p. 4

21. T. C. Skeat, former keeper of manuscripts, to his successor D. P. Waley, Jan. 26, 1974; Waley to Skeat, Jan. 30, 1974; Waley to Cyril E. Wright, Jan. 30, 1974; Wright to Waley, Jan. 30, 1974, BMMD, "Recurrent file—Vinland Map."

22. Skeat To The Principal Keeper, Department of Printed Books, Nov. 9, 1966, BMMD, "Recurrent file—Vinland Map."

23. A. H. Chaplin, principal keeper, the British Museum Department of Printed Books, to Skeat, BMMD, "Recurrent file—Vinland Map."

24. Notes on a meeting of George Painter, Eila Campbell, and Derek Weber, the Savage Club, Sept. 23, 1974, BLML, "Papers of Eila Campbell."

25. Peter Schofield, "Bertram Schofield and the Vinland Map," *Imago Mundi* 53 (2001): 136–39, esp. p. 136. Bertram Schofield was the keeper of manuscripts from 1956 until his retirement in 1961.

26. Witten, "Vinland's Saga," p. xliii.

27. Personal information from conversations with Helen Wallis.

28. Notes of a meeting of A. D. Baynes-Cope, Helen Wallis, Eila Campbell, and Derek Weber, the Savage Club, June 2, 1975, BLML, "Papers of Eila Campbell." The minutes of the meeting were written by Derek Weber, editor of the *Geographical Magazine*.

29. Helen Wallis, F. R. Maddison, G. D. Painter, D. B. Quinn, R. M. Perkins, G. R. Crone, A. D. Baynes-Cope, and Walter C. and Lucy B. McCrone, "The Strange Case of the Vinland Map: A Symposium," *The Geographical Journal* 140, no. 2 (1974): 183–217.

30. Waley to Skeat, Jan. 30, 1974; Wright to Waley, Jan. 31, 1974, BMMD, "Recurrent file—Vinland Map."

31. Skeat to Waley, Feb. 6, 1974, BMMD, "Recurrent file—Vinland Map."

32. Chaplin to Skeat, Dec. 1, 1966, BMMD, "Recurrent file—Vinland Map."

33. Peter Schofield Jr., written communications to author, Jan.–Apr. 2000; Schofield, "Bertram Schofield," pp. 136–39.

34. Neil Ascherson and Joyce Egginton, "Forged map that fooled the world," *The Observer* (London), Jan. 27, 1974, pp. 1–2.

35. Ibid.

36. Washburn, *Proceedings*, p. 4; Wallis et al., "Strange Case," p. 184; Skelton et al., *Vinland Map* (1995 ed.), p. xliii.

37. Skelton et al., *Vinland Map* (1995 ed.), p. xlv.

38. Skelton et al., *Vinland Map* (1995 ed.), pp. 4–14; Witten, "Vrai ou fausse?" pp. 286–313; idem, "Vinland's Saga," pp. xli–lviii.

39. Skelton et al., *Vinland Map* (1995 ed.), pp. xlii–xliii.

40. See Paul Grosz (introduction) and Lynn H. Nichols (preface) in Christie's *Catalogue of the Mauerbach Benefit Sale* of items seized by the Nazis. To be sold in Vienna Oct. 29 and 30, 1996, for the benefit of the victims of the Holocaust. I am grateful to Peter Barber of The British Library Map Library for lending me this catalogue. I am also grateful to Andrew Cook for reminding me about the 1955 change in the political fortunes of Spain.

41. Paul Saenger, "Vinland Re-read" (review article), *Imago Mundi* 50 (1998): 199–202, esp. p. 202; Shailor, *Catalogue*, vol. 2, pp. 183–86.

42. Skelton et al., *Vinland Map* (1995 ed.), p. xlv.

43. Washburn, *Proceedings*, pp. 26–27.

44. Laurence Witten, "Collecting Medieval and Renaissance Manuscripts Today," *Library Trends*, Apr. 1961, pp. 398–405, esp. pp. 400–402.

45. Saenger, "Vinland," p. 200; Saenger noted that three hundred thousand dollars at this time equaled three million dollars in 1997. Washburn, *Proceedings*, p. 26; [Wilcomb E. Washburn] Public Broadcasting Service transcript of interview with Wilcomb Washburn, Feb. 13, 1996.

46. Robert Babcock of the Beinecke Library at Yale, e-mail to author, May 14–15, 2000.

47. Shailor, *Catalogue*, vol. 2, pp. 183–86.

48. Witten, "Vinland's Saga," p. li.

49. Tony Campbell, ed., "Chronicle for 1989," *Imago Mundi* 42 (1990): pp. 120–21.

50. Aliene M. Laws, secretary to Paul Mellon, to author, Oct. 22, 1998. Cited here by kind permission from Mr. Mellon and Ms. Laws.

51. Witten, "Vinland's Saga," pp. xlv, liii, lvii.

52. Saenger, "Vinland," p. 201; Shailor, *Catalogue*, vol. 3, pp. xix–xxvii.

53. Washburn, *Proceedings*, p. 8.

54. Skelton et al., *Vinland Map*, p. 3.

55. Saenger, "Vinland," pp. 201–2.

56. Washburn, *Proceedings*, pp. 19–20, 22.

57. Ibid., p. 26.

58. Shailor, *Catalogue*, vol. 3, p. xix.

59. Skelton et al., *Vinland Map*, p. 3.

60. Washburn, *Proceedings*, p. 5; Witten, "Vinland's Saga," pp. xlvi–xlviii.

61. Washburn, *Proceedings*, p. 7.

62. Witten, "Vinland's Saga," p. xlix.

63. Skelton et al., *Vinland Map*, pp. 3–4.

64. Witten, "Vinland's Saga," p. liii; Washburn, *Proceedings*, pp. 4, 9, 26.

65. Perrott, "Great map forgery," pp. 1–2.

66. The author is most grateful to Andrew Cook for pointing out this aspect of the 1974 Beinecke Library publication and for putting me in possession of the volume.

67. Wallis et al., "Strange Case," p. 194.

Chapter 4

1. Skelton et al., *Vinland Map*, p. 3.

2. Ibid., p. 4.

3. Ibid., pp. 3–5, 12–15.

4. I double-checked this information with A. D. Baynes-Cope, who was quite certain that the map and the "Tartar Relation" were bound together when he examined them in his British Museum Laboratory in 1967.

5. T. C. Skeat to R. A. Skelton, Mar. 1, 1967, BMMD, "Recurrent file— Vinland Map." Quoted here with kind permission.

6. Skelton et al., *Vinland Map*, pp. 24–27.

7. G. D. Painter to Skeat, Jan. 14, 1967, BMMD, "Recurrent file— Vinland Map."

8. Washburn, *Proceedings*, p.7.

9. Skelton et al., *Vinland Map*, p. 5; Kirsten A. Seaver, "The Mystery of the 'Vinland Map' Manuscript Volume," *The Map Collector* 94 (1996): 24–29, esp. p. 24.

10. Seaver, "Mystery," p. 25. Some of these codicological details will be discussed further in the last chapter in connection with an item that turned up at a Swiss auction in 1934 and that is likely to have been an original part of the dilapidated Yale manuscript.

11. Point 6 in P. D. A. Harvey's notes, June 9, 1967. These were later forwarded to Yale, where they remain unavailable. The author is grateful for a copy of the notes, together with other comments, which Professor Harvey sent on Aug. 2, 1999, with permission to quote.

12. T. A. Cahill, R. N. Schwab, B. H. Kusko, R. A. Eldred, G. Möller, D. Dutschke, and D. L. Wick, "Report to Yale University Beinecke Rare Book and Manuscript Library: 'Further Elemental Analyses of the Vinland Map, the *Tartar Relation*, and the *Speculum Historiale*'" [1985], BLML, Helen Wallis files, "Vinland Map File/Current," p. 24.

13. The folio numbers refer to the ones added later, in pencil.

14. P. D. A. Harvey, notes, June 9, 1967. Quoted here with permission.

15. Shailor, *Catalogue*, vol. 2, pp. 184–86; Skelton et al., *Vinland Map*, pp. 4–16, 24–25; Seaver, "Mystery," p. 24.

16. Neil Ker to Skeat, Jan. 4, 1967, BMMD, "Recurrent file—Vinland Map."

17. David B. Quinn, professor of modern history at the University of Liverpool, to Skeat, Jan. 6, 1967, BMMD, "Recurrent file—Vinland Map." Quoted here by permission. In a telephone conversation in 1999, Quinn told me that he had withheld judgment up to that time in 1967, but seeing the original map made him suspect that it was fake.

18. Skelton et al., *Vinland Map*, pp. 11, 109.

19. P. D. A. Harvey, notes dated June 9, 1967, point 1. Quoted here with permission.

20. Skelton et al., *Vinland Map*, p. 5.

21. Shailor, *Catalogue*, vol. 2, pp. 183–86.

22. Skelton et al., *Vinland Map*, p. 109, with reference to an examination of the manuscripts at Yale in 1961 as well as to a description Witten had provided in October of 1958.

23. Washburn, *Proceedings*, pp. 8, 9.

24. Skelton et al., *Vinland Map* (1995 ed.), p. xvi. Painter is the only one of the three original authors to attempt an explanation of how and why the boards were switched back to their supposedly intended position—another interference with this volume that has raised far more questions than it has solved.

25. Washburn, *Proceedings*, pp. 22–23.

26. "Confidential Report on scientific examination of the Vinland Map. Property of Yale University Library," Nov, 22, 1968. Signed by A. E. Werner and A. D. Baynes-Cope. BMMD, "Recurrent file—Vinland Map." Confirmed in personal conversations with A. D. Baynes-Cope and cited with permission from the authors.

27. Shailor, *Catalogue*, vol. 2, pp. 183–86; Witten, "Vinland's Saga," p. xli.

28. Skelton et al., *Vinland Map*, pp. 3–5, 12, quote p. 15.

29. Ibid., p. 12–15; Washburn, *Proceedings*, p. 9.

30. Skelton et al., *Vinland Map*, p. 5.

31. Skeat to H. W. Liebert, Yale University, June 17, 1967, BMMD, "Recurrent file—Vinland Map." Quoted with kind permission from Mr. Skeat.

32. Shailor, *Catalogue*, vol. 2, pp. 183–86.

33. Melvin H. Jackson, "Medieval Conventions of Form and the Vinland

Map," pp. 1, 11–12 (paper, Vinland Map Conference, Smithsonian Institution, 1966), BLML, Helen Wallis files, "Vinland Map File/Current." See also Melvin H. Jackson, "The Vinland Map and the Imperatives of Medieval Form," in Washburn, ed., *Proceedings*, pp. 57–76.

34. A. H. Chaplin, principal keeper, British Museum Department of Printed Books, to Skeat, Dec. 1, 1966, BMMD, "Recurrent file—Vinland Map."

35. Marston, "Vinland Map: Dating," pp. 2–3; Skelton et al., *Vinland Map*, pp. 6–8.

36. Neil Ker to Skeat, Jan. 4, 1967, BMMD, "Recurrent file—Vinland Map."

37. Skeat to Skelton, Feb. 17, 1967, BMMD, "Recurrent file—Vinland Map."

38. Painter to Skeat, Jan. 14, 1967, BMMD, "Recurrent file—Vinland Map."

39. Washburn, *Proceedings*, pp. 41–42.

40. Skeat to Skelton, Feb. 17, 1967, BMMD, "Recurrent file—Vinland Map."

41. P. D. A. Harvey, notes, June 9, 1967. Quoted here with permission.

42. Skeat to Alexander O. Vietor, July 14, 1967; Vietor to Skeat, handwritten note, Aug. 12, 1967, BMMD, "Recurrent file—Vinland Map."

43. Skeat to Skelton, with a handwritten addendum ("Note—Copies of all other letters received sent over to Skelton by hand."), Feb. 17, 1967, BMMD, "Recurrent file—Vinland Map."

44. Skelton, memorandum, Sept. 16, 1966, BMMD, "Recurrent file—Vinland Map."

45. Saenger, "Vinland," pp. 199–200.

46. "Peter" Skelton to R. A. Wilson, principal keeper of printed books at the British Museum, June 9, 1966; F. Francis, director of the British Museum, to Skeat, Dec. 5, 1966; Skelton to Dr. A. E. A. Werner, Research Laboratory, the British Museum, Dec. 14, 1966; Skeat to Skelton, Feb. 17, 1967, BMMD, "Recurrent file—Vinland Map."

47. Skeat to Ker, Jan. 5, 1967, BMMD, "Recurrent file—Vinland Map."

48. Washburn, *Proceedings*, pp. 95, 98.

49. Skelton et al., *Vinland Map*, pp. 9–10. Sample watermarks from both the *Speculum* and the "Tartar Relation" appear in plate V, shown just before the main text in the book.

50. Ibid., pp. 4–6, 9–10, 12–15; Washburn, *Proceedings*, pp. 4, 7.

51. Skelton et al., *Vinland Map*, p. 9.

52. C. M. Briquet, *Les Filigranes: Dictionnaire historique des marques du papier dés leur apparition vers 1282 jusqu'en 1600*, vol. 4 (Leipzig, 1923; facsimile ed. of original 1907 edition), p. 715.

53. P. D. A. Harvey, notes, June 9, 1967, point 3. Cited with kind permission.

54. Washburn, *Proceedings*, p. 98.

55. Marston, "Vinland Map: Dating," pp. 1–5 passim.

56. Allan Stevenson, *The Problem of the* Missale speciale (London: Bibliographical Society, 1967), pp. xi, 5, 271, 331.

57. Skelton et al., *Vinland Map*, pp. 9–10.

58. Allan Stevenson, *Observations on Paper as Evidence* (Lawrence, Kans.: University of Kansas Libraries, 1961), pp. 11–12.

59. Stevenson, *Problem*, p. 27.

60. Ibid., pp. 47–48, 56–64.

61. Ibid., pp.50–54, 69.

62. Skelton et al., *Vinland Map*, pp. 9–10.

63. BLML, Helen Wallis files, "Vinland Map File/Current."

64. Skelton et al., *Vinland Map*, p. 16.

65. Ibid., p. 178.

66. Ibid., p. 230.

67. Shailor, *Catalogue*, vol. 2, pp. 183–84.

68. Skelton et al., *Vinland Map* (1995 ed.), pp. xvi–xvii.

69. Ibid., p. xlviii.

70. Washburn, *Proceedings*, p. 42, 23.

71. Ibid., photos pp. xiv–xv.

72. Ibid., pp. xi–xii.

73. Robert Babcock, curator of the Vínland Map and its related volumes at Yale, personal communication, Apr. 20, 2001. He made a special check while I was at the Beinecke.

74. "Peter" Skelton to Robert A. Wilson, principal keeper of printed books, June 9, 1966; Skelton to Wilson, June 13, 1966; Skelton to Wilson, Aug. 3, 1966, BMMD, "Recurrent file—Vinland Map." On balance, it seems that Skelton (and probably also Painter) was kept poorly informed about what Witten and Marston were doing in New Haven either before or after 1965. Witten's 1989 statement suggests that communications between London and New Haven may indeed have left something to be desired. Witten said that he had almost no contact with either Skelton or Painter. See Skelton et al., *Vinland Map* (1995 ed.), p. li.

75. See especially Skelton to Wilson, June 13, 1966; Skelton to Wilson, Aug. 3, 1966; A. H. Chaplin to F. Francis, director of the British Museum, Dec. 1, 1966, BMMD, "Recurrent file—Vinland Map."

76. See, e.g., Skelton to Dr. A. E. A. Werner, British Museum Research Laboratory, Dec. 14, 1966; Skelton to Skeat, Dec. 14, 1966; Skelton to Skeat, Mar. 3, 1967, BMMD, "Recurrent file—Vinland Map."

77. Skelton to Skeat, Mar. 3, 1967; Skeat to Skelton, Mar. 8, 1967, BMMD, "Recurrent file—Vinland Map."

78. Skelton to Skeat, Mar. 20, 1967, BMMD, "Recurrent file—Vinland Map."

79. John H. Ottemiller, associate university librarian at Yale, to Francis, with a cc. to Vietor, BMMD, "Recurrent file—Vinland Map."

80. Shailor, *Catalogue*, vol. 3: re MS 232 (*Marston Manuscripts*), which had reached Marston through Ferrajoli, Rauch, and Witten.

81. Ibid.

82. A. N. E. D. Schofield, "England and the Council of Basel," in Walter Brandmüller and Remigius Bäumer, eds., *Annuarium Historiae Conciliorum* (Amsterdam, 1973), Heft 1, pp. 1–117, esp. pp. 1–3.

83. Ibid., pp. 3, 27, 92, 105–6; Joachim W. Stieber, *Pope Eugenius IV, the Council of Basel and the Secular and Ecclesiastical Authorities in the Empire* (Leiden: E. J. Brill, 1978), pp. 10–13, 19–26, 40. Eugene's complaint about poor attendance was not unfounded: it had taken time for the delegates to be selected and even longer for them to reach Switzerland from the remoter parts of Europe, and the participants did not necessarily stay long once they had arrived. For example, the English delegation did not reach Basel until late February 1433, having probably set off sometime in December. After 1435 neither church nor crown in England was represented at Basel, chiefly as a protest against what they considered a bias in favor of the French king's interests.

84. Schofield, "England," pp. 6–9, 27–37, 109.

85. Beata Losman, *Norden och reformkonsilierna 1408–1449*, Studia Historica Gothoburgensia 11 (Göteborg, 1970), pp. 123, 152–59 passim, 195.

86. Johannes Haller, ed., *Concilium Basiliense*, vol. 3, *Die Protokolle des Concils von 1434 und 1435 aus dem Manuale des Notars Bruneti und einer Römisches Handschrift* (Basel, 1900), p. 46; Gustav Beckmann, Rudolf Wackernagel, and Giulio Coggiola, eds., *Concilium Basiliense*, vol. 5, *Tagebuchaufzeichnungen 1431–1435 und 1438; Acten der Gesandtschaft nach Avignon und Konstantinopel 1437–1438; Brief des Enea Silvio 1433; Tagebuch des Andrea Gatari 1433–1435* (Basel, 1904), pp. 84, 397.

87. Erik Lönnroth, *Sverige och Kalmarunionen, 1397–1457*, 2nd ed., Studia Historica Gothoburgensia 10 (Göteborg, 1969), pp. 67–69, 72, 121–25; Losman, *Norden*, pp. 113–18, 121–30, 142–46; Seaver, *Frozen Echo*, pp. 158–67 passim, 176–87 passim, 320.

88. Losman, *Norden*, pp. 123, 130, 142–54, 165.

89. Seaver, *Frozen Echo*, pp. 141–58 passim, 174, 186, 188, 197–99, 237–38, 309, 327, 358–59, 365; *DN* 17: 515 (letter dated Sept. 24, 1433, signed by An. de Adria).

90. Washburn, *Proceedings*, pp. 6–7; Skelton et al., *Vinland Map* (1995 ed.), pp. xliv, xlvi–li, 3–5.

91. Skelton et al., *Vinland Map* (1995 ed.), p. xvi, n19 (referring to private information from H. M. Nixon, 1967, on his examination of the *Speculum* binding at the British Museum).

92. Ibid., p. li.

93. Ker to Skeat, Jan. 4, 1967, BMMD, "Recurrent file—Vinland Map."

94. B. W. Langlands, professor of geography, Makerere University, Kampala, Uganda, to George Painter, Oct. 17, 1974, copy, BLML, Helen Wallis files, "Vinland Map File/Current."

Chapter 5

1. Skelton et al., *Vinland Map* (1995 ed.), p. vii.

2. Laurence C. Witten II (class of 1948), "The Wormhole Mystery," *Williams Alumni Review* (Nov. 1965).

3. Washburn, *Proceedings*, pp. 24–25.

4. Ibid., pp. 15–18.

5. Ibid., pp. 15–16.

6. E. G. R. Taylor, typescript draft of article on the Vínland Map, Jan. 1964; Skelton to Taylor, Oct. 21, 1963, BLML, "Papers of Eila Campbell," folders 1 and 2a, b.

7. E. G. R. Taylor, "The Vinland Map," *Journal of the Institute of Navigation* 27, no. 2 (1974): 195–205; Michael W. Richey, "The Vinland Map" (review), *Journal of the Institute of Navigation* 19, no. 1 (1966): 124–25; Michael Richey, "E. G. R. Taylor and the Vinland Map," *The Journal of Navigation* 53, no. 2 (2000): 193–205.

8. David B. Quinn, "Raleigh Ashton Skelton: His Contributions to the History of Discovery," *Imago Mundi* 25 (1971): 13–15; Philip R. Harris, *History of the British Museum Library, 1753–1973* (London: The British Library, 1998), pp. 585n, 593, 610, 646, 667–68.

9. P. R. Harris, ed., *The Library of the British Museum: Retrospective Essays on the Department of Printed Books* (London: The British Library, 1991), p. 257.

10. Alain de Botton, review of *Marcel Proust: A Biography*, by Jean-Yves Tadié, *Sunday Telegraph*, July 2, 2000; Euan Cameron, review of the same work, *Daily Telegraph*, July 22, 2000.

11. George D. Painter is still alive and living in retirement at the time of the present book's completion (2003).

12. Shailor, *Catalogue*, vol. 3, pp. xvii–xviii.

13. Haraldur Sigurðsson, "Vínland Map."

14. *Aftenposten* (Oslo), Oct. 11, 1965.

15. Ibid.

16. *Morgunblaðið*, Reykjavík, Oct. 9, 1965, p. 1.

17. Ingstad, "Vinland ruins," pp. 708–35 passim.

18. I am very grateful to Thorsteinn Hallgrímsson at the National and University Library of Iceland in Reykjavík, and to Karen Arup Seip at the National Library of Norway in Oslo, for providing newspaper articles and other public information resulting from Yale's claims regarding the Vínland Map.

19. Henning Sinding-Larsen's interview with Helge Ingstad, *Aftenposten* (Oslo), Oct. 11, 1965. The translation of the quote is mine.

20. Washburn, *Proceedings*, p. 25.

21. Charles Swithinbank, letter to the editor of Oct. 11, 1965, the *Times*, London, Oct. 13, 1965.

22. Clipping from *New York Times*, Dec. 11, 1965. Amintore Fanfani was also president of the United Nations General Assembly and professor of economic history at the University of Rome. Clipping from *New York Times*, Dec. 14, 1965, BLML, "Papers of Eila Campbell," folder 4.

23. Haraldur Sigurðsson, "Vínland Map"; idem, *Kortasaga Íslands*, vol. 1, pp. 261–62.

24. G. R. Crone, librarian and map curator, Royal Geographical Society, letter to the *Times*, Oct. 14, 1965; Skelton, letter to the *Times*, Oct. 14, 1965, BLML, "Papers of Eila Campbell," folder 4.

25. G. R. Crone, "The Vinland Map Cartographically Considered" (review), *Geographical Journal* 132 (1966): 75–80; Skelton, letter of Apr. 24, 1966, *Geographical Journal* 132 (1966): 336–39; Crone and Skelton, letters, *Encounter* (Apr. 1966). BLML, "Papers of Eila Campbell," folder 4.

26. *New York Times Book Review* 70 (Nov. 7, 1965), p. 7.

27. Clipping from *Times Literary Supplement*, Nov. 25, 1965, BLML, "Papers of Eila Campbell," folder 4.

28. Wilcomb E. Washburn, review of *The Vinland Map and the Tartar Relation*, *American Historical Review* 71 (Apr. 1966): 927–28; Wilcomb E. Washburn, "Examen critique des Amérique," *La découverte de l'Amérique* (Dixième stage international d'études humanistes, Tours, 1966) (Paris, 1968), pp. 77–87, quote from p. 82 ("C'était précisément à l'époque de la carte Vinland, le deuxième quart du quinzième siècle, que les moines de Vienne et de Klosterneuburg commencèrent à créer une projection scientifique, en utilisant les tables astronomiques et autres moyens.").

29. I am grateful to Professor Solveig Zempel at St. Olaf College, Northfield, Minn., for sending along this newspaper article and for other help and support in preparing the present book.

30. Skelton et al., *Vinland Map* (1995 ed.), pp. vii–viii.

31. *American Heritage* 15, no. 6 (Oct. 1965).

32. G. R. Crone, "How Authentic is the 'Vinland Map'?" *Encounter* 26 (Feb. 1966): 75–78; "Is the Vinland Map a forgery?" *Sunday Times*, Mar. 6, 1966, p. 13.

33. "Is the Vinland Map a forgery?" p. 13.

34. Richey, "Vinland Map, pp. 124–25; Richey, "E. G. R. Taylor," p. 197.

35. "Is the Vinland Map a forgery?" p. 13.

36. Taylor, "Vinland Map," pp. 195–205; Eila Campbell, "Verdict on the Vinland Map," *Geographical Magazine* (London), Apr. 1974, pp. 307–12.

37. Clipping, "A find or a fraud?" review of *Proceedings of the Vinland Map Conference*, by W. E. Washburn, *Times Literary Supplement*, Apr. 28, 1972, BLML, "Papers of Eila Campbell."

38. Washburn, *Proceedings*, p. 185; Skelton et al., *Vinland Map* (1995 ed.), p. xxvii.

39. Public Broadcasting Service, *News Hour*, Feb. 13, 1996, "The World before Columbus." Charlayne Hunter Gault interviews Wilcomb Washburn. I taped this interview at the time; a transcript may also be found at http://www.pbs.org/newshour/bb/science/map_2-13.html.

40. Walter McCrone and Kenneth M. Towe, personal communications, Sept.–Oct. 1998; Kenneth M. Towe to Wilcomb E. Washburn, Mar. 4, 1996, cited here with kind permission. See also John Noble Wilford, "Disputed Medieval Map Held Genuine After All," *New York Times*, Feb. 12, 1996; Kirsten A. Seaver, "The Vinland Map: A $3,500 duckling that became a $25,000,000 swan," *Mercator's World* 2, no. 2 (1997): 42–47.

41. Wilford, "Disputed Medieval Map"; [Wilcomb Washburn], PBS *News Hour*, Feb. 13, 1996.

42. Author to John Ryden, Jan. 9, 1997; author to Ralph Franklin, Jan. 28, 1997.

43. For the likely printing history of this map, see Elizabeth Harris, "The Waldseemüller World Map: A Typographical Appraisal," *Imago Mundi* 37 (1987): 30–53.

44. Skelton to Wilson, July 8, 1966; Wilson to Skelton, July 11, 1966, BL, Vinland Map file.

45. Skelton to Wilson, July 25, 1966; Wilson to Francis, July 26, 1966; Francis to Wilson, Aug. 2, 1966; Skelton to Wilson, Aug. 3, 1966; Skelton, memorandum, Sept. 16, 1966, BL, Vinland Map file.

46. Francis to James Tanis, Oct. 20, 1966; A. H. Chaplin (the new principal keeper of printed books) to Francis, Dec. 1, 1966, BL, Vinland Map file.

47. BMMD, "Recurrent file—Vinland Map."

48. Skelton, memorandum, Dec. 14, 1966; Skelton, "Progress Report," Dec. 22, 1966; T. C. Skeat, memo, Dec. 30, 1966, BMMD, "Recurrent file—Vinland Map."

49. Skelton to Skeat, Feb. 2, 1967, BMMD, "Recurrent file—Vinland Map."

50. *Aftenposten* (Oslo), Feb. 22 and 23, 1967.

51. Ibid., Jan. 14, 1967, p. 1. I am very grateful to Karen Arup Seip and Benedicte Gamborg Briså for valuable help, including archival material, from the Map Collection, National Library, Oslo.

52. The New York office of the Bank of Norway confirmed (by telephone, Apr. 2001) that the 1965 value was 7.14 *kroner* to the U.S. dollar.

53. *Morgunblaðid*, Reykjavík, Mar. 15, 1967, pp. 1, 19. I am most grateful to Thorsteinn Hallgrímsson for valuable archival material from the National and University Library of Iceland, and for making further inquiries regarding the matter of insurance, including with the representative for the Ministry of Culture who went to Oslo to fetch the map in 1967. This official does not recall being told about the insurance. The published newspaper information is so far the best source for the amount involved.

54. Ib Kejlbo, "Chronicle," *Imago Mundi* 23 (1969): 109–10.

55. Henrik Dupont, curator of maps and prints, Royal Library, Copenhagen, e-mail to author, Jan. 23, 1997.

56. William W. Fitzhugh, personal communication, Apr. 27, 2000.

Chapter 6

1. Some may wonder about Douglas McNaughton's statements concerning the map's ink; see "A World in Transition: Early Cartography of the North Atlantic," in Fitzhugh and Ward, *Vikings*. The theory has no place in the present discussion because—as McNaughton himself made clear—his analysis contained no new data. It consisted of speculations based on work already done by scientists who dealt with the Vínland Map in their laboratories.

2. "The Vínland Map: A Bibliography," *Pre-Columbiana: A Journal of Long-Distance Contacts* 2, no. 1 (2000): 59–84.

3. Skelton et al., *Vinland Map*, quote p. 177.

4. Washburn, *Proceedings*, pp. 48–56, quote p. 49.

5. Skelton et al., *Vinland Map*, p. 109.

6. Ibid., p. 109.

7. Reflecting on this point some years later, Baynes-Cope came to suspect that the damaged edge was part of a rotted-away gutter that would have made it easier to abstract the two parchment halves. A. D. Baynes-Cope, personal communication, July 2001.

8. Washburn, *Proceedings*, p. 39. A notation accompanying the map in its folder at the Beinecke indicates that ultraviolet light was used for this enhanced black-and-white photograph.

9. Skelton et al., *Vinland Map* (1995 ed.), p. xxix.

10. Werner and Baynes-Cope, "Confidential Report."

11. Baynes-Cope, personal communication.

12. It is important to note the sequence of Baynes-Cope's own disclosures. In his recent article in Fitzhugh and Ward, *Vikings*, Douglas McNaughton presented a version of Baynes-Cope's actions that made it appear as if the British scientist had broken his confidentiality agreement with Yale.

13. Wallis et al., "Strange Case," pp. 208–11.

14. Werner and Baynes-Cope, "Confidential Report." See also Wallis et al., "Strange Case," pp. 208–11.

15. Baynes-Cope, personal communication.

16. Skeat to Skelton, Mar. 1, 1967, BMMD, "Recurrent file—Vinland Map." Quoted here with kind permission from T. C. Skeat.

17. Skelton et al., *Vinland Map*, p. 109.

18. Seaver, "Mystery," p. 24.

19. Baynes-Cope, personal communication.

20. D. J. Donahue, J. S. Olin, G. Harbottle, "Determination of the Radiocarbon Age of the Vinland Map," *Radiocarbon* 44, no. 1 (2002): 45–52.

21. Wallis et al., "Strange Case," p. 211.

22. I am grateful to A. D. Baynes-Cope for valuable help in noting these distinctions.

23. Skelton et al., *Vinland Map*, pp. 4n, 10.

24. Baynes-Cope, personal communication.

25. Werner and Baynes-Cope, "Confidential Report." See also Wallis et al., "Strange Case," pp. 208–11.

26. Cahill et al., "Report."

27. Baynes-Cope, personal communication.

28. Cahill et al., "Report," p. 23.

29. Skelton et al., *Vinland Map*, p. 109.

30. P. D. A. Harvey, notes, June 9, 1967. Quoted with kind permission.

31. In this connection, it is also worth noting that while the map's four parchment corners are to this day dirtier than the main area of the map, except for the center fold, there is no obvious evidence of residual stickiness, suggesting that the parchment had been taped to a work surface.

32. David B. Quinn to T. C. Skeat, Jan. 6, 1967, BMMD, "Recurrent file—Vinland Map." Quoted here with kind permission from Professor Quinn.

33. Neil Ker to Skeat, Jan. 4, 1967, BMMD, "Recurrent file—Vinland Map."

34. Chaplin to Skeat, Dec. 1, 1966, BMMD, "Recurrent file—Vinland Map."

35. Skelton et al., *Vinland Map*, pp. 6, 24.

36. Washburn, *Proceedings*, pp. 41–42, 95, 98.

37. Ker to Skeat, Jan. 4, 1967, BMMD, "Recurrent file—Vinland Map."

38. Skeat to Skelton, Feb. 17, 1967, BMMD, "Recurrent file—Vinland Map." Quoted with kind permission from T. C. Skeat.

39. See Kirsten A. Seaver, "The 'Vinland Map': Who Made It, and Why? New Light on an Old Problem." *The Map Collector* 70 (spring 1995): 32–40.

40. Seaver, "Mystery," p. 29.

41. F. Donald Logan, e-mail to author, Apr. 25, 2001. Quoted with permission.

42. P. D. A. Harvey, notes, June 9, 1967, point 2. Quoted with kind permission.

43. Skelton et al., *Vinland Map*, pp. 4, 16, 24, 26.

44. L.-A. Vigneras, "Greenland, Vinland, and the Yale Map," *Terrae Incognitae* 4 (1972): 53–94, esp. pp. 89–90.

45. Harvey, notes, June 9, 1967, point 2.

46. Skelton et al., *Vinland Map*, p. 3.

47. Skelton et al., *Vinland Map* (1995 ed.), p. xlix. For reference to Witten's illness at that time, see Saenger, "Vinland," p. 200.

48. Shailor, *Catalogue*, vol. 2, pp. 185–86.

49. Harvey, notes, June 9, 1967, point 2.

50. Saenger, "Vinland," p. 200.

51. The author is grateful to F. Donald Logan for permission to cite his suggested interpretations during the summer of 1999 and in the course of e-mail correspondence in the spring of 2001.

52. Wallis et al., "Strange Case," p. 184.

53. Seaver, "Mystery," p. 25.

54. Wallis et al., "Strange Case," p. 194.

55. Skelton et al., *Vinland Map*, p. 109.

56. Ker to Skeat, Jan. 4, 1967, BMMD, "Recurrent file—Vinland Map."

57. Werner and Baynes-Cope, "Confidential Report."

58. Skelton et al., *Vinland Map*, pp. 4–5.

59. Ibid., p. 109.

60. Washburn, *Proceedings*, pp. 30–43, 61.

61. Skeat to A. E. Werner, Dec. 16, 1968, BMMD, "Recurrent file—Vinland Map." Quoted with kind permission from T. C. Skeat.

62. Werner to Skeat, Jan. 6, 1969, BMMD, "Recurrent file—Vinland Map."

63. Ibid. Addendum quoted with kind permission from T. C. Skeat.

64. Typescript to "Travellers to the New World," a BBC Home Service program recorded Aug. 4, 1966, aired Aug. 25. Moderator: Alan Gibson. Speakers: David Quinn, J. R. L. Anderson, L. Witten, R. A. Skelton, G.

Painter, Michael W. Richey. Accessed at BLML, "Papers of Eila Campbell, cat. no. II/3/6, folder II/3/5.

65. Marston, "Vinland Map: Dating," p. 3.

66. Witten, "Wormhole."

67. Prof. Th. DeBeer, Oudt Hollandse Olieverven Makerij, Driebergen, The Netherlands, fax message, Jan. 26, 1999; Ralph Mayer, *The Artist's Handbook of Materials and Techniques*, 5th rev. ed. (New York: Viking, 1991), p. 551.

68. Oak galls or gall nuts are produced by trees reacting to eggs laid by a small, wasplike insect. Gum arabic is a vegetable gum obtained from the Acacia tree native to Egypt and the Levant.

69. Cynthia Karnes (Museum Boijmans Van Beuningen, Rotterdam), "Iron gall ink," http://www.knaw.nl/ecpa/ink/html/intro.html (accessed June 3, 2000).

70. Baynes-Cope, personal communication.

71. Ibid.; Courtauld Gallery (London), information booklet for the exhibition "Material Evidence," Oct. 30, 1998–Jan. 24, 1999.

72. Baynes-Cope, personal communication.

73. Courtauld Gallery, "Material Evidence"; Cornell University Library page images, The Nineteenth Century in Print: Periodicals, "Manufacture of India-Ink" [*Manufacturer and Builder*, vol. 3, no. 5 (May 1871)], p. 102.

74. Evan Lindquist, "Old Writing/Drawing Ink," http://www.clt.astate.edu/elind/oldink.htm (accessed May 13, 2001).

75. Cornell University, "Nineteenth Century," p. 102.

76. Courtauld Gallery, "Material Evidence."

77. Jan Burandt, "An Investigation Toward the Identification of Traditional Drawing Inks" (paper, Book and Paper specialty group session, The American Institute for Conservation 22nd Annual Meeting, June 11, 1994), available on the The American Institute for Conservation Web site (accessed May 14, 2001).

78. "Ink," *Encyclopædia Britannica*, http://Britannica.com (accessed May 13, 2001); Baynes-Cope, personal communication.

79. Mayer, *Artist's Handbook*, pp. 550–51.

80. DeBeer, fax message.

81. Baynes-Cope, personal communication.

82. Jack C. Thompson, message posted on book_arts-listserv.syr.edu, Feb. 6, 1997 (accessed May 13, 2001).

83. Elmer Eusman (Museum Boijmans Van Beuningen, Rotterdam), "Iron gall ink," http://www.knaw.nl/ecpa/ink/html/intro.html (accessed June 3, 2000).

84. Jan Burandt, "An Investigation."

85. Malcolm W. Browne, "Map May Be From Vikings After All," *New York Times*, May 10, 1987, p. 14.

86. *Times* (London), Jan. 20, 1967, BLML, "Papers of Eila Campbell," folder II/3/6.

87. Anne Taylor, "Vinland Map ink puzzles experts," *The Observer* (London), Feb. 5, 1967, BLML, "Papers of Eila Campbell," folder II/3/6. This article mistakenly gives Painter the title of "Assistant Keeper of Manuscripts."

88. *Aftenposten* (Oslo), Feb. 23, 1967, p. 14. From the archives of the Norwegian National Library Map Section, Oslo. The translation of the quote is mine.

89. A. E. Werner and A. D. Baynes-Cope, personal communication, summer 2000.

90. A.D. Baynes-Cope and A. E. Werner, letter to the editors, *Mercator's World* 1, no. 6 (1996): 8.

91. Werner and Baynes-Cope, "Confidential Report." See also Wallis et al., "Strange Case," pp. 208–11.

92. Werner and Baynes-Cope, "Confidential Report." See also Wallis et al., "Strange Case," pp. 208–11.

93. Later, Baynes-Cope experimented with other recipes for inks known to have been used in medieval Europe. In 1969 he demonstrated that the Vínland Map ink has nothing in common with medieval Icelandic inks. A. D. Baynes-Cope, personal communication, 1994.

94. Werner and Baynes-Cope, "Confidential Report." See also Wallis et al., "Strange Case," pp. 208–11.

95. This part of the British Museum is now called the Department of Scientific Research. I wish to thank the present keeper, Dr. Sheridan Bowman, for generous access (July 8 and 9, 1999) to her department's archives with the results of the 1967 Vínland Map investigations performed by A. D. Baynes-Cope and A. E. Werner. I am obliged to A. D. Baynes-Cope for communicating the remark made to him by the photographer.

96. The third photograph is identified as X-Ray no. 364, Record File no. 2693. Ref. Yale University via MSS. Dept. Kodak infrared plate. Type II-N Series 9. I/R Filter 88A Type "B" li. The fourth photograph carries the description "Separation Neg. Type 1, Type B Studio Lights." File no. 2693 also contains some Xeroxed prints made in 1974 from negative 206–6. In print no. 55, the inked outline of the map clearly displays dark outside edges and lighter delineations toward the middle, generally indicating uneven pen pressure. Two more prints made from the same negative similarly display an uneven dispersal of the black pigment.

97. Washburn, *Proceedings*, p. 38.

98. Alexander Vietor to Eila Campbell, May 8, 1974, BLML, "Papers of Eila Campbell."

99. Ibid. See also Walter C. McCrone, "The Vinland Map," *Analytical Chemistry* 60 (1988): 1009–18, esp. p. 1010.

100. McCrone, "Vinland Map," p. 1010; Walter C. McCrone, *Judgment Day for the Turin Shroud* (Chicago: McCrone Research Institute, 1996), p. 41.

101. Wallis et al., "Strange Case," pp. 210–14; Walter C. McCrone Associates, Inc., *Chemical Analytical Study of the Vinland Map*, Report to Yale University Library, Jan. 22, 1974; idem, *Morphology of Ground vs. Precipitated Anatase*, Report to Yale University Library, Aug. 21, 1975; McCrone, "Vinland Map," pp. 1009–18; McCrone, *Judgment Day*, p. 41; Baynes-Cope, personal communication.

102. Walter C. McCrone, personal communication, Palo Alto, Oct. 1998.

103. Walter C. McCrone, "Vinland Map 1999," *Microscope* 42, no. 2 (1999): 71–74.

104. McCrone, *Judgment Day*, p. 41.

105. Perrott, "Great map forgery," pp. 1–2.

106. Notes on a meeting of George Painter, Eila Campbell, and Derek Weber, the Savage Club, Sept. 23, 1974, BLML, "Papers of Eila Cambell"; Skelton et al., *Vinland Map* (1995 ed.), pp. ix–xix, quote p. xvii.

107. Skelton et al., *Vinland Map* (1995 ed.), p. xxvi; Jacqueline S. Olin, "Without Comparative Studies of Inks, What Do We Know about the Vinland Map?" *Pre-Columbiana* 2, no. 2 (2000): 27–36, quote p. 30.

108. Kenneth M. Towe, "The Vinland Map Revisited: An Analysis of the McCrone Reports as an Evaluation of the Problem of the Map's Authenticity," Report to Yale University Library, 1982, p. 12. See also Kenneth M. Towe, "The Vinland Map: Still a Forgery," *Accounts of Chemical Research* 23 (Mar. 1990): 84–87.

109. Towe, "Vinland Map Revisited," p. 9; see also McCrone, *Judgment Day*, pp. 41–42.

110. Cahill et al., "Report."

111. Ibid., pp. 12, 18, 23.

112. Ibid., pp. 1, 3.

113. Skelton et al., *Vinland Map* (1995 ed.), pp. xxix–xxxix, quote p. xxxviii; Cahill et al., "Report"; Thomas A. Cahill, R. N. Schwab, B. H. Kusko, R. A. Eldred, G. Moller, D. Dutschke, D. L. Wick, and A. S. Pooley, "The Vinland Map, Revisited: New Compositional Evidence on Its Inks and Parchments," *Analytical Chemistry* 59 (1987): 829–33.

114. Cahill et al., "Report," p. 6.

115. A. D. Baynes-Cope to Helen Wallis, memorandum, Oct. 19, 1985, BLML, Helen Wallis files, "Vinland Map File/Current." Quoted with A. D.

Baynes-Cope's kind permission. Baynes-Cope explained that the term *crystalline* referred "to the arrangement of atoms in the crystal, not to the visible shape."

116. Walter McCrone to Helen Wallis, Oct. 21, 1985, BLML, Helen Wallis files, "Vinland Map File/Current."

117. Malcolm W. Browne, "Map May Be From Vikings After All," *New York Times*, May 10, 1987, p. 14.

118. McCrone, *Judgment Day*, pp. 46–48.

119. John Noble Wilford, "Disputed Medieval Map Held Genuine After All," *New York Times*, Feb. 12, 1996, pp. B-7 and B-12.

120. Saenger, "Vinland," p. 202.

121. Kenneth M. Towe to Wilcomb E. Washburn, Mar. 4, 1996. Quoted with Towe's kind permission.

122. Katherine L. Brown and Robin J. H. Clark, "Analysis of Pigmentary Materials on the Vinland Map and Tartar Relation by Raman Microprobe Spectroscopy," *Analytical Chemistry* 74 (2002): 3658–61.

123. Baynes-Cope to Wallis, memorandum, Oct. 19, 1985, BLML, Helen Wallis files, "Vinland Map File/Current," quoted with Baynes-Cope's kind permission; Baynes-Cope, personal communication by telephone, Nov. 21, 1998. See also McCrone, *Judgment Day*, pp. 42–43.

124. Towe to Ardell Abrahamson, Nov. 20, 1991. Used here with Towe's kind permission.

125. Rolv Petter Amdam, "Industrikomiteen i New York 1943–45: Ein kanal for kunnskapsoverføring frå USA til Norge," *Historisk Tidsskrift* 1 (2000), http://www.uit.no/ht/art/001.pdf (accessed May 27, 2001).

126. J. Victor Owen, Department of Geology, St. Mary's University, Halifax, Nova Scotia, personal communication, May 23, 2001.

127. Note that this process required the addition of barium carbonate to neutralize the sulfuric acid. *Die Produkt-Entwicklung bei KRONOS*, 1991, p. 5; Truls Tandberg, retired CEO of Kronos Titan A/S, Fredrikstad, Norway, personal communications, Nov. 1998–May 2001; Erik Lund, Lundconsult, Fredrikstad, personal communications, Apr. 2001–Feb. 2002. Personal thanks are also due to my brother, Per-Olaf Andresen of Fredrikstad, Norway, for contacting these invaluable sources of information.

128. Torstein Bryn, Sandefjord, Norway, personal communication by telephone, Apr. 18, 1999.

129. Web site created by Emerick Patterson, http://web1.caryacademy.pvt .k12.nc.us/chemistry/rushin/StudentProjects/ElementWebsites/titanium/ History.htm (accessed May 20, 2001).

130. Titan Company A/S of Fredrikstad, now Kronos Titan A/S, acquired the share majority of Titania in 1916. The National Lead Company (now

called NL Inc.) acquired Titania in 1927 and still owns it through Kronos Norge A/S. Titania A/S Web site, http://fuv.hivolda.no/prosjekt/rekelol /titania.htm (accessed May 27, 2001).

131. Erik Lund, e-mail to author, June 24, 2001.

132. Titan A/S in Fredrikstad was bought in 1927 (along with its mining company Titania) by the American firm National Lead, with which it still is affiliated as Kronos Titan A/S, Fredrikstad. See Amdam, "Industrikomiteen."

133. "Report on the Titan Company's history," p. 8; Tandberg, personal communication; Lund, personal communication.

134. Lund, e-mail.

135. Torstein Bryn, *Vision, Colour, Form: The History of Jotun*, trans. Susannah Finzi and Dorothy Thomas (Sandefjord, Norway: Jotun A/S, 1998), p. 39.

136. Truls Tandberg to Per-Olaf Andresen, Nov. 13, 1998, author's possession. Cited here with kind permission.

137. Tandberg, personal communication; Lund, personal communication; *Die Produktionentwicklung bei Kronos*, 1991, p. 5.

138. Towe, personal communication, June 30, 2001.

139. Lund to Per-Olaf Andresen, Apr. 22, 1999, author's possession. Quoted here with kind permission.

140. Ibid.

141. The anatase samples arrived on Nov. 28, 1998, and on Feb. 12, 1999. My warmest thanks to Per Thoen, the present CEO of Kronos Titan A/S, Fredrikstad, for finding and sending these samples, as well as to Truls Tandberg and to Per-Olaf Andresen for their assistance.

142. J. Victor Owen, personal communication, Aug. 20, 2001. Quoted here with kind permission.

143. Peter Buseck, regents' professor, departments of geology and chemistry/ biochemistry, Arizona State University, Tempe, e-mail to author, Jan. 23, 1999. I am also indebted to Carl Djerassi and Richard Zare of the Stanford University chemistry department for establishing contact with Professor Buseck.

144. Lund to Andresen, Feb. 4, 1999, author's possession.

Chapter 7

1. Norman J. W. Thrower, *Maps and Civilization: Cartography in Culture and Society*, 2nd ed. (Chicago: University of Chicago Press, 1999), pp. 441–43; P. D. A. Harvey, *Medieval Maps* (Toronto and Buffalo: University of Toronto Press, 1991), p. 19–21; Oswald Ashton Wentworth Dilke, *Greek and Roman Maps* (London: Thames and Hudson, 1985), p. 173; Claude Nicolet, *Space, Geography, and Politics in the Early Roman Empire*, Jerome Lectures 19 (Ann Arbor: University of Michigan Press, 1991).

2. J. B. Harley and David Woodward, eds., *The History of Cartography*,

vol. 1, *Cartography in Prehistoric, Ancient, and Medieval Europe and the Mediterranean* (Chicago and London: University of Chicago Press, 1987), p. 263.

3. Ibid., pp. 136, 263, 318–21, 342.

4. Skelton et al., *Vinland Map*, pp. 172–75.

5. Ibid., p. 119.

6. Washburn, *Proceedings*, pp. xi, 56–61.

7. Melvin H. Jackson, review of *The Vinland Map and the Tartar Relation*, by Skelton et al., *The Cartographer* (Ontario; renamed *Canadian Cartographer* in 1967) 3, no. 2 (1966): 14–17. The editors noted that Jackson's article was submitted on Mar. 29, 1966.

8. Leo Bagrow, "The Origin of Ptolemy's Geographia," *Geografiska Annalar* (Stockholm) (1943): 335.

9. Skelton et al., *Vinland Map*, pp. 110–11.

10. Petrus Aillacus [Pierre d'Ailly], *Imago Mundi*, trans. Edwin F. Keever (Wilmington, N.C., 1948), typescript, British Library 10002.i.18., ch. 11.

11. Frank Lestringant, "Îles," in Monique Pelletier, ed., *Géographie du Monde au Moyen Age et à la Renaissance* (Paris: Éditions du C.T.H.S., 1989), pp. 165–67, esp. p. 166. In Book 7, ch. 5, of the *Geographia*, Ptolemy noted that "the most northern parallel is sixty-three degrees north of the equator and is called the parallel passing through the island of Thule." See [Claudius Ptolemæus], *Claudius Ptolemy: The Geography*, trans. Edward L. Stevenson, with an introduction by Josef Fischer (New York: The New York Public Library, 1932), pp. 26, 159–60.

12. Dilke, *Greek*, pp. 33–35; Germain Aujac, "L'Île de Thulé, de Pythéas à Ptolémée," in Pelletier, *Géographie*, pp. 181–90.

13. Dilke, *Greek*, pp. 62–64, 206n40; Harley and Woodward, *History*, vol. 1, pp. 173–75.

14. Skelton et al., *The Vinland Map* (1995 ed.), p. xvii.

15. *DI* 1: 17–19. The joint archbishopric of Hamburg-Bremen had purportedly been in existence since 858 (*DI* 1: 5).

16. Adam of Bremen, *History*, pp. xiii–xvi, xviii–xx, xiv, xxvii, xxxi–ii. See also Werner Trillmich, "Adam von Bremen Bischofsgeschichte der hamburger Kirche," in *Quellen des 9. und 11. Jahrhunderts zur Geschichte der hamburgerischen Kirche und des Reiches* 11 (Berlin, 1961), which uses the 1917 critical edition by Schmeidler and contains a number of useful observations about the *scholia*, or explanatory additions. None of Adam's original manuscripts survive (the one in the Vatican Library dates from 1451), so circumspection is in order not only with regard to both manuscript and printed versions, but also concerning the *scholia*, which do not necessarily represent eleventh-century thinking.

17. A direct reference to a northern abyss (which the Norwegian King

Harold Hardrada supposedly narrowly escaped), often laid at Adam's feet, is a later insertion that J. M. Lappenberg included in his 1846 edition of Adam's *History*. See Adam of Bremen, *History*, pp. xxxii, 210–11 (Book IV, ch. xxxi), 215 (Book IV, ch. xxxv), 219–20 (Book IV, ch. xxxviii); Trillmich, "Adam von Bremen," pp. 476, 482, 488–91.

18. Adam of Bremen, *History*, quotes pp. 91, 134.

19. Ibid., quotes pp. 185, 193–94.

20. Ibid., quotes p. 194.

21. Ibid., quotes pp. 196, 198, 200. See also Trillmich, "Adam von Bremen," Latin quotes pp. 452, 456.

22. Ibid., quotes pp. 196, 200, 202. See p. 206 for Adam's description of the "Rhiphaean Mountains" east of Sweden, "where there is an immense wasteland, the deepest snows, and where hordes of human monsters prevent access to what lies beyond."

23. Ibid., pp. 211, 215–16.

24. Ibid., pp. 216–18. See also Trillmich, "Adam von Bremen," pp. 484–86.

25. See, e.g., Skelton et al., *Vinland Map*, p. 175; James Enterline, "Cryptography in the Yale Vinland Map," *Terrae Incognitae* 23 (1991): 13–27, which claims (pp. 15–16) that Bishop Eirik's supposed return to Greenland "was probably at the behest of an encrypted recall message."

26. The British Library map is catalogued as Cotton MS. Iberius B.V, f56v. A full-page reproduction of the map may be found in P. D. A. Harvey, *Medieval Maps*, p. 26.

27. Adam of Bremen, *History*, p. 218. See also Trillmich, "Adam von Bremen," p. 288: "Sunt autem plures aliae in oceano insulae, quarum non minima [est] Gronland, profundius in oceano sita contra montes Suediae vel Rhiphea inga."

28. *DI* 7: 5, 17–19.

29. Adam of Bremen, *History*, p. 219; Trillmich, "Adam von Bremen," pp. 488–91, where the German translation of the Latin passage reads: "Außerdem erzählte er, viele Männer hätten in diesem Ozean noch eine weitere Insel entdeckt; sie heiße Winland, weil dort wilde Weinstöcke wachsen, die besten Wein bringen." See also Reeves, *Finding*, p. 187. Translating from the Lappenberg Latin edition (1876), Reeves wrote: "Moreover he spoke of an island in that ocean discovered by many, which is called Wineland."

30. Axel Anton Bjørnbo, "Cartographia Groenlandica," *Meddelelser om Grønland* (Copenhagen) 48 (1912): 68–80; Halvdan Koht, "Den eldste Noregshistoria," *Gamalnorske Bokverk* (Oslo) 19 (1921): 9–11, 90–92; *King's Mirror*, pp. 134–36.

31. Saxo Grammaticus, *Den danske Krønike*, trans. Anders Sørensen Vedel,

reprinted by G. F. Wegener. Samfundet til den danske Literaturs Fremme (København, 1851), p. 17 (from Vedel's introduction), Book VIII, pp. clxxxv–cixxxvi; Skelton et al., *Vinland Map*, p. 163 and n75. Skelton's belief was based on Nansen's advice from Saxo's fellow countryman Bjørnbo.

32. Skelton et al., *Vinland Map*, pp. 172–73 and fig. 5.

33. John Dee, "Map of part of the northern hemisphere," BL, Cotton MS Augustus I.i.1; E. G. R. Taylor, "A Letter Dated 1577 from Mercator to John Dee." *Imago Mundi* (Stockholm) 13 (1956): 56–67.

34. Richard Hakluyt, *Principall Navigations of the English Nation*, photo-lithographic facsimile of the 1589 edition with an introduction by David B. Quinn and Raleigh Ashlin Skelton (Cambridge: Cambridge University Press [for the Hakluyt Society], 1965) vol. 1, pp. xxvii, 248–49, 301–4. For a good color reproduction of Mercator's 1569 world map, see Marcel Watelet, ed., *The Mercator Atlas of Europe*, with contributions by James R. Akerman, Peter M. Barber, Arthur Dürst, Mireille Pastoureau, Marcel Watelet (Pleasant Hill, Ore.: Walking Tree Press, 1998), pp. 80–81.

35. Seaver, *Frozen Echo*, pp. 123–24, 132–37, 150, 262; Skelton et al., *Vinland Map*, pp. 179–82.

36. Hakluyt, *Principall Navigations*.

37. Skelton et al., *Vinland Map*, pp. 179–82, quote p. 179.

38. Ibid., p. 179.

39. *DI* 4: 776; also Pope Nicholas V to the bishops of Skalholt and Holar regarding Greenland, Sept. 20, 1448, *DN* 4: 527. See also Seaver, *Frozen Echo*, pp. 96, 132–37, 174–79 passim, 189, 226, 237.

40. Axel Anton Bjørnbo to Fridtjof Nansen, Feb. 18, 1910, NNLO Manuscript Department, Ms. fol. 1924:301$_B$.

41. Skelton et al., *Vinland Map*, p. 180.

42. Ibid., pp. 173, 180.

43. The American scholar Thomas Suárez, for one, considers Ptolemy's world picture as much more sophisticated than Strabo's. Thomas Suárez, *Shedding the Veil: Mapping the European Discovery of America and the World* (London: World Scientific, 1992), pp. 19–20.

44. Marica Milanesi, "Il *De Insulis et earum proprietatibus* di Domenico Silvestri (1385–1406)," *Geographia Antiqua* (Florence; Giunto Gruppo Editoriale) 2 (1993): 133–46, esp. p. 147.

45. Edward Lynam, *The Engraved Atlas of the World: The Cosmographia of Claudius Ptolemaeus* (Bologna, 1477; reprint; Jenkintown, Penn.: Tall Tree Publishers, 1941), pp. 5–6.

46. Leo Bagrow, *History of Cartography*, 2nd ed., rev. and enlarged by R. A. Skelton (Chicago: Precedent Publishing, 1985), p. 34.

47. [Ptolemæus], *Geography*, p. 26.

48. J. Lennart Berggren and Alexander Jones, *Ptolemy's* Geography: *An Annotated Translation of the Theoretical Chapters* (Princeton and Oxford: Princeton University Press, 2000), p. 22.

49. Concerning the African outlines, L.-A. Vigneras notes that the shape of Africa on the Vínland Map is commonly found on fifteenth-century circular maps, including on Bianco's 1436 world map, which furthermore shows the same two bays on the West African coast that are found on the Yale map. However, Vigneras does not believe that the southern truncation of Africa was inspired by a crack or fold in the Bianco map, thus disagreeing with C. R. Crone's claim that this cutoff was sufficient evidence that the map is a fake. Vigneras, "Greenland," p. 75 and n56.

50. [Ptolemæus], *Geography*, p. 159.

51. Skelton et al., *Vinland Map*, pp. 112–14.

52. Washburn, *Proceedings*, p. 47.

53. Ibid., pp. 50–51.

54. Milanesi, *"De Insulis,"* p. 142.

55. Washburn, *Proceedings*, p. 54.

56. Ibid., pp. 48–54; Seaver, *Frozen Echo*, pp. 259–60. Goldstein's chief source of information about Claudius Clavus Swart was Father Josef Fischer, "Claudius Clavus, the First Cartographer of America," *Historical Records* (New York; U.S. Catholic Historical Society) 6 (1911): 81–101.

57. Skelton et al., *Vinland Map*, pp. 154–55. The beautiful map by Henricus Martellus Germanus now hangs on a downstairs wall in Yale's Beinecke Library.

58. This Martellus map (which shows the 1488 discovery of the Cape of Good Hope by Bartolomeo Días) belongs to The British Library, Add. MS. 15760, ff. 68v.–69. See Harvey, *Medieval Maps*, illus. p. 55

59. Axel Anton Bjørnbo and Carl S. Petersen, *Fyenboen Claudius Claussøn Swart (Claudius Clavus): Nordens ældste Kartograf.* Kgl. Danske Videnskabelige Selskabs Skrifter, 6. Række, historisk og filosofisk Afdeling, VI. 2 (Copenhagen, 1904), pp. 47, 49, 98, 101–2, 132. Through the Innsbruck connections of Father Josef Fischer, Bjørnbo's work appeared in German translation in 1909, entitled *Der Däne Claudius Claussøn Swart* (The Dane Claudius Claussøn Swart). Bjørnbo identified the 1427 Nancy MS as "Cod. Nanc. lat. 441" and the two Vienna texts as "Codex Vindelbonensis latinus 5277" and "Codex Vindelbonensis latinus 3227," the latter in his opinion the superior one.

60. Skelton et al., *Vinland Map*, quotes from pp. 116, n23, 176.

61. G. R. Crone, librarian and map curator, Royal Geographical Society, letter to the *Times*, Oct. 14, 1965, BLML, "Papers of Eila Campbell," folder 4.

62. Kirsten A. Seaver, "Albertin de Virga and the Far North," *Mercator's*

World vol. 2, no. 6 (1997): 58–62. The De Virga world map has been lost since 1932.

63. P. D. A. Harvey, *Mappamundi: The Hereford World Map* (London and Toronto: Hereford Cathedral and The British Library, 1996), pp. 22–24, illus. p. 23.

64. Bjørnbo and Petersen, *Fyenboen*, pp. 188, 197–98, 208–15, 223; Bjørnbo, "Cartographia," pp. 101, 108.

65. Skelton et al., *Vinland Map*, p. 176 incl. n129.

66. Axel Anton Bjørnbo to Fridtjof Nansen, Feb. 26, Mar. 2 and 3, 1910, NNLO Manuscript Department; Nansen to Bjørnbo, Feb. 7, 1910; Feb. 15, 1911, RLC, Ny kgl. Samling 2508. 2°, Nansen folder.

67. Bjørnbo, "Cartographia Groenlandica," pp. v–vi, x–xi, 101, 108–16.

68. Ibid., pp. 116–17.

69. Concerning the connection between the cardinals Fillastre and D'Ailly, see John Hine Mundy and Kennerly M. Woody, eds., *The Council of Constance: The Unification of the Church*, trans. Louise Ropes Loomois, Columbia University Records of Civilization Sources and Studies 63 (New York and London: Columbia University Press, 1961), p. 200.

70. [Petrus Aillacus], *Imago*, ch. 11. In *The Vinland Map and the Tartar Relation*, Skelton observed (p. 154n42) that D'Ailly's notions about east-west navigation went back to Roger Bacon's *Opus Majus*.

71. [Petrus Aillacus], *Imago*, ch. 13.

72. Ibid., chs. 13–15, quotes ch. 15.

73. Ibid., chs. 13–15, ch. 26; Skelton et al., *Vinland Map*, p. 129.

74. Ibid., pp. 155, 167.

75. Ibid., p. 117.

76. Ibid., pp. 136 (quote), 151–53.

77. Concerning the cartographical impact of Marco Polo's travels, see John Larner, *Marco Polo and the Discovery of the World* (New Haven and London: Yale University Press, 1999).

78. Vigneras, "Greenland," p. 80; Thomaso Porcacchi da Castiglione, *L'Isole piv famoso del mondo*, arretino e intagliate dá Girolamo Porro (Venetia, 1572), British Library Maps C.7.b.19., p. 109. On this world map, the Caspian Sea is an oval shape shown inland from the Black Sea.

79. Skelton et al., *Vinland Map*, pp. 119–20, 149–50, 153, 155, 231.

80. *Landnámabók*, pp. 2–3.

81. Pulsiano and Wolf, *Medieval Scandinavia*, pp. 110, 163–64; C. J. Brandt, ed., *Lucidarius, en Folkebog fra Middelalderen*, Det nordiske Litteratur-Samfund, Nordiske Oldskrifter 7 (Copenhagen, 1849), pp. i–ii, v. *Lucidarius* succeeded so well that after the Reformation, a suitably retailored version was produced and reprinted right into the eighteenth century.

82. Pulsiano and Wolf, *Medieval Scandinavia*, pp. 163–65; Brandt, *Lucidarius*, pp. iv, xvii–xxi, 42–43, 54.

83. Koht, "Den eldste," pp. 9–11.

84. Ibid., pp. 9–11.

85. Ibid., pp. 9–11; my translation.

86. Janet Bately, ed., *The Old English Orosius*, Early English Text Society S.S. 6 (London: Oxford University Press, 1980), p. 15; Richard Hakluyt, *The Principal Navigations Voyages Traffiques and Discoveries of the English Nation*, vol. 1 (Glasgow: James MacLehose and Sons, 1903), pp. 13–14. For a useful recent article on the Kvens, see Helge Guttormsen, "Did the Kvens Introduce a New Type of Farming to Northern Norway?" In Sigurðsson and Skaptason, *Aspects*, pp. 315–29, with definition of region involved pp. 315–14.

87. *Konge-speilet. Speculum Regale*, p. 16. The most critical passage reads: "That mæla menn ok víst, at Grœnalandi liggi á yztu síðu hemsins til norðrs, ok ætla ek ekki land út or kringlu heimsins frá Grœnalandi, nem hafit mikla, that er umhverfis rennr heiminn, ok that mæla menn, thar sem fróðir eru, at that sund skerist ihjá [alt.: inn hjá]Grœnalandi, er hit tóma haf steypisk inn í landsklofi, ok siðdan skiptisk that með fjörðum ok hafsbotnum allra landa millum, thar sem that nær at renna inn i kringlu heimsins."

88. Ibid., pp. 44–46; quote 1 on p. 44, which also provides the alternative construction *alla kringla*, from another manuscript version; quote 2 on pp. 45–46; quote 3 on p. 45. See also Koht, "Den eldste," pp. 9–11, 90–92; *King's Mirror*, pp. 134–36, 148; Jón Jóhannesson, "Om Haf Innan," *Saga/Sögurít* 24 (1960): 17–28; Rafn and Magnusen, *GHM*, vol. 3, pp. 326–29.

89. Bjørnbo, "Cartographia," pp. 68–85; Koht, "Den eldste," pp. 9–11, 90–92; *King's Mirror*, p. 148; Jóhannesson, "Om Haf," pp. 17–28; Rafn and Magnusen, *GHM*, vol. 3, pp. 326–29.

90. This particular description is from the Arnamagnæan manuscript A.M. 194 8°, written in 1387; these details regarding Vínland do not occur in A.M. 736, I, 4°. Kr. Kålund, *Alfræði íslenzk. Islandsk encyklopædisk Litteratur. I. Cod. Mbr. AM. 194.8vo*. Samfund til Udgivelse af gammel nordisk Litteratur. Københavns Universitet [Editions of Manuscripts], no. 37, Copenhagen, 1908, pp. xix, 8–12; Rafn and Magnusen, *GHM*, vol. 3, pp. 216–19; Jóhannesson, "Om Haf," pp. 17–28.

91. Bjørnbo, "Cartographia," p. 80.

92. Skelton et al., *Vinland Map*, pp. 172–73 and fig. 5.

93. Harley and Woodward, *History*, vol. 1, p. 304.

94. Finn Hødnebø and Hallvard Magerøy, eds., *Snorre Sturluson: Norges kongesagaer*, trans. Anne Holtsmark and Didrik Arup Seip (Oslo: Den norske Bokklubben, 1981), pp. 13–15.

95. Kirsten Hastrup, "Cosmography," in Pulsiano and Wolf, *Medieval Scandinavia*, pp. 108–9.

96. Dilke, *Greek*, pp. 27–29.

97. Anthony Faulkes, ed., *Snorri Sturluson: Edda. Prologue and Gylfaginning* (Oxford: Clarendon Press, 1982), pp. xxvii–xxviii, quote p. xxvii. See also the introduction to Anne Holtsmark and Jón Helgason, eds., *Snorri Sturluson Edda: Gylfaginning og Prosafortellingene av Skáldskaparmál*, Nordisk Filologi, Series A (Copenhagen, 1950).

98. *The Sybil's Prophecy* is the first poem in the *Codex Regius*, which forms a part of the *Poetic Edda*. There is also a rather different version in the early-fourteenth-century Icelandic codex *Hauksbók*. For an English translation of the poem, see Lee M. Hollander, trans. and ed., *The Poetic Edda* (Austin: University of Texas Press, 1962; repr. 1988).

99. Jón Helgason, ed., *Eddadigte. I. Völuspá, Hávamál* (Copenhagen, Oslo, Stockholm, 1951), p. 1.

100. See, e.g., the glossary discussion in Faulkes, ed., *Snorri Sturluson: Edda. Prologue and Gylfaginning*, p. 100.

101. For an English translation of Snorri's *Edda*, see, e.g., Anthony Faulkes, *Snorri Sturluson, Edda* (London and Melbourne: Everyman's Classics, 1987).

102. Snorri's *Edda* consists of four sections: Prologue, *Gylfaginning*, *Skáldskaparmál*, and *Háttatal*.

103. Faulkes, *Snorri Sturluson*.

104. It is doubtful that Skelton was aware that the *Historia Norvegiæ* exists only in a mid-fifteenth-century paper codex that the Norwegian historian P. A. Munch discovered in Edinburgh in 1849. See Asgaut Steinnes, "Ikring Historia Norvegiae," *Historisk Tidsskrift* (Oslo) 34 (1946–48): 1–61.

105. Skelton et al., *Vinland Map*, pp. 173, 180, 201–2, and plate XVIII.

106. Ibid., pp. 201–2 (quote), and plate XVIII.

107. Steenstrup, "Om Østerbygden," pp. 1–53, esp. pp. 42–44 and plate II. The translations of map key texts are mine. See also Seaver, "Renewing," pp. 42–49. Steenstrup's illustration of Thorlaksson's map was copied from Arngrim Jónsson's *Liber de Gronlandia*, catalogued at the Royal Library (Copenhagen) as Gl. kgl. Sml. 4 to Nr. 2876. This version was based on Bishop Thord Thorlaksson's copy of Bishop Gudbrand's own original, which Hans Poulson Resen had owned and annotated.

108. The Latin text and the translation notes are from Peter Hogg's personal communication of July 20, 2000. I am deeply grateful for his help. In translation, the Resen map title reads: "Outline of Greenland and the neighbouring regions towards the north and the west, from a certain old map drawn in a rough manner about a hundred years ago by Icelanders, to whom

that land was then very well known, and from nautical observations made in our time."

109. Peter C. Hogg, "The Prototype of the Stefánsson and Resen Charts," *Historisk Tidskrift* (Oslo) 1 (1989): 3–27. See also Seaver, "Renewing," pp. 42–49.

110. Steenstrup, "Om Østerbygden," pp. 7 (map), 40 (quote). The English translation is mine, based on Bishop Thorlak Thorlaksson's 1669 translation of the text as originally written by Sigurd Stefansson.

111. Ferenc Maron, "A Map, Dating from 1599, Found in Hungary," *Hungarian Review* no. 1 (1967): 20–21; Helge Ingstad, *Vesterveg til Vinland* (Oslo, Gyldendal Norsk Forlag, 1965), color reproduction opposite p. 89; Peter C. Hogg, personal communication, July 2000.

112. Steenstrup, "Om Østerbygden," pp. 1–53 passim.

113. Gustav Storm, "Den danske Geograf Claudius Clavus eller Nicolaus Niger," parts 1 and 2 in *Ymer*, Stockholm, 1889, vol. 9, pp. 129–46; parts III-VI in *Ymer*, Stockholm, 1891, vol. 11, pp. 13–38.

114. Gustav Storm, "Ginnungagap i Mytologien og i Geografien," in Axel Koch, ed., *Arkiv för nordisk Filologi* (Lund, Sweden) 6 (new series, vol. 2) (1890): 342–43. The translation of the quote is mine. The extant Danish MS to which Storm referred is reportedly from about 1434 and found at the Royal Library in Copenhagen, Gl. Saml. 718 fol.

115. Ibid., p. 340.

116. Ibid., pp. 343–44.

117. Ibid., pp. 343–44, 347; Rafn and Magnusen, *GHM*, vol. 1, pp. 79–89; vol. 3, pp. 224 (quote). The translation of the quote is mine.

118. Skelton et al., *Vinland Map*, p. 137.

119. Ibid., pp. 137–38.

120. Armando Cortesão, *The Nautical Chart of 1424* (Coimbra: University of Coimbra, 1954), pp. 39–40; Skelton et al., *Vinland Map*, pp. 137–38. The 1424 nautical chart by Zuane Pizzigano is at the James Ford Bell Library in Minneapolis.

Chapter 8

1. For the documents specifically mentioned, see *DN* 1: 1059; 17: 849, 1184–86, 1260, 1263, 1273.

2. Pope Nicholas V to the bishops of Skálholt and Hólar regarding Greenland, Sept. 20, 1448, *DI* 4: 776; also in *DN* 6: 527. See also Seaver, *Frozen Echo*, pp. 96, 132–37, 174–79 passim, 189, 226, 237; Ludwig Pastor, *The History of the Popes*, 7th ed., ed. Frederick Ignatius Antrobus (London: Paul, Trench, Trübner, and Company, Ltd., 1949), vol. 2, pp. 11–19, 74–75, 86–88, 331–32; *DI* 4: 744, 748–58, 760–61, among others. Translation used here:

L. Rey, "Gardar, the Episcopal Seat of Medieval Greenland," *Arctic* 37, no. 4 (1984): 324–33.

3. Seaver, *Frozen Echo*, pp. 141–58 passim, 174, 186, 188, 197–99, 237–38, 309, 327, 358–59, 365; *DN* 17: 514–15, letter dated Sept. 24, 1433, signed by An. de Adria.

4. *DN* 17: 644–59, 1085. See also Seaver, *Frozen Echo*, pp. 96, 237–38.

5. *DN* 6: 527; Seaver, *Frozen Echo*, pp. 96, 132–37, 174–79 passim, 189, 226, 237.

6. Skelton et al., *Vinland Map*, p. 175, quote p. 196.

7. Vigneras, "Greenland," pp. 61–62; Antoine de la Sale, *Oeuvres Complètes*, vol. 1, *La Salade*, ed. Ferdinand Desonay (Liège and Paris: Bibliothèque de la Faculté de Philosophie et Lettres de l'Université de Liège, 1935). This work was concocted by Antoine de la Sale for the benefit of his pupils, the children of René of Anjou.

8. See, e.g., Skelton et al., *Vinland Map*, pp. 175–76.

9. Skelton et al., *Vinland Map* (1995 ed.), p. xiv.

10. Jón Johannesson, "Reisubók Bjarnar Jórsalafara," *Skírnir* 119 (1945): 68–96. See also Seaver, *Frozen Echo*, pp. 147–51 passim, 154–65 passim, 315–25 passim, 352n38.

11. Samuel Eliot Morison, *The European Discovery of America* (New York: Oxford University Press, 1971), pp. 67–68.

12. W. D. Foulke, *Biography and Correspondence of Arthur M. Reeves* (London: Henry Froude, 1895), pp. ix–xii; Reeves, *Finding*, p. 1.

13. Gabriel Gravier, *Découverte de l'Amérique par les Normands au Xe siècle* (Rouen, 1874), p. xxxvii. According to the front of the volume, only 150 copies were printed, of which The British Library has no. 109 (press mark: 10408.g.9). The library's possession of this volume is probably linked to Gravier's observation (p. xxxviii) that he had undertaken his study because of a letter (Aug. 5, 1872) from Mr. R.-H. Major, the keeper of nautical and geographical maps at the British Museum, asking who those Norse and Breton sailors were who saw America before Columbus, and about whom Gravier had written in his *Découvertes et établissements de Cavalier de la Salle*.

14. Skelton et al., *Vinland Map*, pp. 224–25; *DN* 17 B: 280–86.

15. Pius Bonifacius Gams, *Series episcoparum ecclesiae*, 1873–86, list of Greenland bishops p. 334; Luka Jelic, "L'évangélisation de l'Amérique," *Le Missioni francescane* 8, no. 6 (1897): 556–60, provides his own list of Greenland bishops (revealing a considerable reliance on Gams) and adds to his general observations on this topic made at the 1891 Congress of Americanists.

16. See, e.g., Washburn, *Proceedings*, pp. 109–10, 114, concerning Konstantin Reichard's suggestion that Jelic was linked to the Vínland Map. Referring to early suspicions among members of the Yale History Department, a

London newspaper article brought up Jelic's name in connection with the publication of the McCrones' report on the map's ink. Neil Ascherson and Joyce Egginton, "Forged map that fooled the world," *The Observer*, Jan. 27, 1974, pp. 1–2.

17. Skelton et al., *Vinland Map*, pp. 133 (quote), 135. According to Skelton, the Latin text reads: "Montes inferiores abrupti / In hanc terram primi fratres nostri ordinis iter faciendo ad tartaros / mōgalos samogedos [et] indos transiuerunt nobiscum per obedientiam / et subieccionem tam debitam ˜q' deuotam Iñocentio sanctissimo Patri nostro Pont. max. per totum occidentem et in reliqua parte usque ad mare occeanum orientale." The translation he provides is: "Steep mountains, not very high. The first to cross into this land were brothers of our order, when journeying to the Tartars, Mongols, Samoyeds, and Indians, along with us, in obedience and submission to our most holy father Pope Innocent, given both in duty and in devotion, and through all the west and in the remaining part [of the land] as far as the eastern ocean sea."

18. I am indebted to F. Donald Logan for an independent transcription and translation in which he extends abbreviations and adds capitals as well as punctuation where appropriate. Logan, e-mail to author, May 22, 2002.

19. Skelton et al., *The Vinland Map*, p. 135.

20. Luka Jelic, "L'évangélisation de l'Amérique avant Christophe Colomb," *Compte Rendu du congrès scientificque international des catholiques* (Paris; Sciences Historiques) 2 (1891): 170–84.

21. Ibid., pp. 170, 175.

22. Ibid., p. 170.

23. Skelton et al., *Vinland Map*, p. 129.

24. Ibid.

25. Ibid., pp. 54–55, with English and Latin versions of the "Tartar Relation" text.

26. Anastasius van den Wyngaert, *Sinica Franciscana*, vol. 1, *Itinera et Relationes Fratrum Minorum Saeculi XIII et XIV* (Florence: Qaracchi Ad Claras Aquas, 1929), p. 15.

27. Ibid., pp. 3–26; for biographical data on Friar John, pp. 27–130; for text to the *Ystoria Mongalorum* (longer version), p. 130; for biographical data on Friar Benedict, pp. 133–34; for text to his "Relatio," pp. 135–43.

28. Larner, *Marco Polo*, pp. 23–27.

29. Christopher Dawson, ed., *The Mongol Mission: Narratives and Letters of the Franciscan Missionaries in Mongolia and China in the Thirteenth and Fourteenth Centuries*, trans. by a nun of Stanbrook Abbey (London and New York: Sheed and Ward, 1955), p. 80.

30. Skelton et al., *Vinland Map*, p. 23n6. Painter estimates that the

ultimate *Speculum* edition from Vincent's own hand dates to about or just before 1255.

31. Larner, *Marco Polo*, ch. 7 and appendix 2.

32. Hakluyt, *Principal Navigations* (1903), vol. 1, quote p. liii.

33. Dawson, *Mongol Mission*, p. 2.

34. Wallis et al., *Strange Case*, pp. 187–91.

35. Skelton et al., *Vinland Map*, pp. 21–23, 39–52.

36. Wyngaert, *Sinica Franciscana*, pp. 27–143 passim; Dawson, *Mongol Mission*, p. 2.

37. Skelton et al., *Vinland Map*, pp. 23–24, quote p. 23.

38. Ibid., pp. 21–22; Wyngaert, *Sinica Franciscana*, pp. 42 (quote), 133–43.

39. For the text of Benedict's dictated account, see Wyngaert, *Sinica Franciscana*, pp. 135–43.

40. Skelton et al., *Vinland Map*, p. 40; Casimiro Biernacki, *Speculum Minorum* (Kraków, 1658), pp. 223–24.

41. Quote as translated by Painter in Skelton et al., *Vinland Map*, p. 54.

42. Dawson, *Mongol Mission*, pp. 71–72.

43. Skelton et al., *Vinland Map*, pp. 39–40 and n3; Wyngaert, *Sinica Franciscana*, p. 141.

44. Skelton et al., *Vinland Map*, p. 41.

45. E.-T. Hamy, *Le Livre de la Description des pays de Gilles le Bouvier, dit Berry, Premier Roi d'Armes de Charles VII, roi de France*, vol. 22, *Recueil de Voyages et de Documents pour servir à l'Histoire de la Géographie Depuis le XIIIe jusqu'à la fin du xvie siècle* (Paris, 1908), pp. 4–9.

46. *Monumenta Conciliorum Generalium Seculi Decimi Quinti: Concilium Basiliense Scriptorum* (Vindibonae) 2 (1873): 899.

47. Joseph Paul Bartak, *John Hus at Constance* (Nashville: Cokesbury Press, 1935), pp. 41–45 passim, 65.

48. Biernacki, *Speculum*, pp. 269–71.

49. *Monumenta Conciliorum*, pp. 287–357.

50. *Neue Kronik von Böhmen vom Jahre 530, bis 1780* (Nebst einer geographischen Beschreibung aller Städte, Schlösser und anderer merkwürdigen Orte) (Prague, 1780), pp. 109–72 passim.

51. Schofield, "England," pp. 1–3; Jan Herben, *Huss and his Followers* (London: Geoffrey Bless, 1926), pp. 122–26.

52. *American Catholic Encyclopedia*, vol. 2, Charles G. Herbermann, gen. ed. (New York: Robert Appleton Company, 1907), pp. 334–38.

53. [Petrus Aillacus], *Imago*, chs. 11, 54.

54. Skelton et al., *Vinland Map*, p. 148.

55. Larner, *Marco Polo*, pp. 59, 80–81, 112, 122, 128–31.

56. Vigneras, "Greenland," pp. 79–80.

57. Skelton et al., *Vinland Map*, pp. 132–33.

58. Ibid., pp. 84–86.

59. Ibid., p. 133.

60. Ibid., p. 121.

61. Ibid., pp. 136 (quote), 151–53.

62. Ibid., p. 131–32, quote p. 132.

63. Ibid., p. 131.

64. Cortesão, *History*, vol. 1, pp. 255–75. See also George D. Painter's summary in Skelton et al., *Vinland Map*, pp. 48–49, and Skelton's comments, ibid., p. 131.

65. Skelton et al., *Vinland Map*, pp. 131–32.

66. Ibid., p. 136.

67. Ibid., pp. 66–67.

68. Ibid., pp. 136–37.

69. Vigneras, "Greenland," pp. 53–94, esp. pp. 84–86.

70. *Biskupa sögur* (Copenhagen: Hið íslenzka bókmenntafélag, 1858), vol. 1, p. 795; *GHM*, vol. 3, pp. 13–15; Hermann Pálsson, "Landafundurinn árið 1285," *Saga* 4 (1964): 53–69; *Islandske Annaler*, pp. 142, 196, 383–85. See also Seaver, *Frozen Echo*, pp. 33, 76–77.

71. Skelton et al., *Vinland Map*, p. 137.

72. Ibid., p. 140.

73. Ibid., pp. 135–36, quote p. 135.

74. Ibid., p. 133.

75. Vigneras, "Greenland," pp. 53–94, esp. p. 81.

76. Ibid.

77. Skelton et al., *Vinland Map*, p. 137.

78. Ibid., p. 140.

79. Ibid.

80. Ibid., 255–62.

81. Peter Foote, "On the Legends of the Vínland Map," *Saga-Book* (London; Viking Society for Northern Research) 17 (1966): 73–89, esp. pp. 75–76, 83.

82. Ibid., pp. 75–76.

83. Skelton et al., *Vinland Map*, p. 223.

84. Ibid., pp. 139–40. Please note that not one of these dates has been ascertained.

85. Mads Lidegaard, ed., "Glahns anmærkninger. 1700-tallets Grøn-lændere. Et nærbillede," *Det Grønlandske Selskabs Skrifter* (Copenhagen) 30 (1991).

86. David Crantz, *History of Greenland*, trans. from High Dutch [published as *Historie von Grönland*, 1765], 2 vols. (London, 1767). Printed for

the Brethren Society for the Furtherance of the Gospel among the Heathen. Vol. 1, pp. 254–55.

87. Charles Francis Hall, *Life with the Esquimaux: The Narrative of Captain Charles Francis Hall of the Whaling Barque "George Henry" from the 29th May, 1860, to the 13th September, 1862* (London: Sampson, Low, Son and Marston, 1864), pp. 39–41.

88. Erik Pontoppidan, *Norges Naturlige Historie* (Copenhagen, 1752); idem, *The Natural History of Norway* (London, 1755); Paul Henry Mallet, *Introduction à l'histoire de Dannemarc* (Copenhagen: L. H. Lillie, 1755–56).

89. Lyschander, *Grønlandske*, pp. 14–15, 19–26.

90. Paul Henry Mallet, *Northern Antiquities. A Translation of "Introduction à l'histoire de Dannemarc" [1755–56, 2 vols.]*, w. introd. and added notes by the English translator (London, 1770), pp. 279–83.

91. Arngrim Jónsson, *Grönlandia: Eller Historie om Grønland af Islandske Haandskrevne Historie-Bøger. . . . og først i det Latinske Sprog forfatted af Arngrim Jonsson*, trans. from Latin into Icelandic by Einar Eyjolfsson (1688; repr., Copenhagen, 1732), pp. 43–45.

92. Tormod Torfæus, *Gronlandia antiqua* (Copenhagen, 1706), translated as *Det gamle Grønland* by the author and published in Copenhagen in 1706. Reissued in Oslo, A. W. Brøgger [Oslo Etnografisk Museum], 1947.

93. Pontoppidan, *Natural History*, pp. 228–29.

94. Adam of Bremen, *Adam von Bremen*, pp. 488–91. Trillmich translates this passage as "Außerdem erzählte er, viele Männer hätten in diesem Ozean noch eine weitere Insel entdeckt; sie heiße Winland." An English translation reads: "He spoke also of yet another island of the many found in that ocean." Adam of Bremen, *History*, p. 219.

95. Skelton et al., *Vinland Map*, pp. 62–63 (incl. n11 no. 5), 140.

96. Ibid., p. 140.

97. The author thanks Philippe Buc at Stanford University for verifying this point through an independent translation of the Latin text.

98. Adam of Bremen, *History*, p. 216; and *scholia* 152, 154; p. 219 and *scholium* 159.

99. A passage in *Hungrvaka* concerning the circa 1117 appointment of Bishop Thorlak Runolfsson of Skálholt shows the obvious problems involved in determining even theoretical ecclesiastical superiors in Eirik's case. See *DD*, vol. 2, 43.

100. *Islandske Annaler*, pp. 19, 59, 112, 251–52, 320, 473. See also Seaver, *Frozen Echo*, pp. 32–33.

101. B. Kahle, ed., "Kristnisaga, Tháttr Thorvalds ens Vidförla, Tháttr Ísleifs Biskups Gizurarsonar, Hungrvaka," *Altnordische Saga-Bibliothek*, vol. 11 (Halle a.d. S., 1905), pp. xxiii–v, 102, incl. notes.

102. *DD* 1: 28, 119, 280, 294; 2: 47.

103. *Islandske Annaler*, pp. 20, 59, 112, 113, 252, 320, 473. I will return later to the "floating" Bishop Eirik Gnupsson who preceded Bishop Arnald. Note that the first Icelandic Tithing Law was enacted in 1096. *DI* 1: 22.

104. Adam of Bremen, *History*, Book IV, p. 219 (ch. xxxviii–xxxix).

105. Vigneras, "Greenland," p. 76.

106. Petrus Ailliacus, *Imago*, ch. 31.

107. Adam of Bremen, *History*, quotes p. 194.

108. Skelton et al., *Vinland Map*, pp. 128–29.

Chapter 9

1. *Neue deutsche Biographie*, vol. 5, Der Historischen Kommission bei der Bayerischen Akademie der Wissenschaften (Berlin: Duncker and Humbolt, 1961), article on Josef Fischer by Georg Strassenberger, pp. 194–95; Father Josef Fischer, S.J., to the princess of Waldburg-Wolfegg, telling about his mother's death, Jan. 24, 1902, Archives of Wolfegg Castle. I am grateful to Count Maximilian zu Waldburg-Wolfegg and to his archivist, Dr. Bernd Mayer, for their generosity and kindness in allowing an examination of Father Fischer's letters and a treasure trove of manuscript maps in August 1995, during the Granite Productions filming of a program about Father Fischer and the Vínland Map (shown in the United States on the Discovery Channel ("Arthur C. Clarke's Mysterious Universe"), Jan. 30, 1996. Warm thanks are also due to Dr. Rita Haub, the head archivist at the Jesuit Archives in Munich, for sending me a copy of Wilfried Haller's master's thesis, "Prof. Dr. h.c.P. Josef Fischer S.J.: Leben und Werk" (typescript, ca. 1980), which contained many useful biographical details about Fischer.

2. Josef Fischer, "Autobiographische Darstellung des Lebensganges und des wissenschaftlichen Lebenswerkes," *Imago Mundi* (Berlin) 1 (1933): 58–61, esp. p. 58; Hugo Hassinger, "Josef Fischer," *Almanach der Akademie der Wissenschaffen* (Vienna) (1945): 239–50.

3. My information about Stella Matutina comes partly from printed material that the Stella Matutina Foundation's current administrator, Isolde Listmayer, has provided over time with the greatest generosity; partly from personal correspondence with Frau Listmayer, and partly from Dr. Bernd Mayer, the castle archivist when I was at Wolfegg in August 1995 with Sadie Holland and her Granite Productions team. Concerning Fischer's early contact with Wolfegg, see Fischer, "Autobiographische," pp. 58–61, esp. p. 59.

4. Fischer to the princess of Waldburg-Wolfegg, Apr. 23, 1902, Archives of Wolfegg Castle. I am grateful to Dr. Bernd Mayer for additional information about Fischer's relationship with Princess Sophie, with whom he corresponded for several years. His priesthood stood him in good stead with the princess,

who was a very devout woman, but she must also have been very kind. Fischer's communications to her were invariably respectful, but they also show that he felt free to share some of his private reflections with her.

5. Hassinger, "Josef Fischer," p. 250.

6. [Josef Fischer], *Der deutsche Ptolemaeus aus dem Ende des XV. Jahrhunderts (um 1490) in Faksimiliedrück*, with an introduction by Jos. Fischer (Strasbourg: Heitz and Mündel, 1910).

7. The 1409 map, which belongs to the Bibliothèque Nationale in Paris, is reproduced in Mollat du Jourdin et al., *Sea Charts*, plate 11, text pp. 204–5.

8. [Von Wieser], *Gedenkschrift*, pp. 46–47; Albert Dürst, "Die Weltkarte von Albertin de Virga von 1411 oder 1415," *Cartographica Helvetica* 13 (1966): 18–21; Franz von Wieser, *Die Weltkarte des Albertin de Virga aus dem Anfange des XV. Jahrhunderts in der Sammlung Figdor in Wien* (Innsbruck, 1912), p. 16n1; Seaver, "Albertin de Virga," pp. 58–62. Von Wieser was possibly irked by several oblique criticisms of his own work on Claudius Clavus that Fischer had just published in his 1911 encomium on the Danish mapmaker. Fischer's remarks were respectful as always, but his disagreement with his mentor on certain points was nevertheless evident. Fischer, "Claudius Clavus," pp. 78–79.

9. [Von Wieser], *Gedenkschrift*, pp. 35–37. The translation of the quote (p. 35) is mine.

10. Fischer to Axel Anton Bjørnbo, Jan. 3, 1904, RLC, Ny kgl. Samling 2508. 2°, folder 3. The translation is mine. I am indebted to Henrik Dupont for calling my attention in May of 1995 to this archive in his library.

11. Joseph Fischer, *Die Entdeckungen der Normannen in Amerika*, supp. vol. 21 of *Stimmen aus Maria-Laach* (Freiburg in the Breisgau: *Stimmen*, 1902). This work appeared in English translation the following year.

12. Fischer, *Claudius Clavus*, pp. 73–101.

13. Bjørnbo and Petersen, *Fyenboen*.

14. Fischer to Axel Anton Bjørnbo, postcard, no date, RLC, Ny kgl. Samling 2508. 2°, folder 3. See also Josef Fischer, "Die älteste Karte vom Fürstentum Liechtenstein. Mit einem Faksimilie der Karte." *Jahrbuch d. histor. Vereins von Liechtenstein* (Vadus) 10 (1910).

15. Bjørnbo to Fridtjof Nansen, Feb. 26, Mar. 2 and 3, 1910, NNLO, Ms. fol. 1924:301$_B$; Nansen to Bjørnbo, Feb. 15, 1911, RLC, Ny kgl. Samling 2508. 2°, Nansen folder.

16. Anonymous preface (dated Dec. 1911) to Bjørnbo, "Cartographia," pp. x–xi. The translation is mine.

17. Ibid.

18. Fischer hoped that Nansen's new work would be published in English or French translation. He confided to Bjørnbo: "Die nordischen Sprachen

machen mir zu viele Arbeit." (The Nordic languages are too hard for me.) Fischer to Bjørnbo, Jan. 3, 1911, RLC, Ny kgl. Samling 2508. 2°, folder 3.

19. Bjørnbo, "Cartographia," pp. v–vi, x–xi, 101, 108–17.

20. Nansen to Bjørnbo, Feb. 7, 1910, RLC, Ny kgl. Samling 2508. 2°, Nansen folder.

21. Fischer to Bjørnbo, Jan. 3, 1911, RLC, Ny kgl. Samling 2508. 2°, folder 3; Fischer, "Claudius Clavus," p. 96.

22. Fischer, "Claudius Clavus," pp. 73–101, quotes p. 73.

23. Fischer to Bjørnbo, May 24, 1904, RLC, Ny kgl. Samling 2508. 2°, folder 3.

24. The archivist at Wolfegg, Dr. Bernd Mayer, agreed (Aug. 1995) with my assessment of Father Fischer as a scholarly, pious man with a rather rigid personality. See also Seaver, "Mystery," p. 26.

25. Bjørnbo to Nansen, Feb. 26, 1910, NNLO, Ms. fol. 1924:301$_B$.

26. In his book on the Norse in America, Fischer wrote: "In the translation of the Scandinavian works of Storm and Jónsson Finnur [*sic*], etc., I am much indebted to my colleague in the Society of Jesus, Father H. Klene." Fischer, *Discoveries*, p. vi; Fischer, *Entdeckungen*, p. iv, says only "Jónsson."

27. See, e.g., Fischer, *Discoveries*, p. 2.

28. Gunter Schweikhart, *Der Codex Wolfegg: Zeichnungen nach der Antike von Amico Aspertini* (London: Warburg Institute, 1986), pp. 23–28.

29. Robert Haardt, testimonials to Father Fischer, collected by Robert Haardt and introduced by His Excellency Graf Johannes zu Waldburg Wolfegg, *Der Globusfreund* 7 (Nov. 1958): 26–32. The translation of the quote (p. 26) is mine.

30. Bjørnbo and Petersen, *Fyenboen*, p. 47.

31. Fischer to Bjørnbo, May 25, 1904; July 20, Dec. 12, 1906 (postcards); Dec. 29, 1907; Jan. 28, Apr. 6, 1909, RLC, Ny kgl. Samling 2508. 2°, folder 3.

32. Skelton et al., *Vinland Map*, pp. 176n, 177n, 190–91 (quote p. 191).

33. John Goss, *The Mapping of North America: Three Centuries of Mapmaking, 1500–1860* (Secaucus, N.J.: Wellfleet Press, 1990), pp. 16–20; E. Bernleithner, "Austria's Share in World Cartography," *Imago Mundi* 25 (1971): 65–73, esp. p. 69.

34. [Von Wieser], *Gedenkschrift*, p. 36.

35. Fischer, *Discoveries*, pp. vi–vii.

36. Fischer, "Autobiographische," p. 60.

37. Edward Luther Stevenson and Joseph Fischer, eds., *Map of the World by Jodocus Hondius, 1611* (New York: The American Geographical Society and the Hispanic Society of America, 1907). The volume was dedicated to His Highness Prince Max von Waldburg zu Wolfegg-Waldsee, whose father, Prince Franz, had died in 1906. Professor von Wieser is merely mentioned among

those whom the authors thank for contributing information about Hondius (p. 8). Readers who want to look further into Hondius and his work will find excellent information in Hans Wolff, ed., *America: Early Maps of the New World* (Munich: Prestel, 1992); and Rodney Shirley, *The Mapping of the World: Early Printed World Maps, 1472–1700* (London: New Holland, 1993).

38. Josef Fischer and R. von Wieser, *The Oldest Map with the Name America of the Year 1507 and the Carta Marina of the Year 1516 by M. Waldseemüller (Ilacomilus)* (Innsbruck: Wagner'sche Universitäts-buchhandlung, 1903), pp. 3–5.

39. A retrospective view suggests that Hugo Hassinger may have over-estimated the impact of an article by Fischer, "The Oldest Map with the Name 'America' and How It Was Found," *Benzinger's Magazine* 4 (1902). Hassinger focused almost entirely on the late scholar's interest in the Norse. See Hassinger, "Josef Fischer," pp. 242–43.

40. For a reproduction of the whole map and a succinct overview of Waldseemüller's work, see Hans Wolff, "Martin Waldseemüller: The Most Important Cosmographer in a Period of Dramatic Scientific Change," in Wolff, *America*, pp. 111–26 and fig. 6.

41. In his introduction to the *Cosmographiae*, Waldseemüller wrote: "Yet another, a fourth continent has been discovered by Americus Vesputius, and I do not see who justly could rule out calling it after its discoverer Americus, who is a far-sighted man: Ameriges, so to say Land of Americus, or America." Cited from Bernleithner, "Austria's Share," p. 69.

42. For an good facsimile of the 1516 map, see the BLML Maps *920. (536).

43. Fischer and Von Wieser, *Oldest Map*, p. 22. Waldseemüller (b. 1470) died in 1521.

44. Fischer and Von Wieser, *Oldest Map*, pp. 26–29.

45. For reproductions and discussions of the maps in question, see, e.g., Nebenzahl, *Atlas*, pp. 40–43, 52–55; Wolff, *America*, pp. 45–47, 111–26.

46. Seaver, *Frozen Echo*, pp. 275–80.

47. Fischer and Von Wieser, *Oldest Map*, pp. 25–27.

48. Ibid., pp. 5, 21.

49. Ibid., pp. 5–6. Harris, "Waldseemüller," pp. 30–53. The exhibition at the Smithsonian marked the beginning of the 1983–85 tour of the two Wald-seemüller works, which until then had not left Wolfegg.

50. Fischer to the princess of Waldburg-Wolfegg, Nov. 28, 1904; Mar. 3, 1905, Archives of Wolfegg Castle.

51. Fischer and Von Wieser, *Oldest Map*, p. 29.

52. Ibid., pp. 30–32, quote p. 32. Waldseemüller died in 1521 without having drawn such a map of the North, leaving one to speculate about what

details he might have included, and about what he might have done with his *morsus*—an elephant-like, tusked creature depicted in northern Norway. In the winter of 1519–20, Waldseemüller's friend and collaborator, Albrecht Dürer, saw and drew the salted head of a *morsus* that Archbishop Erik Valkendorf of Norway had sent to the pope as a truly exotic gift. See Seaver, "Very Common."

53. Fischer and Von Wieser, *Oldest Map*, pp. 33–35.

54. Ibid., pp. 34–35.

55. Fischer, *Discoveries*, p. 35.

56. Fischer, "Autobiographische," p. 59. The four early Fischer articles were: "War Pseudo-Donis Benediktiner in Reichenbach?" *Historisch-politische Blätter* (Munich) 126 (1900); "Kann Bischof Johannes aus Irland (gest. 1066) mit Recht als erster Märtyrer Amerikas bezeichnet werden?" *Innsbrucker theologische Zeitschrift* (Innsbruck) 24 (1900); "Die Bedeutung des Ciphus de nuce ultramarina (1327) für eine Besiedelung des Festlandes von Amerika durch die Normannen," *Historisches Jahrbuch der Görresgesellschaft* (Freiburg in the Breisgau) 21 (1900); and "Pseudo-Donis und seine Werke," *Akten des 5. Internationalen Kongresses der Katolischen Gelehrten* (Munich) 1901.

57. Fischer, *Discoveries*, pp. vii–viii.

58. Ibid., pp. 57–58, 69, 105, 107; Fischer, "Claudius Clavus," pp. 79, 81–85.

59. Storm, "Den danske Geograf," parts 1–4.

60. The manuscript was not reliably dated until after the publication of the *Entdeckungen*. See Fischer to Bjørnbo, May 25, 1904, RLC, Ny kgl. Samling 2508. 2°, folder 3.

61. Fischer, *Discoveries*, pp. 58 (quote), 62–69.

62. Ibid., pp. 69–71.

63. Ibid., pp. 69–77, 81–85 (quotes pp. 77, 85). For his 1911 (post-Bjørnbo) views, see Fischer, "Claudius Clavus," p. 94.

64. Fischer, *Discoveries*, pp. 83–85, 93, quote p. 84. Fillastre's Latin text reads: "grolandia . . . est versus insulam tyle magis ad orientem et ita tenet totam illam plagam septentrionalem usque ad terram incognitam, de quibus tholomeus nullam facit mencionem."

65. Ibid., pp. 85–94.

66. Fischer, "Claudius Clavus," pp. 94–95.

67. Fischer, *Discoveries*, p. 94

68. Ibid., p. 97. Fischer reiterated this view a few years later, in his article "America, Pre-Columbian Discovery of," *ACE*, vol. 1, pp. 416–23, esp. p. 419. See also Gustav Storm, *Studies on the Vineland Voyages* (Copenhagen: Thiele, 1889), pp. 36–39.

69. Fischer, *Discoveries*, pp. 2–5, 11–14.

70. Ibid., pp. 2–5. Reeves had already made this Adam of Bremen connection in his 1890 work "Finding," pp. 15–19, 187.

71. Father Fischer corresponded regularly with his translator, Basil Soulsby, during the preparation of the English edition, and he was still doing so in 1904, as he wrote to Bjørnbo. Fischer to Bjørnbo, May 25, 1904, RLC, Ny kgl. Samling 2508. 2°, folder 3. See also Fischer to the princess of Waldburg-Wolfegg, July 2, 1902, Archives of Wolfegg Castle.

72. Fischer, *Discoveries*, pp. 21–22; Fischer, *Entdeckungen,* pp. 21–22.

73. Fischer, *Discoveries*, pp. 25–26, 45.

74. Ibid., pp. 20–21.

75. Ibid., pp. 101–2; Fischer, "Claudius Clavus," p. 93.

76. Fischer, *Discoveries*, pp. 21, 101–2.

77. A recent example of this position concerning the Vatican Archives is in Thor Heyerdahl and Per Lillieström, *Ingen grenser* [Without Borders/Limits] (Oslo: J. M. Stenersens Forlag A/S, 1999), pp. 13, 219–22, 227–28, 278–87 passim, 298, 357. This work, which also defends the authenticity of the Kensington Rune Stone and the Vínland Map, has been publicly criticized by Norwegian scholars for the amount of misinformation it contains in a variety of fields.

78. See N. F. Nørlund, *Islands Kortlægning,* Geodetisk Instituts Publikationer VII (Copenhagen: Munksgaard, 1944), p. 11.

79. Fischer, *Discoveries*, pp. 94– 99, 104–5.

80. Ibid., p. 34.

81. Ibid., pp. 32– 35, citing N. A. E. Nordenskiöld, *Studien und Forschungen veranlasst durch meine Reisen im hohen Norden* (Leipzig, 1885), p. 44.

82. Ibid., pp. 44–46n2, 47.

83. Ibid., pp. 56–57.

84. Ibid., pp. 3–7.

85. Ibid., pp. 95, 97.

86. Ibid., p. 106, quote p. 107.

87. [Fischer], "P. Josef Fischer," *Aus der Stella Matutina* 65 (1948–49): 39–40.

88. Hassinger, "Josef Fischer," pp. 239–50; *Neue deutsche Biographie,* article on Josef Fischer by Georg Strassenberger, pp. 194–95.

89. Fischer, "Autobiographische," pp. 58–61.

90. Teobaldo Fischer, *Facsimiles,* BLML, 8.d. The 1447 planisphere (facsimile 29) is at the Biblioteca Nazionale in Florence.

91. Fischer to the princess of Waldburg-Wolfegg, Oct. 24, Nov. 27, 1903; Jan. 16, 29, 1904, Archives of Wolfegg Castle.

92. See bibliography in Fischer, "Autobiographische," pp. 58–61.

93. Fischer to the princess of Waldburg-Wolfegg, Apr. 7, Aug. 26, 1904, Archives of Wolfegg Castle.

94. Fischer to Bjørnbo, postcards, July 24, Oct. 10, 1904, RLC, Ny kgl. Samling 2508. 2°, folder 3.

95. Joseph Fischer, "Die kartographische Darstellung der Entdeckungen der Normannen in Amerika," *Proceedings*, 14th International Congress of Americanists, 1904, Stuttgart. Stuttgart, 1906, 2 vols., vol. 1, pp. 31–39. The list of members and participants (vol. 1, pp. x–xxi) shows Father Joseph Fischer from Feldkirch (Vorarlberg) as a participating member; Jelic is neither a member nor a participant.

96. Josef Fischer, "The Tithes for the Crusades in Greenland, 1276–1282: A Contribution to Ecclesiastical History of the Northmen in America," *Historical Records and Studies* (New York; U.S. Catholic Historical Society) 3 (1904).

97. Fischer, "America, Pre-Columbian Discovery of," pp. 416–23, quotes pp. 419, 420. Fischer had clearly got his idea about "whale teeth" from his translation of a March 4, 1282, letter from Pope Martin IV to the archbishop of Trondheim, which used the phrase *dentibus et funibus balenarum*.

98. Ibid., pp. 416–23, quote p. 422.

99. Fischer to the princess of Waldburg-Wolfegg, Jan. 4, 1905, Archives of Wolfegg Castle. President Roosevelt's letter was reportedly dated Dec. 19, 1904. See also Josef Fischer, "Die älteste Weltkarte mit dem Namen 'Berlin,' " *Stimmen aus Maria-Laach* 64 (1903).

100. Fischer to the princess of Waldburg-Wolfegg, Sept. 24, 1904, Archives of Wolfegg Castle.

101. Fischer to Bjørnbo, postcards, May 9, Dec. 9, 1908, RLC, Ny kgl. Samling 2508. 2°, folder 3; [Von Wieser], *Gedenkschrift*, p. 4.

102. Agothodaimon map, BL Add. Ms. 19391.

103. Harley and Woodward, *History*, p. 271.

104. Fischer to Bjørnbo, Sept. 18, 1910, RLC, Ny kgl. Samling 2508. 2°, folder 3, which said that Fischer was very busy, among other things because they were building a new school building. Fischer, *Der deutsche*, pp. 7–9, 18–22. Facsimile on p. 10. Fischer had already made his discovery known in a 1906 article published in *Stimmen aus Maria-Laach*, entitled "Der älteste 'deutsche Ptolemaeus' und der älteste gedruckte Planiglobus."

105. Josef Fischer, "Ptolemaeus und Agothodämon," Kaiserliche Akademie der Wissenschaften in Wien, Philosophisch-historische Klasse, *Denkschriften*, vol. 59, Abh. 4, Wien, 1916, pp. 69–93 with two facsimile maps, esp. pp. 72, 84–85.

106. Bagrow, "Origin," p. 320.

107. Fischer, "Ptolemaeus und Agothodämon," p. 73.

108. Josef Fischer, "Der Wolfegger Globusbecher," *Stimmen aus Maria-Laach* 80 (1911). This article also appeared in English translation as "The Globe-Goblet of Wolfegg," *Historical Records and Studies* (U.S. Catholic Historical Society) 6, no. 2 (1913).

109. Josef Fischer, "Die älteste Karte mit dem Namen Brazilien (1512)," *Kölnische Volkszeitung*, Apr. 15, 1912; idem, "Die handschriftliche Überlieferung der Ptolemäuskarten," *Verhandlungen d. 18. Deutschen Geographentages zu Innsbruck* (1912) and in *Petermanns Mitteilungen* 2 (1912): 61–63.

110. Josef Fischer, "An Important Ptolemy-manuscript with Maps in the New York Public Library," *Historical Records and Studies* (U.S. Catholic Historical Society) 6, no. 2 (1913); idem, "Resultados de mis investigaciones cartograficas," *Iberica* (Tortosa) 1 (1913), also published in English translation as "Results of my Cartographical Investigations." *Historical Records and Studies* (U.S. Catholic Historical Society) 7 (1914).

111. Josef Fischer, "Massenas Sturm auf Feldkirch 1799 März 23," Separatabdruck des Gymnasialprograms der Stella Matutina 1913–14. Feldkirch, im Verlage der Anstalt, 1914. I am grateful to Sadie Holland for giving me this publication after we had finished work on the Granite Productions film about the Vínland Map. The pamphlet had been presented to Holland while she was at Stella Matutina researching background for the film.

112. Josef Fischer, "Von alten Kriegskarten," *Stimmen der Zeit* [formerly *Stimmen aus Maria-Laach*] 89 (1915).

113. *Stella Heft* 11, Dec. 1990, p. 33. (An informational publication for Stella Matutina alumni.)

114. *Aus der Stella Matutina* 63/64 (Oct. 1938): 206–7.

115. Haller, "Prof. Dr. h.c.P. Josef Fischer," p. 4.

116. Josef Fischer, "Der russische Zar als 'Kaiser' auf der Carta marina Waldseemüllers vom Jahre 1516," *Stimmen der Zeit* 90 (1916); idem, "Die Straßburger Ptolemäus-Ausgabe vom Jahre 1513," *Stimmen aus Maria-Laach* 86 (1914): 359–60. For excellent reproductions and a modern commentary on both maps, see Wolff, *America*, pp. 117–18.

117. Josef Fischer, "Die Entdeckung Russlands durch Nicolaus Poppel in den Jahren 1486–1489," *Stimmen der Zeit* 89 (1915).

118. Josef Fischer, "Die Carta Marina Martin Waldseemüllers vom Jahre 1516 und die katolischen Missionen. Zur 400–jährigen Gedankfeier," *Katolische Missionen* (Freiburg i. Breisgau) 45 (1916).

119. Josef Fischer, "Zwei verschollene Nürnberger Weltkarten," *Ebenda* (1916).

120. Josef Fischer, "Zur Carta marina Waldseemüllers und der deutschen Bearbeitung derselben durch L. Fries, *Ebenda* (1917); idem, "Dr. Hieronymus Münzer und die Feldkircher St.-Nikolaus-Bibliothek," *Archiv für Geschichte*

und Landeskunde Vorlarlbergs (Bregenz) 1 (1917); idem, "Dr. Hieronymus Münzer und die Feldkircher silberne Monstranz aus dem Jahre 1506," *Vierteljahresschrift für Geschichte und Landeskunde Vorlarlbergs* (Bregenz) 1 (1917); idem, "Der Nürnberger Arzt Dr. Hieronymus Münzer (gest. 1518) aus Feldkirch als Mensch und Gelehrter," *Stimmen der Zeit* 96 (1919): 148–68, esp. p. 148; idem, "Autobiographische," p. 59. For the 1493 Münzer letter, see Richard Hennig, "The Representation on Maps of the Magelhães Strait before their Discovery,"*Imago Mundi* 5 (1948): 33–37, text to letter p. 35.

121. For a concise summary of the Cusanus-Münzer-Waldseemüller connection, see Bagrow, *History*, pp. 147–48.

122. Fischer, "Nürnberger Arzt," pp. 159–63. Concerning the Münzer letter, see also E. P. Goldschmidt, *Hieronymus Münzer und seine Bibliothek* (London: The Warburg Institute, 1938), pp. 46–48.

123. Josef Fischer, "Die Stadtzeichen auf den Ptolemäuskarten" (Vienna) 7 (1918); idem, "Pappus und die Ptolemäuskarten," *Zeitschrift für Erdkunde zu Berlin* (Berlin) (1919); idem, "Ptolemaios als Kartograph," supplement to Konstantin Cebrian, *Geschichte der Kartographie* (*Geographische Bausteine* 10), Gotha, 1922. In his supplement, Father Fischer paid tribute (pp. 108–12) to Cebrian, who had died bravely as an officer in 1914.

124. Josef Fischer, "War der erste Apostel 'der Indischen Inseln' (der Neuen Welt) ein Sohn des heiligen Benediktus oder des heiligen Franziscus?" *Miscellanea Fr. Ehrle* 3, Rome, Biblioteca Vaticana, 1924.

125. Haardt, testimonial to Fischer, p. 26. The translation of the quote is mine.

126. Josef Fischer, "Vier Kartenwerke zur Geschichte der Geographie," *Petermanns Mitteilungen* (Gotha) 11/12 (1928): 336–37; idem, "Der Codex Burneyanus Graecus III. *75 Jahre Stella Matutina*, 3 vols., Feldkirch, Verlag Stella Matutina, 1931, vol. 1, pp. 151–59, ref. to "Sir Warner" on p. 153. Fischer reported (pp. 152–53) that the British Museum printed catalogue dated the map to the end of the fourteenth century or the beginning of the fifteenth, and that "Sir Warner" had later told him that it dated from the end of the fourteenth century. (See also O. A. W. Dilke's comments in Harley and Woodward, *History*, p. 270n64.); idem, "Die Karte des Nicolaus von Kusa (vor 1490). Die älteste Karte von Mitteleuropa," in Bernhardt Brandt, ed., *Kartographische Denkmäler der Sudetenländer* (part 1), Geographisches Institut der Deutschen Universität (Prague, 1930), with a black-and-white reproduction of the map and four pages of text; idem, "Das älteste Stadium," pp. 180–81.

127. For a good reproduction of this map, see Wolff, *America*, p. 163.

128. For a discussion of the Ruysch map, especially in relation to Norse Greenland, see Seaver, *Frozen Echo*, pp. 214–18.

129. [Von Wieser], *Gedenkschrift*, pp. 44–45; Fischer, "Karte des Nicolaus von Kusa," p. 3. More recently, Robert Karrow has provided useful reflections on the lost Cusanus map, and P. D. A. Harvey has observed that the Eichstädt map may in fact not have been completed and used until the 1530s. See Robert Karrow, *Mapmakers of the Sixteenth Century and their Maps* (Chicago: Speculum Orbis Press for the Newberry Library, 1993), p. 131; P. D. A. Harvey in Harley and Woodward, *History*, p. 497.

130. Fischer, "Karte des Nicolaus von Kusa," pp. 3–4. The codex containing the Henricus Martellus map in question was identified as the Magliab. lat. Cl. XIII, no. 16, at the Biblioteca Nazionale in Florence.

131. Ibid.

132. Karrow, *Mapmakers*, pp. 129–30, 132. Karrow also lays out the Cusanus cartographic lineages with which Fischer struggled, but these would take us too far afield here.

133. Ibid., p. 129.

134. Ibid.; Stieber, *Pope Eugenius*, p. 506; *Monumenta Conciliorum Generalium*, vol. 2, p. 899; James MacCaffrey, "Council of Basle," in *ACE*, vol. 11, pp. 60–62.

135. Gustavo Uzielli, *La vita e i tempi di Paolo dal Pozzo Toscanelli* (Rome, 1894), pp. 117–19.

136. Berggren and Jones, *Ptolemy's Geography*, p. 53.

137. Edward Luther Stevenson, trans. and ed., *Geography of Claudius Ptolemy*, with an Introduction by Joseph Fischer (New York: The New York Public Library, 1932), pp. 5–7, 11–12.

138. Berggren and Jones, *Ptolemy's Geography*, p. 46.

139. Josef Fischer, *Claudii Ptolemaei Geographiae Codex Urbinas Graecus 82*. Phototypice depictus consilio et opera curatorum Bibliothecae Vaticanae. Lugduni Batavorum et Lipsiae, 1932.

140. *Aus der Stella Matutina*, Apr. 1934, p. 375.

141. Hassinger, "Josef Fischer," pp. 194–95; Obituary of Joseph Fischer, *Imago Mundi* 5 (1948): 94.

142. "P. Josef Fischer in Rom beim Hl. Vater," *Aus der Stella Matutina*, Apr. 1933, pp. 206–9.

143. *Aus der Stella Matutina* 62, Nov. 1937, pp. 172–73.

144. *Stella Heft* (Feltkirch) 11, Dec. 1990, p. 33.

145. Dürst, "Weltkarte," pp. 18–21. The De Virga map is item no. 56 in Gilhofer and Ranschburg's *Versteigerungskatalog* 8, 1932, Lucerne, which I accessed at the British Library. The auction was to be held June 14–15, 1932, with all the items available on view June 9–13. For more information about Albert Figdor, see Gustav Otruba, "Figdor, Albert," in *Neue Deutsche Biographie*, vol. 5, pp. 143–44; "Figdor, Albert," in *Österreichisches bibliographisches Lexicon*,

1815–1950, Leo Santifaller, gen. ed., Österreichischen Akademie der Wissenschaften, Graz-Köln 1954–57, vol. 1, p. 313; Friedrich Weissensteiner, ed., *Michael Hainisch, 75 Jahre aus bewegter Zeit: Lebenserinnerungen eines österreichischen Staatsmannes*, Vienna-Cologne-Graz, 1978, pp. 105.

146. Ernst Walz (1859–1941) was an honorary professor of jurisprudence at the University of Heidelberg and also a former lord mayor of Heidelberg.

147. Gilhofer and Ranschburg, *Versteigerungskatalog* 8. The price list, which follows p. 158, sets a reserve price of twelve thousand Swiss francs for item number 70, described as one of only four surviving copies of Gerardus Mercator, *Nova et Aucta Orbis Terrae Descriptio ad Usum Navigantium Emendate Accommodata* (Duisburg, 1569).

148. Josef Fischer, "Die Ptolemäushandschrift des Georgius Schbab (nach 1513)," *Zeitschrift für Buchdrück-, Bibliophilie- und Pressegeschichte* (Schweizerisches Gutenbergmuseum) 18 (1932): 212–21; Gilhofer und Ranschburg, *Versteigerungs-Katalog 11*, vol. 2, item 81, BL, 11900.v.2.

149. Seaver, "Albertin de Virga," pp. 58–62 passim.

150. After much legal wrangling and string pulling by the well-connected Frau Becker-Walz, she was able to auction off the bulk of Figdor's artworks and furniture in 1930. These auctions did not include maps and manuscripts. Concerning Albert Figdor, his collections, and the Becker-Walz legal struggle, see *Neue Deutsche Biographie*, vol. 5, pp. 143–44; *Österreichisches bibliographisches Lexicon 1815–1950*, vol. 1, p. 313; Friedrich Weissensteiner, ed., *Michael Hainisch, 75 Jahre aus bewegter Zeit: Lebenserinnerungen eines österreichischen Staatsmannes* (Vienna, Cologne, and Graz, 1978); Otto von Falke, *Der Sammlung Figdor*, auction catalogue, 5 vols. (Vienna and Berlin, 1930); Christian Jansen, "Professoren und Politik: Politisches Denken und Handeln der Heidelberger Hochschullehrer 1914–1935," *Kritische Studien zur Geschichtswissenschaft* (Göttingen) 99 (1992): 109, 229, 247–49.

151. See Paul Grosz (introduction) and Lynn H. Nichols (preface) in Christie's, *Catalogue*.

152. Fischer, "Ptolemäushandschrift," pp. 115–16 and n3, 220–21. For an excellent reproduction of the 1513 Waldseemüller world map, see Wolff, *America*, p. 118, fig. 9.

153. Harley and Woodward, *History*, pp. 198–99.

154. As cited in Wolff, *America*, p. 112.

155. Fischer, "Ptolemäushandschrift," pp. 221.

156. See Chapter 4 concerning Allan Stevenson's reservations about relying solely on Briquet's sketches and interpretations.

157. Beda Dudik, "Handschriften der Fürstlich Dietrichstein'ske Bibliothek zu Nikolsburg in Mähren," *Österreichische Akademie der Wissenschaffen Archiv*

für österreichische Geschichte 39, part 2 (1868): 419–524, esp. p. 492; Gilhofer and Ranschburg, *Versteigerungs-Katalog 1*, vol. 1, for a sale taking place Nov. 21 and 22, 1933, in Lucerne, encompassing the library of Alexander, Prince Dietrichstein of Nikolsburg Castle in the Czech Socialist Republic and "consisting of the collections of the Nuremberger humanist and city physician Hieronymus Münter (Monetarius), 1440–1508, of his son-in-law and heir Hieronymus Holzschuher, a friend of Albrecht Dürer's (1469–1529), and of Ferdinand Hoffmann, Freiherr of Grünpühel and Strechau (1540–1607), and including valuable manuscripts and miniatures from the ninth to the fifteenth centuries."

158. I am grateful to Gerald Nattrass of the British Library German Section for explaining the significance of this description of the binding after he had personally checked the auction catalogue.

159. Stevenson, *Problem*, p. 52. Stevenson cites Briquet as making it clear that in the fifteenth century there were generally two different sizes of paper— small and large, the latter roughly double the size of the smaller. A folio on small paper ranges around thirty centimeters tall, and one on large paper roughly forty centimeters, unless it has been cut deeply. The leaves of the Zurich copy of the *Missale speciale* measured 30.5 by 21.3 centimeters and were derived from sheets that must have measured about 32 by 45 centimeters uncut. The smaller format represented some 90 percent of all paper then used.

160. Gilhofer and Ranschburg, catalogue for auction in Lucerne, June 25 and 26, 1934.

161. Gilhofer and Ranschburg, catalogue for Nov. 21 and 22, 1933.; Gilhofer and Ranschburg, *Catalogue 61* (Vienna) for a combined auction Feb. 27–Mar. 1, 1934, of valuable books and manuscripts from the library of Alexander Fürst Dietrichstein, Nikolsburg, together with the music and theater collection belonging to Dr. August Heymann of Vienna.

162. E. P. Goldschmidt, *Medieval Texts and Their First Appearance in Print*, supplement to the Bibliographical Society's Transactions, no. 16 (Oxford and London: Oxford University Press, 1943), p. 94.

163. Dudik, "Handschriften," p. 483, describing "Cod. Ms. membr. et chart. fol. max. saecul. XV," in a sixteenth-century binding of brown leather.

164. Frederick Schwab of Gilhofer and Ranschburg in Lucerne wrote that the manuscript was not sold at the auction, and that he does not know if it was sold afterward. He also noted that the Prince Dietrichstein Library at Mikulov Castle had been acquired in the 1930s by the Vienna firm (where his father was the managing director), partly outright, partly by auction, so it is possible that the item was returned to Vienna after the Lucerne auction. Upon checking her records, the present head of Gilhofer's in Vienna, Elizabeth Hoffmann, found

only a cypher she could not interpret next to the description of this item. Neither firm had more information about the actual size of the pages.

165. In piecing together the story of Mikulov Castle and its library from 1931 to the present, I have received much valuable help from Eva Handler-Wajntraub in Vienna and her friend Dorothea McEwan at the Warburg Institute in London, as well as from Gilhofer Antiquariat in Vienna, Gilhofer and Ranschburg Antiquariat in Lucerne, the Moravian Public Archives in Brno and the Czech National Library in Prague. Edward Schnayder in Kraków, who sadly died in late 2001, made a number of inquiries on my behalf, and I am also grateful to Olle Ekstedt in Sweden, a former superior court judge with early maps as his avocation, who asked his Central European contacts to help with the search.

166. Gilhofer und Ranschburg, *Versteigerungs-Katalog 11*, vol. 2, item 292.

167. Seaver, "Mystery," pp. 24–29.

168. Dudik, "Handschriften," pp. 420, 424–25.

169. Ibid., p. 420; Goldschmidt, *Hieronymus Münzer*, pp. 3–5.

170. Dudik, "Handschriften," p. 420; Goldschmidt, *Hieronymus Münzer*, pp. 5–7. Before the prince could accept the gift, the emperor ordered the Jesuits in Brünn to examine the collection and weed out heretical items. Goldschmidt reasoned that heretical items might have originated with Hoffmann von Grünbuchel, because he had become a Lutheran and was therefore suspect. The conscientious priests must have weeded out 842 volumes—in 1679, the Prince von Dietrichstein gave them to the Jesuit Kollegium in Brünn. They were later transferred to the Research Library in Olmütz, including a MS signed by Melanchton himself.

171. Goldschmidt, *Hieronymus Münzer*, pp. 3, 7, 10. Goldschmidt provided this example of Münzer's inscriptions: "Jste liber est mei Hieroniimi Monetarii de Feltkirchen. arcium medici negue doctoris, quem mihi comparari Nuremberge in Kalendis septembris 1487." He also described the most characteristic features of the Nuremberg binder's work: a stamp of a bar surrounded by a frame of foliage and with rows of diamonds filling in the central part; there are also large rosettes in the frame as well as on the back. A diamond-shaped stamp with a rising griffon equipped with scaly wings is another characteristic of these bindings.

172. Isolde Listmayer (letter of Sept. 19, 1995) was quite clear about these rules and about the stamping of all material used by the pupils and priests at Stella Matutina. Father Hans Grünewald, S.J., archivist at the Jesuit provincial archive in Munich, also confirmed, in a letter of Dec. 22, 1994, the general Jesuit rules concerning property and also stressed that all the research material that Father Fischer used at Stella Matutina would have been marked with the institutional stamp.

173. Seaver, "Mystery," p. 26.

174. See, e.g., S. Harrison Thomson, *Czechoslovakia in European History*, 2nd ed. (1965), esp. pp. 161–86 passim, 251–76 passim, 331–38, 365–69.

175. Seaver, "Mystery," pp. 24–29.

176. With thanks to Isolde Listmayer at Stella Matutina, who sent me Xeroxed copies of several pictures taken of Father Fischer over the years.

177. *Stella Heft* 11, Dec. 1990, pp. 33–36.

178. Jansen, *Professoren*, pp. 11, 25–27.

179. *Stella Heft* 11, Dec. 1990, p. 36.

180. Johann Neuhäusler, *Kreuz und Hakenkreuz*, vol. 1 (Munich: Katolisches Kirche Bayerns, 1946), pp. 22–27.

181. Ibid., vol. 1, p. 59.

182. Joseph Schröteler, "Volk, Staat, Erziehung," *Stimmen der Zeit* (Freiburg in the Breisgau) 126 (1934): 289–96, esp. 289.

183. Adolf Rieth, *Archaeological Fakes*, trans. Diana Imber (New York: Barrie and Jenkins, 1970).

184. Bagrow, Fischer review, *Petermanns geographische Mitteilungen*, Gotha, Justus Perthes, Vol. 73, no. 1 (1933), review no. 89, pp. 51–52.

185. [Bagrow, Leo] Obituary of Leo Bagrow, with bibliography, *Imago Mundi* 16 (1959): 7–12, quotes 10.

186. L. Bagrow, review of "Fischer, Josephus: *De Cl. Ptolemaei vita operibus Geographia prasentim eiusque fatis*. Leiden-Leipzig 1932," *Imago Mundi* 1 (1935): 777.

187. Bagrow, "Origin," p. 318.

188. Fischer's work was reviewed by W. Kubitschek in the *Göttinger gelehrte Anzeiger*, no. 10 (1935): 369–87.

189. *Stella Heft* 11, Dec. 1990, pp. 36–37. The illustration on p. 37 shows the dignified beauty of a sizable chapel.

190. Campbell, "Verdict," pp. 310–11.

191. Helen Wallis, "The Vinland Map: Fake, forgery or jeu d'ésprit?" *The Map Collector* no. 65 (winter 1990): 2–6.

192. Jeremy Black, *Maps and History: Constructing Images of the Past* (New Haven and London: Yale University Press, 1997), pp. 123–26, quotes p. 123.

193. Mark Monmonier, *How to Lie with Maps*, 2nd ed. (Chicago and London: University of Chicago Press, 1996), p. 99 (quote), p. 107.

194. Ibid., p. 123.

195. Ibid.

196. Rieth, *Archaeological*, pp. 138–71.

197. Isolde Listmayer to the author, May 14, July 26, 1999.

198. Prof. Gerhard Banik, Statliche Akademie der Bildenden Künste, Stuttgart. Contribution to studies on iron-gall ink presented on http://www

.knaw.nl/ecpa/ink/html/intro.html (accessed June 3, 2000). I am grateful to Jacqueline Olin for calling my attention to this informative Web site.

199. RLC Ny kgl. Samling 2508. 2°, folder 3. The translation is mine.

200. I am grateful to the Royal Geographical Society Archives for the opportunity to examine a 1927 letter that Fischer wrote to the society.

201. *Stella Heft* 11, Dec. 1990, pp. 37–38.

202. Josef Fischer, "Abessinien auf dem Globus des Martin Behaim von 1492 und in der Reisebeschreibung des Ritters Arnold von Harff un das Jahr 1498," *Petermanns Mitteilungen* 86 (1940): 371–72; idem, "Die östliche Mittelmeer-Gebiete um 1500. Ein bedeutsammes Fragment einer bisher unbekannten, modernisierten ptolemäischen Weltkarte," *Petermanns Mitteilungen* (1941): 12–15 with facs.; idem, "Eine bisher unbekannte angeblich venezianische Weltkarte aus dem Jahre 1519," *Petermanns Mitteilungen* 87 (1941): 449–51.

203. Neuhäusler, *Kreuz*, vol. 1, p. 83.

204. *Stimmen der Zeit* 139 (Oct. 1946), editor's preface in this first issue published after the war was over.

205. Haardt, Testimonials, p. 26. The translation of the quote is mine.

206. Ibid., p. 26.

207. Countess Frederica zu Waldburg, diaries and letters, BL, Add. Mss. 73025.933 D, diary for 1944 is Add Mss. 74942.

208. Haardt, Testimonials, pp. 26, 30–31.

209. Father Hans Grünewald, S.J., archivist at the Jesuit Provincial Archives in Munich, to author, Dec. 15 and 22, 1994; Dr. Rita Haub, archivist at the Jesuit provincial archive in Munich, e-mails to author, July 11, 25, and 26, 2002.

210. *Aus der Stella Matutina* 63–64 (Oct. 1938): 208–11, 269–80; *Stella Heft* 11, Dec. 1990, pp. 38–45.

211. Grünewald to author, Dec. 22, 1994; Isolde Listmayer to author, July 26, 1999.

212. *Stella Heft* 11, Dec. 1990, pp. 38–41.

213. "1938--Ein Schicksalsjahr für die Stella Matutina." Typescript, 14 pp., prepared for the 1998 *Stella Heft* and provided to the author by Isolde Listmayer.

214. David Woodward, "Could These Italian Maps be Fakes?" *The Map Collector* 67 (July 1994): 2–10, esp. pp. 3–6.

215. Ibid., p. 6.

Bibliography

Primary Sources

Adam of Bremen [Adamus Bremensis]. *History of the Archbishops of Hamburg-Bremen.* Trans. with introduction and notes by Francis J. Tschahn. New York: Columbia University Press, 1959.

——. "Adam von Bremen Bischofsgeschichte der hamburger Kirche." Trans. Werner Trillmich. *Quellen des 9. und 11. Jahrhunderts zur Geschichte der hamburgerischen Kirche und des Reiches,* Vol. 11. Berlin, 1961.

Agothodaimon map, BL Add. Ms. 19391.

Biskupa sögur. Vols. 1–2. Copenhagen: Hið íslenzka bókmenntafélag, 1858.

BL. Vínland Map file, CE2/1.

BLML. Files on the Vínland Map: "The Papers of Eila Campbell (1915–1994)," compiled by Brigid Allen. Cat. no. II/3/1–12.

BLML. Helen Wallis files. "Vinland Map File/Current."

BLML. Helen Wallis files. "Vinland Map File/General."

BMMD. "Recurrent file—Vinland Map."

Cahill, T. A., with R. N. Schwab, B. H. Kusko, R. A. Eldred, G. Möller, D. Dutschke, and D. L. Wick. "Report to Yale University Beinecke Rare Book and Manuscript Library: 'Further Elemental Analyses of the Vinland Map, the *Tartar Relation,* and the *Speculum Historiale.*' " [1985]. (BLML, Helen Wallis files, "Vinland Map File/Current.")

Dee, John. "Map of part of the northern hemisphere." BL, Cotton MS Augustus I.i.1.

Diplomatarium Danicum. Det danske Sprog-og Litteraturselskab. Series I. Vol. 1. Ed. Lauritz Weibull. Copenhagen, 1963; Vol. 2. Ed. C. A. Christensen and Herluf Nielsen. Copenhagen, 1975.

Diplomatarium Islandicum. Vols. 1–16. Copenhagen and Reykjavík, 1857–1959.

Diplomatarium Norvegicum. Vols. 1–21. Oslo, 1849–1970.

Eyrbyggja saga. Trans. Hermann Pálsson and Paul Edwards. Edinburgh: Southside, 1972.

439

440 *Bibliography*

Gilhofer and Ranschburg. *Versteigerungskatalog 8.* Lucerne, for auction of June 14–15, 1932.

———. *Versteigerungskatalog 11.* Vol. 1, Sale taking place Nov. 21–22, 1933. Lucerne; Vol. 2, Sale taking place June 25–26, 1934. Lucerne.

"Grænlendinga tháttr." Ed. Guðni Jónsson. *Islendinga sögur.* Vol. 1. Reykjavík, 1968.

"[Grænlendinga tháttr] The Tale of the Greenlanders." Trans. John Porter, gen. ed. Víðar Hreinsson. *The Complete Sagas of Icelanders,* pp. 372–82. Reykjavík: Leifur Eiríksson Publishing, 1997.

Hauksbók. Udgiven efter De Arnamagnæiske Haandskrifter No. 371, 544 og 675, 40 [Det Kongelige nordiske Oldskrift-Selskab]. Copenhagen, 1892–96.

Hødnebø, Finn, and Hallvard Magerøy, eds. *Snorre Sturluson: Norges kongesagaer.* Trans. Anne Holtsmark and Didrik Arup Seip. Oslo: Den norske Bokklubben, 1981.

Islandske Annaler indtil 1578. Comp. and ed. Gustav Storm. 1888; repr., Oslo: Norsk Historisk Kjeldeskrifts-Institutt, 1977.

Kålund, Kr. *Alfræði íslenzk. Islandsk encyklopædisk Litteratur. I. Cod. Mbr. AM. 194. 8vo.* Samfund til Udgivelse af gammel nordisk Litteratur. Københavns Universitet [Editions of Manuscripts], no. 37. Copenhagen, 1908.

The King's Mirror. Trans. Laurence Marcellus Larson. New York: Twayne, 1917; repr., 1972.

Konge-speilet. Speculum Regale. Konungs-skuggsjá. Trans. and ed. R. Keyser, P. A. Munch, and C. R. Unger. Christiania: Kongeligt Norsk Frederiks Universitet, 1848.

Landnámabók [The Book of Settlements]. Trans. Hermann Pálsson and Paul Edwards. Vol. 1. Winnipeg: University of Manitoba Icelandic Studies, 1972.

———. *Landnåmsboken.* Trans. Liv Kjørsvik Schei, with an introduction by Hermann Pálsson. Oslo: H. Aschehough and Company, 1997.

Lyschander, Claus Christophersen. *Den Grønlandske Chronica.* 1608; repr., Copenhagen, 1726.

Norwegian National Library (Oslo). Manuscript Department. Correspondence between Fridtjof Nansen and Axel Anton Bjørnbo. Ms. fol. 1924: 301B.

Petrus Ailliacus [Pierre d'Ailly, Cardinal]. *Imago Mundi.* Trans. Edwin F. Keever. Wilmington, N.C., 1948. Typescript, BL, 10002.i.18.

Porcacchi da Castiglione, Thomaso [Tommaso]. *L'Isole piu famoso del mondo,* arretino e intagliate dá Girolamo Porro. Venetia, 1572, BL Maps, C.7.b.19.

Ptolemaeus, Claudius. *Geographia.* Rome, 1508, BLML, copies 1 and 2, press marks C.I.d.5 and .6.

RLC. Correspondence between Axel Anton Bjørnbo and Fridtjof Nansen. Ny kgl. Samling 2508. 2° (Nansen folder).

Saxo Grammaticus. *Den danske Krønike.* Trans. Anders Sørensen Vedel. Reprinted by G. F. Wegener. Samfundet til den danske Literaturs Fremme, København, 1851.

Towe, Kenneth M. "The Vinland Map Revisited: An Analysis of the McCrone Reports as an Evaluation of the Problem of the Map's Authenticity." Report to Yale University Library, 1982.

The Vinland Sagas: The Norse Discovery of America. Trans. and ed. Magnús Magnússon and Hermann Pálsson. London: Penguin Books, 1965.

Von Falke, Otto. *Der Sammlung Figdor,* Auction catalogue. 5 vols. Vienna and Berlin, 1930.

[Waldburg] Countess Frederica zu Waldburg. Diaries and letters. BL, Add. Mss. 72931; 73025.933; 72937; 72939; 74942.

Walter C. McCrone Associates, Inc. *Chemical Analytical Study of the Vinland Map.* Report to the Yale University Library, Jan. 22, 1974.

——. *Morphology of Ground vs. Precipitated Anatase.* Report to Yale University Library, Aug. 21, 1975.

Werner, A. E., and A. D. Baynes-Cope. "Confidential Report on Scientific Examination of the Vinland Map. 22nd November, 1968." BMMD, "Recurrent file—Vinland Map."

Wolfegg Castle Archives. Letters from Father Josef Fischer, S.J., to the princess of Waldburg-Wolfegg.

Secondary Sources

Abramowitcz, Zygmunt. "The Expressions "Fish-tooth" and "Lion-Fish" in Turkish and Persian." *Folia Orientalia* (Kraków; Académie Polonaise des sciences, Centre de Cracovie, Commission Orientaliste) 12 (1970): 25–32.

Agnarsdóttir, Anna, ed. *Voyages and Exploration in the North Atlantic from the Middle Ages to the XVIIth Century.* Reykjavík: Institute of History, University of Iceland, 2000.

Amdam, Rolv Petter. "Industrikomiteen i New York 1943–45: Ein kanal for kunnskapsoverføring frå USA til Norge." *Historisk Tidskrift* 1 (2000), http://www.uit.no/ht/art/001.pdf (accessed May 27, 2001).

American Catholic Encyclopedia. 15 vols. Charles H. Herbermann, gen. ed. New York: Robert Appleton Company, 1907.

Andersen, Erik, and Claus Malmros, "Ship's Parts Found in the Viking Settlements in Greenland." In Clausen, ed., *Viking Voyages,* pp. 118–22.

Andreasen, Claus. "Nipaitsoq og Vesterbygden." *Grønland* 30 (1982).

————. "Nordbosager fra Vesterbygden på Grønland." *Hikuin* 6 (1980): 135–46.

Appelt, Martin, with Joel Berglund and Hans Christian Gulløv, eds. *Identities and Cultural Contacts in the Arctic.* Copenhagen: Danish Polar Center, 2000.

Arneborg, Jette. "Contact between Eskimos and Norsemen in Greenland." In Roesdal and Meulengracht Sørensen, *Beretning.*

Arneborg, Jette, and Hans Christian Gulløv, eds. *Man, Culture and Environment in Ancient Greenland: Report on a Research Programme.* Copenhagen: The Danish National Museum and Danish Polar Center, 1998.

Arneborg, Jette, with Jan Heinemeier, Niels Lynnerup, Henrik L. Nielsen, Niels Rud, and Árny E. Sveinbjörnsdóttir. "Change of Diet of the Greenland Vikings Determined from Stable Carbon Isotope Analysis and 14C Dating of Their Bones." *Radiocarbon* 41, no. 2 (1999): 157–58.

Ascherson, Neil, and Joyce Egginton. "Forged map that fooled the world." *The Observer* (London), Jan. 27, 1974, pp. 1–2.

Bagrow, Leo. Fischer review. *Petermanns geographische Mitteilungen* (Gotha, Justus Perthes) 73, no. 1 (1933): 51–52.

————. *History of Cartography.* 2nd ed. Rev. and enlarged by R. A. Skelton. Chicago: Precedent Publishing, 1985.

[————.] Obituary of Leo Bagrow, with bibliography. *Imago Mundi* 16 (1959).

————. "The Origin of Ptolemy's Geographia." *Geografiska Annalar* (Stockholm) (1943).

————. Review of *De Cl. Ptolemaei vita operibus Geographia prasentim eiusque fatis,* by Josephus Fischer. *Imago Mundi* 1 (1935): 777.

Bartak, Joseph Paul. *John Hus at Constance.* Nashville: Cokesbury Press [1935].

Bately, Janet, ed. *The Old English Orosius.* Early English Text Society S.S. 6. London, New York, and Toronto: Oxford University Press, 1980.

Beckmann, Gustav, with Rudolf Wackernagel and Giulio Coggiola, eds. *Concilium Basiliense.* Vol. 5. *Tagebuchaufzeichnungen 1431–1435 und 1438; Acten der Gesandtschaft nach Avignon und Konstantinopel 1437–1438; Brief des Enea Silvio 1433; Tagebuch des Andrea Gatari 1433–1435.* Basel, 1904.

[Beinecke Library, Yale University]. *The Beinecke Rare Book and Manuscript Library.* [New Haven], 1974.

Berggren, J. Lennart, and Alexander Jones. *Ptolemy's Geography: An Annotated Translation of the Theoretical Chapters.* Princeton and Oxford: Princeton University Press, 2000.

Berglund, Joel. "The Decline of the Norse Settlements in Greenland." *Arctic Anthropology* 23 (1986): 109–35.

Bernleithner, E. "Austria's Share in World Cartography." *Imago Mundi* 25 (1971): 65–73.

Biernacki, Casimiro. *Speculum Minorum*. Kraków, 1658.

Bigelow, Gerald F., gen. ed. "The Norse of the North Atlantic." *Acta Archaeologica* 61 (1991).

Bjørnbo, Axel Anton. "Cartographia Groenlandica." *MoG* 48 (1912).

Bjørnbo, Axel Anton, and Carl S. Petersen. *Der Däne Claudius Claussøn Swart (Claudius Clavus) der älteste Kartograph des Nordens*. Innsbruck: Wagner, 1909.

———. *Fyenboen Claudius Claussøn Swart* [Claudius Clavus]: *Nordens ældste Kartograf*. Kgl. Danske Videnskabelige Selskabs Skrifter, 6. Række, historisk og filosofisk Afdeling, VI. 2. Copenhagen, 1904.

Black, Jeremy. *Maps and History: Constructing Images of the Past*. New Haven and London: Yale University Press, 1997.

Blegen, Theodore C. *The Kensington Runestone: New Light on an Old Riddle*. St. Paul: Minnesota Historical Society, 1968.

Bradley, Ray. "1000 Years of Climate Change." *Science* 288 (2000): 1353–55.

Brandt, C. J., ed. *Lucidarius, en Folkebog fra Middelalderen*. Nordiske Oldskrifter 7. Copenhagen: Det nordiske Litteratur-Samfund, 1849.

Briquet, C. M. *Les Filigranes: Dictionnaire historique des marques du papier dés leur apparition vers 1282 jusqu'en 1600*. 4 vols. Leipzig, 1923. Facsimile ed. of original 1907 edition.

Brown, Katherine L., and Robin J. H. Clark. "Analysis of Pigmentary Materials on the Vinland Map and Tartar Relation by Raman Microprobe Spectroscopy." *Analytical Chemistry* 74 (2002): 3658–61.

Brown, Neville. *History and Climate Change: A Eurocentric Perspective*. Routledge Studies in Physical Geography and Environment 3. London and New York: Routledge, 2001.

Bryn, Torstein. *Vision, Colour, Form: The History of Jotun*. Trans. Susannah Finzi and Dorothy Thomas. Sandefjord, Norway: Jotun A/S, 1998.

Buchwald, Vagn Fabritius. "Ancient Iron and Slags in Greenland." *MoG: M&S* 26 (2001).

Cahill, Thomas A., with R. N. Schwab, B. H. Kusko, R. A. Eldred, G. Moller, D. Dutschke, D. L. Wick, and A. S. Pooley. "The Vinland Map, Revisited: New Compositional Evidence on Its Inks and Parchments." *Analytical Chemistry* 59 (1987): 829–33.

Campbell, Eila. "Verdict on the Vinland Map." *Geographical Magazine* (London), Apr. 1974, pp. 307–12.

Carpenter, Edmund. *Norse Penny*. New York: The Rock Foundation, 2003.

Carus Wilson, Eleanora Mary. *The Overseas Trade of Bristol*. London: Merlin Press, 1967.

Christensen, Arne Emil. "The Age of the Vikings." *Scientific American: Discovering Archaeology* 2, no. 4 (2000): 40–47.

Christie's of London. *Catalogue of the Mauerbach Benefit Sale*, Vienna, Oct. 29 and 30, 1996.

Clausen, Birthe L., ed. *Viking Voyages to North America*. Roskilde, Denmark: The Viking Ship Museum, 1993.

Cook, Karen Severud, ed. *Images and Icons of the New World: Essays on American Cartography*. London: British Library Publications, 1996.

Cornelius, James M. *The Norwegian Americans*. New York: Chelsea House Publishers, 1989.

Cortesão, Armando. *The Nautical Chart of 1424*. Coimbra: University of Coimbra, 1954.

Courtauld Gallery (London). Information booklet for the exhibition "Material Evidence," Oct. 30, 1998–Jan. 24, 1999.

Crantz, David. *History of Greenland*. 2 vols. Trans. from High Dutch. London: The Brethren Society for the Furtherance of the Gospel among the Heathen, 1767.

———. *Historie von Grönland*. 2 vols. Leipzig: Barby, 1765.

Crone, G. R., trans. and ed. "How Authentic is the 'Vinland Map'?" *Encounter* 26 (Feb. 1966): 75–78.

———. "The Vinland Map Cartographically Considered." Review. *Geographical Journal* 132 (Mar. 1966): 75–80.

———. *The Voyages of Cadamosto and Other Documents on Western Africa in the Second Half of the Fifteenth Century*. Series 2, Vol. 80. London: Hakluyt Society, 1937.

Dansgaard, Willi. "Bringer luftforureningen torsken tilbage til Grønland?" *Forskning i Grønland/Tusaat* 8, no. 1 (1985): 24–25.

Dawson, Christopher, ed. *The Mongol Mission: Narratives and Letters of the Franciscan Missionaries in Mongolia and China in the Thirteenth and Fourteenth Centuries*. Trans. by a nun of Stanbrook Abbey. London and New York: Sheed and Ward, 1955.

De la Sale, Antoine. *Oeuvres Complètes*. Ed. Ferdinand Desonay. Vol. 1. *La Salade*. Liège and Paris: Bibliothèque de la Faculté de Philosophie et Lettres de l'Université de Liège, 1935.

Dilke, Oswald Ashton Wentworth. *Greek and Roman Maps*. London: Thames and Hudson, 1985.

Donahue, D. J., J. S. Olin, and G. Harbottle. "Determination of the Radiocarbon Age of the Vinland Map." *Radiocarbon* 44, no. 1 (2002): 45–52.

Drever, Charles. *Cod Fishing at Greenland*. The White Fish Authority. Typescript. BL, x.313/380, pp. 1–32.

Dudik, Beda. "Handschriften der Fürstlich Dietrichstein'ske Bibliothek zu Nikolsburg in Mähren." *Österreichische Akademie der Wissenschaffen Archiv für österreichische Geschichte* 39, part 2 (1868): 419–524.

Dürst, Albert. "Die Weltkarte von Albertin de Virga von 1411 oder 1415." *Cartographica Helvetica* 13 (1966): 18–21.

Eden, Richard. *The First Three English Books on America [?1511–1555 AD].* Ed. Edward Arber. Birmingham and Edinburgh: Turnbull and Spears, 1885.

Enghoff, Inge Bødtker. "Hunting, Fishing and Animal Husbandry at The Farm Beneath the Sand, Western Greenland." *MoG: M&S* 28 (2003).

Ettinghausen, Richard. *Studies in Muslim Iconography I: The Unicorn.* Occasional Paper I: 3. Washington, D.C.: Freer Gallery of Art, 1950.

Faulkes, Anthony, ed. *Snorri Sturluson, Edda.* London and Melbourne: Everyman's Classics, 1987.

———. *Snorri Sturluson: Edda. Prologue and Gylfaginning.* Clarendon Press: Oxford, 1982.

Fischer, Josef. "Abessinien auf dem Globus des Martin Behaim von 1492 und in der Reisebeschreibung des Ritters Arnold von Harff un das Jahr 1498." *Petermanns Mitteilungen* 86 (1940): 371–72.

———. "Der älteste 'deutsche Ptolemäus' und der älteste gedruckte Planiglobus." *Stimmen aus Maria-Laach,* 1906.

———. "Die älteste Karte mit dem Namen Brazilien." *Kölnische Volkszeitung,* Apr. 15, 1912.

———. "Die älteste Karte vom Fürstentum Liechtenstein. Mit einem Faksimilie der Karte." *Jahrbuch d. histor. Vereins von Liechtenstein* (Vadus) 10 (1910).

———. "Das älteste Stadium der Weltkarte des Johannes Ruysch (1508)." *Zeitschrift,* Schweizerisches Gutenbergmuseum (Berne) 17, no. 4 (1931): 180–81.

———. "Die älteste Weltkarte mit dem Namen 'Berlin.'" *Stimmen aus Maria-Laach* 64 (1903).

———. "Autobiographische Darstellung des Lebensganges und des wissenschaftlichen Lebenswerkes." *Imago Mundi* (Berlin) 1 (1933): 58–61.

———. "Die Bedeutung des Ciphus de nuce ultramarina (1327) für eine Besiedelung des Festlandes von Amerika durch die Normannen." *Historisches Jahrbuch der Görresgesellschaft* (Freiburg in the Breisgau) 21 (1900).

———. "Die Carta Marina Martin Waldseemüllers vom Jahre 1516 und die katolischen Missionen. Zur 400–jährigen Gedankfeier." *Katolische Missionen* (Freiburg i. Breisgau) 45 (1916).

———. "Claudius Clavus, the First Cartographer of America." *Historical Records* (New York; U.S. Catholic Historical Society) 6 (1911): 81–101.

———. *Claudii Ptolemaei Geographiae Codex Urbinas Graecus 82. Phototypice depictus consilio et opera curatorum Bibliothecae Vaticanae.* 4 vols. Lugduni Batavorum et Lipsiae, 1932.

———. "Der Codex Burneyanus Graecus III." *75 Jahre Stella Matutina.* Vol. I, pp. 151–59. Feldkirch: Verlag Stella Matutina, 1931.

———. *Der deutsche Ptolemäus aus dem Ende des XV. Jahrhunderts (um 1490) in Faksimiliedrück.* Intro. Jos. Fischer. Strassburg: Heitz and Mündel, 1910.

———. *The Discoveries of the Norsemen in America.* Trans. Basil Soulsby. London: Henry Stevens, Son and Stiles, 1903.

———. "Eine bisher unbekannte angeblich venezianische Weltkarte aus dem Jahre 1519." *Petermanns Mitteilungen* 87 (1941): 449–51.

———. "Die Entdeckung Russlands durch Nikolaus Poppel in den Jahren 1486–1489." *Stimmen der Zeit* 89 (1915).

———. *Die Entdeckungen der Normannen in Amerika: Unter besonderer Berücksichtigung der Kartographischen Darstellungen. Stimmen aus Maria-Laach* (Freiburg in the Breisgau) supp. vol. 21 (1902).

———. "The Globe-Goblet of Wolfegg." *Historical Records and Studies* (New York; U.S. Catholic Historical Society) 6, no. 2 (1913).

———. "Die handschriftliche Überlieferung der Ptolemäuskarten." *Verhandlungen d. 18. Deutschen Geographentages zu Innsbruck,* 1912.

———. "Die handschriftliche Überlieferung der Ptolemäuskarten." *Petermanns Mitteilungen* 2 (1912): 61–63.

———. "Dr. Hieronymus Münzer und die Feldkircher St.-Nikolaus-Bibliothek." *Archiv für Geschichte und Landeskunde Vorarlbergs* (Bregenz) 1 (1917).

———. "Dr. Hieronymus Münzer und die Feldkircher silberne Monstranz aus dem Jahre 1506." *Vierteljahresschrift für Geschichte und Landeskunde Vorarlbergs* (Bregenz) 1 (1917).

———. "An Important Ptolemy-manuscript with Maps in the New York Public Library." *Historical Records and Studies* (New York; U.S. Catholic Historical Society) 6, no. 2 (1913).

———. "Kann Bischof Johannes aus Irland (gest. 1066) mit Recht als erster Märtyrer Amerikas bezeichnet werden?" *Innsbrucker theologische Zeitschrift* (Innsbruck) 24 (1900).

———. "Die Karte des Nikolaus von Kusa (vor 1490). Die älteste Karte von Mitteleuropa." In Bernhardt Brandt, ed., *Kartographische Denkmäler der Sudetenländer* (part 1), Geographisches Institut der Deutschen Universität, Prague, 1930 (with a bifold black-and-white reproduction of the map and four pages of text).

———. "Die Kartographische Darstellung der Entdeckungen der normannen in Amerika." *Proceedings,* 14th International Congress of Americanists, 1904, Stuttgart. Vol. I, pp. 31–39. Stuttgart, 1906.

———. "Massenas Sturm auf Feldkirch 1799 März 23." Separatabdruck des

Gymnasialprograms der Stella Matutina 1913–14. Feldkirch, im Verlage der Anstalt, 1914.

————. "Der Nürnberger Arzt Dr. Hieronymus Münzer (gest. 1518) aus Feldkirch als Mensch und Gelehrter." *Stimmen der Zeit* 96 (1919): 148–68.

[————.] Obituary of Joseph Fischer, S.J. *Imago Mundi* 5 (1948): 94.

————. "The Oldest Map with the Name 'America' and How It Was Found." *Benzinger's Magazine* 4 (1902).

————. "Die östliche Mittelmeer-Gebiete um 1500. Ein bedeutsammes Fragment einer bisher unbekannten, modernisierten ptolemäischen Weltkarte." *Petermanns Mitteilungen* 87 (1941): 12–15 with facsimiles.

[————.] "P. Josef Fischer." *Aus der Stella Matutina* 65, 1948–49, pp. 39–40.

[————.] "P. Josef Fischer in Rom beim Hl. Vater." *Aus der Stella Matutina*, Apr. 1933, pp. 206–9.

————. "Pappus und die Ptolemäuskarten." *Zeitschrift für Erdkunde zu Berlin*, Berlin, 1919.

————. "Pseudo-Donis und seine Werke." *Akten des 5. Internationalen Kongresses der Katolischen Gelehrten* (Munich) (1901).

————. "Ptolemaios als Kartograph." Supplement to Konstantin Cebrian, *Geschichte der Kartographie (Geographische Bausteine* 10), Gotha, 1922.

————. "Ptolemäus und Agothodämon." Kaiserliche Akademie der Wissenschaften in Wien, Philosophicsch-historische Klasse, *Denkschriften*, Vol. 59, Abh. 4, Wien, 1916, pp. 69–93 with two facsimile maps.

————. "Die Ptolemäushandschrift des Georgius Schbab (nach 1513)." *Zeitschrift für Buchdrück-, Bibliophilie- und Pressegeschichte* (Schweizerisches Gutenbergmuseum) 18 (1932): 212–21.

————. "Resultados de mis investigaciones cartograficas." *Iberica* (Tortosa) 1 (1913).

————. "Results of my cartographical investigations." *Historical Records and Studies* (New York; U.S. Catholic Historical Society) 7 (1914).

————. "Der russische Zar als "Kaiser" auf der Carta marina Waldseemüllers vom Jahre 1516." *Stimmen der Zeit* 90 (1916).

————. "Die Stadtzeichen auf den Ptolemäuskarten." *Kartographische und Schulgeografische Zeitschrift* (Vienna) 7 (1918).

————. "Die Straßburger Ptolemäus-Ausgabe vom Jahre 1513." *Stimmen aus Maria-Laach* 86 (1914): 359–60.

————. "The Tithes for the Crusades in Greenland, 1276–1282: A Contribution to Ecclesiastical History of the Northmen in America." *Historical Records and Studies* (New York; U.S. Catholic Historical Society) 3 (1904).

————. "Vier Kartenwerke zur Geschichte der Geographie." *Petermanns Mitteilungen* (Gotha) 11/12 (1928): 336–37.

————. "Von alten Kriegskarten." *Stimmen der Zeit* [formerly *Stimmen aus Maria-Laach*] 89 (1915).

————. "War der erste Apostel 'der Indischen Inseln' (der Neuen Welt) ein Sohn des heiligen Benediktus oder des heiligen Franziscus?" *Miscellanea Fr. Ehrle* 3, Rome, Biblioteca Vaticana, 1924.

————. "War Pseudo-Donis Benediktiner in Reichenbach?" *Historisch-politische Blätter* (Munich) 126 (1900).

————. "Der Wolfegger Globusbecher." *Stimmen aus Maria-Laach* 80 (1911).

————. "Zur Carta marina Waldseemüllers und der deutschen Bearbeitung derselben durch L. Fries." *Ebenda* (1917).

————. "Zwei verschollene Nürnberger Weltkarte." *Ebenda*, 1916.

Fischer, Josef, and Franz Ritter von Wieser. *The Oldest Map with the Name America of the year 1507 and the Carta Marina of the year 1516 by M. Waldseemuller (Ilacomilus)*. Innsbruck: Wagner'sche Universitätsbuchhandlung, 1903.

Fitzhugh, William W. "Iron Blooms, Elizabethans, and Politics: The Frobisher Project 1974–1995." *Review of Archaeology* 17, no. 2 (1997): 12–21. (A special issue. Jeffrey P. Brain, ed., *Contributions to the Historical Archaeology of European Exploration and Colonization in North America*.)

————. "A Review of Paleo-Eskimo Culture History in Southern Quebec-Labrador and Newfoundland." *Inuit Studies* 4, nos. 1–2 (1980): 12–21.

Fitzhugh, William W., and Elisabeth I. Ward, eds. *Vikings: The North Atlantic Saga*. Washington, D.C.: Smithsonian Institution Press, 2000.

Fløttum, Sivert. "The Norse *Vika Sjovar* and the Nautical Mile." *Mariner's Mirror* 87, no. 4 (2001): 189–90.

Foote, Peter. "On the Legends of the 'Vinland Map.'" *Saga-Book* (London; Viking Society for Northern Research) 17 (1966): 73–89.

Foulke, W. D. *Biography and Correspondence of Arthur M. Reeves, author of 'The Finding of Wineland the Good.'* London: Henry Froude, 1895.

Fredskild, Bent. "Agriculture in a Marginal Area: South Greenland from the Norse Landnam (AD 985) to the Present (1985)." In Hilary H. Birks, H. J. B. Birks, Peter Emil Kaland, and Dagfinn Moe, eds. *The Cultural Landscape: Past, Present and Future*, pp. 381–94. Cambridge, England: Cambridge University Press, 1988.

————. "Palaeobotanical Investigations of Some Peat Bog Deposits of Norse Age at Quagssiarssuk, South Greenland." *MoG* 204, no. 5 (1978): 1–41.

Gad, Finn. *Grønlands historie*. Vol. I. Copenhagen: Politiken, 1970.

Gams, Pius Bonifacius. *Series episcoparum ecclesiae*. 1873–86.

Gelsinger, Bruce E. *Icelandic Enterprise: Commerce and Economy in the Middle Ages*. Columbia, S.C.: University of South Carolina Press, 1981.

Goldschmidt, E. P. *Hieronymus Münzer und seine Bibliothek*. London: The Warburg Institute, 1938.

———. *Medieval Texts and Their First Appearance in Print*. Supplement to the Bibliographical Society's Transactions, no. 16. Oxford and London: Oxford University Press, 1943.

Goss, John. *The Mapping of North America: Three Centuries of Mapmaking, 1500–1860*. Secaucus, N.J.: Wellfleet Press, 1990.

Gravier, Gabriel. *Découverte de l'Amérique par les Normands au Xe siècle*. Rouen, 1874.

Gulløv, Hans Christian. "The Eskimo Culture in Greenland and the Medieval Norse." In Sigurðsson and Skaptason, *Aspects*, pp. 184–93.

Gunnarsson, Gísli. "Given Good Time, Legs Get Shorter in Cold Weather." In Sigurðsson and Skaptason, *Aspects*, pp. 593–602.

Guttormsen, Helge. "Did the Kvens Introduce a New Type of Farming to Northern Norway?" In Sigurðsson and Skaptason, *Aspects*, pp. 315–29.

Haardt, Robert. "Testimonials to Father Fischer, collected by Robert Haardt and introduced by His Excellency Graf Johannes zu Waldburg Wolfegg." *Der Globusfreund* 7 (Nov. 1958): 26–32.

Hainisch, Michael. *75 Jahre aus bewegter Zeit: Lebenserinnerungen eines österreichischen Staatsmannes*. Veröffentlichungen der Kommission für Neuere Geschichle Österreichs, vol. 64. Ed. and introd. Friedrich Weissensteiner. Vienna, Cologne, and Graz, 1978.

Hakluyt, Richard. *Principall Navigations of the English Nation*. 2 vols. Photolithographic facsimile of the 1589 edition with an introduction by David B. Quinn and Raleigh Ashlin Skelton. Cambridge, England: Cambridge University Press for the Hakluyt Society, 1965.

———. *The Principal Navigations Voyages Traffiques & Discoveries of the English Nation*. Glasgow: James MacLehose and Sons, 1903.

Hall, Charles Francis. *Life with the Esquimaux: The Narrative of Captain Charles Francis Hall of the Whaling Barque "George Henry" from the 29th May, 1860, to the 13th September, 1862*. London: Sampson, Low, Son and Marston, 1864.

Halldórsson, Ólafur. "Einars tháttr Sokkasonar." In Phillip Pulsiano and Kirsten Wolf, eds., *Medieval Scandinavia: An Encyclopedia*. New York and London: Garland Publishing, Inc., 1993.

———. *Grænland í miðaldarítum*. Reykjavík: Sögufélag, 1978.

Haller, Johannes, ed. *Concilium Basiliense*. Vol. 3. *Die Protokolle des Concils von 1434 und 1435 aus dem Manuale des Notars Bruneti und einer Römisches Handschrift*. Basel, 1900.

Haller, Wilfried. "Prof. Dr. h. c. P. Josef Fischer S.J.: Leben und Werk." M.A. thesis. Typescript in the Jesuit Provincial Archives, Munich, circa 1980.

Hamy, E.-T. *Le Livre de la Description des pays de Gilles le Bouvier, dit Berry, Premier Roi d'Armes de Charles VII, roi de France*. Recueil de Voyages et de Documents pour servir à l'Histoire de la Géographie depuis le XIIIe jusqu'à la fin du xvie siècle. Vol. 22. Paris, 1908.

Harley, J. B., and David Woodward, eds. *The History of Cartography*. Vol. 1. *Cartography in Prehistoric, Ancient, and Medieval Europe and the Mediterranean*. Chicago and London: University of Chicago Press, 1987.

Harris, Elizabeth. "The Waldseemüller World Map: A Typographical Appraisal." *Imago Mundi* 37 (1987): 30–53.

Harris, Philip R., ed. *History of the British Museum Library, 1753–1973*. London: The British Library, 1998.

——. *The Library of the British Museum: Retrospective Essays on the Department of Printed Books*. London: The British Library, 1991.

Harp, Elmer. "A Late Dorset Copper Amulet from Southeastern Hudson Bay." *Folk* 16–17 (1975): 33–44.

Harrisse, Henry. *The Discovery of North America*. 2 vols. London: Henry Stevens, 1892.

Harvey, P. D. A. *Mappamundi: The Hereford World Map*. London and Toronto: Hereford Cathedral and The British Library, 1996.

——. *Medieval Maps*. Toronto and Buffalo: University of Toronto Press, 1991.

Hassinger, Hugo. "Josef Fischer." In *Almanach der Akademie der Wissenschaffen*, pp. 239–50. Vienna, 1945.

Hastrup, Kirsten. "Sæters in Iceland, 900–1600." *Acta Borealia* 6 (1989): 72–85.

Helgason, Agnar, with Sigrún Sigurðardóttir, Jeffrey R. Gulcher, Ryk Ward, and Kári Stefánsson. "mtDNA and the Origin of the Icelanders: Deciphering Signals of Recent Population History." *American Journal of Human Genetics* 66 (2000): 999–1016.

Helgason, Jón, ed. *Eddadigte. I. Völuspá, Hávamál. Nordisk filologi* Series A. Copenhagen, Oslo, and Stockholm, 1951.

Hennig, Richard. "The Representation on Maps of the Magelhães Strait before their Discovery." *Imago Mundi* 5 (1948): 33–37.

Herben, Jan. *Huss and his Followers*. London: Geoffrey Bles, 1926.

Hertz, Johannes. "The Newport Tower." In Fitzhugh and Ward, *Vikings*, p. 376.

Hogg, Peter C. "The Prototype of the Stefánsson and Resen charts." *Historisk Tidskrift* (Oslo) 1 (1989): 3–27.

Holand, Hjalmar R. *Explorations in America Before Columbus*. New York: Twayne Publ., 1956.

——. *The Kensington Stone*. Privately printed, 1932.

Hollander, Lee M., trans. and ed. *The Poetic Edda.* 1962; repr., Austin: University of Texas Press, 1988.

Holm Olsen, Inger Marie. "The Helgøy Project: Evidence from Farm Mounds: Economy and Settlement Pattern AD 1350–1600." *Norwegian Archaeological Review* 14 (1981).

Holtsmark, Anne, and Jón Helgason, eds. *Snorri Sturluson Edda: Gylfaginning og Prosafortellingene av Skaldskaparmál. Nordiskfilologi* Series A. Copenhagen, 1950.

Hreinsson, Víðar, gen. ed. *The Complete Sagas of Icelanders.* Reykjavík: Leifur Eiríksson Publishing, 1997.

Ingstad, Helge. *Vesterveg til Vinland.* Oslo: Gyldendal Norsk Forlag, 1965.

———. "Vinland Ruins Prove Vikings Found the New World." *National Geographic Magazine.* Vol. 126 (Nov. 1964): 708–35.

Jackson, Melvin H. "Medieval Conventions of Form and the Vinland Map." Paper, Washington symposium, 1966. Typescript, BLML, Helen Wallis Files, "Vinland Map File/Current."

———. "The Vinland Map and the Imperatives of Medieval Form." In Washburn, *Proceedings,* pp. 57–76.

———. "The Vinland Map and the Tartar Relation: Review Article." *The Cartographer* (renamed *Canadian Cartographer* in 1967) 3, no. 2 (1966): 14–17.

Jackson, Tatjana N. "*Biarmaland* between Norway and Old Rus." In Ingi Sigurðsson and Jón Skaptason, *Aspects,* pp. 113–20.

Jansen, Christian. *Professoren und Politik: Politisches Denken und Handeln der Heidelberger Hochschullehrer 1914–1935.* Vol. 99. Göttingen: Kritische Studien zur Geschichtswissenschaft, 1992.

Jelic, Luka. "L'évangélisation de l'Amérique." *Le Missioni francescane* 8, no. 6 (1897): 556–60.

———. "L'évangélisation de l'Amérique avant Christophe Colomb." *Compte Rendu du congrès scientificque international des catholiques.* Vol. 2, pp. 170–84. Paris: Sciences Historiques, 1891.

Jóhannesson, Jón. "Om Haf Innan." *Saga/Sögurit* 24 (1960): 17–28.

———. "Reisubók Bjarnar Jorsalafara." *Skirnir* 119 (1945): 68–96.

Jónsson, Arngrim. *Grönlandia: Eller Historie om Grønland af Islandske Haandskrevne Historie-Bøger. . . . og først i det Latinske Sprog forfatted af Arngrim Jonsson.* Trans. from Latin into Icelandic by Einar Eyjolfsson in 1688. Copenhagen, 1732.

Jónsson, Finnur. *Det gamle Grønlands Beskrivelse.* Copenhagen: Levin and Munksgaard, 1930.

———. "Grønlands gamle Topografi efter Kilderne: Østerbygden og Vesterbygden." *MoG* 20 (1899).

Kahle, B., ed. "Kristnisaga, Tháttr Thorvalds ens Víðförla, Tháttr Ísleifs Biskups Gizurarsonar, Hungrvaka." *Altnordische Saga-Bibliothek*. Vol. 11. Halle a.d. S., 1905.

Karrow, Robert. *Mapmakers of the Sixteenth Century and Their Maps*. Chicago: Speculum Orbis Press for the Newberry Library, 1993.

Kaups, Matti Enn. "Shifting Vinland—Tradition and Myth." *Terrae Incognitae* 2 (1970): 29–60.

Kejlbo, Ib. "Chronicle." *Imago Mundi* 23 (1969): 109–10.

Kisbye Møller, J. "Isaac de la Peyrère: Relation du Groenlande." *Grønland* 29 (1981): 168–84.

Koht, Halvdan. "Den eldste Noregshistoria." *Gamalnorske Bokverk* (Oslo) 19 (1921).

Kowaleski, Maryanne. "The Expansion of the South-western Fisheries in Late Medieval England." *Economic History Review* 53, no. 3 (2000): 429–54.

———. "The Western Fisheries." In David J. Starkey, Chris Reid, and Neil Ashcroft, eds., *England's Sea Fisheries: The Commercial Sea Fisheries of England and Wales since 1300*, pp. 23–29. London: Chatham Publishing, 2000.

Kristinsson, Axel. "Productivity and Population in Pre-Industrial Iceland." In Sigurðsson and Skaptason, *Aspects*, pp. 270–78.

Kulturhistorisk leksikon for nordisk middelalder. 21 vols. Copenhagen, 1956–78.

Kurlansky, Mark. *Cod: A Biography of the Fish that Changed the World*. New York: Penguin Books, 1997.

Larner, John. *Marco Polo and the Discovery of the World*. New Haven and London: Yale University Press, 1999.

Lebel, Serge, and Patrick Plumet. "Étude Technologique de l'Exploitation des Blocs et des Galets en Métabasalte par les Dorsétiens au Site Tuvaaluk (DIA.4, JfEI-4)." *Journal canadien d'archéologie* 15 (1991).

Lehn, Waldemar H. "Skerrylike Mirages and the Discovery of Greenland." *Applied Optics* 39, no. 2 (2000): 3612–19.

Lidegaard, Mads, ed. "Glahns anmærkninger. 1700-tallets Grønlændere. Et nærbillede." *Det Grønlandske Selskabs Skrifter* 30. [Copenhagen], 1991.

[Lintot, Henry, and John Osborn, eds.]. *A Collection of Voyages and Travels*. Vol. 2. London: Henry Lintot and John Osborn, 1744.

Lönnroth, Erik. *Sverige och Kalmarunionen, 1397–1457*. Studia Historica Gothoburgensia 10. 2nd ed. Göteborg (Sweden), 1969.

Losman, Beata. *Norden och reformkonsilierna, 1408–1449*. Studia Historica Gothoburgensia 11. Göteborg (Sweden), 1970.

Lucas, Frederic W. *The Annals of the Voyages of the Brothers Nicolò and Antonio Zeno in the North Atlantic about the End of the Fourteenth Century and the Claim founded thereon to a Venetian Discovery of America*. London: Henry Stevens and Son, 1898.

Lynam, Edward. *The Engraved Atlas of the World: The Cosmographia of Claudius Ptolemaeus, Bologna, 1477.* Jenkintown, Penn.: Tall Tree Publishers, 1941.

Lynnerup, Niels. "The Greenland Norse: A Biological-Anthropological Study." *MoG: M&S* 24 (1998).

Mallet, Paul Henry. *Introduction à l'histoire de Dannemarc.* 2 vols. Copenhagen: L. H. Lillie, 1755–56.

———. *Northern Antiquities.* Translation of *Introduction à l'Histoire de Dannemarc.* With introduction and notes by the English translator. London, 1770.

Marston, Thomas E. "The Vinland Map: Dating the Manuscript." *The Cartographer* (The Ontario Institute of Chartered Cartographers) 3, no. 2 (1966): 1–5.

Mattox, William G. "Fishing in West Greenland 1910–1966: The Development of a New Native Industry." *MoG* 197, no. 1 (1973).

Mayer, Ralph. *The Artist's Handbook of Materials and Techniques.* 5th rev. ed. New York: Viking, 1991.

McCrone, Walter C. *Judgement Day for the Turin Shroud.* Chicago: McCrone Research Institute, 1996.

———. "The Vinland Map." *Analytical Chemistry* 60 (1988): 1009–18.

———. "Vinland Map 1999." *Microscope* 42, no. 2 (1999): 71–74.

McCullough, Karen, and Peter Schledermann. "Mystery Cairns on Washington Irving Island." *Polar Record* 35 (1999): 289–98.

McGhee, Robert. "Contact Between Native North Americans and the Medieval Norse: A Review of the Evidence." *American Antiquity* 49 (1984): 4–26.

———. "A New View of the Norse in the Arctic." *Scientific American Discovering Archaeology* 2, no. 4 (2000): 54–61.

———. "Radiocarbon Dating and the Timing of the Thule Migration." In Appelt, Berglund, and Gulløv, *Identities,* pp. 181–91.

———. "The Skraellings of *Vínland.*" In Clausen, *Viking Voyages,* pp. 43–53.

McGovern, Thomas H. "Bones, Buildings, and Boundaries: Palæoeconomic Approaches to Norse Greenland." In Christopher D. Morris and D. James Rackham, eds., *Norse and Later Settlement and Subsistence in the North Atlantic,* pp. 193–230. Glasgow: University of Glasgow, Department of Archaeology, 1992.

———. "The Economics of Extinction." In T. M. Wrigley, M. J. Ingram, and G. Farmer, eds. *Climate and History: Studies in Past Climates and Their Impact on Man,* pp. 404–34. Cambridge, England: Cambridge University Press, 1980.

———. "The Economics of Landnám. Animal Bone Evidence from Iceland

and Greenland." Report, The North Atlantic Saga conference, Reykjavík, Iceland, Aug. 9–11, 1999.

McGovern, Thomas, and G. F. Bigelow. "Archaezoology of the Norse Site Ø17a Narssaq District, Southwest Greenland." *Acta Borealia* 1 (1984): 85–101.

McGovern, Thomas, with Gerald F. Bigelow, Thomas Amorosi, James Woollett, and Sophia Perdikaris. "The zooarchaeology of Ø17a." In C. L. Vebæk, "Narsaq," pp. 58–74.

Maron, Ferenc. "A Map, Dating from 1599, Found in Hungary," *Hungarian Review* no. 1 (1967): 20–21.

Milanesi, Marica. "Il *De Insulis et earum proprietatibus* di Domenico Silvestri (1385–1406)." *Geographia Antiqua* (Florence; Giunto Gruppo Editoriale) 2 (1993).

Mollat du Jourdin, Michel, and Monique de la Roncière, with Marie-Madeleine Azard, Isabelle Raynaud-Nguyen, and Marie-Antoinette Vannerau. *Sea Charts of the Early Explorers 13th to 17th Century.* Trans. L. le R. Dethan. New York: Thames and Hudson, 1984.

Monmonier, Mark. *How to Lie with Maps.* 2nd ed. Chicago and London: University of Chicago Press, 1996.

Monumenta Conciliorum Generalium Seculi Decimi Quinti: Concilium Basiliense Scriptorum (Vindibonae) 2 (1873).

Morcken, Roald. *Sjøfartshistoriske artikler gjennom 20 år* [Articles on maritime history through twenty years, with summaries in English]. Bergen: privately published, 1983.

Morison, Samuel Eliot. *The European Discovery of America.* New York: Oxford University Press, 1971.

Munch, Peter Andreas. *Pavelige Nuntiers Regnskabe.* Oslo, 1864.

Mundy, John Hine, and Kennerly M. Woody, eds. *The Council of Constance: The Unification of the Church.* Trans. Louise Ropes Loomois. Columbia University Records of Civilization Sources and Studies 63. New York and London: Columbia University Press, 1961.

Nansen, Fridtjof. *Nord i Taakeheimen.* Oslo, 1911.

———. *In Northern Mists.* 2 vols. London: William Heinemann, 1911.

Nebenzahl, Kenneth. *Atlas of Columbus.* Chicago: Rand McNally and Company, 1990.

Neue deutsche Biographie. Der Historischen Kommission bei der Bayerischen Akademie der Wissenschaften. Vol. 5. Berlin: Duncker and Humbolt, 1961.

Neue Kronik von Böhmen vom Jahre 530, bis 1780 (Nebst einer geographischen Beschreibung aller Städte, Schlösser und anderer merkwürdigen Orte). Prague, 1780.

Neuhäusler, Johann. *Kreuz und Hakenkreuz.* 2 vols. Munich: Katolisches Kirche Bayerns, 1946.

Nicolet, Claude. *Space, Geography, and Politics in the Early Roman Empire.* Jerome Lectures 19. Ann Arbor: University of Michigan Press, 1991.

Nordenskiöld, Nils A. E. *Facsimile Atlas to the Early History of Cartography.* 1889; repr., New York: Kraus, 1961.

Nørlund, N. F. *Islands Kortlægning.* Geodetisk Instituts Publikationer 7. Copenhagen: Munksgaard, 1944.

Nørlund, Poul. "Buried Norsemen at Herjolfsnes." *MoG* 67, no. 1 (1924).

———. "Norse Ruins at Gardar." *MoG* 76, no. 1 (1929).

Nytt fra Norge (Oslo) 44, no. 3.

Ogilvie, A. E. J. "Climatic Changes in Iceland c. AD 865 to 1598." In Gerald F. Bigelow, gen. ed., "The Norse of the North Atlantic." *Acta Archaeologica* 61 (1991): 233–51.

Ogilvie, A. E. J., and T. Jónsson. "'Litte Ice Age' Research: A Perspective from Iceland." In A. E. J. Ogilvie and T. Jónsson, gen. eds., *Climatic Change* 48 (2001), special monograph issue, pp. 1–46.

Olin, Jacqueline S. "Without Comparative Studies of Inks, What Do We Know about the Vinland Map?" *Pre-Columbiana* 2, no. 2 (2000): 27–36.

Österreichisches bibliographisches Lexicon, 1815–1950, Leo Santifaller, gen. ed., *Österreichischen Akademie der Wissenschaften* Graz-Köln, 1954–57.

Pálsson, Hermann. "Landafundurinn árið 1285." *Saga* 4 (1964): 53–69.

Pang, Kevin D. "Climatic Impact of the Mid-Fifteenth Century Cuwae Caldera Formation, as Reconstructed from Historical and Proxy Data." *Eos* 74 (1993): 106.

Pastor, Ludwig. *The History of the Popes.* 7th ed. Ed. Frederick Ignatius Antrobus. London: K. Paul, Trench, Trübner and Company, Ltd., 1949.

Peitz, W. M. "Die Weltkarten Waldseemüllers." *Stimmen aus Maria-Laach* (Freiburg in the Breisgau) 66 (1904): 540–46.

Pelletier, Monique, ed. *Géographie du Monde au Moyen Age et à la Renaissance.* Paris: Editions du C.T.H.S., 1989.

Perrott, Roy. "The great map forgery." *Sunday Times* (London), Feb. 3, 1974, p. 1.

Philbert, Poul-Erik. "Man er hvad man spiser." *Polarfronten* 2 (2002): 12–13.

———. "Tryk på klimaet i Nordatlanteren." *Polarfronten* 1 (2001): 6–7.

Plumet, Patrick. "L'Esquimau: Essai de synthèse de la préhistoire de l'arctique esquimau." *Revista de Arqueología Americana* 10 (1996): 7–51.

———. "Les maisons longues dorsétiennes de l'Ungava." *Géographie Physique et Quaternaire* 36, no. 3 (1982): 253–89.

———. "Le Site de la Pointe aux Bélougas (Qilalugarsiuvik) et les maisons longues dorsétiennes." *Archéologie de l'Ungava* (Montreal), no. 18 (1985).

Pontoppidan, Erik. *The Natural History of Norway.* London, 1755.

———. *Norges Naturlige Historie.* Copenhagen, 1752.

[Ptolemæus, Claudius]. *Claudius Ptolemy: The Geography.* Trans. Edward L. Stevenson, with an introduction by Josef Fischer. New York: Dover Publications, Inc., 1932.

Pulsiano, Phillip, and Kirsten Wolf, eds. *Medieval Scandinavia: An Encyclopedia.* New York and London: Garland Publishing, Inc., 1993.

Quinn, David B. "Raleigh Ashlin Skelton: His Contributions to the History of Discovery" (Obituary). *Imago Mundi* 25 (1971): 13–15.

Rafn, C. C., and Finn Magnusen, comps. and eds. *Antiquitates Americanæ.* Hafniæ: Regia Antiquarium Septentrionalium, 1837.

———. *Grønlands Historiske Mindesmærker.* 3 vols. Copenhagen: Det Kongelige Norske Oldtids-Selskab, 1845.

[Rask, Rasmus, and Finn Magnusen]. "Efterretning om en i Grønland funden Runesteen med dens Forklaring, forfattet af Professor Rask, og nogle dertil hørende Oplysninger ved Professor F. Magnusen." *Antiqvariske Annaler* (Copenhagen) 4, part 2 (1827): 309–43, with an addendum containing a report by the missionary P. Kragh, July, 1826, pp. 367–79.

Reeh, Niels. "Indlandsisen på langsom skrump." *Polarfronten* 3 (2000): 4–5.

Reeves, Arthur Middleton. *The Finding of Wineland the Good: the History of the Icelandic Discovery of America.* London: Henry Frowde, 1890.

Rey, L. "Gardar, the Episcopal Seat of Medieval Greenland." *Arctic* 37, no. 4 (1984): 324–33.

Richey, Michael W. "E. G. R. Taylor and the Vinland Map." *The Journal of Navigation* 53, no. 2 (2000): 193–205.

———. "The Vinland Map." Review in *Journal of the Institute of Navigation* 19, no. 1 (1966): 124–25.

Rieth, Adolf. *Archaeological Fakes.* Trans. Diana Imber. New York: Barrie and Jenkins, 1970.

Roesdahl, Else, and Preben Meulengracht Sørensen, eds. *Beretning fra tolvte tværfaglige vikingesymposium, Aarhus Universitet.* [Aarhus, Denmark]: Aarhus Universitet, 1993.

———. "L'ivoire de morse et les colonies norroises du Groenland." *Proxima Thule, revue d'études nordiques* 3 (spring 1998): 9–48.

Rosenørn, Stig, with Jens Fabricius, Erik Buch, and Svend Aage Horsted. "Isvinter ved Vestgrønland: Klima, vestis, oceanografi og biologi." *Forskning i Grønland/Tusaat* 4, no. 2 (1981): 2–19.

Roussell, Aage. "Sandnes and the Neighbouring Farms." With an Appendix by Erik Moltke, "Greenland Runic Inscriptions 1." *MoG* 88, no. 2 (1936).

Russell, Peter. *Prince Henry 'the Navigator': A Life.* New Haven and London: Yale University Press, 2000.

Sabo, George, and Deborah Sabo. "A Possible Thule Carving of a Viking from Baffin Island N.W.T." *Canadian Journal of Archaeology* 2 (1978): 33–42.

Saenger, Paul. "Vinland Re-read." Review of *The Vinland Map and the Tartar Relation,* 1995 ed. *Imago Mundi* 50, London, 1998, pp. 199–202.

Samson, Ross, ed. *Social Approaches to Viking Studies.* Glasgow: Cruithne Press, 1991.

Schledermann, Peter. "Ellesmere." In Fitzhugh and Ward, *Vikings,* pp. 248–56.

———. "The Norse in the Arctic." *Scientific American Discovering Archaeology* 2, no. 4 (2000): 59.

———. "Norsemen in the High Arctic?" In Clausen, *Viking Voyages,* pp. 54–66.

Schofield, A. N. E. D. "England and the Council of Basel." In Walter Brandmüller and Remigius Bäumer, eds., *Annuarium Historiae Conciliorum,* Amsterdam, 1973, Heft 1, pp. 1–117 (BL reprint, x.100/13076).

Schofield, Peter. "Bertram Schofield and the Vinland Map." *Imago Mundi* 53 (2001): 136–39.

Schröteler, Joseph. "Volk, Staat, Erziehung." *Stimmen der Zeit* (Freiburg in the Breisgau) 126 (1934).

Schweikhart, Gunter. *Der Codex Wolfegg: Zeichnungen nach der Antike von Amico Aspertini,* pp. 23–28. London: The Warburg Institute, 1986.

Seaver, Kirsten A."Albertin de Virga and the Far North." *Mercator's World* 2, no. 6 (1997): 58–62.

———. "Baffin Island Mandibles and Walrus Blooms." In Symons, *Meta Incognita,* Vol. 2, pp. 563–74.

———. "Far and Yet Near: North America and Norse Greenland." *Viking Heritage Newsletter* (Visby, Sweden) 1, no. 1 (2000): 3–5, 23.

———. *The Frozen Echo: Greenland and the Exploration of North America ca. AD 1000–1500.* Stanford: Stanford University Press, 1996.

———. "How Strange Is a Stranger?" In Symons, *Meta Incognita,* Vol. 2, pp. 523–52.

———. "Land of Wine and Forests: The Norse in North America." *Mercator's World* 5, no. 1 (2000): 18–24.

———. "The Mystery of the 'Vinland Map' Manuscript Volume." *The Map Collector* 74 (1996): 24–29.

———. "Norse Greenland on the Eve of Renaissance Exploration." In Agnarsdóttir, *Voyages,* pp. 29–44.

———. "Norumbega and *Harmonia Mundi* in Sixteenth-Century Cartography." *Imago Mundi* 50 (1998): 34–58.

———. "Renewing the Quest for Vínland: The Stefánsson, Resen and Thorláksson maps." *Mercator's World* 5, no. 5 (2000): 42–49.

———. "'A Very Common and Usuall Trade': The Relationship Between Cartographic Perceptions and Fishing in the Davis Strait c. 1500–1550."

British Library Journal (June 1996): 1–26. Also in Karen Severud Cook, ed., *Images and Icons*, pp. 1–26.

————. "The Vinland Map: A $3,500 duckling that became a $25,000,000 swan." *Mercator's World* 2, no. 2 (1997): 42–47.

————. "The 'Vinland Map': Who Made It, and Why? New Light on an Old Problem." *The Map Collector* 70 (spring 1995): 32–40.

Shailor, Barbara. *Catalogue of Medieval and Renaissance Manuscripts in the Beinecke Rare Book and Manuscript Library, Yale University.* Vol. 2. Binghamton, N.Y.: Medieval and Renaissance Texts and Studies, 1987; Vol. 3, *Marston Manuscripts,* 1992.

Shirley, Rodney. *The Mapping of the World: Early Printed World Maps 1472–1700.* London: New Holland, 1993.

Sigurðsson, Gísli. "The Quest for Vinland in Saga Scholarship." In Fitzhugh and Ward, *Vikings,* pp. 232–37.

Sigurðsson, Gísli, and Sigurjón Jóhannesson. *Vikings and the New World.* Exh. cat. Reykjavík: The Culture House, 2000.

Sigurðsson, Haraldur. *Kortasaga Íslands.* Vol. 1. Reykjavík: Menningarsjóður, 1971.

————. "The Vinland Map, its date and origin." *Thjóðdviljinn,* Dec. 24, 1965.

Sigurðsson, Ingi, and Jón Skaptason, eds. *Aspects of Arctic and Sub-Arctic History: Proceedings of the International Congress on the History of the Arctic and Sub-Arctic Region, Reykjavík, 18–21 June 1998.* Reykjavík: University of Iceland Press, 2000.

Skaare, Kolbjørn. "En norsk penning fra 11. årh. funnet på kysten av Maine, U.S.A." *Meddelelser fra Norsk Numismatisk Forening* 2 (May 1979): 2–17.

Skelton, R. A., Thomas E. Marston, and George D. Painter. *The Vinland Map and the Tartar Relation.* New Haven, Conn.: Yale University Press, 1965.

————. *The Vinland Map and the Tartar Relation.* 2nd ed. New Haven, Conn.: Yale University Press, 1995.

Smith, Brian. " 'Earl Henry Sinclair's fictitious trip to America.' " *New Orkney Antiquarian Journal* 2 (2000).

————. "The not-so-secret scroll: Priceless relic or floorcloth?" *The Orcadian,* Mar. 29, 2001, p. 18; may be accessed on http://www.orkneyjar.com/history/historicalfigures/henrysinclair/kirkwallscroll2.htm.

Smith, Kevin P. "Who Lived at L'Anse aux Meadows?" In Fitzhugh and Ward, *Vikings,* p. 217.

Sørensen, Ingrid. "Pollenundersøgelser i møddingen på Niaqussat." *Grønland* 30 (1982): 296–304.

Steenstrup, K. J. V. "Om Østerbygden (1886)." *MoG* 9 (1889): 1–53.

Steinnes, Asgaut. "Ikring Historia Norvegiae." *Historisk Tidsskrift* (Oslo) 34 (1946–48): 1–61.

Stevenson, Allan. *Observations on Paper as Evidence.* Lawrence (Kansas): University of Kansas Libraries, 1961.

———. *The Problem of the* Missale speciale. London: The Bibliographical Society, 1967.

Stevenson, Edward Luther, trans. and ed. *Geography of Claudius Ptolemy.* With an introduction by Joseph Fischer. New York: The New York Public Library, 1932.

Stevenson, Edward Luther, and Joseph Fischer, eds. *Map of the World by Jodocus Hondius, 1611.* New York: The American Geographical Society and the Hispanic Society of America, 1907.

Stieber, Joachim W. "Den danske Geograf Claudius Clavus eller Nicolaus Niger." *Ymer* (Stockholm) 9, parts 1 and 2 (1889): 129–46; 11, parts 3 and 4 (1891): 13–38.

———. "Ginnungagap i Mytologien og i Geografien." In Axel Koch, ed., *Arkiv för nordisk Filologi* (Lund, Sweden) 6 (New series, vol. 2) (1890): 340–50.

———. *Pope Eugenius IV, the Council of Basel and the Secular and Ecclesiastical Authorities in the Empire.* Leiden: E. J. Brill, 1978.

———. *Studies on the Vineland Voyages.* Copenhagen: Thiele, 1889.

Sutherland, Patricia D., and Robert McGhee. "Arktisk Kontakt." *Skalk* (Copenhagen) 3 (1983): 12–15.

———. "The Norse and Native Norse Americans." In Fitzhugh and Ward, *Vikings*, pp. 238–47.

———. "Strands of Culture Contact: Dorset-Norse Interactions in the Eastern Canadian Arctic." In Appelt, Berglund, and Gulløv, *Identities*, pp. 159–69.

Symons, Thomas H. B., ed. *Meta Incognita: A Discourse of Discovery. Martin Frobisher's Arctic Expeditions, 1576–1578.* 2 vols. Mercury Series. Hull, Quebec: Canadian Museum of Civilization, 1999.

Taylor, E. G. R. "A Letter Dated 1577 from Mercator to John Dee." *Imago Mundi* (Stockholm) 13 (1956): 56–67.

———. "The Vinland Map." *Journal of the Institute of Navigation* 27, no. 2 (1974): 195–205.

Thomson, S. Harrison. *Czechoslovakia in European History.* 2nd ed. London: Frank Cass and Company, 1965.

Thór, Jón Th. "Fisheries in the Traditional Icelandic Society." In Sigurðsson and Skaptason, *Aspects*, pp. 611–17.

Thorsteinsson, Ingvi. "The Environmental Effects of Farming in South

Greenland in the Middle Ages and the Twentieth Century." In Sigurðsson and Skaptason, *Aspects*, pp. 258–63.

Thrower, Norman J. W. *Maps and Civilization: Cartography in Culture and Society.* 2nd ed. Chicago: University of Chicago Press, 1999.

Times Literary Supplement. Review of *The Vinland Map and the Tartar Relation*, Nov. 25, 1965.

Torfæus, Tormod. *Det gamle Grønland.* Trans. of *Gronlandia antiqua* by the author. Copenhagen, 1706; repr., Oslo: A. W. Brøgger: [Oslo Etnografisk Museum], 1947.

———. *Gronlandia antiqua.* Copenhagen, 1706.

Tornøe, J. Kr. *Columbus in the Arctic? and the Vineland Literature, etc.* Oslo: Brøgger, 1965.

———. *Norsemen Before Columbus.* Oslo: Universitetsforlaget, 1964.

Towe, Kenneth M. "The Vinland Map: Still a Forgery." *Accounts of Chemical Research* 23 (Mar. 1990): 84–87.

Uzielli, Gustavo. *La vita e i tempi di Paolo dal Pozzo Toscanelli.* Rome, 1894.

Vebæk, C. L. "The Church Topography of the Eastern Settlement and the Excavation of the Benedictine Convent at Narsarsuaq in the Uunartoq Fjord." *MoG: M&S* 14 (1991).

———. "Narsaq—A Norse *landnáma* farm." *MoG: M&S* 18 (1993).

———. "Vatnahverfi: An inland district of the Eastern Settlement in Greenland." *MoG: M&S* 17 (1992).

Vickers, Michael, et al. *Ivory: An International History and Illustrated Survey.* New York: Abrams, 1987.

Vigneras, L.-A. "Greenland, Vinland, and the Yale Map." *Terrae Incognitae* 4 (1972): 53–94.

Villain-Gandossi, Christiane, with Salerno Bussutil and Paul Adam, eds. *Medieval Ships and the Birth of Technological Societies.* Vol. 1. *Northern Europe. European Coordination.* Malta: Centre for Research and Documentation in Social Sciences, Foundation for International Studies, 1989.

Vollan, Odd. "Torskefiske." *Kulturhistorisk leksikon for nordisk middelalder* 18 (1974): cols. 506–10.

Von Wieser, Franz Ritter. *Die Weltkarte des Albertin de Virga aus dem Anfange des XV. Jahrhunderts in der Sammlung Figdor in Wien.* Innsbruck, 1912.

[———.] *Franz Ritter von Wieser, Gedenkschrift.* Heft 5. Innsbruck: Veröffentlichungen des Museums Ferdinandeum in Innsbruck, 1925.

Wahlgren, Erik. *The Vikings and America.* London: Thames and Hudson, 1986.

Wallace, Birgitta Linderoth. "L'Anse aux Meadows, the Western Outpost." In Clausen, *Viking Voyages*, pp. 30–42.

———. "Norse Expansion into North America." Internet report for

Canadian Heritage, Atlantic Region, 1996, http://www/heureka/fi/en/x/
nxwallace.html.
———. "The Norse in the North Atlantic: The L'Anse aux Meadows Settle-
ment in Newfoundland." In Sigurðsson and Skaptason, *Aspects*, pp. 486–
500.
———. "The Vikings in North America: Myth and Reality." In Ross Samson,
ed., *Social Approaches to Viking Studies*, pp. 206–12. Glasgow: Cruithne
Press, 1991.
———. "The Viking Settlement at L'Anse aux Meadows." In Fitzhugh and
Ward, *Vikings*, pp. 209–13.
Wallis, Helen. "The Vinland Map: Fake, forgery or jeu d'ésprit?" *The Map
Collector* (winter 1990): 2–6.
Wallis, Helen, with F. R. Maddison, G. D. Painter, D. B. Quinn, R. M.
Perkins, G. R. Crone, A. D. Baynes-Cope, and Walter C. and Lucy B.
McCrone. "The Strange Case of the Vinland Map: A Symposium."
The Geographical Journal 140, no. 2 (1974): 183–217.
Washburn, Wilcomb E. "Examen critique des Amériques." *La découverte de
l'Amérique*, pp. 77–87. Dixième stage international d'études humanistes,
Tours, 1966. Paris, 1968.
———, ed. *Proceedings of the Vinland Map Conference*. Chicago: University of
Chicago Press, 1971.
[———.] Public Broadcasting Service transcript of interview with Wilcomb
Washburn on Feb. 13, 1996.
———. Review of *The Vinland Map and the Tartar Relation. American Histor-
ical Review* 71 (Apr. 1966): 927–28.
Watelet, Marcel, ed. *The Mercator Atlas of Europe*. Pleasant Hill, Ore.:
Walking Tree Press, 1998.
Weissensteiner, Friedrich, ed. *Michael Hainisch, 75 Jahre aus bewegter Zeit:
Lebenserinnerungen eines österreichischen Staatsmannes*. Veröffentlichungen
der Kommission für Neuere Geschichte Österreichs, vol. 64. Vienna,
Cologne, Graz, 1978.
Wilson, Derek, and Peter Ayerst. *White Gold: The Story of African Ivory*. Lon-
don: Heinemann, 1970.
Witten, Laurence C., II. "Collecting Medieval and Renaissance Manuscripts
Today," *Library Trends*, Apr. 1961, pp. 398–405.
———. "Vinland's Saga Recalled." In Skelton et al., *Vinland Map* (1995
ed.). Reprinted from an account published in the *Yale University Gazette*,
Oct. 1989.
———. "Vrai ou fausse? La saga de la *Carte du Vinland*." *Bulletin du
bibliophile* (Paris) no. 2 (1990): 286–313.
———. "The Wormhole Mystery." *Williams Alumni Review*, Nov. 1965.

Wolff, Hans, ed. *America: Early Maps of the New World*. Munich: Prestel, 1992.

Woodward, David. "Could these Italian maps be fakes?" *The Map Collector* 67 (July 1994): 2–10.

Wyngaert, Anastasius van den. *Sinica Franciscana*. Vol. 1. *Itinera et Relationes Fratrum Minorum Saeculi XIII et XIV*. Florence: Qaracchi Ad Claras Aquas, 1929.

Index

Lightning Source UK Ltd.
Milton Keynes UK
UKHW041605240121
377501UK00014B/537